HANDBOOK OF EMPLOYEE COMMITMENT

To Trudy, Matthew and Samantha
*For helping me to understand the true meaning of commitment
and all that it has to offer*

Handbook of Employee Commitment

Edited by

John P. Meyer

Department of Psychology, Social Science Centre, The University of Western Ontario, Canada and Professor, Curtin Business School, Curtin University, Australia

EE **Edward Elgar**
PUBLISHING

Cheltenham, UK • Northampton, MA, USA

Published by
Edward Elgar Publishing Limited
The Lypiatts
15 Lansdown Road
Cheltenham
Glos GL50 2JA
UK

Edward Elgar Publishing, Inc.
William Pratt House
9 Dewey Court
Northampton
Massachusetts 01060
USA

Paperback edition 2018

A catalogue record for this book
is available from the British Library

Library of Congress Control Number: 2016938602

This book is available electronically in the **Elgar**online
Business subject collection
DOI 10.4337/9781784711740

ISBN 978 1 78471 173 3 (cased)
ISBN 978 1 78471 174 0 (eBook)
ISBN 978 1 78471 175 7 (paperback)

Typeset by Servis Filmsetting Ltd, Stockport, Cheshire
Printed and bound in the United States.
Printed on ECF recycled paper containing 30% Post Consumer Waste.

Contents

PART VI COMMITMENT ACROSS CULTURES

PART VII METHODOLOGICAL ISSUES

CONCLUSION

Figures

Tables

Contributors

Albrecht, Simon L., Deakin University, Australia.

Allen, Natalie J., The University of Western Ontario, Canada.

Anderson, Brittney K., The University of Western Ontario, Canada.

Arciniega, Luis M., ITAM School of Business, Mexico City, Mexico.

Barling, Julian, Queen's University, Canada.

Becker, Thomas E., University of South Florida Sarasota–Manatee, USA.

Bentein, Kathleen, University of Quebec at Montreal, Canada.

Bergman, Mindy E., Texas A&M University, USA.

Bobocel, D. Ramona, University of Waterloo, Canada.

Bremner, Nicholas L., The University of Western Ontario, Canada.

Brinsfield, Chad T., University of St Thomas, USA.

Caesens, Gaëtane, Université catholique de Louvain, Belgium.

Chris, Alexandra C., University of Guelph, Canada.

Clark, Laura, University of Houston, USA.

Cohen, Aaron, University of Haifa, Israel.

Datta, Sumita, S.P. Jain Institute of Management and Research, India.

Dhir, Vidyut Lata, S.P. Jain Institute of Management and Research, India.

Dineen, Olivia J., Deakin University, Australia.

Eisenberger, Robert, University of Houston, USA.

Espinoza, Jose A., The University of Western Ontario, Canada.

Felfe, Jörg, Helmut Schmidt University, Germany.

Gagné, Marylène, The University of Western Australia, Australia.

Gallagher, Daniel G., James Madison University, USA.

Gellatly, Ian R., University of Alberta, Canada.

Griep, Yannick, University of Calgary, Canada.

Hamstra, Melvyn R.W., Maastricht University, The Netherlands.

Hansen, Samantha D., University of Toronto, Canada.

Hedberg, Leanne M., University of Alberta, Canada.

Holtom, Brooks C., Georgetown University, USA.

Horsman, Patrick, Saint Mary's University, Canada.

Howard, Joshua, The University of Western Australia, Australia.

Jean, Vanessa A., Texas A&M University, USA.

Jiang, Kaifeng, University of Notre Dame, USA.

Kelloway, E. Kevin, Saint Mary's University, Canada.

Klein, Howard J., The Ohio State University, USA.

Koen, Jessie, University of Amsterdam, The Netherlands.

Laschinger, Heather K., The University of Western Ontario, Canada.

Maltin, Elyse R., JMW Consultants.

Marcus, Bernd, University of Hagen, Germany.

Meyer, John P., The University of Western Ontario, Canada.

Morelli, Neil A., The Cole Group, USA.

Morin, Alexandre J.S., Australian Catholic University, Australia.

Mu, Frank, University of Waterloo, Canada.

Newman, Alex, Deakin University, Australia.

Park, Hee Man, The Ohio State University, USA.

Read, Emily, The University of Western Ontario, Canada.

Roe, Robert A., Maastricht University, The Netherlands.

Solinger, Omar N., VU University Amsterdam, The Netherlands.

Stanley, David J., University of Guelph, Canada.

Stinglhamber, Florence, Université catholique de Louvain, Belgium.

Trivisonno, Melissa, Queen's University, Canada.

Van Dick, Rolf, Goethe University Frankfurt, Germany, and Work Research Institute (AFI), Oslo, Norway.

Van Olffen, Woody, Tilburg University, The Netherlands.

Van Vianen, Annelies E.M., University of Amsterdam, The Netherlands.

Vandenberg, Robert J., The University of Georgia, USA.

Vandenberghe, Christian, HEC Montréal, Canada.

Wang, Dan, Monash University, Australia.

Wasti, S. Arzu, Sabanci University, Turkey.

Wombacher, Jörg, University of Applied Sciences Northwestern Switzerland, Switzerland.

Zhu, Junhong, The University of Western Ontario, Canada.

Preface

Little did I know when I agreed to supervise Natalie Allen's dissertation on commitment more than 30 years ago that the investigative journey would be so long, yet enjoyable, and help to connect me to such a committed international network of scholars. As I contemplated the structure of this book and who I might contact to contribute chapters, I was struck by the breadth of interest in, and applications of, commitment in the fields of organizational psychology, organizational behavior, and management. From its beginnings as an 'attitude' toward one's organization that helped to reduce turnover, it has expanded to other targets, including unions, occupations, supervisors, teams, customers, goals, and change initiatives, to name but a few, and has been linked to a wide variety of important outcomes for both organizations (job performance, successful implementation of change, financial performance) and their employees (health and well-being). It has been incorporated into a broad range of theories including leadership, strategic human resource management, organizational trust and justice, employee engagement, stress and coping, and the like as a key outcome, moderator and/or mediator. It has been studied at multiple levels of analysis – individual, group, unit, and organization – and in numerous countries around the world. It has stimulated numerous debates, including those pertaining to the nature of the construct itself, its distinction from related constructs, its unique contributions to the understanding and prediction of work behavior and organizational effectiveness, and its continued relevance in the ever changing world of work.

My objective in putting this *Handbook* together was to provide readers with a flavor of all of the above. To accommodate as much breadth as possible, I asked authors to write chapters that were much shorter than what they were capable of, and probably would have liked. I also asked them to address their topics in such a way that they would be of interest to both academic and practitioner audiences, and I believe they have been successful in doing so. Consequently, I believe there is something for everyone with an interest in commitment in this *Handbook*. For those who are new to the field, there is both history (for context) and up-to-date reviews of the latest developments in theory and research. For those looking for research ideas, the experts in the field outline what they consider to be the biggest gaps in our understanding of commitment and describe the latest tools at our disposal for addressing those gaps. For practitioners interested in understanding the 'business case' for investments in commitment and/or looking for guidance in developing an evidence-based approach to fostering commitment, there are sections devoted to both the outcomes and drivers of commitment. Finally, for those curious about how well the theory holds, and/or the practical implications generalize, outside North America, there is a section focused specifically on the implications of culture on commitment.

There are many people I want to thank for their help in making this *Handbook* a reality. First and foremost, I want to thank the authors who agreed to contribute chapters to this volume, and continued to participate even after I informed them that they would need to convey their wealth of knowledge in approximately 7000 words. I also want to thank the broader community of commitment scholars who contributed indirectly to the content of this book, with special thanks to my graduate students and collaborators over the years; it was the stimulating and enjoyable interactions with you that kept things fresh and helped to sustain my attention for such a lengthy period of time. Finally, I want to extend my thanks to Edward Elgar Publishing for the invitation to edit this *Handbook*, and in particular to Francine O'Sullivan, Amber Watts, and Chloe Mitchell who were the faces of Edward Elgar Publishing for me and so ably guided me through the production process.

John P. Meyer

28 April 2016

INTRODUCTION

1. Employee commitment: an introduction and roadmap
John P. Meyer

Commitments are important. To wit, when politicians want to convince voters that they are serious about an issue, they make commitments. Similarly, businesses pledge their commitment to whatever quality they believe is important to customers in order to sell their products or services. And of course, couples make commitments to one another through the bonds of matrimony, often accompanied by elaborate celebrations by friends and family. As further testament to their importance, commitments can be frightening and sometimes politicians, businesses, and couples are reluctant to make them. Why do we seek, celebrate, and resist commitments? It is because commitments convey a sense of permanence. We want others to make commitments because it implies that they will persist in a course of action that will serve to benefit us in the future. We are reluctant to make commitments when we have reservations about whether we want to maintain a relationship or persist in a course of action in an uncertain future. Of course commitments can be broken and are sometimes made without a true intention to follow through. However, there is a stigma attached to breaking commitments, and lack of sincerity in making commitment breeds cynicism. This would not be the case if commitments were not important.

This book is about employee commitment, and the wealth of theory and research described in its pages attest to the fact that it too is important. The commitment of employees is only one aspect of workplace commitments more generally. Employers also make commitments to their employees, unions, customers, shareholders, regulatory bodies, and the like, and these commitments are also important. However, the vast majority of theory and research has focused on employee commitments, beginning initially with commitment to their organizations but extending to other entities (for example, occupation, union, team, supervisor, customer) or courses of action (for example, goals, decisions, policies, programs, change initiatives). Therefore, this book focuses on employee commitments and their implications for the targets of these commitments and the employees who make them.

Interest in employee commitment to organizations (that is, organizational commitment) began in earnest in North America, particularly the United States, in the 1960s and 1970s, although its roots can be traced back even further. This interest continues today, but the 1980s saw a branching of theory and research to include other targets of commitment. In the 1990s studies conducted in other parts of the world began to appear more regularly in the literature, and this trend burgeoned in the new millennium and shows no sign of waning. I will refrain from providing a more detailed historical review here because these are available elsewhere (e.g., Klein et al., 2009; Meyer et al., 2008; Mowday et al., 1982), including in Chapters 2, 3, and 4 in Part I of the current volume. Instead, I will focus on a few key issues that served as the impetus for this book and provide a roadmap to the content herein.

THE CONCEPTUALIZATION OF COMMITMENT

Despite its importance in our everyday lives, few of us stop to ask what 'commitment' really means. I would hazard a guess that most organizational leaders, despite agreeing that they would like a committed workforce, have also rarely given serious thought to its definition. That is the job of academics, and many of us have been at it for a long time. Hence one might expect that there is a consensus on the definition and measurement of commitment. Not so! From the beginning, commitment has been examined from different disciplinary perspectives, using different methodologies and analytical procedures, and with different objectives. This continues to be the case today. Although some might argue that this failure to reach consensus reflects a lack of progress, I think the contents of this book belie that perspective. Indeed, we have learned a lot about commitment over the last 50-plus years that can and should be used to guide practice, despite academic disagreements. However, the disagreements themselves suggest that we still have much to learn, and should serve to fuel future investigation.

The authors of Part I of this *Handbook*, 'Conceptualization of Commitment', are thought leaders and have been actively involved in theory development and research for many years. Each has had a major impact on the field, both directly and indirectly through the large bodies of research they have stimulated. However, there are some fundamental differences in the approaches they have taken to the study of employee commitment. This is most evident in the divergence of opinion on the dimensionality of commitment, with Howard Klein and his student Hee Man Park arguing the case for unidimensionality in Chapter 2, and Natalie Allen stating the case for a multidimensional perspective in Chapter 3. Both chapters trace the historical roots of the differing perspectives, describe how it has guided research, and discuss its practical implications. Thomas Becker (Chapter 4) takes the less controversial perspective that employees can be committed to various work-relevant entities and/or courses of action. Although not contentious itself, the potential for multiple commitments raises questions about compatibility and conflict as well as the relative importance of these commitments as predictors of important outcomes. Addressing these questions requires a decision about how commitment should be conceptualized and measured, and the dimensionality issue again becomes front and center. The discussion of commitment in the remaining chapters of this book reflects how the issues of dimensionality and focus have been addressed by researchers as they investigate various substantive issues, including the development and consequences of commitment and the generalizability of theory and research findings across cultures. In the concluding chapter, I return to this issue, not with the objective of resolution, but to suggest how the energy generated by the debate might serve to guide future research.

RELATED CONSTRUCTS

Another challenge for both academics and practitioners is distinguishing commitment from related constructs (for example, motivation, engagement, embededdness, identification, and psychological contracts). What makes these constructs 'related', and why might they be considered a 'challenge' to those with an interest in commitment? I will have more to say on this issue in the concluding chapter, but the short answer for now is that they all relate to – and arguably influence – the same outcomes, including retention, attendance, job performance, citizenship behavior, counterproductive behavior, and/or well-being. The potential for construct redundancy is probably of greater concern for academics than it is for practitioners or their client organizations, but even the latter might find the terminology confusing, and this is arguably not conducive to the promotion of an evidence-based approach to management.

The authors of Part II, 'Related Constructs', have all been actively involved in theory development and research pertaining to these constructs and are well positioned to discuss the similarities to, differences from, and relations with commitment. Theory and research pertaining to work motivation has a longer history than commitment and it is legitimate to question whether there is really a difference between a committed and a motivated workforce. In Chapter 5, Gagné and Howard compare the two constructs from a self-determination theory (SDT) perspective and, although they distinguish the constructs primarily on the basis of focus (task versus organization), they also explain how key concepts within SDT (for example, need satisfaction) can be used to explain the motivating properties of commitments. Albrecht and Dineen discuss the similarities and differences between employee commitment and engagement in Chapter 6. Of the related constructs discussed in Part II, engagement is arguably the most controversial among commitment theorists. Purportedly introduced and popularized by human resources consulting firms (Macey and Schneider, 2008), some academics question whether it is simply 'old wine in new bottles', whereas others have embraced it and initiated elaborate programs of research designed, among other things, to demonstrate its unique contribution to understanding, predicting, and enhancing important organization- and employee-relevant outcomes.

In Chapter 7, Holtom describes theory and research pertaining to job embeddedness. Although introduced relatively recently in an effort to explain why employees stay with an organization, like commitment, job embeddedness also has implications for what employees do while on the job (for example, performance, citizenship behavior) as well as why they leave. The same is true of organizational identification, as discussed by Van Dick in Chapter 8, and psychological contracts, as discussed by Hansen and Griep in Chapter 9. Although there might be less concern in the latter cases with construct redundancy per se, there is some uncertainty about the nature and direction of their relations with commitment. The authors describe some interesting new developments in research pertaining to these constructs that have implications for their links to commitment. They also describe new and interesting research strategies that might be adapted in future commitment research (for example, use of manipulations to increase the salience of identities, or contract-relevant inducements that could have a bearing on the nature and/or focus of employees' commitments).

MULTIPLE FOCI OF COMMITMENT

Although commitment to the organization (that is, the employer) has been, and continues to be, the primary focus of research, it has long been recognized that employees can, and do, develop commitments to many different constituencies within the organization (for example, unit, supervisor, team) or outside it (occupation, union, clientele) (Becker, 1992;

Morrow, 1983: Reichers, 1985; for more detail, see Chapter 4, this volume). These constituencies are typically individuals or groups with whom the employee interacts or belongs, but employees can also commit to a particular course of action (Becker, 1960; Kiesler, 1971; Salancik, 1977), or a proximal impetus to that action (for example, goal, decision, project, program, change initiative; see Neubert and Wu, 2009). Such commitments are of interest in their own right because of their implications for the relevant target (for example, participation in union activities; occupational retention and involvement; goal attainment; change effectiveness), but are often studied because of their implications for organizations. Acknowledging the multiple targets of commitment raises questions concerning the potential for conflict, compatibility, or synergy. Therefore, understanding the conditions that contribute to these different possibilities is of considerable importance for organizations and their employees. Organizations will want to minimize potential conflicts (for example, with unions or professions) and, where possible, strive for compatibility or synergy. In this era of instability and change, some organizations may find it difficult to establish long-term commitments with their employees and may seek substitutes such as commitment to supervisors, teams, or goals as a way of aligning employees' interests with their own (Meyer, 2009). Likewise, employees should benefit from alignment of goals and values among the targets of their commitment. Finally, as more research is conducted outside North America, and Western countries more generally, it is becoming apparent that cultural values and traditions can have an influence on the relative importance of commitment to targets within the organization (for example, supervisor, team) or outside it (for example, family, personal career). Therefore, understanding the foci of commitments, their interactions, and their influences is of importance to organizations operating internationally and/or with culturally diverse workforces.

The authors of Part III, 'Foci of Commitment', review theory and research pertaining to targets of commitment other than the organization. In Chapter 10, Meyer and Espinoza discuss commitment to one's occupation, or 'line of work', including both professional and non-professional occupations, and in Chapter 11, Vandenberghe examines social commitments to targets including supervisors, teams, and customers. In Chapter 12, Horsman, Gallagher, and Kelloway trace the history of theory and research pertaining to union commitment. The targets of commitment discussed in these chapters are all 'entities' with varying connections to the organization. Some (for example, supervisors and teams) are nested within the organization whereas others (for example, occupation, union, and customers) are external, but all are somewhat interrelated and create the potential for conflict, compatibility, or synergy with commitment to the organization. Finally, in Chapter 13, Meyer and Anderson review theory and research pertaining to action commitments; that is, commitment to a specific course of action, or to initiatives (for example, goals, policies, changes) that serve as the impetus to action. Although action commitments have generally received less attention than organizational, occupational, and social commitments, Meyer and Anderson argue that managing these commitments effectively might be particularly important under turbulent conditions that preclude the establishment of long-term relationships with an organization or social foci embedded within the organization. Although commitments to non-work foci (for example, family) are not specifically addressed in this section, they are discussed in several of the chapters in the section in Part VI on 'Commitment across Cultures'.

CONSEQUENCES OF COMMITMENT

As noted above, commitments are important because they have implications for behavior. Interest in organizational commitment was arguably stimulated by its implications for retention (Mowday et al., 1982): employees who are committed to the organization should be less likely to leave voluntarily. Of course, keeping employees is not sufficient for organizations to be effective. Those employees must also attend regularly, perform their tasks effectively, contribute to a positive social milieu, and avoid engaging in behaviors that are counterproductive. Therefore, commitment theory and research gradually evolved to place more emphasis on on-the-job behavior and performance. Indeed, the impetus for the development of some of the multidimensional models discussed by Allen (Chapter 3 in this volume) was the notion that, regardless of how it is conceptualized, commitment to the organization should reduce turnover, but the implications for on-the-job behavior will vary depending on how it is experienced. Even more recently, researchers have begun to consider the implications of commitment, and its different forms and foci, for employees' own well-being (Meyer and Maltin, 2010).

Because the consequences of employee commitment are so central to interest in the construct itself, they are discussed to some extent in most of the chapters in this *Handbook*. However, the authors in Part IV, 'Consequences of Commitment', focus specifically on theory and research pertaining to the implications of commitments for the targets and the employees who make them. In Chapter 14, Gellatly and Hedberg focus on implications for employee withdrawal in the forms of turnover and absenteeism. As noted above, turnover has long been a focus of commitment researchers, but attendance is also important for organizations to achieve the full benefit of employment. In Chapter 15, Stanley and Meyer review the findings pertaining to two well-established forms of performance: task performance and organizational citizenship behavior. They also address the question of whether the nature of the commitment matters with regard to its implications for performance. In Chapter 16, Marcus looks at the flip-side of performance, namely counterproductive work behavior. Although of more recent interest, the implications of commitment, and the way it is experienced, on behaviors that are harmful to organizations and/or their employees is no less important. In the final two chapters in this section, the authors focus more on outcomes of relevance to employees themselves. In Chapter 17, Chris, Maltin, and Meyer consider implications for employees' physical and psychological well-being. In Chapter 18, Klein and Brinsfield address the role(s) that affect plays in the commitment process. They illustrate how employees' affective experiences can be impacted by their commitment, but acknowledge that they are probably implicated more broadly in the commitment process. The authors argue that affect has not received sufficient attention to date in commitment theory and research, and make important recommendations for how this situation might be rectified.

DRIVERS OF COMMITMENT

If commitment is important, then it is natural for scientists and practitioners to want to know how it develops. This is a tall order because there are arguably many factors that can contribute to the development of commitment. Despite the attention it has been given, early research conducted in the search for 'antecedents' was largely unsystematic and therefore uninformative. Indeed, Reichers (1985) referred to the variables included in early studies as a 'laundry list', and this was also apparent in early meta-analytic reviews (e.g., Mathieu and Zajac, 1990). A practitioner surveying this literature for clues as to how to foster stronger commitment would be hard-pressed to find anything meaningful. Fortunately, that situation has changed as theory and research have become more systematic and focused around basic principles that are arguably more generalizable and useful in guiding intervention strategies.

The chapters in Part V, 'Drivers of Commitment', are structured around broad themes or categories with inherent underlying principles. In Chapter 19, Bergman and Jean focus on the role(s) that individual differences can play in the development of commitment. It is perhaps not surprising that much of Bergman and Jean's discussion of individual differences focuses on how they interact with situational factors to influence commitment. Van Vianen, Hamstra, and Koen pick up on this theme in Chapter 20 and elaborate on the importance of person–environment (P–E) fit in its many forms (for example, person–job, person–organization, person–supervisor, person–team). The message in both of these chapters is that practitioners need to attend to both selection and work conditions, and to achieving a good match between the two. The remaining chapters in Part V focus more specifically on the work context. In Chapter 21, Jiang reviews theory and research pertaining to strategic human resource management (SHRM) practices, and more specifically on the implications of high-performance work systems (HPWSs) on commitment. Interestingly, much of the research in this tradition is conducted at an organizational level of analysis and makes a strong case for commitment as a mediator between HPWSs and various indices of organizational effectiveness. In Chapter 22, Trivisonno and Barling address the important role that leadership at various levels throughout the organization plays in shaping commitment. Among the many ways that leaders can foster commitment is by empowering employees, a practice addressed in more detail by Laschinger, Read, and Zhu in Chapter 23. In Chapter 24, Stinglhamber, Caesens, Clark, and Eisenberger discuss what has arguably been identified as one of the most important drivers of employee commitment, namely perceived organizational support (POS). Stinglhamber et al. note that organizational support is analogous to the commitment of the organization to its employees and that the strong relation between POS and employee commitment reflects the importance of social exchange and reciprocity. Importantly, they argue that supervisors can also contribute to the development of commitment, both directly through their own supportive behavior (perceived supervisor support), and indirectly by helping to foster POS. Finally, in Chapter 25, Bobocel and Mu explain the important role that justice perceptions have on the development and maintenance of employee commitment. Their treatment of justice provides an excellent example of how a set of principles firmly established in one domain (organizational justice) can help to inform another (organizational commitment). That is, having established a strong relation between fair treatment and commitment, practitioners can draw upon an extensive body of justice theory and research to guide the design and implementation of HRM systems.

COMMITMENT ACROSS CULTURES

Most theory and the bulk of research on employee commitment originated in North America (the United States and Canada). Not surprisingly, the earliest expansion was to other Western countries. However, since the turn of the millennium, the picture has changed and published research is now coming regularly from other parts of the world. Admittedly, there is still far less research being conducted in non-Western than in Western countries, and there are large parts of the world for which there is still very little published research. Moreover, the research that does exist has largely been guided by Western theory; there is little in the way of new commitment theory being generated outside of the West (at least, theory that is easily accessible to those in the West who might be interested in new perspectives). Consequently, the authors in Part VI of this *Handbook*, 'Commitment across Cultures', were invited to write chapters with three objectives in mind. One was to provide a summary or representative sample of the commitment research conducted in a particular region of the world. Admittedly, this was a very challenging task because the regions selected were very large. A second objective was to identify ways that the culture(s) within these regions differ from the culture(s) in North America and might have a bearing on the nature, development or consequences of employee commitment. This task was also very challenging because, like North America, each region can be meaningfully divided into sub-regions with their own cultures, and even within these sub-regions there may be culture differences associated with language, ethnic origin, religion, economic conditions, climate, geography, and so on. The final objective was to identify gaps in existing theory and research that might be addressed in future research.

Wasti opens Part VI with Chapter 26 on the state of cross-cultural commitment research, and an astute analysis of the issues and challenges confronting researchers interested in examining commitment across countries and cultures. In Chapter 27, Felfe and Wombacher take on the challenging task of reviewing the commitment literature in Europe. As noted above, the challenge here is in synthesizing research coming from many different European countries with their multiple languages, histories, political systems, economies, and cultures. The task was perhaps facilitated to some degree by the fact that European researchers are well versed in the commitment literature and adept at conducting research. They also publish in journals that are easily accessible, many in English. In contrast, Newman and Wang (Chapter 28) and Dhir, Bremner and Datta (Chapter 29) not only took on the two most populous nations in the world – China and India, respectively – but also were confronted with situations where the amount of readily accessible published research is limited, there are multiple regions with different subcultures, and there are strong pressures for cultural change. In Chapter 30, Cohen faced similar obstacles in reviewing the literature in the Middle East; a region that is currently in turmoil and the focus of little published research. Most of the available research including Arab samples was conducted with Israeli Arabs who work under conditions that are quite unique in several respects. Finally, in Chapter 31, Arciniega provides a sampling of studies conducted in various countries within the large Latin American region. Although these countries differ in many ways, Arciniega points to some commonalities in cultural values, most notably high power distance and collectivism (Hofstede et al., 2010), and addresses the question of whether these differences from North American (that is, United

States and Canadian) culture are reflected in the strength and nature of commitment as well as the effectiveness of HRM practices imported from North America.

METHODOLOGICAL ISSUES IN COMMITMENT RESEARCH

It is not uncommon for the complexities of the theories we develop, and the research questions we ask, to exceed the capacity of the methodological and analytic tools we have available to address them. This has certainly been the case with commitment theory and research. Fortunately, there are methodologists and statisticians who make it their business to develop new and better research tools. Importantly, there are others who bridge the two worlds and are able to apply the latest developments in methodology and analysis to address important substantive issues, and to share their expertise with others. The authors of Part VII of this *Handbook* are such individuals.

In Chapter 32, Vandenberg and Morelli provide a critique and update of Vandenberg and Lance's (2000) earlier recommendations for assessing measurement invariance across groups and/or over time. This is an important issue because many of the recommendations for future research offered throughout this *Handbook* involve the use of multi-wave longitudinal research intended to address causal relations proposed, but too seldom tested, within commitment theory. Other recommendations require the comparison of different groups (for example, cultural) with regard to the strength, development, or consequences of commitment. Providing meaningful answers to questions about changes over time or differences across groups requires some assurance that the instruments being used are measuring the same constructs in the same ways (that is, are invariant) over time and group.

Many of the most interesting questions we ask about employee commitment have to do with its development and consequences. Both imply causality, but very rarely do we, or are we able to, use the powerful experimental designs required to test causal hypotheses. More often than not we use non-experimental methods to detect covariation, one of the minimal requirements for causal inference. Occasionally we use longitudinal designs that allow for detection of covariation over time and partial control of extraneous variables. Fortunately, there have been a number of new developments in analytic procedures that can get us even closer to understanding how and why commitment develops and exerts its influence on behavior and well-being. In Chapter 33, Bentein describes how latent growth modeling (LGM) analyses can be applied to multi-wave longitudinal data to test a variety of the hypotheses implicit in our theories of commitment (for example, expectations prior to entry will influence the initial level of commitment that new employees experience, as well as the trajectory of change in their commitment over time; changes in commitment over time will be associated with changes in thoughts of quitting, and these changes, and perhaps the rate of change, will predict actual turnover).

In Chapter 34, van Olffen, Solinger, and Roe call for an even greater emphasis on time in the investigation of commitment. More specifically, they suggest how recent developments in temporal process research might be applied in the study of commitment. Further, they explain how taking a temporal process 'mindset' can have wide-ranging implications for commitment research, beginning with the conceptualization and measurement of the construct through to strategies for data collection and analysis. Although the approach is still very new and involves procedures that are likely to be somewhat controversial, it is a good illustration how new developments in methodology not only allow us to conduct better tests of existing theory, but can also challenge the status quo and stimulate us to think about the same phenomena from different perspectives.

Finally, early theories pertaining to multiple forms (for example, mindsets) and/or foci of commitment often included hypotheses concerning how these forms and foci might combine to influence behavior or other outcomes of interest. In the absence of analytic techniques well suited to testing these hypotheses, researchers often focus on the individual components (for example, mindsets or foci), or use analytic tools (for example, moderated multiple regression, median-split profile comparisons) that get closer to addressing the research question but have important limitations. In Chapter 35, Morin discusses new developments in person-centered research strategies that can be used to identify the different ways that commitment mindsets and/or foci combine to form profiles and interact to influence important outcomes. Like the temporal process approach discussed by van Olffen et al. in Chapter 34, taking a person-centered approach requires a different 'mindset' (Zyphur, 2009), but opens up a wide range of new research opportunities.

All of the analytic strategies described in Part VII are complex, but the authors provide clear descriptions of the underlying rationale and objectives, provide illustrative examples, and direct the reader to other sources for more details on the procedures required to use them. In short, they provide an excellent complement to the many useful recommendations for research offered throughout this book.

A GUIDE FOR READERS

Each of the chapters in this *Handbook* stands alone in providing a good overview of what we know about specific issues pertaining to employee commitment. However, the reader might find it helpful to consult the chapters in Part I on the conceptualization of commitment for the historical context surrounding these issues. Most authors also discuss how what we currently know can be used as a guide to practice, but also point to the gaps in our knowledge and identify important questions to be addressed in future research. The authors in Part VII describe some of the latest developments in methodology and analyses that can be used to address these questions. So I hope there will be something in the pages of this *Handbook* for all readers with an interest in the important topic of employee commitment, whether it is to get an up-to-date overview of theory and research, ideas for future research, or suggestions for building a more committed workforce. I will offer my attempt at a synthesis on all three counts in the concluding chapter.

REFERENCES

Becker, H.S. (1960). Notes on the concept of commitment. *American Journal of Sociology*, 66(1), 32–40.
Becker, T.E. (1992). Foci and bases of commitment: Are they distinctions worth making? *Academy of Management Journal*, 35(1), 232–244.
Hofstede, G., Hofstede, G.J. and Minkov, M. (2010). *Cultures and Organizations: Software of the Mind* (3rd edition). New York: McGraw-Hill.

Kiesler, C. (1971). *The Psychology of Commitment*. New York: Academic Press.

Klein, H.J., Molloy, J.C. and Cooper, J.T. (2009). Conceptual foundations: Construct definitions and theoretical representations of workplace commitments. In H.J. Klein, T.E. Becker and J.P. Meyer (eds), *Commitment in Organizations: Accumulated Wisdom and New Directions* (3–36). New York: Routledge/Taylor & Francis.

Macey, W.H. and Schneider, B. (2008). The meaning of employee engagement. *Industrial and Organizational Psychology: Perspectives on Science and Practice*, *1*, 3–30.

Mathieu, J.E. and Zajac, D.M. (1990). A review and meta-analysis of the antecedents, correlates, and consequences of organizational commitment. *Psychological Bulletin*, *108*, 171–194.

Meyer, J.P. (2009). Commitment in a changing world of work. In H.J. Klein, T.E. Becker and J.P. Meyer (eds), *Commitment in Organizations: Accumulated Wisdom and New Directions* (37–68). Florence, KY: Routledge/Taylor & Francis Group.

Meyer, J.P. and Maltin, E.R. (2010). Employee commitment and well-being: A critical review, theoretical framework and research agenda. *Journal of Vocational Behavior*, *77*(2), 323–337.

Meyer, J.P., Jackson, T.A. and Maltin, E.R. (2008). Commitment in the workplace: Past, present, and future. In C.L. Cooper and J. Barling (eds), *Handbook of Organizational Behavior* (Vol. 1, 35–53). Thousand Oaks, CA: Sage Publications.

Morrow, P.C. (1983). Concept redundancy in organizational research: The case of work commitment. *Academy of Management Review*, *8*, 486–500.

Mowday, R.T., Porter, L.W. and Steers, R. (1982) *Organizational Linkages: The Psychology of Commitment, Absenteeism, and Turnover*. San Diego, CA: Academic Press.

Neubert, M.J. and Wu, C. (2009). Action commitments. In H.J. Klein, T.E. Becker and J.P. Meyer (eds), *Commitment in Organizations: Accumulated Wisdom and New Directions* (179–213). New York: Routledge/Taylor & Francis Group.

Reichers, A.E. (1985). A review and reconceptualization of organizational commitment, *Academy of Management Review*, *10*, 465–476.

Salancik, G. (1977). Commitment and the control of organizational behavior and belief. In B. Staw and G. Salancik (eds), *New Directions in Organizational Behavior* (1–54). Chicago, IL: St Clair.

Vandenberg, R.J. and Lance, C.E. (2000). A review and synthesis of the measurement invariance literature: Suggestions, practices and recommendations for organizational research. *Organizational Research Methods*, *3*, 4–70.

Zyphur, M. (2009). When mindsets collide: Switching analytical mindsets to advance organizational science. *Academy of Management Review*, *34*, 677–688.

PART I

CONCEPTUALIZATION OF COMMITMENT

2. Commitment as a unidimensional construct
Howard J. Klein and Hee Man Park

Commitment has a rich and long multidisciplinary history and has been examined from a variety of perspectives (for example, economic, behavioral, psychological) and conceptualized in a variety of ways. This chapter presents the case for viewing commitment as a unidimensional construct.

HISTORICAL BASIS FOR A UNIDIMENSIONAL CONSTRUCT

We begin by providing a historical basis for viewing commitment as a unidimensional construct. We do so because seeing where and why single versus multiple dimensions have been used in the past is helpful in understanding what may be most useful in the future. We discuss various commitment conceptualizations in chronological order and then present most recent models of uni- and multidimensional commitment conceptualization.

Early Commitment Conceptualizations

In early commitment research, as noted by Becker (1960), the construct was rarely defined. Yet in reading these earliest works, which focused on understanding loyalty and collective action (e.g., Roethlisberger and Dickson, 1939), commitment was implicitly discussed as a singular construct. The 1960s saw the emergence of the behavioral perspective on commitment. Again here, dimensionality was not explicitly addressed, but the construct was generally discussed as being singular, largely focusing on employee loyalty to employers. From the behavioral perspective, commitment is the propensity to engage in consistent lines of activity (e.g., Becker, 1960; Kiesler, 1971). Specifically, side-bets and prior choices bind the individual to future actions consistent with those prior choices. Early multidimensional views appeared around the same time, including Gouldner's (1960) distinction between cosmopolitan integration and organizational introjection, based on different commitment targets, and Etzioni's (1961) typology of involvement based upon use of power and organizational control. The final example here is Kanter's (1968) model of control, continuance, and cohesive commitment. Although Kanter described three distinct types of commitment, it should be noted that she also defined commitment singularly as 'the willingness of social actors to give their energy and loyalty to social systems' (p. 499).

The 1970s saw a continuation of the unidimensional behavioral perspective (e.g., Salancik, 1977). At this time the attitudinal view of commitment emerged and rose to prominence (e.g., Porter et al., 1974). Porter et al. defined commitment as identification with and involvement in a particular organization and further asserted that commitment is characterized by three factors: belief in and acceptance of goals and values; willingness to exert effort; and strong desire to maintain membership. Although described using multiple terms and indicators, this view presented commitment as unidimensional.

Furthermore, the measure based on this perspective, the Organizational Commitment Questionnaire (Mowday et al., 1979) was designed to be unidimensional. During this time, additional multidimensional models were also put forth, for example Buchanan's (1974) model of identification, involvement, and loyalty as components of commitment.

Even though commitment to the employing organization dominated the early study of commitment in work contexts, as indicated by most of the above research, it has long (e.g., Simon et al., 1950) been recognized that individuals have multiple commitment targets in the workplace (for example, supervisor, team, organization). Research on some of the other workplace commitment targets developed largely independently from research on organizational commitment. Examples here include escalation of commitment in the decision-making literature (e.g., Staw, 1981), goal commitment in the motivation literature (e.g., Locke, 1968), and occupational commitment in the career literature (e.g., Hall, 1971). In all these cases, a unidimensional conceptualization is the norm. The exception here is union commitment, which is widely examined as multidimensional (e.g., Gordon et al., 1980). For other workplace targets, conceptualizations were largely adapted from the work on organizational commitment. For these targets, some have largely been unidimensional (for example, team and career commitment; Bishop and Scott, 2000; Blau, 1985), others multidimensional (for example, supervisor commitment; Becker, 1992), and still others both, depending on the author (for example, commitment to change efforts; Herscovitch and Meyer, 2002; Neubert and Cady, 2001).

In the mid-1980s commitments to multiple targets were rediscovered as a research focus. Some conceptualizations proposed commitment as multidimensional based on different commitment targets (e.g., Reichers, 1985), or a combination of bases and targets (e.g., Becker, 1992; Morrow, 1983). Empirical efforts exploring the dimensionality of commitment across targets often find more than one dimension, but such research has not yielded a consistent structure across targets (for example, supervisor commitment sometimes loads as a separate factor from organizational commitment, sometimes it does not; Redman and Snape, 2005), or evidence of a hierarchical structure (for example, organizational commitment has not consistently been found to be a higher order-factor with commitments to more specific workplace targets such as supervisor or team, being lower-order factors; Becker et al., 1996). Thus, multidimensional frameworks have and continue to largely reflect multiple bases for, rather than targets of, commitment.

Recent Multidimensional Models

More recent multidimensional frameworks include the taxonomy offered by O'Reilly and Chatman (1986), which proposed compliance, identification, and internalization as three forms of psychological attachment underlying commitment and the three-component model (TCM) introduced by Meyer and Allen (1991). The TCM model (presented and discussed in Chapter 3, this volume), holds that commitment is experienced as one or more of three commitment mindsets (affective, normative, and continuance), each resulting from different bases of commitment. It is worth noting that, parallel to Kanter (1968), the TCM model holds that commitment is experienced as multidimensional mindsets, but the core essence of commitment is unidimensional, defined most recently as 'an internal force that binds an individual to a target (social or nonsocial) and/or to a course of action of relevance to that target' (Meyer, 2009, p. 39). Other more recent multidimensional models include that of Cohen (2007), who specified two bases of organizational commitment (that is, instrumental or psychological attachment) that can occur pre- or post-entry.

The Klein, Molloy, and Brinsfield Unidimensional Model

The most recent unidimensional perspective is that proposed by Klein, Molloy and Brinsfield. Klein et al. (2012) redefined commitment based on three primary objectives: (1) conceptualizing commitment as a unique type of psychological attachment or bond to highlight the distinctiveness of the commitment construct; (2) doing so in a manner applicable to all commitment targets; and (3) drawing the construct boundaries narrowly to exclude perceived confounds in prior definitions. Based on their analysis, Klein et al. (2012) concluded that commitment is 'a volitional psychological bond reflecting dedication to and responsibility for a particular target' (p. 137). Defining commitment as a particular type of bond is not just relabeling or excluding some of the TCM mindsets. The Klein et al. definition is distinct from the TCM core essence of commitment in three ways. First, commitment is defined as a type of bond rather than as a binding force (see Klein et al., 2009 for more on this distinction). Second, commitment is defined as a particular bond type, eliminating the need for ancillary mindsets. Finally, there is no reference to 'a course of action'. This unidimensional definition is also distinct from each of the TCM mindsets as discussed by Klein et al. (2012).

The Klein et al. (2012) model, shown in Figure 2.1, proposes two proximal outcomes (continuation and motivation), with action and the results of those actions (for example, performance) being more distal outcomes. In short, committed individuals are less likely

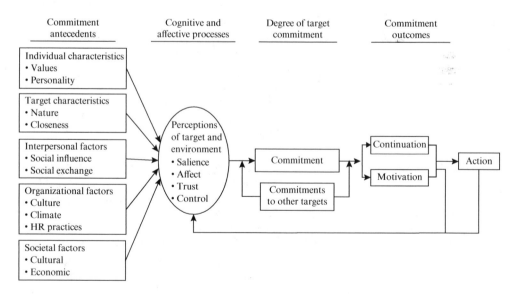

Source: Reprinted from H.J. Klein, Molloy, J.C. and Brinsfield, C.T. (2012). Reconceptualizing workplace commitment to redress a stretched construct: Revisiting assumptions and removing confounds. *Academy of Management Review*, 37(1), 139. Copyright (2012), with permission from Academy of Management.

Figure 2.1   Klein et al. (2012) process model of commitment to any workplace target

to withdraw from the target of that commitment. In terms of motivation, high commitment results in individuals allocating more effort and resources in support of the target, and being more willing to make trade-offs in favor of the target when allocating constrained resources such as time and attention (Klein et al., 2012). In terms of antecedents, the Klein et al. model suggests that four perceptual evaluations (that is, salience, positive affect, trust, and perceived control) are the immediate determinants of commitment. A wide range of more distal antecedents, organized by level (for example, individual, target, interpersonal, organizational level), influence the development of commitment through the four proximal states (Klein et al., 2012).

To summarize this historical review, prior commitment conceptualizations include both uni- and multidimensional perspectives, with both represented with the employing organization as the target, and the unidimensional perspective being more prevalent for other targets. For the remainder of the chapter, in contrasting uni- versus multidimensional conceptualizations, we focus on the Klein et al. (2012) and TCM models and the recommended measures corresponding to each (Klein et al., 2014; Meyer et al., 1993). The next section provides a conceptual basis for comparing these two commitment models by discussing the nature of construct definitions.

CONSTRUCT DIMENSIONALITY

Whether a construct is uni- or multidimensional is a theoretical issue, because the dimensionality of a construct is based on theory and specified in the construct definition. Related to dimensionality is the issue of how coarse- versus fine-grained a construct is defined. A fine-grained definition is not necessarily superior to a coarse one, nor is a unidimensional conceptualization of a construct necessarily better than a multidimensional one (Bagozzi and Edwards, 1998). Problems arise, however, when: (1) ambiguity exists regarding the boundaries and structure of a construct (Molloy and Ployhart, 2012); (2) those boundaries partly or wholly incorporate other constructs thought to be antecedents and/or outcomes of the focal construct creating contamination and overestimating true relationships (Jaros, 2009); and/or (3) the construct is defined so broadly that the concept becomes 'stretched' beyond usefulness for scientific or practical purposes (Osigweh, 1989).

In comparing the TCM and Klein et al. construct definitions, one is not necessarily more complex than the other, and the person-centered approach (see Chapter 35, this volume) can be used with either, as the unidimensional conceptualization can be examined across multiple commitment targets or with other types of bonds. Rather, the main differences between the two definitions are narrowness and specificity. In terms of narrowness, Klein et al. (2012) took a selective approach, defining commitment as a particular type of bond whereas the TCM was designed to be inclusive, integrating prior conceptualizations of commitment. To account for the variation in the way different types of attachment are experienced, the concept of mindsets was used. In more narrowly defining commitment as a particular type of bond, the Klein et al. (2012) perspective eliminates the need for the ancillary mindsets.

Klein et al. (2012) essentially argue that the commitment literature has lumped bond types together under the label of commitment when they should be split; and split targets when they should have been lumped. Lumping and splitting each have a role to play in scientific advancement, but both can also be dysfunctional (Klein and Delery, 2012). Lumping is warranted when existing constructs are redundant or when a combination of constructs results in something unique from its parts or from anything else in the literature. Otherwise, lumping creates a 'jingle fallacy' (using the same term to represent quite distinct phenomena; Block, 1957), in this case using the term commitment to represent multiple types of psychological bonds. Even though different modifiers are used for the different TCM mindsets, there is a jingle fallacy if they should not all be considered commitment. Splitting is appropriate when meaningful conceptual and verifiable distinctions can be made (Tepper and Henle, 2011). If such distinctions cannot be made, splitting unnecessarily creates a 'jangle fallacy' (using different terms to refer to the same thing; Block, 1957). Jangle fallacies are problematic because they inhibit scientific progress by introducing confusion, violating the law of parsimony, impeding theory-building, and making the literature difficult to integrate or summarize (Cole et al., 2012).

In terms of specificity, Klein et al. (2012) devote considerable attention to fully articulating a complete conceptual definition of commitment. For the TCM, although subsequent writings and revisions have provided some additional clarity, ambiguities remain about the exact nature and structure of the construct definition (Jaros, 1997). Conceptual definitions for multidimensional constructs need to clearly and precisely define each dimension as well as the overall structure of the construct. That is, the case needs to be made for structural validity, the extent to which a set of variables fit together as indicators of a single higher-order multidimensional construct (Johnson et al., 2012). In addition, that definition should specify the nature of the relationship between the higher-order construct and the dimensions of the construct. That is, whether the overall essence of commitment is an aggregate versus superordinate construct (sometimes termed formative versus reflective) relative to the commitment mindsets. Finally, conceptual definitions for multidimensional constructs require precise inclusion criteria so it is clear: (1) what should be included and excluded from those dimensions; and (2) how to model the higher-order construct (Johnson et al., 2012).

Construct validation can demonstrate that the conceptual space and dimensionality of a measure is consistent with the conceptual definition that measure is intended to capture. There is not, however, an empirical test for evaluating whether a conceptual definition is appropriate, or whether one conceptual definition is better than another. The accumulated empirical evidence can only point to one theory, and hence the conceptual definition that is part of the theory, being more defensible or useful than another. That is, the field, through the wisdom of the crowd in terms of usage, accumulated empirical support, and citations ultimately determines what conceptual definitions and accompanying measures are most valuable. We next make the conceptual and empirical case for using a unidimensional conceptualization.

CONCEPTUAL BASIS FOR A UNIDIMENSIONAL CONSTRUCT

We believe there are three conceptual arguments that favor viewing commitment as a unidimensional construct: parsimony, consistency, and confounds. First, the scientific law of parsimony suggests that a construct should be considered unidimensional unless there is compelling conceptual or empirical evidence to the contrary. An issue related to providing that compelling conceptual case that multiple dimensions are needed is the question of how the different dimensions together reflect or combine to represent the overall strength of the commitment (Brown, 1996). In the case of the TCM, an explicit nomological network has not been put forth explicating the expected relationships among the different mindsets (Bergman, 2006), or between the mindsets (or profiles of mindsets) and the singular core essence of commitment. In addition, as pointed out by Gonzalez and Guillen (2008), there is no theoretical justification for there being three distinct mindsets as opposed to some other number.

A second conceptual issue is consistency. Given the evidence that the commitment construct is largely the same regardless of the target (Klein et al., 2012), why is a unidimensional definition sufficient for some targets but not others? As noted earlier, when the target is the employing organization, or for targets that borrowed from that literature, one finds a mix of uni- and multidimensional definitions. Yet the definitions of commitment have typically been unidimensional when developed independently of the organizational commitment literature. The third conceptual issue, confounds, relates to the conceptual and empirical basis for concluding that commitment is multidimensional. Specifically, the different dimensions in multidimensional models nearly all reflect different targets, types of psychological bonds, antecedents of psychological bonds, or indicators of a psychological bond. Klein and colleagues (Klein, 2013; Klein et al., 2012) present arguments for why different targets and types of bond should not be considered different types or forms or dimensions of commitment. In terms of different antecedents and indicators, these are usually distinct constructs that arguably lie outside of the construct boundary. This third conceptual issue is further discussed in the next section.

Confounded Elements in Multidimensional Frameworks

We assert that the conclusion that multiple dimensions are necessary results from construct boundaries being drawn too broadly. Specifically, we articulate below how the inclusion of related but distinct constructs, and the distinct types of psychological bonds, have contributed to commitment being unnecessarily viewed as multidimensional.

Inclusion of distinct constructs

In many cases, commitment conceptualizations include concepts that can and should be distinguished from commitment, including antecedents or outcomes of commitment. Incorporating these elements results in the overestimation of the empirical relationships between commitment and those antecedents and outcomes. Determinants of commitment included in some prior commitment conceptualizations include exchanges and/or investments, and goal and/or value congruence (Klein et al., 2009). The accrual of investments and exchanges can lead to a psychological bond with a target, and that bond may be experienced as commitment, but those received, promised, or accrued benefits are antecedents to commitment and not commitment itself. Examples of conceptualizations that reflect the incorporation of these antecedents include Etzioni's (1961) calculative involvement, Kanter's (1968) continuance commitment, and O'Reilly and Chatman's (1986) compliance dimension. In terms of the congruence between the goals or values of the individual and the commitment target, examples include Etzioni's (1961) moral involvement dimension and O'Reilly and Chatman's (1986) internalization dimension. Again here, we view value and/or goal congruence as an antecedent of commitment, rather than as commitment itself.

Prior commitment conceptualizations have similarly included elements that we believe should be viewed as consequences of commitment. These include motivation or behavioral intentions as well as continuation with the target. Motivation is typically defined as a set of forces that initiate behavior and determine its form, direction, intensity, and duration (Pinder, 1998). Some authors have similarly defined commitment as a force (e.g., Brown, 1996; Meyer and Herscovitch, 2001). In terms of behavioral implications, some definitions explicitly include intentions, whereas others use more implicit language, referring to desires, obligations, or the need to act, or to a specific course of action. Finally, many conceptualizations of commitment equate commitment with continuation with the target. In sum, it is our position that many multidimensional conceptualizations are multidimensional because the boundary of the construct is drawn too broadly, including distinct constructs that fall out into separate dimensions.

Inclusion of distinct types of bonds
Individuals form numerous psychological bonds in the workplace and those bonds can be differentiated by both target and the type of attachment. The second way in which overly broad definitions of commitment have resulted in multiple dimensions is by equating commitment with attachment or staying. That is, some multidimensional commitment frameworks represent distinct types of bonds, all of which are termed commitment despite reflecting distinct psychological phenomena. For example, identification has been included in many prior conceptualizations, definitions, and measures of commitment, but identification is now generally recognized as conceptually and empirically distinct from commitment (e.g., Meyer et al., 2006).

Because different bond types arise from differing circumstances and have different psychological and behavioral implications, they should not all be lumped together and called commitment. Klein et al. (2012) provide conceptual arguments for splitting distinct bond types (for example, acquiescence, instrumental) and treating them as distinct constructs rather than different types or forms of commitment. If commitment is synonymous with 'staying', then incorporating all of the different bonds that hold people to a target is appropriate. If, however, commitment is more than just staying, then not all bonds should be viewed as commitment. When commitment is defined more narrowly, including only the psychological state reflecting a commitment bond rather than all types of attachments, the resulting concept is unidimensional. In sum, when distinct concepts and other types of bonds are stripped away, leaving only what is uniquely commitment, what remains is unidimensional. Commitment only becomes multidimensional when extraneous constructs and/or additional bond types are included in the conceptualization.

EMPIRICAL BASIS FOR A UNIDIMENSIONAL CONSTRUCT

In addition to the above conceptual arguments, there is also empirical evidence that both calls multidimensional frameworks into question, and is supportive of a unidimensional viewpoint. In this section we do not claim to provide a comprehensive review of the extensive research based on the TCM framework, but rather point out the concerns and limitations that have been raised in the literature. Despite widespread usage, measures reflecting multidimensional conceptualizations have been criticized (e.g., Bayazit et al., 2004; Jaros, 2009; Klein et al., 2014) in terms of both structure and confounded content. Starting with structure, there are mixed empirical results regarding the three-dimensional structure, as a number of studies support alternative models (Meyer and Herscovitch, 2001). Although the proposed structure has been supported in some studies, several other studies have found that: (1) normative and affective mindsets overlap substantially (Allen and Meyer, 1990; Bergman, 2006); (2) the continuance mindset consists of two separate dimensions: high investments versus few alternatives (e.g., Cooper-Hakim and Viswesvaran, 2005; Meyer et al., 1990); and (3) the normative mindset can be experienced as either a 'moral imperative' or 'indebted obligation' (e.g., Gellatly et al., 2006). Similarly, the Gordon et al. (1980) union commitment scale was written to reflect a six-factor conceptualization, but is commonly treated as either three or four factors (e.g., Tetrick et al., 1989). The inability to demonstrate clear and consistent multiple dimensions suggests that an alternative approach may be more appropriate.

Related to the concerns that multidimensional commitment measures do not reflect the proposed structure, are criticisms of the content and construct validity of the measures (e.g., Jaros, 2009). For example, as part of a content validation process, Klein et al. (2014) found that subject matter experts sorted the TCM affective mindset items as identification, rather than commitment, 64 percent of the time. Others have similarly decomposed the TCM scales into constructs other than commitment (Jaros, 2007, 2012). Likewise some dimensions of the union commitment scale have been critiqued as reflecting antecedents (for example, belief in unionism) or outcomes of commitment (for example, willingness to serve), rather than commitment itself (Jaros, 2009). Many multidimensional commitment scales have undergone revisions to attempt to address these problems. However, these 'fixes' have largely been unsuccessful, leading scholars (e.g., Gonzalez and Guillen, 2008; Jaros, 2009; Klein et al., 2012; Solinger et al., 2008) to conclude that measurement refinements alone will not resolve these problems because of the underlying conceptual issues discussed above.

Another empirical issue is the extent to which theoretically expected substantive relationships have been observed using measures reflecting multidimensional perspectives. On the one hand, there is no question that multidimensional models of commitment have generated a considerable amount of empirical findings, many of which are consistent with commitment theory. That said, in the case of the TCM, the predictive validity for some dimensions has been criticized (e.g., Cohen, 1996). In addition, given the above concerns about definitions and measures, including aspects of the very independent and dependent variables examined along with commitment, it is reasonable to question whether the accumulated estimates of the strength of those relationships is overstated (Klein et al., 2014). A final observation about the accumulated empirical evidence from multidimensional perspectives is that in many empirical studies, only a single dimension is examined, not the full multidimensional model. For example, recent meta-analyses (Cooper-Hakim and Viswesvaran, 2005; Meyer et al., 2012) indicate that the affective mindset has been studied three times more often than the normative mindset. That is, researchers have frequently worked from the TCM model, but examined just the affective mindset, though there are other times, particularly outside North America, where researchers have only examined the normative mindset. It thus appears that many researchers either do not accept that commitment is multidimensional or do not believe it is necessary to capture all of its dimensions in order to understand the concept.

The recommended unidimensional measure has only been in the literature a short time and as such, does not have the same empirical base available to support or refute its validity or substantive operation relative to other constructs. However, the study introducing the Klein et al. unidimensional, target-free measure of commitment (Klein et al., 2014) presented a constellation of evidence in support of the measure. Specifically, this study demonstrated: (1) strong content validity evidence supporting the relationships between items and the theoretical construct; (2) that the measure's psychometric properties operated as expected across multiple targets, samples, and settings; and (3) that the measure demonstrated convergent, discriminant, and predictive validity with measures of constructs within the nomological network. In terms of the psychometrics, the measure demonstrated clear, singular dimensionality and high internal consistency reliability (median alpha = .95) across multiple targets. It was also shown that the measure was sensitive enough to detect differences in participants' commitment strength across targets.

Two other advantages of the unidimensional approach, and the Klein et al. (2014) measure in particular, are parsimony and direct comparability across targets. The brevity of the measure, only four items, makes it well suited for studies assessing multiple commitment targets or examining within-person variations in commitment over time. With respect to assessing multiple commitments, the measure was designed to be easily adapted to any target, whereas multidimensional frameworks were initially developed around a particular commitment target and are not easily modified for all other targets. Initial findings are promising but additional research is needed to further demonstrate the measure's equivalence (see Chapter 32, this volume) across both targets and cultures.

IMPLICATIONS OF TREATING COMMITMENT AS A UNIDIMENSIONAL CONSTRUCT

We next turn to exploring the implications of taking a unidimensional approach. Beginning with implications for theory, there are two primary areas for future conceptual development highlighted by taking a unidimensional approach. The first is to develop a more complete theory of workplace bonds or attachments. This comes from viewing commitment as a particular type of bond (versus including a wide range of bonds under the umbrella of commitment; see Klein et al., 2012 for other types of workplace bonds) while recognizing that other bond types are also important constructs for understanding and predicting organizational behavior. Klein et al. (2012) explicate the nature of commitment bonds, but only suggest the nature of other workplace bonds. Creating a broader theory of bonds would require more completely identifying the range of workplace bond types and the factors that distinguish, trigger, and alter each bond type. The second conceptual need, highlighted by the 'target-free' emphasis of the unidimensional view, is for a logically meaningful and parsimonious typology for categorizing commitment targets. Such a framework would ideally also yield predictions about the interdependencies and interplay among simultaneously held workplace commitments and their potentially synergistic or detrimental effects.

Turning to future research implications, taking a unidimensional view generates a number of empirical questions relating to multiple types of bonds and commitment targets. In terms of bonds, there are measurement issues to be addressed for each of the other identified bond types. Klein et al. (2014) provide a validated measure for commitment bonds, but other bond types, previously included in broader conceptualizations of commitment, need to be revisited. Identification is an established, distinct construct with established measures, but for others (for example, acquiescence and instrumental bonds) it is unclear whether existing measures adequately capture these constructs or whether new measures need to be developed. Additional research opportunities include verifying the proposed differential outcomes for different bond types, identifying the key factors that influence the formation of one bond type over another, and taking a person-centered approch to examining the extent to which individuals simultaneously hold different types of bonds to a single or multiple targets. A final future research need involves understanding the 'tipping points' for altering the bond type (versus the strength of the bond). That is, research is needed to identify the key factors and processes that, over time, change one's primary attachment to a target from one bond type to another (for example, from an instrumental to a commitment bond, or vice versa).

Regarding multiple targets, the unidimensional perspective facilitates the simultaneous examination of multiple commitments, creating opportunities to integrate fractured commitment literatures. Commitment scholarship has been largely target-driven, with different researchers studying the antecedents and consequences of commitment to different targets. Research is needed to both verify the generalizability of the Klein et al. (2012) model across targets and identify key differences unique to given targets or contexts. The model in Figure 2.1 identifies general antecedents, processes, and outcomes common to all workplace commitment targets, but research is needed to identify the context and target specific variations within those broad categories. For example, how might the relative importance of the antecedents and outcomes vary across targets (might social influence be more important for interpersonal targets such as a co-worker, than they are for intra-individual targets such as a decision)? What specific influences and outcomes are most relevant for particular targets and contexts? Are there systematic differences in the development, maintenance, or dissipation of commitment over time across targets (for example, are commitments to targets with a predetermined end, such as project teams or goals, more susceptible to decline than ongoing targets such as one's career or values)? The strength of cultural influences on the patterns, consistency, and interrelationships among commitments also warrant investigation. Another future research issue is better understanding what workplace commitment targets are most relevant, in terms of driving desired organizational outcomes, for different types of positions, structures, employment relationships, and organizational forms (for example, should policies for contract workers focus on facilitating commitment to a project or values rather than the organization or supervisor?).

In addition to the above-noted future research examining the similarities and differences among workplace commitment targets, the unidimensional perspective also facilitates future research aimed at better understanding the interdependencies and potential conflicts among simultaneously held commitments. For example, do those interdependencies vary in different contexts? Under what conditions does commitment to a given target facilitate or interfere with commitment to other targets? How are priorities determined among competing commitments? How are conflicts among competing commitments resolved? A final research stream facilitated by the unidimensional perspective comes from the explicit recognition given to temporality and commitment malleability. These insights, coupled with a short, target-free measure, open opportunities for longitudinal within-person studies (see Chapters 33 and 34, this volume, for relevant procedures) to examine the dynamic reciprocal relationships depicted in Figure 2.1. For example, what moderating factors influence how commitment outcomes, over time, reciprocally influence perceptions of the commitment target and environment and, subsequently, commitment? Such research would help to map how commitment develops, is maintained, and declines over time. It would also be helpful if this research identified critical inflection points in the development or dissipation of commitment, and potentially different patterns for different commitment targets.

CONCLUSION

This chapter has presented the case for viewing commitment as a unidimensional construct. After briefly reviewing the history of commitment research, we review the role of construct definitions, provide conceptual and empirical evidence for taking a unidimensional approach, and put forth a future research agenda. Specificity and narrowness are the primary differences between the recent unidimensional view of Klein et al. (2012) and the mostly widely used multidimensional TCM framework; reflecting the selective versus inclusive approaches taken in developing the two perspectives. In our opinion, the narrower unidimensional view of commitment provides: (1) a more concise definition with clearer boundaries that better differentiates commitment as a unique construct; (2) greater applicability across the full array of workplace targets, addressing issues of redundancy and criticisms of relevancy; (3) greater coherence, convergence, and synergy across the currently fragmented study of different workplace commitments; and (4) a parsimonious conceptualization that eliminates the need for ancillary concepts to account for different types of bonds. When there are alternative conceptualizations of a construct, the relative validity of the measures used to operationalize those conceptualizations can be compared, but doing so does not reveal which is the more accurate or useful conceptualization. That determination will be made by the consensus of the field, based on the perceived theoretical and empirical utility of each approach.

REFERENCES

Allen, N.J. and Meyer, J.P. (1990). The measurement and antecedents of affective, continuance and normative commitment to the organization. *Journal of Occupational Psychology*, 63(1), 1–18.
Bagozzi, R.P. and Edwards, J.R. (1998). A general approach to representing constructs in organizational research. *Organizational Research Methods*, 1, 45–87.
Bayazit, M., Hammer, T. and Wazeter, D. (2004). Methodological challenges in union commitment studies. *Journal of Applied Psychology*, 89, 738–747.

Becker, H.S. (1960). Notes on the concept of commitment. *American Journal of Sociology*, 66(1), 32–40.
Becker, T.E. (1992). Foci and bases of commitment: Are they distinctions worth making? *Academy of Management Journal*, 35(1), 232–244.
Becker, T.E., Billings, R.S., Eveleth, D.M. and Gilbert, N.L. (1996). Foci and bases of employee commitment: Implications for job performance. *Academy of Management Journal*, 39, 464–482.
Bergman, M.E. (2006). The relationship between affective and normative commitment: Review and research agenda. *Journal of Organizational Behavior*, 27, 645–663.
Bishop, J.W. and Scott, K.D. (2000). An examination of organizational and team commitment in a self-directed team environment. *Journal of Applied Psychology*, 85(3), 439–450.
Blau, G.J. (1985). The measurement and prediction of career commitment. *Journal of Occupational Psychology*, 58(4), 277–288.
Block, J. (1957). Three tasks for personality psychology. In L.R. Bergman, and L. Nystedt (eds), *Developmental Science and the Holistic Approach* (155–164). New York: Psychological Press.
Brown, R.B. (1996). Organizational commitment: Clarifying the concept and simplifying the existing construct typology. *Journal of Vocational Behavior*, 49, 230–251.
Buchanan, B. (1974). Building organizational commitment: The socialization of managers in work organizations. *Administrative Science Quarterly*, 19(4), 533–546.
Cohen, A. (1996). On the discriminant validity of the Meyer and Allen measure of organizational commitment: How. *Educational and Psychological Measurement*, 56(3), 494.
Cohen, A. (2007). Commitment before and after: An evaluation and reconceptualization of organizational commitment. *Human Resource Management Review*, 17, 336–354.
Cole, M.S., Walter, F., Bedeian, A.G. and O'Boyle, E.H. (2012). Job burnout and employee engagement: A meta-analytic examination of construct proliferation. *Journal of Management*, 38(5), 1550–1581.
Cooper-Hakim, A. and Viswesvaran, C. (2005). The construct of work commitment: Testing an integrative framework. *Psychological Bulletin*, 131(2), 241–259.
Etzioni, A. (1961). *A Comparative Analysis of Complex Organizations*. New York: Free Press.
Gellatly, I.R., Meyer, J.P. and Luchak, A.A. (2006). Combined effect of the three commitment components on focal and discretionary behaviors: A test of Meyer and Herscovitch's propositions. *Journal of Vocational Behavior*, 69, 331–345.
Gonzalez, T.F. and Guillen, M. (2008). Organizational commitment: A proposal for a wider ethical conceptualization of 'normative commitment'. *Journal of Business Ethics*, 78(3), 401–414.
Gordon, M.E., Philpot, J.W., Burt, R.E., Thompson, C.A. and Spiller, W.E. (1980). Commitment to the union: Development of a measure and an examination of its correlates. *Journal of Applied Psychology*, 65(4), 479–499.
Gouldner, H.P. (1960). Dimensions of organizational commitment. *Administrative Science Quarterly*, 4(4), 468–490.
Hall, D.T. (1971). A theoretical model of career subidentity development in organizational settings. *Organizational Behavior and Human Performance*, 6, 50–76.
Herscovitch, L. and Meyer, J.P. (2002). Commitment to organizational change: Extension of a three-component model. *Journal of Applied Psychology*, 87(3), 474–487.
Jaros, S. (1997). An assessment of Meyer and Allen's three-component model of organizational commitment and turnover intentions. *Journal of Vocational Behavior*, 51, 319–337.
Jaros, S.J. (2007). Measurement issues in the Meyer and Allen model of organizational commitment. *Journal of Organizational Behavior*, 6, 7–25.
Jaros, S.J. (2009). Measurement of commitment. In H. Klein, T. Becker, and J. Meyer (eds), *Commitment in Organizations: Accumulated Wisdom and New Directions* (347–381). Mahwah, NJ: Lawrence Erlbaum.
Jaros S.J. (2012). Evaluating the 'few alternatives' dimension of continuance commitment: A comment on Johnson, Chang, and Yang (2010). *Journal of Leadership, Accountability and Ethics*, 9(4), 63–71.
Johnson, R.E., Rosen, C.C., Chang, C.H., Djurdjevic, E. and Taing, M.U. (2012). Recommendations for improving the construct clarity of higher-order multidimensional constructs. *Human Resource Management Review*, 22(2), 62–72.
Kanter, R.M. (1968). Commitment and social organization: A study of commitment mechanisms in utopian communities. *American Sociological Review*, 33(4), 499–517.
Kiesler, C.A. (1971). *The Psychology of Commitment: Experiments Linking Behavior to Belief*. New York: Academic Press.
Klein, H.J. (2013). Distinguishing commitment bonds from other attachments in a target-free manner. In J.K. Ford, J.R. Hollenbeck, and A.M. Ryan (eds) *The Nature of Work: Advances in Psychological Theory, Methods, and Practice* (117–146). Washington, DC: American Psychological Association Press.
Klein, H.J., Cooper, J.T., Molloy, J.C. and Swanson, J.A. (2014). The assessment of commitment: Advantages of a unidimensional, target-free approach. *Journal of Applied Psychology*, 99, 222–238.

Klein, H.J. and Delery, J.E. (2012). Construct clarity in human resource management research: Introduction to the special issue. *Human Resource Management Review*, *22*, 57–61.

Klein, H.J., Molloy, J.C. and Brinsfield, C.B. (2012). Reconceptualizing workplace commitment to redress a stretched construct: Revisiting assumptions and removing confounds. *Academy of Management Review*, *37*, 130–151.

Klein, H.J., Molloy, J.C. and Cooper, J.T. (2009). Conceptual foundations: Construct definitions and theoretical representations of workplace commitments. In H.J. Klein, T.E. Becker, and J.P. Meyer (eds), *Commitment in Organizations: Accumulated Wisdom and New Directions* (3–36). New York: Routledge/Taylor & Francis.

Locke, E.A. (1968). Toward a theory of task motivation and incentives. *Organizational Behavior and Human Performance*, *3*(2), 157–189.

Meyer, J.P. (2009). Commitment in a changing world of work. In H.J. Klein, T.E. Becker, and J.P. Meyer (eds), *Commitment in Organizations: Accumulated Wisdom and New Directions* (37–68). New York: Routledge/Taylor & Francis.

Meyer, J.P. and Allen, N.J. (1991). A three-component conceptualization of organizational commitment. *Human Resource Management Review*, *1*(1), 61–89.

Meyer, J.P., Allen, N.J. and Gellatly, I.R. (1990). Affective and continuance commitment to the organization: evaluation of measures and analysis of concurrent and time-lagged relations. *Journal of Applied Psychology*, *75*, 710–720.

Meyer, J.P., Allen, N.J. and Smith, C.A. (1993). Commitment to organizations and occupations: Extension and test of a three-component conceptualization. *Journal of Applied Psychology*, *78*(4), 538–551.

Meyer, J.P., Becker, T.E. and van Dick, R. (2006). Social identities and commitments at work: Toward an integrative model. *Journal of Organizational Behavior*, *27*, 665–683.

Meyer, J.P. and Herscovitch, L. (2001). Commitment in the workplace: Toward a general model. *Human Resource Management Review*, *11*(3), 299–326.

Meyer, J.P., Stanley, D.J., Jackson, T.A., McInnis, K.J., Maltin, E.R. and Sheppard, L. (2012). Affective, normative, and continuance commitment levels across cultures: A meta-analysis. *Journal of Vocational Behavior*, *80*(2), 225–245.

Molloy, J.C. and Ployhart, R.E. (2012). Construct clarity: multidisciplinary considerations and an illustration using human capital. *Human Resource Management Review*, *22*(2), 152–156.

Morrow, P.C. (1983). Concept redundancy in organizational research: The case of work commitment. *Academy of Management Review*, *8*(3), 486–500.

Mowday, R.T., Steers, R.M. and Porter, L.W. (1979). The measurement of organizational commitment. *Journal of Vocational Behavior*, *14*, 224–247.

Neubert, M.J. and Cady, S.H. (2001). Program commitment: A multi-study longitudinal field investigation of its impact and antecedents. *Personnel Psychology*, *54*(2), 421–448.

O'Reilly, C. and Chatman, J. (1986). Organizational commitment and psychological attachment: The effects of compliance, identification, and internalization on prosocial behavior. *Journal of Applied Psychology*, *71*(3), 492–499.

Osigweh, C.A.B. (1989). Concept fallibility in organizational science. *Academy of Management Review*, *14*(4), 579–594.

Pinder, C.C. (1998). *Motivation in Work Organizations*. Upper Saddle River, NJ: Prentice Hall.

Porter, L.W., Steers, R.M., Mowday, R.T. and Boulian, P.V. (1974). Organizational commitment, job satisfaction, and turnover among psychiatric technicians. *Journal of Applied Psychology*, *59*(5), 603–609.

Redman, T. and Snape, E. (2005). Unpacking commitment: Multiple loyalties and employee behaviour. *Journal of Management Studies*, *42*, 301–328.

Reichers, A.E. (1985). A review and reconceptualization of organizational commitment. *Academy of Management Review*, *10*(3), 465–476.

Roethlisberger, F.J. and Dickson, W.J. (1939). *Management and the Worker*. Cambridge, MA: Harvard University Press.

Salancik, G.R. (1977). Commitment and the control of organizational behavior and belief. In B.M. Staw and G.R. Salancik (eds). *New Directions in Organizational Behavior* (1–54). Chicago, IL: St Clair Press.

Simon, H.A., Smithburg, D.W. and Thompson, V.A. (1950). *Public Administration*. New York: Knopf.

Solinger, O.N., van Olffen, W. and Roe, R.A. (2008). Beyond the three-component model of organizational commitment. *Journal of Applied Psychology*, *93*(1), 70–83.

Staw, B.M. (1981). The escalation of commitment to a course of action. *Academy of Management Review*, *6*(4), 569.

Tepper, B.J. and Henle, C.A. (2011). A case for recognizing distinctions among constructs that capture interpersonal mistreatment in work organizations. *Journal of Organizational Behavior*, *32*, 487–498.

Tetrick, L.E., Thacker, J.W. and Fields, M.W. (1989). Evidence for the stability of the four dimensions of the commitment to the union scale. *Journal of Applied Psychology*, *74*(5), 819.

3.   Commitment as a multidimensional construct
Natalie J. Allen

Many years ago, I interviewed several dozen long-term volunteers, from different community organizations, about the various social causes to which they directed their efforts and, in particular, their motivations for beginning volunteer activity with their chosen organization. They were an enthusiastic group with lots to say about their initial motives and I learned a great deal about the problems they sought to solve, injustices they hoped to reverse, and people they wanted to help. Some volunteers described their involvement as extremely enjoyable and personally rewarding, while others emphasized stressful times when they thought it was 'too much' or 'maybe not worth it'. Yet all had been with their organizations for a very long time. At the time, my attention was focused on learning *why* the volunteers joined their respective organizations. Had I listened more carefully, however, or asked more incisive questions, I might also have learned something about what *sustained* their organizational involvement, even when the work became more difficult or less appealing. In short, I might have learned something about commitment.

If understanding commitment to volunteer organizations had been my goal, however, I would also have learned that social scientific research examining organizational commitment was, prior to 1980, in an interesting and fairly confusing state of play. Drawing as it did from 'different foundational literatures' (Klein et al., 2009, p. 9), theoretical work in the two decades prior (e.g., Etzioni, 1961; Kanter, 1968) had been rich and varied, foreshadowing the conceptual complexity that was to come. By the 1980s, although there was no shortage of empirical commitment research, the overall body of work was characterized by many challenges. Most notably, the construct itself was conceptualized in numerous ways. In their now classic book on employee–organization linkages, Mowday et al. (1982) drew from key studies in the literature to illustrate ten 'wildly divergent definitions' of commitment (p. 20), and numerous other scholars commented on the various commitment definitions in the research literature. Given this, it is not surprising that the measurement of employee commitment also varied considerably, thus limiting how easily researchers could draw general conclusions about commitment's development, correlates, or consequences. Moreover, although some of these measures appeared to fit their expressed conceptualizations well, many others did not. Relatedly, measure development and construct validation work had been undertaken in a somewhat uneven way, with some researchers attending much more closely to psychometric issues than others. Perhaps not surprisingly, the conceptual fragmentation, confounded measures, and a proliferation of constructs produced a fair amount of confusion in the literature, prompting one prominent researcher to call for more rigorous conceptualization, measurement, and validation efforts and for a moratorium on the explication of new commitment constructs (Morrow, 1983).

During the 1980s and 1990s, however, two general – and important – trends emerged within commitment research. First, researchers considerably widened their focus.

Although much of the early research examined employee commitment to organizations (Etzioni, 1975; Hrebiniak and Alutto, 1972; Kanter, 1968), increased attention was extended to other workplace domains such as unions (e.g., Gordon et al., 1980), management and supervisors (e.g., Becker and Billings, 1993), and occupations and professions (e.g., Blau, 1985, 1989; Blau and Lunz, 1998; Wallace, 1993, 1995). This research (see Chapter 4, this volume) seemed motivated by an interest in providing a fuller picture of commitment in the workplace (e.g., Becker, 1992; Morrow, 1983, 1993; Reichers, 1985) and by questions about interactions among multiple commitment foci, potential commitment compatibilities (or 'dual allegiances') among commitment foci (e.g., union–organization; occupation–organization) and the challenges that individuals potentially faced as they navigated among them. Could one be strongly committed to both the union and the employing organization? Did commitment to one's profession align well with commitment to the organization? And, if two or more foci to which a person was strongly committed had contradictory expectations, how might an understanding of multiple commitments inform our understanding of the person's behavior?

The second and, arguably, more critical trend involved changes in the way in which the commitment construct itself was conceptualized. Common to almost all views, of course, was the notion that commitment represented a tie that bound individuals to the organization, such that strongly committed employees were more likely to stay with the organization than were those with weak commitment. Beyond that, however, early views – and measures – of commitment varied considerably, reflecting, one might argue, the complexity and nuanced nature of the construct. Although there were exceptions and, unquestionably, some instances of conceptual and measurement ambiguity (e.g., Alutto et al., 1973; Hrebiniak and Alutto, 1972; Ritzer and Trice, 1969), most empirical researchers appeared to conceptualize commitment as a singular, or unidimensional, construct and they assessed it accordingly. Wiener (1982; Wiener and Vardi, 1980), for example, forwarded a view of commitment in which emphasis was placed on the responsibility, or sense of duty and obligation, that individuals felt toward the focus of their commitment. Despite their description of commitment as an attitude made up of acceptance of the organization's values, willingness to exert effort at work, and desire to remain with the organization, the Organizational Commitment Questionnaire (OCQ) developed by Mowday et al. (1982) – and used by hundreds of researchers – also treats commitment as a singular (unidimensional) affective construct. Cook and Wall (1980) took a similar approach, arguing that 'organizational commitment refers to a person's affective reaction to characteristics of his [and presumably her] employing organization' (p. 40). Like the OCQ, Cook and Wall's British Organizational Commitment Scale (BOCS) assessed commitment as a unidimensional construct.

As the body of commitment research grew, and researchers were challenged with a complex and somewhat confusing set of findings, approaches to commitment began to change. In particular, among commitment scholars working during the 1980s and 1990s, these findings seemed to prompt more nuanced thinking about the construct itself and gave rise to models of commitment that explicitly described and assessed the construct as being multidimensional in nature. Some of these models are summarized below.

SELECTED MULTIDIMENSIONAL COMMITMENT MODELS

Although multidimensional constructs are commonly used in social scientific work, multidimensionality itself is conceptualized in numerous ways (Edwards, 2001; Law and Wong, 1999). In the following overview, I use the term 'multidimensional' in the manner that is most typical within the commitment literature. Broadly, multidimensional models of commitment describe, and differentiate empirically among, the psychological bases of commitment to a particular focus. Put another way, they attempt to characterize the nature of the 'ties that bind' individuals to the focus of their commitment. In contrast to what might be considered an ambiguously dimensional approach taken by OCQ users, the explicitly multidimensional models outlined below treat each commitment dimension as a separate construct that, subsequently, could be considered singly or in concert with the other commitment dimensions.

Extending Etzioni's (1975) largely macro-level model of organizational involvement to the study of employee commitment to the organization, Penley and Gould (1988) posited a three-dimensional model of commitment and, foreshadowing the notion of a commitment profile, argued that these dimensions could be found 'singly or in combination among individuals' (p. 48). 'Moral commitment' was described as an affective connection with the organization 'characterized by the acceptance and identification with organizational goals . . . [that] may be thought of as a kind of organizational identification' (p. 45). Penley and Gould conceptualized 'alienative commitment' as commitment that, like moral commitment, is affective in nature but is based on rewards and punishments that 'may seem random' and prompt a perceived 'lack of control'. Employees who experienced alienative commitment remain with the organization largely due to losses that may ensue if they leave. Finally, 'calculative commitment' referred to commitment based on various inducements the employee anticipates for their contributions to the organization. Penley and Gould developed measures of each dimension and evaluated the model using several samples. Factor analytic evidence and correlations with work outcomes supported the distinction among dimensions; subsequently, however, the model received little research attention.

Drawing from the distinction that March and Simon (1958) made between motivation to produce and motivation to participate, and based on subsequent measurement work by Schechter (1985), Mayer and Schoorman (1992) proposed a two-dimensional model of organization commitment. 'Value commitment' was conceptualized as a 'belief in and acceptance of organizational goals and values and a willingness to exert considerable effort on behalf of the organization' (p. 673). Mayer and Schoorman argued that the stronger one's value commitment, the more one would be motivated to produce for the organization. 'Continuance commitment' was conceptualized as 'the desire to remain in the organization'; thus, Mayer and Schoorman argued that employees with strong continuance commitment would express strong intention to remain with the organization. Confirmatory factor analyses provided support for the proposed two-dimensional structure of commitment, and links between the two dimensions and outcomes were generally in accord with predictions. In subsequent research, Mayer and Schoorman (1998) theorized, and found evidence consistent with the idea, that the two dimensions developed on the basis of different personal and job attitude variables. Thereafter, however, the model generated little additional empirical work.

O'Reilly and colleagues (O'Reilly and Chatman, 1986; O'Reilly et al., 1991) also drew from early notions about commitment (Etzioni, 1975; Kanter, 1968) and, more directly, from Kelman's (1958) work on attitude and behavior change. In doing so, they conceptualized commitment as having three bases – compliance, internalization, and identification – and suggested that each would have differing implications for behavior. 'Compliance' refers to commitment arising from the employee's interest in acquiring rewards that the organizational membership offers. 'Internalization' focuses on the employee's pride in belonging to the organization. Finally, 'identification' refers to commitment based on attitudes and values that the employee shared with the organization. Although questions have been raised about the distinction between the identification and internalization dimensions (e.g., Becker et al., 1995; Vandenberg et al., 1994), prompting the combination of the two in some studies (e.g., Caldwell et al., 1990), the model generated a considerable amount of research that focused attention on the value of examining commitment from a multidimensional perspective.

Particularly noteworthy is research conducted by Becker and Billings (1993), who examined commitment in terms of both its dimensions (bases) and the foci to which the commitment was directed. Using cluster analysis, they identified four distinct commitment profiles, conceptualized in terms of compliance, internalization, and identification, and associated with each of four foci (supervisor, workgroup, top management, organization); for simplicity, Becker and Billings chose profile labels that reflected commitment foci, rather than commitment bases). Results showed that the profiles were associated with different behavioral and attitudinal variables in general accordance with theory. For example, employees in the 'globally committed' profile – those whose strongest commitment was directed to top management and the overall organization – exhibited high levels of compliance, particularly in contrast to employees identified as 'locally committed'. As its name implies, this latter profile was characterized by strong commitment to the supervisor and work group and lower commitment to the overall organization and its top management.

THE THREE-COMPONENT MODEL

Thus far, the multidimensional view of commitment that has received the most sustained theoretical and empirical attention, and consequent refinement, is that which forms the core of the three-component model (TCM) (Allen and Meyer, 1990, 1996; Meyer and Allen, 1991, 1997). This model was developed in an attempt to help draw together and integrate several prevailing streams of commitment theory and research that, taken together, seemed to paint a discrepant picture of what 'commitment' meant, and that in some cases paid scant attention to construct articulation, construct measurement, or both. As noted, some theorists characterized commitment in terms of the individual's emotional ties to the organization, while others emphasized loyalty and obligation. Still others seemed to view commitment as the psychological recognition of the costs that would be incurred if one left the organization. Drawing from this body of work, and with an initial focus on the organization, TCM researchers identified three distinct components (or dimensions) of commitment, each characterized by a different underlying 'mindset', and they developed self-report measures to assess each. 'Affective commitment' refers to the employee's emotional attachment to the organization, characterized by enjoyment of the organization and a desire to stay. Employees with strong affective commitment remain with the organization because they want to do so. 'Continuance commitment' refers to the extent to which the employee perceives that leaving the organization would be costly. Employees with strong continuance commitment remain because they feel that they have to do so. 'Normative commitment' refers to the employee's feelings of obligation to the organization and the belief that staying with it is the right thing to do. Employees with strong normative commitment remain because they feel that they ought to do so.

According to the TCM, affective, continuance, and normative commitment develop on the basis of somewhat different work experiences and perceptions. Further, an individual's commitment is best characterized not in terms of the components considered individually, but as a profile made up of all three. Thus, employees with different affective–continuance–normative (ACN) commitment profiles are theorized to have different relationships with their organizations and to behave and react accordingly.

Over the past 25 years, aspects of the TCM have been examined extensively, in a wide variety of settings. Further, the model has undergone theoretical, measurement, and methodological refinements and its focus has been extended beyond the organization to numerous work-related foci. In the remainder of the chapter, my goal is not to evaluate the TCM against other possible commitment models but, rather, to draw on this extensive body of work to describe how the evaluation of a commitment model that explicitly conceptualizes commitment as multidimensional construct has been approached. In what follows, therefore, I focus on the evidence that is of particular relevance to the multidimensional nature of commitment, identify some challenges that remain, and discuss the practical implications associated with taking this approach.

THE CASE FOR MULTIDIMENSIONALITY

Perhaps not surprisingly, early empirical TCM research focused on the development and refinement of reliable measures of each of the three commitment components or dimensions (e.g., Allen and Meyer, 1990; Meyer et al., 1993) and the evaluation of the construct validity associated with each (e.g., Allen and Meyer, 1996, 2000; Meyer and Allen, 1984, 1991, 1997; Meyer et al., 1990; Meyer and Parfyonova, 2010; Powell and Meyer, 2004). Over the years, these multiple-item measures, typically referred to as the Affective Commitment Scale (ACS), Continuance Commitment Scale (CCS), and the Normative Commitment Scale (NCS) have been used by hundreds of researchers. Some research has focused specifically on evaluating the measures themselves and modifying them to suit particular research needs. Other research has examined TCM theorizing regarding the development and consequences of commitment. Taken together, this activity has resulted in a rich repository of research upon which to base an examination of this particular multidimensional view of commitment.

In accordance with theory, several studies have provided factor analytic, and other, evidence suggesting that affective, continuance, and normative commitment are distinct dimensions (e.g., Allen and Meyer, 1990; Hackett et al., 1994; Tayyab, 2007; Xu and Bassham, 2010; but see Bergman, 2006; McGee and Ford, 1987). Further, dozens of studies have examined the links among the three commitment components and their relations with their theoretically expected 'antecedent' and 'consequence' correlates. Most of these studies provide evidence that is consistent with theory, although there are some exceptions (e.g., Jaros, 1997; Whitener and Walz, 1993). As recent research on replications makes clear, however, it is critically important to examine the preponderance of evidence over the results of any given study (Stanley and Spence, 2014). Accordingly, meta-analytic examination (Meyer et al., 2002) has established that the three components were related to differing work experience variables or 'antecedents' (see Part V, this volume). Also supportive of the dimensionality claim, and consistent with TCM theory, is meta-analytic evidence (Meyer et al., 2002) that each commitment dimension is negatively related to turnover intention and turnover behavior (see Chapter 14, this volume), but differentially related to various other employee reactions, intentions, and behaviors. For example, in accordance with TCM predictions, affective and normative commitment correlated positively with job performance and organizational citizenship behavior (OCB), but continuance commitment correlated negatively with performance and was unrelated to OCB (see Chapter 15, this volume). Meta-analytic work also suggests that the three components resonate meaningfully with employees across cultures and, interestingly, that cultural variation itself predicts levels of affective commitment and normative commitment (Meyer et al., 2012a).

In sum, a large body of evidence supports the fundamental premises of the TCM and, hence, the multidimensional nature of the commitment construct. Specifically, this evidence suggests that: (1) the three components are distinct; (2) they develop on the basis of different work experiences and processes; and (3) although differentially related to several work-related behaviors and reactions, each component is linked meaningfully to employee intention to stay and to retention-related behavior, arguably the most cogent manifestations of workplace commitment.

Commitment Profiles

Recall, however, that a key proposition of this model is that employee commitment is best considered not in terms of the separate commitment dimensions but, rather, with respect to the individual's affective–continuance–normative (ACN) commitment profile. Thus, the determination of the types of commitment profiles that typically develop, and the examination of the patterns of work-related behavior and reactions that are associated with each, are both of particular importance. As might be expected, however, evaluation of this aspect of the model has faced both theoretical and methodological challenges.

Some theoretical challenges stemmed from the fact that early discussions of the TCM had relatively little to say about which types of commitment profiles might be most likely to develop in employee samples, and how particular ACN profiles might shape workplace behaviors and other commitment outcomes. In 2001, however, Meyer and Herscovitch advanced a general theoretical model of workplace commitment. Specifically, they conceptualized commitment as a binding force characterized by the 'multiple mindsets' of desire, perceived costs, and obligation that underlie affective, continuance, and normative commitment, respectively, and that, taken together, reflect an individual's commitment profile. Further, they distinguished between commitment-related behaviors that are expected, on the basis of the terms of the individual's commitment (focal behaviors, such as staying with the organization), from those that a committed individual might choose, but not be expected, to do (discretionary behaviors, such as 'citizenship' or 'extra-role' work behavior). Based on this, they provided valuable guidance to researchers by identifying eight potential commitment profiles and offering hypotheses regarding the behavioral patterns associated with each. For example, they predicted that employees with the 'affective-dominant' profile, characterized by high affective, low continuance, and low normative commitment, would be most likely to remain with their organizations and to exhibit discretionary work behavior. In contrast, those with a 'continuance-dominant' profile would be likely to remain with the organization, though somewhat less so, and would be very unlikely to engage in discretionary behavior. This general model was useful in that it provided a framework within which commitment researchers could think about, and test, specific hypotheses about the emergence of particular profiles and their behavioral manifestations and it guided much research.

Researchers interested in assessing profile predictions, however, also faced methodological challenges. Initial attempts to evaluate profile effects largely relied on variable-centered approaches and, as such, assessed links between commitment variables (dimensions) and various employee behaviors using correlational, moderated multiple regression, and structural equation modeling techniques. Although details vary across studies and samples, results from this line of research generally suggest that the level of one commitment component tempers the effects of the other components. In an early study, for example, Somers (1995) examined the link between commitment and annexed absences (that is, absence linked to long weekends or holidays) and found that affective commitment (AC) and continuance commitment (CC) interacted such that the positive relation between annexed absence and CC was greater among employees with weak AC. Gellatly et al. (2006) examined the interactions among all three components and also found some support for the idea that the manner in which one commitment dimension is experienced provides a context in which the others are experienced and expressed. For example, they reported that the relation between AC and organizational citizenship behavior was stronger among employees whose levels of CC and normative commitment (NC) were low, rather than high. Taken together, this and other similar research (e.g., Johnson et al., 2009; McNally and Irving, 2010; Meyer et al., 1989) provide evidence consistent with the idea that the dimensions of commitment operate jointly to shape employee behavior.

Although much has been learned from this line of research, the variable-centered approach is not considered optimally suited to the challenge of identifying and assessing commitment profiles (e.g., Vandenberg and Stanley, 2009). Not surprisingly, therefore, the past few years have seen calls for, and increased use of, person-centered strategies – which allow researchers to identify subgroups within a population whose members have similar sets of characteristics – to complement this earlier work (e.g., Meyer et al., 2013b; Chapter 35, this volume).

Some researchers who take this approach rely on cluster analysis to determine how commitment components combine, within a particular sample, to form distinct profiles. Once profiles are identified, they examine how employees who share a particular profile differ, on key outcome measures, from those with other profiles. Wasti (2005) took this approach and determined that employees in her sample formed six commitment profile clusters. Among these, the most desirable behaviors (strong job performance) were exhibited by employees with profiles characterized by high levels of affective commitment and the least desirable behaviors were associated with either the 'non-committed' profile (low on all three dimensions) or the profile in which continuance was the dominant dimension. Using a similar approach, Somers (2010) identified seven of the eight profiles described by Meyer and Herscovitch (2001); consistent with other research (Meyer et al., 2013a; Meyer et al., 2012b; Stanley et al., 2013) only the 'normative-dominant' profile was not observed. Somers compared each profile group with respect to turnover intention, turnover, and absence, finding some support for the notion that how one commitment dimension is experienced, and expressed behaviorally, can be affected by the levels of the other two. More specifically, he reported that intention to remain with the organization was strongest among employees in the 'highly committed' profile (high on all three dimensions) and the affective-dominant or the normative-dominant profile. Although effects on actual turnover were less consistent, highly committed employees were significantly more likely to remain in the organization than were those with low commitment or continuance-dominant profiles. Interestingly, absence was unrelated to commitment profile. Somers noted, however, that the absence measure did not differentiate between voluntary and involuntary absence, and that this may have affected the results. Finally, using a somewhat smaller sample, Tsoumbris and Xenikou (2010) used cluster analysis to examine the emergence of ACN profiles that reflected commitment to both the organization and the occupation. Interestingly, consistent with other research and theory, they found that employees in the cluster defined by high levels of all three dimensions of commitment, directed to both foci, reported the highest levels of organizational citizenship behavior and expressed the weakest intention to leave their organization and occupation.

More recently, researchers have examined commitment profiles using latent profile analysis (LPA). As several authors have noted (e.g., Meyer et al., 2013b; Chapter 35, this volume; Vandenberg and Stanley, 2009), this more powerful person-oriented strategy appears to be particularly effective at discerning the homogeneous subgroups (profiles) that exist within a sample and is better able to handle situations involving numerous interactions. Like cluster analysis studies, this body of work provides evidence regarding the emergence and characteristics of specific commitment profiles. Meyer et al. (2012b), for example, used LPA to identify commitment profiles in a sample drawn from employees in three health and social services agencies and reported evidence of six organizational commitment profiles. Further, they provided evidence that these profile groups were associated with different patterns of employee behavior and well-being and that these patterns were in general accord with theoretical expectations (Meyer and Herscovitch, 2001; Meyer and Maltin, 2010). For example, discretionary work performance (that is, citizenship behavior) was most common, and general health was strongest, among those employees with either 'fully committed' profiles (high on all three dimensions) or affective-dominant profiles. Meyer et al. (2013a) also used LPA to identify organizational commitment profiles within a large sample of Canadian military personnel and to assess both antecedents and outcomes of the identified profiles. Again, six organizational commitment profiles emerged, and outcome variables were generally consistent with expectations. Particularly noteworthy is that both the 'uncommitted' profile and the CC-dominant profiles were associated with the lowest levels of psychological well-being (anxiety, depression). Further, these researchers provide valuable evidence relevant to how particular profiles develop. Importantly, they showed that the more 'desirable' profiles (AC-dominant, AC/NC-dominant) were related to perceived organizational support, job satisfaction, and satisfaction with leadership.

Finally, LPA has been used to examine work commitment profiles based on both commitment dimensions and commitment foci (Meyer et al., 2015; Morin et al., 2015). In one such study, Morin et al. (2015) assessed teachers' affective, continuance, and normative commitment to the organization (school) and to the teaching occupation. Their analyses identified seven distinct dual (organization–occupational) commitment profiles and revealed that these were associated with distinct patterns of employee well-being, intention to stay with the organization, and intention to stay with teaching. Given the multidimensional, dual-focus aspect of this work, these observed patterns are necessarily complex, but are in accordance with predictions for both employment intentions and well-being. For example, Morin et al. reported that both intention to stay with the teaching occupation and well-being were highest among the teachers with one of two commitment profiles: (1) AC-dominant organizational commitment and AC/NC-dominant occupational commitment and (2) strong NC-dominant organizational commitment and fully committed to occupation.

Clearly, examination of multidimensional commitment profiles based on TCM theorizing is on an upward trajectory and, although still at an early stage, profile research shows much promise. Based on this, and the extensive body of earlier TCM work, it seems reasonable to make the following general observations about what has been learned about the value of taking a multidimensional approach to commitment, some research challenges that remain, and the implications of this work for practitioners interested in developing stable, productive, and healthy workforces.

RESEARCH CONSIDERATIONS

First, it appears that some consensus is emerging regarding the types and prevalence of commitment profiles observed across studies and settings. This observation is based, however, on the relatively modest number of studies that have examined TCM profiles explicitly. Clearly, our picture of commitment profiles and their distribution, within and across foci, will be greatly enhanced as multidimensional commitment research extends to a wider array of workplaces, work units, occupations, and cultures. Also valuable will be the widespread adoption of person-centered approaches to conduct profile analysis, accompanied by consistency with respect to profile labeling and reporting practices (Chapter 35, this volume).

Second, the nature of commitment matters. Research to date strongly suggests that the components (or dimensions) of commitment – and the profiles they form – are linked meaningfully to different patterns of employee behavior, intentions, and other variables, and in a manner generally in accordance with theory. Thus, existing evidence suggests that the multidimensional approach to commitment is improving our understanding of, and ability to predict, various employee reactions to the workplace. Although many researchers have tended to focus on turnover variables (intention, actual) and self-reports or peer reports of prescribed and discretionary work performance, research examining health and well-being variables is also increasing (see Chapter 17, this volume). To add to this important work, a valuable direction for future research, perhaps, would be studies examining how different workplace commitment profiles influence the conflict, or the synergies, between work and home and family life.

Third, as noted above, and reviewed in detail elsewhere (see Part V, this volume), we know a great deal about the factors – both personal and organizational – that shape employee commitment. Much of this research focuses on the work experiences and characteristics that are associated with the separate dimensions of commitment and most is cross-sectional in nature. Some research, however, has examined how these variables might combine, or compile, to shape specific commitment profiles. For example, Gellatly et al. (2009) reported that the presence of 'development-oriented' practices, such as skills training, feedback, and opportunities for personal development, characterized more employees whose profiles included high levels of AC and fewer employees with low AC, high CC profiles. Taken together, research of this sort has much to offer practitioners interested in selecting, developing, and maintaining a workforce with a desirable commitment profile.

Fourth, most research examining the development of commitment is cross-sectional in nature. In one of the few studies examining commitment profiles over time, however, Kam et al. (2015) examined the impact, over an eight-month period, of a complex organizational change initiative. Interestingly, they reported substantial stability, over time, in employees' commitment profiles and noted that any observed change in profile membership appeared limited to the effects of changes in employees' perceived trustworthiness of top management. Although this does not mean that established commitment profiles do not change, it may suggest that such effects will be modest, especially if the change initiatives themselves are subtle. Indeed, Kam et al. suggested that the change initiative they examined may not have been as 'dramatic or turbulent' (p. 20) as other workplace events that drive profile change. Somewhat consistent with this is longitudinal research conducted by Arciniega et al. (2013), who examined employee commitment before and after events that most certainly would be considered both dramatic and turbulent. In this study, employee commitment was assessed twice at a production plant in Venezuela. During the six months that followed the initial assessment, the company that owned the plant was subjected to a series of direct operational and military threats by the country's then president, Hugo Chavez. In response to these threats, senior management stood up to Chavez by launching a lawsuit against the government. Hours later, in a prime-time broadcast on state television, Chavez threatened the organization with national expropriation. Commitment was assessed again, thus allowing Arciniega et al. to examine the potential impact of these events on commitment profiles. They reported change in more than 60 percent of the employee profiles. Most changes involved greater differentiation among the levels of the three components (for example, changes from all-low, or all-high, TCM profiles to those in which the levels of AC, NC, and CC varied); further, significant increases in both NC and AC were observed. Possibly, the dramatic nature of the events prompted employees to think more intently, and/or in a more nuanced manner, about their relationship with their organization. Further, Arciniega et al. suggested that management's strong response to the threats may have signalled that it could be trusted to stand up for employees and the organization, even under very risky political conditions, and that this aroused greater feelings of obligation to, and pride in, the organization.

Taken together, the admittedly limited evidence to date suggests that altering established commitment profiles may be challenging. On the positive side, this suggests that the commitment dimensions are not tenuous, constantly fluctuating phenomena that change rapidly in response to 'everyday' workplace events. Less positively, perhaps, it suggests that changing established undesirable employee commitment profiles may prove difficult. In what follows, I discuss how practitioners interested in developing and maintaining stable, productive, and healthy workforces might approach this challenge.

IMPLICATIONS FOR PRACTITIONERS

Considerable research suggests that different TCM commitment profiles are linked to different behavioral patterns. Moreover, research points to numerous ways in which the dimensions of commitment, and hence, commitment profiles, can be shaped and maintained. Organizations interested in optimizing the commitment profiles of their employees might well begin by conducting a 'commitment audit' (Allen, 2010). Broadly, this includes: (1) an assessment of the employee commitment profile(s) that the organizations seeks to develop; (2) an assessment of existing employee commitment profiles using established commitment measures; and (3) a plan to minimize the discrepancy between the two and to evaluate these efforts.

Reaping benefits of any commitment strategy requires, of course, that the organization has a clear sense of what sorts of employee behaviors and reactions – and hence what types of commitment profiles – it sees as most valuable. While such decisions are best made in consultation with senior managers, human resource professionals, and other stakeholders familiar with organizational operations, it is quite likely that identified profile(s) will include those described as 'desirable' profiles in the growing body of TCM research (for example, AC-dominant, AC/NC-dominant). A multidimensional employee commitment survey is essential, of course, to evaluate the current profiles within the organization and, subsequently, to serve as a benchmark against which progress can be evaluated. Finally, guided by the abundant TCM research on the development and correlates of the dimensions of commitment, and an examination of existing organizational policies and practices, it ought to be possible for practitioners to offer relevant 'designing for commitment' advice. Naturally, much attention will focus on the existing workforce. The organizational newcomer literature (e.g., Bauer and Erdogan, 2011), however, suggests the critical importance of setting the stage for desired employee outcomes as early as possible. Thus, attention to the newest employees – and commitment initiatives associated with recruitment, selection, onboarding, training, and early-stage supervision – may pay particular dividends and should not be overlooked.

Finally, it must be acknowledged that although the TCM has been examined by numerous researchers in a wide variety of settings, it and other multidimensional models of commitment are most certainly not without their critics (see Chapter 2, this volume; Klein et al., 2014; Klein et al., 2012; Solinger et al., 2008). As is likely rather obvious, my view is that a multidimensional approach to workplace commitment well befits the inherent psychological complexity associated with the ties that bind people to their work, and that such an approach has practical value. Ultimately, of course, the value of any conceptualization of commitment, whether it involves single or multiple dimensions, lies with its ability to help us better understand how people behave in the workplace.

REFERENCES

Allen, N.J. (2010). Organizational commitment: An evidence-based challenge for healthcare organizations. In A.V. Ciurea, C.L. Cooper, and E. Avram (eds), *Management of Healthcare Systems and Organizations* (pp. 361–376). Bucharest: Editura Universitaria Carol Davila.

Allen, N.J. and Meyer, J.P. (1990). The measurement and antecedents of affective, continuance, and normative commitment to the organization. *Journal of Occupational Psychology*, *63*, 1–18. doi:10.1111/j.2044-8325.1990.tb00506.x.

Allen, N.J. and Meyer, J.P. (1996). Affective, continuance, and normative commitment to the organization: An examination of construct validity. *Journal of Vocational Behavior*, *49*, 252–276. doi:10.1006/jvbe.1996.0043.

Allen, N.J. and Meyer, J.P. (2000). Construct validation in organizational behavior research: The case of organizational commitment. In R.D. Goffin and E. Helmes (eds), *Problems and Solutions in Human Assessment: Honoring Douglas N. Jackson at Seventy* (pp. 285–314). New York: Kluwer Academic/Plenum Publishers.

Alutto, J.A., Hrebiniak, L.G., and Alonso, R.C. (1973). On operationalizing the concept of commitment. *Social Forces*, *51*, 448–454.

Arciniega, L.M., Allen, N.J., and González. L. (2013). Don't mess with my company. Poster presented at the annual conference of the Society for Industrial and Organizational Psychology, Houston, TX.

Bauer, T.N. and Erdogan, B. (2011). Organization socialization: The effective onboarding of new employees. In S. Zedeck (ed.), *APA Handbook of Industrial and Organizational Psychology* (Vol. 1, pp. 51–63). Washington, DC: American Psychological Association.

Becker, T.E. (1992). Foci and bases of commitment: Are they distinctions worth making? *Academy of Management Journal*, *35*, 232–244. doi:10.2307/256481.

Becker, T.E. and Billings, R.S. (1993). Profiles of commitment: An empirical test. *Journal of Organizational Behavior*, *14*, 177–190. doi:10.1002/job.4030140207.

Becker, T.E., Randall, D.M., and Riegel, C.D. (1995). The multidimensional view of commitment and the theory of reasoned action: A comparative evaluation. *Journal of Management*, *21*, 617–638. doi:10.1177/014920639502100402.

Bergman, M.E. (2006). The relationship between affective and normative commitment: Review and research agenda. *Journal of Organizational Behavior*, *27*, 645–663. doi.org/10.1002/b.372.

Blau, G. (1985). The measurement and prediction of career commitment. *Journal of Occupational Psychology*, *58*, 277–288. doi:10.1111/j.2044-8325.1985.tb00201.x.

Blau, G. (1989). Testing the generalizability of a career commitment measure and its impact on employee turnover. *Journal of Vocational Behavior*, *35*, 88–103. doi:10.1016/0001-8791(89)90050-X.

Blau, G. and Lunz, M. (1998). Testing the incremental effect of professional commitment on intent to leave one's profession beyond the effects of external, personal and work-related variables. *Journal of Vocational Behavior*, *52*, 260–269. doi:10.1006/jvbe.1997.1601.

Caldwell, D.F., Chatman, J.A., and O'Reilly, C.A. (1990). Building organizational commitment: A multifirm study. *Journal of Occupational Psychology*, *63*, 245–261. doi:10.1111/j.2044-8325.1990.tb00525.x.

Cook, J. and Wall, T. (1980). New work attitude measures of trust, organizational commitment and personal need non-fulfillment. *Journal of Occupational Psychology*, *53*, 39–52. DOI: 10.1111/j.2044-8325.1980.tb00005.x.

Edwards, J.R. (2001). Multidimensional constructs in organizational behavior research: An integrative analytical framework. *Organizational Research Methods*, *4*, 144–192. doi:10.1177/109442810142004.

Etzioni, A. (1961). *A Comparative Analysis of Complex Organizations: On Power, Involvement, and their Correlates*. New York: Free Press.

Etzioni, A. (1975). *A Comparative Analysis of Complex Organizations: On Power, Involvement and their Correlates*. New York: Free Press.

Gellatly, I.R., Hunter, K.H., Currie, L.G., and Irving, P.G. (2009). HRM practices and organizational commitment profiles. *International Journal of Human Resource Management*, *20*, 869–884. doi:10.1080/09585190902770794.

Gellatly, I.R., Meyer, J.P., and Luchak, A.A. (2006). Combined effects of the three commitment components on focal and discretionary behaviors: A test of Meyer and Herscovitch's propositions. *Journal of Vocational Behavior*, *69*, 331–345. doi:10.1016/j.jvb.2005.12.005.

Gordon, M.E., Philpot, J.W., Burt, R.E., Thompson, C.A., and Spiller, W.E. (1980). Commitment to the union: Development of a measure and an examination of its correlates. *Journal of Applied Psychology*, *65*, 479–499. doi: 10.1037/0021-9010.65.4.479.

Hackett, R.D., Bycio, P., and Hausdorf, P.A. (1994). Further assessments of Meyer and Allen's (1991) three-component model of organizational commitment. *Journal of Applied Psychology*, *79*, 15–23. doi:10.1037/0021-9010.79.1.15.

Hrebiniak, L.G. and Alutto, J.A. (1972). Personal and role-related factors in the development of organizational commitment. *Administrative Science Quarterly*, *17*, 555–573. doi:10.2307/2393833.

Jaros, S.J. (1997). An assessment of Meyer and Allen's (1991) three-component model of organizational commitment and turnover intentions. *Journal of Vocational Behavior*, *51*, 319–337. doi.10.1006/jvbe.1995.1553.

Johnson, R.E., Groff, K.W., and Taing, M.U. (2009). Nature of the interactions among organizational commitments: Complementary, competitive, or synergistic? *British Journal of Management*, *20*, 431–447. doi:10.1111/j.1467-8551.2008.00592.x.

Kam, C., Morin, A.J.S., Meyer, J.P., and Topolnytsky, L. (2015). Are commitment profiles stable and predictable? A latent transition analysis. *Journal of Management*. Advance online publication. doi:10.1177/0149206313503010.

Kanter, R.M. (1968). Commitment and social organization: A study of commitment mechanisms in utopian communities. *American Sociological Review*, *33*, 499–517. doi: http://dx.doi.org/10.2307/2092438.

Kelman, H.C. (1958). Compliance, identification, and internalization: Three processes of attitude change. *Journal of Conflict Resolution*, *2*, 51–60. doi:10.1177/002200275800200106.

Klein, H.J., Cooper, J.T., Molloy, J.C., and Swanson, J.A. (2014). The assessment of commitment: Advantages of a unidimensional, target-free approach. *Journal of Applied Psychology*, *99*, 222–238. doi:10.1037/a0034751.

Klein, H.J., Molloy, J.C., and Brinsfield, C.T. (2012). Reconceptualizing workplace commitment to redress a stretched construct: revisiting assumptions and removing confounds. *Academy of Management Review*, *37*(1), 130–151. doi:10.5465/arma.2010.0018.

Klein, H.J., Molloy, J.C., and Cooper, J.T. (2009). Conceptual foundations: Construct definitions and theoretical foundations of workplace commitments. In H.J. Klein, T.E. Becker, and J.P. Meyer (eds), *Commitment in Organizations: Accumulated Wisdom and New Directions* (pp. 3–36). New York: Routledge/Taylor.

Law, K.S. and Wong, C.S. (1999). Multidimensional constructs in structural equation analysis: An illustration using the job perception and job satisfaction constructs. *Journal of Management*, *25*, 143–160. doi:10.1016/S0149-2063(99)80007-5.

March, J.G. and Simon, H.A. (1958). *Organizations*. Oxford: Wiley.

Mayer, R.C. and Schoorman, F.D. (1992). Predicting participation and production outcomes through a two-dimensional model of organizational commitment. *Academy of Management Journal*, *35*, 671–684. doi:10.2307/256492.

Mayer, R.C. and Schoorman, F.D. (1998). Differentiating antecedents of organizational commitment: A test of March and Simon's model. *Journal of Organizational Behavior*, *19*, 15–28. doi:10.1002/(SICI)1099-1379(199801)19:1.

McGee, G.W. and Ford, R.C. (1987). Two (or more?) dimensions of organizational commitment: Reexamination of affective and continuance commitment scales. *Journal of Applied Psychology*, *72*, 638–641. doi.org/10.1037/0021-9010.72.4.638.

McNally, J.J. and Irving, P.G. (2010). The relationship between university student commitment profiles and behavior: Exploring the nature of context effects. *Journal of Leadership and Organizational Studies*, *17*, 201–215. doi:10.1177/1548051810363810.

Meyer, J.P. and Allen, N.J. (1984). Testing the 'side-bet theory' of organizational commitment: Some methodological considerations. *Journal of Applied Psychology*, *69*, 372–378. doi:10.1037/0021-9010.69.3.372.

Meyer, J.P. and Allen, N.J. (1991). A three-component conceptualization of organizational commitment. *Human Resource Management Review*, *1*, 61–89. doi:10.1016/1053-4822(91)90011-Z.

Meyer, J.P. and Allen, N.J. (1997). *Commitment in the Workplace: Theory, Research, and Application*. Thousand Oaks, CA: Sage Publications.

Meyer, J.P., Allen, N.J., and Gellatly, IR. (1990). Affective and continuance commitment to the organization: Evaluation of measures and analysis of concurrent and time-lagged relations. *Journal of Applied Psychology*, *75*, 710–720. doi:10.1037/0021-9010.75.6.710.

Meyer, J.P., Allen, N.J., and Smith, C.A. (1993). Commitment to organizations and occupations: Extension and test of a three-component conceptualization. *Journal of Applied Psychology*, *78*, 538–551. doi:10.1037/0021-9010.78.4.538.

Meyer, J.P. and Herscovitch, L. (2001). Commitment in the workplace: Toward a general model. *Human Resource Management Review*, *11*, 299–326. doi:10.1016/S1053-4822(00)00053-X.

Meyer, J.P., Kam, C., Goldenberg, I., and Bremner, N.L. (2013a). Organizational commitment in the military: Application of a profile approach. *Military Psychology*, *25*, 381–401. doi:10.1037/mil0000007.

Meyer, J.P. and Maltin, E.R. (2010). Employee commitment and well-being: A critical review, theoretical framework and research agenda. *Journal of Vocational Behavior*, *77*, 323–337. doi:10.1016/j.jvb.2010.04.007.

Meyer, J.P., Morin, A.J.S., and Vandenberghe, C. (2015). Dual commitment to organization and supervisor: A person-centered approach. *Journal of Vocational Behavior*, *88*, 56–72. doi: 10.1016/j.jvb.2015.02.001.

Meyer, J.P. and Parfyonova, N.M. (2010). Normative commitment in the workplace: A theoretical analysis and re-conceptualization. *Human Resource Management Review*, *20*, 283–294. doi:10.1016/j.hrmr.2009.09.001.

Meyer, J.P., Paunonen, S.V., Gellatly, I.R., Goffin, R.D., and Jackson, D.N. (1989). Organizational commitment and job performance: It's the nature of the commitment that counts. *Journal of Applied Psychology, 74*, 152–156. doi:10.1037/0021-9010.74.1.152.

Meyer, J.P., Stanley, D.J., Herscovitch, L., and Topolnytsky, L. (2002). Affective, continuance and normative commitment to the organization: A meta-analysis of antecedents, correlates, and consequences. *Journal of Vocational Behavior, 61*, 20–52. doi:10.1006/jvbe.2001.1842.

Meyer, J.P., Stanley, D.J., Jackson, T.A., McInnis, K.J., Maltin, E.R., and Sheppard, L. (2012a). Affective, normative and continuance commitment levels across cultures: A meta-analysis. *Journal of Vocational Behavior, 80*, 225–245. doi:10.1016/j.jvb.2011.09.005.

Meyer, J.P., Stanley, L.J., and Parfyonova, N.M. (2012b). Employee commitment in context: The nature and implication of commitment profiles. *Journal of Vocational Behavior, 80*, 1–16. doi:10.1016/j.jvb.2011.07.002.

Meyer, J.P., Stanley, L.J., and Vandenberg, R.J. (2013b). A person-centered approach to the study of commitment. *Human Resource Management Review, 23*, 190–202. doi:10.1016/j.hrmr.2012.07.007.

Morin, A.J.S., Meyer, J.P., McInerney, D.M., Marsh, H.W., and Ganotice, F.A., Jr. (2015). Profiles of dual commitment to the occupation and organization: Relations to well-being and turnover intentions. *Asia Pacific Journal of Management, 32*, 717–744. doi:10.1007/s10490-015-9411-6.

Morrow, P.C. (1983). Concept redundancy in organizational research: The case of work commitment. *Academy of Management Review, 8*, 486–500. doi:10.2307/257837.

Morrow, P.C. (1993). *The Theory and Measurement of Work Commitment.* Greenwich, CT: JAI Press.

Mowday, R.T., Porter, L.W., and Steers, R.M. (1982). *Employee–Organization Linkages: The Psychology of Commitment, Absenteeism, and Turnover.* New York: Academic Press.

Mowday, R.T., Steers, R.M., and Porter, L.W. (1979). The measurement of organizational commitment. *Journal of Applied Psychology, 14*, 224–247. doi:10.1016/0001 8791(79)90072-1.

O'Reilly, C. and Chatman, J. (1986). Organizational commitment and psychological attachment: The effects of compliance, identification, and internalization on prosocial behavior. *Journal of Applied Psychology, 71*, 492–499. doi:10.1037/0021-9010.71.3.492.

O'Reilly, C.A., Chatman, J., and Caldwell, D.F. (1991). People and organizational culture: A profile comparison approach to assessing person–organization fit. *Academy of Management Journal, 34*, 487–516. doi:10.2307/256404.

Penley, L.E. and Gould, S. (1988). Etzioni's model of organizational involvement: A perspective for understanding commitment to organizations. *Journal of Organizational Behavior, 9*, 43–59. doi:10.1002/job.4030090105.

Powell, D.M. and Meyer, J.P. (2004). Side-bet theory and the three-component model of organizational commitment. *Journal of Vocational Behavior, 65*, 157–177. doi:10.1016/S0001-8791(03)00050-2.

Reichers, A.E. (1985). A review and reconceptualization of organizational commitment. *Academy of Management Review, 10*, 465–476. doi:10.2307/258128.

Ritzer, G., and Trice, H.M. (1969). An empirical study of Howard Becker's side-bet theory. *Social Forces, 47*, 475–479.

Schechter, D.S. (1985). Value and continuance commitment: A field test of a dual conceptualization of organizational commitment. Unpublished master's thesis. University of Maryland, College Park, MD.

Solinger, O.N., van Olffen, W., and Roe, R.A. (2008). Beyond the three-component model of organizational commitment. *Journal of Applied Psychology, 93*, 70–83. doi:10.1037/0021-9010.93.1.70.

Somers, M.J. (1995). Organizational commitment, turnover and absenteeism: An examination of direct and interaction effects. *Journal of Organizational Behavior, 16*, 49–58. doi:10.1002/job.4030160107.

Somers, M.J. (2010). Patterns of attachment to organizations: Commitment profiles and work outcomes. *Journal of Occupational and Organizational Psychology, 83*, 443–453. doi:10.1348/096317909X424060.

Stanley, D.J. and Spence, J.R. (2014). Expectations for replications: Are yours realistic? *Perspectives on Psychological Science, 9*, 305–318. doi:10.1177/1745691614528518.

Stanley, L., Vandenberghe, C., Vandenberg, R., and Bentein, K. (2013). Commitment profiles and employee turnover. *Journal of Vocational Behavior, 82*, 176–187. doi:10.1016/j.jvb.2013.01.011.

Tayyab, S. (2007). An empirical assessment of organizational commitment measures. *Pakistan Journal of Psychological Research, 22*, 1–21. http://search.proquest.com/docview/89070690?accountid=15115.

Tsoumbris, P. and Xenikou, A. (2010). Commitment profiles: The configural effect of the forms and foci of commitment on work outcomes. *Journal of Vocational Behavior, 77*, 401–411. doi:10.1016/j.jvb.2010.07.006.

Vandenberg, R.J., Self, R.M., and Seo, J.H. (1994). A critical examination of the internalization, identification, and compliance commitment measures. *Journal of Management, 20*, 123–140. doi:10.1177/014920639402000106.

Vandenberg, R.J. and Stanley, L.J. (2009). Statistical and methodological challenges for commitment researchers: Issues of invariance, change across time, and profile differences. In H.J. Klein, T.E. Becker, and J.P. Meyer (eds), *Commitment in Organizations* (pp. 383–416). New York: Routledge/Taylor.

Wallace, J.E. (1993). Professional and organizational commitment compatible or incompatible? *Journal of Vocational Behavior, 42*(3), 333–349. doi:10.1006/jvbe.1993.1023.

Wallace, J. E. (1995). Organizational and professional commitment in professional and nonprofessional organizations. *Administrative Science Quarterly, 40*(2), 228–255. doi:10.2307/2393637.

Wasti, S.A. (2005). Commitment profiles: Combinations of organizational commitment forms and job outcomes. *Journal of Vocational Behavior, 67*, 290–308. doi:10.1016/j.jvb.2004.07.002.

Whitener, E.M. and Walz, P.M. (1993). Exchange theory determinants of affective and continuance commitment and turnover. *Journal of Vocational Behavior, 42*, 265–281. doi.org/10.1006/jvbe.1993.1019.

Wiener, Y. (1982). Commitment in organizations: A normative view. *Academy of Management Review, 7*, 418–428. doi:10.2307/257334.

Wiener, Y. and Vardi, Y. (1980). Relationships between job, organization, and career commitments and work outcomes: An integrative approach. *Organizational Behavior and Human Performance, 26*, 81–96. doi.org/10.1016/0030-5073(80)90048-3.

Xu, L. and Bassham, L.S. (2010). Reexamination of factor structure and psychometric properties of the three-component model of organizational commitment. *North American Journal of Psychology, 12*, 297–311. https://www.lib.uwo.ca/cgi-bin/ezpauthn.cgi?url=http://search.proquest.com/docview/861789456?accountid=151.

4. Multiple foci of workplace commitments
Thomas E. Becker

It has long been known that employees can be psychologically attached to multiple workplace targets. As early as 1950, Herbert Simon and his colleagues recognized that commitment to an organization as a whole is distinguishable from commitment to its specific values or policies (Simon et al., 1950). In 1957, Gouldner published his ground-breaking work demonstrating that some employees ('locals') are tied more to groups within the organization while others ('cosmopolitans') identify more with their occupations. Subsequent research supported Gouldner's distinction by showing that, compared to locals, cosmopolitans are less likely to express loyalty to a particular community and more likely to participate in occupational organizations (Gouldner, 1958). Also, locals are more responsive than cosmopolitans to immediate primary group pressures, while cosmopolitans are more sensitive to a broader range of demands (Merton, 1957). The relevance of Gouldner's work for the study of multiple commitments was not recognized for some time. The bulk of the theory and research on commitment during the 1970s and 1980s focused on commitment to the organization (Mowday et al., 1982). To be sure, there were exceptions. For example, several investigators studied how commitment to a union is related to commitment to employing organizations, and others discussed escalation of commitment to a course of action and goal commitment. However, the great majority of published work on commitment during this time focused exclusively on the organization as the target.

Reichers (1985) took a quantum leap forward by developing a theoretical foundation upon which a multiple commitments perspective could be based. She argued that in order to specify the foci of multiple commitments, the various groups that are relevant to an organization must be identified. Reichers used Gouldner's work on reference groups and research on role theory to suggest that many organization members are aware of and committed to sets of goals and values held by multiple groups. She discussed potential commitment foci within the organization, including co-workers and top management, and external to the organization, including clients, customers, professional associations, unions, and the community. In sum, Reichers made a strong argument that a multiple commitments approach is more precise and meaningful than an approach focused on global conceptions of organizational commitment.

In the early 1990s I published a paper that examined whether certain distinctions among foci and bases (motives) of commitment are worth making (Becker, 1992). A central result was that commitments to top management, supervisors, and work groups explained variance in job satisfaction, the intent to quit and prosocial organizational behaviors, over and above that accounted for by commitment to organizations. Later my colleagues and I demonstrated the applicability of a multiple commitments approach to tardiness and job performance (Becker et al., 1996; Becker et al., 1995). A host of other researchers identified additional foci of commitment and provided evidence of their theoretical and practical relevance. Among these were commitments to divisions within an organization and foci external to it, including professions, careers, subsidiaries, and joint ventures (Vandenberghe, 2009). In addition, a mass of new research was conducted on commitments to interpersonal foci, including supervisors, peers, work teams, top management, and customers (Becker, 2009). Finally, theorists and researchers attempted to link commitments more closely to behavior by studying 'action commitments', including commitments to goals and values, group norms, and organizational change efforts (Neubert and Wu, 2009).

Concomitant to work identifying and evaluating commitment foci was research on antecedents and consequences of these commitments. Antecedents included individual-level factors such as demographic variables and personality (Bergman et al., 2009); social influences such as leader–member exchange, perceived organizational support, and psychological contracts (Wayne et al., 2009); and organizational-level antecedents such as structure, climate, and culture (Wright and Kehoe, 2009). More recent work has identified other antecedents, including Machiavellianism (Zettler et al., 2011), self-esteem (Panaccio and Vandenberghe, 2011), social climate (Rice, 2009), and human resource practices such as training opportunities and empowerment in decision-making (Wasti and Can, 2008).

In addition to in-role and extra-role job performance and withdrawal behaviors, researchers have examined the impact of multiple commitments on creativity, employee well-being, and bottom-line outcomes such as sales volume and market share (see Chapter 17, this volume; Klein et al., 2009). Recent research has further documented the link between multiple commitments and in-role and extra-role job performance (Veurink and Fischer, 2011) and withdrawal behaviors (Askew et al., 2013), and identified other relevant outcomes, including burnout (Morin et al., 2013), proactive behavior (Belschak and Hartog, 2010), team proficiency (Strauss et al., 2009), and customer loyalty (Jones et al., 2008).

OTHER KEY IDEAS AND FINDINGS

Other central issues attracting research attention include the discriminant validity of multiple commitments, the notion that particular foci of commitment can be 'matched' to certain behaviors, and the possibility of conflicting commitments. Investigations of more complex relationships between multiple commitments and outcomes have also been conducted.

Discriminant Validity

To be useful, distinctions among various commitment foci must be conceptually meaningfully and empirically supported. Early work supported discriminant validity among foci of commitment (Becker et al., 1996; Bishop and Scott, 2000) and later research has added to the evidence. This evidence includes confirmatory factor analyses supporting the existence of different commitment foci, and confirmation that different foci often have different antecedents and consequences (Becker and Kernan, 2003; Belschak and Hartog, 2010; Panaccio and Vandenberghe, 2011; Vandenberghe and Bentein, 2009).

The Matching Hypothesis

The principle of compatibility was originally proposed by Fishbein and Ajzen (1977) and holds that attitudes are reasonably accurate predictors of behavior, to the extent that the attitudes are defined in relation to the behavior. When applied to multiple commitments this principle, sometimes called the matching hypothesis, is that commitment to a given target is a good predictor of a behavior, to the extent that the behavior is of concern to the target and the target has the opportunity to influence the behavior. For example, commitment to supervisors is a better predictor of job performance than is commitment to organizations, because supervisors are usually directly accountable for the performance of their reports and have the opportunity to influence performance in a number of ways (appraisal, monitoring, verbal recognition). On the other hand, commitment to organizations is a better predictor of citizenship behavior directed toward the organization, because such behaviors are of central concern to organizations and reinforcement often comes from higher-level representatives of the organization. Older research generally supported the matching hypothesis (Becker and Kernan, 2003; Cheng et al., 2003; Siders et al., 2001), as has more recent work (Belschak and Hartog, 2010; Veurink and Fischer, 2011). However, support is not universal (Tsoumbris and Xenikou, 2010; Wasti and Can, 2008), and it is not clear that the most relevant target or targets can always be accurately specified a priori.

Conflicting and Compatible Commitments

Reichers (1985) originally proposed the possibility of conflicts among commitment to different foci, and she later demonstrated it in a study of commitments to top management, funding agencies, clients, and professions (Reichers, 1986). She called differences in the endorsements (commitments) of one target over another, 'intrapsychic conflict', and differences between individuals' endorsements of the foci and the perceived endorsements of top management, 'psychosocial conflict'. While intrapsychic conflict did not have significant relations with other variables, psychosocial conflict appeared to decrease job satisfaction and commitment to the overall organization. Later work examined commitment conflicts among expatriates returning home (Gregersen and Black, 1990), members of directorial boards (Golden-Biddle and Rao, 1997), and management teams involved in joint ventures (Johnson, 1999). Recent work has also demonstrated that commitments sometimes can and do conflict (Jones et al., 2008; Kinnie and Swart, 2012), though sometimes they also complement each other (Tsoumbris and Xenikou, 2010). We do not yet have a strong theory of the nature of commitment conflicts and when multiple commitments are likely to be conflicting versus complementary.

Complex Relationships among Commitment Foci

Much of the work on commitment has examined simple linear relationships between multiple commitments and their outcomes. However, recent research has begun to describe and document more complex relationships including curvilinear effects (Morin et al., 2013) and interactive effects among commitment foci (Askew et al., 2013). In addition, investigation of within-person commitments has begun (Becker et al., 2013) and some researchers have taken a person-centered approach to dual commitments (Meyer et al., 2015; Morin et al., 2015). Finally, an integrative theory of commitment and motivation, hereafter referred to as the MBV model (Meyer, Becker, Vandenberg), has been proposed (Meyer et al., 2004) and partially tested (Becker et al., forthcoming).

So, much has been accomplished and much has yet to be learned. The following section contains my evaluation of the current status of the multiple commitments literature.

ASSESSMENT OF THE CURRENT STATE OF THE LITERATURE

My strengths, weaknesses, opportunities, threats (SWOT) analysis involves assessing the strengths and weaknesses of the literature, and appraisal of opportunities and threats in the environment. In this context, the environment consists of theorists and researchers outside the community of commitment scholars. Based on the quality of the literature, these constituencies will decide whether to make use of or ignore work in the area. A summary of the analysis is provided in Table 4.1.

Strengths

One strength of the literature is the provision of clear evidence for the multi-foci perspective. There is now convincing evidence that a number of potential targets of commitment exist, and that many employees are committed to some degree to one or more of these targets. In addition, there is convincing support for other central hypotheses in the area. Among them are that: (1) distinguishing among commitments often contributes to understanding and predicting important work behaviors, and this is particularly true when the foci of commitment and behavior 'match'; (2) profiles of commitment foci can be created and this may further deepen comprehension and behavioral forecasting; and (3) conflicts among commitments sometimes occur and, when they do, they can have negative consequences for employee attitudes and action. Thus, while there is certainly

Table 4.1   Swot analysis of the literature on multiple foci of commitment

Strengths	*Weaknesses*
Clear evidence for multiple commitments	Proliferation of commitment foci
Support for central ideas	Redundant research questions
Practical relevance	Failure to address important theoretical issues
Advancing knowledge	Weak research designs
Opportunities	*Threats*
Linking commitment to other OB topics	Paradigm underdevelopment
Linking commitment to other human resources topics	Perceived concept redundancy
Needs of 'external' scholars for better explanations of behaviors and outcomes	Fads and fashions of scholarly concepts
Practitioner needs for tools to diagnose, predict, and influence behavior and outcomes	Publish or perish versus scientific advancement

room for additional debate and development, there is a solid core of reliable knowledge and a credible foundation for further growth.

Another strength is the practical relevance of the literature. Even with increased job mobility and alternative work arrangements, organizations still need a committed workforce. Withdrawal behaviors, in-role and extra-role job performance, deviance, and creativity will continue to be consequential for organizations, and managing these outcomes must often include managing employee commitments. For instance, although voluntary turnover may occur for a number of reasons, commitments to organizational foci often play a key role. Employees quit because commitment to their manager has been demolished by abusive supervision, commitment to the organization has been eroded by violation of the psychological contract, or dysfunctional dynamics in their team have led to alienation from rather than commitment to their teams. Managers who understand these relationships can influence commitment by becoming better leaders, preserving psychological contracts and building more effective teams. The matching hypothesis is useful because it suggests to managers which commitments can be expected to affect a given behavior. If job performance is a problem, then commitment to supervisors might be the focus of development. If team cohesiveness is an issue, then fostering commitment to the team is more pertinent. If the goal is to promote greater volunteerism on behalf of the organization, then commitment to the organization should be emphasized.

A final strength is that knowledge is advancing in the area and progress can be expected to continue. For instance, there is still a great deal to be known about within-person variability in commitments and, while there is now a sound theory linking multiple commitments to motivation, behaviors and outcomes (Meyer et al., 2004), MBV theory has yet to be fully tested.

In addition, given the changing nature of work and organizations, it may be more difficult than ever for employees to commit long term to organizations, because organizations cannot make such a commitment to employees. A fascinating question, thus, is: to what targets (for example, supervisors, teams, projects) can or should employees commit, and what, if anything, can management do to promote commitment to these substitutes for organizational commitment? Advancing knowledge indicates a vital and promising line of science and scholars in the area have formed a community to promote advancement. They meet every few years at a conference at Ohio State, USA to discuss new ideas, argue philosophical points and identify paths forward. This has produced valuable books such as Klein et al. (2009) and this one, as well as several special journal issues on commitment topics, including multiple commitments (see the 2013 special issue on understanding workplace commitments in the *Human Resource Management Review*, and the May, 2016 special issue in the *Journal of Organizational Behavior*).

Weaknesses

One potentially serious weakness is the proliferation of commitment foci. This problem is reminiscent of the explosion in the proposed number of human needs in the 1960s and 1970s, whereby virtually every behavior was explained via a corresponding need. The result was transforming an originally useful notion into an increasingly multitudinous, narrow and, ultimately, tautological concept. To avoid a similar fate, commitment researchers need to ensure that distinctions among foci are theoretically and empirically worth making. At this point there is ample evidence of discriminant validity for some foci, but less evidence for others. Further, there is little in the way of a meaningful framework for classifying commitment foci or a theory explaining changes in the salience and influence of particular foci. Without theory and data on these issues the proliferation of foci could create a confusing mishmash of targets.

Another weakness in the area is the pursuit of answers to questions for which we already have reliable answers. Although replication is an important aspect of science, continuing to ask redundant questions past a certain point holds back progress. We do not need more studies showing that multiple commitments exist in a particular company, industry, sample, or geographical location; nor do we need more evidence that various commitments are correlated with performance or withdrawal criteria. It may be tempting to implement such studies because they have a ready theoretical basis, are easy to conduct, can be expected to produce significant findings, and can probably be published somewhere. However, they contribute little to existing knowledge and undermine our credibility by making it seem that we have nothing new to say.

The flipside of this coin is a failure to address important theoretical issues. For example, MBV theory suggests that commitment to social foci have specific causal effects on goal regulation and goal commitment and, through these, on direction, effort, persistence, task strategies, and behavior. More than ten years following publication of the theory, there is little sound research examining these relationships. Other theoretical issues in pressing need of empirical investigation are: the development of a meaningful typology of commitment foci and profiles of foci; work on different kinds of commitment conflicts and their causes, consequences, and resolution; a more precise mapping of which foci 'match' which behaviors and outcomes (and why); and detailed examination of the nature and implications of within-person variation in multiple commitments.

A final weakness is the shaky research designs used in much multiple commitments research. In my review of recent studies (2008–2015) the majority of investigations were cross-sectional, with most or all data based on self-report. I suspect that such designs are more prevalent because they are easier to carry out than stronger designs. Further, academic tenure and promotion systems often reinforce doing publishable work that does not take too long, and journal standards sometimes value elaborate statistical techniques more than sound methods of data collection. This is not to be cynical: some research has utilized rigorous designs including experiments (Jones et al., 2008) and data drawn from multiple sources (Askew et al., 2013). However, that these constitute a minority of published studies does count as a weakness.

Opportunities

Scholars in other areas of organizational behavior (OB) and human resource management comprise one audience in the 'environment' of multiple commitments research, and opportunities exist for making connections to these areas. This has already happened in OB to an extent, with work on multiple commitments being tied to theory and research on motivation, leadership, and team dynamics. Other connections are feasible especially in the domain of organizational processes. For instance, commitment to the employer could play a moderating role in the effect of organizational structure on strategy, such that top managers are more likely to align structure and strategy if they are highly committed to the employer, and lower-level employees are more likely to implement the strategy if they are similarly committed. Commitment to more local foci would presumably be less relevant in this case. In some instances commitment may be an antecedent, as when commitment to a decision-making group encourages broadening the decision frame, needed to make effective decisions. In other instances commitment might be a mediator, as when participation increases commitment to one's work team, which in turn fosters information-sharing and the distribution of knowledge.

There are additional connections that could be made in the area of human resource management both in terms of commitment's effects on human resources and vice versa. The following are some examples:

- The consequences of supervisors' commitments to the organization and direct reports on reported Equal Employment Opportunity Commission (EEOC) violations and charges of adverse impact.
- The influence of commitments of compensation committees to the chief executive officer (CEO) and shareholders on executive salaries, bonuses, and stock options.
- The role of team composition and reward practices on commitment to teams.
- The impact of the contingent workforce on the levels, bases, and foci of commitment and its outcomes.

More broadly, industrial-organizational psychologists and OB scholars have long borrowed concepts and theories from other disciplines such as social and clinical psychology, and this is certainly true of work in the multiple commitments area. It would be nice to see the field contribute back to these disciplines, and there are undoubtedly opportunities to do so. For instance, in social psychology the MBV model could be used to more thoroughly explicate the role of multiple commitments in promotion and prevention processes as described in regulatory focus theory (Higgins, 1998). Also, perhaps the process of interpersonal attraction could be better understood if the relative commitment to the target of attraction and commitment to peer groups (which may define and reinforce notions of attractiveness) were taken into account (see Berscheid and Reis, 1998).

In clinical psychology a deeper understanding of teen anxiety and dysfunctional defiance might be gained by considering conflicting commitments to parents, peers, and role models (Greene et al., 2002). Further, work on adult attachment styles could be advanced by recognizing that work-related commitments, in addition to other foci, may drive attachment-related behaviors (see Bartholomew and Horowitz, 1991). The nature of multiple commitments even poses broad questions for evolutionary psychology (see Buss, 1999, 2005): is there something in our evolutionary history that has produced a set of genes that interacts with the environment to produce a tendency toward multiple commitments? What survival value, if any, is there to possessing conflicting commitments? Commitments to what foci are most crucial to species well-being, and under what circumstances? For example, perhaps there is a predisposition to become more committed to leaders and groups (proximal foci) than to abstract, psychologically distal collectives (for example, society) because for much of human history the former have promoted greater safety and defense than the latter.

A final opportunity resides in practitioner needs for tools to diagnose, predict, and affect workplace behavior and outcomes. Although it is common for articles on multiple commitments to conclude with implications for practice, not much has been done to turn those implications into practice. A proactive approach would involve focusing research and consulting on 'how-to' topics related to measuring and managing multiple commitments. For instance, researchers could create and validate simple, practical scales aimed at identifying key foci and bases of commitment (along the lines suggested by Becker, 1992 and Cohen, 2003). Consultants could then ensure that these measures get into the hands of managers by including the measures in commitment workshops. Such workshops could also include discussions of the nature and consequences of multiple commitments and how to address commitment conflicts, match commitments to behaviors and outcomes, and enhance commitment to relevant foci.

Threats

Debate and discussion are part of healthy discourse in science and, by these criteria, commitment theory and research have been healthy indeed. However, there is a danger that if a community of scholars cannot agree on basic issues their credibility may suffer. Pfeffer (1993) argued that to compete successfully with adjacent social sciences in the contest for resources, organizational science must demonstrate a certain level of paradigm development. This requires achieving and projecting a consensus on basic concepts and technical certainty necessary for obtaining resources (for example, government funding, business participation in research) and fostering collaborations among people in the field. Funding and collaboration in turn enhance subsequent development of the field.

In the current case the threat is that external constituencies may come to believe that work on multiple commitments cannot be taken seriously. For instance, these audiences might conclude that if after decades of study commitment researchers cannot even agree on the meaning and measurement of commitment, then work on multiple commitments is of little value. Is commitment a broad term for a psychological bond with organizational foci (Becker, 2009; O'Reilly and Chatman, 1986) or, rather, a force that binds (Meyer and Allen, 1991; Meyer and Herscovitch, 2001)? Or is it a specific type of bond to workplace targets (Brown, 1996; Klein et al., 2012)? Or is it a job attitude (Mowday et al., 1982; Solinger et al., 2008) or part of a general job attitude (Harrison et al., 2006)? The definition of commitment is the most basic issue in the field and as yet there is no consensus. In fact, there is less consensus now than in the past. Definitional disagreements translate into disagreements over measurement because the measures are predicated on the presumed meaning of commitment. Because measures enable data collection, entire bodies of research rest upon the adopted definition. Hence, the current path in commitment research leads to largely non-comparable bodies of work that cannot be cumulated because they rest on different foundations.

These definitional and measurement issues are highly relevant to the current chapter because to study multiple commitments we must know what commitment means and how to evaluate it. To obtain consensus on these issues I believe leaders in the commitment area must put aside short-term self-interests and agree to work toward a common definition and measures. One possibility is to use an Ohio State Commitment Conference or another forum as an opportunity to discuss and debate definitions and measures. After all the relevant parties have presented their perspectives the community of commitment scholars in attendance would vote and the prevailing definition and measures would become the recognized position of the commitment community. Scholars would remain free to study whatever they like, and the official position could be revisited from time to time if compelling reasons are identified. In the meantime, members of the community would agree to abide by the official position in their theoretical and empirical pursuits.

A related problem is concept redundancy, a difficulty that has accompanied commitment research for years (Morrow, 1983). There are a number of variables that involve employee attachments, including commitment, identification, job satisfaction, job involvement, engagement, and embeddedness. Considerable progress has been made in terms of discriminant validity with support for distinctions between commitment and some of these variables. For example, job satisfaction is primarily evaluative in nature with the job as the central target, while commitment is more a matter of attachment than evaluation with many possible foci. Identification is an assessment of self ('Who am I?') while commitment is an assessment of relationships ('What is my attachment to [a given target]?'). As such, identification is an antecedent of commitment in that one must have a sense of self-identity before considering relationships to other individuals, groups, or organizations (Meyer et al., 2006). Despite the tenability of such distinctions, my sense is that people outside the commitment community do not know a great deal about differences among the variables. A lack of information and evidence can make these people susceptible to undue influence by vocal champions of notions like engagement and embeddedness. It is our job as professionals to inform and rationally persuade individuals outside our community that commitment is not just another job attitude but, rather, a key concept essential to understanding employee motivation and behavior.

I have taken several potshots at engagement and embeddedness and this is because fads and fashions of OB concepts constitute another threat. Abrahamson (1996) identified the role of scholarly fashion-setters (those creating new concepts, theories, and techniques) in foisting ideas on gullible managers and others. Successful fashion-setters must sense the emergent collective preferences of relevant constituencies, develop rhetorics that describe their ideas as the forefront of scholarly or management progress, and disseminate these rhetorics back to managers and other stakeholders. 'Fashion setters that fall behind in this race are condemned to be perceived as lagging rather than leading management progress' (Abrahamson, 1996, p. 254). Abrahamson and Fairchild (1999) later described the life cycle of academic fads and fashions. Early stages of the cycle are characterized by emotionally charged, enthusiastic, and often unreasoned discourse. Later stages, typically signaling the end of a fad or fashion, are characterized by reasoned, unemotional, qualified discussions. Unfortunately, the mature concepts are not necessarily recognized as such and are not necessarily adopted by future theorists, researchers, and practitioners. Rather, new fads and fashions enter the arena of ideas and take their turn in the spotlight while the mature concepts are relegated to the intellectual dustbin.

I contend that the concepts of engagement and embeddedness are fashions or at least began as fashions, and still have something of a faddish nature. The idea of engagement appears to have been created by management consultants and to have been heavily marketed to clients in the early 2000s (Macey and Schneider, 2008). The life cycle of the engagement concept has progressed and more reputable, scientific work has recently been conducted (see Meyer, 2013; Chapter 6 in this volume). A similar cycle can be seen with the notion of job embeddedness (see Chapter 7 in this volume). Although some research on construct validity has now been done (Crossley et al., 2007), earlier work was trendy in nature, with embeddedness having considerable conceptual overlap with commitment. Embeddedness researchers have further blurred the distinction by borrowing the idea of multiple foci (Kiazad et al., 2015). My point here is not that engagement and embeddedness are necessarily useless concepts but that the process producing the concepts – the churning mill of fads and fashions – is one that threatens the longevity of the more venerable work on employee commitment, including multiple commitments. Scholars and practitioners interested in multiple commitments need to broadcast the legitimate strengths of their concepts, theories, and research. There is an important difference between the zealotry that often accompanies fads and fashions, and the confidence that can and should accompany scientific knowledge. The confidence associated with scientific knowledge is based on sound theoretical and empirical support, while the zealotry accompanying fads and fashions is based on unreasoned enthusiasm and, often, self-promotion. Champions are needed to ensure the continuing advancement of multiple commitments research.

A final threat is the sometimes opposing goals of obtaining academic tenure and contributing meaningfully to science. While scientific contribution is presumably a requirement for publication, there are other criteria which dilute standards of scientific advancement. An example is the pressure inherent in many promotion and tenure systems to publish a certain number of papers in a given time. This pressure probably leads some scholars to address simpler, redundant research questions using quicker though less rigorous research methods, rather more complex, newer questions using more time-consuming but more rigorous methods. The same pressure encourages a focus on scholarly fashions. In the early 2000s, for instance, one might have been tempted to conduct a cross-sectional survey on employee engagement rather than carry out a longitudinal study of an important but less flashy multiple commitments topic. We can hope that assistant professors will conduct important, meaningful work (many do), but granting promotion and tenure on the basis of the quantity of publications on current scholarly fads does nothing to encourage this end. To combat this threat, commitment scholars serving on promotion and tenure committees should serve as advocates for rigorous research on meaningful topics.

SUMMARY

To summarize promising paths forward identified in the SWOT analysis, future work in the multiple commitments area should build on current strengths by extending recent advancements, including examination of the matching hypotheses (which foci go with which behaviors and why?); developing deeper theory regarding the nature of commitment conflicts and when they are likely to occur; and conducting additional research on complex relationships (for example, non-linear, interactive). In addition, theorists and researchers in the area should work to overcome current weaknesses by avoiding unnecessary proliferation of commitment foci and pursuing questions for which there are already clear answers (for example: do multiple commitments exist?). Instead, I recommend pursuing important though more difficult questions on the interplay among commitments, within-person variation in commitments, and the accuracy and boundary conditions of MBV theory; and investigating these topics via research that uses rigorous research methods. Scholars should also exploit opportunities by making new connections between the notion of multiple commitments and OB and human resources concepts, and topics outside the field, and along the way, meeting practitioner needs. Finally, we need to address threats related to paradigm underdevelopment, perceived concept redundancy, fads and fashions, and the effects of the 'publish-or-perish' system.

The chapters on specific commitments in this volume will address topics related to their particular target. My purpose here has been to provide an overview and broad assessment of the multiple commitments literature and to suggest several fruitful paths to progress. If I have been preachy in places it is not due to a lack of respect for the work that has been done or those who have done it. Rather, it is my hope that we who work in the area continue to act in accordance with Galileo's commandment: contribute to science..

REFERENCES

Abrahamson, E. (1996). Management fashion, *Academy of Management Review*, 21, 254–285.

Abrahamson, E. and G. Fairchild (1999). Management fashion: Lifcycles, triggers, and collective learning processes, *Administrative Science Quarterly*, 44, 708–740.

Askew, K., M.U. Taing and R.E. Johnson (2013). The effects of commitment to multiple foci: An analysis of relative influence and interactions, *Human Performance*, 26, 171–190.

Bartholomew, K. and L.M. Horowitz (1991). Attachment styles among young adults: A test of a four-category model, *Journal of Personality and Social Psychology*, 61, 226–244.

Becker, T.E. (1992). Foci and bases of commitment: Are they distinctions worth making? *Academy of Management Journal*, 35, 232–244.

Becker, T.E. (2009). Interpersonal commitments, in H.J. Klein, T.E. Becker, and J.P. Meyer (eds), *Commitment in Organizations*, New York: Routledge, pp. 137–178.

Becker, T.E., R.S. Billings, D.M. Eveleth and N.W. Gilbert (1996). Foci and bases of commitment: Implications for performance, *Academy of Management Journal*, 39, 464–482.

Becker, T.E. and M.C. Kernan (2003). Matching commitment to supervisors and organizations to in-role and extra-role performance, *Human Performance*, 16, 327–348.

Becker, T.E., M.C. Kernan, K.D. Clark and H.J. Klein (forthcoming). Dual commitments to organizations and professions: Different motivational pathways to productivity. *Journal of Management*.

Becker, T.E., D.M. Randall and C.D. Riegel (1995). The multidimensional view of commitment and the theory of reasoned action: A comparative evaluation, *Journal of Management*, 21, 617–638.

Becker, T.E., Ullrich, J. and R. Van Dick (2013). Within-person variation in employee commitment: Where it comes from and why it matters, *Human Resource Management Review*, 23, 131–147.

Belschak, F.D. and D.N.D. Hartog (2010). Pro-self, prosocial, and pro-organizational foci of proactive behavior: Differential antecedents and consequences, *Journal of Occupational and Organizational Psychology*, 83, 475–498.

Bergman, M.E., J.K. Benzer and J.B. Henning (2009). The role of individual differences as contributors to the development of commitment, in H.J. Klein, T.E. Becker, and J.P. Meyer (eds), *Commitment in Organizations*, New York: Routledge, pp. 217–252.

Berscheid, E. and H.T. Reis (1998). Attraction and close relationships, in G. Lindsey, D. Gilbert and S.T. Fiske (eds), *The Handbook of Social Psychology*, Oxford: Oxford University Press, pp. 193–281.

Bishop, J.W. and K.D. Scott (2000). An examination of organizational and team commitment in a self-directed team environment, *Journal of Applied Psychology*, 85, 439–450.

Brown, R.B. (1996). Organizational commitment: Clarifying the concept and simplifying the existing construct typology, *Journal of Vocational Behavior*, 49, 230–251.

Buss, D.M. (1999). *Evolutionary Psychology: The New Science of the Mind*, Boston, MA: Allyn & Bacon.

Buss, D.M. (2005). *The Handbook of Evolutionary Psychology*, Hoboken, NJ: Wiley.

Cheng, B., Jiang, D. and J.H. Riley (2003). Organizational commitment, supervisory commitment, and employee outcomes in the Chinese context: Proximal hypothesis or global hypothesis?, *Journal of Organizational Behavior*, 24, 373–334.

Cohen, A.C. (2003). *Multiple Commitments in the Workplace*, Mahwah, NJ: Lawrence Erlbaum.

Crossley, C.D., R.J. Bennett, S.M. Jex and J.L. Burnfield (2007). Development of a global measure of job embeddedness and integration into a traditional model of voluntary turnover, *Journal of Applied Psychology*, 92, 1031–1042.

Fishbein, M. and I. Ajzen (1977). Attitude–behavior relations: A theoretical analysis and review of empirical research, *Psychological Bulletin*, 84, 888–918.

Golden-Biddle, K. and H. Rao (1997). Breaches in the boardroom: Organizational identity and conflicts of commitment in a nonprofit organization, *Organizational Science*, 8, 593–611.

Gouldner, A.W. (1957). Cosmopolitans and locals: Toward an analysis of latent social roles – I, *Administrative Science Quarterly*, 2, 281–306.

Gouldner, A.W. (1958). Cosmopolitans and locals: Toward an analysis of latent social roles – II, *Administrative Science Quarterly*, 2, 444–480.

Greene, R.W., J. Biederman, S. Zerwas, M.C. Monuteaux, J.C. Goring and S.V. Faranone (2002). Psychiatric comorbidity, family dysfunction, and social impairment in referred youth with oppositional defiant disorder, *American Journal of Psychiatry*, 159, 1214–1224.

Gregersen, H.B. and J.S. Black (1990). A multifaceted approach to expatriate retention in international assignments, *Group and Organization Studies*, 15, 461–484.

Harrison, D.A., D.A. Newman and P.L. Rother (2006). How important are job attitudes? Meta-analytic comparisons of integrative behavioral outcomes and time sequences, *Academy of Management Journal*, 49, 305–325.

Higgins, E.T. (1998). Promotion and prevention: Regulatory focus as a motivational principle, in M.P. Zanna (ed.), *Advances in Experimental Psychology*, New York: Academic Press, Vol. 30, pp. 1–45.

Johnson, J.P. (1999). Multiple commitments and conflicting loyalties in international joint venture management teams, *International Journal of Organizational Analysis*, 7, 54–71.

Jones, T., S.F. Taylor and H.S. Bansal (2008). Commitment to a friend, a service provider, or a service company – are they distinctions worth making?, *Journal of the Academy of Marketing Science*, 36, 473–487.

Kiazad, K., B.C. Holtom, P.W. Hom and A. Newman (2015). Job embeddedness: A multifoci theoretical extension, *Journal of Applied Psychology*, 100, 641–659.

Kinnie, N. and J. Swart (2012). Committed to whom? Professional knowledge worker commitment in cross-boundary organizations, *Human Resource Management Journal*, 22, 21–38.

Klein, H.J., T.E. Becker and J.P. Meyer (2009). *Commitment in Organizations: Accumulated Wisdom and New Directions*, New York: Routledge.

Klein, H.J., J.C. Molloy and C.T. Brinsfield (2012). Reconceptualizing workplace commitment to redress a stretched concept: Revisiting assumptions and removing confounds, *Academy of Management Review*, 37, 130–151.

Macey, W.H. and B. Schneider (2008). The meaning of employee engagement, *Industrial and Organizational Psychology*, 1, 3–30.

Merton, R.K. (1957). *Social Theory and Social Structure*. Glencoe, IL: Free Press.

Meyer, J.P. (2013). The science–practice gap and employee engagement: It's a matter of principle, *Canadian Psychology*, 4, 235–245.

Meyer, J.P. and N.J. Allen (1991). A three-component conceptualization of organizational commitment, *Human Resource Management Review*, 1, 61–89.

Meyer, J.P., Becker, T.E., and Dick, R. (2006). Social identities and commitments at work: Toward an integrative model, *Journal of Organizational Behavior*, 27, 665–683.

Meyer, J.P., T.E. Becker and C. Vandenberghe (2004). Employee commitment and motivation: A conceptual analysis and integrative model, *Journal of Applied Psychology*, 89, 991–1007.

Meyer, J.P. and L. Herscovitch (2001). Commitment in the workplace: Toward a general model, *Human Resource Management Review*, 11, 299–326.

Meyer, J.P., J.S. Morin and C. Vandenberghe (2015). Dual commitment to organization and supervisor: A person-centered approach, *Journal of Vocational Behavior*, 88, 56–72.

Morin, A.J.S., Meyer, J.P., McInerney, D.M., Marsh, H.W. and F.A. Ganotice, Jr. (2015). Profiles of dual commitment to the occupation and organization: Relations to well-being and turnover intentions, *Asia Pacific Journal of Management*, 32, 717–744.

Morin, A.J.S., C. Vandenberghe, M. Turmel, I. Madore and C. Maïano (2013). Probing into commitment's nonlinear relationships to work outcomes, *Journal of Managerial Psychology*, 28, 202–223.

Morrow, P.C. (1983). Concept redundancy in organizational research: The case of work commitment, *Academy of Management Review*, 8, 486–500.

Mowday, R.T., L.W. Porter and R.M. Steers (1982). *Employee–Organization Linkages: The Psychology of Commitment, Absenteeism, and Turnover*, New York: Academic Press.

Neubert, M.J. and C. Wu (2009). Action commitments, in H.J. Klein, T.E. Becker, and J.P. Meyer (eds), *Commitment in Organizations*, New York: Routledge, pp. 179–213.

O'Reilly, C. and J. Chatman (1986). Organizational commitment and psycholocial attachment: The effects of compliance, identification, and internalization on prosocial behavior, *Journal of Applied Psychology*, 71, 492–499.

Panaccio, A. and C. Vandenberghe (2011). The relationships of role clarity and organization-based self-esteem to commitment to supervisors and organizations and turnover intentions, *Journal of Applied Social Psychology*, 41, 1455–1485.

Pfeffer, J. (1993). Barriers to the advance of organizational science: Paradigm development as a dependent variable, *Academy of Management Review*, 18, 599–620.

Reichers, A.E. (1985). A review and reconceptualization of organizational commitment, *Academy of Management Review*, 10, 465–476.

Reichers, A.E. (1986). Conflict and organizational commitments, *Journal of Applied Psychology*, 71, 508–514.

Rice, N.C. (2009). *Examining Predictors of Organizational Commitment: The Influence of Social Climate in a Juvenile Justice Setting*, University of Louisville, ProQuest, Louisville, KY: UMI Dissertations Publishing, 3370038.

Siders, M.A., G. George and R. Dharwadkar (2001). The relationship of internal and external commitment foci to objective job performance measures, *Academy of Management Journal*, 44, 570–579.

Simon, H.A., D.W. Smithburg and V.A. Thompson (1950). *Public Administration*, New York: Knopf.

Solinger, O., W. Van Olffen and R.A. Roe (2008). Beyond the three-component model of organizational commitment, *Journal of Applied Psychology*, 93, 70–83.

Strauss, K., M.A. Griffin and A.E. Rafferty (2009). Proactivity directed toward the team and organization: The role of leadership, commitment and role-breadth self-efficacy, *British Journal of Management*, 20, 279–291.

Tsoumbris, P. and A. Xenikou (2010). Commitment profiles: The configural effect of the forms and foci of commitment on work outcomes, *Journal of Vocational Behavior*, 77, 401–411.

Vandenberghe, C. (2009). Organizational commitments, in H.J. Klein, T.E. Becker, and J.P. Meyer (eds.), *Commitment in Organizations*, New York: Routledge, pp. 99–135.

Vandenberghe, C. and K. Bentein (2009). A closer look at the relationship between affective commitment to supervisors and organizations and turnover, *Journal of Occupational and Organizational Psychology*, 82, 331–348.

Veurink, S.A. and R. Fischer (2011). A refocus on foci: A multidimensional and multi-foci examination of commitment in work contexts, *New Zealand Journal of Psychology*, 40, 160–167.

Wasti, S.A. and Ö. Can (2008). Affective and normative commitment to organization, supervisor, and coworkers: Do collectivist values matter?, *Journal of Vocational Behavior*, 73, 404–413.

Wayne, S.J., J.A.M. Coyle-Shapiro, R. Eisenberger, R.C. Liden, D.M. Rousseau and L.M. Shore (2009). Social influences, in H.J. Klein, T.E. Becker, and J.P. Meyer (eds), *Commitment in Organizations*, New York: Routledge, pp. 253–284.

Wright, P.M. and R.R. Kehoe (2009). Organization-level antecedents and consequences of commitment, in H.J. Klein, T.E. Becker, and J.P. Meyer (eds), *Commitment in Organizations*, New York: Routledge, pp. 285–307.

Zettler, I., N. Friedrich and B.E. Hilbig (2011). 'Dissecting work commitment: The role of Machiavellianism', *Career Development International*, 16, 20–35.

PART II

RELATED CONSTRUCTS

5. A motivational model of employee attachment to an organization

Marylène Gagné and Joshua Howard

Research in management has increasingly come to recognize that there is a gap in our knowledge regarding the effects of workplace initiatives on employee and organizational outcomes. As management scholars have increasingly recognized that an organization's internal resources (including human resources) are a source of competitive advantage (Barney, 1991), there has been growing interest in filling this gap. This problem has been referred to as the 'black box' due to our lack of understanding of the mechanisms that explain relations between the implementation of a new job design initiative or human resources management (HRM) practice and outcomes (Edgar and Geare, 2009). In particular, organizations are often concerned with the attraction and retention of talent, which in part explains the large bodies of research on engagement and turnover.

Interestingly, Wright et al. (1994) have argued that though human resource tools (for example, selection procedures, compensation systems) are important in predicting turnover and performance (Huselid, 1995), they do not constitute the most proximal cause of competitive advantage, because they can easily be copied by competitors. Instead, Wright et al. (1994) argued that it is the human capital itself in an organization that makes the organization competitive. This human capital, if it is to be competitive, is highly skilled and highly motivated. In light of this, it appears that organizations need to attract a workforce with a certain set of skills, and the job of the organization thereafter is to keep this workforce motivated and attached to the organization.

The purpose of this chapter is to build a new understanding of how this can be achieved. Integrating job embeddedness theory, self-determination theory, and the tripartite model of commitment, new propositions are put forth with the goal to enhance our understanding of the forces that engage and attach individuals to organizations.

SELF-DETERMINATION THEORY

Self-determination theory (SDT) (Deci and Ryan, 1985) is a theory of human motivation that is particularly well suited to linking workplace initiatives to outcomes. SDT, at its core, distinguishes intrinsic from extrinsic motivation. Intrinsic motivation represents engagement in an activity out of interest and enjoyment. Extrinsic motivation refers to engaging in an activity for instrumental reasons, such as obtaining a reward or avoiding a punishment, preserving or enhancing one's self-esteem, and pursuing a meaningful goal. One of these extrinsic motives is considered to be volitionally driven, or autonomous: 'identified regulation' represents engagement in an activity out of meaning and importance. The other forms of extrinsic motivation are considered to be regulated out of external or internal pressure: 'external regulation' represents engagement in an activity in order to obtain a reward or avoid a punishment, while 'introjected regulation' represents engagement in an activity out of ego-involvement.

Because research has found that the autonomous types of motivation, namely intrinsic and identified, yielded more positive results in terms of performance, persistence, and well-being than controlled forms of motivation, namely external and introjected (Deci and Ryan, 2008), it makes more sense to differentiate motivations using a control versus autonomy dichotomy rather than the intrinsic versus extrinsic one. However, it is still arguably more meaningful to analyze the effects of the discrete types of motivation as it has been shown in some cases that identified regulation and intrinsic motivation predicted different outcomes, and that introjection and external regulation also predicted different outcomes (e.g., Koestner and Losier, 2002).

There is indeed a strong body of evidence showing that autonomous motivation is associated with greater task performance than controlled motivation on complex tasks and tasks that require creativity (Grant and Berry, 2011; Grolnick and Ryan, 1987; McGraw and McCullers, 1979). Likewise, the amount of effort an individual is willing to exert has been shown to be more strongly associated with autonomous motivation than controlled motivation (De Cooman et al., 2013). Proactive workplace behavior and organizational citizenship behaviors are also much more likely to occur in autonomously motivated individuals (Parker et al., 2010). Likewise, employee turnover and absenteeism have been shown to be negatively related to autonomous motivation and positively related to controlled motivation (Gillet et al., 2013; Kuvaas et al., 2015; Richer et al., 2002), as has burnout (Van den Broeck et al., 2013).

In light of the well-understood positive outcomes of autonomous work motivation, it becomes important to know how we can promote this motivational orientation to work. SDT proposes that when people feel competent, autonomous, and related to others at work, they are more likely to experience intrinsic motivation and to internalize the importance of work tasks, which increases the identified regulation of extrinsic motivation (Deci and Ryan, 2000). The satisfaction of these needs in work organizations can be acquired through motivational job design (e.g., Gagné et al., 1997), transformational leadership (Hetland et al., 2011; Gagné et al., 2015), adequate training and development (Dysvik and Kuvaas, 2014), best practice HR systems (Marescaux et al., 2013), and through compensation systems that do not pressure employees (Kuvaas et al., 2015). We argue that organizational factors that influence the satisfaction of the psychological needs may be the same as those that would influence the development of organizational commitment.

Need Satisfaction and Commitment

The tripartite model of organizational commitment (Allen and Meyer, 1990; Chapter 3 in this volume) describes three types of commitment. The first one, labelled 'affective commitment', describes affective ties that an individual has to the organization. It describes a deep emotional attachment to the organization, often characterized by identifying with the organization and caring for it. The second one, labelled 'normative commitment', describes feelings of loyalty, obligation, and indebtedness towards the organization. The third, 'continuance commitment', describes instrumental ties that an individual may have to the organization, such as perceived sacrifices that would result from leaving the organization, and perceived lack of alternative employment. Continuance commitment is sometimes split into these two components which have been shown to lead to different, and at times opposite outcomes (Bentein et al., 2005; Vandenberghe and Panaccio, 2012). Perceived sacrifice has also been described as an approach-based form of continuance commitment, while lack of alternatives has been described as an avoidance-based form. As a result, perceived sacrifice is often associated with more positive outcomes than lack of alternatives (Vandenberghe and Panaccio, 2012).

Meyer et al. (2004) proposed an integrative model of commitment and motivation which has garnered attention in subsequent years. One point to grow from this model is that need satisfaction has been suggested as a common antecedent to both commitment and motivation (Meyer and Maltin, 2010). Just as mounting evidence shows that need satisfaction is more highly related to autonomous than to controlled motivation, there is also accumulating evidence that need satisfaction is highly related to affective organizational commitment. Van den Broeck et al. (2010) found that affective commitment was highly positively related to the satisfaction of the need for autonomy, followed by relatedness and competence. Similarly, Sheldon and Bettencourt (2002) found that both autonomy and relatedness satisfaction were related to commitment to a social group, whereas Greguras and Diefendorff (2009) found that all three needs were equally positively related to organizational commitment. Marescaux et al. (2013) showed that best-practice HR systems were positively related to the satisfaction of autonomy and relatedness, which were in turn associated with greater affective organizational commitment. Finally, in a person-centred analysis, Meyer et al. (2012) concluded that profiles higher in affective commitment were associated with greater need satisfaction.

Motivation and Commitment

Given similarity in the outcomes of motivation and commitment, and given that both seem to be affected similarly by need satisfaction, it becomes easy to link different forms of motivation with different commitment mindsets. This has indeed been quite reliably demonstrated. Intrinsic and identified motivation are typically positively related to affective commitment, while introjected regulation is typically positively related to normative commitment (Battistelli et al., 2013). Relations with continuance commitment seem to depend on the subscales used. High sacrifice seems to be related to both introjected and external regulation, while lack of alternatives is only related to external regulation (Battistelli et al., 2013).

While commitment and motivation are conceptually similar (Meyer et al., 2004), they are clearly distinguishable in that they are directed at different targets: the target of commitment being an entity (for example, organization), and the target of motivation being a course of action (for example, work tasks; Gagné et al. (2008)). However, the temporal positioning of motivation and commitment has hindered their differentiation. Some research has assumed that work motivation would serve as a mediator between need satisfaction and commitment (e.g., Graves and Luciano, 2013; Eby et al., 1999), while other research has assumed that work motivation would serve as a mediator between commitment and work outcomes, such as turnover intentions (Battistelli et al., 2013). However, this research has remained largely cross-sectional, which opens the door to alternative directions of influence between these constructs. Meyer et al. (2004) predicted that affective commitment would lead to the development of autonomous work motivation, while normative commitment would lead to the development of introjected regulation, and continuance commitment to the development of external regulation. However, Gagné et al. (2008) argued that work motivation would instead lead to the development of organizational commitment, based on the idea that it is through the process of internalization that employees become tied to their organization. The process of internalization reflects the taking-in of external regulations so that they become autonomously regulated (that is, identified regulation; Ryan, 1995).

Research by Gagné et al. (2008) supported this position and found, in cross-lagged analyses, that autonomous motivation predicted increases in affective organizational commitment, and that introjected regulation predicted increases in normative organizational commitment. However, the hypothesis that external regulation would predict continuance commitment was not supported. Instead, they found that while a lack of alternatives (the second component of continuance commitment) predicted increases in external regulation, perceived sacrifice did not relate to external regulation. In a cross-lagged study of school principals, Fernet et al. (2012) recently replicated the direction of causality found by Gagné et al. between autonomous work motivation and occupational affective commitment. They did not measure the other forms of commitment. There might also be the possibility that, though autonomous motivation and affective commitment are quite highly related (approx. $r = .40$), they sometimes interact to predict certain outcomes. For example, a person could be highly intrinsically motivated to do a type of work, yet not be committed to a particular employer. In such a case, would intrinsic motivation be as highly related to, say, organizational citizenship behaviour? Such moderating effects of commitment on relations between motivation and outcomes have not been tested, to our knowledge.

Though these studies have found that the 'internalized' forms of motivation (autonomous and introjected) lead to changes in two of the forms of commitment – namely affective and normative – lending credence to the importance of internalization in this process, it is still possible that there may be recursive effects over time. No research, to our knowledge, has examined this possibility. However, Meyer et al. (1991) followed newly graduated university students' organizational commitment development in the first year of their employment. Though they measured pre-entry predictors, such as job choice, pressure from others, and employment irrevocability, none of these influenced subsequent affective commitment at six and 11 months of employment. Only post-entry perceptions of motivational job design positively predicted these outcomes. Job choice negatively predicted continuance commitment at six months, while perceptions of alternative employment options predicted continuance commitment at six and 11 months. These results seem to indicate that the same factors that have been shown to influence autonomous motivation, such as job design (Gagné et al., 1997), are also among the most influential in the development of affective commitment, while perceived employment options seem to affect the development of continuance commitment. More stringent tests of these ideas need to be undertaken to ascertain these effects. We propose that job embeddedness theory can help build our understanding of how people become attached to their job and organization.

JOB EMBEDDEDNESS THEORY

Job embeddedness is a relatively new construct in organizational psychology that offers an alternative view on turnover (Chapter 7 in this volume; Lee et al., 2004; Mitchell et al., 2001). Rather than focus on factors that cause employees to leave an organization, such as job satisfaction or stress (Griffeth et al., 2000), job embeddedness theory (JET) (Mitchell et al., 2001) focuses on factors that dispose an employee to stay. It is often likened to how attached, stuck, or enmeshed an employee is within a social, and perhaps financial, system. Job embeddedness was initially conceptualized as a formative construct determined by three components that cut across the organization and the community in which the organization exists: links, fit, and sacrifice.

As explained in detail by Holtom (Chapter 7 in this volume), 'links' are connections that employees form between themselves and the organization, with other organizational members, and with the community in which the organization operates (Lee et al., 2004; Mitchell et al., 2001). These links can be formal in the case of a supervisory chain, or informal as exemplified by belonging to social and community groups (for example, a social committee at work). According to JET, the number of links and their relative strength (for example, tenure) will influence how strongly the employee is bound to the job. Likewise, the degree to which employees perceive themselves as compatible with the organization and surrounding community will influence any decision to stay or leave (Lee et al., 2004; Mitchell et al., 2001). This is referred to as 'fit' (Chapter 20 in this volume), and includes the degree to which the employee's personal values, knowledge, skills, and abilities are congruent with those of the organization and the community. 'Sacrifice' refers to the psychological, social, and material costs associated with leaving the organization and the community (Lee et al., 2004; Mitchell et al., 2001), such as a loss of a steady income and other job-related perks, and the loss of friends in the organization and in the community.

While JET recognizes workplace and community factors as distinct and independently important factors (Lee et al., 2004), we will focus more on organizationally focused embeddedness and how organizations can promote it in order to foster engagement and retention. To do so, we dig deeper into how job embeddedness is likely to influence motivational processes that have been shown to influence organizational commitment.

ORGANIZATIONAL COMMITMENT AND JOB EMBEDDEDNESS

Holtom (Chapter 7 in this volume) describes the similarities and differences between the components of job embeddedness and the different organizational commitment mind-sets. In short, whereas job embeddedness is operationalized as the links, fit, and sacrifices associated with being a member of an organization and community, organizational commitment is generally defined as the ties that bind an individual to an organization (Meyer et al., 2006). The difference lies in JET's focus on more objective environmental factors that influence ties, in contrast with the tripartite model of commitment focusing on perceptions and emotions that tie a person to an organization.

In a meta-analytic investigation of JE and its nomological network, Jiang et al. (2012)

estimated that composite embeddedness within an organization is moderately related to affective commitment ($r = .55$, sample size adjusted $r = .61$). Unfortunately, insufficient research linking these two concepts meant that the other components of commitment were not included. However, a single study by Ng and Feldman (2010) estimated the zero-order correlations between JE (which was a composite of links, fit, and sacrifice) and all three components of commitment. While affective commitment correlated moderately at .41, normative commitment and continuance commitments were only weakly associated ($r = .27$ and .16, respectively). As predicted this research indicated that higher levels of job embeddedness were associated with what are considered to be the more positive forms of commitment.

Several aspects of these relations remain unknown. For one, are the links, fit, and sacrifice aspects of job embeddedness equally related to each commitment mindset? Would the sacrifice component, for example, be more strongly linked to continuance commitment when considered alone (as suggested by Holtom, Chapter 7 in this volume)? Secondly, do the quality of links, the sources of fit, and the types of sacrifice differentially predict different commitment mindsets? In order to predict how this would happen, self-determination theory is used.

USING SELF-DETERMINATION THEORY TO INTEGRATE JOB EMBEDDEDNESS AND COMMITMENT

Going back to our speculations regarding how links, fit, and sacrifice will relate to the different forms of commitment, using the concept of need satisfaction may allow us to make more precise predictions. As noted earlier, JET predicts that number of links, as well as link strength, determine attachment to an organization. As noted by Zhang et al. (2012), the quality of links is indeed as important as the quantity. So far, JET research has operationalized link strength or quality in terms of tenure in the organization, in a position, and on committees. We instead view link quality in terms of the extent to which a link would satisfy the three psychological needs for autonomy, competence, and relatedness. This implies that we could examine the extent to which links, but also fit and sacrifices, influence the satisfaction of each psychological need. The prediction would be that links that satisfy psychological needs are more likely to lead to greater affective commitment, links that do not satisfy psychological needs are more likely to lead to continuance commitment, and no links would lead to no commitment at all. Having too many links, especially when an insufficient number of them satisfy psychological needs, may foster normative commitment through felt obligations.

With regards to fit, we could follow predictions and findings by Greguras and Dienfendorff (2009), who found that person–organization fit was related to the three psychological needs, while person–group fit was related to the relatedness need, and person–job fit was related to the competence need. This clearly demonstrates that different types of fit will be related to different psychological needs. With regards to sacrifices, we could again examine how each sacrifice would influence the thwarting of psychological needs, to predict whether they would lead to reductions in affective, normative, or continuance commitment. In each case, the different forms of work motivation could be examined as potential mediators between need satisfaction and organizational commitment.

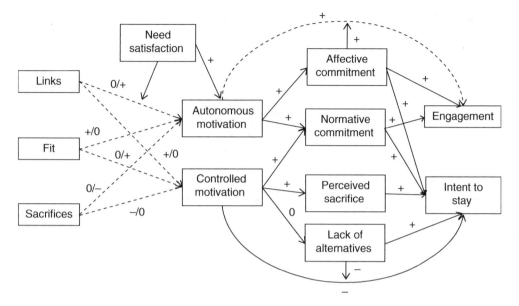

Note: Dashed lines represent moderated links. Values before the backslash are for conditions of low need satisfaction, while values after the dash are for conditions of high need satisfaction.

Figure 5.1 Motivational model of attachment to the organization

Taken together, these predictions would lead to the model depicted in Figure 5.1. In this model, links that satisfy psychological needs (for example, good friends) would lead to greater autonomous motivation and consequently greater affective and, to a lesser extent, normative commitment; whereas links that do not satisfy psychological needs (for example, owning a house in the community) would lead to greater controlled motivation and consequently greater continuance commitment based on perceived sacrifice (based on Gagné et al., 2008). Fit that satisfies psychological needs (for example, good fit between organizational and well internalized personal values) would also increase autonomous motivation and consequently affective and, to a lesser extent, normative commitment. An interesting caveat to this proposal, however, comes from a subtheory within SDT that argues for the unequal effects of extrinsic over intrinsic values on general well-being (Vansteenkiste et al., 2010). Indeed, it has been shown that people who hold more extrinsic values, such as financial success, image, and popularity, report lower well-being than people who hold more intrinsic values, such as affiliation, community, and self-acceptance (Grouzet et al., 2005; Kasser and Ryan, 1993, 1996). The reason why extrinsic values lead to lower well-being than intrinsic values is that they are less likely to satisfy the basic psychological needs (Ryan et al., 1996). In light of this, it can be argued that affective commitment might be less heavily influenced by fit between an extrinsic personal and organizational value, and that perhaps continuance commitment would instead be promoted by fit of extrinsic values, due to satisfaction of needs. Finally, when leaving the organization would mean making sacrifices that lead to a reduction of need satisfaction (for example, interesting work), staying to avoid this sacrifice will be associated with greater affective and, to a lesser extent, normative commitment. Whereas when leaving would mean making sacrifices that would not reduce need satisfaction (for example, a pension fund), staying to avoid this sacrifice may instead promote continuance commitment.

In this model, we focus on two important workplace outcomes that have previously been linked to both motivation and commitment, as discussed previously: namely, work engagement and intent to stay. Work engagement is defined as a combination of vigour, absorption, and dedication to the task (Schaufeli, 2012; Schaufeli and Salanova, 2011). We view these two outcomes as good indicators of a person's quality of attachment and dedication to an organization. Based on the reviewed research, we propose that autonomous motivation would have a positive effect on work engagement, at least partially through affective and, to a lesser extent, normative commitment; whereas controlled motivation typically has no effect on work engagement (Gagné et al., 2015). Alternatively, and as proposed earlier, we could predict a possible moderating effect of affective commitment on the effect of autonomous motivation on work engagement. This is based on the possibility that people may be willing to work hard for an organization only when they have internalized the value of the tasks in combination with an affective attachment to the organization.

We also predict that autonomous motivation would have a positive effect on intent to stay in the organization through affective and, to a lesser extent, normative commitment, even so far as to suggest complete mediation (Meyer et al., 2012). However, controlled motivation would have a negative effect on intent to stay (Kuvaas et al., 2015), but it might be moderated by continuance commitment such that highly controlled employees may wish to leave the organization but be unable to, due to perceived sacrifices and few alternatives.

Through this discussion, we have remained rather vague about the role of normative commitment. This is in part because normative commitment has been neglected, compared to affective and continuance commitment, by researchers. More recently, Meyer and Parfyonova (2010) have noted this neglect and investigated further the role of normative commitment. They found that ambiguous and heterogeneous effects with normative commitment found in past research may be due to the fact that normative commitment has differential effects on outcomes depending on whether it is coupled with high affective commitment or high continuance commitment. When normative commitment is coupled with affective commitment, it represents a sense of moral duty towards the organization; however, when it is coupled with continuance commitment, it represents a sense of indebtedness towards the organization.

IMPLICATIONS FOR RESEARCH

Adequately testing a model such as the one presented in Figure 5.1 would require longitudinal research to examine prospective effects of one variable in the sequence over the next one. It would also ideally involve organizational newcomers, so that we can examine the development of both work motivation and organizational commitment over time as a function of the development of job embeddedness. Well-validated measures exist to assess work-related need satisfaction (Van den Broeck et al., 2010), work motivation (Gagné et al., 2015), organizational commitment (Meyer et al., 1993), work engagement

(Schaufeli et al., 2002), and intent to stay (Meyer et al., 1993). However, current measures of job embeddedness (Crossley et al., 2007; Holtom et al., 2013; Mitchell et al., 2001) would not allow us to properly test the proposed model because they do not allow for the separation of fit, links, and sacrifice into subscales. An alternative measurement model could be developed to address this issue, and this has been called for by researchers using JET (Zhang et al., 2012).

CONCLUSION

This chapter has reviewed the literature linking commitment to motivation as defined by SDT and highlighted several key issues in the literature still to be addressed. Past research indicates that motivation and commitment are closely linked constructs, yet they also display discriminant validity, indicating the usefulness of maintaining them as separate concepts. A key difference lies in the target of work motivation being the work itself, and the target of organizational commitment being the employer or organization. The direction of influence between motivation and commitment also requires further examination, and we have proposed some possible avenues in this regard.

The inclusion of job embeddedness in the proposed motivational model of attachment to the organization allows for a closer examination of factors that may influence both motivation and commitment. By examining how links, fit, and sacrifices may influence the satisfaction of basic psychological needs, and consequently work motivation and organizational commitment, we will be able to provide more concrete and precise advice on how to design human resource management practices, such as recruitment and selection procedures, training programs, performance management and compensation systems, that will maximize autonomous motivation and affective (and perhaps normative) organizational commitment.

REFERENCES

Allen, N.J. and Meyer, J. (1990). The measurement and antecedents of affective, continuance, and normative commitment to the organization. *Journal of Occupational Psychology*, 63, 1–18.

Barney, J. (1991). Firm resources and sustained competitive advantage. *Journal of Management*, 17, 99–120.

Battistelli, A., Galletta, M., Portoghese, I. and Vandenberghe, C. (2013). Mindsets of commitment and motivation: Interrelationships and contribution to work outcomes. *Journal of Psychology*, 147(1), 17–48.

Bentein, K., Vandenberg, R.J., Vandenberghe, C. and Stinglhamber, F. (2005). The role of change in the relationship between commitment and turnover: A latent growth modeling approach. *Journal of Applied Psychology*, 90, 468–482.

Crossley, C.D., Bennett, R.J., Jex, S.M. and Burnfield, J.L. (2007). Development of a global measure of job embeddedness and integration into a traditional model of voluntary turnover. *Journal of Applied Psychology*, 92, 1031–1042.

Deci, E.L. and Ryan, R.M. (1985). *Intrinsic Motivation and Self-Determination in Human Behavior*, New York: Plenum Press.

Deci, E.L. and Ryan, R.M. (2000). The 'what' and 'why' of goal pursuits: Human needs and the self-determination of behaviour. *Psychological Inquiry*, 11(4), 227–268.

Deci, E.L. and Ryan, R.M. (2008). Facilitating optimal motivation and psychological well-being across life's domains. *Canadian Psychology*, 49, 14–23.

De Cooman, R., Stynen, D., Van den Broeck, A., Sels, L. and De Witte, H. (2013). How job characteristics relate to need satisfaction and autonomous motivation: Implications for work effort. *Journal of Applied Psychology*, 43(6), 1342–1352, DOI: 10.1111/jasp.1214.

Dysvik, A. and Kuvaas, B. (2014). SDT and workplace training and development. In Marylene Gagné (ed.), *Oxford Handbook of Work Engagement, Motivation and Self-Determination Theory* (218–228). New York: Oxford University Press.

Eby, L., Freeman, D., Rush, M. and Lance, C. (1999). Motivational bases of affective organizational commitment: A partial test of an integrative theoretical model. *Journal of Occupational and Organizational Psychology*, 72, 463–483.

Edgar, F. and Geare, A. (2009). Inside the 'black box' and 'HRM'. *International Journal of Manpower*, 30(3), 220–236. DOI 10.1108/01437720910956736.

Fernet, C., Austin, S. and Vallerand, R. (2012). The effects of work motivation on employee exhaustion and commitment: An extension of the JD-R model. *Work and Stress*, 26(3), 213–229. DOI:10.1080/02678373.2012.713202.

Gagné, M., Chemolli, E., Forest, J. and Koestner, R. (2008). A temporal analysis of the relationship between organisational commitment and work motivation. *Psychologica Belgica*, 48(2–3), 219–241.

Gagné, M., Forest, J., Vansteenkiste, M., Crevier-Braud, L., Van den Broeck, A., et al. (2015). The multidimensional work motivation scale: Validation evidence in seven languages and nine countries. *Journal of Work and Organizational Psychology*, DOI: http://dx.doi.org/10.1080/1359432X.2013.877892.

Gagné, M., Senécal, C. and Koestner, R. (1997). Proximal job characteristics, feelings of empowerment, and intrinsic motivation: a multidimensional model. *Journal of Applied Social Psychology*, 27, 1222–1240.

Gillet, N., Gagné, M., Sauvagère, S. and Fouquereau, E. (2013). The role of supervisor autonomy support, organizational support, and autonomous and controlled motivation in predicting employees' satisfaction and turnover intentions. *European Journal of Work and Organizational Psychology*, 22(4), 450–460, DOI:10.1080/1359432X.2012.665228.

Grant, A.M. and Berry, J. (2011). The necessity of others is the mother of invention: Intrinsic and prosocial motivations, perspective-taking, and creativity. *Academy of Management Journal*, 54, 73–96, DOI:10.5465/AMJ.2011.59215085.

Graves, L. and Luciano, M. (2013). Self-determination at work: Understanding the role of leader–member exchange. *Motivation and Emotion*, 37, 518–536. DOI 10.1007/s11031-012-9336-z.

Greguras, G.J. and Diefendorff, J.M. (2009). Different fits satisfy different needs: linking person–environment fit to employee commitment and performance using self-determination theory. *Journal of Applied Psychology*, 94(2), 465.

Griffeth, R.W., Hom, P.W., and Gaertner, S. (2000). A meta-analysis of antecedents and correlates of employee turnover: Update, moderator tests, and research implications for the next millennium. *Journal of Management*, 26(3), 463–488.

Grolnick, W.S. and Ryan, R. (1987). Autonomy in children's learning: An experimental and individual difference investigation. *Journal of Personality and Social Psychology*, 52, 890–898.

Grouzet, F.M., Kasser, T., Ahuvia, A., Dols, J.M.F., Kim, Y., Lau, S., et al. (2005). The structure of goal contents across 15 cultures. *Journal of Personality and Social Psychology*, 89(5), 800–816.

Hetland, H., Hetland, J., Andreassen, C.S., Pallesen, S. and Notelaers, G. (2011). Leadership and fulfillment of the three basic psychological needs at work. *Career Development International*, 16, 507–523.

Holtom, B.C., Tidd, S.T., Mitchell, T.R. and Lee, T.W. (2013). A demonstration of the importance of temporal considerations in the prediction of newcomer turnover. *Human Relations*, 66(10), 1337–1352.

Huselid, M.A. (1995). The impact of human resource management practices on turnover, productivity, and corporate financial performance. *Academy of Management Journal*, 38(3), 635–672.

Jiang, K., Liu, D., McKay, P., Lee, P. and Mitchell, T. (2012). When and how is job embeddedness predictive of turnover? A meta-analytic investigation. *Journal of Applied Psychology*, 97(5), 1077–1096, DOI: 10.1037/a0028610.

Kasser, T. and Ryan, R.M. (1993). A dark side of the American dream: correlates of financial success as a central life aspiration. *Journal of Personality and Social Psychology*, 65(2), 410.

Kasser, T. and Ryan, R.M. (1996). Further examining the American dream: Differential correlates of intrinsic and extrinsic goals. *Personality and Social Psychology Bulletin*, 22(3), 280–287.

Koestner, R. and Losier, G.F. (2002). Distinguishing three ways of being highly motivated: A closer look at introjection, identification, and intrinsic motivation. In Edward L. Deci and Richard M. Ryan (eds), *The Handbook of Self-Determination Theory Research* (101–121). Rochester, NY: University of Rochester Press.

Kuvaas, B. Buch, R., Gagné, M. and Dysvik, A. (2015). Do you get what you pay for? Sales incentives, motivation, and employee outcomes. Unpublished manuscript, BI School of Management.

Lee, T.W., Mitchell, T.R., Sablynski, C.J., Burton, J.P. and Holtom, B.C. (2004). The effects of job embeddedness on organizational citizenship, job performance, volitional absences, and voluntary turnover. *Academy of Management Journal*, 47, 711–722.

Marescaux, E., De Winne, S. and Sels, L. (2013). HR practices and HRM outcomes: The role of basic need satisfaction. *Personnel Review*, 42(1), 4–27, DOI:10.1108/00483481311285200.

McGraw, K. and McCullers, J. (1979). Evidence of a detrimental effect of extrinsic incentives on breaking a mental set. *Journal of Experimental Social Psychology*, 15(3), 285–294. DOI: 10.1016/0022-1031(79)90039-8.

Meyer, J.P., Becker, T.E. and Vandenberghe, C. (2004). Employee commitment and motivation: a conceptual analysis and integrative model. *Journal of Applied Psychology*, 89, 991–1007.

Meyer, J.P., Becker, T.E. and Van Dick, R. (2006). Social identities and commitments at work: toward an integrative model. *Journal of Organizational Behavior*, 27, 665–683.

Meyer, J.P., Bobocel, D.R. and Allen, N.J. (1991). Development of organizational commitment during the first year of employment: A longitudinal study of pre- and post-entry influences. *Journal of Management*, 17, 717–733.

Meyer, J.P. and Maltin, E. (2010). Employee commitment and well-being: A critical review, theoretical framework and research agenda. *Journal of Vocational Behavior*, 77, 323–337.

Meyer, J.P., Meyer, J.P., Allen, N.J. and Smith, C.A. (1993). Commitment to organizations and occupations: Extension and test of a three-component conceptualization. *Journal of Applied Psychology*, 78(4), 538–351.

Meyer, J.P. and Parfyonova, N.M. (2010). Normative commitment in the workplace: A theoretical analysis and re-conceptualization. *Human Resource Management Review*, 20(4), 283–294.

Meyer, J.P., Stanley, L. and Parfyonova, N. (2012). Employee commitment in context: The nature and implication of commitment profiles. *Journal of Vocational Behavior*, 80, 1–16, DOI:10.1016/j.jvb.2011.07.002.

Mitchell, T., Holtom, B., Lee, T., Sablynski, C. and Erez, M. (2001). Why people stay: Using job embeddedness to predict voluntary turnover. *Academy of Management Journal*, 44, 1102–1122.

Ng, T. and Feldman, D. (2010). The impact of job embeddedness on innovation-related behaviors. *Human Resource Management*, 49(6), 1067–1087, DOI: 10.1002/hrm.20390.

Parker, S.K., Bindl, U. and Strauss, K. (2010). Making things happen: A model of proactive motivation. *Journal of Management*, 36(4), 827–856, DOI: 10.1177/0149206310363732.

Porter, L.W. and Edward, L.E. (1968). *Managerial Attitudes and Performance*. Homewood, IL: Richard D. Irwin.

Richer, S.F., Blanchard, C. and Vallerand, R.J. (2002). A motivational model of work turnover. *Journal of Applied Social Psychology*, 32, 2089–2113.

Ryan, R.M. (1995). Psychological needs and the facilitation of integrative processes. *Journal of Personality*, 63, 397–427.

Ryan, R.M., Sheldon, K.M., Kasser, T. and Deci, E.L. (1996). All goals are not created equal: An organismic perspective on the nature of goals and their regulation. In Peter M. Gollwitzer and John A. Bargh (eds), *The Psychology of Action: Linking Cognition and Motivation to Behavior* (7–26). New York: Guilford Press

Schaufeli, W.B. (2012). The measurement of work engagement, In Robert R. Sinclair, Mo Wang and Lois E. Tetrick (eds), *Research Methods in Occupational Health Psychology: Measurement, Design, and Data Analysis* (138–153). New York: Routledge.

Schaufeli, W.B. and Salanova, M. (2011). Work engagement: On how to better catch a slippery concept. *European Journal of Work and Organizational Psychology*, 20, 39–46, DOI: 10.1080/1359432X.2010.515981.

Schaufeli, W.B., Salanova, M., Gonzalez-Romá, V. and Bakker, A.B. (2002). The measurement of engagement and burnout: A confirmative analytic approach. *Journal of Happiness Studies*, 3(1), 7–92. DOI:10.1023/A:1015630930326.

Sheldon, K.M. and Bettencourt, B.A. (2002). Psychological need-satisfaction and subjective well-being within social groups. *British Journal of Social Psychology*, 41, 25–38.

Vandenberghe, C. and Panaccio, A. (2012). Perceived sacrifice and few alternatives commitments: The motivational underpinnings of continuance commitment's subdimensions. *Journal of Vocational Behavior*, 81, 59–72, DOI:10.1016/j.jvb.2012.05.002.

Van den Broeck, A., Lens, W., De Witte, H. and Van Coillie, H. (2013). Unraveling the importance of the quantity and the quality of workers' motivation for well-being: A person-centered perspective. *Journal of Vocational Behavior*, 82, 69–78, DOI:10.1016/j.jvb.2012.11.005.

Van den Broeck, A., Vansteenkiste, M., De Witte, H., Soenens, B. and Lens, W. (2010). Capturing autonomy, relatedness and competence at work: Construction and validation of a work-related basic need satisfaction scale. *Journal of Occupational and Organizational Psychology*, 83(4), 981–1002.

Vansteenkiste, M., Niemiec, C.P. and Soenens, B. (2010). The development of the five mini-theories of self-determination theory: An historical overview, emerging trends, and future directions. *Advances in Motivation and Achievement*, 16, 105–166.

Wright, P., McMahan, G. and McWilliams, A. (1994). Human resources as a source of sustained competitive advantage. *International Journal of Human Resource Management*, 5, 299–324.

Zhang, M., Fried, D. and Griffeth, R. (2012). Review of job embeddedness: Conceptual, measurement issues, and directions for future research. *Human Resource Management Review*, 22, 220–231, DOI:10.1016/j.hrmr.2012.02.004.

6. Organizational commitment and employee engagement: ten key questions
Simon L. Albrecht and Olivia J. Dineen

In today's highly competitive business environment, organizations are increasingly recognizing that a committed and motivated workforce is critical to business success (Albrecht et al., 2015). As such, developing an understanding of the nature, causes, and consequences of employees' psychological connection with their work remains an important focus for researchers and practitioners (Bakker et al., 2011; Schaufeli and Taris, 2014).

Traditionally, job satisfaction, organizational commitment, and job involvement have been considered the three 'classic' or core barometers of the individual–organization relationship (Newman et al., 2010; Schohat and Vigoda-Gadot, 2010). More recently, employee engagement has also been recognized as an important indicator of the individual–organization relationship (Albrecht, 2012; Bakker et al., 2011). Given ongoing debate regarding the uniqueness of engagement in relation to the three core work attitudes (e.g., Newman et al., 2010; Rigg, 2013), this chapter aims to clarify distinctions between engagement and organizational commitment, establish the direction of the relationship, and set an agenda for future research. To do so, we address ten key questions.

HOW ARE COMMITMENT AND ENGAGEMENT DEFINED?

Organizational Commitment

Commitment has variously been defined in terms of an employee's psychological attachment to (Meyer and Allen, 1991), attitude towards (Roe et al., 2009), bond with (Chapter 2 in this volume), and identification with their organization (e.g., Mowday et al., 1982). Other definitions have framed the concept in terms of value or goal congruence (e.g., O'Reilly and Chatman, 1986), an investment or exchange relationship (e.g., Becker, 1960), turnover intention (Mowday et al., 1982), and the motivational propensity to achieve organizational success (Mowday et al., 1979). Solinger et al. (2008), in an attempt to reconcile the differing conceptualizations, referred to commitment as 'an attitude of an employee vis-à-vis the organization, reflected in a combination of *affect* (emotional attachment, identification), *cognition* (identification and internalisation of goals, norms and values) and *action-readiness* (a generalised behavioural pledge to serve and enhance the organization's interests)' (p. 134).

Meyer and Allen (1991), in what is arguably the most commonly cited definition of organizational commitment, defined it as 'a psychological state that characterises the employee's relationship with the organization and has implications for their decision to continue or discontinue membership' (p. 4). Meyer and Allen's 'three-component model' (TCM) (Allen and Meyer, 1990; Meyer and Allen, 1991; Chapter 3 in this volume) conceptualizes commitment as consisting of affective, continuance, and normative components. Affective commitment refers to an employee's emotional attachment to, identification with, and involvement in the organization. Continuance commitment refers to an employee's awareness of the costs associated with leaving their organization. Normative commitment refers to an employee's feeling of obligation to continue employment.

Employee Engagement

Kahn (1990), in one of the first published papers on the topic, defined employee engagement as 'the simultaneous expression and employment of a person's "preferred self" in their work task, thereby promoting connections to work and to others, personal presence (physical, cognitive and emotional) and active, full role performances' (p. 700). Other academics have also conceptualized engagement as containing cognitive, emotional, and behavioural dimensions (e.g., May et al., 2004; Rich et al., 2010). In their widely cited definition, Schaufeli et al. (2002, p. 74) defined engagement as 'a positive, fulfilling, work related state of mind characterised by vigour, dedication and absorption'. Vigour refers to high levels of energy and mental resilience while working. Dedication refers to being strongly involved in one's work and experiencing a sense of significance, enthusiasm and pride. Absorption refers to being fully concentrated and happily engrossed in one's work.

Within the more practitioner-oriented literature, engagement and commitment are often confused or used interchangeably. Shaw (2005, p. 8), for example, defined engagement as 'the emotional and intellectual commitment to the organization'. Similarly, the Corporate Leadership Council (2004, p. 4) defined engagement as 'the extent to which employees commit to something or someone in their organization and how hard they work and how long they stay as a result of that commitment'. Within the academic domain it has also been questioned whether engagement is nothing more than a 'repackaging' of well-established work-related psychological constructs; nothing more than 'old wine in new bottles'. Consistent with this view, Newman et al. (2010) argued that engagement might better be conceptualized as an indicator of a higher-order attitude factor, or 'A-factor', also consisting of job satisfaction, affective organizational commitment, and job involvement. In support of their argument, Newman et al. reported engagement loaded strongly on the A-factor ($\lambda = .72$).

In contrast to 'old wine, new bottle' arguments, it has also been claimed there is enough evidence to debunk the notion that engagement is nothing more than a conceptual cocktail of established work-related psychological constructs (Christian et al., 2011; Hallberg and Schaufeli, 2006; Schaufeli and Bakker, 2010). Hallberg and Schaufeli, for example, provided confirmatory factor analytic evidence to show that engagement, job involvement, and organizational commitment are distinct but related constructs. Importantly, Christian et al.'s meta-analysis, drawn from more than 3000 respondents, showed that engagement predicted significant amounts of variance in both in-role and extra-role performance beyond that predicted by organizational commitment.

WHAT ARE THE KEY SIMILARITIES AND DIFFERENCES IN HOW COMMITMENT AND ENGAGEMENT ARE DEFINED?

A number of researchers have compared and contrasted organizational commitment and employee engagement along a number of dimensions (e.g., Byrne et al., 2014; Schohat and Vigoda-Gadot, 2010). The constructs are similar in that they both refer to positive psychological states that are adaptive for employee well-being and performance; have affective, cognitive, and behavioural dimensions; and involve job and organizational identification and involvement. There are also key differences, as follows.

Target of the Psychological State

Organizational commitment generally references an attachment to the organization as a whole, whereas engagement references the work role or work itself (Barnes and Collier, 2013; Christian et al., 2011). Engagement reflects the energy an employee invests in their work (Schaufeli et al., 2002), whereas commitment reflects an employee's attachment to, or intention to remain at, their organization (Mowday et al., 1982). Although Saks (2006) proposed the notion of 'organizational engagement', the majority of engagement research has focused on job-related experiences (Schaufeli and Taris, 2014). The most frequently cited model of engagement, the job-demands resources (JD-R) model (Bakker and Demerouti, 2014b) emphasizes job resources, rather than organizational resources, as the key antecedents of engagement.

Level of Arousal

With reference to well-established theoretical models of job-related affect (e.g., Russell, 1980; Inceoglu and Fleck, 2010), employee engagement is generally expressed through more-activated, high-arousal positive affective states such as energy and enthusiasm. In contrast, commitment is characterized by less-activated positive affective states such as contentment and comfort.

Stability over Time

Engagement was originally conceptualized as a relatively stable and enduring psychological state (e.g., Schaufeli et al., 2002). However, more recently, diary studies have shown that engagement fluctuates within individuals over short time periods (e.g., Ouweneel et al., 2012). Given that 30 to 70 per cent of the variance in engagement can be attributed to within-person variation, the momentary and transient fluctuations from minute to minute, hour to hour, and day to day need to be recognized (Sonnentag et al., 2010).

Organizational commitment is generally regarded as a stable construct that develops slowly over time (Mowday et al., 1979). Day-to-day job-related experiences are less likely to cause employees to seriously re-evaluate their overall attachment to their organization (Mowday et al., 1979). Instead, changes in commitment are more likely to be influenced by organizational-level events such as changes in company policy or practices, which generally occur infrequently (Becker et al., 2013). Although most empirical research has demonstrated commitment to be moderately stable over time (e.g., Sturges et al., 2002),

Solinger et al. (2014) recently reported fluctuations in individual commitment over 25 weekly measurements. As such, further diary research is required to better understand the extent to which within-person commitment fluctuates over hourly, daily, weekly, and monthly intervals.

Components and Dimensions as Constituents

Another key distinction between engagement and commitment centres on the nature of their constituent elements. Meyer and Allen (1991) explained that affective, continuance, and normative commitments are 'components' of commitment because an employee can experience all three to varying degrees, and the components may be influenced by different antecedents. The very modest meta-analytic correlations between affective and continuance commitment, for example, attest to their independence (Meyer et al., 2002). In contrast, employees must experience all constituent engagement dimensions (vigour, dedication, and absorption) to be considered engaged (Schaufeli et al., 2002). Consistent with this view, Schaufeli and Bakker (2010) reported correlations between the three dimensions ranging from .80 to .90.

Overall, we conclude that there is obvious conceptual overlap between employee engagement and organizational commitment. Both refer to positive work-related psychological states. However, the constructs can be differentiated in terms of the target of the psychological state; the level of arousal typically associated with each construct; the degree to which they may fluctuate within different people over differing time periods; and the nature of their constituent parts.

WHAT THEORETICAL PERSPECTIVES AND MODELS UNDERPIN EACH CONSTRUCT?

Theoretical platforms used to explain the emergence and maintenance of commitment and engagement have included social exchange theory (Blau, 1964), self-determination theory (Deci and Ryan, 2000), social identity theory (Tajfel, 1974), role theory (Kahn, 1990), the broaden and build theory of positive emotion (Fredrickson, 2001), job characteristics theory (Hackman and Oldham, 1980), and conservation of resources theory (Hobfoll, 2002). Below we briefly review the theories most commonly used to explain commitment and engagement.

Organizational Commitment

Social exchange theory (SET) and self-determination theory (SDT) are the dominant theories used to explain the relationship between commitment and its antecedents and outcomes. According to SET, obligations are generated through a series of interactions between two parties who are in a state of reciprocal interdependence. Based on this premise it has been suggested that employees offer commitment in return for the receipt (or anticipated receipt) of rewards from the organization (Oliver, 1990). Alternatively, in SDT terms (Deci and Ryan, 2000), work environments that facilitate the satisfaction of three basic psychological needs (autonomy, relatedness, and competence) therefore promote organizational commitment and other positive psychological and behavioural outcomes (Meyer et al., 2004).

Employee Engagement

As previously noted, the JD-R model (Bakker and Demerouti, 2007) is the most widely accepted model of engagement. The JD-R model theorizes two processes: (1) a health impairment process in which the experience of job demands leads to exhaustion and burnout; and (2) a motivational process in which the availability of job resources relates to engagement. Job demands are physical, psychological, social, or organizational aspects of a job that require sustained effort and are therefore associated with physiological and/or psychological costs. Job resources are physical, psychological, social, or organizational aspects of work that may reduce the health-impairing impact of job demands, are functional in achieving work goals, and stimulate personal growth or learning.

Integrated Models of Organizational Commitment and Employee Engagement

Although theorizing and research about commitment and engagement have largely run on separate paths, some researchers have proposed models to explain their association. Saks (2006), drawing from social exchange theory, tested a model showing organizational commitment as an outcome of both job and organizational engagement. Meyer et al. (2010), drawing from SDT and the TCM, suggested that levels of engagement (disengagement, contingent engagement, and full engagement) are differentially associated with different forms of motivation (intrinsic or extrinsic) and commitment (normative, continuance, and affective). Meyer et al. argued that the key to moving employees from disengaged and not committed, to fully engaged and committed, is to create a work environment that allows for the satisfaction of employees' basic psychological needs (autonomy, relatedness, competence). Meyer et al.'s model has yet, however, to be widely tested and, more generally, additional research is needed to test theoretically derived models that integrate JD-R and TCM constructs.

HOW ARE COMMITMENT AND ENGAGEMENT MEASURED?

Organizational Commitment

A number of different measures of organizational commitment can be found in the academic literature and practitioner domains. The Organizational Commitment Questionnaire (OCQ) (Mowday et al., 1979) and Allen and Meyer's (1990) measures of affective, normative, and continuance commitment are most commonly used. Although criticisms have been raised regarding the construct validity of continuance commitment, and the discriminant validity between normative and affective commitment (Solinger et al., 2008), recent studies have shown that different combinations of components, operationalized as different commitment profiles, differentially predict well-being, behavioural, and performance outcomes (see Meyer et al., 2012). Irrespective of criticisms and evidence to support profiles, affective commitment remains the most strongly validated component, and is therefore the measure most often included in commitment-related research.

Employee Engagement

A range of engagement measures can be sourced from both the academic and practitioner domains. Commonly cited academic measures include Rich et al.'s (2010) Job Engagement Scale, the Utrecht Work Engagement Scale (UWES) (Schaufeli et al., 2002), and scales developed by May et al. (2004), Rothband (2001), Saks (2006), and Soane et al. (2012). The UWES-9 (Schaufeli et al., 2006), measuring the subscales of vigour, dedication, and absorption, is widely used in academic research. Example items include: 'At work I feel bursting with energy' (vigour), 'My job inspires me' (dedication), and 'I am immersed in my work' (absorption). It should be noted that some researchers have suggested that absorption should be considered a consequence of work engagement, rather than a core component (e.g., Salanova and Schaufeli, 2008).

The debate regarding whether engagement and commitment are distinct has largely centred on measurement of the constructs. Some researchers have argued that measures of engagement include items that are too similar to items used to measure commitment. Newman and Harrison (2008), for example, argued that the UWES-9 item, 'I am proud of the work I do', is very similar to the OCQ item, 'I am proud to tell others that I am part of this organization' (Mowday et al., 1979). Similarly for the UWES item, 'My job inspires me', and the OCQ item, 'This organization really inspires the very best in me in the way of job performance'. We argue, however, that the UWES items target attitudes toward the work role, whereas the OCQ items target attitudes towards the organization. As mentioned previously, the target of the psychological state is a key differentiator between engagement and commitment (e.g., Crawford et al., 2010; Hallberg and Schaufeli, 2006).

WHAT IS THE STRENGTH OF THE RELATIONSHIP BETWEEN COMMITMENT AND ENGAGEMENT?

We have argued that engagement and commitment are distinct constructs. Table 6.1 provides a summary of empirical studies published in English language peer-reviewed journals from 1990 that have reported the strength of the association between the two constructs.

As shown in Table 6.1, correlations between overall commitment and engagement ranged from $r = .40$ to $r = .71$, with the average correlation of $r = .57$ suggesting a medium to large effect size (Cohen, 1992). The average effect translates as 32 per cent shared variance between the constructs. The 68 per cent of variance not shared supports the proposition that engagement and commitment are distinct.

As suggested by Table 6.1, some research has focused on understanding how the dimensions of engagement (vigour, dedication, and absorption) relate to the components of commitment (affective, normative, and continuance). Moderate to strong associations between affective commitment and vigour, dedication, and absorption have been reported (e.g., Viljevac et al., 2012; Barnes and Collier, 2013). The correlations with

Table 6.1 Studies reporting associations between commitment and engagement

Author and year of study	Study design and method of data collection	Sample characteristics (Sample location)	Measure of employee engagement	Measure of organizational commitment	Effect size (Pearson's r)
Albrecht and Andreetta (2011)	Cross-sectional; Self-report survey	158 employees of a community health service; 89% were full-time employees (Australia)	UWES-9	Allen and Meyer (1990) – ACS	$r = .58$
Barnes and Collier (2013)	Cross-sectional; Self-report survey	Study 1: 401 high customer contact employees Study 2: 304 low customer contact service employees (USA)	UWES	Mowday et al. (1979) – short form	Study 1 AC and VIG: $r = .53$ AC and DED: $r = .63$ AC and ABS: $r = .44$ Study 2 AC and VIG: $r = .59$ AC and DED: $r = .62$ AC and ABS: $r = .47$
Biswas and Bhatnagar (2013)	Cross-sectional; Self-report survey	276 full-time employees (North-Central India)	Saks (2006)	Rhoades et al. (2001)	$r = .47$
Brunetto et al. (2012)	Cross-sectional; Self-report survey	193 police officers (Australia)	UWES-9	Allen and Meyer (1990) – ACS	$r = .62$
Christian et al. (2011)	Meta-analysis	Meta-analytic sample of 11 449 participants	6 ENG measures (e.g. UWES, UWES-9); Saks (2006), May et al. (2004)	ACS included in studies that met the meta-analytic criteria; Mean reliability estimate $\alpha = .80$	$Mp = .59$
Dalal et al. (2012)	Cross-sectional; Self-report survey	191 full-time and part-time employees (USA)	UWES-9	A composite scale of Meyer et al. (1993) and Mowday et al. (1979)	$r = .60$

Study	Design	Sample	Engagement measure	Commitment measure	Result
De Beer et al. (2012)	Cross-sectional; Self-report survey	15 663 employees from a range of organizations and industry sectors (South Africa)	South African Employee Health and Wellness Survey (SAEHWS)	SAEHWS	r = .61
Demerouti et al. (2001)	Cross-sectional; Self-report survey	381 insurance company employees	UWES	Mowday et al. (1979)	AC and VIG: r = .49 AC and DED: r = .59 AC and ABS: r = .45
Ferrer and Morris (2013)	Cross-sectional; Self-report survey	664 business academics in public funded universities (Australia)	UWES	Allen and Meyer (1990) – ACS	Elite university sample: r = .37 Non-elite university sample: r = .42
Field and Buitendach (2011)	Cross-sectional; Self-report survey	123 university employees	UWES	Allen and Meyer (1990) – ACS	r = .60
Karatepe (2011)	1-week time lag; Self-report and supervisor rating surveys	143 full-time frontline hotel employees and their immediate supervisors (Nigeria)	UWES	Mowday et al. (1979) – 5 items	r = .67
Karatepe (2013)	1-week time lag; Self-report and supervisor rating surveys	231 full-time frontline hotel employees (Iran)	UWES	Allen and Meyer (1990) – ACS	r = .60

Table 6.1 (continued)

Author and year of study	Study design and method of data collection	Sample characteristics (Sample location)	Measure of employee engagement	Measure of organizational commitment	Effect size (Pearson's *r*)
Karatepe and Aga (2012)	2-week time lag; Self-report survey	195 full-time frontline bank employees (North Cyprus)	UWES	Mowday et al. (1979)	$r = .40$
Karatepe et al. (2014)	2-week time lag; Self-report and supervisor rating surveys	195 full-time frontline hotel employees and their supervisors (North Cyprus)	UWES-9	Mowday et al. (1979)	$r = .42$
Parzefall and Hakanen (2010)	Cross-sectional; Self-report survey	178 employees from a public sector organization (Finland)	UWES (vigour and dedication scales)	Allen and Meyer (1990) – ACS	AC and VIG: $r = .18$ AC and DED: $r = .33$
Poon (2013)	Cross-sectional; Self-report survey	115 full-time employees enrolled as part-time students on graduate courses at a large public university (Malaysia)	UWES	Meyer et al. (1993) – ACS	$r = .65$
Saks (2006)	Cross-sectional; Self-report survey	102 employees working in a variety of jobs and organizations (Canada)	Saks (2006)	Rhoades et al. (2001)	$r = .53$
Shuck et al. (2011)	Cross-sectional; Self-report survey	283 workers in the service, manufacturing, professional and non-profit industries (USA)	May et al. (2004)	Rhoades et al. (2001)	$r = .71$

Study	Design	Sample	Measure	Measure	Results
Simons and Buitendach (2013)	Cross-sectional; Self-report survey	106 call centre employees (South Africa)	UWES	Allen and Meyer (1990)	OC total: $r = .63$ AC and VIG: $r = .64$ AC and DED: $r = .65$ AC and ABS: $r = .54$ NC and VIG: $r = .62$ NC and DED: $r = .57$ NC and ABS: $r = .52$ CC and VIG: $r = .27$ CC and DED: $r = .69$ CC and ABS: $r = .41$
Yalabik et al. (2013)	1-year cross-lagged design; Self-report survey	199 clerical employees in the specialist lending division of a bank (UK)	UWES-9	Allen and Meyer (1990) – ACS	Time 1 AC and time 1 ENG: $r = .68$ Time 1 AC and time 2 ENG: $r = .58$ Time 2 AC and time 1 ENG: $r = .55$ Time 2 AC and time 2 ENG: $r = .73$
Scrima (2014)	Cross-sectional design; Self-report survey	405 full-time working Italian adults from the manufacturing, public and retail sector (Italy)	UWES (Italian version)	Allen and Meyer (1990) – ACS, Italian version	AC and VIG: $r = .26$ AC and DED: $r = .53$ AC and ABS: $r = .34$

Table 6.1 (continued)

Author and year of study	Study design and method of data collection	Sample characteristics (Sample location)	Measure of employee engagement	Measure of organizational commitment	Effect size (Pearson's *r*)
Vigoda-Gadot et al. (2012)	Cross-sectional; Self-report survey	593 from public and private sector organizations (Israel)	UWES-9	Allen and Meyer (1990) – ACS, short form	AC and VIG: *r* = .57 AC and DED: *r* = .70 AC and ABS: *r* = .50
Viljevac et al. (2012)	Cross-sectional; Self-report survey	139 employees from call centres of two finance institutions (New Zealand)	UWES	Allen and Meyer (1990) – ACS	AC and VIG: *r* = .48 AC and DED: *r* = .52 AC and ABS: *r* = .54
Wefald et al. (2011)	Cross-sectional; Self-report survey	382 employees and managers from a midsized financial institution (USA)	UWES-9	Allen and Meyer (1990) – ACS, short form	*r* = .53
Richardsen et al. (2006)	Cross-sectional; Self-report survey	150 police officers mostly full time (96%) (Norway)	UWES-9	OCQ – short form (Mowday et al., 1979)	*r* = .55
Yalabik et al. (2014)	Cross-sectional; Self-report survey	375 employees from a global PSF (mostly UK)	UWES	Meyer et al. (1993) – ACS	AC and VIG: *r* = .49 AC and DED: *r* = .53 AC and ABS: *r* = .22

Note: ACS = Affective Commitment Scale, AC = Affective Commitment, VIG = Vigour, DED = Dedication, ABS = Absorption, ENG = Engagement, OC = Organizational Commitment, PSF = Professional Service Firms.

vigour ranged from $r = .26$ to $r = .64$; with dedication ranging from $r = .18$ to $r = .70$; and absorption ranging from $r = .22$ to $r = .54$. There is very limited research evidence as to the strength of the relationships between normative and continuance commitment and the three engagement dimensions. Further research is needed to determine the strength of these associations.

DOES ENGAGEMENT PREDICT COMMITMENT OR DOES COMMITMENT PREDICT ENGAGEMENT?

While there is sufficient evidence to conclude that engagement and commitment are independent constructs, there have been mixed findings regarding their causal relationship. Most researchers have modelled engagement as an antecedent to commitment (e.g., Albrecht and Andreetta, 2011; Field and Buitendach, 2011; Saks, 2006). Drawing on social exchange theory, Biswas and Bhatnagar (2013) argued that engaged employees feel obliged to be socio-emotionally attached to the source of their engagement (that is, their organization), thereby creating commitment. Although engagement has been found to be an antecedent of commitment in a number of longitudinal and cross-lagged studies (e.g., Karatepe, 2011, 2013), the majority of studies demonstrating this relationship have been cross-sectional in design (e.g., Albrecht, 2012; Parzefall and Hakanen, 2010; Field and Buitendach, 2011). As cross-sectional research designs cannot confirm causation, further longitudinal research is necessary to confirm the causal ordering of the constructs.

A limited number of researchers have modelled commitment as an antecedent to engagement. Drawing from social identity theory (Tajfel, 1974), Barnes and Collier (2013) argued that as employees become committed to their organization, they have a greater interest in ensuring organizational success, thereby becoming more engaged in their job. Similarly, Yalabik et al. (2013) argued that employees who have affection for their employers are more likely to approach their work in a manner consistent with the wishes of their employer, and perform in the spirit of the job rather than simply working to rule. Yalabik et al. (2013), using longitudinal data, reported a moderately positive association from affective commitment to work engagement one year later ($\beta = .45$). It is noteworthy, however, that in a subsequent cross-sectional study, Yalabik et al. (2014) modelled and demonstrated a strong positive association from engagement to affective commitment ($\beta = .60$). Additional longitudinal research is required to clarify the causal associations and potential reciprocal effects.

WHAT ARE THE KEY DRIVERS OF COMMITMENT AND ENGAGEMENT?

Although research has demonstrated that commitment and engagement are distinct constructs, they share common antecedents. Studies have shown, for example, that task autonomy, skill utilization, job feedback, supervisor support, and transformational leadership independently predict both constructs (Bakker et al., 2010; Crawford et al., 2010; Saks, 2006; Van den Broeck et al., 2008; Wefald et al., 2011). Additionally, individual difference variables such as self-efficacy, extraversion, and positive affect have been

Table 6.2   Meta-analytic effect sizes for antecedents and outcomes of commitment and engagement (k** > 10)

Commitment*	Effect Size**	Engagement	Effect Size
Antecedents	p = .63[1]	*Antecedents*	p = .39[4], .37[5]
Organizational Support		Autonomy	
Person–Organizational Fit	p = .51[2]	Feedback	p = .33[4], .35[5], .27[6]
Perceived Supervisor Support	p = .48[3]	Social Support	p = .32[4], .33[5], .35[6]
Distributive Justice	p = .40[1]	Work Climate	p = .28[5]
Role Ambiguity	p = −.39[1]	Workload	p = .13[4]
Procedural Justice	p = .38[1]	Role Conflict	p = −.20[4]
Perceived Co-worker Support	p = .28[3]	Task Variety	p = .53[4], .53[5]
		Task Significance	p = .51[4]
Self-Efficacy	p = .11[1]	Self-Efficacy	p = .59[6]
		Conscientiousness	p = .42[4], .33[5], .35[6]
		Optimism	p = .44[6]
		Positive Affect	p = .43[4], .33[5], .35[6]
Outcomes		*Outcomes*	
Withdrawal Cognitions	p = −.56[1]	Turnover Intention	p = −.26[6]
Overall Absence	p = −.15[1]	Task Performance	p = .43[4], .36[6]
Job Performance Self Rated	p = .12[1]	Contextual Performance	p = .34[4]
Job Pfmce Supervisor Rated	p = .17[1]	Health	p = .20[6]
Organizational Citizenship	p = .32[1]		
Work–Family Conflict	p = −.20[1]		
Job Involvement	p = −.53[1]		
Job Satisfaction	p = −.65[1]		
Engagement	p = .38[6]	Commitment	p = .38[6]

Notes and sources:

*   affective commitment only; ** p = corrected correlation and included only if number of
   correlations used for meta-analyses >10.
1.   Meyer et al. (2002).
2.   Kristof-Brown et al. (2005).
3.   Ng and Sorensen (2008).
4.   Christian et al. (2011).
5.   Crawford et al. (2010).
6.   Halbesleben (2010).

shown to be associated with both commitment and engagement (Christian et al., 2011; Halbesleben, 2010; Panaccio and Vendenberghe, 2012; Thoreson et al., 2003). These findings, for the most part, have been derived from single studies that have not included both engagement and commitment in the analyses. Table 6.2 summarizes the antecedents, outcomes, and corresponding effect sizes for commitment and engagement as reported in selected meta-analyses.

As demonstrated in Table 6.2, despite some commonality across predictors, organizationally focused factors such as organizational support have stronger relationships with organizational commitment, while job-focused factors such as task variety have stronger relationships with engagement. These findings are broadly consistent with the compatibility principle (Ajzen, 2005), suggesting that prediction of an attitude or behaviour is strongest when the specificity of predictors and outcomes are consistent. Table 6.2 also shows that self-efficacy has a substantially stronger association with engagement than commitment. Given that self-efficacy influences both the activities that people pursue and how much effort they allocate to these activities (Bandura, 1977), it is not surprising that the effects are stronger for a more proximal job-focused construct such as engagement, as opposed to a more distal organizationally focused construct such as commitment.

WHAT ARE THE KEY CONSEQUENCES OF COMMITMENT AND ENGAGEMENT?

Individual research studies have shown that both commitment and engagement predict productivity, innovation, customer satisfaction (Langford, 2010), organizational citizenship (Saks, 2006; Meyer et al., 2002), psychological and physical health (Grawitch et al., 2007; Siu, 2002), overall life satisfaction (Hakanen and Schaufeli, 2012), and positive affect (Thoresen et al., 2003; Bakker et al., 2010). More compellingly, as shown in Table 6.2, meta-analyses demonstrate that both commitment and engagement have relatively strong associations with outcomes such as job performance, withdrawal cognitions, turnover intention, and absenteeism. Consistent with the notion that engagement is more job-focused, while commitment is more organizationally focused, Table 6.2 shows that engagement has a stronger association with task or job performance, while commitment has a stronger association with turnover intention. However, given that Halbesleben (2010), on the basis of 8623 responses from 14 unique samples, reported a corrected correlation of $r = .38$ for engagement as a predictor of commitment, commitment may also mediate some of the influence of engagement on performance and turnover intention. Further research incorporating both constructs is needed in order to better establish the strength and configuration of the associations.

WHAT INTERVENTIONS HELP DEVELOP COMMITMENT AND ENGAGEMENT?

Irrespective of the academic arguments surrounding the distinction between the constructs, it is important that researchers and practitioners provide guidance to organizations seeking to implement interventions to develop or enhance commitment and engagement. JD-R theory (Bakker and Demerouti, 2014a), at a broad level, suggests that the provision of job resources, the development of personal resources, and the management of job demands are fundamental to developing and sustaining engagement. As such, organizations should create a culture or climate for engagement by ensuring policies, practices, and procedures support the provision of quality job resources and the appropriate management of job demands. Albrecht et al. (2015) argued for the importance of moving beyond the routine administration of annual engagement surveys and for the need to embed engagement in human resource management (HRM) policies and practices such as personnel selection, socialization, performance management, and training and development. Job redesign, work training, career management, and leadership development programmes have also been suggested (Schaufeli and Salanova, 2010; Vincent-Hoeper et al., 2012).

Drawing from a JD-R perspective, Bakker (2015) suggested two interventions. The first 'top-down' intervention is essentially a survey feedback process (Golombiewski and Hilles, 1979). The process entails: (1) conducting interviews with stakeholders to determine which job demands and resources are potentially most important for engagement; (2) operationalizing the relevant job demands and resources and administering a self-report survey to all employees; (3) based on survey results, prioritizing the job demands and resources that will be targeted through interventions; and (4) readministering the survey post-intervention to assess the impact on engagement. Bakker (2015) also suggested job crafting, whereby employees craft their own jobs, as a 'bottom-up' approach to enhance engagement.

Bakker's 'top-down' and 'bottom-up' interventions are in line with Kahn and Fellows' (2013) recommendations that engagement be enhanced by: (1) creating contextual conditions that make it likely for employees to engage in their jobs (for example, involving employees in decisions); and (2) 'enabling' workers: treating employees in ways that elevate and make noble the meanings of their work (for example, job crafting, developmental reviews, and building connectedness). Interventions to improve the personal resources of employees by developing self-efficacy (Carter et al., 2010), coaching (Crabb, 2011), increasing psychological capital (PsyCap; Luthans et al., 2007), increasing positive affect, and developing emotional intelligence (Bakker et al., 2011) have also been recommended.

Organizational Commitment

Interventions to improve commitment largely overlap with those designed to improve engagement. The importance of providing role clarity, organizational dependability, and cohesiveness has been acknowledged (Allen and Meyer, 1990). Furthermore, leadership development (Albrecht and Andreetta, 2011), and creating trust between employees and their organization, have also been recommended to increase both commitment and engagement (Agarwal and Bhargava, 2013; Bal et al., 2013).

Generally, commitment interventions are targeted at enhancing the individual–organizational relationship, while engagement interventions focus on enhancing the individual–job relationship. Given that meta-analyses have shown that perceptions of organizational support (POS) (Rhoades et al., 2001) are strongly associated with commitment, interventions broadly aimed at demonstrating to employees that the organization values them, cares about their welfare, and investing in them will likely be effective. Interventions that support and develop employee experiences of organizational justice, organizational identification, and person–organization fit (Becker et al., 2009) will also be effective. More specific commitment interventions have focused on stress reduction strategies (e.g., Pignata et al., 2014) and caring intervention strategies (Grdinovac and Yancey, 2012). Additional ideas and strategies for organizational commitment interventions can be sourced from Part V, 'Drivers of Commitment', in this volume.

WHAT ARE THE KEY QUESTIONS FOR FURTHER RESEARCH?

Throughout this chapter we have noted opportunities for further research. We have argued there is a need for researchers to further clarify the unique and shared influence of engagement and commitment on employee well-being and individual and organizational performance. We have suggested the need for additional longitudinal studies that include both commitment and engagement in theoretically based research models. Research using the JD-R, for instance, could accommodate consideration of the antecedents and outcomes associated with both constructs and how they interrelate. We also recommend further diary research to more clearly determine whether, how, and why within-persons organizational commitment, like engagement, fluctuates over hourly, daily, weekly, and monthly intervals. We also suggest research that builds on the idea of commitment profiles to examine how the dimensions of commitment and components of engagement interact to predict important individual, team, and organizational outcomes. Importantly, given that we already know a considerable amount about the antecedents and outcomes associated with the two constructs, a clear focus on intervention research and efficacy is needed. That is, we need to understand what interventions successfully improve engagement and commitment, and under what circumstances.

SAME OR DIFFERENT: A SUMMARY AND CONCLUSION

We have argued that there is sufficient conceptual, theoretical, and empirical evidence to demonstrate that commitment and engagement are positively related, yet distinct constructs. The constructs can be differentiated in terms of the target of the psychological state; the level of arousal typically associated with each construct; the degree to which they fluctuate within different people over differing time periods; and the nature of their constituent parts. We have argued for further research and for intervention studies. Importantly, initiatives and interventions designed to develop commitment and engagement need to be strategically embedded and supported across selection, socialization, performance management, and training and development practices, processes, and systems.

REFERENCES

Agarwal, U.A. and Bhargava, S. (2013), 'Effects of psychological contract breach on organizational outcomes: Moderating role of tenure and educational levels', *Vikalpa: The Journal for Decision Makers, 38* (1), 13–25.

Ajzen, I. (2005), *Attitudes, Personality and Behavior* (2nd edn). Milton Keynes: Open University Press.

Albrecht, S.L. (2012), 'The influence of job, team and organizational level resources on employee well-being, engagement, commitment and extra-role performance: Test of a model', *International Journal of Manpower, 33* (7), 840–885.

Albrecht, S.L. and Andreetta, M. (2011), 'The influence of empowering leadership, empowerment and engagement on affective commitment and turnover intentions in community health service workers: Test of a model', *Leadership in Health Services, 24* (3), 228–237.

Albrecht, S.L., Bakker, A.B., Gruman, J.A., Macey, W.H., and Saks, A.M. (2015), 'Employee engagement, human resource management practices and competitive advantage', *Journal of Organizational Effectiveness: People and Performance, 2* (1), 7–35.

Allen, N.J. and Meyer, J.P. (1990), 'The measurement and antecedents of affective, continuance and normative commitment to the organization', *Journal of Occupational Psychology*, *63* (1), 1–18.

Bakker, A.B. (2015), 'Top-down and bottom-up interventions to increase work engagement', in P.J. Hartung, M.L. Savickas, and W.B. Walsh (eds), *APA Handbook of Career Intervention, Volume 2: Applications*, Washington, DC: American Psychological Association, pp. 427–438.

Bakker, A.B., Albrecht, S., and Leiter, M.P. (2011), 'Key questions regarding work engagement', *European Journal of Work and Organizational Psychology*, *20* (1), 4–28.

Bakker, A.B. and Demerouti, E. (2007), 'The job demands–resources model: state of the art', *Journal of Managerial Psychology*, *22* (3), 309–328.

Bakker, A.B and Demerouti, E. (2014a), 'Job demands–resources theory', in P.Y. Chen and C.L. Cooper (eds), *Work and Wellbeing* (Vol. 3), Chichester, UK: Wiley-Blackwell, pp. 37–64.

Bakker, A.B. and Demerouti, A.I. (2014b), 'Burnout and work engagement: The JD–R approach', *Annual Review of Organizational Psychology and Organizational Behavior*, *1*, 389–411.

Bakker, A.B., van Veldhoven, M., and Xanthopoulou, D. (2010), 'Beyond the demand-control model: Thriving on high job demands and resources', *Journal of Personnel Psychology*, *9* (1), 3–16.

Bal, P.M., Kooij, D.T.A.M., and De Jong, S.B. (2013), 'How do developmental and accommodative HRM enhance employee engagement and commitment? The role of psychological contract and SOC Strategies', *Journal of Management Studies*, *50* (4), 545–572.

Bandura, A. (1977), 'Self-efficacy: Toward a unifying theory of behavioral change', *Psychological Review*, *84* (2), 191–215.

Barnes, D.C. and Collier, J.E. (2013), 'Investigating work engagement in the service environment', *Journal of Services Marketing*, *27* (6), 485–499.

Becker, H.S. (1960), 'Notes on the concept of commitment', *American Journal of Sociology*, *66* (1), 32–40.

Becker, T.E., Klein, H.J., and Meyer, J.P. (2009), 'Commitment in organizations: Accumulated wisdom and new directions', in H. Klein, T.E. Becker, J.P. Meyer (eds), *Commitment in Organizations: Accumulated Wisdom and New Directions*, New York: Routledge/Taylor & Francis, pp. 419–452.

Becker, T.E., Ullrich, J., and Van Dick, R. (2013), 'Within-person variation in affective commitment to teams: Where it comes from and why it matters', *Human Resource Management Review*, *23* (1), 131–147.

Biswas, S. and Bhatnagar, J. (2013), 'Mediator analysis of employee engagement: Role of perceived organizational support, P–O fit, organizational commitment and job satisfaction', *Journal for Decision Makers*, *38* (1), 27–40.

Blau, P.M. (1964), *Exchange and Power in Social Life*, New York: Wiley.

Brunetto, Y., Teo, S.T.T., Shacklock, K., and Farr-Wharton, R. (2012), 'Emotional intelligence, job satisfaction, well-being and engagement: Explaining organisational commitment and turnover intentions in policing', *Human Resource Management Journal*, *22* (4), 428–441.

Byrne, Z.S., Peters, J.M., and Drake, T. (2014), 'Measurement of employee engagement: The Utrecht Work Engagement Scale versus the Job Engagement Scale', unpublished manuscript.

Carter, R., Nesbit, P., and Joy, M. (2010), 'Using theatre-based interventions to increase employee self-efficacy and engagement', in S.L. Albrecht (ed.), *Handbook of Employee Engagement: Perspectives, Issues, Research and Practice*, Cheltenham, UK and Northampton, MA, USA: Edward Elgar Publishing, pp. 416–424.

Christian, M.S., Garza, A.S., and Slaughter, J.E. (2011), 'Work engagement: A quantitative review and test of its relations with task and contextual performance', *Personnel Psychology*, *64*, 89–136.

Cohen, A. (1992), 'Antecedents of organizational commitment across occupational groups: A meta-analysis', *Journal of Organizational Behavior*, *13*, 539–558.

Corporate Leadership Council (2004), 'Driving performance and retention through employee engagement', Washington DC.

Crabb, S. (2011), 'The use of coaching principles to foster employee engagement', *Coaching Psychologist*, *7* (1), 27–34.

Crawford, E.R., LePine, J.A., and Rich, B.L. (2010), 'Linking job demands and resources to employee engagement and burnout: a theoretical extension and meta-analytic test', *Journal of Applied Psychology*, *95* (5), 834–848.

Dalal, R.S., Baysinger, M., Brummel, B.J., and LeBreton, J.M. (2012), 'The relative importance of employee engagement, other job attitudes, and trait affect as predictors of job performance', *Journal of Applied Social Psychology*, *42*, 295–325.

De Beer, L., Rothmann Jr, S., and Pienaar, J. (2012), 'A confirmatory investigation of a job demands–resources model using a categorical estimator', *Psychological Reports*, *111* (2), 528–544.

Deci, E.L. and Ryan, R.M. (2000), 'The "what" and "why" of goal pursuits: Human needs and the self-determination of behavior', *Psychological Inquiry*, *11* (4), 227–268.

Demerouti, E., Bakker, A.B., de Jonge, J., Janssen, P.M., and Schaufeli, W.B. (2001), 'Burnout and engagement at work as a function of demands and control', *Scandinavian Journal of Work, Environment and Health*, *27* (4), 279–286.

Ferrer, J.L. and Morris, L. (2013), 'Engaging élitism: The mediating effect of work engagement on affective commitment and quit intentions in two Australian university groups', *Higher Education Quarterly*, 67 (4), 340–357.

Field, L.K. and Buitendach, J.H. (2011), 'Happiness, work engagement and organisational commitment of support staff at a tertiary education institution in South Africa', *SA Journal of Industrial Psychology*, 37 (1), 1–10.

Fredrickson, B.L. (2001), 'The role of positive emotions in positive psychology: The broaden- and-build theory of positive emotions', *American Psychologist*, 56 (3), 218–226.

Golombiewski, R.T. and Hilles, R.J. (1979), *Toward the Responsive Organization: The Theory and Practice of Survey Feedback*, Salt Lake City, UT: Brighton.

Grawitch, M.J., Trares, S., and Kohler, J.M. (2007), 'Healthy workplace practices and employee outcomes', *International Journal of Stress Management*, 14 (1), 275–293.

Grdinovac, J.A. and Yancey, G.B. (2012), 'How organizational adaptations to recession relate to organizational commitment', *Psychologist-Manager Journal*, 15 (1), 6–24.

Hackman, J.R. and Oldham, G.R. (1980), *Work Re-design*, Reading, MA: Addison-Wesley.

Hakanen, J.J. and Schaufeli, W.B. (2012), 'Do burnout and work engagement predict depressive symptoms and life satisfaction? A three-wave seven-year prospective study', *Journal of Affective Disorders*, 141 (2–3), 415–424.

Halbesleben, J.R.B. (2010), 'A meta-analysis of work engagement: Relationships with burnout, demands, resources, and consequences', in A.B. Bakker and M.P. Leiter (eds), *Work Engagement: A Handbook of Essential Theory and Research*, New York: Psychology Press, pp. 102–117.

Hallberg, U.E. and Schaufeli, W.B. (2006), '"Same same" but different? Can work engagement be discriminated from job involvement and organizational commitment?', *European Psychologist*, 11 (2), 119–127.

Hobfoll, S.E. (2002), 'Social and psychological resources and adaptation', *Review of General Psychology*, 6 (4), 307–324.

Inceoglu, I. and Fleck, S. (2010), 'Engagement as a motivational construct', in S.L. Albrecht (ed.), *Handbook of Employee Engagement: Perspectives, Issues, Research and Practice*, Cheltenham, UK and Northampton, MA, USA: Edward Elgar Publishing, pp. 74–86.

Kahn, W.A. (1990), 'Psychological conditions of personal engagement and disengagement at work', *Academy of Management Journal*, 33 (4), 692–724.

Kahn, W.A. and Fellows, S. (2013), 'Employee engagement and meaningful work', in B.J. Dik, Z.S. Byrne, and M.F. Steger (eds), *Purpose and Meaning in the Workplace*, Boston, MA: American Psychological Association, pp. 105–126.

Karatepe, O.M. (2011), 'Procedural justice, work engagement, and job outcomes: Evidence from Nigeria', *Journal of Hospitality Marketing and Management*, 20 (8), 855–878.

Karatepe, O.M. (2013), 'Perceptions of organizational politics and hotel employee outcomes: The mediating role of work engagement', *International Journal of Contemporary Hospitality Management*, 25 (1), 82–104.

Karatepe, O.M. and Aga, M. (2012), 'Work engagement as a mediator of the effects of personality traits on job outcomes: A study of frontline employees', *Services Marketing Quarterly*, 33 (4), 343–362.

Karatepe, O.M., Beirami, E., Bouzari, M., and Safavi, H.P. (2014), 'Does work engagement mediate the effects of challenge stressors on job outcomes? Evidence from the hotel industry', *International Journal of Hospitality Management*, 36, 14–22.

Kristof-Brown, A., Zimmerman, R., and Johnson, E. (2005), 'Consequences of individuals' fit at work: A meta-analysis of person–job, person–organization, person–group, and person–supervisor fit', *Personnel Psychology*, 58, 281–342.

Langford, P.H. (2010), 'Benchmarking work practices and outcomes in Australian universities using an employee survey', *Journal of Higher Education Policy and Management*, 32 (1), 41–53.

Luthans, F., Youssef, C.M., and Avolio, B.J. (2007), *Psychological Capital: Developing the Human Competitive Edge*, Oxford: Oxford University Press.

May, D.R., Gilson, R.L., and Harter, L.M. (2004), 'The psychological conditions of meaningfulness, safety and availability and the engagement of the human spirit at work', *Journal of Occupational and Organizational Psychology*, 77 (1), 11–37.

Meyer, J.P. and Allen, N.J. (1991), 'A three-component conceptualization of organizational commitment', *Human Resource Management Review*, 1 (1), 61–89.

Meyer, J.P., Allen, N.J., and Smith, C.A. (1993), 'Commitment to organizations and occupations: Extension and test of a three-component conceptualization', *Journal of Applied Psychology*, 78, 538–551.

Meyer, J.P., Becker, T.E., and Vandenberghe, C. (2004), 'Employee commitment and motivation: A conceptual analysis and integrative model', *Journal of Applied Psychology*, 89 (1), 991–1007.

Meyer, J.P., Gagné, M., and Parfyonova, N.M. (2010), 'Toward an evidence-based model of engagement: What we can learn from motivation and commitment research', in S.L. Albrecht (ed.), *Handbook of Employee*

Engagement: Perspectives, Issues, Research and Practice, Cheltenham, UK and Northampton, MA, USA: Edward Elgar Publishing, pp. 62–73.

Meyer, J.P., Stanley, D.J., Herscovitch, L., and Topolnytsky, L. (2002), 'Affective, continuance, and normative commitment to the organization: A meta-analysis of antecedents, correlates, and consequences', *Journal of Vocational Behavior*, *61* (1), 20–52.

Meyer, J.P., Stanley, L.J., and Parfyonova, N.M. (2012), 'Employee commitment in context: The nature and implication of commitment profiles', *Journal of Vocational Behavior*, *80* (1), 1–16.

Mowday, R.T., Porter, L.W., and Steers, R.M. (1982), *Employee–Organisation Linkages: The Psychology of Commitment, Absenteeism, and Turnover*, New York: Academic Press.

Mowday, R.T., Steers, R.M., and Porter, G. (1979), 'The measurement of organizational commitment', *Journal of Vocational Behavior*, *14* (1), 224–247.

Newman, D.A. and Harrison, D.A. (2008), 'Been there, bottled that: Are state and behavioural work engagement new and useful construct 'wines'?', *Industrial and Organizational Psychology: Perspectives on Science and Practice*, *1* (1), 31–35.

Newman, D.A., Joseph, D.L., and Hulin, C.L. (2010), 'Job attitudes and employee engagement: considering the attitude "A-factor"', in S.L. Albrecht (ed.), *Handbook of Employee Engagement*, Cheltenham, UK and Northampton, MA, USA: Edward Elgar, pp. 43–61.

Ng, T. and Sorensen, K. (2008), 'Toward a further understanding of the relationships between perceptions of support and work attitudes: A meta-analysis', *Group and Organization Management*, *33* (3), 243–268.

Oliver, N. (1990), 'Rewards, investments, alternatives and organizational commitment: Empirical evidence and theoretical development', *Journal of Occupational Psychology*, *63* (1), 19–31.

O'Reilly, C. and Chatman, J. (1986), 'Organizational commitment and psychological attachment: The effects of compliance, identification and internalization on prosocial behaviour', *Journal of Applied Psychology*, *71* (3), 492–499.

Ouweneel, E., Le Blanc, P.M., Schaufeli, W.B., and van Wijhe, C.I. (2012), 'Good morning, good day: A diary study on positive emotions, hope, and work engagement', *Human Relations*, *65* (9), 1129–1154.

Panaccio, A. and Vendenberghe, C. (2012), 'Five-factor model of personality and organizational commitment: The mediating role of positive and negative affective states', *Journal of Vocational Behavior*, *80* (3), 647–658.

Parzefall, M-R. and Hakanen, J. (2010), 'Psychological contract and its motivational and health-enhancing properties', *Journal of Managerial Psychology*, *25* (1), 4–21.

Pignata, S., Boyd, C., Gillespie, N., Provis, C., and Winefield, A.H. (2014), 'Awareness of stress-reduction interventions: The impact on employees' well-being and organizational attitudes', *Stress and Health*. DOI: 10.1002/smi.2597.

Poon, J.M.L. (2013), 'Relationships among perceived career support, affective commitment, and work engagement', *International Journal of Psychology*, *48* (6), 1148–1155.

Rhoades, L., Eisenberger, R., and Armeli, S. (2001), 'Affective commitment to the organization: The contribution of perceived organizational support', *Journal of Applied Psychology*, *86* (5), 825–836.

Rich, B.L., LePine, J.A., and Crawford, E.R. (2010), 'Job engagement: Antecedents and effects on job performance', *Academy of Management Journal*, *53* (3), 617–635.

Richardsen, A.M., Burke, R.J., and Martinussen, M. (2006), 'Work and health outcomes among police officers: The mediating role of police cynicism and engagement', *International Journal of Stress Management*, *13* (4), 555–574.

Rigg, J. (2013), 'Worthwhile concept or old wine? A review of employee engagement and related constructs', *American Journal of Business and Management*, *2* (1), 31–36.

Roe, R., Solinger, O., and van Olffen, W. (2009), 'Shaping organizational commitment', in S. Clegg and C. Cooper (eds), *The SAGE Handbook of Organizational Behavior: Volume II – Macro Approaches*, London: SAGE Publications, pp. 130–150.

Rothband, N.P. (2001), 'Enriching or depleting? The dynamics of engagement in work and family roles', *Administrative Science Quarterly*, *46* (1), 655–684.

Russell, J.A. (1980), 'Circumplex model of affect', *Journal of Personality and Social Psychology*, *39* (1), 1161–1178.

Saks, A.M. (2006), 'Antecedents and consequences of employee engagement', *Journal of Managerial Psychology*, *21* (7), 600–619.

Salanova, M. and Schaufeli, W.B. (2008), 'A cross-national study of work engagement as a mediator between job resources and proactive behaviour', *International Journal of Human Resource Management*, *19* (1), 116–131.

Schaufeli, W.B. and Bakker, A.B. (2010), 'Defining and measuring work engagement; bringing clarity to the concept', in A.B. Bakker and M.P. Leiter (eds), *Work Engagement*, New York: Psychology Press, pp. 10–24.

Schaufeli, W.B., Bakker, A.B., and Salanova, M. (2006), 'The measurement of work engagement with a short questionnaire: A Cross-National Study', *Educational and Psychological Measurement*, *66* (4), 701–716.

Schaufeli, W.B. and Salanova, M. (2010), 'How to improve work engagement?' in S.L. Albrecht (eds), *Handbook of Employee Engagement: Perspectives, Issues, Research and Practice*, Cheltenham, UK and Northampton, MA, USA: Edward Elgar Publishing, pp. 399–415.

Schaufeli, W.B., Salanova, M., González-Romá, V., and Bakker, A.B. (2002), 'The measurement of engagement and burnout: A two sample confirmatory factor analytic approach', *Journal of Happiness Studies*, 3, 71–92.

Schaufeli, W.B. and Taris, T.W. (2014), 'A critical review of the job demands–resources model: Implications for improving work and health', in G.F. Bauer and O. Hämmig (eds), *Bridging Occupational, Organizational and Public Health: A Transdisciplinary Approach*, New York: Springer Science + Business Media, pp. 43–68.

Schohat, L.M. and Vigoda-Gadot, E. (2010), '"Engage me once again": is employee engagement for real, or is it "same lady – different dress?"' in S.L. Albrecht (ed.), *Handbook of Employee Engagement*, Cheltenham, UK: Edward Elgar Publishing, pp. 98–107.

Scrima, F. (2014), 'The mediating role of work engagement on the relationship between job involvement and affective commitment', *Human Resource Management*, 25 (15), 2159–2173.

Shaw, K. (2005), 'An engagement strategy process for communicators', *Strategic Communication Management*, 9 (3), 26–29.

Shuck, B., Reio, T.G., and Rocco, T.S. (2011), 'Employee engagement: an examination of antecedent and outcome variables', *Human Resource Development International*, 14(4), 427–445.

Simons, J.C. and Buitendach, J.H. (2013), 'Psychological capital, work engagement and organisational commitment amongst call centre employees in South Africa', *SA Journal of Industrial Psychology*, 39 (2), 1–12.

Siu, O.L. (2002), 'Occupational stressors and well-being among Chinese employees: The role of organisational commitment', *Applied Psychology: An International Review*, 51 (4), 527–544.

Soane, E., Truss, C., Alfes, K., Shantz, A., Rees, C., and Gatenby, M. (2012), 'Development and application of a new measure of employee engagement: The ISA Engagement Scale', *Human Resource Development International*, 15 (5), 529–547.

Solinger, O.N., Hofmans, J., and van Olffen, W. (2014), 'The dynamic microstructure of organizational commitment', *Journal of Occupational and Organizational Psychology*, 88, 773–796.

Solinger, O.N., van Olffen, W., and Roe, R. A. (2008), 'Beyond the three-component model of organizational commitment', *Journal of Applied Psychology*, 93 (1), 70–83.

Sonnentag, S., Dormann, C., and Demerouti, E. (2010), 'Not all days are created equal: The concept of state work engagement', in A.B. Bakker and M. Leiter (eds), *Work Engagement: The Essential in Theory and Research*, New York: Psychology Press, pp. 25–38.

Sturges, J., Guest, D., Conway, N., and Davey, K. (2002), 'A longitudinal study of the relationship between career management and organizational commitment among graduates in the first ten years at work', *Journal of Organizational Behavior*, 23, 731–748.

Tajfel, H. (1974), 'Social identity and intergroup behaviour', *Social Science Information/sur les sciences sociales*, 13 (2), 65–93.

Thoresen, C.J., Kaplan, S.A., Barsky, A.P., Warren, C.R., and de Chermont, K. (2003), 'The affective underpinnings of job perceptions and attitudes: A meta-analytic review and integration', *Psychological Bulletin*, 129 (6), 914–945.

Van den Broeck, A., Vansteenkiste, M., De Witte, H., and Lens, W. (2008), 'Explaining the relationships between job characteristics, burnout, and engagement: The role of basic psychological need satisfaction', *Work and Stress*, 22 (3), 277–294.

Vigoda-Gadot, E., Eldor, L., and Schohat, L.M. (2012), 'Engage them to public service: Conceptualization and empirical examination of employee engagement in public administration', *American Review of Public Administration*, 43 (5), 518–538.

Viljevac, A., Cooper-Thomas, H.D., and Saks, A.M. (2012), 'An investigation into the validity of two measures of work engagement', *International Journal of Human Resource Management*, 23 (17), 3692–3709.

Vincent-Hoeper, S., Muser, C., and Janneck, M. (2012), 'Transformational leadership, work engagement, and occupational success', *Career Development International*, 17 (6–7), 663–682.

Wefald, A.J., Reichard, R.J., and Serrano, S.A. (2011), 'Fitting engagement into a nomological network: The relationship of engagement to leadership and personality', *Journal of Leadership and Organizational Studies*, 18 (4), 522–537.

Yalabik, Z.Y., Popaitoon, P., Chowne, J.A., and Rayton, B.A. (2013), 'Work engagement as a mediator between employee attitudes and outcomes', *International Journal of Human Resource Management*, 24 (14), 2799–2823.

Yalabik, Z.Y., Rossenberg, Y.V., Kinnie, N., and Swart, J. (2014), 'Engaged and committed? The relationship between work engagement and commitment in professional service firms', *International Journal of Human Resource Management*, 26 (12), 1–20.

7. Job embeddedness, employee commitment, and related constructs

Brooks C. Holtom

Compared to organizational commitment, job embeddedness theory (Mitchell et al., 2001) is a relative newcomer to the employee attachment arena. However, over the past 15 years a sizeable amount of research based on the construct has been published (see meta-analysis by Jiang et al., 2012) and it has gained the attention of researchers (Holtom et al., 2008) and practitioners (Holtom et al., 2006). Perhaps the biggest difference between job embeddedness and other constructs is that rather than being developed to explain why people voluntarily leave organizations, it was formulated to explain why people stay in organizations (Lee et al., 2014). Notwithstanding this distinctive origin, it shares considerable construct space in the nomological network with organizational commitment, job satisfaction, organizational identification, and other concepts.

In the following pages, I review the theoretical foundation of job embeddedness. Then, I explore its conceptual connections to employee commitment and related constructs. Next, I examine the ways in which job embeddedness has been measured and the empirical relationships that have been observed among related constructs, as well as the contribution that job embeddedness makes in explaining important organizational outcomes such as job performance, organizational citizenship behaviors, absenteeism, and voluntary turnover. Finally, I provide ideas for future research and practical implications of job embeddedness theory.

JOB EMBEDDEDNESS THEORY

In our early deliberations regarding a 'staying construct', my colleagues and I were determined to focus less on affect or affect-saturated constructs (for example, satisfaction, commitment or involvement) and more on contextual factors that influence staying. In specifying the construct space for job embeddedness, we (Mitchell et al., 2001, p. 1104) described job embeddedness as follows:

> Job embeddedness represents a broad constellation of influences on employee retention . . . [W]e can describe job embeddedness as like a net or a web in which an individual can become stuck. One who is highly embedded has many links that are close together (not highly differentiated). Moreover, the content of the parts may vary considerably, suggesting that one can be enmeshed or embedded in many different ways. It is this overall level of embeddedness, rather than specific elements of embeddedness, that is our central focus. The critical aspects of job embeddedness are (1) the extent to which people have links to other people or activities, (2) the extent to which their jobs and communities are similar to or fit with the other aspects in their life spaces, and, (3) the ease with which links can be broken – what they would give up if they left, especially if they had to physically move to other cities or homes. We labeled these three dimensions 'links,' 'fit,' and 'sacrifice,' and they are important both on and off the job.

In sum, job embeddedness is conceptualized as the combination of forces that keep a person from leaving their job. It captures a broad set of factors that influence retention. The overall construct is broken down into three dimensions: links, fit, and sacrifice. Each dimension has two subdimensions: 'on the job' (sometimes called 'organizational embeddedness') and 'off the job' (sometimes called 'community embeddedness'). Job embeddedness is measured as the aggregate of these six subdimensions. Each of the subdimensions contributes unique understanding and predictive power to the overall job embeddedness concept.

'Links' refer to the connections people have both on and off the job. These connections can be to institutions (for example, non-profit boards of directors) or people (for example, mentors). The number of links contributes to a general sense of embeddedness. The higher the number of links between the person and the web in which they are embedded, the more they are bound to the job, organization, and community.

'Fit' refers to an employee's perceived compatibility with an organization and the community. This sense of compatibility may contain both affective reactions and non-affective judgments. Fit in the organization relates to the alignment with the job itself, personal values, career goals, and future plans. Fit in the community includes one's compatibility with the local weather, culture of the community, entertainment, political and religious activities. The better the fit, the more likely people will feel professionally and personally tied to their job and organization.

'Sacrifice' is the perceived cost of material or psychological benefits that may be forfeited by leaving a job. For example, leaving a job likely entails leaving colleagues, perks, and projects. Additionally, many switching costs may also factor into the decision (for example, new healthcare or pension plans, stock options) as well as opportunities for job stability or advancement. Community sacrifices are mostly an issue when people consider relocating. Leaving a safe, comfortable community where you have many family and friends can be very difficult. But even changing organizations within the same region may entail sacrifices such as an easy commute, carpool arrangements, or flextime agreements. In sum, the more one has to give up, the more difficult it is to break from the current job. Based on this definition, I will now explain similarities and differences between job embeddedness and related constructs.

SIMILARITIES AND DIFFERENCES WITH OTHER CONSTRUCTS

At the most general level, it is important to recognize that the term 'embeddedness' has been used in the sociological literature for many years to describe how social relationships may influence or constrain economic actions (e.g., Granovetter, 1985; Uzzi, 1997). The major similarity with job embeddedness is the notion that social networks act as a constraint (in this case on job mobility). The major differences are the units of analysis and variables of interest. Whereas sociologists like Granovetter and Uzzi examine groups, organizations, and wide-ranging economic actions, my colleagues and I are focused narrowly on individuals staying in jobs.

Another important difference at a very general level is the fact that job embeddedness assesses both organizational as well as community linkages. Traditional turnover

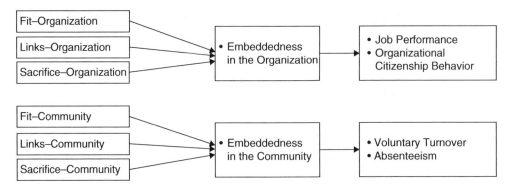

Note: Key findings: after controlling for job satisfaction and organizational commitment: (1) embeddedness in the organization predicts job performance and organizational citizenship behavior; and (2) embeddedness in the community predicts voluntary turnover and absenteeism (Lee et al., 2004).

Figure 7.1   Antecedents and consequences of job embeddedness

predictors such as job satisfaction focus primarily on organizational factors influencing leaving (for example, satisfaction with supervisor, satisfaction with pay, satisfaction with the work itself, and so on). In contrast, job embeddedness includes both organizational and community considerations. Indeed, in 2004, Lee and colleagues found that, after controlling for job satisfaction and organizational commitment, embeddedness in the community predicts voluntary turnover and absenteeism (see Figure 7.1). Thus, a primary difference is the unique explanatory variance that accrues from measuring the community component of attachment.

Additionally, it is important to note that the original measurement of job embeddedness was largely non-affective. Mitchell et al. (2001) posited that job embeddedness is best represented as a formative measure, meaning that the measures cause the construct; rather than as a reflective measure, where the construct is the 'real' underlying characteristic and a measure is simply a reflection of that characteristic (see the Appendix for examples of the job embeddedness items). Whereas affective commitment (Allen and Meyer, 1990) reflects one's liking for a job and emotional attachment to an organization, job embeddedness was developed with little affective content. For example, the measurement of links is primarily about things that can be counted (for example, how many work teams a person is on, how many colleagues they regularly interact with, how long they have been employed by the organization). It is similarly important to note that the fit-in-the-organization component as operationalized followed Cable and Parsons's notion that it 'represents a cognitive belief rather than an emotional response' (Cable and Parsons, 1999: 24). Having made these high-level comparisons, in the following pages, I will now describe the many similarities and differences at the subdimension level.

Sacrifice–Organization Subdimension

The dimension of job embeddedness that is most like other constructs in the field is the sacrifice–organization composite. Four similar ideas will be discussed: side bets, continuance commitment, cost of quitting, and job investments.

In 1960, Becker laid foundation stones for the organizational commitment construct when he introduced the notion of side bets. He stated that side bets occur when an employee 'staked something of value to him, something originally unrelated to his present line of activity' (p. 35). Jaros and colleagues described this idea as 'the investments or side bets, an employee makes in an organization, such as time, job effort, and the development of work friendships, organization-specific skills, and political deals' (Jaros et al., 1993, p. 953). The idea of side bets as 'sunk costs' is similar to our notion that job embeddedness reflects how 'stuck' one feels.

Continuance commitment as developed by Allen and Meyer (1990, p. 4) reflects 'the magnitude and/or number of investments (or side-bets) individuals make and a perceived lack of alternatives'. The sacrifice–organization factor and the continuance commitment idea clearly share the notions of 'sunk cost' and reluctance to give up things by leaving. However, the measure of sacrifice–organization includes specific items referring to perks, respect, compensation, benefits (retirement and healthcare), and promotional opportunities which are not included in continuance commitment.

In 1977, Mobley introduced the idea of cost of quitting, stating that 'the cost of quitting would include such considerations as loss of seniority, loss of vested benefits, and the like' (p. 238). He also included the expected utility of search, which of course leads to turnover. The original measure of sacrifice–organization explicitly incorporated the perceived costs of leaving the organization.

In 1981, based on equity and exchange ideas, Farrell and Rusbult developed their job investment model. According to these authors (1981, p. 431):

> Investments in a job may consist of resources that are intrinsic to the job (e.g., years of service, non-portable training, non-vested portions of retirement programs) or resources that are extrinsic, but inextricably connected to the job (e.g., housing arrangements that facilitate travel to and from work, friends at work, extraneous benefits uniquely associated with a particular job).

In their model, commitment was seen as the antecedent to turnover and 'commitment is said to increase with increases in job rewards, decreases in job costs, increases in investment size and decreases in alternative quality' (Rusbult and Farrell, 1983, p. 430). So, although the general idea of job-investment is similar to sacrifice–organization, it is operationalized and analyzed differently.

Links–Organization Subdimension

One of the key conceptual contributors to our thinking around links in the organization was Reichers's (1985) notion of constituency commitment. She notes that 'commitment is a process of identification with the goals of an organization's multiple constituencies' (p. 465). She includes top management, customers, unions, and/or the public at large. In 1992, Becker tested this concept using the following question: 'How attached are you to the following people and groups (top management, supervisor and work group)?' Note that this item assesses the degree to which one is attached. In contrast, the links–organization measure simply assesses the number of attachments people had in terms of their length of time in a job or organization, and the number of co-workers, teams, and committees with which they are involved. It is a completely non-affective measure.

Constituency commitment implies goal identification and attachment to these groups, which may be affective in nature.

Fit–Organization Subdimension

The fit–organization dimension is similar to the person–job, person–supervisor, person–group, and person–organization fit constructs (Kristof, 1996; Chapter 20 in this volume). It is also related to the organizational identification literature (Chapter 8 in this volume). The principal difference is that the fit–organization subdimension seeks to parsimoniously capture the breadth of these concepts.

Person–organization fit addresses compatibility or 'congruence of the personality traits, beliefs and values of individual persons with the culture, strategic needs, norms and values of organizations' (Netemeyer et al., 1997, p. 88). Similarly, congruence of knowledge, skills, and abilities with one's job constitutes person–job fit (Saks and Ashforth, 1997). The job embeddedness notion of fit in the organization was designed to extend beyond both person–organization and person–job fit. Consequently, the original formative measure assesses how well employees perceive they fit with their co-workers, groups, jobs, companies, and cultures. In addition, because of the confusion in the literature about the bases of fit (or congruence) with personality, values, needs, and goals, the measure simply asked for an overall fit perception without referring to needs.

Mael and Ashforth (1992, p. 103) define organizational identification as 'a perceived oneness with an organization and the experience of the organization's success and failures as one's own'. In other words, 'the individual defines him or herself in terms of the organization(s) in which he or she is a member' (p. 104). The construct of organizational identification is fundamentally different from fit–organization in that organizational identification at the personal level is involved with self-definition. Ashforth (1998) says organizational identification involves the fusion of self and organization.

Links–Community Subdimension

While there are very few constructs that are similar to the sacrifice and fit in the community dimensions, there are a couple of constructs that are related to links with the community. First is the notion of kinship responsibility. In their theory of turnover, Price and Mueller (1981) suggest that kinship responsibilities may be an important reason why people stay in a job. Blegen et al. (1988, p. 402) define kinship responsibility as 'the degree of an individual's obligations to relatives in the community in which the individual resides'. They used simple indicators such as marital status and number of relatives in the community to measure kinship responsibility.

The literature on relocation and repatriation also focuses on links to the community, especially one's spouse, as determinants of job-related decisions. For example, Miller (1976), Spitz (1986), and Turban et al. (1992) suggest that relocation (taking a job in another city but staying with the company) is severely hindered if a spouse does not want to move. Turban et al. (1992) use a measure that is very much like the Price and Mueller (1981) kinship responsibility measure. In addition, they measured adjustment to the move.

For repatriation, the relationship with one's spouse and family is also seen as important. Black (1988) and Shaffer and Harrison (1998), for example, used the kinship responsibility measure of Blegen et al. (1988) and some additional items to assess spouse's adjustment. They also asked questions about satisfaction with living conditions. These ideas are very similar to the links–community factor, but are different in that job embeddedness does not have a normative or ethical dimension like kinship responsibility.

Global Reflective Measure of Job Embeddedness

In 2007, Crossley et al. published an article that 'developed and tested a global, reflective measure of job embeddedness' that they argue 'overcomes important limitations and serves as a companion to the original composite measure' (p. 1031). As these authors correctly note:

> [T]he composite measure of job embeddedness (Mitchell et al., 2001) is formed when one adds together equally weighted facets, assuming that the whole is equal to the sum of its parts. In contrast, a global measure of embeddedness would assume that the whole is greater than the sum of its parts and assess overall impressions of attachment by asking general questions. This approach suggests that some sort of mental processing occurs and simply asks for the end product. During this process, respondents subjectively weigh various facets and may even incorporate additional relevant information that might have been omitted from facet-level scales. (Crossley et al., 2007, p. 1032)

Thus motivated, they created a seven-item global reflective measure. The measure proved reliable and predictive of withdrawal behaviors including intention to search, intention to quit, and actual voluntary turnover. Moreover, the global measure predicted turnover after controlling for job satisfaction, perceived alternatives, and intentions to search. Over time, researchers have used the original formative measure (Mitchell et al., 2001), a revised, shortened formative measure (Felps et al., 2009), and the global reflective measure (Crossley et al., 2007) to produce a generally similar pattern of results (Jiang et al., 2012). Representative items for these measures are provided in the Appendix.

ANTECEDENTS AND CONSEQUENCES OF JOB EMBEDDEDNESS

In the past decade many studies have examined job embeddedness as an antecedent to a variety of consequences including voluntary and involuntary turnover, absenteeism, as well as in-role and extra-role performance. More recently a number of studies have explored the antecedents to job embeddedness and others have explored job embeddedness as a mediator or moderator. Given some degree of conceptual overlap between job embeddedness and organizational commitment, it is not surprising that they predict similar outcomes. In this section, I review key findings that help us better understand the nomological network surrounding job embeddedness.

Empirical Relationship between Job Embeddedness and Related Constructs

In their meta-analysis, Jiang et al. (2012) reported the following mean sample size weighted corrected correlations between organizational embeddedness and: community embeddedness ($r_c = .31$), actual turnover ($r_c = -.19$), turnover intentions ($r_c = -.48$), job performance ($r_c = .18$), affective commitment ($r_c = .61$), and job satisfaction ($r_c = .64$). In general, and not surprisingly, the correlations between community embeddedness and the same constructs were smaller: actual turnover ($r_c = -.12$), turnover intentions ($r_c = -.22$), job performance ($r_c = .10$), affective commitment ($r_c = .16$), and job satisfaction ($r_c = .22$). It is worth noting as well that the same meta-analysis reports the following pattern for affective commitment: actual turnover ($r_c = .22$), turnover intentions ($r_c = -.44$), job performance ($r_c = .18$), and job satisfaction ($r_c = .68$). Job satisfaction also demonstrated significant correlations with these key variables as follows: actual turnover ($r_c = -.16$), turnover intentions ($r_c = -.52$), and job performance ($r_c = .19$). Thus, it is clear that job embeddedness correlates with important organizational outcomes such as voluntary turnover and in-role performance at approximately the same level as affective commitment and job satisfaction. However, as the meta-analysis also makes clear, job embeddedness explains unique variance over and above job satisfaction, affective commitment, job alternatives, and job search behaviors. One conclusion that can be drawn from this pattern of results is that job embeddedness is not necessarily a more robust predictor than job satisfaction or organizational commitment. However, it captures unique variance and thus has value to both researchers and practitioners.

The meta-analysis also reviewed possible moderators of the job embeddedness–turnover relationship. Only one moderator achieved statistical significance. The relationship between organizational embeddedness and turnover is stronger in public ($r_c = -.27$) than in private ($r_c = -.19$) organizations. However, this was not true of the community embeddedness–turnover relationship. National culture and gender were both tested but the relationships were non-significant. This may be due to the low number of studies of subjects outside of the United States (US). Given significant differences in retirement and pension systems between the US and other countries (such as Germany, where such benefits come from the state rather than an employing organization), it seems likely that perceptions about the potential sacrifices of leaving an employer would be muted.

Theorists explain that one reason why individuals invest resources such as effort and time (Halbesleben et al., 2014) into extra-role behaviors (for example, socializing newcomers, attending outside-work functions, helping colleagues) is to accumulate more resources and in the process become more embedded (Halbesleben and Wheeler, 2015; Ng and Feldman, 2012; Podsakoff et al., 2009). Thus, one might act altruistically towards superiors or colleagues to build goodwill and reciprocity to repay such kindness (earning them higher performance reviews, including favorable 360 degree feedback), with the ultimate effect being deeper job embeddedness. This suggests reciprocal causality, or what practitioners might call a virtuous cycle.

Further, as regards task performance, high-performing employees can expect greater extrinsic benefits (for example, favorable reviews, pay raises, promotions) and intrinsic benefits (for example, feeling valuable and competent) (Lanaj et al., 2012; Rotundo and Sackett, 2002; Salamin and Hom, 2005). Thus, it is reasonable to expect that people embedded in occupations, organizations, and jobs should thus be motivated to invest time and effort towards superior task performance to meet professional goals. Also, because job-embedded incumbents have the requisite demands–abilities job fit (Kristof, 1996) and links (social capital from high-density colleague networks; Sparrowe et al., 2001) to reach high performance standards, on-the-job embeddedness should promote high job performance. Finally, because counterproductive work behaviors (for example, Internet surfing, abusing colleagues) can lead to termination, lost opportunities for advancement, or a tarnished reputation (Feldman et al., 2012; Lee et al., 2004; Rotundo and Sackett, 2002), it is not surprising that people who are highly embedded in their organizations are less likely to engage in such behaviors.

As noted previously, Lee et al. (2004) found that off-the-job embeddedness decreased the probability of turnover and absenteeism, whereas on-the-job embeddedness increased the probability of organizational citizenship behaviors (OCBs) and better job performance. Subsequent research extended those findings, demonstrating that on-the-job embeddedness is correlated with workplace attitudes (turnover intentions, job satisfaction, affective commitment) and behaviors (job search, performance) more strongly than off-the-job embeddedness (Allen, 2006; Ng and Feldman, 2014; Wheeler et al., 2012). Demonstrating buffering effects, Burton et al. (2010) also observed that job-embedded employees do not react with worse performance or lower organizational citizenship behaviors when experiencing negative job shocks, such as poor performance reviews or low pay raises. In sum, a solid body of evidence demonstrates the utility of the construct and how it complements existing concepts that are adjacent in the nomological network.

INNOVATIONS AND EXTENSIONS OF JOB EMBEDDEDNESS THEORY

In the original formulation of job embeddedness, Mitchell et al. (2001) conceived two prime foci – the job and the community – within which employees become embedded. Recent theoretical extensions highlight other embedding foci for individuals (Feldman and Ng, 2007) and their families (Feldman et al., 2012; Ramesh and Gelfand, 2010). The different embeddedness foci appear to be empirically distinct and to differentially affect outcomes (staying, performance, work–family conflict; Lee et al., 2004; Ng and Feldman, 2009, 2012; Ramesh and Gelfand, 2010). Building on the work of Kiazad et al. (2015), I now review the emerging literature on multi-foci job embeddedness below.

On-the-Job and Organizational Embeddedness

In 2007, Ng and Feldman first distinguished between on-the-job and organizational embeddedness. Whereas Mitchell et al. (2001) assume that people embedded in jobs are also embedded in organizations, Ng and Feldman (2007) reason that incumbents can be embedded in one but not necessarily the other. They note that an employee may fit job demands, have multiple ties to colleagues in local work environs, and sacrifice a corner office upon leaving a job. However, these employees may lack fit with corporate values, have few links to employees outside work units, and possess few organizational perks (for example, pension) that would be forfeited by leaving. So, they may be embedded in a particular job but not in the organization. Because jobs are nested within firms, on-the-job embeddedness often translates into higher workplace retention. Job-embedded incumbents may nonetheless quit if their employer reassigns (or promotes) them to a different job that they find less fulfilling or perform less proficiently (Ng and Feldman, 2007). Despite the ways in which on-the-job and organizational embeddedness can differ, job embeddedness researchers have largely treated them synonymously. It is likely that following the recommendation of Ng and Feldman (2007) to separate these two embedding foci will advance understanding as they may differentially affect work outcomes.

Occupational Embeddedness

In 2007, Feldman and Ng also introduced 'occupational embeddedness' – or 'the totality of forces that keep people in their present occupations' (p. 353) – to clarify why incumbents remain in occupational fields and may even leave companies to hone or practice their professional skills elsewhere (Feldman and Ng, 2007). In contrast to the original job embeddedness construct, this form of embeddedness may not promote staying in an organization. Feldman and Ng (2007) further conceptualize that people are embedded in occupations via links. In an initial test, Ng and Feldman (2009) found that occupational embeddedness explains unique variance in task performance, counterproductive work behaviors (CWBs), and creativity after controlling organizational embeddedness.

Family Embeddedness in the Community

A number of researchers have sought to advance a reconceptualization of outside-work forces keeping individuals bound to their current locale (Feldman et al., 2012; Ramesh and Gelfand, 2010). Defining off-the-job embeddedness 'as the cumulative forces of an individual's family, community, and non-work activities which bind an individual to his/her current location' (p. 215), Feldman et al. (2012) differentiate what personally embeds an individual in the community (for example, recreational pursuits) from that which embeds an individual indirectly through their family (for example, domestic partner and other relatives living in the household). As an example, an employee's family may be embedded in a geographic area (for example, spouse owns a local business, teenagers attend magnet schools), thereby embedding the employee. However, such 'embeddedness by proxy' (or 'family embeddedness in community') should not be confused with community attachment. Similarly, Hom et al. (2012) also theorize that felt extrinsic constraints (that is, family pressure) can emanate from family embeddedness and drive different withdrawal states that are distinct from other embedding forces.

Finally, Ramesh and Gelfand (2010) also promulgated the concept of 'family embeddedness'. This is defined as families becoming embedded within workplaces. This occurs when family members favorably appraise firms, befriend other employees, and personally partake of job benefits. Hence an employee may feel compelled to stay in a job or community they misfit because their families prefer that they stay or receive benefits from their employment (for example, health insurance, family status). In support, Ramesh and Gelfand (2010) demonstrated that family embeddedness in the organization explains additional variance in turnover beyond that of on-the-job and community embeddedness.

FUTURE RESEARCH

Finally, there are many exciting avenues for future research to pursue. Following are a few ideas to stimulate further development of the field.

Non-Work Embeddedness: Moderating Effects

According to Feldman et al. (2012), the effects of work-focused embeddedness on work outcomes should be highest when employees also have high off-the-job embeddedness. Since March and Simon (1958), organizational scholars have differentiated organizational contributions based on their association with the decision to stay (participate) or perform. Whereas withdrawal behaviors such as voluntary turnover and work avoidance (Harrison and Newman, 2013) reflect employees' motivation to (not) stay, OCBs and task performance reflect motivation to perform (Hanisch and Hulin, 1991; Hom et al., 2012; Lee et al., 2004). Because off-the-job embeddedness principally compels 'the desire to remain in the present location – and the necessity of maintaining employment to do so' (Feldman et al., 2012, p. 227), it should increase work-focused embeddedness effects on behaviors reflecting the desire to stay. Conversely, although off-the-job resources (for example, community social capital) could allow an employee to stay at work longer, they would not necessarily facilitate better work performance since they are less instrumental in the work context (Halbesleben, 2006). For example, off-the-job links might help employees to meet work performance obligations (for example, relatives help to alleviate work–family conflict), yet such support is less useful for enabling exceptional work performance (for example, formulating work-role or organizational improvements). In fact, individuals may feel compelled to reinvest into supportive non-work relationships to continue acquiring resources from those sources (Halbesleben and Wheeler, 2015). As resources are finite and 'a heavy investment of time in the personal life domain is likely to cut into time which can be spent at work' (Feldman et al., 2012, pp. 225–226), individuals will have less time and energy to invest in work performance. This suggests that off-the-job embeddedness should attenuate the beneficial impact of work-focused embeddedness on OCBs and in-role performance.

Measuring Job Embeddedness

Kiazad et al.'s (2015) model brings a new perspective on the issue of whether embeddedness should be measured as a global gestalt variable (Crossley et al., 2007) or an equally weighted composite (Mitchell et al., 2001). Both the global and composite indices have strengths and shortcomings (Zhang et al., 2012). In terms of strength, the global measure recognizes that different embedding facets and dimensions may be more or less important to different people depending on their personal circumstances. Thus, respondents can subjectively weigh different forces binding them to the firm or community based on their importance. However, unlike the composite, the global scale focuses on the feeling or motivational state of being embedded (Hom et al., 2012; Meyer et al., 2012) rather than explicitly referencing antecedents of this condition, such as links, fit, and sacrifices. Yet these dimensions help to differentiate job embeddedness from related constructs and best match Mitchell et al.'s (2001) initial conceptualization of a formative-indicator construct defined by its dimensions. Building on the work by Lee et al. (2004) as well as Kiazad et al. (2015), researchers who employ the composite measure and thereby model the unique contribution of fit, links, and sacrifices may develop deeper understanding of their differential associations with antecedents and outcomes than those obtained by using the global reflective measure.

Time Dynamics

Researchers are encouraged to adopt longitudinal methods to test the hypothesis that resource–context fit may underlie job embeddedness fluctuations over time (Ng and Feldman, 2013). With a few exceptions (Ng and Feldman, 2007, 2010, 2013), time issues have not been adequately addressed in job embeddedness scholarship. Ng and Feldman (2007) captured very well a number of these time issues, describing how different embedding factors or resources yield embedding influence at different career stages. Building on these ideas, researchers should test the impact of resource usefulness over time to capture changes in job embeddedness over time. Since the value of resources depends on their utility in a given context, people should become increasingly embedded over time if the resources they accumulate persist in satisfying their particular needs or goals (Halbesleben et al., 2014). However, resources might become less embedding should they no longer meet individuals' particular needs or goals. For example, nightlife and outdoor opportunities might embed a young couple in their neighborhood, yet such embedding force might diminish once they have children and their needs change.

PRACTICAL IMPLICATIONS

While experienced scholars and practitioners know there are no magic bullets for retaining employees, job embeddedness theory points to a number of potential ways to increase the odds of retention which go beyond traditional organization-focused approaches. For example, by recruiting most heavily in the neighborhoods surrounding retail locations, organizations can improve the chances that applicants will 'fit in the community'. Similarly, locating new offices near the largest concentrations of existing employees would serve to leverage this pre-existing 'fit'. Further, a number of firms provide employees with paid time off to volunteer in their communities or serve on non-profit boards (Holtom et al., 2006). This creates opportunities to develop closer ties or 'links in the community'. Finally, providing local transportation or home-buying assistance can serve to increase the 'sacrifice' associated with leaving an employer in a given community. These are just a few practical ideas to improve the odds of keeping valued employees that grow out of job embeddedness theory.

CONCLUSION

In this chapter I have sought to describe job embeddedness and the ways in which this construct is similar to and different from others in the field. Generally speaking, it explains unique variance in organizational outcomes such as voluntary turnover, absenteeism, and in-role as well as extra-role performance. It is correlated with job satisfaction, organizational commitment, and organizational identification, yet distinct in a number of ways, in particular its measurement. Given the importance of identifying how to increase the odds of encouraging employees to remain in the organization and perform at high levels, job embeddedness is a valuable complement to organizational commitment and related constructs. Not surprisingly, research extending understanding of this promising construct is vibrant.

REFERENCES

Allen, D. (2006). Do organizational socialization tactics influence newcomer embeddedness and turnover? *Journal of Management, 32*, 237–256.

Allen, N. and Meyer, J. (1990). The measurement and antecedents of affective, continuance, and normative commitment to the organization. *Journal of Occupational Psychology, 63*, 1–18.

Ashforth, B.E. (1998). Epilogue: What does the concept of identity add to organization science. In D. Whetten and P.G. Godfrey (eds), *Identity in Organizations: Building Theory through Conversations* (273–294). Thousand Oaks, CA: Sage.

Becker, H. (1960). Notes on the concept of commitment. *American Journal of Sociology, 66*, 32–42.

Becker, T. (1992). Foci and bases of commitment: Are there distinctions worth making? *Academy of Management Journal, 35*, 232–244.

Black, J. (1988). Work role transitions: A study of American expatriate managers in Japan. *Journal of International Business Studies, 19*, 277–294.

Blegen, M., Mueller, C., and Price, J. (1988). Measurement of kinship responsibility for organizational research. *Journal of Applied Psychology, 73*, 402–409.

Burton, J., Holtom, B., Sablynski, C., Mitchell, T., and Lee, T. (2010). The buffering effects of job embeddedness on negative shocks. *Journal of Vocational Behavior, 76*, 42–51.

Cable, D. and Parsons, C. (1999). Establishing person–organization fit during organizational entry. Paper presented at the Annual Meetings of the Academy of Management, Chicago, USA.

Crossley, C., Bennett, R., Jex, S., and Burnfield, J. (2007). Development of a global measure of job embeddedness and integration into a traditional model of voluntary turnover. *Journal of Applied Psychology, 92*, 1031–1042.

Farrell, E. and Rusbult, C. (1981). Exchange variables as predictors of job satisfaction, job commitment, and turnover: The impact of rewards, costs, alternatives, and investments. *Organizational Behavior and Human Performance, 28*, 78–95.

Feldman, D. and Ng, T. (2007). Careers: Mobility, embeddedness, and success. *Journal of Management, 33*, 350–377.

Feldman, D., Ng, T., and Vogel, R. (2012). Off-the-job embeddedness: A reconceptualization and agenda for future research. *Research in Personnel and Human Resources Management, 31*, 209–251.

Felps, W., Mitchell, T., Hekman, D., Lee, T., Harman, W., and Holtom, B. (2009). Turnover contagion: how coworkers' job embeddedness and coworkers' job search behaviors influence quitting. *Academy of Management Journal, 52*, 545–561.

Granovetter, M. (1985). Economic action and social structure: the problems of embeddedness. *American Journal of Sociology, 91*, 481–510.

Halbesleben, J. (2006). Sources of social support and burnout: a meta-analytic test of the conservation of resources model. *Journal of Applied Psychology, 91*, 1134–1145.

Halbesleben, J., Neveu, J., Paustian-Underdahl, S., and Westman, M. (2014). Getting to the 'COR': Understanding the role of resources in conservation of resources theory. *Journal of Management, 40*, 1334–1364.

Halbesleben, J.R. and Wheeler, A. (2015). To invest or not? The role of coworker support and trust in daily reciprocal gain spirals of helping behavior. *Journal of Management, 41*, 1628–1650.

Hanisch, K. and Hulin, C. (1991). General attitudes and organizational withdrawal: An evaluation of a causal model. *Journal of Vocational Behavior, 39*, 110–128.

Harrison, D. and Newman, D. (2013). Absence, lateness, turnover and retirement: Narrow and broad understandings of withdrawal and behavioral engagement. In N. Schmitt and S. Highhouse (eds), *Handbook of Psychology: Industrial and Organization Psychology* (Vol. 12, 262–291). Hoboken, NJ: Wiley.

Holtom, B., Mitchell, T., and Lee, T. (2006). Increasing human and social capital by applying job embeddedness theory. *Organizational Dynamics, 35*, 316–331.

Holtom, B., Mitchell, T., Lee, T., and Eberly, M. (2008). Turnover and retention research: A glance at the past, a closer review of the present, and a venture into the future. *Academy of Management Annals, 2*, 231–274.

Holtom, B., Tidd, S., Mitchell, T., and Lee, T. (2013). Temporal dependency in the prediction of newcomer turnover. *Human Relations, 66*, 1337–1352.

Hom, P., Mitchell, T., Lee, T., and Griffeth, R. (2012). Reviewing employee turnover: Focusing on proximal withdrawal states and an expanded criterion. *Psychological Bulletin, 138*, 831–858.

Jaros, S., Jermier, J., Koehler, J., and Sincich T. (1993). Effects of continuance, affective, and moral commitment on the withdrawal process: An evaluation of eight structural equation models. *Academy of Management Journal*, *36*, 951–995.

Jiang, K., Liu, D., McKay, P., Lee, T., and Mitchell, T. (2012). When and how is job embeddedness predictive of turnover? A meta-analytic investigation. *Journal of Applied Psychology*, *97*, 1077–1096.

Kiazad, K., Holtom, B., Newman, A., and Hom, P. (2015). Job embeddedness: An integrative review and research agenda. *Journal of Applied Psychology*, *100*, 641–659.

Kristof, A. (1996). Person–organization fit: an integrative review of its conceptualizations, measurement, and implications. *Personnel Psychology*, *49*, 1–49.

Lanaj, K., Chang, C., and Johnson, R. (2012). Regulatory focus and work-related outcomes: A meta-analysis. *Psychological Bulletin*, *138*, 998–1034.

Lee, T., Burch, T., and Mitchell, T. (2014). The story of why we stay: A review of job embeddedness. *Annual Review of Organizational Psychology and Organizational Behavior*, *1*, 199–216.

Lee, T., Mitchell, T., Sablynski, C., Burton, J., and Holtom, B. (2004). The effects of job embeddedness on organizational citizenship, job performance, volitional absences, and voluntary turnover. *Academy of Management Journal*, *47*, 711–722.

Mael, F. and Ashforth, B. (1992). Alumni and their alma mater: A partial test of the reformulated model of organizational identification. *Journal of Organizational Behavior*, *13*, 103–123.

March, J. and Simon, H. (1958). *Organizations*. Oxford: Wiley.

Meyer, J., Stanley, L., and Parfyonova, N. (2012). Employee commitment in context: the nature and implication of commitment profiles. *Journal of Vocational Behavior*, *8*, 1–16.

Miller, S. (1976). Family life cycle, extended family orientations, and aspirations as factors in the propensity to migrate. *Sociological Quarterly*, *17*, 323–335.

Mitchell, T., Holtom, B., Lee, T., Sablynski, C., and Erez, M. (2001). Why people stay: using job embeddedness to predict voluntary turnover. *Academy of Management Journal*, *44*, 1102–1121.

Mobley, W. (1977). Intermediate linkages in the relationship between job satisfaction and employee turnover. *Journal of Applied Psychology*, *62*, 237–240.

Netemeyer, R., Boles, J., McKee, D., and McMurrian, R. (1997). An investigation into the antecedents of organizational citizenship behaviors in a personal selling context. *Journal of Marketing*, *61*, 85–98.

Ng, T. and Feldman, D. (2007). Organizational embeddedness and occupational embeddedness across career stages. *Journal of Vocational Behavior*, *65*, 336–351.

Ng, T. and Feldman, D. (2009). Occupational embeddedness and job performance. *Journal of Organizational Behavior*, *30*, 863–891.

Ng, T. and Feldman, D. (2010). The effects of organizational embeddedness on development of social capital and human capital. *Journal of Applied Psychology*, *95*, 696–712.

Ng, T. and Feldman, D. (2012). Employee voice behavior: A meta-analytic test of the conservation of resources framework. *Journal of Organizational Behavior*, *33*, 216–234.

Ng, T. and Feldman, D. (2013). Changes in perceived supervisor embeddedness: Effects on employee embeddedness, organizational trust, and voice behavior. *Personnel Psychology*, *66*, 645–685.

Ng, T. and Feldman, D. (2014). Community embeddedness and work outcomes: The mediating role of organizational embeddedness. *Human Relations*, *67*, 71–103.

Podsakoff, N., Whiting, S., Podsakoff, P., and Blume, B. (2009). Individual- and organizational-level consequences of organizational citizenship behaviors: A meta-analysis. *Journal of Applied Psychology*, 94, 122–141.

Price, J. and Mueller, C. (1981). A causal model of turnover for nurses. *Academy of Management Journal*, *24*, 543–565.

Ramesh, A. and Gelfand, M. (2010). Will they stay or will they go? The role of job embeddedness in predicting turnover in individualistic and collectivistic cultures. *Journal of Applied Psychology*, *95*, 807–823.

Reichers, A. (1985). A review and reconceptualization of organizational commitment. *Academy of Management Review*, *10*, 465–476.

Rotundo, M. and Sackett, P. (2002). The relative importance of task, citizenship, and counterproductive performance to global ratings of job performance: A policy capturing approach. *Journal of Applied Psychology*, *87*, 66–80.

Rusbult, C. and Farrell, D. (1983). A longitudinal test of the investment model: the impact on job satisfaction, job commitment, and turnover of variations in rewards, costs, alternatives, and investments. *Journal of Applied Psychology*, *68*, 429–438.

Saks, A. and Ashforth, B. (1997). A longitudinal investigation of the relationships between job information sources, applicant perceptions of fit, and work outcomes. *Personnel Psychology*, *50*, 395–426.

Salamin, A. and Hom, P. (2005). In search of the elusive u-shaped performance–turnover relationship: Are high performing Swiss bankers more liable to quit? *Journal of Applied Psychology*, *90*, 1204–1216.

Shaffer, M. and Harrison, D. (1998). Expatriates psychological withdrawal from international assignments: Work, nonwork, and family influences. *Personnel Psychology*, *51*, 87–118.

Sparrowe, R., Liden, R., Wayne, S., and Kraimer, M. (2001). Social networks and the performance of individuals and groups. *Academy of Management Journal, 44*, 316–325.

Spitz, G. (1986). Family migration largely unresponsive to wife's employment. *Sociology and Social Research, 70*, 231–234.

Turban, D., Campion, J., and Eyring, A. (1992). Factors relating to relocation decisions of research and development employees. *Journal of Vocational Behavior, 41*, 183–199.

Uzzi, B. (1997). Social structure and competition in interfirm networks: the paradox of embeddedness. *Administrative Science Quarterly, 42*, 33–67.

Wheeler, A., Harris, K., and Sablynski, C. (2012). How do employees invest abundant resources? The mediating role of work effort in the job-embeddedness/job–performance relationship. *Journal of Applied Social Psychology, 42*, 244–266.

Zhang, M., Fried, D., and Griffeth, R. (2012). Job embeddedness: A review of conceptualization and measurement issues. *Human Resource Management Review, 22*, 220–231.

APPENDIX: REPRESENTATIVE ITEMS FROM MEASURES OF JOB EMBEDDEDNESS

Original (Formative) Model of Job Embeddedness (Mitchell et al., 2001)

Fit–Community
'This community is a good match for me.'
'I think of the community where I live as home.'
'The area where I live offers the leisure activities that I like.'

Fit–Organization
'My coworkers are similar to me.'
'My job utilizes my skills and talents well.'
'I fit with the company's culture.'

Links–Community
'Are you currently married?'
'If you are married, does your spouse work outside the home?'
'Do you own the home you live in?'

Links–Organization
'How long have you worked for this company?'
'How many coworkers do you interact with regularly?'
'How many work teams are you on?'

Sacrifice–Community
'Leaving this community would be very hard.'
'People respect me a lot in my community.'
'My neighborhood is safe.'

Sacrifice–Organization
'My promotional opportunities are excellent here.'
'I am well compensated for my level of performance.'
'The benefits are good on this job.'

Revised (Formative) Job Embeddedness Measure (Holtom et al., 2013)

Fit–Community
'The place where I live is a good match for me.'
'The area where I live offers the leisure activities that I like (sports, outdoor activities, cultural events and arts).'

Fit–Organization
'My job utilizes my skills and talents well.'
'I feel like I am a good match for my organization.'

Links–Community
'My family roots are in this community.'

'I am active in one or more community organizations (for example, churches, sports teams, schools, etc.).'

Links–Organization
'I am a member of an effective work group.'
'I work closely with my coworkers.'

Sacrifice–Community
'Leaving the community where I live would be very hard.'
'If I were to leave the area where I live, I would miss my neighborhood.'

Sacrifice–Organization
'I would sacrifice a lot if I left this job.'
'I believe the prospects for continuing employment with my organization are excellent.'

Global (Reflective) Measure of Job Embeddedness (Crossley et al., 2007)

'It would be difficult for me to leave this organization.'
'I'm too caught up in this organization to leave.'
'I feel tied to this organization.'
'It would be easy for me to leave this organization.'
'I am tightly connected to this organization.'

8. Organizational identification
Rolf van Dick

INTRODUCTION AND HISTORY OF OI RESEARCH

Organizational identification (OI) is a powerful concept that has been shown to relate to a myriad of other work-related attitudes and behaviors. OI is, as I will show in more detail later, predictive of employees' satisfaction, turnover intentions, and extra- and in-role performance, amongst other things. OI is closely related to organizational commitment, and I will outline the overlap and differences later in this chapter.

OI has been studied for more than 50 years, with first research by Brown (1969), Cheney (1983), Lee (1969), Hall and Schneider (1972), and Rotondi (1975). These early attempts, however, lacked theoretical development and their operationalizations were very close to related concepts such as job involvement, organizational commitment, or turnover intentions. From the late 1970s onwards, the social identity approach provided a fruitful theoretical background for conceptualizing social identification with groups. This approach was applied to organizational identification as early as 1978 by Rupert Brown, but it took until 1989, when Ashforth and Mael introduced the concept to the wider management literature in their seminal *Academy of Management Review* article, before the concept became one of the classic job attitudes studied not only in social psychological literatures but also in industrial/organizational (I/O) and management research and as a regular component of employee attitude surveys in many organizations. I will, therefore, start this chapter with a brief overview of the social identity approach.

THE SOCIAL IDENTITY APPROACH

The social identity approach comprises two closely related theories: the social identity theory (SIT, Tajfel and Turner, 1979) and the self-categorization theory (SCT, Turner et al., 1987). Henri Tajfel and his colleagues developed SIT to understand negative intergroup attitudes and intergroup conflict. According to the theory, group membership defines at least part of its members' identity: their social identity. The main predictions of SIT can be summarized in three assumptions (Tajfel and Turner, 1979, p. 16): (1) people strive for the establishment or enhancement of positive self-esteem; (2) a part of the person's self-concept – their social identity – is based on the person's group memberships; (3) to maintain a positive social identity, the person strives for positive differentiation between their ingroup and relevant outgroups. Tajfel and colleagues conducted a series of so-called minimal group experiments to test these assumptions (Tajfel et al., 1971). In these experiments, participants were randomly assigned to one of two groups and were then asked to allocate points or small amounts of money to members of their own group (other than themselves) and members of the other group. The main result was the demonstration of an ingroup bias; that is, participants distributed more rewards to ingroup members compared to outgroup members and, sometimes, participants even accepted a lower absolute amount of points for the members of their own group when this helped to increase the relative positive difference to the members of the other group. This finding is explained as a result of the participants' desire to achieve a positive social identity.

Turner et al. (1987) developed SCT to specify the processes within groups; especially contextual influences on identification. SCT states that individuals can categorize themselves at three levels of abstraction: on a subordinate level as an individual person (who compares themself with other individuals), on an intermediate level as a member of a certain group (which then is compared with relevant outgroups), or on a superordinate level as a human being. SIT and SCT describe two preconditions for the emergence of self-categorization and group behavior: identification and category salience. Identification means that the individual sees themself as a member of a specific category (that is, perceives this category as relevant for their identity; Wagner, 1994). The concept of category salience connects these processes with situational influence. Salience depends on both the accessibility of a category within a person's cognitive repertoire, and the fit of the category to the situation. Salience increases, for example, if a category is specifically mentioned (Hogg and Turner, 1985), if the category is set into a context of relevant other categories (Turner et al., 1987, p. 112), and especially if the category is set into conflict with other categories (Wagner and Ward, 1993). If self-categorization takes place on the intermediate level, the above-mentioned conditions would render group membership and social identity more salient and therefore more relevant than personal identities.

As will be explained in more detail below, the social identity approach helps in distinguishing the concept of OI from organizational commitment (OC) for (at least) two reasons. First, the concept of salience helps in understanding why OI is sometimes more and sometimes less relevant for employee attitudes and behaviors, which goes beyond traditional OC research. Second, whereas OC is defined as a bond between the person and the (external) organization, OI is the perceived overlap between the person and the organization or the integration of the organization into the self. To illustrate what this means, I will provide an overview of the most commonly used measures of OI in the following.

THE MEASUREMENT OF OI

Identity has been defined as that part of an individual's self-concept that stems from their memberships in social groups. Identification can thus be defined as the degree to which the respective social identities are important to the individual, and organizational identification refers to this degree as far as organizational groupings are concerned. In a narrower sense, OI is the degree of perceived overlap between oneself and the organization (for example, company) one works for. In a wider sense, OI could also refer to other foci in organizational contexts such as the occupational group, one's team, department, organizational network, and so on. I will discuss these different foci below in more detail. Here, I will look into the most common ways to measure OI. Mael and Ashforth (1992) have provided a six-item scale that is certainly the most frequently used instrument. The six items are as follows:

1. When someone criticizes my organization, it feels like a personal insult.
2. When I talk about my organization, I usually say 'we' rather than 'they'.
3. I am interested in what others think of the organization I work for.
4. I view the organization's successes as my successes.
5. When someone praises my organization, it feels like a personal compliment.
6. If a story in the media criticized my organization, I would feel embarrassed.

As can be seen, the items cover several dimensions and are most suitable for measuring OI in real-world contexts. An alternative, also frequently used and an item-based measure, is the scale developed by social psychologists Doosje et al. (1995) which comprises the following four items:

1. I define myself as a member of this organization.
2. I am pleased to be a member of this organization.
3. I feel strong ties with members of this organization.
4. I identify with other members of this organization.

This scale has been used in field research but also in laboratory studies with simulated organizations or groups in which the individuals were members only for the duration of the experiment. Finally, van Dick et al. (2004) have developed an instrument that is provided to participants in the form of a table with each column representing a different focus such as team, division, organization, or occupation and the rows representing the following items:

- I identify myself as a member of . . ..
- Being a member of . . . reflects my personality well.
- I like to work for . . .
- I think reluctantly of . . . (recoded).
- Sometimes I rather don't say that I'm a member of . . . (recoded).
- I am actively involved in . . .

The presentation in the form of a table allows a time- and space-saving assessment of multiple foci. All the scales presented here have demonstrated good psychometric properties in terms of reliability and validity.

An alternative way to assess OI has been developed by Bergami and Bagozzi (2000) in the form of a Venn diagram, as depicted in Figure 8.1. Participants are instructed to indicate to which degree their self-image would overlap with the image of their organization by selecting one of the eight possibilities; typically, the participants tick the alternative that suits them most by marking one of the lines on the left, but the alternatives could also be numbered and the participant asked to write down the number.

This Venn diagram has also been shown to deliver valid assessment of OI. Finally, the Organizational Identification Questionnaire (OIQ) (Cheney, 1983) should be mentioned: this instrument comprises 25 items and was frequently used in the 1980s but has since been replaced by the above-mentioned scales because of its very large overlap with other concepts such as OC or job involvement.

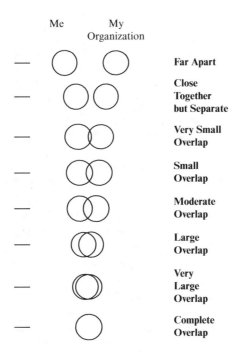

Figure 8.1   *Graphical instrument to measure OI*

RELATIONS BETWEEN OI AND OTHER WORK-RELATED CONCEPTS

OI has repeatedly been found to positively relate to important work-related concepts. A meta-analysis by Riketta (2005) found a relation between OI and job satisfaction of $r = .54$ based on 38 studies. A detailed analysis showed that the correlation between job satisfaction and OI measured with the OIQ was considerably stronger ($r = .68$) than for OI measured using the Mael and Ashforth (1992) scale ($r = .47$). Correlations with organizational satisfaction ($r = .59$) or job involvement ($r = .61$) were also very high. The meta-analysis also revealed significant average relations with important outcome variables such as intention to leave ($r = -.48$), in-role performance ($r = .17$), and citizenship behavior ($r = .35$), whereas no relation was found for absenteeism ($r = -.01$, based on six samples). OI thus proves to be an important concept for management research. For the present discussion, it is necessary to take a look at the relations between OI and OC. In his meta-analysis, Riketta found a very strong average correlation between the two concepts of $r = .78$ (based on 16 studies). The relation was a little weaker when OC was measured with the Meyer and Allen (1997) affective commitment scale ($r = .71$) and even stronger when OI was measured with the OIQ and OC measured with the Organizational Commitment Questionnaire (OCQ) (Mowday et al., 1979) ($r = .94$). Riketta also calculated the differential predictive value of the two concepts and found – to give but two examples – that OI related more strongly to job involvement than OC (.61 versus

.53), whereas OC related more strongly to job satisfaction (.65 versus .54) or turnover intentions (−.56 versus −.48). These differences were significant and indicate that despite the very strong overlap between the two concepts, OC and OI seem to have some unique predictive value – albeit minor.

To further explore the overlap and to show the distinctiveness of the two concepts, two studies have been conducted. First, Gautam et al. (2004) surveyed a heterogeneous sample of 450 employees in Nepal using the OIQ, the Meyer and Allen's affective commitment (AC), normative commitment (NC) and continuance commitment (CC) scales and the OCQ. Using expert ratings, the OIQ was revised by reducing it to those items that measured OI most closely. Confirmatory factor analyses showed that, for each of the combinations of the revised OIQ and one of the OC measures, the proposed (correlated) two-factor models fit the data better than unidimensional models. The correlations between OI were largest for the OCQ ($r = .80$), followed by NC ($r = .67$) and AC ($r = .65$), whereas the relation between OI and CC was moderate with $r = .29$.

Similarly, van Knippenberg and Sleebos (2006), in a study of 133 university staff, showed a strong correlation between OI (using Mael and Ashforth's scale) and OC (using the AC scale by Meyer and Allen) of $r = .67$. Again, confirmatory factor analysis confirmed the superiority of a two-factor model over a unidimensional model. Moreover, and in line with the authors' hypotheses, OC was more strongly related to perceived organizational support (as an exchange-based variable that was predicted to be closer to the OC concept than to OI), whereas OI was more strongly related to a single-item measure of self-reference ('When I think about myself, I often think about myself as a member of this organization').

To summarize, the meta-analysis and individual studies show a clear and strong overlap of OI and OC. Riketta (2005) argued, however, that even correlations of about .70 leave an unshared variation of 50 percent. Moreover, the confirmatory factor analyses and the (slightly) distinctive patterns of correlations in the nomological net support the view that OC and OI are related but not redundant.

INTEGRATING ORGANIZATIONAL IDENTIFICATION AND ORGANIZATIONAL COMMITMENT

As seen in the previous section, the two concepts of identification and commitment have been found to be extremely closely related on the one hand, but they also seem to carry unique aspects. Theoretically, as was briefly touched upon above, OI can best be defined as the integration of the organization into the self or the employee's perception of overlap between themself and the organization. OC, on the other hand, is an attitude of the person towards an (external) object. Even if this attitude is extremely positive and characterizes a strong bond between person and organization, it does not carry the self-referential nature that OI does. Secondly, OC – particularly affective commitment as closest to OI – mainly develops out of perceptions that the organization provides benefits for the employee, such as good human resource management in terms of training and development, pay, feedback, and so on. OI, on the other hand, develops out of perceptions that person and organization share the same characteristics (including goals), and OI gets stronger the more the employees feel that they are (proto-)typical for what the organization stands for. Finally, the concept of salience helps to explain theoretically why OI is not predictive of work-related attitudes and behaviors at all times. Only when a shared identity is salient in a given moment does OI lead to positive behaviors on behalf of the organization; this concept of salience has not been considered in OC research in such explicit terms.

Meyer et al. (2006) developed an integrative model of the two concepts. They distinguish commitment into value-based aspects (that is, affective commitment and normative commitment as moral imperative) on the one hand, and exchange-based aspects (that is, continuance commitment and normative commitment as indebted obligation) on the other. Value-based commitment predicts motivation and behavior that is characterized by autonomous regulation (discretionary and non-discretionary work behavior), whereas exchange-based commitment predicts mainly non-discretionary behavior driven by external regulation. Rousseau (1998) distinguished between situated identity and deep-structure identity. Whereas the former is short-lived and arises when the situation makes the common interests of the individual and the group salient, the latter refers to the long-term incorporation of the collective into the individual's self-concept. These two forms of identity form the basis of commitment and Meyer and colleagues suggest that exchange-based commitment is predicted by situated identity, whereas deep-structure identity precedes value-based commitment.

Stinglhamber et al. (2015) recently provided evidence for the causal pathway from OI to OC in three studies. In the first, a longitudinal study across a four-month interval, they conducted cross-lagged analyses and found a weak but significant relation between OI measured at the beginning of the study and changes in affective commitment from time 1 to time 2, whereas the reversed path from commitment at time 1 on changes in identification over time was not significant. In their second study they showed that job autonomy, leader–member exchange and perceived organizational support predicted identification, which in turn predicted commitment. Finally, in the third study they found a relation between identification and actual turnover, which was mediated by commitment. Thus, the three studies in total show that certain aspects of the job predict organizational identification, which predicts commitment, which in turn predicts job-related outcomes.

RECENT DEVELOPMENTS IN OI RESEARCH

Foci of Identification

Similar to research on organizational commitment (see Becker, 1992; Chapter 4 in this volume), OI researchers have considered the possibility of identification with various targets or foci. The first study in this respect was conducted by van Knippenberg and van Schie (2000) who looked into employee identification with both the larger focus of the organization as a whole, and the team as a smaller focus. In two different samples, they found that team identification was stronger than organizational identification and, in line with their predictions, that it was also more predictive of other work-related attitudes (satisfaction, motivation, involvement, and turnover intentions). Ullrich et al. (2007) challenged the prediction that team identification would always be more closely related to criteria but instead formulated the 'identity-matching principle' according to which the respective focus of identification would be more closely related to the theoretically corresponding criterion. This was confirmed in their study for the two foci of organizational identification (which was related to customer-oriented behavior) and corporate identification (which was related to corporate citizenship behavior). This matching principle was further supported by a meta-analysis conducted by Riketta and van Dick (2005). They collapsed studies of commitment and identification in an analysis of 'attachment in organizations' and identified 38 samples in which team and organizational identification were measured simultaneously and with similar scales, and found that overall team attachment was stronger than attachment to the organization. But the analyses also showed that team attachment (compared to organizational attachment) was more closely related to the corresponding variables of, for instance, team satisfaction, team climate, or helping behavior towards colleagues. Organizational attachment, on the other hand, was (compared to team attachment) more closely related to, for instance, turnover intentions or general job satisfaction.

Van Dick et al. (2004) extended team and organizational identification by two more foci. They added occupational identification as a broader focus of social identification and identification with one's own career to measure the importance of an employee's personal identity. Van Dick et al. (2004) found, across three samples, that these four foci could indeed be differentiated and had unique predictive power for a range of related attitudes. Team identification, for instance, was most closely related to perceptions of a positive team climate. Organizational identification was related to organization-based citizenship behavior, and career identification was related to voluntary activities such as taking additional training. Van Dick et al. (2005) provided further evidence for the existence of identification with these foci and could also experimentally show that the situational salience influences the strength of these identifications. In their study, teachers who were told that their results would be compared with results from other schools to render the school identity more salient indeed identified more strongly with their schools than teachers who were told that the comparison would be with individual teachers (personal identity condition) or teachers with other professional groups (occupational identity condition). Teachers in the professional groups condition, on the other hand, identified more strongly with their occupational group than in the other conditions. This is perfectly in line with predictions from self-categorization theory (Oakes, 1987; Oakes et al., 1991) that highlight the fit of the respective group-based identity to the situation for individual processes of identification and identification-based behavior.

Finally, two studies looked into the interaction of the two foci of team and organizational identification. Van Dick et al. (2008) found that the two foci produced an augmented effect on criteria: employees with both high team and organizational identification reported the most job satisfaction and citizenship behavior compared to those who were only identified with one of the foci. Similarly, Richter et al. (2006) conducted a team-level analysis of 40 teams in British hospitals. They found that the possible negative effects of team identification on conflicts with members of other teams were moderated by high organizational identification. When team members identified with both foci (team and organization), teams worked productively together. This supports the suggestion of West et al. (2004) that effective teamwork needs both bonding (within the team) and bridging (across the team boundaries).

New Forms of Organizational Identification

In 2004, Kreiner and Ashforth, building on the work of Elsbach (1999), developed a model and provided empirical evidence for the existence of new forms of organizational identification. More specifically, their notion of an 'expanded model of organizational identification' suggests three possibilities to define the relation between the employee and the organization in addition to the classic overlap, that is, OI. These forms are: (1) feelings of disidentification (sample items: 'I have tried to keep the organization I work for a secret from people I meet', 'I find this organization to be disgraceful'); (2) ambivalent identification (sample items: 'I have mixed feelings about my affiliation with this organization', 'I'm torn between loving and hating this organization'; and (3) neutral identification (sample items: 'It really doesn't matter to me what happens to this organization', 'I don't have many feelings about this organization at all').

Disidentification develops when an employee learns about aspects of an organization that contrast with their own values and norms. Under these conditions, the act of separating the self from the organization would then contribute to the employee's identity. Kreiner and Ashforth (2004) noted that disidentification is not merely the opposite of identification. An absent (or very low) identification would result in absenteeism or low performance, whereas high disidentification might result in sabotage or whistleblowing activities. Another possibility is that the employee has both positive and negative feelings about their relationship to the organization. This would result in ambivalent identification. This concept could be useful as a moderator that helps to explain why the link between OI and certain outcomes is sometimes stronger, sometimes weaker. When people are highly identified and at the same time low in ambivalence, the links to positive work-related behaviors should be especially strong. When people feel highly identified but at the same time also have some mixed feelings, the link should be weaker. Schuh et al. (in press), for instance, have shown across several samples that the link between OI and extra-role behavior is particularly strong when ambivalent identification is low. Finally, some employees may feel neither attachment nor separation in relation to the organization. Being in such a state means that, on the one hand, an individual avoids behaviors that could build up commitment (for example, organizational citizenship behavior), but on the other hand, has no tendency to leave the organization or talk negatively about it. Kreiner and Ashforth (2004) refer to such a state as neutral identification, which is a lack of both identification and disidentification.

Egold and van Dick (2015) recently tested the expanded model. They found, as expected, that OI was negatively related to the other three forms (−.35 to disidentification, −.37 to ambivalent, and −.47 to neutral identification). The other three forms were all positively linked with correlations between .63 and .82. Results further showed that each of the forms was related to criteria as one would expect: OI predicted job satisfaction, engagement, and well-being positively, whereas each of the other three forms were negatively related. Furthermore, intra-role conflict and role ambiguity were negatively related to OI but positively related to each of the other forms.

Identification, Stress, and Overidentification

Haslam (2004) has presented the social identity approach to stress, which proposes that people have better well-being and are better able to cope with stress when they identify with groups and when the shared social identity with others is salient. A number of studies have indeed provided evidence for positive relations between organizational identification and various indicators of employee well-being (van Dick and Haslam, 2012). Van Dick and Wagner (2002), for instance, found that teachers who identified more strongly with their schools reported less burnout and fewer physical symptoms such as headaches. This was also confirmed in a school setting for both teachers and students by Bizumic et al. (2009), who found negative associations between school identification and clinical conditions such as anxiety and depression. Haslam et al. (2005) showed that a shared identity helps in normalizing and coping with stress even in atypically dangerous occupations such as bomb disposal officers.

According to the social identity approach to stress, social support is a key variable that translates shared identity into better well-being because, in a context of shared identities, social support is more readily provided to members of the ingroup, and it is accepted more readily because it is interpreted in a positive spirit and not with mistrust and concerns of not being able to reciprocate the help one receives. And indeed, Haslam et al. (2005) found that, for both bar staff and bomb disposal officers, organizational identification was related to the experience of less stress, and that this relationship was mediated by higher social support. Avanzi et al. (2015), in a sample of schoolteachers, showed that the link between OI and burnout is serially mediated, firstly by social support, and secondly by collective self-esteem. In a longitudinal five-phase study with members of a theatre production team, Haslam et al. (2009) showed that OI at the beginning of the production was positively related to citizenship behavior at the end of the production, mediated by lower burnout in the middle of the study.

There is also evidence from the laboratory that confirms the positive relation between identification and well-being and suggests that this link is indeed causal from OI to well-being. Haslam et al. (2004), in line with the predictions of the social identity approach, found that participants who worked on a stressful arithmetic task interpreted the task as less stressful when they received a message that the task was (positively) challenging rather than (negatively) stressful; but only when the message came from another participant who belonged to the focal participants' ingroup, and not when the message came from an outgroup member. Wegge et al. (2012) invited trained call-center employees into the laboratory and had them communicate with fake customers who were either friendly or markedly unfriendly. Those participants who identified more strongly with their organization showed lower symptoms of stress (measured by immunoglobulin A) when interacting with unfriendly customers, compared to the less-identified participants. Häusser et al. (2012) conducted a laboratory study with student participants who came into the lab in groups of three. The researchers first manipulated a shared versus non-shared identity by having the students briefly discuss commonalities (versus differences), took a group picture (versus individual pictures) and gave the participants a group name (versus individual names) for the duration of the following stress manipulation, which consisted of the Trier Social Stress Test (TSST). The TSST is a standard protocol for inducing short-term stress by having participants take a mock job interview and perform an arithmetic task. As expected, participants who had developed a shared identity showed less signs of stress (measured by cortisol) compared to participants who had not developed a shared group identity. Research in the field and in the laboratory thus seems to provide clear evidence for the predictions of the social identity approach to stress.

However, one could argue that organizational identification could also have some downsides and may lead people to exhaust themselves on behalf of their organization and to ignore their individual needs (for example, for short-term recovery and work–life balance in general). And indeed, there is at least one study that provides evidence for the possibility of overidentification. Avanzi et al. (2012) tested curvilinear effects of organizational identification on well-being (measured with the general health questionnaire) in a cross-sectional study with law court employees and in a longitudinal study with schoolteachers. They found, across both samples, that identification led to better well-being only up to a certain level, and once this level was exceeded, more identification related to lower well-being. This curvilinear relation was mediated by workaholism: too-strong identification caused participants to concentrate on work more than was healthy. Following the integrative model by Meyer et al. (2006), one could assume that too-high levels of identification lead to overcommitment which drives the curvilinear effects on workaholism and health in this study.

However, despite anecdotal evidence and rare studies such as the above, Steffens et al. (in press) recently conducted a meta-analysis across 63 effect sizes and more than 16 000 participants. The results showed a clear link between OI and well-being with an average correlation of $r = .28$. Thus, in summary, identification is likely to protect employee health rather than to reduce it.

CONCLUSION AND DIRECTIONS FOR FUTURE RESEARCH

As this chapter has shown, OI has developed from a distinctive and powerful theoretical framework, the social identity approach. According to this approach, social identification helps to satisfy individual needs of affiliation and belonging. However, which of the many groups are relevant for the individual's thinking, feeling, and behavior depends on the salience of the respective identity at any given moment. Despite this unique theoretical foundation, the measurement of identification and commitment often shows strong empirical correlations between the two concepts, which is evidence for their conceptual similarity. Several studies, however, have demonstrated that OI and OC have not only commonalities but also distinct aspects and, therefore, models which assume that the two concepts are related but different seem to be superior than models that treat the concepts as interchangeable. There is also reason and evidence to assume that identification is a precursor of commitment. The chapter has presented evidence for the value of studying different foci of identification, and that the identity-matching principle helps in understanding which of these identifications is the best predictor for certain criteria. Finally, recent theories were presented that differentiate identification into the new forms of ambivalent, neutral, and disidentification, and propose that that identification is an important variable for coping with stressful situations insofar as a shared identity helps in activating social support in teams.

One question that has not been addressed by empirical research so far is whether identification is always stable across days or weeks, or whether it can fluctuate. Becker et al. (2013) recently suggested a model in which they propose that commitment to a team is not necessarily stable, but that it can vary within individuals and that the degree of variation influences the predictive power of commitment for other work-related concepts. Becker et al. explicitly state that their model can also be applied to the variation of other job attitudes such as team identification. Theoretically, there is good reason to assume that it also generalizes to other foci of identification such as the organization. Applying Becker et al.'s (2013) model to OI, it would propose first, and in line with the findings on the relations between OI and outcomes as discussed above (Riketta, 2005), that the level of the individual employees' OI predicts their behavior such as in-role and extra-role performance or intentions to remain in the organization. However, and key in Becker et al.'s theory, an individual's identification is thought of as variable and the degree of variation (which can be different between individuals) moderates the predictive power of the level of OI. To illustrate, consider the example of two employees whose OI is measured on a daily basis. Employee 1's average level of identification is medium, but there are large variations over the course of the week, with high OI on Monday, much reduced OI on Tuesday, high OI again on Wednesday, and so forth. Employee 2's OI is also medium but very stable with almost identical scores each day. Typically, we assess OI only at one point in time (such as in an annual staff survey), which would result in an accurate prediction of employee 2's average OI. For employee 1, however, it would not result in a precise assessment of their OI. If we surveyed OI more often, we would also have the opportunity to determine OI variation, which we could include, for instance, in analyses predicting employee behavior from their OI.

Becker et al. (2013) further specify the sources for individual variation in employee attitudes and suggest that it may result from both internal and external factors. For employees high in moodiness or those who have relatively low self-esteem stability, one would also assume more variation in OI. Similarly, variations in OI can result from situational factors such as the daily hassles (for example, an unfriendly customer) or uplifts (for example, recognition received by one's supervisor) which decrease or increase OI on a daily basis. This would also follow from self-categorization theory's notion of category salience, which predicts that certain identities can be switched 'on' and 'off' by situational influences; which is an important aspect that distinguishes OI from OC research.

For both organizational research and practice a desirable approach in the future would be to more clearly differentiate between the way in which OI and OC are measured. As discussed above, the items of current OI scales are rather similar to at least some of the items used to measure affective commitment. Strengthening the self-referential part of OI (for example, 'I see myself as a member of my organization') and not including the affective or behavioral aspects of the current measures, would be a good way forward to further empirically separate the constructs.

In sum, although OI is certainly a very close relative of OC, it also carries unique features which help in differentiating between the concepts. And although there is certainly a lot of overlap between OI and affective commitment, the discussion of additional forms of OI and the differentiation of OC into different forms beyond AC and its profiles show that there is room left for the further development of each of the two concepts.

REFERENCES

Ashforth, B.E. and Mael, F. (1989). Social Identity Theory and the organization. *Academy of Management Journal*, *14*, 20–39.

Avanzi, L., Schuh, S., Fraccaroli, F., and van Dick, R. (2015). Why does organizational identification relate to reduced employee burnout? The mediating influence of social support and collective efficacy. *Work and Stress*, *29*, 1–10.

Avanzi, L., van Dick, R., Fraccaroli, F., and Sarchielli, G. (2012). The downside of organizational identification: Relationships between identification, workaholism and well-being. *Work and Stress*, *26*, 289–307.

Becker, T.E. (1992). Foci and bases of commitment: Are they distinctions worth making? *Academy of Management Journal*, *35*, 232–244.

Becker, T.E., Ullrich, J., and van Dick, R. (2013). Within-person variation in affective commitment to teams: Where it comes from and why it matters. *Human Resource Management Review*, *23*, 131–147.

Bergami, M. and Bagozzi, R.P. (2000). Self-categorization, affective commitment and group self-esteem as distinct aspects of social identity in the organization. *British Journal of Social Psychology*, *39*, 555–577.

Bizumic, B., Reynolds, K.J., Turner, J.C., Bromhead, D., and Subasic, E. (2009). The role of the group in individual functioning: School identification and the psychological well-being of staff and students. *Applied Psychology: An International Review*, *58*, 171–192.

Brown, M.E. (1969). Identification and some conditions of organizational involvement. *Administrative Science Quarterly*, *14*, 346–355.

Brown, R.J. (1978). Divided we fall: Analysis of relations between different sections of a factory workforce. In H. Tajfel (ed.), *Differentiation between Social Groups: Studies in the Social Psychology of Intergroup Relations* (pp. 395–429). London: Academic Press.

Cheney, G. (1983). On the various and changing meanings of organizational membership: A field study of organizational identification. *Communication Monographs*, *50*, 342–362.

Doosje, B., Ellemers, N., and Spears, R. (1995). Perceived intragroup variability as a function of group status and identification. *Journal of Experimental Social Psychology*, *31*, 410–436.

Egold, N. and Van Dick, R. (2015). Career and organizational identification: Expanding the extended model of identification. In A. De Vos and B. Van der Heiden (eds), *Handbook of Research on Sustainable Careers: Aims, Approach and Outline* (pp. 99–115). Cheltenham, UK and Northampton, MA, USA: Edward Elgar Publishing.

Elsbach, K.D. (1999). An expanded model of organizational identification. *Research in Organizational Behavior*, *21*, 163–200.

Gautam, T., Van Dick, R., and Wagner, U. (2004). Organizational identification and organizational commitment: Distinct aspects of two related concepts. *Asian Journal of Social Psychology*, *7*, 301–315.

Häusser, J.A., Kattenstroth, M., van Dick, R., and Mojzisch, A. (2012). 'We' are not stressed: Social identity in groups buffers neuroendocrine stress reactions. *Journal of Experimental Social Psychology*, *48*, 973–977.

Hall, D.T. and Schneider, B. (1972). Correlates of organizational identification as a function of career pattern and organizational type. *Administrative Science Quarterly*, *17*, 340–350.

Haslam, S.A. (2004). *Psychology in Organizations: The Social Identity Approach*. London: Sage Publications.

Haslam, S.A., Jetten, J., O'Brien, A.T., and Jacobs, E. (2004). Social identity, social influence, and reactions to potentially stressful tasks: Support for the self-categorization model of stress. *Stress and Health*, *20*, 3–9.

Haslam, S.A., Jetten, J., and Waghorn, C. (2009). Social identification, stress, and citizenship in teams: A five-phase longitudinal study. *Stress and Health*, *25*, 21–30.

Haslam, S.A., O'Brien, A.T., Jetten, J., Vormedal, K., and Penna, S. (2005). Taking the strain: Social identity, social support and the experience of stress. *British Journal of Social Psychology*, *44*, 355–370.

Hogg, M.A. and Turner, J.C. (1985). When liking begets solidarity: an experiment on the role of interpersonal attraction in psychological group formation. *British Journal of Social Psychology*, *24*, 267–281.

Kreiner, G.E. and Ashforth, B.E. (2004). Evidence toward an expanded model of organizational identification. *Journal of Organizational Behavior*, *25*, 1–27.

Lee, S.M. (1969). Organizational identification of scientists. *Academy of Management Journal*, *12*, 327–337.

Mael, F. and Ashforth, B.E. (1992). Alumni and their alma mater: A partial test of the reformulated model of organizational identification. *Journal of Organizational Behavior*, *13*, 103–123.

Meyer, J.P. and Allen, N.J. (1997). *Commitment in the Workplace*. Thousand Oaks, CA: Sage.

Meyer, J.P., Becker, T.E., and Van Dick, R. (2006). Social identities and commitments at work: Toward an integrative model. *Journal of Organizational Behavior*, *27*, 665–683.

Mowday, R.M., Steers, R.T., and Porter, L.W. (1979). The measurement of organizational commitment. *Journal of Vocational Behavior*, *14*, 224–247.

Oakes, P.J. (1987). The salience of social categories. In J.C. Turner, M.A. Hogg, P.J. Oakes, S.D. Reicher, and M.S. Wetherell (eds), *Rediscovering the Social Group* (pp. 117–141). Oxford: Blackwell.

Oakes, P.J., Turner, J.C., and Haslam, S.A. (1991). Perceiving people as group members: The role of fit in the salience of social categorizations. *British Journal of Social Psychology*, *30*, 125–144.

Richter, A., West, M.A., Van Dick, R., and Dawson, J.F. (2006). Boundary spanners' identification, intergroup contact and effective intergroup relations. *Academy of Management Journal*, *49*, 1252–1269.

Riketta, M. (2005). Organizational identification: A meta-analysis. *Journal of Vocational Behavior*, *66*, 358–384.

Riketta, M. and van Dick, R. (2005). Foci of attachment in organizations: A meta-analysis comparison of the strength and correlates of work-group versus organizational commitment and identification. *Journal of Vocational Behavior*, *67*, 490–510.

Rotondi, T. (1975). Organizational identification: Issues and implications. *Organizational Behavior and Human Performance*, *13*, 95–109.

Rousseau, D.M. (1998). Why workers still identify with organizations. *Journal of Organizational Behavior*, *19*, 217–233.

Schuh, S.C., Van Quaquebeke, N., Göritz, A., Xin, K.R., De Cremer, D., and Van Dick, R. (in press). Mixed feelings, mixed blessing? How ambivalence in organizational identification relates to employees' regulatory focus and citizenship behaviors. *Human Relations*.

Steffens, N.K., Haslam, S.A., Schuh, S.C., Jetten, J., and Van Dick, R. (in press). A meta-analytic review of social identification and health in organizational contexts. *Personality and Social Psychology Review*.

Stinglhamber, F., Marique, G., Caesens, G., Desmette, D., Hansez, I., Hanin, D., and Bertrand, F. (2015). Employees' Organizational Identification and Affective Organizational Commitment: An Integrative Approach. *PLoS ONE*, 10(4): e0123955. doi: 10.1371/journal.pone.0123955.

Tajfel, H., Billig, M.G., Bundy, R., and Flament, C. (1971). Social categorization and intergroup behavior. *European Journal of Social Psychology*, *1*, 149–178.

Tajfel, H. and Turner, J.C. (1979). An integrative theory of intergroup conflict. In W.G. Austin, and S. Worchel (eds), *The Social Psychology of Intergroup Relations* (pp. 33–47). Monterey: Brooks/Cole.

Turner, J C., Hogg, M.A., Oakes, P.J., Reicher, S.D., and Wetherell, M.S. (1987). *Rediscovering the Social Group*. Oxford: Blackwell.

Ullrich, J., Wieseke, J., Christ, O., Schulze, J., and Van Dick, R. (2007). The identity matching principle: Corporate and organizational identification in a franchising system. *British Journal of Management*, *18*, 29–44.

Van Dick, R. and Haslam, S.A. (2012). Stress and well-being in the workplace: Support for key propositions from the social identity approach. In J. Jetten, C. Haslam, and S.A. Haslam (eds), *The Social Cure: Identity, Health, and Well-being* (pp. 175–194). Hove, UK and New York, USA: Psychology Press.

Van Dick, R., van Knippenberg, D., Kerschreiter, R., Hertel, G., and Wieseke, J. (2008). Interactive effects of work group and organizational identitification on job satisfaction and extra-role behavior. *Journal of Vocational Behavior*, *72*, 388–399.

Van Dick, R. and Wagner, U. (2002). Social identification among schoolteachers: Dimensions, foci, and correlates. *European Journal of Work and Organizational Psychology*, *11*, 129–149.

Van Dick, R., Wagner, U., Stellmacher, J., and Christ, O. (2004). The utility of a broader conceptualization of organizational identification: Which aspects really matter? *Journal of Occupational and Organizational Psychology*, *77*, 171–191.

Van Dick, R., Wagner, U., Stellmacher, J., and Christ, O. (2005). Category salience and its effects on organizational identification. *Journal of Occupational and Organizational Psychology*, *78*, 273–285.

Van Knippenberg, D. and Sleebos, E. (2006). Organizational identification versus organizational commitment: Self-definition, social exchange, and job attitudes. *Journal of Organizational Behavior*, *27*, 571–584.

Van Knippenberg, D. and van Schie, E.C.M. (2000). Foci and correlates of organizational identification. *Journal of Occupational and Organizational Psychology*, *73*, 137–147.

Wagner, U. (1994). *Sozialpsychologie der Intergruppenbeziehungen* (Social psychology of intergroup relations). Göttingen: Hogrefe.

Wagner, U. and Ward, P.L. (1993). Variation of outgroup presence and evaluation of the in-group. *British Journal of Social Psychology*, *32*, 241–251.

Wegge, J., Schuh, S.C., and Van Dick, R. (2012). I feel bad – We feel good!? Emotions as a driver for personal and organizational identity and organizational identification as a resource for serving unfriendly customers. *Stress and Health*, *28*, 123–136.

West, M.A., Hirst, G., Richter, A., and Shipton, H. (2004). Twelve steps to heaven: Successfully managing change through developing innovative teams. *European Journal of Work and Organizational Psychology*, *13*, 269–299.

9.   Psychological contracts
Samantha D. Hansen and Yannick Griep

In recent years there has been a significant increase in organizations' need to adapt to technological advances and remain competitive globally, resulting in various cost-cutting practices including restructuring, downsizing, and mergers (Frese, 2000). Further, as competition to attract and retain highly skilled and committed workers continues to increase, employees are demanding more opportunities for career advancement, skill development, social interaction, and work–life balance from their organization in exchange for their contributions (De Hauw and De Vos, 2010). Such pressures have created a highly dynamic work environment, necessitating changes in the ways employers manage their exchange relationship with employees. Although some of these changes have benefited employees (for example, flex-time), other changes have been detrimental (for example, reduced job security), resulting in unfavorable consequences for both employees and employers (for example, reduced commitment to the organization). As such, it is prudent that organizations devote significant thought and effort to managing their employees' psychological contracts.

The psychological contract (PC) is 'an individual's beliefs regarding the terms and conditions of a reciprocal exchange agreement between the focal person and another party' (Rousseau, 1989, p. 123). In the employment context, the PC represents the employee's mental model or cognitive schema about the exchange relationship with the employer. This schema comprises the employee's perceived mutual obligations (that is, own and organization's obligations). Obligations represent a sense of duty to provide particular resources to another. Perceived organizational obligations develop primarily based on interactions with the organization and its agents, policies, and procedures (Rousseau, 2001). The PC influences the employee's interpretation of employer actions (or nonactions) and guides employee attitudes (for example, commitment) and behavior (for example, organizational citizenship behaviors) toward the organization. Decades of research have shown that perceived PC fulfillment is associated with positive employee attitudes and behaviors, whereas perceived PC breach is associated with negative such reactions (Zhao et al., 2007).

The primary goal of this chapter is to provide a broad overview of the refinement of the PC construct and supporting theory, with special attention given to links between organizational commitment and PCs. Generally, organizational commitment has garnered a fair amount of theoretical interest and empirical attention as an outcome variable in the study of PCs (e.g., Coyle-Shapiro and Kessler, 2013; Johnson and O'Leary-Kelly, 2003; Kickul, 2001; Ng et al., 2010; Sturges et al., 2005; Tomprou et al., 2012). Although 'commitment' sometimes loosely refers to the contents of the PC (for example, employer commitments), we begin this chapter by clarifying that commitment and PCs are two distinct but related constructs.

DISTINGUISHING BETWEEN ORGANIZATIONAL COMMITMENT AND PCs

According to Meyer and Allen (1991), organizational commitment is a psychological state that characterizes an employee's relationship with the organization, with implications for intentions to remain. Similarly, Mowday et al. (1979) believed that it reflected the strength of an employee's identification with and involvement in the organization, influencing intentions to stay. As discussed elsewhere (Chapter 3 in this volume), Meyer and Allen (1991, 1997) identified three commitment components: affective commitment (AC) – affective attachment to the organization; normative commitment (NC) – obligation to stay with the organization; and continuance commitment (CC) – perceived costs associated with leaving the organization. Most research linking organizational commitment and PCs has focused on either Mowday et al.'s (1979) conceptualization or one of Allen and Meyer's (1990) components, most often AC, despite the apparent conceptual overlap between PCs and NC.

Although theoretically organizational commitment has been conceptualized as part of the relationship between employees and their organization (Rousseau, 1995), commitment is not conceptualized as part of the PC (Rousseau, 1989). The PC is an employee's cognitive schema, comprised of perceived employee and employer obligations to engage in certain behaviors (Rousseau et al., 2016). Employer obligations include delivery of inducements (for example, competitive compensation, support, developmental opportunities) and employee obligations include behavioral contributions (for example, performing job duties, accepting new roles, assisting co-workers). Feeling a sense of belongingness and attachment to the organization (AC) and believing that one must remain at the organization due to the costs of leaving (CC) are not examples of such behavioral obligations. However, an obligation to remain with the organization (NC), a behavioral contribution, may contribute to the PC schema. It is important to note that the PC is comprised of a multitude of perceived obligations, thus making NC and the PC distinct constructs. Despite the conceptual overlap between PCs and NC, organizational commitment has typically been situated as an important consequence of PCs (Meyer and Herscovitch, 2001).

Social exchange theory (Blau, 1964) helps to explain the relationship between PCs and the bond between employee and organization reflected in organizational commitment. It suggests that when both parties fulfill their obligations, employees feel valued and respected, and are likely to respond with increased emotional engagement in, and commitment to, the organization. However, when employees fulfill their obligations but the organization does not, employees tend to feel undervalued and disrespected and believe that they cannot trust the organization to fulfill future obligations (Robinson, 1995). This perceived discrepancy between perceived employer obligations and delivered inducements is a 'PC breach', which can cause negative affect such as anger, frustration, and disappointment, collectively known as 'feelings of violation' (Morrison and Robinson, 1997). These feelings, in turn, dissolve employees' emotional bond with, and commitment to, the organization (Robinson, 1996).

In the following section, we offer a brief review of the major points of focus in contemporary PC research. Particular attention is paid to connections between PCs and organizational commitment.

CONTEMPORARY CONCEPTUALIZATION AND STUDY OF PCs

Systematic investigation of the PC began with Rousseau's (1989, 1995) seminal work introducing psychological contract theory (PCT). Central to PCT, PC obligations were promissory in nature (made in exchange for some consideration or contribution of the other party). For the most part, research in the subsequent two decades focused on two research areas: outcomes associated with PC types and with PC evaluation.

PC Types

A variety of types of PCs have been identified in the literature (for example, relational, transactional, balanced, transitional, ideological). However, the distinction between relational and transactional has been most prominent (e.g., Rousseau, 1995). Research has explored PC types in terms of differences in features and content.

From a features perspective, PC types can be contrasted based on particular attributes such as tangibility, scope, stability, and time-frame (e.g., Rousseau and McLean Parks, 1993). Relational contracts are described as relationship-oriented, intangible, subjective, flexible, long-lasting, and requiring significant emotional investment. In contrast, transactional contracts are described as being economic or materialistic, tangible, specific, static, short-term in nature, with minimal emotional investment (Morrison and Robinson, 1997). Recent work has identified additional features (explicitness, negotiation, formality), implying that the make-up of certain types of contracts is changing in concert with the nature of work (McInnis et al., 2009).

From a content perspective, PCs are categorized based on the particular types of employer obligations that comprise the contract. Although not entirely consistent (Arnold, 1996), evidence indicates that such obligations tend to load onto distinct factors reflecting relational and transactional contracts (Rousseau, 1989, 1990). The former include items such as developmental opportunities and personal support, whereas the latter include items relating to compensation and job security (Rousseau, 1990, 1995).

Conjecture exists with regard to how PC type, particularly relational and transactional contracts, relates to important employee and organizational outcomes (e.g., McLean Parks et al., 1998). However, few studies have tested such differences empirically (e.g., Arnold, 1996). Research indicates that relational PCs are associated positively with job commitment, organizational commitment (overall organizational commitment, AC, and CC), intentions to remain, and job satisfaction (e.g., Raja et al., 2004; Shore et al., 2006). Transactional PCs are either related negatively or unrelated to these same outcome variables, and further, are related positively to CC (Hughes and Palmer, 2007). With regard to less frequently studied types, McInnis et al. (2009) found that balanced PCs (favoring employee and employer interests) related positively, and organization-centered PCs (favoring organizational interests) related negatively, to AC and NC, and that individualized PCs (favoring employee interests) related positively to NC.

PC Evaluation

It is one thing to hold a highly valued PC (that is, employer obligations to provide desirable inducements) with one's employer. However, whether that employer fulfills those obligations is an entirely different, and arguably more significant, issue. Indeed, meta-analytic evidence indicates that PC breach is associated negatively with satisfaction, organizational trust, commitment, in-role performance, organizational citizenship behavior (OCB), and intent to remain, and that such reactions are stronger for relational than for transactional breaches (e.g., Bal et al., 2008; Zhao et al., 2007). Further, as proposed by Rousseau (1995) and Morrison and Robinson (1997), perceptions of breach have the potential to elicit feelings of violation, which ultimately erode the employment relationship (Rousseau, 1995). Indeed, Zhao et al. (2007) found that violation feelings mediated the effects of breach on employee attitudes and behaviors. Other work also demonstrated that, although conceptually lying on the same continuum, direct measures of breach perceptions (defined as a deficiency or unfulfilled promises) have stronger effects on outcomes, including overall commitment (e.g., Conway et al., 2011), compared to direct measures of fulfillment perceptions. As with other phenomena, the effects of a negative experience appear to carry greater weight than the effects of a positive experience (Baumeister et al., 2001; Taylor, 1991).

Interesting findings have emerged with regard to PC evaluation and commitment. Not surprisingly, perceptions of breach related negatively to overall organizational commitment (e.g., Flood et al., 2001), AC (e.g., Kickul, 2001), NC, and CC (Giannikis and Nikandrou, 2013). Several studies found that feelings of violation partially mediated the relationship between breach perceptions and overall organizational commitment (e.g., Suazo, 2009), AC (e.g., Dulac et al., 2008), and CC (Cassar and Briner, 2011). Perceptions of fulfillment related positively to AC and NC (Gakovic and Tetrick, 2003; Sturges et al., 2005), whereas they were inconsistently related to CC (sometimes positively: Sturges et al., 2005; sometimes negatively: Conway and Briner, 2002). Recent work with commitment profiles may help to explain this inconsistency. Such research demonstrates that the effect of a particular form of commitment on outcome variables differs depending on how it combines with other commitment components (Gellatly et al., 2006; Meyer et al., 2012). Although independently high CC tends to relate negatively to desirable employee behaviors (for example, OCB), when combined with high AC and high NC, high levels of CC relate positively to such behaviors (Meyer et al., 2012). Further research is needed to explore the implications of commitment profiles for PCs.

CHALLENGES FACED IN THE STUDY OF PCs

As with any construct and associated body of literature, the study of PCs is not without its challenges and shortcomings. Below we identify issues that have stimulated change in the theorizing and study of PCs. Following that, we detail such advances.

Inconsistency in the Conceptual Definition of the PC

Variability exists in the definition of the PC, particularly with regard to the form of beliefs it encompasses. Early conceptualizations of the PC as employees' expectations (for example, from industry standards) about their work experiences (e.g., Levinson et al., 1962) persist in some contemporary work, either in theorizing or in operationalization of PCs (e.g., Rousseau and Greller, 1994). Rousseau's (1989, 1995) conceptualization emphasizing the 'promissory nature of perceived obligations' spawned an empirical focus on both perceived employer promises (for example, from policies, procedures, supervisors) and obligations (e.g., Deery et al., 2006; Lambert et al., 2003; Lester et al., 2007; Suazo, 2009). Complicating matters further, some empirical works theorize about one belief source (for example, promises) yet measure another (for example, expectations). This is problematic because these belief sources may be related to variables in different ways. For instance, because promises are affect-laden, it is conceivable that AC is more strongly related to these beliefs than to general expectations. Indeed, although equivalency among obligations, promises, and expectations is implicitly assumed, empirical work suggests that these are distinct, but related, constructs (Roehling, 2008). Therefore, these constructs are not interchangeable and a need exists to clarify the relations among them.

Challenges to Psychological Contract Theory

Although well formulated and generally well supported, several tenets and assumptions of PCT (Rousseau, 1995) have been challenged by unexpected research findings. Moreover, advances in related literatures draw attention to portions of the theory that could better account for real-world phenomena and processes. First, although originally framed as the central belief comprising the PC (Rousseau, 1989, 1990), empirical evidence now suggests that promises may not be as critical to the employment relationship, and to PCs, as once believed (e.g., Lambert et al., 2003; Montes and Zweig, 2009). Such findings indicate that employees may care more about what the organization actually delivers, suggesting that some modification to PCT may be in order.

Second, research has implicitly assumed that PCs relate to outcomes in a linear and uniform way. For instance, most methodological and analytic approaches presumed that only under-fulfillment of the PC was associated with negative reactions. However, research examining non-linear relations of breach components (for example, promised and delivered inducements) showed that sometimes delivering more skill development than initially promised is associated with increased feelings of violation (Montes and Irving, 2008). Similarly, Griep et al. (2016a) found that, contrary to presumptions, excessive leader support is sometimes associated with an increased tendency to perceive PC breach. Such findings demonstrate that the simple linear relations implied by PCT do not accurately reflect real exchange relationships.

Third, findings suggest that the role of affect was underdeveloped in PCT. Affect, in the form of violation feelings, was positioned as an outcome of breach (e.g., Morrison and Robinson, 1997) and meta-analytic evidence indicates that it is an important mediator in the relations between breach and employee reactions, including commitment (Zhao et al., 2007). However, recent findings suggest a broader role of affect in the employment relationship (see Chapter 18 in this volume). For example, when an employee experiences happiness and excitement because of an excellent performance evaluation, these positive emotions can trigger a desire to negotiate revisions (for example, a promotion or pay rise, training opportunities) to the employment agreement (e.g., Isen, 2001). As such, PCT may give a somewhat limited, and largely negative, view of the role of affect.

Overlooking the Dynamic Nature of PCs

Despite agreement that the PC is a dynamic construct (e.g., Ng et al., 2010; Schalk and Roe, 2007), as in the commitment literature (Chapter 34 in this volume), most empirical work has overlooked this dynamism. Multiple forces put the employee–employer relationship in a constant state of flux. Such change can substantially affect the employer's ability to fulfill the PC as well as affect the employee's perceptions of the PC itself (for example, as personal goals change, so too do perceived obligations).

Widely held assumptions that failed to account for the dynamic nature of PCs have limited our ability to accurately reflect real-world phenomena and produce valid insights for management practice. First, research has assumed that the relationships among relevant PC variables are static: a given variable holds the same relationship with the PC at any given point in time. For example, certain variables (such as organizational promises) have been typecast as antecedents whereas other variables (such as organizational commitment) have been typecast as outcomes of PCs. Little regard has been given to the notion that what is an important predictor at one point in time may, in fact, be an important consequence at a different point in time, and vice versa. For instance, commitment may impact employees' perceptions of what the organization is obligated to provide to them (for example, perceived obligations may be more significant, the higher the employee's AC), serving as an antecedent of PCs.

Second, research has assumed that particular variables are relevant throughout the employment relationship, with no recognition that relevance may change depending on the phase the relationship is in. For instance, promises may not matter to an employee who has settled into a comfortable and predictable period of exchange with the employer. However, promises might matter a great deal to an employee who has just experienced a significant PC breach and is working to repair the employment relationship.

Finally, although PCT acknowledged that employees could change the PC through significant direct effort (Rousseau, 1995), it did not account for the influence of continuously changing personal goals, which are known to influence perception, recall, and use of information (e.g., Carver and Scheier, 1990; Lord et al., 2010). Nor did it directly account for the finding that employee perceptions of the PC change over time as a function of the actual exchange of contributions and inducements (Lambert, 2011; Lee et al., 2011).

In the following section we discuss recent efforts to revise PCT to better account for the aforementioned advances and inconsistencies in the literature and to better understand and address the dynamic employee–employer relationship.

RECENT THEORETICAL ADVANCES

PCT 2.0

Drawing on self-regulation theory (Carver and Scheier, 2001; Lord et al., 2010), Rousseau et al. (2016) developed a phase-based model of PC processes (commonly referred to as PCT 2.0) to better account for the dynamic nature of the employment relationship and to overcome shortcomings of PCT. Consistent with past work, PCT 2.0 takes the employee perspective (that is, it focuses on employees' perceptions of their own and their organization's obligations). However, it acknowledges that accommodations can be made to explore the employer perspective. PCT 2.0 specifies how an employee's PC is created, maintained, and changed over the course of the employment relationship. It names perceived employee and employer obligations as the central beliefs comprising the PC and recognizes that various sources of information (for example, employer promises, general expectations, contributions) play a crucial role in establishing, maintaining, and changing perceived obligations, depending on what phase of the employment relationship the employee is in. The four phases – creation, maintenance, repair, and renegotiation – operate according to distinct goal-related dynamics, with relevant variables and their interrelations differing across the phases. Affect (both positive and negative) plays a key role in transitions between the phases.

In addition to its potential significant theoretical impact, PCT 2.0 has important practical implications. In particular, it calls attention to the importance of employee goals in establishing, maintaining, and revising the PC to promote a positive employee–employer relationship. This is consistent with Locke (1976) and Meyer and Allen (1997), who recognized that employees' organizational commitment varies as a function of how well their job promotes the attainment of personal goals. Indeed, there are many reasons why management and human resources (HR) professionals should learn about and attend to employee goals. For instance, goal-consistent promises are likely to be accepted and relied upon, and delivery (or delivery failure) of goal-consistent inducements is likely to be noticed. According to PCT 2.0, PC dynamism is influenced by changing employee goals; the same is likely true of commitment.

PCT 2.0 asserts that, upon organizational entry, the newcomer enters the creation phase, wherein the aim is to develop a PC that will enable the pursuit of personal goals while satisfying organizational goals (e.g., De Vos et al., 2003; Rousseau, 1990). General expectations (for example, from prior experience, societal norms) inform preliminary perceived employee and employer obligations, which are evaluated and adjusted according to organization-specific information encountered (for example, employer promises). Generally, information that is consistent with the employee's personal goals is salient, generates positive affect, and is readily incorporated into the PC. Once a relatively stable PC is established, the employee transitions into the maintenance phase.

The maintenance phase reflects the 'status quo' (Rousseau, 1995) of the relationship. Although the PC remains relatively stable during this phase, employees monitor organizational inducements and their own contributions relative to perceived obligations at a subconscious level (Lee et al., 2011). Indeed, contributions and employer inducements are highly salient, causing factors such as previous employer promises to become less relevant during this phase. This monitoring process reflects a self-regulatory feedback loop used to detect discrepancies between a standard (the PC schema) and an environmental cue (delivered inducements) (Carver and Scheier, 2001). Minor discrepancies are either unnoticed or become assimilated effortlessly into the PC, because such processes operate with minimal cognitive effort (Lord and Levy, 1994). In contrast, major discrepancies that either impede or facilitate goals will create a disruption that generates a strong affective reaction, triggering greater cognitive effort (Chang et al., 2010; Forgas and George, 2001; Johnson et al., 2013). When the disruption is perceived to obstruct goal attainment (for example, an obligated promotion was not delivered) it generates negative affect and the employee shifts into the repair phase. When the disruption is perceived to facilitate goal attainment (for example, employee receives an unexpected but valued promotion), it generates positive affect and the employee shifts into the renegotiation phase.

Whether in the renegotiation or the repair phase, the employee works to create a revised set of obligations that facilitates goal attainment. In renegotiation, obligations reflect the new work agreement and may come from the exchange of new promises. The employee moves back into the maintenance phase when a clear understanding of the revised obligations is established. In the repair phase, the employee may attempt to restore the PC to its original state or attempt to create a revised one. In doing so, perceived obligations may be affected by new employer promises and inducements (for example, remedies, restitution), particularly those that are consistent with the employee's personal goals. According to PCT 2.0, the employee will re-enter the maintenance phase when the negative affect associated with the disruption has subsided.

Post-Violation Model

Expanding on the ideas in PCT 2.0, Tomprou et al. (2015) developed a model of post-violation processes in which they detail how violation victims cope with, and attempt to move past, a PC violation (that is, a severe breach) over time. As in PCT 2.0, self-regulation processes play a critical role in resolving the negative affect associated with a perceived violation. The actions of both parties (for example, employee coping style, organizational responsiveness and restitution) and the speed of resolution impact the type of PC the employee will ultimately hold. Specifically, the employee may conclude with a PC that is the same as the (pre-violation) original ('reactivation'), more favorable to the employee than the original ('thriving'), or more unfavorable to the employee than the original ('impairment'). In each case, the employee returns to the maintenance phase. However, the post-violation model notes that, in some cases, the employee may fail to form a functional PC, and disengage behaviorally and/or mentally. In this case, labeled 'dissolution', although the negative affect associated with the violation may dissipate over time, it is replaced by cynicism, rumination, and careful monitoring of employer actions, increasing the likelihood to perceive future breaches. This brief summary of PCT 2.0 and the post-violation model demonstrates that these theories overcome many of the shortcomings of PCT and stimulate research that better aligns with real employee–employer relationships.

FUTURE DIRECTIONS FOR THE STUDY OF PCs AND COMMITMENT

The introduction of PCT 2.0 (Rousseau et al., 2016) and the post-violation model (Tomprou et al., 2015) will serve as strong catalysts for creative and novel research foci, particularly the relations between PCs and commitment. Although not explicitly discussed in either theory, there are several interesting links between commitment and PC processes for future research to explore. Further, the commitment literature suggests some exciting new research avenues for PCs.

PCT 2.0 and Change in Organizational Commitment

PCT 2.0 phases may coincide with the development of, and fluctuation in, organizational commitment over time. Creation marks the start of an employee's commitment to the organization. However, research suggests that there may be distinct temporal patterns (trajectories) to a newcomer's early commitment formation. Solinger et al. (2013) examined newcomers' development of organizational commitment during their first 25 weeks of employment and found five distinct patterns. The majority of newcomers developed some level of commitment over the duration of the study, with most demonstrating immediate strong commitment to their organization (34.5 percent), and others demonstrating only moderate (12.5 percent) or low (11.5 percent) levels of commitment. Others appeared to need more time to develop a highly committed relationship with their organization (16.5 percent), and some actually de-committed from their organization (25 percent) within these first 25 weeks. It would be interesting to explore how these patterns map onto employees' transition into the maintenance phase.

More generally, it would be interesting to explore whether changes in organizational commitment accompany all PC phase shifts. Although minor breaches are not likely to stimulate change in commitment, significant breaches that shift employees from the maintenance phase into the repair phase will likely have detrimental effects on commitment. In fact, in cases of dissolution, employees who do not return to a functional maintenance phase may remain in a steady state of CC, staying with the organization despite the breach because the costs associated with leaving are too high.

In addition to exploring change in overall commitment, future research might also explore how commitment profiles change over time in conjunction with the changing nature of the employee–employer relationship. For instance, it is conceivable that the experience of repeated breaches over time might change an employee's commitment profile, for instance from a 'pure affective' profile (high AC, low NC, low CC) to a 'pure continuance' profile (low AC, low NC, high CC). Such changes would have significant ramifications for organizational effectiveness.

Post-Violation Model and Change in Organizational Commitment

The post-violation model has implications for exploring commitment restoration following violation. Preliminary evidence supports this connection. Griep et al. (2016b) and Solinger et al. (2016) explored commitment trajectories (that is, how commitment unfolds) following PC breach and resultant violation feelings. They found that employees sometimes re-committed to their organization (resembling reactivation), and sometimes their new level of commitment exceeded original levels (resembling thriving). However, not all employees fully re-committed; some only partially re-committed (resembling impairment) and some continued to de-commit from the organization (resembling dissolution). Consistent with the post-violation model, organizational efforts (for example, support) had a positive impact on the extent to which employees re-committed.

The Role of Time in the Study of PCs and Organizational Commitment

Whether exploring change in PCs or change in commitment, time will be a crucial factor in future research. In PCT 2.0, speed of promise-making and inducement delivery impact how quickly employees transition between phases. In addition, congruence between actual and expected speeds of employer promises and delivered inducements impact affect and perceptions of PC fulfillment, respectively. Similarly, in the post-violation model, the speed of violation resolution has implications for the type of PC outcome that is achieved, with slower resolution associated with less favorable outcomes. Commitment research noted above suggests that changes in commitment follow similar patterns (for example, Griep et al., 2016b). Further, time becomes an important factor in understanding how the PC itself and employee reactions (such as commitment) to it change. Indeed, some changes may be immediate, some may unfold over time; some may be temporary, some may be permanent.

Conventional methods used to investigate static research questions demonstrate only the average reaction of a group of employees, leaving the dynamic nature of the relationship between the PC and outcomes like commitment unknown. Thus, we propose that future research designs reflect the time dependence of PC processes both between and within individuals, with the ultimate goal of mapping time-contingent process of, for example, breach (Ployhart and Vandenberg, 2010). For instance, future research could adopt high-density (high number of repeated measures) and high-temporal (hourly, daily, or weekly) research designs to assess how quickly perceived breach and its accompanying violation feelings influence changes in organizational commitment (see Griep et al., 2016b; Solinger et al., 2016). Further, longitudinal research designs could assess processes that are slower to unfold over time (for example, violation resolution).

Lessons from the Organizational Commitment Literature

Just as developments in PC theory may inspire new avenues of research for commitment, intriguing findings and methods in the organizational commitment literature may also inspire future research on PCs. First, although PCT 2.0 and the post-violation model underscore the roles of both employee and organization in developing and maintaining a positive, committed relationship, these theories are unclear as to who the employer is and whether the 'acting' organizational agent in a particular exchange episode affects PC processes. Drawing on findings in the commitment literature, future research may explore whether the perceived obligations, inducements, and contributions exchanged between employees and their organization differ as a function of the organizational agent (for example, supervisors, recruiters). Just as differential effects of commitment foci

(Chapter 4 in this volume) have demonstrated differential relations among key variables (Meyer and Allen, 1991, 1997), so too might different agents or targets of PC obligations. For example, the strength of employee obligations to the organization may vary depending on who they perceive they have that obligation to (for example, to their team member, direct supervisor, or executive management). Indeed, Tomprou and Nikolaou (2011) proposed important differences in perceived contract fulfillment of direct (for example, supervisor) versus indirect (for example, co-workers) agents of the organization.

Also drawing on the commitment literature, future research might better capture real employee–employer relationships by adopting a person-centered approach (Meyer et al., 2013; Chapter 35 in this volume). This approach involves identifying subgroups within a sample based on having similar patterns of focal variables (for example, particular profiles), and using that membership as a variable itself when exploring relationships with other variables. For example, in their examination of commitment profiles, Gellatly et al. (2006) found that a particular component (for example, NC) can be experienced differently depending on the levels of the other commitment components, and further, that people with these differential profiles can demonstrate different intentions and behaviors toward the organization. The person-centered approach could offer an interesting avenue for examining employee experiences of their PC types and for exploring how different levels of relational and transactional elements within individuals' PCs influence organizational commitment and other important outcome variables.

CONCLUSIONS

Like the organizational commitment literature, the PC literature is an important resource to organizations as they endeavor to create and maintain positive relationships with their employees. The extant PC literature has demonstrated that employee perceptions of obligations have a significant impact on how they think about, feel about, and behave toward their organization. Although some overlap exists between research on PCs and commitment, recent theoretical advances highlighting the dynamic nature of PCs will undoubtedly spark additional empirical work that will expand our understanding of PC processes and their relations with organizational commitment in exciting ways.

REFERENCES

Allen, N.J. and Meyer, J.P. (1990). The measurement and antecedents of affective, continuance and normative commitment. *Journal of Occupational Psychology*, *63*, 1–18.

Arnold, J. (1996). The psychological contract: A concept in need of closer scrutiny? *European Journal of Work and Organizational Psychology*, *5*, 511–520.

Bal, M.P., De Lange, A.H., Jansen, P.G.W., and Van Der Velde, M.E.G. (2008). Psychological contract breach and job attitudes: A meta-analysis of age as a moderator. *Journal of Vocational Behavior*, *72*, 143–158.

Baumeister, R.F., Finkenauer, C., and Vohs, K.D. (2001). Bad is stronger than good. *Review of General Psychology*, *5*, 323–370.

Blau, P.M. (1964). *Exchange and power in social life*. New York: Wiley.

Carver, C.S. and Scheier, M.F. (1990). Origins and functions of positive and negative affect: A control-process view. *Psychological Review*, *97*, 19–35.

Carver, C.S. and Scheier, M.F. (2001). *On the Self-Regulation of Behavior*. Cambridge: Cambridge University Press.

Cassar, V. and Briner, R.B. (2011). The relationship between psychological contract breach and organizational commitment: Exchange imbalance as a moderator of the mediating role of violation. *Journal of Vocational Behavior*, *78*, 283–289.

Chang, C-H., Johnson, R.E., and Lord, R.G. (2010). Moving beyond discrepancies: The importance of velocity as a predictor of satisfaction and motivation. *Human Performance*, *23*, 58–80.

Conway, N. and Briner, R.B. (2002). Full-time versus part-time employees: Understanding the links between work status, the psychological contract, and attitudes. *Journal of Vocational Behavior*, *61*, 279–301.

Conway, N., Guest, D., and Trenberth, L. (2011). Testing the differential effects of changes in psychological contract breach and fulfillment. *Journal of Vocational Behavior*, *79*, 267–276.

Coyle-Shapiro, J.A-M. and Kessler, I. (2013). The employment relationship in the U.K. public sector: a psychological contract perspective. *Journal of Public Administration Research and Theory*, *13*, 213–230.

Deery, S.J., Iverson, R.D., and Walsh, J.T. (2006). Toward a better understanding of psychological contract breach: a study of customer service employees. *Journal of Applied Psychology*, *91*, 166–175.

De Hauw, S. and De Vos, A. (2010). Millennials' career perspective and psychological contract expectations: Does the recession lead to lowered expectations? *Journal of Business and Psychology*, *25*, 293–302.

De Vos, A., Buyens, D. and Schalk, R. (2003). Psychological contract development during organizational socialization: Adaptation to reality and the role of reciprocity. *Journal of Organizational Behavior*, *24*, 537–559.

Dulac, T., Coyle-Shapiro, J.A.M., Henderson, D.J., and Wayne, S.J. (2008). Not all responses to breach are the same: The interconnection of social exchange and psychological contract processes in organizations. *Academy of Management Journal*, *51*, 1079–1098.

Forgas, J.P. and George, J.M. (2001). Affective influences on judgments, decision making and behavior in organizations: An information processing perspective. *Organizational Behavior and Human Decision Processes*, *86*, 3–34.

Flood, P.C., Turner, T., Ramamoorthy, N., and Pearson, J. (2001). Causes and consequences of psychological contracts among knowledge workers in the high technology and financial services industries. *International Journal of Human Resource Management*, *12*, 1152–1165.

Frese, M. (2000). The changing nature of work. In N. Chmiel (ed.), *An Introduction to Work and Organizational Psychology* (pp. 424–439). Oxford: Blackwell.

Gakovic, A. and Tetrick, L.E. (2003). Perceived organizational support and work status: A comparison of the employment relationships of part-time and full-time employees attending university classes. *Journal of Organizational Behavior*, *24*, 649–666.

Gellatly, I.R., Meyer, J.P., and Luchak, A.A. (2006). Combined effects of the three commitment components of focal and discretionary behaviors: A test of Meyer and Herscovitch's propositions. *Journal of Vocational Behavior*, *69*, 331–345.

Giannikis, S. and Nikandrou, I. (2013). The impact of corporate entrepreneurship and high-performance work systems on employees' job attitudes: Empirical evidence from Greece during the economic downturn. *International Journal of Human Resource Management*, *24*, 3644–3666.

Griep, Y., Vantilborgh, T., Baillien, E., and Pepermans, R. (2016a). The mitigating role of leader-member exchange in reaction to psychological contract violation: A diary study among volunteers. *European Journal of Work and Organizational Psychology*, *25*, 254–271. DOI: 10.1080/1359432X.2015.1046048.

Griep, Y., Tomprou, M., Vantilborgh, T., Hansen, S.D., Hofmans, J., Rousseau, D.M., and Pepermans, R. (2016b). Prototypical stories of commitment in the aftermath of violation: The role of perceived organizational support. Paper presented at the 76th Annual Meeting of the Academy of Management, Anaheim, CA, August.

Hughes, L.W. and Palmer, D.K. (2007). An investigation of the effects of psychological contract and organization-based self-esteem on organizational commitment in a sample of permanent and contingent workers. *Journal of Leadership and Organizational Studies*, *14*, 143–156.

Isen, A. (2001). An influence of positive affect on decision making in complex situations: Theoretical issues with practical implications. *Journal of Consumer Psychology*, *11*, 75–85.

Johnson, J.L. and O'Leary-Kelly, A.M. (2003). The effects of psychological contract breach and organizational cynicism: Not all social exchange violations are created equal. *Journal of Organizational Behavior*, *24*, 627–647.

Johnson, R.E., Howe, M., and Chang, C-H. (2013). The importance of velocity, or why speed may matter more than distance. *Organizational Psychology Review*, *3*, 62–85.

Kickul, J. (2001). Promises made, promises broken: An exploration of employee attraction and retention practices in small business. *Journal of Small Business Management*, *39*, 320–335.

Lambert, L.S. (2011). Promised and delivered inducements and contributions: An integrated view of psychological contract appraisal. *Journal of Applied Psychology*, *96*, 695–712.

Lambert, L.S., Edwards, J.R், and Cable, D.M. (2003). Breach and fulfillment of the psychological contract: A comparison of traditional and expanded views. *Personnel Psychology*, *56*, 895–934.

Lee, C., Liu, J., Rousseau, D.M., Hui, C., and Chen, Z.X. (2011). Inducements, contributions, and fulfillment in new employee psychological contracts. *Human Resource Management*, *50*, 201–226.

Lester, S.W., Kickul, J.R., and Bergmann, T.J. (2007). Managing employee perceptions of the psychological contract over time: The role of employer social accounts and contract fulfillment. *Journal of Organizational Behavior*, *28*, 191–208.

Levinson, H., Price, C.R., Munden, K.J., and Solley, C.M. (1962). *Men, Management, and Mental Health*. Cambridge, MA: Harvard University Press.

Locke, E.A. (1976). The nature and causes of job satisfaction. In M.D. Dunnette (ed.), *Handbook of Industrial and Organizational Psychology* (pp. 1297–1349). Chicago, IL: Rand McNally.

Lord, R., Diefendorff, J., Schmidt, A., and Hall, R. (2010). Self-regulation at work. *Annual Review of Psychology*, *61*, 543–568.

Lord, R. and Levy, P.E. (1994). Moving from cognition to action: A control theory perspective. *Applied Psychology: An International Review*, *43*, 335–367.

McInnis, K.J., Meyer, J.P., and Feldman, S. (2009). Psychological contracts and their implications for commitment: A feature-based approach. *Journal of Vocational Behavior*, *74*, 165–180.

McLean Parks, J., Kidder, D.L., and Gallagher, D.G. (1998). Fitting square pegs into round holes: Mapping the domain of contingent work arrangements onto the psychological contract. *Journal of Organizational Behavior*, *19*, 697–730.

Meyer, J.P. and Allen, N.J. (1991). A three-component conceptualization of organizational commitment. *Human Resource Management Review*, *1*, 61–89.

Meyer, J.P. and Allen, N.J. (1997). *Commitment in the Workplace: Theory, Research, and Application*. Thousand Oaks, CA: Sage.

Meyer, J.P. and Herscovitch, L. (2001). Commitment in the workplace. Towards a general model. *Human Resource Management Review*, *11*, 299–326.

Meyer, J.P., Stanley, L.J., and Parfyonova, N.M. (2012). Employee commitment in context: The nature and implication of commitment profiles. *Journal of Vocational Behavior*, *80*, 1–16.

Meyer, J.P., Stanley, L.J., and Vandenberg, R.J. (2013). A person-centered approach to the study of commitment. *Human Resource Management Review*, *23*, 190–202.

Montes, S.D. and Irving, P.G. (2008). Disentangling the effects of promised and delivered inducements: Relational and transactional contract elements and the mediating role of trust. *Journal of Applied Psychology*, *93*, 1367–1381.

Montes, S.D. and Zweig, D. (2009). Do promises matter? An exploration of the role of promises in psychological contract breach. *Journal of Applied Psychology*, *94*, 1243–1260.

Morrison, E.W. and Robinson, S.L. (1997). When employees feel betrayed: A model how psychological contract develops. *Academy of Management Review*, *22*, 226–256.

Mowday, R.T., Steers, R.M., and Porter, L.W. (1979). The measurement of organizational commitment. *Journal of Vocational Behavior*, *14*, 224–247.

Ng, T.W.H., Feldman, D.C., and Lam, S.S.K. (2010). Psychological contract breaches, organizational commitment, and innovation-related behaviors: A latent growth modeling approach. *Journal of Applied Psychology*, *95*, 744–751.

Ployhart, R.E. and Vandenberg, R.J. (2010). Longitudinal research: The theory, design, and analysis of change. *Journal of Management*, *36*, 94–120.

Raja, U., Johns, G., and Ntalianis, F. (2004). The impact of personality on psychological contracts. *Academy of Management Journal*, *47*, 350–367.

Robinson, S.L. (1995). Violation of psychological contracts: Impact on employee attitudes. In L.E. Tetrick and J. Barling (eds), *Changing Employment Relations: Behavioral and Social Perspectives* (pp. 91–108). Washington, DC: APA.

Robinson, S.L. (1996). Trust and breach of the psychological contract. *Administrative Science Quarterly*, *41*, 574–599.

Roehling, M.V. (2008). An empirical assessment of alternative conceptualizations of the psychological contract construct: Meaningful differences or "much to do about nothing"?. *Employee Responsibility and Rights Journal*, *20*, 261–290.

Rousseau, D.M. (1989). Psychological and implied contracts in organizations. *Employee Responsibilities and Rights Journal*, *2*, 121–139.

Rousseau, D.M. (1990). New hire perceptions of their own and their employer's obligations: A study of psychological contracts. *Journal of Organizational Behavior*, *11*, 389–400.

Rousseau, D.M. (1995). *Psychological Contracts in Organizations: Understanding Written and Unwritten Agreements*. Thousand Oaks, CA: Sage.

Rousseau, D.M. (2001). Schema, promise, and mutuality: The building blocks of the psychological contract. *Journal of Occupational and Organizational Psychology*, *74*, 511–541

Rousseau, D.M. and Greller, M.M. (1994). Human resource practices: Administrative contact makers. *Human Resource Management*, *33*, 385–402.

Rousseau, D.M., Hansen, S.D., and Tomprou, M. (2016). Psychological contract theory 2.0. Unpublished manuscript.

Rousseau, D.M. and McLean-Parks, J. (1993). The contracts of individuals and organizations. *Research in Organizational Behavior*, *15*, 1–43.

Schalk, R. and Roe, R.E. (2007). Towards a dynamic model of the psychological contract. *Journal for the Theory of Social Behavior*, *37*, 167–182.

Shore, L.M., Tetrick, L.E., Lynch, P., and Barksdale, K. (2006). Social and economic exchange: Construct development and validation. *Journal of Applied Social Psychology*, *36*, 837–867.

Solinger, O.N., Hofmans, J., Bal, P.M., and Jansen, P.G.W. (2016). Bouncing back from psychological contract breach: How commitment recovers over time. *Journal of Organizational Behavior*, *37*, 494–514. DOI: 10.1002/job.2047.

Solinger, O.N., van Olffen, W., Roe, R.A., and Hofmans, J. (2013). On becoming (un)committed: A taxonomy and test of newcomer onboarding scenarios. *Organization Science*, *24*, 1640–1661.

Sturges, J., Conway, N., Guest, D., and Liefooghe, A. (2005). Managing the career deal: The psychological contract as a framework for understanding career management, organizational commitment and work behavior. *Journal of Organizational Behavior*, *26*, 821–838.

Suazo, M.M. (2009). The mediating role of psychological contract violation on the relations between psychological contract breach and work-related attitudes and behaviors. *Journal of Managerial Psychology*, *24*, 136–160.

Taylor, S.E. (1991). Asymmetrical effects of positive and negative events: The mobilization-minimization hypothesis. *Psychological Bulletin*, *110*, 67–85.

Tomprou, M. and Nikolaou, I. (2011). A model of psychological contract creation upon entry. *Career Development International*, *16*, 342–363.

Tomprou, M., Nikolaou, I., and Vakola, M. (2012). Experiencing organizational change in Greece: the framework of psychological contract. *International Journal of Human Resource Management*, *23*, 385–405.

Tomprou, M., Rousseau, D.M., and Hansen, S.D. (2015). The psychological contracts of violation victims: A post-violation model. *Journal of Organizational Behavior*, *36*, 561–581.

Zhao, H., Wayne, S.J., Glibkowski, B.C., and Bravo, J. (2007). Impact of psychological contract breach on work-related outcomes: A meta-analysis. *Personnel Psychology*, *60*, 647–680.

PART III

FOCI OF COMMITMENT

10. Occupational commitment
John P. Meyer and Jose A. Espinoza

Although interest in workplace commitment focused initially on commitment to the organization, Reichers (1985) noted that employees can commit to multiple constituencies within (for example, supervisors, teams) or outside (for example, occupation, union) the organization. Interest in these other commitments has increased in recent years due in part to concerns about the relevance of organizational commitment in an era of change (Blau, 2001; Meyer, 2009). In their efforts to increase efficiencies in the face of increasing global competition, and to remain flexible in the uncertain economy of the 1990s, organizations began to cut their workforces and/or rely increasingly on contractual or temporary employees (Emshoff, 1994). Although this situation served to undermine the basis for a long-term commitment on the part of employers and employees (Baruch, 1998), it did not mitigate the importance of commitment per se. Indeed, commitment has implications for more than the longevity of a relationship; it can also have an impact on organizational effectiveness and employee well-being (Meyer and Allen, 1997; Meyer and Maltin, 2010).

In this chapter we focus on the occupation as another important target of workplace commitment. We use the term 'occupation' here in a generic sense to refer to one's line of work, but acknowledge that the terms 'profession' and 'career' are often used as well. We view professions as specialized occupations with, among other things, stringent requirements for entry, accepted standards of practice, shared identity and sense of social importance (Hall, 1968; Van Maanen and Barley, 1984), and acknowledge the distinction where appropriate. We eschew use of the term 'career' in this context to avoid confusion with its alternate interpretation as a pattern of work-related decisions and activities within and across organizations and occupations over an individual's lifetime (Arthur et al., 1989; Greenhaus, 1987).

The theoretical framework guiding our review of the occupational commitment literature is depicted in Figure 10.1. We begin by reviewing theory pertaining to the construct of occupational commitment and then discuss the nature of its relation with organizational commitment. Next, we discuss the implications of occupational commitment for three potential stakeholders: occupations (including associations, regulatory bodies, and other members), organizations, and the individuals themselves. Although our focus is on the implications of occupational commitment (solid arrows in Figure 10.1), we also acknowledge that these implications can reflect the interplay between organizational and occupational commitment (as reflected in the broken arrows in Figure 10.1). We then turn our attention to the development of occupational commitment to set the stage for a discussion of management strategies. We conclude by discussing directions for future research.

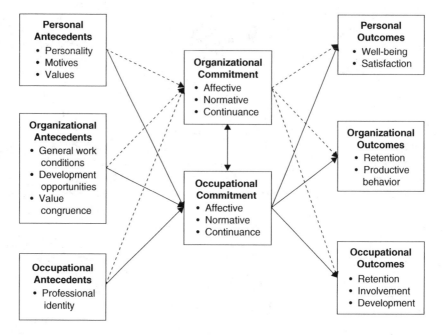

Figure 10.1   Model of organizational and occupational commitment and their relations with antecedents and outcomes

DEVELOPMENT AND EVOLUTION OF OCCUPATIONAL COMMITMENT THEORY

Issues of occupation or career choice, development, and mobility have a long history (see Blau, 1985). Hall (1971, p. 59) was one of the first to define career commitment as 'the strength of one's motivation to a chosen career role' and to distinguish it from related constructs. However, definition and measurement problems persisted until Blau (1985, p. 278) redefined the construct as an 'attitude toward one's profession or vocation' and developed a reliable measure that was shown to be distinct from related constructs such as job involvement, work involvement, and organizational commitment (Blau, 1985, 1988, 1989). Although he used the term 'career commitment' initially, he later adopted the term 'occupational commitment' for the reasons noted above (Blau, 2001, 2003).

In contrast to Blau's (1985) unidimensional conceptualization, two multidimensional models were subsequently introduced. Meyer et al. (1993) adapted the three-component model (TCM) of organizational commitment developed by Allen and Meyer (1990; Meyer and Allen, 1991) to the study of occupational commitment. According to the TCM, commitments can be characterized by different psychological states, or 'mindsets', that have implications for the way they are enacted (see Chapter 3 in this volume). 'Affective commitment' (AC) is characterized by positive emotional attachment, 'normative commitment' (NC) by a sense of obligation, and 'continuance commitment' (CC) by the perceived cost of severing a relationship or discontinuing a course of action. Carson et al. (1995) proposed an alternative three-dimensional model of a related construct they called 'career entrenchment'. The three dimensions – career investments, emotional costs, and limited alternatives – shared much in common with the Meyer et al. model, and Blau (2003) has since proposed an integrated four-dimensional framework by reconceptualizing CC to reflect the accumulated costs and limited alternatives dimensions identified by Carson et al.

Research through the 1980s and 1990s and into the new millennium demonstrated that occupational commitment could be reliably measured and that it related to occupation-relevant behavior (for example, retention, involvement). Although clearly distinguishable from organizational commitment, occupational commitment was also found to account for unique variance in organization-relevant outcomes such as retention and job performance (Lee et al., 2000). Although most research focused on AC or AC-like measures of occupational commitment, studies that included measures of the other dimensions often demonstrated different patterns of relations with occupation- and organization-relevant outcomes (e.g., Blau and Holladay, 2006; Meyer et al., 1993).

Although there have been few major developments in occupational commitment theory per se within the last decade, there have been developments in commitment theory more generally that have implications for occupational commitment. For example, Meyer and Herscovitch (2001) developed a more generic version of the TCM and offered a set of propositions concerning how the three components of commitment – AC, NC, and CC – combine to form commitment profiles, and how these profiles are likely to influence behavior. This development served as the impetus for a growing body of person-centered research (see Meyer et al., 2013; Chapter 35 in this volume) designed to identify and compare groups of individuals with different profiles. Although most of this research focused on organizational commitment (e.g., Meyer et al., 2012; Wasti, 2005), the person-centered approach has recently been applied to the study of occupational commitment as well (Morin et al., 2015). It has also been applied to investigate profiles of commitments to multiple targets, including occupational commitment (e.g., Morin et al., 2011; Morin et al., 2015; Tsoumbris and Xenikou, 2010). The implications of this line of research are discussed in more detail in the next and subsequent sections of this chapter.

RELATIONSHIP BETWEEN OCCUPATIONAL AND ORGANIZATIONAL COMMITMENT

As more professionally trained individuals began to work in large professional organizations (for example, law or accounting firms), or to be employed in staff positions by large non-professional organizations, there was some concern that professional and bureaucratic values would come into conflict (see Wallace, 1995). This could result in employees being forced to commit to either their profession or their organization (Gouldner, 1957). However, modern research consistently finds a moderate positive correlation between AC to the organization and the occupation or profession (Cooper-Hakim and Viswesvaran, 2005; Lee et al., 2000; Wallace, 1993). This positive correlation seems to hold for non-professionals and professionals, and for professionals working in professional and non-professional organizations. Nevertheless, the magnitude of the correlation is modest and does not preclude the possibility of conflict for some employees or under some conditions. Therefore, investigators began to explore the nature of these dual commitments in more detail.

Gouldner (1957) first made the distinction between 'locals' – professional employees who identified more strongly with the organization – and 'cosmopolitans' – those who identified more strongly with the profession. Interestingly, he did not address the possibility that some professionals might develop loyalties to both the organization and the profession, and that others might have little loyalty to either. Researchers interested in the local–cosmopolitan distinction as it pertains to commitment generally considered all four possibilities (e.g., Carson et al., 1999; Somers and Birnbaum, 2000). That is, using a midpoint split approach, they created four groups with varying combinations of high and low scores on occupational and organizational commitment. These studies generally reported the most positive outcomes (for example, job satisfaction, job performance) for the dually committed, and the most negative outcomes for the uncommitted. Differences between locals and cosmopolitans were generally small, but scores tended to be slightly more favorable for the locals. These findings suggest that strong commitment to the occupation can be beneficial to organizations, and that there might be some synergy when employees are committed to both the organization and the occupation. It is important to note, however, that these groups were created artificially (that is, using midpoint splits) and may not accurately reflect the true heterogeneity of commitment profiles within a sample (see Meyer et al., 2013; Morin, this volume). More recently, studies have been conducted using cluster analysis (Tsoumbris and Xenikou, 2010) or latent profile analysis (LPA; Morin et al., 2011, 2015) to identify naturally occurring configurations of occupational and organizational commitment.

Morin et al. (2011) measured AC to the organization and occupation as well as five other targets. They found that levels of commitment to the organization and occupation were quite similar across seven profile groups. Tsoumbris and Xenikou (2010) obtained similar findings across four profile groups obtained with teachers in Greece. In this case, the researchers measured AC, NC, and CC to both targets and found that, although the mindset pattern differed across the profile groups, it was very similar for the two targets within a profile. Thus, both studies suggest that commitment to the organization and occupation are generally compatible (that is, increase or decrease together). In contrast to the midpoint split studies, they provide little evidence of conflict (that is, strong commitment to one target and weak commitment to the other).

More recently, Morin et al. (2015) measured AC, NC, and CC to the occupation and organization in a sample of teachers in Hong Kong. Using LPA, they identified seven profiles reflecting varying levels of AC, NC, and CC to the two targets. For three of these profiles, the mindset pattern for both targets was similar (that is, CC to both targets was dominant in two profiles, and AC to both was dominant in another). This again suggests that the strength and/or nature of employees' commitment to the two targets can move in parallel. For example, positive work experiences might strengthen AC to both the occupation and organization, whereas negative experiences could have the opposite effect. Similarly, poor economic conditions might restrict opportunities to change both occupations and organizations, thereby strengthening CC to both. However, in the remaining four profiles, Morin et al. (2015) found evidence for dissimilarity in the mindset configuration. For example, in one of the profiles, teachers had strong AC, NC, and CC (that is, a fully committed profile) to the occupation, but their commitment to the organization was dominated by NC. In another profile, AC, NC, and CC to the occupation were in the moderate range, but again NC to the organization was dominant. One possible explanation for these differing mindset configurations was provided by Meyer and Allen (1997).

Building on Lawler's (1992) notion of nested commitments, Meyer and Allen (1997) proposed that dependencies can develop among commitments to different targets. Consequently, commitment to one target might influence not only the strength but also the nature of commitment to another. In the case of organizational and occupational commitment, a dependency might exist when maintaining employment in an organization (for example, school, law firm) requires that one continue in an occupation. Thus, in the absence of strong AC to the occupation, strong commitment to the organization could create strong CC to the occupation by increasing the cost of changing fields. Similarly, employees who are highly committed to their occupation but have limited opportunities to practice elsewhere might develop a strong CC to the organization, even when AC and/or NC are low. Interestingly, rather than finding that strong commitment to the profession was accompanied by strong CC to the organization as Meyer and Allen proposed, Morin et al. (2015) found strong NC to the organization. Although we can only speculate at this point, it is possible that the elevation of NC (obligation) rather than CC (personal cost) reflects the collectivist values held by Hong Kong teachers.

There are still too few studies examining profiles of occupational and organizational commitments to draw any firm conclusions, but it appears that conflict may be the exception rather than the rule. Nevertheless, the possibility remains that the nature of employees' commitment to their occupation and organization might be different and that this could have implications for target-relevant behavior. We address these implications in more detail in the following section.

IMPLICATIONS OF OCCUPATIONAL COMMITMENT

The nature and strength of individuals' commitment to an occupation can have implications for the occupational groups to which they belong, the organizations in which they work, and their own personal well-being. In this section we address each of these in turn.

Implications for the Occupation or Profession

As was the case for organizational commitment, interest in occupational commitment was stimulated initially by concerns regarding retention, in this case retention of members within an occupation or profession. Indeed, intention to remain in the occupation was the major outcome variable in Blau's (1985, 1988, 1989) research as well as in studies conducted to test the multidimensional frameworks developed by Meyer et al. (1993) (e.g., Irving et al., 1997; Snape and Redman, 2003) and Carson et al. (1995) (e.g., Carson et al., 1996). Lee et al. (2000) provided meta-analytic evidence of a strong link between occupational AC and intention to leave the occupation ($\rho = -.621$). Nevertheless, researchers have continued to examine the relation, often within a particular occupational group (for example, nurses: Chang et al., 2007; pharmacists: Jones and McIntosh, 2010; psychologists: Carless and Bernath, 2007), and/or under unique conditions (for example, preparation for retirement: Jones and McIntosh, 2010), and/or in different cultures (e.g., Chang et al., 2007). Overall, the evidence is consistent in demonstrating that individuals who are committed to their occupation are less likely to change occupations. Studies examining relations with the different components of commitment identified in the TCM generally find the strongest negative relation for occupational AC, followed by NC and CC respectively (Chang et al., 2007; Meyer et al., 1993; Snape and Redman, 2003).

Surprisingly little attention has been paid to occupation-relevant outcomes other than retention in relation to occupational commitment. Meyer et al. (1993) found that nurses' AC and NC to the profession correlated positively with self-reported professional involvement (for example, taking courses, subscribing to journals), but CC was unrelated. Similarly, Snape and Redman (2003) found that, among human resource management (HRM) specialists in the United Kingdom, AC and NC were positively related to intentions to participate in the Chartered Institute of Personnel and Development (for example, contributing to the newsletter, attending conferences or workshops); CC was unrelated. Blau and Holladay (2006) found that AC related positively to self-reported professional activity (for example, holding office in a professional organization; providing clinical instruction) among medical technologists; neither NC nor accumulated costs commitment correlated significantly, but limited alternatives commitment correlated negatively.

Together, these studies suggest that individuals with a strong AC and/or NC to their occupation are not only more likely to remain within the occupation, but are also more likely to engage in activities that support the occupation and its members, and/or continue to develop their occupation-relevant knowledge and skills. CC generally relates negatively to intention to leave the occupation, appears to carry no added benefit, and may indeed relate negatively to occupational involvement.

Implications for Organizations

In their meta-analysis, Lee et al. (2000) found that AC to the occupation correlated negatively with intention to leave the organization ($\rho = -.247$) and actual turnover ($\rho = -.121$), and positively with supervisor-rated performance ($\rho = .146$). They further observed that the relation between occupational AC and intention to leave the organization was mediated by intention to leave the occupation. That is, employees who had a stronger AC to their occupation were less likely to intent to leave the occupation which, in turn, reduced the likelihood that they would leave the organization. More recently, studies have demonstrated that occupational commitment is positively related to a variety of other organization-relevant outcomes, including knowledge-sharing among employees in public service firms (Swart et al., 2014), research productivity in tenured faculty (Becker et al., forthcoming), and creativity among employees in advertising firms (Madjar et al., 2011). Much less attention has been paid to the implications of occupational NC and CC for organization-relevant outcomes. However, as has been demonstrated in organizational commitment research (e.g., Gellatly et al., 2006; Meyer et al., 2012; Wasti, 2005) the implications of NC and CC for behavior can vary depending on how they combine with the other components in a commitment profile. Therefore, it is important to consider the findings of the few recent profile studies involving occupational commitment.

In their study of Greek teachers described earlier, Tsoumbris and Xenikou (2010) found that those who were fully committed to their occupation (that is, strong AC, NC, and CC) or had an AC/NC-dominant profile were least likely to intend to leave the organization. Recall, however, that Tsoumbris and Xenikou found that the mindset configuration for occupational and organizational commitment was the same across profiles, so it is impossible to tell whether it was commitment to one or both of the targets that explains intentions to remain with the organization. Morin et al. (2015) found the lowest intentions to leave among Hong Kong teachers who were fully committed to teaching, or had an AC/NC-dominant occupational commitment profile, and this was true whether their commitment to the organization reflected strong AC (desire to remain) or NC (obligation to remain). These findings provide further evidence that occupational AC contributes to intention to remain in the organization, and suggest that NC, and even CC, might have synergistic effects. Unfortunately, no other organization-relevant outcomes were included in these profile studies, so it is impossible to determine at this point how the profiles might differ beyond their implications for retention.

Implications for Employees

Although commitment theory and research to date has focused largely on implications for the target of that commitment, more attention has been given recently to the implications for employees' own well-being (see Chapter 17 in this volume). Most of this research has focused on organizational commitment, and presents findings suggesting that the different mindsets of commitment are differentially related to indices of both physical and psychological health, with AC having the strongest positive relations, followed by NC; CC has been found to be negatively related.

Research examining the implications of occupational commitment for health and well-being are limited and generally restricted to AC. Consistent with findings pertaining to organizational commitment, AC to the occupation has been found to relate negatively to various symptoms of stress and burnout (e.g., Reilly, 1994; Yeh et al., 2007). More recently, Baruch et al. (2014) tested a model in which occupational commitment was included as a predictor of 'professional vitality', defined as 'a characteristic possessed by individuals who are able to consistently perform the work of their chosen profession with passion, vigor, facility, and satisfaction' (Harvey, 2002, p. 35). Professional vitality was found to mediate the relations between occupational commitment and both career and life satisfaction.

In their study of dual-commitment profiles, Morin et al. (2015) found that teachers with fully committed or AC/NC-dominant occupational commitment profiles reported the highest levels of well-being. Indeed, when teachers were strongly committed to teaching, they reported high levels of well-being even when their commitment to the organization was NC-dominant (that is, obligation-based). Although preliminary, this suggests that, at least from the standpoint of well-being, strong commitment to one's occupation can substitute for commitment to the organization. Again, the lowest levels of well-being were reported when teachers had weak commitment to both targets, or felt trapped (strong CC) in one or both.

DEVELOPMENT OF OCCUPATIONAL COMMITMENT

Given that occupational commitment has been found to have implications for individuals, their occupations, and their organizations, it is interesting to consider the role(s) that each might play in its development.

Personal Antecedents

Individual differences and demographic variables have generally received little attention as predictors of occupational commitment. Overall, meta-analytic studies report relatively weak relations between demographic variables and commitment to the organization and occupation (e.g., Lee et al., 2000; Meyer et al., 2002). The only dispositional variable with a sufficient number of studies to be included in Lee et al.'s (2000) meta-analysis of occupational commitment was locus of control. They found a modest negative correlation between AC and external locus of control. This finding was replicated by Blau (2003), and Yousaf et al. (2013) found a positive correlation with a related construct, proactive personality. Lin et al. (2013) recently observed modest, albeit significant, correlations between emotional intelligence and both AC and NC to the occupation.

Other individual difference variables that have received attention can be categorized as motivational, and include work ethic (Lee et al., 2000), self-efficacy (Klassen and Chiu, 2011), and motives for entering the occupation (Fokkens-Bruinsma and Canrinus, 2012, 2015). Although research is limited, and focuses almost exclusively on teachers, the findings from these studies paint a picture of the affectively committed teacher as one who views teaching as an intrinsically interesting profession and who perceives him/herself as capable of meeting the challenges and making a difference. Whether the same applies to other occupational groups remains to be determined. Although treated here as individual differences, at least some of these motivational variables can be influenced during the occupational or professional socialization process and/or by the experiences they have within an organization.

Organizational Antecedents

By far the greatest attention to antecedents of occupational commitment has been focused on work conditions within organizations. This may be due to general interest in the potential for conflict between organizational and occupational commitments as discussed earlier, and/or concern that organizations will require a substitute as commitment to the organization itself declines. Our objective here is to provide a sampling of the organizational factors that have been linked to occupational commitment, particularly AC. It is important to note that the bulk of the research has been cross-sectional and therefore it is impossible to establish causality.

In their meta-analysis, Lee et al. (2000) identified a number of work context factors that relate positively with occupational AC, including supervisor and co-worker support, participation in decision-making, and autonomy. They also identified a number of factors that correlated negatively, including job stress, role ambiguity, role conflict, and organization–occupation conflict. These and related variables (for example, growth opportunities, work–family support, justice perceptions) continue to be identified as predictors of occupational AC in more recent research (e.g., Jørgensen and Becker, 2014; Klassen and Chiu, 2011; Major et al., 2013). This pattern of findings, combined with evidence that occupational AC also correlates positively with job satisfaction, job involvement, and organizational AC (Lee et al., 2000), suggests that employees' experiences within a particular organization might have either a positive or a negative impact on their occupational commitment. However, to our knowledge, there has been little systematic investigation of the mechanisms by which these 'background' experiences exert their influence on occupational commitment.

More recently, researchers have begun to address organizational policies and practices that might be of direct relevance to the development of occupational commitment. Indeed, these policies and practices might be introduced with the expressed purpose of strengthening employees' commitment to their occupation. For example, Arora and Rangnekar (2015) found that the availability of career mentoring by supervisors was positively related to occupational commitment for Indian employees from various occupational groups. Knudsen et al. (2013) found that the quality of clinical supervision given to addiction counsellors was positively related to their occupational AC. Weng and McElroy (2012) found that managers from various occupations in China had stronger occupational AC when the organization provided career growth opportunities, including the opportunity to meet career goals, develop occupation-relevant skills, and advance with regard to position and remuneration.

Another theme in research regarding organizational antecedents is the alignment of organizational and occupational values. English (2008) found that Australian police officers, particularly those early in their careers, were more committed to policing when the organization demonstrated a commitment to ethics. Similarly, Kim and Mueller (2011) found that perceptions of the organization's service orientation were positively related to occupational commitment in a national sample of Korean employees. Osinsky and Mueller (2004) found that, with the increasing bureaucratization of Russian organizations, the commitment of specialists to their occupation was greater in organizations that maintained a professional culture (that is, professional autonomy, collegiality, responsibility).

In sum, it appears that organizations have the potential to influence their employees' occupational commitment in several ways: by providing satisfying work experiences in general, facilitating the development of occupation-relevant knowledge and skills, and developing policies and practices that align with occupational values.

Occupational Antecedents

Despite the potential benefits that occupational or professional groups might derive from committed members, relatively little attention has been paid to investigating occupational influences on commitment. This is not to say that there has been little interest in ways to increase occupational retention or involvement, but rather that occupational commitment has not figured predominantly as a key variable. This may change as labor shortages within various occupations (for example, teaching: Fokkens-Bruinsma and Canrinus, 2012; information technology; and science, technology, engineering and mathematics, STEM: Major et al., 2013) become problematic.

One might expect that as employee–organization relationships become more tenuous, there may be a natural movement toward more commitment to the occupation as a source of support and security. However, McAulay et al. (2006) found that this is not necessarily the case. Using data obtained from members of three occupational groups, human resource practitioners, corporate lawyers, and computer programmers, they found that job insecurity was negatively related to AC and NC to the organization, but was unrelated to occupational commitment. This suggests that, while concerns about future employment in an organization provide a push away from the organization, they do not necessarily push employees in the direction of the occupation. In contrast, AC, NC, and CC to the occupation were positively related to the perceived professionalization of the occupation. That is, respondents were more committed to the occupation when they viewed it as having those characteristics commonly associated with traditional professions, including requirements for entry, standards of practice, shared identity, and sense of social importance. According to McAulay et al., it is the perceived professionalization that pulls individuals to commit to the occupation. Consistent with this finding is evidence that occupational commitment tends to be stronger among professionals than among non-professionals (Kim and Mueller, 2011) and, to a lesser extent, among professionals working in professional organizations compared to non-professional organizations (Wallace, 1995). The latter finding might be due to the fact that professionals working in non-professional organizations are less likely to interact with other professionals who trigger their professional identity or reaffirm their sense of social purpose.

PRACTICAL IMPLICATIONS

Although it has received far less attention than organizational commitment, the pattern of findings concerning potential consequences of occupational commitment is very similar. Occupational and professional associations, their members, and their clientele serve to benefit from strong occupational commitment, particularly strong AC and NC. The benefits of CC are less desirable, particularly when CC is the primary basis for continuation in the occupation. The benefits for individuals in terms of health and well-being show a similar pattern. Interestingly, the organizations that employ these individuals can also benefit from the right kinds of occupational commitment. Therefore, it is important to consider how each of these potential beneficiaries can contribute to the development of occupational commitment.

It appears from the personal antecedent research that individuals are more likely to experience a positive commitment to their occupation when they have a proactive personality and are intrinsically motivated. Together, these findings suggest that, to the extent that it is possible, individuals should play an active role in identifying and managing their career objectives. Admittedly, this can be difficult under tough economic conditions and when admission to occupations, particularly the higher-level professions, is highly regulated and competitive. Nevertheless, active investigation of opportunities accompanied by efforts to gain educational and practical experiences related to carefully planned long-term objectives should eventually pay off. Selecting the right organizations in which to work can also be important; ideally they will be ones that provide career development opportunities and have compatible values and ethical standards.

Perhaps the most noteworthy findings of relevance to occupational intervention are

McAulay et al.'s (2006) findings that employees are not necessarily pushed toward occupational commitment when organizational commitment declines. Rather, employees must be pulled to the occupation, and this pull is stronger when they view the occupation as highly professionalized. This condition exists almost by definition for the traditional professions (for example, law, accountancy, medicine), but the finding might provide an important message for less well-established occupational groups (for example, HR professionals, financial advisors). It is occupations such as this that might suffer from low involvement in general (for example, lapsed membership, minimal efforts to upgrade knowledge and skill, unwillingness to take on administrative responsibilities). According to McAulay et al. (2006, p. 590), occupations can become more professionalized by developing a formal occupational association that provides 'a range of services: periodic meetings, a website that helps in networking, training and certification programs, a job exchange, job-related literature, help with technical problems, etc.'. With the establishment of a professional identity and provision of such supports, an occupation is more likely to be viewed as a target of commitment independent of the organizations in which its members work. As a result, members should be more likely to maintain membership, even if they change organizations, and to become more involved in association activities.

As noted earlier, organizations can influence employees' occupational commitment through the quality of work experiences they provide, by supporting opportunities for the development of occupation-relevant knowledge and skills, and by appreciating and accepting occupational values and ethical standards. Although there might be a natural reluctance to invest in the development of generic occupational qualifications that employees can take elsewhere, evidence consistently demonstrates that there is a strong positive correlation between occupational and organizational AC. Thus, the investment in occupational development is likely to foster AC to the organization as well as the occupation. Moreover, in situations where organizations are not in a position to establish long-term relationships with employees, commitment to the occupation can serve as a substitute that has benefits in terms of performance and employee well-being. Indeed, as the psychological contract between organizations and their employees shifts to include employability rather than long-term employment as the organization's inducement (Baruch, 2001), efforts to develop generic occupation-relevant knowledge and skills will help to compel employees to perform effectively as fulfillment of their part of the contract.

DIRECTIONS FOR FUTURE RESEARCH

Although we have reasonable confidence in the recommendations made in the previous section, there are still many gaps in our understanding of the development and consequences of occupational commitment. The boxes in Figure 10.1 are populated by only a few of the many personal, organizational, and occupational characteristics involved in the development of occupational commitment. A more systematic investigation of the independent and combined effects of these characteristics, ideally guided by theory, is needed. Among the theories that might serve as a useful guide are self-determination theory (Ryan and Deci, 2000), regulatory focus theory (Higgins, 1998), and social identity theory (Tajfel and Turner, 1985), all of which have been applied in recent years as the basis for understanding the nature and development of organizational commitment (e.g., Johnson et al., 2010; Meyer et al., 2004; Meyer et al., 2006).

Researchers continue to focus more on AC than they do on NC and CC. It is now becoming increasingly apparent from research on organizational commitment that we can achieve a richer understanding of the nature, development, and consequences of commitment when all three mindsets are considered together, particularly in person-centered studies conducted to identify mindset profiles (see Meyer et al., 2013; Chapter 35 in this volume). It is only recently that profile analyses have been applied to the study of occupational commitment (Morin et al., 2015) or dual commitment to the occupation and organization (Morin et al., 2015; Tsoumbris and Xenikou, 2010). Thus, this is a promising area of investigation that warrants more attention.

Finally, the arrows in Figure 10.1, and our discussion throughout this chapter, imply causal effects of the antecedent variables on commitment and of commitment on personal, organizational, and occupational outcomes. It has also been argued that occupational and organizational commitments can influence one another and combine to influence the various outcomes. However, the vast majority of the research cited in support of these causal connections comes from cross-sectional research. Consequently, there is a need for more experimental, quasi-experimental, and/or longitudinal research to examine how these relations play out over time and to investigate the potential mediating mechanisms suggested by the theories identified above.

CONCLUSION

Theory and research pertaining to occupational or professional commitment has a relatively long history, but it has received considerably less attention than has organizational commitment. As long-term commitment to organizations becomes less viable in increasingly turbulent times, and as temporary contracts and similar arrangements become more prevalent, the occupation is well positioned to become a dominant target of commitment with implications for the well-being of the occupation itself, its members, and the organizations that employ them. To capitalize on this potential, more systematic research is needed. Many of the research methods and analytic tools required to conduct this systematic investigation are described in the chapters in Part VII, 'Methodological Issues', in this volume.

REFERENCES

Allen, N.J. and Meyer, J.P. (1990). The measurement and antecedents of affective, continuance and normative commitment to the organization. *Journal of Occupational Psychology*, 63(1), 1–18.

Arora, R. and Rangnekar, S. (2015). The joint effects of personality and supervisory career mentoring in predicting occupational commitment. *Career Development International*, 20(1), 63–80.

Arthur, M.B., Hall, D.T., and Lawrence, B.S. (1989). Generating new directions in career theory: The case for a transdisciplinary approach. In M.B. Arthur, D.T. Hall, and B.S. Lawrence (eds), *Handbook of Career Theory* (pp. 7–25). New York: Cambridge University Press.

Baruch, Y. (1998). The rise and fall of organizational commitment. *Human Systems Management*, 17(2), 135–143.

Baruch, Y. (2001). Employability: A substitute for loyalty. *Human Resource Development International*, 4(4), 543–566.

Baruch, Y., Grimland, S., and Vigoda-Gadot, E. (2014). Professional vitality and career success: Mediation, age and outcomes. *European Management Journal, 32*(3), 518–527.

Becker, T.E., Kernan, M.C., Clark, K.D., and Klein, H.J. (forthcoming). Dual commitments to organizations and professions: Different motivational pathways to productivity. *Journal of Management.* Available at http://jom. sagepub.com/content/early/2015/09/02/0149206315602532.full.pdf+html. DOI: 10.1177/0149206315602532.

Blau, G.J. (1985). The measurement and prediction of career commitment. *Journal of Occupational Psychology, 58*(4), 277–288.

Blau, G.J. (1988). Further exploring the meaning and measurement of career commitment. *Journal of Vocational Behavior, 32*(3), 284–297.

Blau, G.J. (1989). Testing the generalizability of a career commitment measure and its impact on employee turnover. *Journal of Vocational Behavior, 35,* 88–103.

Blau, G.J. (2001). On assessing the construct validity of two multidimensional constructs: Occupational commitment and occupational entrenchment. *Human Resource Management Review, 11*(3), 279–298.

Blau, G.J. (2003). Testing for a four-dimensional structure of occupational commitment. *Journal of Occupational and Organizational Psychology, 76*(4), 469–488.

Blau, G.J., and Holladay, B.E. (2006). Testing the discriminant validity of a four-dimensional occupational commitment measure. *Journal of Occupational and Organizational Psychology, 79*(4), 691–704.

Carless, S.A. and Bernath, L. (2007). Antecedents of intent to change careers among psychologists. *Journal of Career Development, 33*(3), 183–200.

Carson, K.D., Carson, P.P., and Bedeian, A.G. (1995). Development and construct validation of a career entrenchment measure. *Journal of Occupational and Organizational Psychology, 68*(4), 301–320.

Carson, K.D., Carson, P.P., Roe, C.W., Birkenmeir, B.J., and Phillips, J.S. (1999). Four commitment profiles and their relationships to empowerment, service recovery, and work attitudes. *Public Personnel Management, 28*(1), 1–13.

Carson, K.D., Carson, P.P., Roe, C.W., and Phillips, J.S. (1996). A career entrenchment model: Theoretical development and empirical outcomes. *Journal of Career Development, 22*(4), 273–286.

Chang, H.-T., Chi, N.-W., and Miao, M.-C. (2007). Testing the relationship between three-component organizational/occupational commitment and organizational/occupational turnover intention using a non-recursive model. *Journal of Vocational Behavior, 70*(2), 352–368.

Cooper-Hakim, A., and Viswesvaran, C. (2005). The construct of work commitment: Testing an integrative framework. *Psychological Bulletin, 131*(2), 241–259.

Emshoff, J.R. (1994). How to increase employee loyalty while you downsize. *Business Horizons, 37*(2), 49–57.

English, B. (2008). Climate for ethics and occupational–organisational commitment conflict. *Journal of Management Development, 27*(9), 963–975.

Fokkens-Bruinsma, M. and Canrinus, E.T. (2012). Adaptive and maladaptive motives for becoming a teacher. *Journal of Education for Teaching, 38*(1), 3–19.

Fokkens-Bruinsma, M. and Canrinus, E.T. (2015). Motivation and degree completion in a university-based teacher education programme. *Teaching Education, 26,* 1–14.

Gellatly, I.R., Meyer, J.P., and Luchak. A.A. (2006). Combined effects of the three commitment components on focal and discretionary behaviors: A test of Meyer and Herscovitch's propositions. *Journal of Vocational Behavior, 69*(2), 331–345.

Gouldner, A.W. (1957). Cosmopolitans and locals: Toward an analysis of latent social roles. *Administrative Science Quarterly, 68*(3), 281–306.

Greenhaus, J.H. (1987). *Career Management.* Hinsdale, IL: Dryden Press.

Hall, D.T. (1971). A theoretical model of career subidentity development in organizational settings. *Organizational Behavior and Human Performance, 6*(1), 50–76.

Hall, R.H. (1968). Professionalization and Bureaucratization. *American Sociological Review, 33*(1), 92–104.

Harvey, T. A. (2002). *Professional vitality and the principalship: A construct validity study.* University of Maine.

Higgins, E.T. (1998). Promotion and prevention: Regulatory focus as a motivational principle. *Advances in Experimental Social Psychology, 30,* 1–46.

Irving, P.G., Coleman, D.F., and Cooper, C.L. (1997). Further assessments of a three-component model of occupational commitment: Generalizability and differences across occupations. *Journal of Applied Psychology, 82*(3), 444–452.

Johnson, R.E., Chang, C.-H.D., and Yang, L.-Q. (2010). Commitment and motivation at work: The relevance of employee identity and regulatory focus. *Academy of Management Review, 35*(2), 226–245.

Jones, D.A. and McIntosh, B.R. (2010). Organizational and occupational commitment in relation to bridge employment and retirement intentions. *Journal of Vocational Behavior, 77*(2), 290–303.

Jørgensen, F. and Becker, K. (2014). Balancing organizational and professional commitments in professional service firms: The HR practices that matter. *International Journal of Human Resource Management, 26*(1), 23–41.

Kim, S.-W. and Mueller, C.W. (2011). Occupational and organizational commitment in different occupational contexts: The case of South Korea. *Work and Occupations*, *38*(1), 3–36.

Klassen, R.M. and Chiu, M.M. (2011). The occupational commitment and intention to quit of practicing and pre-service teachers: Influence of self-efficacy, job stress, and teaching context. *Contemporary Educational Psychology*, *36*(2), 114–129.

Knudsen, H.K., Roman, P.M., and Abraham, A.J. (2013). Quality of clinical supervision and counselor emotional exhaustion: The potential mediating roles of organizational and occupational commitment. *Journal of Substance Abuse Treatment*, *44*(5), 528–533.

Lawler, E.J. (1992). Affective attachments to nested groups: A choice-process theory. *American Sociological Review*, *57*(3), 327–339.

Lee, K., Carswell, J.J., and Allen, N.J. (2000). A meta-analytic review of occupational commitment: Relations with person- and work-related variables. *Journal of Applied Psychology*, *85*(5), 799–811.

Lin, S.-H., Huang, L.-C., Chang, C.-C., Lin, C.-S., Chang, P.-C., and Chen, P.-F. (2013). The role of person and organizational variables in the three component model of occupational commitment. *Canadian Journal of Administrative Sciences*, *30*(2), 115–126.

Madjar, N., Greenberg, E., and Chen, Z. (2011). Factors for radical creativity, incremental creativity, and routine, noncreative performance. *Journal of Applied Psychology*, *96*(4), 730–743.

Major, D.A., Morganson, V.J., and Bolen, H.M. (2013). Predictors of occupational and organizational commitment in information technology: Exploring gender differences and similarities. *Journal of Business and Psychology*, *28*(3), 301–314.

McAulay, B.J., Zeitz, G., and Blau, G. (2006). Testing a 'push–pull' theory of work commitment among organizational professionals. *Social Science Journal*, *43*(4), 571–596.

Meyer, J.P. (2009). Commitment in a changing world of work. In H.J. Klein, T.E. Becker, and J.P. Meyer (eds), *Commitment in Organizations: Accumulated Wisdom and New Directions* (pp. 37–68). New York: Routledge/ Taylor & Francis.

Meyer, J.P. and Allen, N.J. (1991). A three-component conceptualization of organizational commitment. *Human Resource Management Review*, *1*(1), 61–89.

Meyer, J.P. and Allen, N.J. (1997). *Commitment in the Workplace: Theory, Research, and Application*. Thousand Oaks, CA: Sage Publications.

Meyer, J.P., Allen, N.J., and Smith, C.A. (1993). Commitment to organizations and occupations: Extension and test of a three-component conceptualization. *Journal of Applied Psychology*, *78*(4), 538–551.

Meyer, J.P., Becker, T.E., and Vandenberghe, C. (2004). Employee commitment and motivation: A conceptual analysis and integrative model. *Journal of Applied Psychology*, *89*(6), 991–1007.

Meyer, J.P., Becker, T.E., and Van Dick, R. (2006). Social identities and commitments at work: Toward an integrative model. *Journal of Organizational Behavior*, *27*(5), 665–683.

Meyer, J.P. and Herscovitch, L. (2001). Commitment in the workplace: Toward a general model. *Human Resource Management Review*, *11*(3), 299–326.

Meyer, J.P. and Maltin, E.R. (2010). Employee commitment and well-being: A critical review, theoretical framework and research agenda. *Journal of Vocational Behavior*, *77*(2), 323–337.

Meyer, J.P., Stanley, D.J., Herscovitch, L., and Topolnytsky, L. (2002). Affective, continuance, and normative commitment to the organization: A meta-analysis of antecedents, correlates, and consequences. *Journal of Vocational Behavior*, *61*(1), 20–52.

Meyer, J.P., Stanley, L.J., and Parfyonova, N.M. (2012). Employee commitment in context: The nature and implication of commitment profiles. *Journal of Vocational Behavior*, *80*(1), 1–16.

Meyer, J.P., Stanley, L.J., and Vandenberghe, R.J. (2013). A person-centered approach to the study of commitment. *Human Resource Management Review*, *23*(2), 190–202.

Morin, A.J.S., Meyer, J.P., McInerney, D.M., Marsh, H.W., and Ganotice, F.A. (2015). Profiles of dual commitment to the occupation and organization: Relations to well-being and turnover intentions. *Asia Pacific Journal of Management*, *32*, 717–744.

Morin, A.J.S., Morizot, J., Boudrias, J.-S., and Madore, I. (2011). A multifoci person-centered perspective on workplace affective commitment: A latent profile/factor mixture analysis. *Organizational Research Methods*, *14*(1), 58–90.

Osinsky, P. and Mueller, C.W. (2004). Professional commitment of Russian provincial specialists. *Work and Occupations*, *31*(2), 193–224.

Reichers, A.E. (1985). A review and reconceptualization of organizational commitment. *Academy of Management Review*, *10*(3), 465–476.

Reilly, N.P. (1994). Exploring a paradox: Commitment as a moderator of the stressor-burnout relationship. *Journal of Applied Social Psychology*, *24*(5), 397–414.

Ryan, R.M. and Deci, E.L. (2000). Self-determination theory and the facilitation of intrinsic motivation, social development, and well-being. *American Psychologist*, *55*(1), 68–78.

Snape, E. and Redman, T. (2003). An evaluation of a three-component model of occupational commitment:

Dimensionality and consequences among United Kingdom human resource management specialists. *Journal of Applied Psychology*, *88*(1), 152–159.

Somers, M.J. and Birnbaum, D. (2000). Exploring the relationship between commitment profiles and work attitudes, employee withdrawal, and job performance. *Public Personnel Management*, *29*(3), 353–366.

Swart, J., Kinnie, N., van Rossenberg, Y., and Yalabik, Z.Y. (2014). Why should I share my knowledge? A multiple foci of commitment perspective. *Human Resource Management Journal*, *24*(3), 269–289.

Tajfel, H. and Turner, J.C. (1985). The social identity theory of intergroup behavior. In S. Worchel and W.G. Austin (eds), *Psychology of Intergroup Relations* (pp. 7–24). Chicago, IL: Nelson-Hall.

Tsoumbris, P. and Xenikou, A. (2010). Commitment profiles: The configural effect of the forms and foci of commitment on work outcomes. *Journal of Vocational Behavior*, *77*(3), 401–411.

Van Maanen, J. and Barley, S.R. (1984). Occupational communities: Culture and control in organizations. *Research in Organizational Behaviour*, *6*, 287–365.

Wallace, J.E. (1993). Professional and organizational commitment: Compatible or incompatible? *Journal of Vocational Behavior*, *42*(3), 333–349.

Wallace, J.E. (1995). Organizational and professional commitment in professional and nonprofessional organizations. *Administrative Science Quarterly*, *40*(2), 228–255.

Wasti, S.A. (2005). Commitment profiles: Combinations of organizational commitment forms and job outcomes. *Journal of Vocational Behavior*, *67*(2), 290–308.

Weng, Q. and McElroy, J.C. (2012). Organizational career growth, affective occupational commitment and turnover intentions. *Journal of Vocational Behavior*, *80*(2), 256–265.

Yeh, Y.-J.Y., Ko, J.-J.R., Chang, Y.-S., and Chen, C.-H.V. (2007). Job stress and work attitudes between temporary and permanently employed nurses. *Stress and Health*, *23*(2), 111–120.

Yousaf, A., Sanders, K., and Shipton, H. (2013). Proactive and politically skilled professionals: What is the relationship with affective occupational commitment? *Asia Pacific Journal of Management*, *30*(1), 211–230.

11. Social commitments
Christian Vandenberghe

The objective of this chapter is to review and integrate empirical research on social commitments, which are defined as commitments to the exchange partners employees are in contact with while completing their tasks in the workplace. They encompass commitment to supervisors (SUPC), teams and workgroups (TEAMC), and customers (CUSTC). I first review accumulated evidence regarding the antecedents and consequences of these commitments. I then review evidence regarding interaction effects among social commitments. Next, I report and comment on an integrated model of social commitments at the team and individual levels of analysis.

Research on social commitments has generally focused on the affective component of commitment. A component reflects a rationale used by the employee to make sense of their relationship with the organization: 'affective commitment' involves an emotional rationale, 'normative commitment' an obligation-based rationale, and 'continuance commitment' a cost-based rationale (Chapter 3 in this volume). A few attempts have nonetheless addressed multiple components as related to SUPC (e.g., Becker, 1992; Becker et al., 1996; Becker and Kernan, 2003; Chan et al., 2011; Clugston et al., 2000; Landry and Vandenberghe, 2009, 2012; Landry et al., 2014; Stinglhamber et al., 2002; Wasti and Can, 2008), TEAMC (Becker and Kernan, 2003; Chan et al., 2011; Clugston et al., 2000; Stinglhamber et al., 2002; Vandenberghe et al., 2001; Wasti and Can, 2008), and CUSTC (Stinglhamber et al., 2002; Valéau et al., 2013; Vandenberghe et al., 2007).

While some of the above studies have reported evidence that non-affective social commitments incrementally predict organizational turnover intentions (Valéau et al., 2013) and service performance (Stinglhamber et al., 2002), there are simply not enough findings accumulated that would provide a case for a viable model including multiple foci and components of social commitments. Moreover, researchers need to answer the question as to whether, for instance, the three-component model (Meyer and Allen, 1991) is applicable to social commitments, and hence determine whether affective, continuance, and normative components have isomorphic meaning across targets and reflect bonds that are similar to what they refer to when applied to the organization. Therefore, this chapter essentially addresses research on affective social commitments.

ANTECEDENTS AND CONSEQUENCES OF SOCIAL COMMITMENTS

Commitment to Supervisors

Redundancy of antecedents with organizational commitment
As the supervisor formally acts on behalf of the organization (Eisenberger et al., 2002), one can expect the antecedents of organizational commitment (ORGC) to be associated

to some extent to SUPC as well. Several studies support this contention. Indeed, some predictors that are inherently tied to the organization's actions towards employees have been found to relate to SUPC. For example, organization-focused procedural, informational, and interpersonal justice dimensions were reported to correlate positively with SUPC (Liao and Rupp, 2005). Similarly, perceived organizational support (POS) has been reported to relate positively (Stinglhamber and Vandenberghe, 2003), and organizational cynicism negatively (Neves, 2012), to SUPC. In a time-lagged study of newcomers, Lapointe et al. (2013) also found psychological contract breach to be negatively related to SUPC.

Relationship with the supervisor and individual differences as specific antecedents
Empirical research has also identified antecedents that were more specific to SUPC. For instance, leader–member exchange (LMX) was found to be a positive predictor of SUPC (Vandenberghe et al., 2004). Relatedly, in a study involving Taiwanese organizations, van Vianen et al. (2011) found that employee perceptions of subjective person–supervisor fit positively predicted SUPC. Moreover, LMX mediated the positive relationship between both employee and supervisor perceptions of subjective person–supervisor fit and SUPC. Likewise, an individual-level measure of collectivism was found to be positively related to SUPC (Clugston et al., 2000). In a Turkish context, Wasti and Can (2008) found satisfaction with the supervisor and empowerment to be positively associated with SUPC. Other studies found perceived supervisor support to act as an antecedent of SUPC (Neves, 2012; Stinglhamber and Vandenberghe, 2003). Finally, an emerging line of research has looked at the relationships between SUPC and individual traits. For instance, positive affectivity has been shown to be positively, and negative affectivity negatively, related to SUPC (Clugston et al., 2000; Den Hartog and Belschak, 2007), while the 'big-five' trait of extraversion has been reported to be positively, and Machiavellianism negatively, related to SUPC (Zettler et al., 2011).

Incremental prediction of job performance and extra-role behavior
Much more research has been conducted on SUPC's consequences. Becker's (1992) study represents a pioneering work that demonstrated for the first time that the supervisor, as a source of commitment among other internal foci, predicted attitudinal (that is, job satisfaction and turnover intention) and behavioral (for example, altruism and conscientiousness) outcomes, over and above ORGC. Since then, other studies have consistently shown that SUPC accounts for unique variance in supervisor-rated job performance (Askew et al., 2013; Becker et al., 1996; Becker and Kernan, 2003; Chen et al., 2002; Cheng et al., 2003; Landry and Vandenberghe, 2012; Redman and Snape, 2005; Vandenberghe et al., 2004) and objective job performance (Siders et al., 2001), over and above ORGC.

Similarly, SUPC has been found to be predictive of discretionary or organizational citizenship behavior (OCB), most of the time incremental to ORGC. Considering only supervisor ratings, SUPC has been positively associated with prosocial behavior (Becker, 1992), altruism (Becker, 1992; Snape et al., 2006), conscientiousness (Becker, 1992; Chen et al., 2002; Snape et al., 2006), non-idleness (Becker, 1992), OCB directed toward the group (Askew et al., 2013; Bentein et al., 2002), OCB directed toward the supervisor (Askew et al., 2013; Wasti and Can, 2008), OCB directed toward the organization (Askew et al., 2013; Morin et al., 2011; Redman and Snape, 2005), OCB directed toward customers (Morin et al., 2011), OCB directed toward individuals (Redman and Snape, 2005), sportsmanship (Redman and Snape, 2005), courtesy (Becker and Kernan, 2003), general OCB (Cheng et al., 2003), boosterism (that is, a form of OCB; Chen et al., 2002), interpersonal facilitation (Law et al., 2004; Snape et al., 2006), job dedication (Law et al., 2004), identification with the company (Snape et al., 2006), protecting the company resources (Snape et al., 2006), and extra-role performance (Neves, 2012).

Incremental prediction of job attitudes, strain, and withdrawal propensity
Finally, controlling for ORGC, a number of studies found positive associations of SUPC with job satisfaction (Becker, 1992; Chen, 2001; Cheng et al., 2003) and work engagement (Chughtai, 2013), and negative associations between SUPC and organizational withdrawal cognitions (Askew et al., 2013; Becker, 1992; Chan et al., 2006; Chen, 2001; Cheng et al., 2003; Snape et al., 2006; Stinglhamber et al., 2002; Vandenberghe and Bentein, 2009; Vandenberghe et al., 2004) and union withdrawal cognitions (Chan et al., 2006). SUPC has also been shown to be negatively associated with task and relational conflicts with the supervisor (Landry and Vandenberghe, 2009) as well as employee job stress (Wasti and Can, 2008). Finally, a handful of studies have reported a negative association between SUPC and turnover, controlling for ORGC (Stinglhamber and Vandenberghe, 2003; Vandenberghe and Bentein, 2009; Vandenberghe et al., forthcoming).

Concluding remarks
One conclusion that can be drawn from the findings reported above is that the pattern of relationships between SUPC and presumed antecedents and consequences does not follow a perfect target similarity framework (Lavelle et al., 2007). For instance, SUPC has antecedents reflecting the organization's actions toward employees (that is, justice, support, psychological contract breach, or organizational cynicism) but also has specific antecedents that refer to value-based predictors, LMX, or individual difference variables. Similarly, SUPC has consequences that are of relevance not only to the supervisor, but also to the organization, co-workers, and customers. This is likely due to the fact that the supervisor is a central referent in the employee's exchange network and that the supervisor role involves promoting the employee's contributions to a variety of constituencies. For example, the supervisor may be rewarded for preventing their employees from leaving the organization.

Commitment to Co-Workers, the Workgroup, or Team

In this section, I will consider commitment to co-workers, workgroups, and teams (TEAMC) as being interchangeable, essentially because researchers have not provided a framework that allows distinguishing between these types of commitment.

Team-level studies: structural and relational characteristics as antecedents and team performance criteria as outcomes
At the team level, TEAMC has been positively linked to team empowerment (Kirkman and Rosen, 1999), goal-setting structure in a virtual-team context (Huang et al., 2002), teams' learning orientation (Porter, 2005), teams' performance orientation, particularly under high task performance conditions (Porter, 2005), team diversity and reflexiv-

ity (Schippers et al., 2003), leader emphasis on teamwork and perceived team support (Pearce and Herbik, 2004), and team virtuousness (Rego et al., 2013).

In terms of outcomes, if one retains only externally rated outcomes, team-level commitment has been associated with increased team innovativeness (West and Wallace, 1991), team-level productivity, proactivity, and customer service (Kirkman and Rosen, 1999), team performance and team learning (van der Vegt and Bunderson, 2005), and team citizenship behavior (Pearce and Herbik, 2004). Moreover, team-level commitment has been linked to decreased team anti-social behavior (Pearce and Giacalone, 2003).

Individual-level studies: perceived social relations and task structure, and individual differences as antecedents

More studies have been conducted on TEAMC measured as an individual-level variable. In terms of antecedents, TEAMC has been reported to be positively linked to task interdependence (Bishop and Scott, 2000; de Jong and Bal, 2014; Jehn et al., 1999; van der Vegt et al., 2000) (particularly under high outcome interdependence; van der Vegt et al., 2000), job complexity (van der Vegt et al., 2000), asymmetrical task dependence under high task interdependence conditions (de Jong and Bal, 2014), extraversion (Zettler et al., 2011), perceived team support (Bishop et al., 2000; Bishop et al., 2005; Howes et al., 2000), teamwork processes (Park et al., 2005), intersender conflict (that is, 'incompatible requests from two or more people'; Bishop and Scott, 2000), satisfaction with co-workers (Bishop and Scott, 2000; Wasti and Can, 2008), group value-based fit (Seong and Kristof-Brown, 2012), procedural fairness of the workgroup (Lavelle et al., 2009), perceived group cohesiveness (Vandenberghe et al., 2004; Zaccaro and Dobbins, 1989), task-liking (Zaccaro and Dobbins, 1989), work group social interaction (Heffner and Rentsch, 2001), individualized collectivism (Clugston et al., 2000), training opportunities (Wasti and Can, 2008), empowerment (Wasti and Can, 2008), media richness and cognitive style (that is, preference for working in groups, structured work, and abstract information) in the context of virtual teams (Workman et al., 2003), unit-level team-member exchange (Liu et al., 2011), high-status job title (Lucas, 1999), prior overtime work (Ellemers et al., 1998), and leader's attention and leader climate strength (Sanders et al., 2011). TEAMC has also been found to be negatively related to informational dissimilarity when there was incongruence between task and goal interdependence (van der Vegt et al., 2003), value diversity and relationship conflict (Jehn et al., 1999), and Machiavellianism (Zettler et al., 2011).

Individual-level studies: job performance and extra-role behavior, and withdrawal propensity as specific outcomes

In terms of outcomes, controlling for ORGC, individual-level TEAMC has been reported to positively predict a variety of work behaviors, as rated by supervisors: general OCB (Bishop et al., 2000), job performance (Bishop et al., 2000; Seong and Kristof-Brown, 2012), contextual and overall performance (Ellemers et al., 1998), altruism (Cohen, 2006), OCB directed towards co-workers and customers (Morin et al., 2011), and self-initiative, that is, a disposition towards proactive behavior (Den Hartog and Belschak, 2007); self-rated work behaviors: extra-role behavior (Lee and Olshfski, 2002), OCB directed toward individuals (Lavelle et al., 2009), helping and loyal behavior (van der Vegt et al., 2003), job performance (van Steenbergen and Ellemers, 2009), altruism (Chan et al., 2006;

Chan et al., 2011; Redman and Snape, 2005), conscientiousness (Chan et al., 2006), civic virtue (Redman and Snape, 2005), union citizenship behavior targeted at individuals and organization (Chan et al., 2006), intention to share knowledge (Liu et al., 2011), intention to help co-workers (Ellemers et al., 1998), self-initiative (Den Hartog and Belschak, 2007); and peer-rated OCB directed toward individuals (Lavelle et al., 2009). In one study, controlling for ORGC, TEAMC was found to be positively related to organizational turnover intentions (Askew et al., 2013). Controlling for ORGC, TEAMC has also been reported to be negatively related to organizational withdrawal cognitions (Snape et al., 2006) and intended and actual internal mobility (van Steenbergen and Ellemers, 2009). One study also reported a negative association between TEAMC and supervisor-rated job performance (Redman and Snape, 2005), controlling for ORGC. This finding may be due to respondents in that study working individually.

Concluding remarks
The evidence reviewed above tends to suggest that TEAMC can operate at both the team and the individual level. At the team level, TEAMC's processes seem compatible with a team effectiveness framework where structural inputs lead to group processes (that is, emerging states, including TEAMC), and ultimately team outcomes (Mathieu et al., 2008). At the individual level, TEAMC seems to be generated by individual perceptions of the environment (for example, task characteristics) and would lead to both focal (for example, job performance) and discretionary (for example, OCB) behaviors.

Commitment to Customers

Service performance and organizational turnover intention as specific outcomes
Little research has addressed CUSTC. The few studies that examined CUSTC looked at the potential consequences of CUSTC using an individual level of analysis. For instance, Siders et al. (2001) found that CUSTC predicted job performance criteria that had relevance to and were rewarded by customers, namely market share and product breadth. In a sample of hospital nurses, Stinglhamber et al. (2002) found CUSTC to be positively associated with organizational turnover intention, controlling for ORGC components. In another study, Vandenberghe et al. (2007) found that, controlling for ORGC components, CUSTC was positively related to customer-rated service performance (self-presentation and helping behavior). Similarly, controlling for ORGC, Morin et al. (2011) found that CUSTC was positively linked to supervisor-rated OCB directed towards co-workers and customers. Redman and Snape (2005), also controlling for ORGC, reported CUSTC to be positively related to supervisor- and self-rated customer service, and to self-rated conscientiousness and civic virtue. Finally, in a study of multiple commitments among volunteers, Valéau et al. (2013) reported normative commitment to service recipients to be negatively related to organizational turnover intention, over and above OC components.

These results tend to demonstrate that CUSTC is particularly predictive of outcomes that are reflective of the customer's perspective (Siders et al., 2001; Vandenberghe et al., 2007). These findings seem compatible with 'choice-process theory' (Lawler, 1992), which predicts that local attachments foster positive emotions because they strengthen individuals' sense of control over their environment, and ultimately influence their behavior. Morin et al.'s (2011) and Redman and Snape's (2005) findings further demonstrate that CUSTC's effects on customer service and OCB are observable by supervisors as well. The question arises however as to whether CUSTC's workings are entirely compatible with the organization's priorities. For instance, Stinglhamber et al. (2002) reported a positive association between CUSTC and organizational turnover intention in a sample of nurses, which can be explained by the fact that hospitals' top management is often perceived to prioritize resource efficiency at the expense of service quality, resulting in nurses with high CUSTC willing to leave the organization.

Lack of research on the antecedents of commitment to customers

Virtually no research has addressed CUSTC's antecedents. Although speculative at this point, several variables would be worth investigating as drivers of, or obstacles to, CUSTC. For instance, given what we know of the psychology of POS (Eisenberger et al., 2002), and following a target similarity framework (Lavelle et al., 2007), it would make sense to expect support from customers (as expressed through supportive words and communication, or praise for good service and help given) to increase employees' CUSTC. Similarly, customer orientation, which is an individual difference variable reflecting an employee's willingness to meet customers' expectations and needs (Allen et al., 2010), has been subjected to much research, particularly in respect to its contribution to customer satisfaction. As such, it seems reasonable to expect customer orientation to act upon customer satisfaction through fostering service contact employees' CUSTC. Customer orientation has also been used to characterize a firm's practice that 'emphasizes, in multiple ways, meeting customer needs and expectations for service quality' (Schneider et al., 1998, p. 153). Customer orientation defined this way has been treated as a central component of a 'climate for service' (Schneider et al., 1998). I would thus propose that climate for service is a unit-level variable that is positively related to employees' CUSTC.

On the other hand, following a social exchange perspective (Cropanzano and Mitchell, 2005), the quality of employee–customer exchange relationships (which can be defined, following the words of Liden et al., 1993, p. 662, as the extent to which the relationship is 'characterized by mutual trust, respect, liking, and mutual influence') should be positively related to CUSTC. Finally, CUSTC may also be negatively affected by customer incivility, aggression, and mistreatment, all of them being liable to induce interpersonal injustice perceptions (Skarlicki et al., 2008), ultimately reducing CUSTC. Although this may suggest that CUSTC is customer-specific, it remains that social exchange relations between employees and customers are not disconnected from the exchanges with the organization, as employees' relationships to customers are exerted in the name and context of the organization. Hence, some interdependence may exist between ORGC and CUSTC.

INTERACTION EFFECTS INVOLVING SOCIAL COMMITMENTS

A few studies have examined interactions involving social commitments. Following Johnson et al. (2009), interactions among commitments can display different patterns, that is, 'compensatory', 'synergistic', and 'competitive'. A compensatory interaction occurs when being high on one commitment is sufficient to bring about the outcome (whatever the level on the other commitment). A synergistic interaction accounts for situations where two commitments have multiplicative effects on the outcome of interest (that is, they combine their effects synergistically). Finally, a competitive interaction describes situations where two commitments display incompatible effects, which may happen among commitments directed towards constituencies that have competing values.

Vandenberghe and Bentein (2009) found that affective SUPC interacted with affective ORGC such that it was more strongly and negatively associated with intended and actual turnover under conditions of low ORGC, illustrating a compensatory form of interaction between the two dimensions. Similarly, Snape et al. (2006) showed that affective SUPC was a stronger positive predictor of two dimensions of OCB rated by supervisors, protecting company resources and interpersonal harmony, when affective TEAMC was low, again revealing a compensatory form of interaction between the two commitments. In a time-lagged study of newcomers, Lapointe et al. (2013) found that affective ORGC was more strongly and negatively related to subsequent turnover intention and emotional exhaustion when employees experienced low affective SUPC. Likewise, Valéau et al. (2013) found that affective and normative commitments to service recipients were more negatively related to organizational turnover intention when affective ORGC was low. In another study, Landry and Vandenberghe (2012) reported that affective SUPC was more strongly and positively related to supervisor-rated performance when the supervisor reported low affective, normative, and continuance (sacrificed investments subdimension) commitments to the employee.

Finally, one study (Vandenberghe, 2015) reported interactions that pertained to two different patterns described by Johnson et al. (2009). Specifically, normative ORGC was more negatively related to turnover when affective TEAMC was high, while few alternatives commitment (that is, a subdimension of continuance commitment) was more negatively related to turnover when continuance commitment to the group was high (that is, a synergistic model of interactions). In contrast, normative ORGC was more strongly and negatively associated with turnover when normative TEAMC was low (that is, a pattern consistent with the compensatory model).

In sum, the evidence accumulated thus far seems to suggest that components of social commitments and ORGC are likely tied through a compensatory mechanism, whereby one commitment can compensate for the weakness of another. Moreover, although evidence in support for the compensatory model has accrued in regard to prediction of focal attitudes and behaviors (for example, withdrawal cognitions, turnover, and job performance; e.g., Landry and Vandenberghe, 2012; Vandenberghe and Bentein, 2009), as was proposed by Johnson et al. (2009), there is also evidence that the prediction of discretionary behaviors (OCB; Snape et al., 2006) and health-related outcomes (emotional exhaustion; Lapointe et al., 2013) is sensitive to compensatory mechanisms among commitments. A next step in this research would be to determine whether compensatory processes vary across components of commitment.

A GENERAL FRAMEWORK OF SOCIAL COMMITMENTS' ANTECEDENTS AND OUTCOMES

A general model of social commitments at the unit level is proposed in Figure 11.1 while a general model of individual-level social commitments is represented in Figure 11.2.

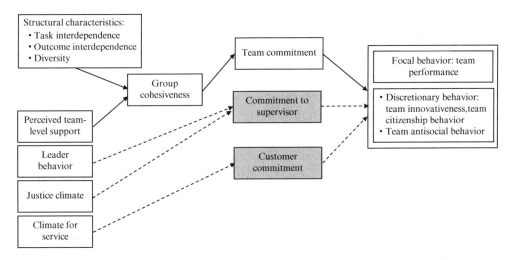

Figure 11.1 A general model of unit-level social commitments

Given the scarcity of research on multiple components of social commitments, the two figures focus only on the affective component of SUPC, TEAMC, and CUSTC. I developed these models from several considerations. First, the two models incorporate and summarize the major antecedents and outcomes that have been identified in the social commitments literature, as reviewed above. Second, additional constructs and paths were incorporated in the models based on related research and/or for theoretical reasons. For example, SUPC and CUSTC are added as unit-level commitments in Figure 11.1 while empirical evidence regarding their validity is lacking (for this reason, the boxes for these constructs appear in grey). Despite this, I argue that these constructs make sense and can emerge through social information processing. Links in the models that have not been investigated but make theoretical sense, or that need more supportive evidence, appear as dotted lines (see Figures 11.1 and 11.2). Third, an assumption is made that social commitments do not necessarily operate in the same manner at the unit and individual level of analysis. For example, at the team level, models of team effectiveness such as Mathieu et al.'s (2008) inputs–processes–outputs framework can be used to build a viable model including both the antecedents and the outcomes of social commitments. At the individual level, the model differs, essentially because it is based on individual perceptions of the environment, individual difference variables, value fit components, and specific exchange relationships with supervisors and customers.

Team-Level Social Commitments

Regarding the team-level model of social commitments (Figure 11.1), I make the assumption that SUPC, TEAMC, and CUSTC can all be aggregated at the team level owing to the operation of social information processing (Salancik and Pfeffer, 1978) within teams. Although aggregating individual commitment data at the unit level has rarely been done in the past, evidence has been reported that ORGC can be shared among employees working for the same business units (Harter et al., 2002) and firms (Gong et al., 2009).

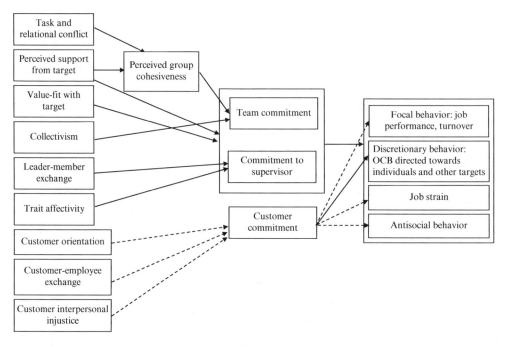

Figure 11.2   A general model of individual-level social commitments

On the side of antecedents of team-level commitment, Figure 11.1 includes structural characteristics of teams such as task interdependence (e.g., Jehn et al., 1999) and outcome interdependence (van der Vegt et al., 2000) as positive predictors, and diversity (in terms of demographics and skills; e.g., Schippers et al., 2003) as a negative predictor, of team cohesiveness, which in turn positively influences TEAMC. Following Mathieu et al.'s (2008) inputs–processes–outputs framework, the three structural characteristics would act as inputs impacting team cohesiveness (that is, a process variable or emerging state) because they facilitate the interpersonal aspects of team functioning (DeChurch and Mesmer-Magnus, 2010). Team cohesiveness would then induce a sense of collective belonging to the team, as expressed through TEAMC. Perceived team support is another antecedent that positively relates to team cohesiveness and through it to TEAMC. Although team support has been essentially studied at the individual level (e.g., Bishop and Scott, 2000; Bishop et al., 2000), there is evidence that support perceptions can aggregate at the group level (Vandenberghe et al., 2007).

SUPC at the team level would have two specific antecedents: leader behavior and justice climate. Leader behavior would represent a climate variable indicating that a leader provides consistent attention (task-oriented and supportive leadership; Sanders et al., 2011) to members of the team such that team-level affective SUPC would naturally ensue. Similarly, supervisor-focused procedural and interpersonal justice climates have been shown to positively predict individual-level SUPC (Liao and Rupp, 2005). Assuming that SUPC can aggregate at the group level, one may speculate that these climates also positively impact team-level SUPC. Finally, climate for service would be an antecedent unique to team-level CUSTC. Climate for service refers to shared perceptions among employees regarding the practices, procedures, and behaviors that support and reward service to customers (Schneider et al., 1998). Such a climate should provide the motivational impetus for a team-level CUSTC.

On the side of consequences, team-level social commitments should relate positively to team performance (that is, a focal behavior for social commitments), which could refer to attainment of group goals, service quality as assessed by customers, or service perform-ance. Moreover, one can expect team-level social commitments to contribute positively to discretionary behaviors such as team innovativeness (West and Wallace, 1991) and team citizenship behavior (Pearce and Herbik, 2004). In addition, team-level social commit-ments should reduce the occurrence of team anti-social behavior (Pearce and Giacalone, 2003) as all of these commitments should facilitate the emergence of positive interper-sonal relationships and cooperative behaviors among teammates.

Individual-Level Social Commitments

Figure 11.2 depicts a model of social commitments at the individual level. As regards TEAMC, two antecedents are thought to indirectly relate to it through perceived group cohesiveness, namely task and relational conflict (Bishop and Scott, 2000; Jehn et al., 1999) and perceived team support (Bishop and Scott, 2000; Bishop et al., 2000; Howes et al., 2000). These variables are defined as antecedents at the individual level because there is likely much variance in the exposure to task conflict across individuals, as a function of the nature of their work, and in perceptions of support, which partly depend on individuals' perceptual biases. Perceived group cohesiveness would be a more proximal determinant of TEAMC (Vandenberghe et al., 2004; Zaccaro and Dobbins, 1989) because both constructs speak to interpersonal aspects of attachment to co-workers. Note that perceived team support may also exert a direct effect on TEAMC as both constructs' theoretical basis indicates a social exchange relationship (Cropanzano and Mitchell, 2005; Lavelle et al., 2007) that has little in common with perceived group cohesiveness. Group value-based fit (Seong and Kristof-Brown, 2012) and individual-ized collectivism (Clugston et al., 2000) represent two additional antecedents that have direct effects on TEAMC. Value fit with the group is thought to influence TEAMC because it instills a sense of closeness to and identification with the group, while the influence of collectivism may be understood as a sense of openness to the group's well-being. As these variables inherently address individuals' own psychological standing with regard to their group, their influence should not be mediated by perceived group cohesiveness.

Value fit (van Vianen et al., 2011) with and perceived support (Neves, 2012; Stinglhamber and Vandenberghe, 2003) from the supervisor are thought to act as ante-cedents of SUPC. As argued above, value fit likely exerts its effect on SUPC because it creates a sense of closeness to and identification with the target, while perceived supervisor support presumptively predicts SUPC because it induces a social exchange relationship with the supervisor. Similarly, LMX, which also indicates the operation of a social exchange relationship in the employee–supervisor dyad (Liden et al., 1993) and has demonstrated differentiation within teams (Henderson et al., 2008), is expected to lead to increased SUPC (Vandenberghe et al., 2004). Finally, trait positive and negative affectivity should be, respectively, positively and negatively associated with SUPC (Clugston et al., 2000; Den Hartog and Belschak, 2007) as both traits have an affective underpinning that is likely involved in the emergence of emotional attachment to specific individuals such as supervisors.

The identification of antecedents to CUSTC is speculative at this point, given the dearth of research in this area. First, customer orientation (Allen et al., 2010) should positively relate to CUSTC. Such disposition likely expresses a fundamental need of the individual to view self-development as being tied to serving others. As such, customer orientation may be closely related to a prosocial or other-orientation that drives behavior benefiting others. The other two proposed predictors of CUSTC are indicators of a social exchange relationship between the customer and the service provider. Customer–employee exchange would qualify a relationship with the customer that is based on respect, mutual trust, and liking. Such exchange is similar in nature to what LMX refers to within employee–supervisor dyads (Liden et al., 1993). This may happen particularly in relationship service contexts, which characterize situations where the service takes place within an enduring relationship allowing the partners to get to know each other over time (for example, financial services provided in bank branches). Finally, customer interpersonal injustice would happen when the customer engages in aggressive behavior toward the service provider (Skarlicki et al., 2008), which would result in lower CUSTC.

All three social commitments would lead to focal behavior, such as higher job performance and a lower propensity to leave the supervisor (SUPC), the work-group (TEAMC), or the customer service job (CUSTC). In addition, these commitments are likely to foster discretionary behavior, such as OCB directed towards supervisors (SUPC), co-workers (TEAMC), and customers (CUSTC). However, as the research reviewed above suggests, there might be spillover effects on OCB towards other foci (including the organization). Finally, social commitments may be associated with fewer health-related symptoms (Landry et al., 2014; Wasti and Can, 2008) and reduced antisocial behavior (Pearce and Giacalone, 2003).

CONCLUSION

Research has provided evidence that social commitments are linked to distinguishable antecedents and incrementally predict a variety of outcomes, over and above the effects of ORGC. Based on extant research and theoretical arguments, a unit-level model and an individual-level model of social commitments are proposed. These models depict only partial homology in the nomological network of social commitments across levels. Past research has also largely focused on the affective component of social commitments. Therefore, additional work is needed to clarify the role that other components of commitment (for example, continuance, normative) might play in the enactment of social commitments. For example, affective ORGC may create continuance TEAMC because work teams are nested within the organization. It is also worth noting that the study of antecedents to CUSTC is virtually non-existent. Inquiry in this area is obviously warranted in order to further establish CUSTC's discriminant validity. Finally, the emergence of research on interaction effects among social commitments is promising and supports the relevance of a compensatory model of interactions across foci and components. Additional research is, however, needed in order to more firmly establish the relevance of social commitments in the workplace.

REFERENCES

Allen, J., Pugh, D., Grandey, A., and Groth, M. (2010). Following display rules in good or bad faith? Customer orientation as a moderator of the display rule-emotional labor relationship. *Human Performance*, *23*, 101–115.

Askew, K., Taing, M.U., and Johnson, R.E. (2013). The effects of commitment to multiple foci: An analysis of relative influence and interactions. *Human Performance*, *26*, 171–190.

Becker, T.E. (1992). Foci and bases of commitment: Are they distinctions worth making? *Academy of Management Journal*, *35*, 232–244.

Becker, T.E., Billings, R.S., Eveleth, D.M., and Gilbert, N.L. (1996). Foci and bases of employee commitment: Implications for job performance. *Academy of Management Journal*, *39*, 464–482.

Becker, T.E. and Kernan, M. (2003). Matching commitment to supervisors and organizations to in-role and extra-role performance. *Human Performance*, *16*, 327–348.

Bentein, K., Stinglhamber, F., and Vandenberghe, C. (2002). Organization-, supervisor-, and workgroup-directed commitments and citizenship behaviours: A comparison of models. *European Journal of Work and Organizational Psychology*, *11*, 341–362.

Bishop, J.W. and Scott, K.D. (2000). An examination of organizational and team commitment in a self-directed team environment. *Journal of Applied Psychology*, *85*, 439–450.

Bishop, J.W., Scott, K.D., and Burroughs, S.M. (2000). Support, commitment, and employee outcomes in a team environment. *Journal of Management*, *26*, 1113–1132.

Bishop, J.W., Scott, K.D., Goldsby, M.G., and Cropanzano, R. (2005). A construct validity study of commitment and perceived support variables: A multifoci approach across different team environments. *Group and Organization Management*, *30*, 153–180.

Chan, A., Snape, E., and Redman, T. (2011). Multiple foci and bases of commitment in a Chinese workforce. *International Journal of Human Resource Management*, *22*, 3290–3304.

Chan, A.W., Tong-qing, F., Redman, T., and Snape, E. (2006). Evaluating the multi-dimensional view of employee commitment: A comparative UK-Chinese study. *International Journal of Human Resource Management*, *17*, 1873–1887.

Chen, Z. (2001). Further investigation of the outcomes of loyalty to supervisor: Job satisfaction and intention to stay. *Journal of Managerial Psychology*, *16*, 650–660.

Chen, Z.X., Tsui, A.S., and Farh, J.-L. (2002). Loyalty to supervisor vs. organizational commitment: Relationships to employee performance in China. *Journal of Occupational and Organizational Psychology*, *75*, 339–356.

Cheng, B.-S., Jiang, D.-Y., and Riley, J.H. (2003). Organizational commitment, supervisory commitment, and employee outcomes in the Chinese context: Proximal hypothesis or global hypothesis? *Journal of Organizational Behavior*, *24*, 313–334.

Chughtai, A.A. (2013). Linking affective commitment to supervisor to work outcomes. *Journal of Managerial Psychology*, *28*, 606–627.

Clugston, M., Howell, J.P., and Dorfman, P.W. (2000). Does cultural socialization predict multiple bases and foci of commitment? *Journal of Management*, *26*, 5–30.

Cohen, A. (2006). The relationship between multiple commitments and organizational citizenship behavior in Arab and Jewish culture. *Journal of Vocational Behavior*, *69*, 105–118.

Cropanzano, R. and Mitchell, M.S. (2005). Social exchange theory: An interdisciplinary review. *Journal of Management*, *31*, 874–900.

DeChurch, L.A. and Mesmer-Magnus, J.R. (2010). The cognitive underpinnings of effective teamwork: A meta-analysis. *Journal of Applied Psychology*, *95*, 32–53.

de Jong, S.B. and Bal, P.M. (2014). How asymmetrical task dependence and task interdependence interact. *Journal of Managerial Psychology*, *29*, 1115–1132.

Den Hartog, D.N. and Belschak, F.D. (2007). Personal initiative, commitment and affect at work. *Journal of Occupational and Organizational Psychology*, *80*, 601–622.

Eisenberger, R., Stinglhamber, F., Vandenberghe, C., Sucharski, I., and Rhoades, L. (2002). Perceived supervisor support: Contributions to perceived organizational support and employee retention. *Journal of Applied Psychology*, *87*, 565–573.

Ellemers, N., de Gilder, D., and van den Heuvel, H. (1998). Career-oriented versus team-oriented commitment and behavior at work. *Journal of Applied Psychology*, *83*, 717–730.

Gong, Y., Law, K.S., Chang, S., and Xin, K.R. (2009). Human resources management and firm performance: The differential role of managerial affective and continuance commitment. *Journal of Applied Psychology, 94*, 263–275.

Harter, J.K., Schmidt, F.L., and Hayes, T. L. (2002). Business-unit-level relationship between employee satisfaction, employee engagement, and business outcomes: A meta-analysis. *Journal of Applied Psychology, 87*, 268–279.

Heffner, T.S. and Rentsch, J.R. (2001). Organizational commitment and social interaction: A multiple constituencies approach. *Journal of Vocational Behavior, 59*, 471–490.

Henderson, D.J., Wayne, S.J., Shore, L.M., Bommer, W.H., and Tetrick, L.E. (2008). Leader-member exchange, differentiation, and psychological contract fulfillment: A multilevel examination. *Journal of Applied Psychology, 93*, 1208–1219.

Howes, J.C., Cropanzano, R., Grandey, A.A., and Mohler, C.J. (2000). Who is supporting whom? Quality team effectiveness and perceived organizational support. *Journal of Quality Management, 5*, 207–223.

Huang, W.W., Wei, K.-K., Watson, R.T., and Tan, B.C.Y. (2002). Supporting virtual team-building with a GSS: An empirical investigation. *Decision Support Systems, 34*, 359–367.

Jehn, K.A., Northcraft, G.B., and Neale, M.A. (1999). Why differences make a difference: A field study of diversity, conflict, and performance in workgroups. *Administrative Science Quarterly, 44*, 741–763.

Johnson, R.E., Groff, K.W., and Taing, M.U. (2009). Nature of the interactions among organizational commitments: Non-existent, competitive, or synergistic? *British Journal of Management, 20*, 431–447.

Kirkman, B.L. and Rosen, B. (1999). Beyond self-management: Antecedents and consequences of team empowerment. *Academy of Management Journal, 42*, 58–74.

Landry, G. and Vandenberghe, C. (2009). Role of commitment to the supervisor, leader–member exchange and supervisor-based self-esteem in employee–supervisor conflicts. *Journal of Social Psychology, 149*, 5–27.

Landry, G. and Vandenberghe, C. (2012). Relational commitments in employee-supervisor dyads and employee job performance. *Leadership Quarterly, 23*, 293–308.

Landry, G., Vandenberghe, C., and Ben Ayed, A.K. (2014). Supervisor commitment to employees: Does agreement among supervisors' and employees' perceptions matter? *Leadership Quarterly, 25*, 885–900.

Lapointe, E., Vandenberghe, C., and Boudrias, J.-S. (2013). Psychological contract breach, affective commitment to organization and supervisor, and newcomer adjustment: A three-wave moderated mediation model. *Journal of Vocational Behavior, 83*, 528–538.

Lavelle, J.J., Brockner, J., Konovsky, M.A., Price, K., Henley, A., Taneja, A., and Vinekar, V. (2009). Commitment, procedural fairness, and organizational citizenship behavior: A multifoci analysis. *Journal of Organizational Behavior, 30*, 337–357.

Lavelle, J.J., Rupp, D.E., and Brockner, J. (2007). Taking a multifoci approach to the study of justice, social exchange, and citizenship behavior: The target similarity model. *Journal of Management, 33*, 841–866.

Law, K.S., Wong, C.S., and Song, L.J. (2004). The construct and criterion validity of emotional intelligence and its potential utility for management studies. *Journal of Applied Psychology, 89*, 483–496.

Lawler, E.J. (1992). Affective attachment to nested groups: A choice process theory. *American Sociological Review, 57*, 327–339.

Lee, S.-H., and Olshfski, D. (2002). Employee commitment and firefighters: It's my job. *Public Administration Review, 62*, 108–114.

Liao, H. and Rupp, D.E. (2005). The impact of justice climate and justice orientation on work outcomes: A cross-level multifoci framework. *Journal of Applied Psychology, 90*, 242–256.

Liden, R.C., Wayne, S.J., and Stilwell, D. (1993). A longitudinal study on the early development of leader-member exchanges. *Journal of Applied Psychology, 78*, 662–674.

Liu, Y., Keller, R.T., and Shih, H.-A. (2011). The impact of team-member exchange, differentiation, team commitment, and knowledge sharing on R&D project team performance. *R&D Management, 41*, 274–287.

Lucas, J.W. (1999). Behavioral and emotional outcomes of leadership in task groups. *Social Forces, 78*, 747–778.

Mathieu, J., Maynard, M.T., Rapp, T.L., and Gilson, L. (2008). Team effectiveness 1997–2007: A review of recent advancements and a glimpse into the future. *Journal of Management, 34*, 410–476.

Meyer, J.P. and Allen, N.J. (1991). A three-component conceptualization of organizational commitment. *Human Resource Management Review, 1*, 61–89.

Morin, A.J.S., Vandenberghe, C., Boudrias, J.-S., Madore, I., Morizot, J., and Tremblay, M. (2011). Affective commitment and citizenship behaviors across multiple foci. *Journal of Managerial Psychology, 26*, 716–738.

Neves, P. (2012). Organizational cynicism: Spillover effects on supervisor-subordinate relationships and performance. *Leadership Quarterly, 23*, 965–976.

Park, S., Henkin, A.B., and Egley, R. (2005). Teacher team commitment, teamwork and trust: Exploring associations. *Journal of Educational Administration, 43*, 462–470.

Pearce, C.L. and Giacalone, R.A. (2003). Teams behaving badly: Factors associated with anti-citizenship behavior in teams. *Journal of Applied Social Psychology*, *33*, 58–75.

Pearce, C.L. and Herbik, P.A. (2004). Citizenship behavior at the team level of analysis: The effects of team leadership, team commitment, perceived team support, and team size. *Journal of Social Psychology*, *144*, 293–310.

Porter, C.O.L.H. (2005). Goal orientation: Effects on backing up behavior, performance, efficacy, and commitment in teams. *Journal of Applied Psychology*, *90*, 811–818.

Redman, T. and Snape, E. (2005). Unpacking commitment: Multiple loyalties and employee behaviour. *Journal of Management Studies*, *42*, 301–328.

Rego, A., Vitória, A., Magalhães, A., Ribeiro, N., and Cunha, M.P.E. (2013). Authentic leadership predicting team potency: The mediating role of team virtuousness and affective commitment. *Leadership Quarterly*, *24*, 61–79.

Salancik, G.R. and Pfeffer, J. (1978). A social information processing approach to job attitudes and task design. *Administrative Science Quarterly*, *23*, 224–253.

Sanders, K., Geurts, P., and van Riemsdijk, M.V. (2011). Affective commitment within supermarkets in Eastern Europe: Consider the leadership climate strength. *Small Group Research*, *42*, 103–123.

Schippers, M.C., Den Hartog, D.N., Koopman, P.L., and Wienk, J.A. (2003). Diversity and team outcomes: The moderating effects of outcome interdependence and group longevity and the mediating effect of reflexivity. *Journal of Organizational Behavior*, *24*, 779–802.

Schneider, B., White, S.S., and Paul, M.C. (1998). Linking service climate and customer perceptions of service quality: Test of a causal model. *Journal of Applied Psychology*, *83*, 150–163.

Seong, J.Y. and Kristof-Brown, A.L. (2012). Testing multidimensional models of person-group fit. *Journal of Managerial Psychology*, *27*, 536–556.

Siders, M.A., George, G., and Dharwadkar, R. (2001). The relationship of internal and external commitment foci to objective job performance measures. *Academy of Management Journal*, *44*, 570–579.

Skarlicki, D.P., van Jaarsveld, D.D., and Walker, D.D. (2008). Getting even for customer mistreatment: The role of moral identity in the relationship between customer interpersonal injustice and employee sabotage. *Journal of Applied Psychology*, *93*, 1335–1347.

Snape, E., Chan, A.W., and Redman, T. (2006). Multiple commitments in the Chinese context: Testing compatibility, cultural, and moderating hypotheses. *Journal of Vocational Behavior*, *69*, 302–314.

Stinglhamber, F., Bentein, K., and Vandenberghe, C. (2002). Extension of the three-component model of commitment to five foci: Development of measures and substantive test. *European Journal of Psychological Assessment*, *18*, 123–138.

Stinglhamber, F. and Vandenberghe, C. (2003). Organizations and supervisors as sources of support and targets of commitment: A longitudinal investigation. *Journal of Organizational Behavior*, *24*, 251–270.

Valéau, P., Mignonac, K., Vandenberghe, C., and Gatignon-Turnau, A.-L. (2013). A study of the relationships between volunteers' commitments to organizations and beneficiaries and turnover intentions. *Canadian Journal of Behavioural Science*, *45*, 85–95.

Vandenberghe, C. (2015). The role of interactions among multiple commitments in the prediction of turnover. *Relations Industrielles/Industrial Relations*, *70*, 62–85.

Vandenberghe, C. and Bentein, K. (2009). A closer look at the relationship between affective commitment to supervisors and organizations and turnover. *Journal of Occupational and Organizational Psychology*, *82*, 331–348.

Vandenberghe, C., Bentein, K., Michon, R., Chebat, J.-C., Tremblay, M., and Fils, J.-F. (2007). An examination of the role of perceived support and employee commitment in employee-customer encounters. *Journal of Applied Psychology*, *92*, 1177–1187.

Vandenberghe, C., Bentein, K., and Panaccio, A. (forthcoming). Affective commitment to organizations and supervisors and turnover: A role theory perspective. *Journal of Management*.

Vandenberghe, C., Bentein, K., and Stinglhamber, F. (2004). Affective commitment to the organization, supervisor, and work group: Antecedents and outcomes. *Journal of Vocational Behavior*, *64*, 47–71.

Vandenberghe, C., Stinglhamber, S., Bentein, K., and Delhaise, T. (2001). An examination of the cross-cultural validity of a multidimensional model of commitment in Europe. *Journal of Cross-Cultural Psychology*, *32*, 322–347.

van der Vegt, G.S. and Bunderson, J.S. (2005). Learning and performance in multidisciplinary teams: The importance of collective team identification. *Academy of Management Journal*, *48*, 532–547.

van der Vegt, G.S., Emans, B., and van de Vliert, E. (2000). Team members' affective responses to patterns of intragroup interdependence and job complexity. *Journal of Management*, *26*, 633–655.

van der Vegt, G.S., van de Vliert, E., and Oosterhof, A. (2003). Informational dissimilarity and organizational citizenship behavior: The role of intrateam interdependence and team identification. *Academy of Management Journal*, *46*, 715–727.

van Steenbergen, E.F. and Ellemers, N. (2009). Feeling committed to work: How specific forms of work-commitment predict work behavior and performance over time. *Human Performance, 22*, 410–431.

van Vianen, A.E., Shen, C.-T., and Chuang, A. (2011). Person–organization and person–supervisor fits: Employee commitments in a Chinese context. *Journal of Organizational Behavior, 32*, 906–926.

Wasti, S.A. and Can, O. (2008). Affective and normative commitment to organization, supervisor, and coworkers: Do collectivist values matter? *Journal of Vocational Behavior, 73*, 404–413.

West, M.A. and Wallace, M. (1991). Innovation in health-care teams. *European Journal of Social Psychology, 21*, 303–315.

Workman, M., Kahnweiler, W., and Bommer, W. (2003). The effects of cognitive style and media richness on commitment to telework and virtual teams. *Journal of Vocational Behavior, 63*, 199–219.

Zaccaro, S.J. and Dobbins, G.H. (1989). Contrasting group and organizational commitment: Evidence for differences among multilevel attachments. *Journal of Organizational Behavior, 10*, 267–273.

Zettler, I., Friedrich, N., and Hilbig, B.E. (2011). Dissecting work commitment: The role of Machiavellianism. *Career Development International, 16*, 20–35.

12. The rise, decline, resurrection, and growth of union commitment research
Patrick Horsman, Daniel G. Gallagher and E. Kevin Kelloway

'Will you be a union man or thug for J.H. Claire?' These words from the 1930s labor anthem, 'Which Side Are You On?', posed a clear choice. In the context of a bitter labor conflict, Florence Reece (the wife of a union organizer for the United Mine Workers in Harlan County, Kentucky in the United States) articulated the view that workers needed to declare on which side of the organizing battle they were going to place their allegiance. In many ways questions about workers' allegiance, loyalty, or commitment have under-pinned the behavioral study of union–member relationships. As noted in Mrs. Reese's lyrics, and with the renewed growth of union membership following World War II, union membership was taken as evidence of a commitment to workers' rights and opposition to capitalist interests.

During this period a central question for researchers was the extent to which workers could be 'loyal' to both the employer and union organizations. Academic interest in this question paralleled the larger societal debate about whether one could be loyal to both country and alternate political views during the Cold War period. The general conclusion was that the vast majority of unionized workers were supportive of the interests of both their employer organization and the union representing them (Kerr, 1954; Stagner, 1954); a conclusion consistent with later research dealing with the multiple foci of commitment (e.g., Morrow, 1983; Reichers, 1985).

The growth of research on organizational commitment, and the recognition of multiple foci for such commitment, provided the foundation for Gordon et al.'s (1980) monograph in the *Journal of Applied Psychology* in which they introduced both a theory and a measure of commitment to the union. Their explicit goal was to provide a criterion that could be used in behavioral research on unions and to stimulate a resurgence of union research. To a large extent, these goals were met and much of the subsequent behavioral research on union members focused on the nature, predictors, correlates, and outcomes of members' commitment to the union.

In this chapter, we provide an overview of union commitment research which is primarily subsequent to the Gordon et al. (1980) article. We: (1) review the development of the construct of union commitment; (2) review and assess the current state of knowledge regarding the antecedents, consequences, and correlates of union commitment; and (3) articulate an agenda for further research on members' commitment to the union. In doing so, we hope to reinvigorate the study of union–member relations, believing that such research informs our understanding both of the union movement and of the nature of union commitment.

THE MEASUREMENT OF UNION COMMITMENT

Gordon et al.'s (1980) measure was based on the work of Porter and Smith who defined organizational commitment as: '(1) a strong desire to remain a member of the particular organization, (2) a willingness to exert high levels of effort on behalf of the organization, and (3) a definite belief in and acceptance of the values and goals of the organization' (cf. Gordon et al., 1980, p. 480). They provided empirical support for a measure that largely reflected this definition and provided empirical evidence linking commitment to individual difference, socialization, and role variables. Perhaps most importantly, Gordon et al. (1980) identified union commitment as a predictor of important union-relevant behaviors (for example, participation in union activities) and length of union affiliation; the former findings were to provide a behavioral focus for most subsequent research on union commitment.

Gordon et al.'s (1980) original measure comprised four factors: union loyalty (a sense of pride in the union and awareness of its instrumentality), responsibility to the union (willingness to fulfill day-to-day duties), willingness to work for the union (willingness to work for and expend energy on behalf of the union), and the belief in unionism (positive regard for the concept of unions and how they operate). A replication study conducted by Ladd et al. (1982) concluded that the four-factor structure was generalizable and consistent.

Friedman and Harvey (1986) reanalyzed the correlation matrix presented by Gordon et al. (1980) and concluded that a two-factor, oblique solution comprising union attitudes and pro-union behavioral intentions offered a simpler solution. A flurry of subsequent studies focused on the factor structure of the original measure (e.g., Fullagar, 1986; Klandermans, 1989; Kuruvilla and Iverson, 1993; Shore et al., 1994; Tetrick et al., 1989; Thacker et al., 1989). In reviewing this literature, Kelloway et al. (1992) noted that researchers had used different sets of items, and different samples to test competing models of the factor structure. Kelloway et al. (1992) provided empirical support for a shortened 13-item measure of union commitment assessing three factors: union loyalty, responsibility to the union, and willingness to work for the union. The three-factor solution has largely been accepted and used in subsequent studies of union commitment. Indeed, in many studies only the union loyalty scale has been employed, with the remaining factors dropped, much like affective commitment has been used as the primary factor in organizational commitment research (e.g., Klandermans, 1989; McElroy et al., 1997).

Sverke and Kuruvilla (1995) proposed an alternative measure based on a model that distinguished between ideological and instrumental attachment to the union. While a great deal of research has been conducted using this instrument in a Swedish context (Alivin and Sverke, 2000; Sjoberg and Sverke, 2001; Sverke et al., 2002; Sverke et al., 2004), the measure has not been widely used outside of Sweden. Although we will return to this suggestion in the latter part of this chapter, it is possible that the widespread reliance on Gordon et al.'s (1980) work led to a stagnation in the definition and measurement of union commitment.

DUAL COMMITMENT

A further and very visible side-effect of Gordon et al.'s (1980) development of the union commitment measure, and subsequent refinements by other researchers, has been the re-emergence of research on the previously noted topic of 'dual loyalty' or 'dual allegiance' which was popular in the 1950s. As noted by McElroy et al. (1997), union and organizational commitment can be related in one of three ways. First, as reflected in early labor anthems, the two constructs can be opposite ends of a single continuum in which one can be either committed to the union or committed to the organization. Second, the two constructs may simply be independent of each other, with each having unique determinates and consequences. Third, the two constructs may be complementary, with similar predictors leading to both commitment to the union and commitment to the organization.

Meta-analytic studies by Reed et al. (1994), Johnson et al. (1999), and Cooper-Harkim and Viswesvaran (2005) demonstrated a small to moderate positive association between union and employer commitment (Reed et al., $r = .43$; Johnson et al., $r = .32$; Cooper-Harkim and Viswesvaran, $r = .15$). Although the general pattern is that union commitment and organizational commitment are positively correlated, the range of empirical findings ($-.25$ to $.77$) suggests the need for a more complex view of the relationship between union and organizational commitment. For the most part, researchers have focused on the nature of the union–management relationship as a potential moderator with stronger relationships emerging between organizational and union commitment under cooperative union–management relationships (Magenau et al., 1988; Snape et al., 2000).

Fukami and Larson (1984) introduced the 'parallel models approach' that sought to address the extent to which union and organizational commitment were driven by common or unique determinants. They found that while traditional models of commitment worked to predict commitment to the company, they were not as effective in predicting commitment to the union. Similarly, Barling et al. (1990) found that job involvement, job satisfaction, and organizational climate were all significant predictors of organizational commitment, as predicted by the model, but only union tenure was a significant predictor of union commitment, marking the need for purposefully constructed models of union commitment. This cause was later championed by Barling et al. (1992a) and Tetrick (1995), and eventually taken up by Bamberger et al. (1999) resulting in what they termed the integrative model of commitment.

To date, the literature is collectively supportive of the finding that organizational and union commitments have more unique than common determinates. Most notably, for the same workers in the same organization, commitment to the organization is associated with individual characteristics as well as work-related experiences. In contrast, union commitment is more associated with performance of the union, most notably the effectiveness of its grievance systems. As such, the findings of Sverke and Sjoberg (1994) and Chan et al. (2011) reaffirm that divergent models of union and organizational commitment have prevailed.

From an even broader perspective is the challenge offered by Gordon and Ladd (1990) as to whether or not the concept of 'dual commitment' has any meaning or value. Most notable is the question of what, if anything, does dual commitment independently add to our knowledge of the union–management relationship? In taking up this challenge a few researchers, most notably Bemmels (1995), offered a study of union shop stewards which indicated that, as a construct, 'dual commitment' added significant explanatory power to the understanding of steward behaviors, above and beyond what was accounted for by separate measures on union and organizational commitment. A similar finding appears to have been obtained in Robinson et al.'s (2012) study of South Korean electronics employees. Union commitment research has also turned to questions of whether or not there is evidence that dual commitment can be interpreted as having an 'additive' or 'multiplicative' or 'interactive' effect on relevant outcomes (Snape et al., 2006). To date, this question seems to be underexplored.

THE CURRENT STATE OF UNION COMMITMENT RESEARCH

Research on the predictors of union commitment has generally focused on three overlapping processes: (1) the socialization of new members into the union; (2) the role of union leaders and, in particular, transformational leadership; and (3) the role of instrumentality beliefs about the benefits of unionization. In terms of the consequences of union commitment, much of the research has been conducted with a goal of understanding why members participate in the formal activities of the union (with implications for union democracy). Other outcomes (for example, attitudinal and behavioral militancy, union citizenship behaviors) have also consistently emerged as correlates of union commitment.

Antecedents

Gallagher and Clark (1989) summarized four core antecedent categories which had established relationships with union commitment: demographics (gender, age, job tenure, and level of education), work-related experience (commitment to the organization, satisfaction), union experience (for example, socialization; experience with the union), and the labor relations climate. Ng (1989) examined demographics and work-related experiences in a university faculty context and found that dissatisfaction with the university administration fostered increased union commitment, whereas demographics had little impact. Union experience variables have also been shown to impact union commitment. For instance, individual appraisals of the grievance system and the process that is followed have been shown to positively relate to union commitment. In particular, union loyalty is reported as higher when the process followed in a grievance is positively evaluated (Clark et al., 1990).

Pro-union attitudes have long been examined as a key antecedent of union commitment (Viswesvaran and Deshpande, 1993). Studies have identified the family socialization process as playing a central role in the development of pro-union attitudes (Huszczo, 1983). Barling et al. (1991) developed a model of family socialization which in turn was replicated and extended by Kelloway and Watts (1994) to include Marxist work beliefs in the prediction of pro-union attitudes along with perception of parental union attitudes. There is also some evidence that the relationship between perceptions of parental attitudes and one's own union attitudes are moderated by identification with the parents (Kelloway et al., 1996). Fullagar et al. (1994) found that individual socialization, which was random, informal, and variable, had the largest effect on pro-union attitudes which in turn predicted union commitment. Similarly, Kuruvilla et al. (1993) investigated union-entry socialization variables and found that new member orientation, newsletters sent to the home, and union-conducted activities acted as information distribution and socialization which in turn promoted higher levels of union commitment, although it had no such impact on union satisfaction.

Union leaders have been identified as socialization agents (Barling et al., 1992a) important to the development of union commitment. Fullagar et al. (1992) tested a path model relating the transformational leadership characteristics of socialization agents in unions, and the process followed to member union attitudes and subsequently union loyalty. Kelloway and Barling (1993) replicated this association between leadership and union loyalty.

It is also important to note that union commitment research has again benefited from theoretical and measurement-related gains in the area of organizational commitment. Most notably, Tetrick et al. (2007) have taken and reconstructed the Eisenberger et al. (1986) based construct of perceived organizational support and recast the construct in the parallel framework of perceived union support.

Outcomes

Despite the variety of interesting outcomes examined over the years, perhaps the most thoroughly studied, and likewise the most important to union leadership, has been union participation (Barling et al., 1992a). Union participation is in essence a behavioral manifestation of union commitment and includes voting, holding office, and pro-union behavior as well as the more mundane participation in day-to-day events (Parks et al., 1995). Parks et al. have amplified the concept of participation from a unidimensional construct to that of three dimensions: participation in administrative duties, participation in activities or events, and supportive participation for other members of the union. Yet others (e.g., Kelloway and Barling, 1993) have argued that participation is best understood as a unidimensional and cumulative construct whereby level of participation can be placed on a gradient with simple tasks such as reading union literature on one end, and full participation such as holding office at the other. Further, they found statistical support for a structural model relating union commitment to union participation, which in turn was predicted by both loyalty towards and responsibility to the union. Union loyalty has been shown to predict voting in favor of the union incumbent in union elections (Martin and Sherman, 2005) and has been related to support in representational elections (Catano, 2010).

Another often-examined outcome of commitment has been strike behavior, including strike propensity, strike voting, and actual engagement in collective action. Union loyalty and strike propensity have been shown to be strongly related, even after controlling for union tenure (Barling et al., 1992b). In faculty members, union commitment is related to the more risky forms of behavioral militancy while on strike, such as picketing and voting to defy a court injunction (McClendon and Klaas, 1993). Internal to the union, Dalton and Tudor (1982) found union commitment statistically predicted whether union stewards would facilitate the grievance process for union personnel. Similarly Kelloway et al. (1995) found that union commitment was correlated with union shop stewards' participation in the union, the number of hours per week spent on union activities, strike propensity, and the number of days willing to be on strike.

Martin and Sinclair (2001) have used an aggregated model of union relations, which included union loyalty, participation, and union performance, to predict strike propensity. Aggregated models generally have more explanatory power and allow us to incorporate what is known of existing union commitment relationships. A recent meta-analysis by Monnot et al. (2010) further suggests that the antecedents of militant and non-militant union participation were greatly moderated by status-based group membership (that is, white- versus blue-collar). Using 15 published meta-analyses, Bamberger et al. (1999) compiled estimates relating organizational commitment, job satisfaction, pro-union attitudes, union instrumentality, union commitment, and union participation. Using these data they were able to test four competing models whereby each of the first four variables predicted union commitment, which in turn predicted union participation. Their final integrative model was a strong fit to the data and resulted in a path model where the relation between instrumentality and commitment was partially mediated by pro-union attitudes, and the relation between job satisfaction and union commitment was partially mediated by organizational commitment. More importantly, the meta-analysis demonstrated that the relationship between pro-union attitudes was strong and consistent, as were the relationships between both participation and instrumentality with union commitment. For many, Bamberger et al.'s meta-analysis marks the end of classic union commitment research, as it established in one document how the relationships between the most often explored antecedents and consequences of union commitment are established and stable.

POST-2000 UNION COMMITMENT RESEARCH

In some respects, the post-2000 research on union commitment may be seen as a period of stagnation with little further development of the construct. Researchers have continued to explore questions around dual commitment (e.g., Kim and Rowly, 2006; Lee, 2004; Snape and Chan, 2000; Snape and Redman, 2007) and the relationship between union commitment and members' participation in the union (e.g. Fullagar et al., 2004; Martin and Sherman, 2005; Tetrick et al., 2007) which is largely the same research conducted up until this point. However, this pessimistic assessment is mitigated by the substantial evidence that research has moved beyond the North American, and even European focus that has dominated much of the early research. Recent investigations have drawn on samples from a wide variety of countries extending the application of union commitment theory across cultures. In particular, union commitment research has been applied in Asian countries including Singapore (Tan and Aryee, 2002), Korea (Kim and Rowly, 2006), and Hong Kong (Chan et al., 2004).

Theoretically, the literature has increasingly drawn on mobilization theory (Klandermans, 1989) to understand why union members become committed to the union. Thus, researchers have identified predictors such as perceived injustice as a predictor of union behavior (e.g., Aryee and Chay, 2001) including members' commitment to the union (e.g., Morrow and McElroy, 2006). The focus on injustice has also extended to a consideration of psychological contract breach (Turnley et al., 2004). The other major trend has been the examination of 'systemic' influences on union commitment. Thus, for example, Bacharach and Bamberger (2004) examined the influence of diversity within the union on union commitment. As a reflection of the economic climate, researchers (e.g., Bernston et al., 2010) have examined associations between job insecurity and members' commitment to the union in answer to Sverke et al.'s (2002) call for more research in this area. A parallel research stream has examined union commitment in the context of union mergers and restructuring (Sverke et al., 2004; Baraldi et al., 2006, 2010).

EVALUATING UNION COMMITMENT RESEARCH

The new millennium has marked a major shift in both how we conduct research and how we evaluate the quality of research. The proposition of any new construct often requires the examination of at least one of three pieces of evidence: (1) its temporal stability and impact on other variables over time via longitudinal research; (2) consideration of context or explanation of the mechanism by which the construct acts on other variables via moderation and mediation analysis; and (3) its stability across cultures. Given these requirements, it is important to objectively evaluate how union commitment research has addressed each historically.

Sjoberg and Sverke (2001) reported on the temporal stability of their scales of ideological and instrumental commitment to the union based on longitudinal data, and have found them to be quite stable. In an initial 12-month assessment of institutional and individual socialization practices among recently hired and unionized letter carriers, Fullagar et al. (1995) found that individual socialization practices had a positive time-lagged impact on union commitment. In a follow-up study of the same group of union members, Fullagar et al. (2004) found that early union commitment was able to predict participation in the union ten years later, and that reciprocal or reverse models were not significant.

Buttigieg et al. (2007) used event history analysis to develop a model of union joining and leaving over a five-year period. While they did not measure union commitment directly, joining and leaving can be viewed as a simplified, dichotomous commitment behavior. They noted that procedural justice influenced both joining and leaving; instrumentality also influenced joining, and having an individualistic orientation impacted leaving. Buttigieg et al. (2014) have also studied the willingness of union members to take industrial action, again measuring justice and collectivist orientations, and whether the relationship between satisfaction and union participation is moderated by union loyalty.

Several studies have addressed mediators and moderators of union commitment. Early work has shown that the relationship between union loyalty and strike propensity is moderated by inter-role conflict such that lower role conflict results in a higher strike propensity (Barling et al., 1992b). Deery et al. (2014) have demonstrated that union loyalty mediated the relationship between each of instrumentality and pro-union attitudes and union citizenship behaviours.

Cross-cultural research, outside the prototypical North American and British settlements (for example, the United Kingdom, Australia, and so on), is unfortunately less common. Klandermans (1989) examined union commitment in a Dutch sample. He found that union loyalty was, as expected, a better predictor of intent to withdraw from the union than union satisfaction. The aforementioned study by Kuruvilla et al. (1993) demonstrated that Swedish and Canadian samples behaved similarly in how the distribution of information by the union during socialization was positively related to union commitment. Cohen and Kirchmeyer (1994) conducted a comparative study using native-born Israeli and Eastern European immigrants and found that immigrants were largely more committed to their union. Other work has examined union issues, such as union membership outcomes, in an Israeli context, but has not explicitly examined union commitment (Harel et al., 2000).

Not surprisingly, some of the best research produced in the union commitment literature incorporates all three. An early study by Fullagar and Barling (1989) examined the moderating effect of race in a South African union sample over an eight-month period as part of an effort to build a model of antecedents and consequences of union loyalty. Instrumentality, dissatisfaction, and socialization experiences were predictive of union loyalty, which in turn predicted participation. Race emerged as a moderator of the antecedent relationships, and instrumentality also moderated the relationship between loyalty and participation.

THE FUTURE OF UNION COMMITMENT RESEARCH

Articulating an agenda for future research on union commitment is a daunting task; in attempting to do so we are conscious of the historical trend for union commitment research to wax and wane in response to societal and economic pressures. To some extent, union commitment is currently at an ebb and this may provide the opportunity to articulate future research directions to invigorate the field. We believe that two such directions are immediately apparent, relating to the measurement of union commitment and the need for greater methodological rigor in the study of union commitment.

The Measurement of Union Commitment

The seminal contribution of Gordon et al. (1980) and measures derived from their work (e.g., Kelloway et al., 1992) have largely dominated the study of union commitment. As a result, union commitment remains largely rooted in early definitions of organizational commitment and has not kept pace with contemporary developments. Organizational commitment research is now largely defined in terms of the Allen and Meyer (1990) three-component model of organizational commitment that comprises affective, normative and continuance commitment (for more, see Chapter 3 in this volume). In contrast, union commitment research focuses on union loyalty (arguably a measure of affective commitment to the union) and two dimensions which may be more properly viewed through the lens of today as behavioral intentions that are outcomes of union commitment (see, e.g., Kelloway and Barling, 1993).

The three-component model does seem to be applicable to the study of unions. Sverke's work on ideological commitment may provide a basis for understanding members' normative commitment to the union. A substantial literature on the benefits of unionization (for a review, see Barling et al., 1992a) suggests that members may experience considerable costs to leaving the union. Moreover, the presence of 'union shop' agreements in some jurisdictions that mandate union membership, may lead to the perception that everyone has no option but to be a union member. These observations suggest the relevance of continuance commitment to the study of members' commitment to the union and thus beg whether the three-component model may be a more appropriate framework.

Research Design

The vast majority of research dealing with union commitment has relied on cross-sectional survey data. The longitudinal studies that have been conducted have established that commitment does precede participation in the union (Fullagar et al., 2004) and that union commitment is a temporally stable attitude (Sjoberg and Sverke, 2001). It is likely that longitudinal research may lead to different or more complex understandings of union commitment. Thus, for example, Zacharewisz et al. (2016) found that perceptions of instrumentality and union support were outcomes, rather than predictors, of union loyalty in their longitudinal study of shop stewards. Kelloway et al. (2007) found that union loyalty was both a predictor and an outcome of participation in a day of protest.

The empirical stability of union commitment (Sjoberg and Sverke, 2001) also poses a challenge to longitudinal research in this area. In the absence of change, longitudinal data are little better than cross-sectional data for inferring temporal order or causality. We believe that there are two viable options for union commitment researchers. One is that researchers explicitly focus on the development of interventions to enhance union commitment. By trying to purposely change union commitment we may derive a greater understanding of the processes that lead to greater commitment. Another option is to consider naturally occurring changes that may shed light on the processes underlying commitment to the union. Catano and Kelloway (1997) took advantage of a union-sponsored political action campaign to examine changes in union commitment. Kelloway et al. (2007) examined commitment to a student union before and after a union-led 'day of protest'. In these examples, an event likely to change members' commitment provided the impetus for studying the processes that underlie the development of union commitment. Although such research is, of necessity, opportunistic, it is also a valuable approach when examining a construct that is stable over time.

UNION COMMITMENT: SUMMARY AND CONCLUSION

Union commitment research has a long history dating from the early studies on dual commitment to the present day. Research on the construct was invigorated by Gordon et al.'s (1980) development of a multidimensional measure of union commitment. Union commitment emerged as a predictor of union-relevant criteria such as members' participation in the union, union citizenship behaviors, militancy and strike propensity, as well as intent to leave the union. Although largely conducted in North America and Europe, recent research has extended these findings to other cultures and countries. In general, replicated findings suggest the generalizability and centrality of union commitment to understanding union–member relationships and union behaviors.

Despite this generally positive conclusion, there is a clear need for union commitment research to re-evaluate the definition and measurement of the construct in light of Allen and Meyer's (1990) three-component model of union commitment. Stronger, longitudinal research designs are required to evaluate the correlational findings that predominate in the literature. Although we began this review with the impression that union commitment research had largely stagnated post-2000, we were heartened to find a considerable number of researchers still interested in the construct and its role in understanding union behaviors. We look forward to the next decade of research that, we hope, will continue to expand our understanding of members' commitment to the union.

REFERENCES

Alivin, M. and Sverke, M. (2000). Do new generations imply the end of solidarity? Swedish unionism in the era of individualization. *Economic and Industrial Democracy*, *21(1)*, 71–95. doi: 10.1177/0143831X00211004.

Allen, N.J. and Meyer, J.P. (1990). The measurement and antecedents of affective, continuance, and normative commitment to the organization. *Journal of Occupational and Organizational Psychology*, *63(1)*, 1–18.

Aryee, S. and Chay, Y.W. (2001). Workplace justice, citizenship behavior, and turnover intentions in a union context: Examining the mediating role of perceived union support and union instrumentality. *Journal of Applied Psychology*, *86*(1), 154–160.

Bacharach, S.B. and Bamberger, P.A. (2004). Diversity and the union: The effect of demographic dissimilarity on members' union attachment. *Group and Organization Management*, *29*(3), 385–418.

Bamberger, P.A., Kluger, A.N., and Suchard, R. (1999). The antecedents and consequences of union commitment: A meta-analysis. *Academy of Management Journal*, *42*(3), 304–18.

Baraldi, S., Sverke, M., and Chaison, G. (2006). The difficulty of implementing union mergers: Investigating the role of members' merger orientation, *Economic and Industrial Democracy*, *27*, 485–504.

Baraldi, S., Sverke, M., and Chaison, G. (2010). Union absorptions in times of restructuring: the importance of attitude towards merger in predicting post-merger attachment levels. *Industrial Relations Journal*, *41*(1), 52–73.

Barling, J., Fullagar, C., and Kelloway, E.K. (1992a). *The Union and Its Members: A Psychological Approach*. New York: Oxford University Press.

Barling, J., Fullagar, C., McElvie, L., and Kelloway, E.K. (1992b). Union loyalty and strike propensity. *Journal of Social Psychology*, *132*, 581–590.

Barling, J., Kelloway, E.K., and Bremermann, E.H. (1991). Preemployment predictors of union attitudes: The role of family socialization and work beliefs. *Journal of Applied Psychology*, *76*, 725–731.

Barling, J., Wade, B., and Fullagar, C. (1990). Predicting employee commitment to company and union: Divergent models. *Journal of Occupational Psychology*, *63*(1), 49–61.

Bemmels, B. (1995). Dual commitment: Unique construct or epiphenomenon? *Journal of Labour Research*, *16*, 401–422.

Bernston, E., Naswall, K., and Sverke, M. (2010). The moderating role of employability in the association between job insecurity and exit, voice, loyalty and neglect. *Economic and Industrial Democracy*, *31*(2), 215–230.

Buttigieg, D.M., Deery, S.J., and Iverson, R.D. (2007). An event history analysis of union joining and leaving. *Journal of Applied Psychology*, *92*(3), 829–839.

Buttigieg, D.M., Deery, S.J., and Iverson, R.D. (2014). Voice within trade unions? A test of the voice and loyalty hypothesis. *Journal of Industrial Relations*, *56*(1), 3–23.

Catano, V.M. (2010). Union members' attitudes and perceptions about their union: Winning a representational election following a merger of four hospitals. *Economic and Industrial Democracy*, *31*(4), 579–592.

Catano, V.M. and Kelloway, E.K. (1997). Evaluating the effectiveness of a political action campaign on union members. In M. Sverke (ed.), *The Future of Trade Unionism: International Perspectives on Emerging Union Structures* (pp. 361–375). Aldershot: Ashgate.

Chan, A.W., Snape, E., and Redman, T. (2004). Union commitment and participation among Hong Kong firefighters: A development of an integrative model. *International Journal of Human Resource Management*, *15*(3), 533–548.

Chan, A.W., Snape, E., and Redman, T. (2011). Multiple foci and bases of commitment in a Chinese workforce. *The International Journal of Human Resource Management*, *22*(16), 3290–3304.

Clark, P.F., Gallagher, D.G., and Pavlak, T.J. (1990). Member commitment in an American union: The role of the grievance procedure. *Industrial Relations Journal*, *21*(2), 147–157.

Cohen, A. and Kirchmeyer, C. (1994). Unions and ethnic diversity: The Israeli case of East European immigrants. *Journal of Applied Behavioral Science*, *30*(2), 141–158.

Cooper-Harkim, A. and Viswesvaran, C. (2005). The construct of work commitment: Testing an integrative framework. *Psychological Bulletin*, *131*(2), 241–259.

Dalton, D.R. and Tudor, W.D. (1982). Antecedents of grievance filing behavior: Attitude/behavioral consistency and the union steward. *Academy of Management Journal, 25*(1), 158–169.

Deery, S.J., Iverson, R.D., Buttigieg, D.M., and Zatzick, C.D. (2014). Can union voice make a difference? The effect of union citizenship behavior on employee absence. *Human Resource Management, 53*(2), 211–228.

Eisenberger, R., Hutington, R., Hutchison, S., and Sowa, D. (1986). Perceived organizational support. *Journal of Applied Psychology, 71*(3), 500–507.

Friedman, L. and Harvey, R.J. (1986). Factors of union commitment: The case for lower dimensionality. *Journal of Applied Psychology, 71*, 371–376.

Fukami, C.V. and Larson, E.W. (1984). Commitment to company and union: parallel models. *Journal of Applied Psychology, 69*(3), 367–371.

Fullagar, C. (1986). A factor analytic study on the validity of a union commitment scale. *Journal of Applied Psychology, 71*(1), 129–136.

Fullagar, C. and Barling, J. (1989). A longitudinal test of a model of the antecedents and consequences of union loyalty. *Journal of Applied Psychology, 74*, 213–227.

Fullagar, C., Clark, P.F., Gallagher, D.G., and Carroll (2004). Union commitment and participation: A 10-year longitudinal study. *Journal of Applied Psychology, 89*(4), 730–737.

Fullagar, C., Clark, P.F., Gallagher, D.G., and Gordon, M.E. (1994). A model of the antecedents of early union commitment: the role of socialization experiences and steward characteristics. *Journal of Organizational Behaviour, 15*, 517–533.

Fullagar, C., Gallagher, D.G., Gordon, M.E., and Clark, P.F. (1995). Impact of early socialization on union commitment and participation: A longitudinal study. *Journal of Applied Psychology, 80*, 147–157.

Fullagar, C., McCoy, D., and Shull, C. (1992). The socialization of union loyalty. *Journal of Organizational Behavior, 13*, 13–26.

Gallagher, D.G. and Clark, P.F. (1989). Research on union commitment: Implications for labor. *Labor Studies Journal, 14*, 52–71.

Gordon, M.E. and Ladd, R.T. (1990). Dual allegiance: Renewal, reconsideration and recantation. *Personnel Psychology, 43*, 36–69.

Gordon, M.E., Philpot, J.W., Burt, R.E., Thompson, C.A., and Spiller, W.E. (1980). Commitment to the union: Development of a measure and an examination of its correlates. *Journal of Applied Psychology, 65*, 479–499.

Harel, G., Tzafrir, S., and Bamberger, P. (2000). Institutional change and union membership: A longitudinal analysis of union membership determinants in Israel. *Industrial Relations, 39*(3), 460–485.

Huszczo, G.E. (1983). Attitude and behavioral variables related to participation in union activities. *Journal of Labor Research, 4*, 289–297.

Johnson, W.R., Johnson, G.J., and Patterson, C.R. (1999). Moderators of the relationship between company and union commitment: A meta-analysis. *Journal of Psychology: Interdisciplinary and Applied, 133*(1), 85–103.

Kelloway, E.K. and Barling, J. (1993). Members' participation in local union activities: Measurement, prediction and replication. *Journal of Applied Psychology, 78*, 262–279.

Kelloway, E.K., Barling, J., and Agar, S. (1996). Preemployment predictors of children's union attitudes: The moderating role of identification with parents. *Journal of Social Psychology, 136*(3), 413–415.

Kelloway, E.K., Catano, V.M., and Carroll, A.E. (1995). The nature of member participation in local union activities. In L.E. Tetrick and J. Barling (eds), *Changing Employment Relations: Behavioral and Social Perspectives* (pp. 333–347). Washington, DC: American Psychological Association.

Kelloway E.K., Catano V.M., and Southwell, R.S. (1992). The construct validity of union commitment: Development and dimensionality of a shorter scale. *Journal of Occupational and Organizational Psychology, 65*, 197–211.

Kelloway, E.K., Francis, L., Catano, V.M., and Teed, M. (2007). Predicting protest. *Basic and Applied Social Psychology, 29*, 13–22.

Kelloway, E.K. and Watts, L. (1994). Preemployment predictors of union attitudes: Replication and extension. *Journal of Applied Psychology, 79*, 631–634.

Kerr, W.A. (1954). Dual allegiance to union and management (a symposium). 3. Dual allegiance and emotional acceptance–rejection in industry. *Personnel Psychology, 7*, 59–66.

Kim, J. and Rowly, C. (2006). Commitment to company and labour union: Empirical evidence from South Korea. *International Journal of Human Resource Management, 17*(4), 673–692.

Klandermans, B. (1989). Union commitment: Replications and tests in the Dutch context. *Journal of Applied Psychology, 74*(6), 869–875.

Kuruvilla, S., Gallagher, D.G., and Wetzel, K. (1993). The development of members' attitudes toward their unions: Sweden and Canada. *Industrial and Labor Relations, 46*, 499–514.

Kuruvilla, S. and Iverson, R.D. (1993). A confirmatory factor analysis of union commitment in Australia. *Journal of Industrial Relations, 35*, 436–452.

Ladd, R.T., Gordon, M.E., Beauvais, L.L., and Morgan, R.L. (1982). Union commitment: Replication and extension. *Journal of Applied Psychology*, *67*(5), 640–644.

Lee, J. (2004). Company and union commitment: evidence from an adversarial industrial relations climate at a Korean auto plant. *International Journal of Human Resource Management*, *15*(8), 1463–1480.

Magenau, J.M., Martin, J.E., and Peterson, M.M. (1988). Dual and unilateral commitment among stewards and rank-and-file union members. *Academy of Management Journal*, *31*(2), 359–376.

Martin, J.E. and Sherman, M.P. (2005). Voting in an officer election: Testing a model in a multi-site local. *Journal of Labour Research*, *24*(2), 281–297.

Martin, J.E. and Sinclair, R.R. (2001). A multiple motive perspective on strike propensities. *Journal of Organizational Behavior*, *22*(4), 387–407.

McClendon, J.A. and Klaas, B. (1993). Determinants of strike-related militancy: An analysis of a university faculty strike. *Industrial and Labor Relations Review*, *46*(3), 560–573.

McElroy, J.C., Morrow, P.C., and Crum, M.R. (1997). Organizational and union commitment among railroad employees. *Transpn Res. E.*, *33*(3), 211–221.

Monnot, M.J., Wagner, S., and Beehr, T.A. (2010). A contingency model of union commitment and participation: Meta-analysis of the antecedents of militant and nonmilitant activities. *Journal of Organizational Behavior*, *32*, 1127–1146.

Morrow, P.C. (1983). Concept redundancy in organizational research: The case of work commitment. *Academy of Management Review*, *8*(3), 486–500.

Morrow, P.C. and McElroy, J.C. (2006). Union loyalty antecedent: A justice perspective. *Journal of Labor Research*, *27*(1), 75–87.

Ng, I. (1989). Determinants of union commitment among university faculty. *Relations Industrielles*, *44*(4), 769–784.

Parks, J.M., Gallagher, D.G., and Fullagar, C.J.A. (1995). Operationalizing the outcomes of union commitment: The dimensionality of participation. *Journal of Organizational Behavior*, *16*(Spec Issue), 533–555.

Porter, L.W., Crampon, W.J., and Smith, F.J. (1976). Organizational commitment and managerial turnover: A longitudinal study. *Organizational Behavior and Human Performance*, *15*(1), 87–98.

Reed, C.S., Young, W.R., and McHugh, P.P. (1994). A comparative look at dual commitment: An international study. *Human Relations*, *47*(10), 1269.

Reichers, A.E. (1985). A review and reconceptualization of organizational commitment. *Academy of Management Review*, *10*, 465–476.

Robinson, S.D. Griffeth, R.W., Allen, D.G., and Lee, M.B. (2012). Comparing operationalizations of dual commitment and their relationships with turnover intentions. *International Journal of Human Resource Management*, *23*(7), 1342–1359.

Shore, L.M., Tetrick, L.E., Sinclair, R.R., and Newton, L.A. (1994). Validation of a measure of perceived union support. *Journal of Applied Psychology*, *79*, 971–977.

Sjoberg, A. and Sverke, M. (2001). Instrumental and ideological union commitment: longitudinal assessment of construct validity. *European Journal of Psychological Assessment*, *17*(2), 98–111.

Snape, E. and Chan, A.W. (2000). Commitment to the company and the union: Evidence from Hong Kong. *Industrial Relations*, *39*(3), 445–459.

Snape, E., Chan, A.W., and Redman, T. (2006). Multiple commitments in the Chinese context, Testing compatibility and moderating hypotheses, *Journal of Vocational Behavior*, *69*(2), 302–314.

Snape, E. and Redman, T. (2007). The nature and consequences of organizational–employee and union member exchange: An empirical analysis. *Journal of Labor Research*, *28*(2), 359–374.

Snape, E., Redman, T., and Chan, A. W. (2000). Commitment to the union: A survey of research and the implications for industrial relations and trade unions. *International Journal of Management Reviews*, *2*, 205–230.

Stagner, R. (1954). Dual allegiance as a problem in modern society. *Personnel Psychology*, *7*, 41–47.

Sverke, M., Chaison, G., and Sjoberg, A. (2004). Do union mergers affect the members? Short-and long-term effects on attitudes and behavior. *Economic and Industrial Democracy*, *25*(1), 103–124.

Sverke, M., Hellgren, J., and Näswall, K. (2002). No security: A meta-analysis and review of job insecurity and its consequences. *Journal of Occupational Health Psychology*, *7*(3), 242–264.

Sverke, M. and Kuruvilla, S. (1995). A new conceptualization of union commitment: Development and test of an integrated theory. *Journal of Organizational Behavior*, *16*, 505–532.

Sverke, M. and Sjoberg, A. (1994). Dual commitment to company and union in Sweden: An examination of predictors and taxonomic spilt methods. *Economic and Industrial Democracy*, *15*(4), 531–564.

Tan, H.H. and Aryee, S. (2002). Antecedents and outcomes of union loyalty: A constructive replication and an extension. *Journal of Applied Psychology*, *87*, 715–722.

Tetrick, L.E. (1995). Developing and maintain union commitment: A theoretical framework. *Journal of Organizational Behavior*, *16*, 583–595.

Tetrick, L.E., Shore, L.M., McClurg, L.N., and Vandenberg, R.J. (2007). A model of union participation: The impact of perceived union support, union instrumentality, and union loyalty. *Journal of Applied Psychology*, *92*, 820–828.

Tetrick, L.E., Thacker, J.W., and Fields, M.W. (1989). Evidence of the stability of the four dimensions of the commitment to union scale. *Journal of Applied Psychology*, *74*, 819–822.

Thacker, J.W., Fields, M.W., and Tetrick, L.E. (1989). The factor structure of union commitment: An application of confirmatory factor analysis. *Journal of Applied Psychology*, *74*, 228–232.

Turnley, W.H., Bolino, M.C., Lester, S.W., and Bloodgood, J.M. (2004). The effects of psychological contract breach on union commitment. *Journal of Occupational and Organizational Psychology*, *77*(3), 421–428.

Viswesvaran, C. and Deshpande, S.P. (1993). Are conclusions of union commitment robust to empirical techniques employed? *Relations Industrelles / Industrial Relations*, *48*(3), 539–538.

Zacharewisz, T., Martinez, D., and Kelloway, E.K. (2016). A longitudinal study of shop stewards' union commitment and perceptions of union instrumentality and support. *Applied Psychology*, *65*(1), 160–182. doi: 10.1111/apps.12052.

13. Action commitments
John P. Meyer and Brittney K. Anderson

The majority of research on workplace commitments has focused on commitment to an entity, most often the organization but also including occupation, union, supervisor, team, customer, and so on. Far less attention is given to what Neubert and Wu (2009) referred to as 'action commitments'. Of course, the interest in 'entity commitments' is due in large part to their implications for action, or behavior, but in this case the behavior is viewed as an outcome, or as a means to a more distal outcome (for example, organizational effectiveness, customer satisfaction). Here we treat the action itself, or at least a more proximal impetus for action (for example, goal, change initiative), as the focus of the commitment. Although we acknowledge that entity commitments can contribute to the development of action commitments, action commitments can exist in the absence of commitment to any particular entity.

Neubert and Wu (2009) noted that action commitments can take many forms, which they classified according to level (individual versus group or organization) and tangibility (tangible versus intangible) of the target. Examples include goal commitment (individual, tangible), commitment to change (organizational, tangible), values commitment (individual, intangible) and group norm commitment (group, intangible). Note that although these examples reflect commitments made by individuals, commitments can also be conceptualized and measured at a collective level (for example, team goal commitment). Neubert and Wu noted that the majority of published research addresses tangible commitments at the individual or group level, but they also discussed other forms of commitment from a theoretical perspective with suggestions for future research. We refer readers to their review for guidance in this direction.

Our objective in this chapter is to provide an updated review of research pertaining to tangible action commitments, most notably commitment to goals and change initiatives. We focus on these commitments because we see them as important complements to, and potential substitutes for, the well-studied entity commitments. One reason we believe that action commitments are particularly important in the modern workplace is because conditions are making it increasingly difficult for the formation of long-term commitments to organizations (Baruch, 1998). However, organizations continue to need assurances that employees will perform effectively and behave in a manner consistent with organizational norms, values, and policies (Meyer, 2009). Thus, even when – and perhaps especially when – commitment to a specific entity is not possible, action commitments continue to be important and warrant more attention.

We begin our review by addressing some conceptual issues. We then provide a structural framework to guide our review and set direction for future research. Finally, we discuss some practical implications of what we know and what we hope to learn about the nature, development, and consequences of action commitments.

CONCEPTUAL ISSUES

As noted elsewhere in this book (for example, Chapters 2 and 3), commitment has been, and continues to be, conceptualized in different ways. Therefore, it is important to be clear about how it is defined within a particular context. To this end, we address some important conceptual issues as a preamble to the development of our working definition.

Our distinction between entity and action commitments is reminiscent of, but not the same as, the distinction between attitudinal and behavioral commitment that was popular in the 1970s and 1980s (Mowday et al., 1982; Salancik, 1977). Attitudinal commitments were considered to reflect a psychological bond that an individual develops toward an entity, typically the organization, and that has implications for how they behave with regard to that entity. In contrast, behavioral commitments were considered to reflect a situation whereby engaging in a course of action leads to a continuation of that course of action. That is, commitment is the continuation of the behavior and can exist beyond conscious awareness. Although research in the behavioral tradition continues, particularly as it pertains to the 'escalation of commitment' to a failing course of action (e.g., Hsieh et al., 2015; Schultze et al., 2012), for the purposes of this chapter we treat action commitments not simply as the continuation of a course of action, but as a psychological state that an individual holds with regard to that course of action.

By viewing action commitments as reflecting a psychological state, we are treating them similarly to entity commitments. This is in line with arguments that commitment should be conceptualized consistently regardless of target (Klein et al., 2012; Meyer and Herscovitch, 2001). How, then, are entity and action commitments distinct? We use the term 'action' to refer to specific behaviors (for example, working toward a goal, implementing a change), but also to any proximal impetus for that action (for example, goal, change initiative). Although a goal or change initiative is not an action per se, it calls for a course of action, and individuals can arguably commit to pursuing that course of action or not. Admittedly, the entities we described above can be the source of goals or change initiatives, in which case we consider them to be a distal impetus. In our conceptual model, we illustrate how entity commitments can influence action commitments, but for present purposes, we consider action commitments as distinct from entity commitments.

Finally, there continues to be a lack of consensus on whether commitment is unidimensional (Chapter 2 in this volume) or multidimensional (Chapter 3 in this volume), and/or is best conceptualized as an attitude (Solinger et al., 2008), bond (Klein et al., 2012), or motivational force (Meyer and Herscovitch, 2001). Although it is impossible to capture the full essence of these different approaches in a working definition, we tried to develop a definition that would emphasize the commonalities and minimize the discrepancies. Therefore, for present purposes, we define action commitment as: *a psychological state characterizing an individual's orientation toward a course of action that contributes to persistence in that course of action.* The psychological state (whether an attitude, bond, or mindset) is conscious, or available to consciousness; has as its focus a course of action, and possibly the immediate impetus for that action (for example, goal, change initiative); and should increase the likelihood that the individual will engage in the focal behavior. Note that the behavior itself is not part of the commitment construct, but rather a primary outcome. Other outcomes might include behaviors other than those prescribed by the impetus (for example, creative problem-solving to achieve the desired end state) or employee well-being. The definition does not make specific reference to potential personal or situational antecedents; these also fall outside the construct.

With this definition in place, we now present a framework to guide our review. It is important to note that, despite our efforts to focus on commonalities in our definition, we acknowledge differences in conceptualization and measurement within and across research pertaining to different action commitments. Indeed, we present the theoretical models, measures, and findings as they were reported by the authors, without attempting to impose a common theoretical structure. We return to a discussion of this issue in the context of directions for future research.

A CONCEPTUAL MODEL

The model we developed to guide our review is presented in Figure 13.1. Note that this model is different from that proposed by Neubert and Wu (2009). Their review focused more than we do on the theoretical mechanisms involved in the formation and consequences of commitment. It is for this reason that we refer to ours as a conceptual rather than a theoretical model. Our intention is to focus attention on what we know about the implications of action commitments for behavior, as well as factors that can foster such commitments. For this same reason, following the presentation of our model, we focus primarily on the few action commitments for which there is a substantial body of research (that is, goal commitment, commitment to organizational change). We discuss

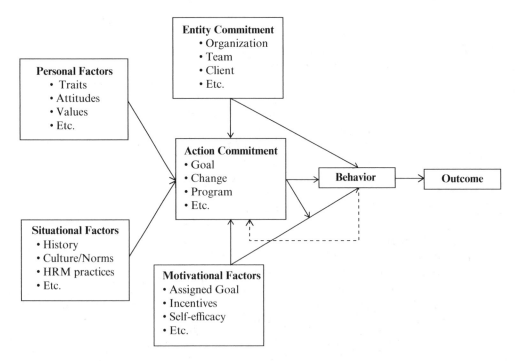

Figure 13.1   Conceptual model of action commitments

the implications of the model for other action commitments in the context of future research.

At the center of the model is action commitment, as defined earlier. Recall that this commitment reflects a psychological state pertaining to a course of action, and possibly its immediate impetus. The behavior itself is identified as an outcome of the commitment and a mediator between the commitment and the ultimate outcomes desired (for example, goal attainment). Action commitments can play multiple roles in determining behavior and its consequences. We discuss each of these in turn with examples, and provide supporting empirical evidence in our review.

Also included in Figure 13.1 as antecedents of behavior are a number of other motivational factors. These factors (for example, self-efficacy, assigned goals, incentives) are included to acknowledge that behavior is multiply determined and not all behaviors are driven by commitments. For example, an employee can work effectively on a task without making any form of commitment. Commitments are generally reserved for important situations where effort must be invested over a period of time and possibly in competition with other demands on the same resources (for example, when commitment to a deadline requires giving up time with family). Note that action commitments can have direct effects on behavior, but can also moderate the effects of other motivational factors. Perhaps the best example of the latter is the moderating effect of goal commitment on the impact of assigned goals on performance (Locke and Latham, 1990). It should also be noted that the effect of action commitments on behavior is likely to be indirect through behavioral intention. However, for simplicity, we did not include behavioral intention in the model and will refer to direct effects in subsequent discussion without repeating this qualification.

The other major category of proximal antecedents of behavior in the figure is entity commitment. Commitments to various entities can have direct effects on behavior or indirect effects mediated by action commitments. For example, employees committed to the organization are more likely than uncommitted employees to do what they judge to be in the best interests of the organization. If they are assigned specific goals or asked to modify their behavior in accord with a change initiative, the effect of their organizational commitment is likely to be channeled through the relevant action commitment.

Although our primary focus is on the prospective (conscious) effects of action commitments on behavior, the model also includes a feedback link between behavior and action commitment. This is to acknowledge evidence that engaging in a course of action under some conditions (for example, volition, irrevocability, visibility) can influence attitudes toward the behavior itself and the target to which it is directed (for example, through retrospective rationalization or dissonance reduction: Kiesler, 1971; Salancik, 1977).

The remaining elements in the figure include personal and situational antecedents to action commitment. These will differ depending on the nature of the action commitment, and we will address specific antecedents for some of these action commitments in the literature review to follow. However, among the personal antecedents are personality, attitudes, and values. Some specific examples might be teamwork orientation in the case of team goals, cynicism in the case of change initiatives, and personal values in the case of organizational policy. Situational antecedents might include the organization's history with regard to a particular situation (for example, managing change), organizational culture or group norms (for example, regarding absenteeism), or human resource management (HRM) practices (for example, involvement in decision-making).

With this conceptual model in place, we turn now to a brief review of research pertaining to goal and change commitments. These were selected because they are among the most well-researched action foci and provide the best opportunity to illustrate the connections depicted in Figure 13.1. We also identify a few other action commitments that have received less attention.

THE CASE OF GOAL COMMITMENT

Goal commitment has long been considered a key element in goal-setting theory (Locke and Latham, 1990; see Klein et al., 2013, for a more extensive review). Goal commitment has typically been conceptualized as a unidimensional construct (e.g., Hollenbeck et al., 1989), and considerable research has been conducted to investigate its antecedents and consequences.

Interest in goal commitment was stimulated by its implications for task performance, and it was expected to have a direct positive effect as well as to moderate the effect of assigned goals. That is, assigning specific and difficult goals was expected to have a greater positive effect when goal commitment was strong versus weak. In their meta-analysis, Klein et al. (1999) found a positive relation between goal commitment and performance ($r = .23$), and similar findings have been reported in more recent research (e.g., Porter and Latham, 2013). Goal commitment has also been found to relate positively to other outcomes that are potential mediators of its effects on performance, including effort, persistence, job satisfaction, and positive affect (e.g., Erez and Judge, 2001; Häsänen et al., 2011). Evidence for a goal level by commitment interaction has been mixed, but is generally found where there is sufficient variability in both goal level and commitment (see Klein et al., 2013).

Conflicting evidence has been obtained with regard to the relation between goal commitment and organizational citizenship behaviors (OCBs), with Häsänen et al. (2011) finding a significant positive relation and Piccolo and Colquitt (2006) finding a non-significant relation. The inconsistency might be explained by the fact that one of the functions of goal-setting is to narrow one's focus on task-relevant behavior. Thus, whether goal commitment relates positively or negatively with OCB might depend on whether the behaviors contribute to or detract from the attainment of the goal (Klein et al., 2013).

Among the potential antecedents of goal commitment are other motivational factors that can influence task behaviors and performance. Klein et al. (2013) divided these into two categories: the first pertaining to the expectancy, and the second to the attractiveness, of goal attainment. In their meta-analysis, Klein et al. (1999) demonstrated that both self-efficacy or expectancy ($r = .36$) and the attractiveness of the goal attainment ($r = .29$) correlate positively with goal commitment. These findings have been replicated in subsequent studies (e.g., De Clercq et al., 2009). Yet another motivational factor likely to contribute to task performance is the use of incentives, but research findings pertaining to their effects on goal commitment have been mixed and vary as a function of reward type and structure (see Klein et al., 2013).

A second category of antecedents includes situational factors pertaining to the nature of the goal and the manner in which it is introduced. It has consistently been demonstrated that the assignment of specific difficult goals leads to higher performance than easy, ambiguous, or no goals (Locke and Latham, 1990), but only specificity has been consistently found to relate positively to goal commitment ($r = .17$: Klein et al., 1999; $p = .36$: Miloslavic, 2014. Note that r indicates an uncorrected average correlation, whereas p reflects an average correlation corrected for unreliability). The relation between goal difficulty and commitment varies across studies and has been found to be negative in some cases (e.g., Wright, 1992). Several other contextual factors have also been found to relate to goal commitment. For example, in their meta-analysis, Klein et al. (1999) found a positive correlation between goal commitment and supervisor supportiveness ($r = .38$). In a more recent meta-analysis, Miloslavic (2014) found a positive correlation between goal commitment and both social support ($p = .35$) and group cohesion ($p = .45$).

There is also meta-analytic evidence demonstrating modest relations between goal commitment and several individual difference variables. For example, Klein et al. (1999) found positive correlations between goal commitment and Type A personality ($r = .12$), need for achievement ($r = .17$), and conscientiousness ($r = .17$). Miloslavic (2014) found positive correlations between goal commitment and performance approach goal orientation ($p = .14$), general self-efficacy ($p = .34$), and positive affect ($p = .29$); and a negative correlation with performance avoidance goal orientation ($p = -.25$).

Finally, research suggests that goal commitment relates positively to entity commitments, particularly commitment to the organization ($r = .20$; Klein et al., 1999). Klein et al. (2014) found a positive correlation using the Klein unidimensional target-free measure, and suggested that similar 'spillover effects' are likely for other commitment foci (for example, supervisor, team). The correlations are relatively modest, however, suggesting that entity commitments may not be required for goal commitment.

Although much of the research on goal commitment has been conducted at the individual level, it has also been studied at the team level. Many of the findings parallel those at the individual level. For example, studies have generally found that team goal commitment relates positively to team performance (e.g., Hoegl and Parboteeah, 2006), and many of the predictors of individual goal commitment such as leadership, participation in goal-setting, efficacy, and feedback have also been found to relate positively to team goal commitment (Klein et al., 2013). There are also some findings that are unique to team goal commitment. For example, group norms for performance and group cohesion have been found to relate positively to team goal commitment (e.g., Durham et al., 1997; Mulvey and Klein, 1998). Finally, findings regarding some of the factors expected to influence team commitment, such as team size, and task and outcome interdependence, have been mixed, perhaps due to the many factors involved in setting and working toward team goals (see Klein et al., 2013).

THE CASE OF COMMITMENT TO CHANGE

In contrast to goal commitment, there is more variability in the way commitment to organizational change has been conceptualized and measured, with some researchers treating it as multidimensional (e.g., Cunningham, 2006) and others as unidimensional (e.g., Sverke et al., 2008). In several studies, Caldwell and colleagues (Caldwell et al.,

2004; Fedor et al., 2006; Herold et al., 2007) used a behavioral measure as a proxy for commitment to the change. Of those taking a multidimensional perspective, most used Herscovitch and Meyer's (2002) measures of affective (desire: want to), normative (obligation: ought to) and continuance (perceived cost: have to) commitment. Still other studies included only one of these measures, most commonly affective commitment (e.g., Herold et al., 2008).

Among the most commonly studied outcomes are compliance with the change, discretionary support for the change, and employee retention. Compliance refers to doing what is asked by the organization in terms of behavior change. Meyer et al. (2007) distinguished between general compliance and 'mere compliance' (that is, doing exactly what is asked but no more). Compliance does not preclude discretionary support (that is, going beyond what is required in order to make the changes work), whereas mere compliance does. In the case of complex change where it is difficult to specify all of the behavior changes that are required and employees must 'learn as they go', mere compliance could seriously undermine the success of the change. Finally, retention has been examined as a potential outcome of commitment to a change because the unanticipated turnover of key employees could undermine its success.

In a preliminary test of the three-component model of commitment to change, Herscovitch and Meyer (2002) found that nurses' affective and normative commitment correlated positively with both compliance and discretionary support for the change, whereas continuance commitment correlated positively with compliance but negatively with discretionary support. Similar findings were obtained in subsequent studies (e.g., Baraldi et al., 2010; Meyer et al., 2007; Michaelis et al., 2009: see Bouckenooghe et al., 2015, for a meta-analytic review). Interestingly, Meyer et al. (2007) found that continuance commitment correlated positively with mere compliance, whereas affective and normative commitment correlated negatively.

As noted above, retention of key employees under conditions of change is important, as is their happiness and health. Several studies found that affective commitment correlated positively with job satisfaction (Hinduan et al., 2009; Rafferty and Restubog, 2010; Sverke et al., 2008) and negatively with turnover intentions (Cunningham, 2006; Hinduan et al., 2009; Neves and Caetano, 2009; Rafferty and Restubog, 2010; Sverke et al., 2008) and emotional exhaustion (Ning and Jing, 2012). Rafferty and Restubog's findings are particularly interesting because they used a longitudinal design to examine reactions to a merger. They found that affective commitment to the change at the time of the merger announcement was positively correlated with job satisfaction and negatively correlated with turnover intentions seven months later during implementation. Moreover, job satisfaction and turnover intentions during implementation predicted voluntary turnover behavior after the merger was complete. Research has also found normative commitment to a change to be negatively related to turnover intention (Cunningham, 2006; Hinduan et al., 2009) and emotional exhaustion (Ning and Jing, 2012). Less attention has been paid to continuance commitment, but Cunningham (2006) found a positive correlation with turnover intention and Ning and Jing (2012) found a positive correlation with emotional exhaustion.

Efforts to identify factors contributing to the development of commitment to change are increasing but still somewhat unsystematic (Meyer and Hamilton, 2013). Of the motivational factors identified in Figure 13.1, self-efficacy has received the most attention and has generally been found to relate positively with change commitment (e.g., Herold et al., 2007; Hornung and Rousseau, 2007). Interestingly, Herold et al. found that this positive relation was strongest when employees were experiencing a number of overlapping changes; what they described as 'change turbulence'. It is possible that turbulence increases the demand on employees and makes differences in self-efficacy beliefs more relevant.

Among the personal factors linked to change commitment are locus of control, cynicism, and tolerance for ambiguity. Chen and Wang (2007) found that internal locus of control was positively associated with affective and normative commitment to a change, and negatively associated with continuance commitment. Bernerth et al. (2007) found that cynicism about organizational change in general was negatively related to affective commitment, and Walker et al. (2007) found that this relation was mediated by tolerance for ambiguity.

Research pertaining to situational factors can be divided into two categories: context and process. We focus here on five contextual factors: change history, uncertainty, trust in management, leadership, and expected impact of the change. Rafferty and Restubog (2010) found that among employees undergoing a merger, those who reported having a poor change history in the organization had lower affective commitment than did those reporting a more positive history. Herold et al. (2007) found that change turbulence (overlapping changes) was not associated with commitment overall, but that it was negatively associated with commitment for employees with low self-efficacy.

Sverke et al. (2008) found that affective commitment to change among hospital workers experiencing a merger was negatively related to several indices of uncertainty, including job insecurity, role ambiguity, and role conflict. Baraldi et al. (2010) found that job insecurity and role ambiguity correlated negatively with affective and normative commitment, and positively with continuance commitment, for employees involved in a restructuring effort. Thus, under conditions of uncertainty, employees may feel that they have little option but to comply with the requirements for change, but are unlikely to embrace it. Interestingly, Kalyal et al. (2010) found that the negative relation with affective commitment was buffered by perceptions of employability.

Given the level of uncertainty surrounding large-scale change, trust in management becomes another important contextual factor. Neves and Caetano (2006) found that affective commitment to the change was positively related to trust in supervisor. Similarly, Michaelis et al. (2009, 2010) found that trust in top management correlated positively with both affective and normative commitment to the change. Beyond trust, leadership in general has been found to relate to change commitment. Both transformational (Herold et al., 2008; Seo et al., 2012) and charismatic (Michaelis et al., 2009) leadership have been found to relate positively with affective commitment to change. In a study conducted with Irish health services workers, Conway and Monks (2008) found that transactional leadership correlated negatively with affective commitment to a change. However, Hinduan et al. (2009) found that, among Indonesian bank employees, both transactional and transformational leadership correlated positively with normative commitment to a change, but not with affective commitment, suggesting the possibility of culture differences in the leadership–commitment relationship.

Finally, and not surprisingly, the expected impact of the change has been found to relate to commitment. Shin et al. (2012) found that employees who expected to benefit from a change initiative had higher levels of both affective and normative commitment than those who did not. Fedor et al. (2006) found that employees were more committed when the change was seen as having benefits for the unit with minimal impact on their own jobs. Ning and Jing (2012) found that affective and normative commitment to a change correlated positively with expectation of positive outcomes, whereas continuance commitment correlated negatively.

Among the process variables that have been studied are justice, employee input, and communication. In a change context, employees are generally responsive to three forms of justice: distributive – the perceived fairness of outcomes or resources; procedural – the perceived fairness of the policies and procedures by which an allocation decision is made; and interactional – the perceived fairness of the interpersonal treatment received when procedures are communicated and implemented (see Oreg and van Dam, 2009). All three forms of justice have been found to have strong positive relations with affective commitment to change (e.g., Bernerth et al., 2007; Foster, 2010). Bernerth et al. (2007) found that affective commitment was highest when both interactional and procedural justice were high, or when both interactional and distributive justice were high. Foster (2010) found that perceived justice related positively with both affective and normative commitment, but negatively with continuance commitment.

Sverke et al. (2008) found a positive relation between participation in decision-making and affective commitment to change resulting from a merger. Similarly, Cook et al. (2008) found that having input into the change correlated positively with affective commitment and negatively with continuance commitment to the change. Conway and Monks (2008) found that employees' satisfaction with HRM practices relating to communication was positively related to affective commitment. Likewise, Rafferty and Restubog (2010) found a strong positive correlation between perceptions of the quality of merger-related information and affective commitment to the change among employees of the low-status merging partner.

Finally, there is evidence to suggest that employees who have stronger affective commitment to the organization undergoing a change are more likely to experience affective and/or normative commitment to the change (e.g., Herold et al., 2008; Herscovitch and Meyer, 2002; Meyer et al., 2007). There is also evidence that continuance commitment to the organization relates negatively to affective commitment to the change (Herscovitch and Meyer, 2002; Meyer et al., 2007). It is important to note, however, that the nature of the relation between commitment to the organization and commitment to a change might depend on whether the change is considered to be in the best interests of the organization and its employees (see Meyer and Hamilton, 2013).

OTHER ACTION COMMITMENTS

As noted earlier, there are many other action commitments that might be of relevance to organizations, or other entities such as unions or professional organizations (see Neubert and Wu, 2009), but these have received far less attention than commitment to goals and change initiatives. Among those that have received attention are commitment to programs (e.g., Neubert and Cady, 2001), strategies (e.g., Ford et al., 2003), and projects (e.g., Ehrardt et al., 2014; Hoegl et al., 2004). Evidence suggests that these commitments relate positively to behavioral support and/or various indicators of success. Albeit limited, findings pertaining to personal and situational factors involved in the development of these action commitments are generally consistent with those observed for change commitment (Neubert and Wu, 2009). Therefore, these and other potential action commitments warrant more attention in both research and practice.

IMPLICATIONS FOR PRACTICE

To date, research on action commitments is limited and largely focused on two targets: goals and change initiatives. We offer several suggestions for future research below, but draw attention here to how existing findings can inform practice. First, commitment to both goals and change initiatives have been found to relate positively with affective organizational commitment. This suggests that efforts to foster a broader commitment to the organization are likely to facilitate efforts to instill commitment to a goal or a change that is of benefit to the organization. However, the correlation is sufficiently weak to suggest that commitment to the organization is not a requirement for fostering commitment to a goal or change; these commitments can be managed independently.

Research concerning change commitment suggests that affective and/or normative commitment may be required if organizations want employees to exert discretionary effort in support of the change. Employees with strong continuance commitment may restrict their efforts to what is required and clearly specified. As discussed earlier, this might not be enough. Whether this applies to other action commitments remains to be determined; in many cases, these commitments have been examined from a unidimensional perspective.

Most of the research we reviewed looked at the commitment of individuals, but there is some evidence from the goal commitment literature that commitment to team goals can contribute to team performance. However, it should be kept in mind that when goals are set at a team level they must be considered in conjunction with the goals of individual team members, and this raises the issues of coordination, compatibility and conflict.

Research pertaining to both goal and change commitment provides some guidance with regard to strengthening commitment. On the personal side, self-efficacy was found to be a positive predictor of both goal and change commitment. This stands to reason given that action commitments have a specific behavioral referent that makes efficacy salient. When the action involves uncertainty, as it does in the case of change commitment, individual differences such as locus of control, tolerance for uncertainty, insecurity and cynicism are likely to play a role. Although these might reflect stable dispositions to some extent, they are also subject to change through careful attention to contextual factors (for example, change history, leadership style) and process factors (for example, fairness, communication, involvement).

In sum, the research suggests that goal and change commitment can complement, and possibly even substitute for, organizational commitment, but these commitments must be managed carefully to ensure that, among other things, the objectives of the action target and organization align and are sufficiently overlapping. Where this is not the case, it might be possible to broaden the focus of action commitments, such as commitment to customer service or to large-scale projects that have implications for a wider array of organization-relevant behaviors, but this is an issue that requires future research.

AGENDA FOR FUTURE RESEARCH

Although the research pertaining to goal and change commitment helps to illustrate their potential importance, action commitments continue to be under-investigated. Indeed, some potentially important action commitments (for example, policy, values, ethics, corporate social responsibility initiatives) have received relatively little attention to date. Thus, there is still much research to be done. Perhaps one of the most important considerations as research moves forward is how commitment should be conceptualized and measured. There continue to be differences in perspective on this, as is apparent from the chapters on the unidimensional (Chapter 2) and multidimensional (Chapter 3) approaches in this volume. Whether the field would benefit most from a unified perspective or from continued application of different approaches is itself a matter for debate (see the concluding Chapter 36 in this volume). For present purposes, we argue that much has been, and can be, learned from both approaches. Therefore, we start by suggesting how each might be applied going forward.

The unidimensional approach has been dominant in goal commitment research, and Klein et al. (2013) suggested that as this approach is applied in the future, there might be benefits to using the new Klein unidimensional target-free measure (Klein et al., 2014). In addition to some evidence for the superiority of its psychometric properties compared to earlier goal commitment measures, an added advantage is that the same measure can be used to gauge other commitments in multi-foci research. As research using this measure across foci accumulates, it will be interesting to determine whether the psychometric properties (for example, factor loadings) are invariant (that is, if the commitment bond is experienced similarly across targets; see Chapter 32 in this volume), and whether relations involving antecedents and consequences are generalizable and/or focus-specific.

The multidimensional approach has been applied with some success in research pertaining to commitment to organizational change. Here the assumption is that employees can experience their commitments in different ways and that the nature of the commitment has implications for whether employees merely comply with the requirements for change or exert discretionary effort to ensure that the initiative succeeds. It would be interesting to see whether this approach would similarly help to predict differential outcomes associated with other action commitments. Also, most studies taking a multidimensional perspective have examined relations involving the individual mindsets. Only a few (e.g., Herscovitch and Meyer, 2002; Meyer et al., 2007) have taken a person-centered approach to examine commitment profiles. The application of a person-centered approach to the study of commitment mindsets has generated some interesting new insights that might also be explored with regard to other action commitments (also see Meyer et al., 2013; Vandenberg and Stanley, 2009).

Regardless of which approach researchers take, there are a number of other important directions for future research. For example, it is important to gain a better understanding of how action commitments combine with entity commitments in shaping behavior to determine when and how action commitments can be used to complement or substitute for entity commitments. We have learned a great deal about factors contributing to the development of goal and change commitments, so it would also be interesting to determine how these findings generalize to other action commitments. Finally, most research to date has focused on individual commitments, so there is a need for more research looking at action commitments at higher levels (for example, team, unit) and how they interact with individual-level commitments. Understanding how to manage commitments across levels is particularly important with the increasing emphasis on teamwork in the modern workplace. In short, there is still much to be learned about the nature, development, and consequences of action commitments and we hope this chapter will serve as a stimulus to action.

REFERENCES

Baraldi, S., Kalyal, H.J., Berntson, E., Naswall, K., and Sverke, M. (2010). The importance of commitment to change in public reform: An example from Pakistan. *Journal of Change Management, 10,* 347–368.

Baruch, Y. (1998). The rise and fall of organizational commitment. *Human Systems Management, 17,* 135–143.

Bernerth, J.B., Armenakis, A.A., Field, H.S., and Walker, H.J. (2007). Justice, cynicism, and commitment: A study of important organizational change variables. *Journal of Applied Behavioral Science, 43,* 303–326.

Bouckenooghe, D., Schwarz, G.M., and Minbashian, A. (2015). Herscovitch and Meyer's three-component model of commitment to change: Meta-analytic findings. *European Journal of Work and Organizational Psychology, 24,* 578–595.

Caldwell, S.D., Herold, D.M., and Fedor, D.B. (2004). Toward an understanding of the relationships among organizational change, individual differences, and changes in person–environment fit: A cross-level study. *Journal of Applied Psychology, 89,* 868–882.

Chen, J. and Wang, L. (2007). Locus of control and the three components of commitment to change. *Personality and Individual Differences, 42,* 503–512.

Conway, E. and Monks, K. (2008). HR practices and commitment to change: An employee-level analysis. *Human Resource Management Journal, 18,* 72–89.

Cook, A.L., Horner, M.T., and Payne, S.C. (2008). In search of the antecedents of commitment to organizational change. Paper presented at the annual meeting of the Society for Industrial and Organizational Psychology, San Francisco, CA, April.

Cunningham, G.B. (2006). The relationships among commitment to change, coping with change, and turnover intentions. *European Journal of Work and Organizational Psychology, 15*(1), 29–45.

De Clercq, D., Menzies, T.V., Diochon, M., and Gasse, Y. (2009). Explaining nascent entrepreneurs' goal commitment: An exploratory study. *Journal of Small Business and Entrepreneurship, 22,* 123–139.

Durham, C., Knight, D., and Locke, E.A. (1997). Effects of leader role, team-set goal difficulty, efficacy, and tactics on team effectiveness. *Organizational Behavior and Human Decision Processes, 72,* 203–231.

Ehrardt, K., Miller, J., Freeman, S.J., and Hom, P.W. (2014). Examining project commitment in cross-functional teams: Antecedents and relationship with team performance. *Journal of Business Psychology, 29,* 443–461.

Erez, A., and Judge, T.A. (2001). Relationship of core self-evaluations to goal setting, motivation, and performance. *Journal of Applied Psychology, 86,* 1270–1279.

Fedor, D.B., Caldwell, S., and Herold, D.M. (2006). The effects of organizational changes on employee commitment: A multilevel investigation. *Personnel Psychology, 59,* 1–29.

Ford, J.K., Weissbein, D.A., and Plamondon, K.E, (2003). Distinguishing organizational from strategy commitment: Linking officer's commitment to community policing to job behaviors and satisfaction. *Justice Quarterly, 20,* 159–185.

Foster, R.D. (2010). Resistance, justice, and commitment to change. *Human Resource Development Quarterly, 21,* 3–39.

Häsänen, L., Hellgren, J., and Hansson, M. (2011). Goal setting and plant closure: When bad things turn good. *Economic and Industrial Democracy, 32,* 135–156.

Herold, D.M., Fedor, D.B., and Caldwell, S.D. (2007). Beyond change management: A multilevel investigation of contextual and personal influences on employees' commitment to change. *Journal of Applied Psychology, 92,* 942–951.

Herold, D.M., Fedor, D.B., Caldwell, S., and Liu, Y. (2008). The effects of transformational and change leadership on employees' commitment to a change: A multilevel study. *Journal of Applied Psychology*, *93*, 346–357.

Herscovitch, L. and Meyer, J.P. (2002). Commitment to organizational change: Extension of a three-component model. *Journal of Applied Psychology*, *87*, 474–487.

Hinduan, Z.R., Wilson-Evered, E., Moss, S., and Scannell, E. (2009). Leadership, work outcomes and openness to change following an Indonesian bank merger. *Asia Pacific Journal of Human Resources*, *47*, 59–78.

Hoegl, M. and Parboteeah, K.P. (2006). Team goal commitment in innovative projects. *International Journal of Innovation Management*, *10*, 299–324.

Hoegl, M., Weinkauf, K., and Gemueden, H. G. (2004). Interteam coordination, project commitments, and teamwork in multiteam RandD projects: A longitudinal study. *Organization Science*, *15*(1), 38–55.

Hollenbeck, J.R., Klein, H.J., O'Leary, A.M., and Wright, P.M. (1989). Investigation of the construct validity of a self-report measure of goal commitment. *Journal of Applied Psychology*, *74*, 951–956.

Hornung, S. and Rousseau, D.M. (2007). Active on the job – proactive in change: How autonomy at work contributes to employee support for organizational change. *Journal of Applied Behavioral Science*, *43*, 401–426.

Hsieh, K.-Y., Tsai, W., and Chen, M.-J. (2015). If they can do it, why not us? Competitors as reference points for justifying escalation of commitment. *Academy of Management Journal*, *58*, 38–58.

Kalyal, H.J., Berntson, E., Beraldi, S., Näswall, K., and Sverke, M. (2010). The moderating role of employability on the relationship between job insecurity and commitment to change. *Economic and Industrial Democracy*, *31*, 327–344.

Kiesler, C. (1971). *The Psychology of Commitment*. New York: Academic Press.

Klein, H.J., Cooper, J.T., Molloy, J.C., and Swanson, J.A. (2014). The assessment of commitment: Advantages of a unidimensional, target-free approach. *Journal of Applied Psychology*, *99*(2), 222–238.

Klein, H.J., Cooper, J.T., and Monahan, C.A. (2013). Goal commitment. In E.A. Locke and G.P. Latham (eds), *New Developments in Goal Setting and Task Performance* (65–89). New York: Routledge/Taylor & Francis.

Klein, H.J., Molloy, J.C., and Brinsfield, C.T. (2012). Reconceptualizing workplace commitment to redress a stretched construct: Revisiting assumptions and removing confounds. *Academy of Management Review*, *37*, 130–151.

Klein, H.J., Wesson, M.J., Hollenbeck, J.R., and Alge, B.J. (1999). Goal commitment and the goal setting process: conceptual clarification and empirical synthesis. *Journal of Applied Psychology*, *84*, 885–896.

Locke, E.A. and Latham, G.P. (1990). *A Theory of Goal Setting and Task Performance*. Englewood Cliffs, NJ: Prentice Hall.

Meyer, J.P. (2009). Commitment in a changing world of work. In H.J. Klein, T.E. Becker, and J.P. Meyer (eds), *Commitment in Organizations: Accumulated Wisdom and New Directions* (37–68). Florence, KY: Routledge/Taylor & Francis.

Meyer, J.P. and Hamilton, L.K. (2013). Commitment to organizational change: Theory, research, principles, and practice. In S. Oreg, A. Michel, and R.T. By (eds), *The Psychology of Organizational Change: Viewing Change from the Recipient's Perspective* (43–64). Cambridge: Cambridge University Press.

Meyer, J.P. and Herscovitch, L. (2001). Commitment in the workplace: Toward a general model. *Human Resource Management Review*, *11*, 299–326.

Meyer, J.P., Srinivas, E.S., Lal, J.B., and Topolnytsky, L. (2007). Employee commitment and support for an organizational change: Test of the three-component model in two cultures. *Journal of Occupational and Organizational Psychology*, *80*, 185–211.

Meyer, J.P., Stanley, L.J., and Vandenberg, R.J. (2013). A person-centered approach to the study of commitment. *Human Resource Management Review*, *23*(2), 190–202.

Michaelis, B., Stegmaier, R., and Sonntag, K. (2009). Affective commitment to change and innovation implementation behavior: The role of charismatic leadership and employees' trust in top management. *Journal of Change Management*, *9*, 399–417.

Michaelis, B., Stegmaier, R., and Sonntag, K. (2010). Shedding light on followers' innovation implementation behavior: The role of transformational leadership, commitment to change, and climate for innovation. *Journal of Managerial Psychology*, *25*, 408–429.

Miloslavic, S.A. (2014). Antecedents and consequences of goal commitment: A meta-analysis. Unpublished doctoral dissertation, Florida Institute of Technology, Florida.

Mowday, R.T., Porter, L.W., and Steers, R. (1982) *Organizational linkages: The psychology of commitment, absenteeism, and turnover*. San Diego, CA: Academic Press.

Mulvey, P.W. and Klein, H.J. (1998). The impact of perceived loafing and collective efficacy in group goal processes and group performance. *Organizational Behavior and Human Decision Processes*, *74*(1), 62–87.

Neubert, M.J. and Cady, S. (2001). Program commitment: A multi-study longitudinal field investigation. *Personnel Psychology*, *54*, 421–448.

Neubert, M.J. and Wu, C. (2009). Action commitments. In H.J. Klein, T.E. Becker, and J.P. Meyer (eds), *Commitment in Organizations: Accumulated Wisdom and New Directions* (179–213). New York: Routledge/Taylor & Francis.

Neves, P. and Caetano, A. (2006). Social exchange processes in organizational change: The roles of trust and control. *Journal of Change Management*, 6, 351–364.

Neves, P. and Caetano, A. (2009). Commitment to change: Contributions to trust in the supervisor and work outcomes. *Group and Organization Management*, 34, 623–644.

Ning, J. and Jing, R. (2012). Commitment to change: Its role in the relationship between expectations and change outcome and emotional exhaustion. *Human Resource Development Quarterly*, 23(4), 461–485.

Oreg, S., and van Dam, K. (2009). Organisational justice in the context of organizational change. *Netherlands Journal of Psychology*, 65(4), 127–135.

Piccolo, R. and Colquitt, J. (2006). Transformational leadership and job behaviors: The mediating role of core job characteristics. *Academy of Management Journal*, 49(2), 327–340.

Porter, R.L. and Latham, G.P. (2013). The effect of employee learning goals and goal commitment on departmental performance. *Journal of Leadership and Organizational Studies*, 20(1), 62–68.

Rafferty, A.E. and Restubog, S.L.D. (2010). The impact of change process and context on change reactions and turnover during a merger. *Journal of Management*, 36, 1309–1338.

Salancik, G. (1977). Commitment and the control of organizational behavior and belief. In B. Staw and G. Salancik (eds), *New Directions in Organizational Behavior* (1–54). Chicago, IL: St. Clair.

Schultze, T., Pfeiffer, F., and Schulz-Hardt, S. (2012). Biased information processing in the escalating paradigm: Information search and information evaluation as potential mediators of escalating commitment. *Journal of Applied Psychology*, 97, 16–32.

Seo, M.-G., Taylor, M.S., Hill, N.S., Zhang, X., Tesluk, P.E., and Lorinkova, N.M. (2012). The role of affect and leadership during organizational change. *Personnel Psychology*, 65, 121–165.

Shin, J., Taylor, M.S., and Seo, M.-G. (2012). Resources for change: The relationships of organizational inducements and psychological resilience to employees' attitudes and behaviors toward organizational change. *Academy of Management Journal*, 55, 727–748.

Solinger, O.N., van Olffen, W., and Roe, R.A. (2008). Beyond the three-component model of organizational commitment. *Journal of Applied Psychology*, 93, 70–83.

Sverke, M., Hellgren, J., Näswall, K., Göransson, S., and Öhrming, J. (2008). Employee participation in organizational change: Investigating the effects of proactive vs. reactive implementation of downsizing in Swedish hospitals. *Zeitschrift für Personalforschung*, 22, 111–129.

Vandenberg, R.J. and Stanley, L.J. (2009). Statistical and methodological challenges for commitment researchers: Issues of invariance, change across time, and profile differences. In H.J. Klein, T.E. Becker, and J.P. Meyer (eds), *Commitment in Organizations: Accumulated Wisdom and New Directions* (383–416). New York: Routledge/Taylor & Francis.

Walker, H.J., Armenakis, A.A., and Bernerth, J.B. (2007). Factors influencing organizational change efforts: An integrative investigation of change content, context, process, and individual differences. *Journal of Organizational Change Management*, 20, 761–773.

Wright, P.M. (1992). An examination of the relationships among monetary incentives, goal level, goal commitment, and performance. *Journal of Management*, 18, 677–693.

PART IV

CONSEQUENCES OF COMMITMENT

14. Employee turnover and absenteeism
Ian R. Gellatly and Leanne M. Hedberg

In this chapter our primary objective is to summarize some of the new approaches to employee commitment, employee turnover, and absenteeism, and to consider what these developments mean for how withdrawal behaviors are (and could be) managed within organizations. The chapter is organized as follows. We begin with an overview of some past and current thinking with respect to employee commitment. We then provide brief reviews of how perspectives of employee turnover and absenteeism have evolved over time, and attempt to reconcile these developments with what we see as parallel developments within commitment theory and research. We then focus attention on how withdrawal behaviors have been managed by organizations and their agents, emphasizing new directions.

ORGANIZATIONAL COMMITMENT

Concept Definitions

Meyer and Allen (Allen and Meyer, 1990; Meyer and Allen, 1991, 1997) proposed three distinct forms of organizational commitment: one that reflects a deeply personal and emotional bond with the organization (AC: affective commitment); one that reflects a logical and rational evaluation of one's circumstances, opportunities, and the costs associated with leaving the organization (CC: continuance commitment); and one that reflects a sense of obligation, duty, and fulfilling expectations (NC: normative commitment). The major difference between these three conceptualizations of commitment concerns the nature of the mindset associated with each of the three components (Meyer, 2009; Meyer and Herscovitch, 2001). These mindsets are generally described as a psychological state (or commitment experience) comprised of one's perceptions, beliefs, and feelings with respect to the commitment object. For instance, the mindset associated with AC has been characterized by strong emotional attachment to, identification with, and personal involvement with the organization. Employees who experience strong AC remain with the organization because they want to. In sharp contrast, the mindset associated with CC is characterized by one's awareness of the lack of alternatives and/or the personal cost of leaving the organization. Employees who experience strong CC stay because they believe they have to – they have no choice. Finally, the mindset associated with NC is characterized by a perceived obligation to remain in the organization. Employees with strong NC stay because they feel it is the right or moral thing to do. In other words, they ought to. Although all three commitment mindsets are thought to bind employees to their organizations, differences are believed to be evident when outcomes other than turnover are considered. Overall, these differential predictions have received strong empirical support (Cooper-Hakim and Viswesvaran, 2005; Meyer et al., 2002).

Evolving Perspectives

An emerging trend in the literature has been to adopt a configuration-based perspective. Rather than focus on individual commitment mindsets, researchers have started to examine the various ways in which the three components combine to create a unique overall experience, and have looked at the cognitive, affective, and behavioral properties associated with different component configurations or profiles (e.g., Gellatly et al., 2006; Meyer and Herscovitch, 2001; Meyer et al., 2012; Sinclair et al., 2005; Somers, 2009, 2010; Wasti, 2005). An early review of this work has revealed that four profiles seem to consistently appear across studies (Meyer et al., 2012). Two of these profiles reflect quantitative differences in the three components ('All Low' and 'All High'), and two of these profiles reflect qualitative differences in the three components. The 'AC–NC-Dominant' profile, for example, refers to a mindset where an individual experiences high levels of AC and NC relative to CC. Conversely, the 'CC-Dominant' profile refers to a mindset where the individual experiences strong feelings of CC relative to the other two components. The notion of component configurations will appear throughout the chapter but now we focus on two forms of employee withdrawal: employee turnover and absenteeism.

EMPLOYEE TURNOVER

Concept Definition

The idea that employee turnover is an intentional, discretionary act can be found in some of the earliest writings on employee withdrawal (for a discussion of this topic and the difficulties of defining turnover, see Hom et al., 2012). Voluntary turnover refers to one's choice to physically withdraw from the organization and does not reflect other forms of termination such as formal dismissal, layoff, or retirement (Hom and Griffeth, 1995). It is this form of discretionary turnover that we are most interested in understanding and considering as a consequence of organizational commitment.

Evolving Perspectives

Some of the earliest conceptualizations of the turnover process viewed staying or leaving as a function of work attitudes. Feelings of overall or facet satisfaction, for instance, were believed to evoke cognitive (for example, thinking about quitting), behavioral (for example, actively seeking for alternative employment), and/or motivational (for example, intentions) responses, which in turn would lead to a decision to leave, providing the individual was able to make the change (e.g., Mobley, 1977; Mobley et al., 1978; Mobley et al., 1979). Although most of the early emphasis was on job satisfaction, the concept of organizational commitment emerged as an attitude closer, conceptually speaking, to intentions to leave and actual quit decisions (e.g., Porter et al., 1974; Price and Mueller, 1986; Rusbult and Farrell, 1983).

The body of empirical evidence, thus far, confirms that measures of organizational commitment are negatively correlated with turnover intentions and with actual turnover, with the relations to turnover intentions being stronger than for actual turnover.

Meta-analytic studies have reported that measures of AC correlate negatively with turnover intentions ($p = -.58$, Cooper-Hakim and Viswesvaran, 2005; $p = -.44$, Jiang et al., 2012b; $p = -.52$, Mathieu and Zajac, 1990; $p = -.51$, Meyer et al., 2002; $p = -.54$, Tett and Meyer, 1993) and actual turnover ($p = -.20$, Cooper-Hakim and Viswesvaran, 2005; $p = -.23$, Griffeth et al., 2000; $p = -.22$, Jiang et al., 2012b; $p = -.28$, Mathieu and Zajac, 1990; $p = -.17$, Meyer et al., 2002). Although substantially lower in magnitude, negative relations have been found between measures of CC and both turnover intentions ($p = -.19$, Cooper-Hakim and Viswesvaran, 2005; $p = -.22$, Mathieu and Zajac, 1990; $p = -.17$, Meyer et al., 2002) and actual turnover ($p = -.25$, Cooper-Hakim and Viswesvaran, 2005; $p = -.25$, Mathieu and Zajac, 1990; $p = -.10$, Meyer et al., 2002). Although far fewer primary studies have included measures of NC, two meta-analyses reported negative relations between this component and turnover intentions ($p = -.37$, Cooper-Hakim and Viswesvaran, 2005; $p = -.39$, Meyer et al., 2002) and actual turnover ($p = -.16$, Cooper-Hakim and Viswesvaran, 2005; $p = -.16$, Meyer et al., 2002). If we take these corrected population estimates at face value it would appear that differences between the three components of commitment are most prevalent for turnover intentions, with AC having the strongest relationship, followed in turn by NC and then CC. With respect to actual turnover, differences between the three components are less evident, with NC showing weaker relations than we see for the other two components.

A long-standing frustration, however, has been the inability of attitude–intention–behavior models to explain more than 15–19 percent of the variance in voluntary turnover decisions (Hom et al., 2012; Jiang et al., 2012b; Russell, 2013). In the early 1990s, this issue led turnover researchers to expand and develop their understanding of why people decide to leave or remain in their organizations. Lee and Mitchell's (1994) 'unfolding model' represented a qualitative change in thinking. At the heart of the traditional process models is the notion that employees choose to quit after engaging in a very thorough, careful, and reasoned analysis. Alternatively, Lee and Mitchell (1994) proposed that this process is not necessarily gradual and ongoing, but rather is triggered by a 'shock', such as a negative work experience or an unsolicited job offer that disrupts or jars employees enough that they began to immediately consider leaving. Furthermore, Lee and Mitchell proposed that the circumstances surrounding the 'shock' provide an important context for the turnover decision process, effectively leading them down different shock-induced decision paths (paths 1–3): ranging from automatic, scripted quitting (that is, if this situational occurs, then I leave) to decision processes that require more deliberation and consideration of what the shock means to the individual (for example, how does the event relate to my past experiences?; cost–benefit analysis of staying versus leaving). The unfolding model also allowed for non-shock leaving (path 4), whereby turnover decisions tracked the traditional attitude–intention–behavior models mentioned earlier (e.g., Hom and Griffeth, 1991). In the early 2000s, the concept of 'embeddedness' was introduced within the unfolding model (e.g., Mitchell et al., 2001; Mitchell and Lee, 2001). Preliminary results have been encouraging and suggest not only that embedded employees (that is, incumbents who are closely tied to their jobs, organizations, and communities) are less likely to leave, but also that one's experience of embeddedness appears to explain variance in voluntary turnover above the level that is explained by traditional decision process measures (Chapter 7 in this volume; Jiang et al., 2012b).

A promising new development for turnover theory has been to move away from specific, narrowly defined attitude path concepts and their measures towards a broader under-standing of the 'withdrawal mindsets' that characterize different turnover scenarios faced by individuals (Hom et al., 2012). Introduced as a new antecedent construct, proximal withdrawal states have been described as overall cognitive states that capture individuals' desire to stay or leave the organization as well as their perceptions of control (that is, the extent to which an individual believes they are free to act on their preference). Hom et al. proposed four primary withdrawal mindsets: (1) 'enthusiastic leaving' (employees want to leave; are free to act on their preference either because they can stay or leave, or because the employer pressures them to leave); (2) 'reluctant leaving' (employees want to stay; are not free to act on their preference and are forced out by their employer or by their cir-cumstances); (3) 'reluctant staying' (employees want to leave; are not free to act on their preference, either because the cost of leaving is too high or because the employer will not release them from a contractual arrangement); and (4) 'enthusiastic staying' (employees want to stay; are free to act on their preference, either because they can stay or leave or because the employer pressures them to stay).

The parallels with commitment mindsets are striking. In their seminal article, Hom et al. (2012) began to connect different withdrawal mindsets with different commitment com-ponent configurations. For instance, it has been suggested that the enthusiastic leaving mindset potentially shares features, by inference, with a commitment mindset where emo-tional investment in the organization or its members is low. In this case, employees want to leave, so if there is emotional attachment, it is likely directed toward the goal of leaving rather than commitment to the organization (see Meyer and Herscovitch, 2001). Feeling unfettered and free to act on one's preferences suggests, again by inference, that the cost of leaving is not prohibitive and that there are no strong feelings of obligation to stay. Employees who exhibit an enthusiastic-leaving mindset will likely direct effort and atten-tion toward activities that will be instrumental in helping them achieve their goal (for example, actively seeking exit opportunities), rather than focusing too much on in-role and extra-role activities, other than meeting minimum standards. Thus, it would appear that the enthusiastic-leaving mindset could overlap with the All Low commitment profile.

It would seem that one difference, from a commitment perspective, between enthusias-tic leaving and enthusiastic staying is the object of the emotional attachment. For enthu-siastic leaving the attachment object is a different job or organization, and one's desire to remain in the current job or organization is low. For enthusiastic stayers, however, the attachment object is the current job or organization. Not only will these employees feel drawn toward the attachment object, but they do so wholeheartedly, feeling free to enact their preferences (that is, perceived control is high). It would seem that enthusi-astic staying maps to a commitment mindset where AC is prominent (AC-Dominant, AC–NC-Dominant, AC–CC-Dominant, All High). The withdrawal mindset, reluctant staying, suggests feelings of entrapment (employees want to go but are constrained from leaving) and appears to map well to a commitment mindset where CC is strong and desire to stay is low (CC-Dominant, CC–NC-Dominant). As alluded to earlier, feeling forced to remain in a situation against one's will may lead to some dysfunctional behaviors (Gellatly et al., 2006), including absenteeism, that allow for a temporary escape from a difficult situation. Finally, the withdrawal mindset, reluctant leaving, has no obvious cor-responding commitment mindset, in part because we are talking about involuntary turn-over (Hom et al., 2012) which falls outside the scope of commitment theory. The notion of reluctantly having to leave a job, organization, or relationship implies the presence of an emotional bond. It also implies very little personal control over the change in events. Research is only now starting to refine and substantiate some of these ideas and to test whether turnover decisions are manifestations of more general withdrawal mindsets that correspond to commitment mindsets (e.g., Li et al., 2015).

ABSENTEEISM

Concept Definitions

Absenteeism has been defined, simply, as not showing up for work as scheduled (Johns, 2002). Like turnover, absenteeism represents clear-cut acts that have important consequences for both the employee and the organization (e.g., Johns and Nicholson, 1982). Rather than permanently severing ties, choosing not to attend work on a given day represents a temporary and shorter-term form of withdrawal. As with turnover, it is common to distinguish between voluntary and involuntary forms of the behavior, and this is reflected in the way that absence is often measured (Chadwick-Jones et al., 1982). Involuntary (unavoidable) absences occur when individuals want to attend work but are unable to do so (for example, injury, personal illness). From the organization's perspective, voluntary absences are generally viewed as avoidable, culpable acts that need to be regulated by formal attendance control policies. From our perspective, of the two different forms of absenteeism, voluntary decisions to attend or be absent from work on any given day should be most sensitive to organizational commitment.

Evolving Perspectives

The early models of absenteeism followed the same traditional lines of thinking as voluntary turnover, including a myriad of personal (for example, age), job content and work experiences, and organizational factors (summarized in Steers and Rhodes, 1978). Much of the early absence research focused on attitudinal precursors, such as job satisfaction (Fitzgibbons, 1992; Rhodes and Steers, 1990). Unfortunately, both narrative (e.g., Muchinsky, 1977; Steers and Rhodes, 1978) and meta-analytic reviews of the absence literature have revealed, at best, weak and inverse relations between job satisfaction measures and absence criteria (e.g., Farrell and Stamm, 1988; Hackett, 1989; Hackett and Guion, 1985; Johns, 2008). Organizational commitment was also featured in early models of voluntary absenteeism (e.g., Mowday et al., 1982; Steers and Rhodes, 1978). As with job satisfaction, meta-analytic reviews of this literature confirmed weak and inconsistent negative relations between measures of organizational commitment and absence ($p = -.10$, Mathieu and Zajac, 1990), and between measures of AC and both overall absence ($p = -.15$; Meyer et al., 2002) and voluntary absence ($p = -.22$, Meyer et al., 2002).

Frustrated with their inability to explain more than a modest degree of the variance in absence behavior, researchers have looked for explanations beyond individual work attitudes (Chadwick-Jones et al., 1982; Johns and Nicholson, 1982; Nicholson and Johns, 1985). While absenteeism is still viewed as a response to negative work experiences and attitudes, current thinking tends to be broader in scope, incorporating a wider range of potential influences such as personal factors (demographics, personality, attitudes), perceived work experiences, health status, stress and strain experiences, normative pressures within one's work situation to attend or be absent, perceptions of absence legitimacy, non-work pressures (for example, family responsibilities), and cultural influences (Addae et al., 2013; Darr and Johns, 2008; Johns 1997, 2008). Along with evolving views of absenteeism, interest has emerged around the related phenomenon of 'presenteeism'. In stark contrast to absenteeism, presenteeism refers to a situation in which an employee decides to attend work when, in fact, they should not, due to illness or a medical condition (Johns, 2010, 2011). While one might think initially that attending work when one is ill is a virtue and something managers might want to encourage, there are indications that this form of behavior is dysfunctional and has serious implications for productivity loss (Johns, 2010, 2011).

Although we do not see explicit reference to 'withdrawal mindsets' with absenteeism theory, the notion of 'absence culture' probably comes closest to Hom et al.'s (2012) idea (for more extensive discussion of absence cultures, see Harrison and Martocchio, 1998; Johns, 1997, 2008; Johns and Nicholson, 1982; Nicholson and Johns, 1985; Rentsch and Steel, 2003). To the extent that one's experience of 'absence culture' resides within individuals (that is, perceived absence culture), reflecting the totality of one's observations, memories, perceptions, beliefs, and understandings with respect to acceptable levels of absence, then the notion of a mindset makes some sense. Although far from being exhaustive, empirical work has confirmed the importance of absence-related cognition (for example, normative perceptions) in shaping individual behavior (e.g., Bamberger and Biron, 2007; Gellatly, 1995; Gellatly and Allen, 2012; Harrison and Shaffer, 1994; Johns, 1994; Martocchio, 1994; Mathieu and Kohler, 1990). Recent work has also examined the importance of legitimacy beliefs regarding absenteeism across national cultures (Addae et al., 2013).

How might recent developments within commitment and turnover theories influence how we think about employee absenteeism and presenteeism? We can easily imagine a scenario where employees might experience a mindset characterized as 'reluctant absence' (that is, they want to attend but are unable to do so). In effect, reluctant absence reflects an imposed circumstance that effectively prevents employees from attending work. Or employees might experience a withdrawal mindset characterized as 'enthusiastic absence'. Here the decision to be absent would be intentional, voluntary, and associated with strong passion (that is, employees desire to be absent and feel free to act on their preferences; see Hom et al., 2012). In effect, employees want to be absent and feel free to act on this preference. Freedom to be absent might reflect the lack of external situational constraints so that individuals are free to act on their intentions or preferences (for example, Type I and Type III absence cultures; Nicholson and Johns, 1985), or it could reflect the 'press' of a strong and salient absence culture that encourages members to 'band together' and protect each other from punitive company policies by exhibiting similar levels of absence (for example, Type II or Type IV absence culture; Nicholson and Johns, 1985).

At first glance, it would seem that the notion of presenteeism might be consistent with a withdrawal mindset characterized as 'reluctant attendance'. Before linking presenteeism with the various commitment mindsets, it is important to sort through and consider the reasons why people feel they have no choice but to attend work when sick (Johns,

2010, 2011). We suspect that when the reasons involve financial necessity, punitive attendance control policies, fear of job loss, and unavailability of a replacement to do one's work, the CC-Dominant mindset will be strong. Whereas when the reasons involve, for instance, workaholism, feeling guilty, not wanting to let the team down, and others or clients are depending on the employee, we suspect that the underlying commitment mindset will emphasize the AC and/or NC component(s) (for example, AC-Dominant, NC-Dominant, AC–NC-Dominant, All High).

Future research is clearly needed to refine and substantiate some of these ideas and test whether absence decisions are manifestations of a more general withdrawal mindset that corresponds to commitment mindsets. We now turn our attention to some of the ways that organizations have leveraged 'commitment-enhancing' strategies to lower withdrawal behaviors.

COMMITMENT-ENHANCING MANAGEMENT POLICIES AND PRACTICES: IMPLICATIONS FOR EMPLOYEE TURNOVER AND ABSENTEEISM

Regardless of whether we adopt a firm-level or individual-level perspective, the body of research evidence suggests that enacting 'commitment-enhancing' management practices can be potent ways of increasing employee commitment, reducing voluntary turnover, and to a lesser extent, reducing absenteeism. Rather than focus on a single policy or management practice, it has been far more common for research to look at how mutually supporting bundles of management practices influence employee commitment and/ or withdrawal behaviors (e.g., Batt and Colvin, 2011; Gong et al., 2009; Wood and de Menezes, 1998; Youndt et al., 1996: also see Chapter 21 in this volume). Huselid (1995), for instance, famously demonstrated that companies implementing a set of progressive, high-performance management practices (for example, use of job analysis, careful selection, use of dispute resolution procedures, quality of work–life programs, frequent performance appraisals, performance-contingent rewards) experienced almost 40 percent less turnover than did firms which did not implement these work practices. Years later, this pattern of effects was confirmed using meta-analysis (e.g., Jiang et al., 2012a).

Over the years it has been debated how many practice categories exist, or which activities fall within each category (for a discussion on this issue, see Posthuma et al., 2013). Jiang et al. (2012a) organized management practices into three categories: skill-enhancing practices (for example, comprehensive recruitment, rigorous selection, extensive training), motivation-enhancing practices (for example, development-oriented performance management practices, competitive compensation, incentives and rewards, benefits, promotion and career development), and opportunity-enhancing practices (for example, flexible job design, work teams, employee involvement, information-sharing). Using meta-analytic structural equation modeling techniques, Jiang et al. (2012a) tested and found support for the mediating role of human capital (that is, a composition of employees' knowledge, skills, and abilities) and employee motivation (that is, effort, positive work attitudes such as job satisfaction, organizational commitment, and perceived organizational support) on relations between the three categories of management practices and voluntary turnover and operational outcomes (for example, productivity). Of these three categories, Jiang et al. (2012a) found that it was the motivation-enhancing and opportunity-enhancing practices that had the strongest effects on employee motivation and work attitudes, which in turn explained 18 percent of the variance in voluntary turnover (see Hom et al., 2012; Russell, 2013).

As interesting and relevant as this research might be, an overall limitation has been the tendency to retain an antiquated view of employee commitment as a unidimensional concept. Commitment-enhancing policies and management are considered efficacious to the extent that they increase the level of overall commitment and lower the level of withdrawal behavior within a firm. Failure to recognize different forms of employee commitment in this research precludes our ability to assess how different management practices, either alone or in combination with other practices, affect the likelihood of profile membership and the commitment-withdrawal mindsets associated with different component configurations. That being true, there has been some initial theoretical and empirical work looking at how the three forms of commitment are influenced by policies and management practices.

Meyer and Allen (1997) theorized that human resource policies and practices that increase employees' perceptions of self-worth should influence the mindset associated with AC and its resultant behavior (for example, lower turnover; higher attendance) via social exchange processes. Indeed, there seems to be support for this notion. Individual practices such as participation in decision-making, performance appraisals, equitable rewards, and career development opportunities have been shown, for instance, to strengthen emotional-based attachment indirectly through their effects on employee perceptions of organizational support (e.g., Allen et al., 2003; Meyer and Smith, 2000). With respect to CC, Meyer and Allen (1997) proposed that individual human resource policies and practices that (inadvertently) increased individuals' awareness of the personal costs and risks associated with leaving the organization would strengthen economically based commitment. The available evidence is consistent with the proposition that increased personal investments in one's organization over time (Becker, 1960), such as high relative pay, non-transferable seniority-related benefits, generous benefit packages that might not be replicated elsewhere, and possible loss of employer's contribution to pension plans, strengthen rather than weaken CC (e.g., Allen and Meyer, 1990; Powell and Meyer, 2004). Although very little empirical work has specifically linked company policies and management practices to NC, Meyer and Allen (1997) hypothesized that, like AC, we could understand this relationship through a social exchange framework. Drawing on a recent meta-analytic review of the perceived organizational support literature (Kurtessis et al., forthcoming), it would appear that company policies and management practices that convey to employees that the organization cares about their well-being (for example, company offers development opportunities, job security, flexibility with schedules, family-supportive practices, autonomy, and participation in decision-making) might indeed evoke within employees feelings of obligation to reciprocate this goodwill through their attitudes and behavior (Eisenberger et al., 2001; Chapter 24 in this volume).

One of the very few studies reporting relations among perceived high-performance (high-involvement) work practices, AC, and behaviors was conducted by Kehoe and Wright (2013). In their study, Kehoe and Wright assessed the extent to which food-service employees believed that 12 management practices (reflecting the same three categories used by Jiang et al., 2012a) existed within their job group. Specifically, the authors wanted to test whether employee perceptions of management practices influenced AC, citizenship behavior, turnover intentions, and attendance. The findings confirmed previous work showing positive relations between commitment-enhancing practices and AC (Allen et al., 2003; Meyer and Smith, 2000). Consistent with Jiang et al.'s (2012a) firm-level, meta-analytic findings, Kehoe and Wright found that AC completely mediated the effects of management practices on turnover intentions, but did not mediate the effects of management practices on attendance.

MOVING FORWARD: LEARNING HOW TO INFLUENCE 'COMMITMENT WITHDRAWAL' MINDSETS

While all three forms of organizational commitment are inversely related to withdrawal behaviors (Cooper-Hakim and Viswesvaran, 2005; Meyer et al., 2002), a slightly different story emerges when we consider profiles of components. Not surprisingly, profile groups that exhibit the lowest level of turnover intentions are those where the AC component is high rather than low (All High, AC–NC-Dominant, and AC-Dominant) (Gellatly et al., 2014; Somers, 2009; Wasti, 2005). It would seem that having a strong emotional bond, whether experienced as a dominant mindset or as a hybrid mindset reflecting obligation-based and/or cost-based influences, effectively acts as a 'trump card' with respect to turnover decisions. Furthermore, the mindsets characterized by strong emotional attachment may have 'spillover' effects to other kinds of relationships within the workplace. For instance, in their study of staff nurses, Gellatly et al. (2014) found that nurses who belonged to the All High and AC-Dominant profile groups were not only the least likely to leave but they also perceived higher-quality relations with other nurses (for example, on my unit, most interpersonal staff relationships are positive and supportive) than did nurses who belonged to profile groups where affective commitment was low. Indeed, nurses who belonged to profile groups where the AC and NC components were both low (All Low and CC-Dominant) experienced the greatest risk of leaving; a pattern that has been reported elsewhere (e.g., Somers, 2009; Wasti, 2005).

　As this literature moves forward it will be important to consider how individual or bundled management practices influence the commitment withdrawal mindsets discussed in this chapter. Once we know how different commitment-enhancing management practices affect AC, CC, and NC we can begin to understand and predict how combinations of practices will affect the likelihood of profile membership and the nature of the commitment withdrawal minds associated with each. An example of this approach was conducted by Gellatly et al. (2009). Employee perceptions of development-oriented practices (for example, offering meaningful and interesting work, greater responsibility and autonomy), stability-oriented practices (for example, offering job security, stable wages), and reward-oriented practices (for example, performance-based incentives, opportunities to earn high pay), were reconciled with the likelihood of different combinations of AC and CC. As expected, perceptions of development-oriented practices increased the likelihood of belonging to a profile group where AC was strong (High AC, Low CC; High AC, High CC) and decreased the likelihood of belonging to a profile group where CC was strong (High CC, Low AC) or when both components were low. Stability-oriented practices increased the likelihood of profiles where CC was strong (High CC, Low AC; High CC, High AC), and decreased the likelihood of the All Low profile. Reward-oriented practices were found to increase the likelihood of the emotionally attachment profile (High AC, Low CC) and decrease the likelihood of an All Low profile.

More work along these lines, extending to the full range of AC, CC, and NC configurations, as well as research that includes measures that more fully capture the nature of the underlying commitment withdrawal mindsets, would help managers to fine-tune their human resource systems and retention strategies. For instance, we know that the potentially negative effects of a CC-Dominant or CC–NC-Dominant mindset can be offset by increasing the strength of AC. Practices known to elevate CC might include retention bonuses and generous, non-portable benefits. An organization that uses economic policies as the primary retention strategy might want to consider bundling these with management practices aimed at strengthening social–emotional ties to others and the organization as a whole, effectively fostering a less adverse AC–CC-Dominant or All High mindset. Clearly we are at the very beginning, and much research is needed to understand how the human resource system can be configured to produce not only productive employees but employees who want to stay.

REFERENCES

Addae, H.M., Johns, G., and Boies, K. (2013). The legitimacy of absenteeism from work: a nine nation exploratory study. *Cross Cultural Management: An International Journal*, *20*(3), 402–428.

Allen, D.G., Shore, L.M., and Griffeth, R.W. (2003). The role of perceived organizational support and supportive human resource practices in the turnover process. *Journal of Management*, *29*(1), 99–118.

Allen, N.J. and Meyer, J.P. (1990). The measurement and antecedents of affective, continuance and normative commitment to the organization. *Journal of Occupational Psychology*, *63*(1), 1–18.

Bamberger, P. and Biron, M. (2007). Group norms and excessive absenteeism: The role of peer referent others. *Organizational Behavior and Human Decision Processes*, *103*(2), 179–196.

Batt, R. and Colvin, A.J. (2011). An employment systems approach to turnover: Human resources practices, quits, dismissals, and performance. *Academy of Management Journal*, *54*(4), 695–717.

Becker, H.S. (1960). Notes on the concept of commitment. *American Journal of Sociology*, *66*(1), 32–40.

Chadwick-Jones, J.K., Nicholson, N., and Brown, C. (1982). *Social Psychology of Absenteeism*. New York: Prager.

Cooper-Hakim, A. and Viswesvaran, C. (2005). The construct of work commitment: Testing an integrative framework. *Psychological Bulletin*, *131*(2), 241.

Darr, W. and Johns, G. (2008). Work strain, health, and absenteeism: a meta-analysis. *Journal of Occupational Health Psychology*, *13*(4), 293.

Eisenberger, R., Armeli, S., Rexwinkel, B., Lynch, P.D., and Rhoades, L. (2001). Reciprocation of perceived organizational support. *Journal of Applied Psychology*, *86*(1), 42.

Farrell, D. and Stamm, C.L. (1988). Meta-analysis of the correlates of employee absence. *Human Relations*, *41*(3), 211–227.

Fitzgibbons, D.E. (1992). A critical reexamination of employee absence: the impact of relational contracting, the negotiated order, and the employment relationship. *Research in Personnel and Human Resources Management*, *10*, 73–120.

Gellatly, I.R. (1995). Individual and group determinants of employee absenteeism: Test of a causal model. *Journal of Organizational Behavior*, *16*(5), 469–485.

Gellatly, I.R. and Allen, N.J. (2012). Group mate absence, dissimilarity, and individual absence: Another look at 'monkey see, monkey do'. *European Journal of Work and Organizational Psychology*, *21*(1), 106–124.

Gellatly, I.R., Cummings, G.G., and Cowden, T.L. (2014). Staff nurse commitment, work relationships, and turnover intentions: A latent profile analysis. *Nursing Research*, *63*(3), 170–181.

Gellatly, I.R., Hunter, K.H., Currie, L.G., and Irving, P.G. (2009). HRM practices and organizational commitment profiles. *International Journal of Human Resource Management*, *20*(4), 869–884.

Gellatly, I.R., Meyer, J.P., and Luchak, A.A. (2006). Combined effects of the three commitment components on focal and discretionary behaviors: A test of Meyer and Herscovitch's propositions. *Journal of Vocational Behavior*, *69*(2), 331–345.

Gong, Y., Law, K.S., Chang, S., and Xin, K.R. (2009). Human resources management and firm performance: The differential role of managerial affective and continuance commitment. *Journal of Applied Psychology*, *94*(1), 263.

Griffeth, R.W., Hom, P.W., and Gaertner, S. (2000). A meta-analysis of antecedents and correlates of employee turnover: Update, moderator tests, and research implications for the next millennium. *Journal of Management*, *26*(3), 463–488.

Hackett, R.D. (1989). Work attitudes and employee absenteeism: A synthesis of the literature. *Journal of Occupational Psychology*, *62*(3), 235–248.

Hackett, R.D. and Guion, R.M. (1985). A reevaluation of the absenteeism–job satisfaction relationship. *Organizational Behavior and Human Decision Processes*, *35*(3), 340–381.

Harrison, D.A. and Martocchio, J.J. (1998). Time for absenteeism: A 20-year review of origins, offshoots, and outcomes. *Journal of Management*, *24*(3), 305–350.

Harrison, D.A. and Shaffer, M.A. (1994). Comparative examinations of self-reports and perceived absenteeism norms: Wading through Lake Wobegon. *Journal of Applied Psychology*, *79*, 240–251.

Hom, P.W. and Griffeth, R.W. (1991). Structural equations modeling test of a turnover theory: Cross-sectional and longitudinal analyses. *Journal of Applied Psychology*, *76*(3), 350.

Hom, P.W. and Griffeth, R.W. (1995). *Employee Turnover*. Cincinnati, OH: South-Western College Publishing.

Hom, P.W., Mitchell, T.R., Lee, T.W., and Griffeth, R.W. (2012). Reviewing employee turnover: focusing on proximal withdrawal states and an expanded criterion. *Psychological Bulletin*, *138*(5), 831–858.

Huselid, M.A. (1995). The impact of human resource management practices on turnover, productivity, and corporate financial performance. *Academy of Management Journal*, *38*(3), 635–672.

Jiang, K., Lepak, D., Hu, J., and Baer, J. (2012a). How does human resource management influence organizational outcomes? A meta-analytic investigation of mediating mechanisms. *Academy of Management Journal*, *55*(6), 1264–1294.

Jiang, K., Liu, D., McKay, P.F., Lee, T.W., and Mitchell, T.R. (2012b). When and how is job embeddedness predictive of turnover? A meta-analytic investigation. *Journal of Applied Psychology*, *97*(5), 1077–1096.

Johns, G. (1994). How often were you absent? A review of the use of self-reported absence data. *Journal of Applied Psychology*, *79*(4), 574.

Johns, G. (1997). Contemporary research on absence from work: Correlates, causes and consequences. *International Review of Industrial and Organizational Psychology*, *12*, 115–174.

Johns, G. (2002). Absenteeism and mental health. In J.C. Thomas, and M. Hersen (eds), *Handbook of Mental Health in the Workplace* (437–455). Thousand Oaks, CA: Sage.

Johns, G. (2008). Absenteeism and presenteeism: Not at work or not working well. In C.L. Cooper and J. Barling (eds), *The Sage Handbook of Organizational Behavior* (Vol. 1, 160–177). London: Sage.

Johns, G. (2010). Presenteeism in the workplace: A review and research agenda. *Journal of Organizational Behavior*, *31*(4), 519–542.

Johns, G. (2011). Attendance dynamics at work: The antecedents and correlates of presenteeism, absenteeism, and productivity loss. *Journal of Occupational Health Psychology*, *16*(4), 483.

Johns, G. and Nicholson, N. (1982). The meanings of absence: New strategies for theory and practice. *Research in Organizational Behavior*, *4*, 127–172.

Kehoe, R.R. and Wright, P.M. (2013). The impact of high-performance human resource practices on employees' attitudes and behaviors. *Journal of Management*, *39*(2), 366–391.

Kurtessis, J.N., Eisenberger, R., Ford, M.T., Buffardi, L.C., Stewart, K.A., and Adis, C.S. (forthcoming). Perceived organizational support a meta-analytic evaluation of organizational support theory. *Journal of Management*.

Lee, T.W. and Mitchell, T.R. (1994). An alternative approach: The unfolding model of voluntary employee turnover. *Academy of Management Review*, *19*(1), 51–89.

Li, J., Lee, T.W., Mitchell, T.R., Hom, P.W., and Griffeth, R.W. (2015). The effects of proximal withdrawal states on job attitudes, job search, intent to leave and voluntary employee turnover. Paper presented at 75th Annual Meeting of the Academy of Management, Vancouver, August

Martocchio, J.J. (1994). The effects of absence culture on individual absence. *Human Relations*, *47*(3), 243–262.

Mathieu, J.E. and Kohler, S.S. (1990). A test of the interactive effects of organizational commitment and job involvement on various types of absence. *Journal of Vocational Behavior*, *36*(1), 33–44.

Mathieu, J.E. and Zajac, D.M. (1990). A review and meta-analysis of the antecedents, correlates, and consequences of organizational commitment. *Psychological Bulletin*, *108*(2), 171.

Meyer, J.P. (2009). Commitment in a changing world of work. In H.J. Klein, T. Becker, and J.P. Meyer (eds),

Commitment in Organizations: Accumulated Wisdom and New Directions (37–68). London: Routledge/Taylor & Francis.

Meyer, J.P. and Allen, N.J. (1991). A three-component conceptualization of organizational commitment. *Human Resource Management Review*, *1*(1), 61–89.

Meyer, J.P. and Allen, N.J. (1997). *Commitment in the Workplace: Theory, Research, and Application*. Thousand Oaks, CA: Sage Publications.

Meyer, J.P. and Herscovitch, L. (2001). Commitment in the workplace: Toward a general model. *Human Resource Management Review*, *11*(3), 299–326.

Meyer, J.P. and Smith, C.A. (2000). HRM practices and organizational commitment: Test of a mediation model. *Canadian Journal of Administrative Sciences/Revue Canadienne Des Sciences De L'Administration*, *17*(4), 319–331.

Meyer, J.P., Stanley, D.J., Herscovitch, L., and Topolnytsky, L. (2002). Affective, continuance, and normative commitment to the organization: A meta-analysis of antecedents, correlates, and consequences. *Journal of Vocational Behavior*, *61*(1), 20–52.

Meyer, J.P., Stanley, L.J., and Parfyonova, N.M. (2012). Employee commitment in context: The nature and implication of commitment profiles. *Journal of Vocational Behavior*, *80*(1), 1–16.

Mitchell, T.R., Holtom, B.C., Lee, T.W., Sablynski, C.J., and Erez, M. (2001). Why people stay: Using job embeddedness to predict voluntary turnover. *Academy of Management Journal*, *44*(6), 1102–1121.

Mitchell, T.R. and Lee, T.W. (2001). The unfolding model of voluntary turnover and job embeddedness: Foundations for a comprehensive theory of attachment. *Research in Organizational Behavior*, *23*, 189–246.

Mobley, W.H. (1977). Intermediate linkages in the relationship between job satisfaction and employee turnover. *Journal of Applied Psychology*, *62*(2), 237.

Mobley, W.H., Griffeth, R.W., Hand, H.H., and Meglino, B.M. (1979). Review and conceptual analysis of the employee turnover process. *Psychological Bulletin*, *86*(3), 493.

Mobley, W.H., Horner, S.O., and Hollingsworth, A.T. (1978). An evaluation of precursors of hospital employee turnover. *Journal of Applied Psychology*, *63*(4), 408.

Mowday, R.T., Porter, L.W., and Steers, R.M. (1982). *Employee–Organization Linkages: The Psychology of Commitment, Absenteeism, and Turnover*. New York: Academic Press.

Muchinsky, P.M. (1977). Employee absenteeism: A review of the literature. *Journal of Vocational Behavior*, *10*(3), 316–340.

Nicholson, N. and Johns, G. (1985). The absence culture and psychological contract – Who's in control of absence? *Academy of Management Review*, *10*(3), 397–407.

Porter, L.W., Steers, R.M., Mowday, R.T., and Boulian, P.V. (1974). Organizational commitment, job satisfaction, and turnover among psychiatric technicians. *Journal of Applied Psychology*, *59*(5), 603.

Posthuma, R.A., Campion, M.C., Masimova, M., and Campion, M.A. (2013). A high performance work practices taxonomy: Integrating the literature and directing future research. *Journal of Management*, *39*(5), 1184–1220.

Powell, D.M. and Meyer, J.P. (2004). Side-bet theory and the three-component model of organizational commitment. *Journal of Vocational Behavior*, *65*(1), 157–177.

Price, J.L. and Mueller, C.W. (1986). *Absenteeism and Turnover of Hospital Employees*. Greenwich, CT: JAI Press.

Rentsch, J.R. and Steel, R.P. (2003). What does unit-level absence mean? Issues for future unit-level absence research. *Human Resource Management Review*, *13*(2), 185–202.

Rhodes, S.R. and Steers, R.M. (1990). *Managing Employee Absenteeism*. Reading, MA: Addison-Wesley.

Rusbult, C.E. and Farrell, D. (1983). A longitudinal test of the investment model: The impact on job satisfaction, job commitment, and turnover of variations in rewards, costs, alternatives, and investments. *Journal of Applied Psychology*, *68*(3), 429.

Russell, C.J. (2013). Is it time to voluntarily turn over theories of voluntary turnover? *Industrial and Organizational Psychology*, *6*(2), 156–173.

Sinclair, R.R., Tucker, J.S., Cullen, J.C., and Wright, C. (2005). Performance differences among four organizational commitment profiles. *Journal of Applied Psychology*, *90*(6), 1280.

Somers, M.J. (2009). The combined influence of affective, continuance and normative commitment on employee withdrawal. *Journal of Vocational Behavior*, *74*(1), 75–81.

Somers, M.J. (2010). Patterns of attachment to organizations: Commitment profiles and work outcomes. *Journal of Occupational and Organizational Psychology*, *83*(2), 443–453.

Steers, R.M. and Rhodes, S.R. (1978). Major influences on employee attendance: A process model. *Journal of Applied Psychology*, *63*(4), 391.

Tett, R.P. and Meyer, J.P. (1993). Job satisfaction, organizational commitment, turnover intention, and turnover: path analyses based on meta-analytic findings. *Personnel Psychology*, *46*(2), 259–293.

Wasti, S.A. (2005). Commitment profiles: Combinations of organizational commitment forms and job outcomes. *Journal of Vocational Behavior*, *67*(2), 290–308.

Wood, S. and De Menezes, L. (1998). High commitment management in the UK: Evidence from the workplace industrial relations survey, and employers' manpower and skills practices survey. *Human Relations*, *51*(4), 485–515.

Youndt, M.A., Snell, S.A., Dean, J.W., and Lepak, D.P. (1996). Human resource management, manufacturing strategy, and firm performance. *Academy of Management Journal*, *39*(4), 836–866.

15. Employee commitment and performance
David J. Stanley and John P. Meyer

Commitment in the organizational context has been the focus of thousands of journal articles. Although interest was stimulated initially by its implications for employee retention, questions about its effects on performance also arose, particularly when it was acknowledged that commitment to an organization can be experienced in different ways (Meyer and Allen, 1991, 1997). Theory and research pertaining to the commitment–performance relationship has increased in complexity over the years due in part to the complexity of the constructs themselves. Commitment can not only be experienced in different ways, but can also be directed at different foci (see Chapter 4 in this volume) and can be measured at different levels (for example, individual, unit, organization). Performance can also be defined and operationalized in different ways and measured at different levels. Consequently, we begin by elaborating on some of this complexity to set the stage for our review of the research literature. The objective of our review is to identify what we currently know about the commitment–performance relationship and the implications for practice, but also to point out the gaps in our knowledge and offer recommendations for future research.

PERFORMANCE

Job performance is a construct central to industrial-organizational psychology and has been studied with a variety of methods over a long period of time (Austin and Villanova, 1992). Correspondingly, many different taxonomic structures have evolved focusing on different parts of job performance with greatly varying numbers of dimensions (cf., Campbell, 1990; Katz and Kahn, 1978; Murphy, 1989; Organ, 1988; Tett et al., 2000). Given the proliferation of taxonomies, it is not surprising that there are often overlapping definitions and behavioral categories (Rotondo and Sackett, 2002). In an attempt to build conceptual consensus based on an extensive review of the literature, Rotondo and Sackett suggested that performance-related behaviors could be clustered into three broad categories: task behaviors, citizenship behaviors, and counterproductive work behaviors. This taxonomy is helpful for reviewing the commitment literature because it is generally consistent with how commitment researchers have conceptualized and measured performance (that is, a focus on broad rather than narrow categories). In this chapter we focus on two of the three performance categories identified by Rotondo and Sackett (2002) – task behaviors and citizenship behaviors – henceforth using the umbrella term 'performance' to refer to both of these types of behaviors. The third category, counterproductive work behavior, is covered in Chapter 16 in this volume.

We use the term 'task performance' to describe the extent to which employees effectively perform organizational behaviors that implement core processes or provide such processes with needed materials or services (Borman and Motowidlo, 1993, 1997). A variety of taxonomies have been proposed for task performance (e.g., Bernardin and Beatty, 1984; Campbell, 1990; Murphy, 1989). However, commitment research typically focuses on overall task performance for parsimony.

The distinction between task performance and organizational citizenship behavior (OCB) used by Rotondo and Sackett (2002) was popularized by Organ and colleagues (e.g., Smith et al., 1983) and parallels work by Borman and Motowidlo (1993) on task versus contextual performance. A common element of the OCB definitions suggested by Organ (1997), Borman and Motowidlo (1993), and Rotondo and Sackett (2002) is that they all focus on behaviors that maintain and enhance the social and psychological context that scaffolds task performance. This approach to defining OCB avoids earlier problems, outlined by Morrison (1994), associated with thinking about the task–OCB distinction in terms of required versus discretionary behaviors. Morrison noted that there is considerable variability in perceptions of whether OCB is discretionary as previously suggested by Organ (1990). In any case, the conceptual distinction between OCBs and task performance has empirical support: they are related but distinguishable; this is evidenced by the fact that they only have 36 percent shared variance ($\rho = .60$: Podsakoff et al., 2009).

A number of OCB taxonomies have been suggested. Initially, Smith et al. (1983) proposed two OCB dimensions: altruism and generalized compliance. Altruism was defined by behaviors intended to benefit a specific person, whereas generalized compliance was defined by behaviors related to observing the norms defining a good employee. Subsequently, Organ (1988) suggested a five-dimensional taxonomy that included three additional dimensions, namely, sportsmanship, courtesy, and civic virtue. Both the altruism and the generalized compliance dimensions were retained (but narrowed), and generalized compliance was renamed conscientiousness (LePine et al., 2002). Others have suggested different multidimensional OCB frameworks (e.g., Morrison, 1994; Van Dyne et al., 1994; Williams and Anderson, 1991).

For purposes of this review, we view OCBs through the lens of the broad OCB-Organization (OCB-O) and OCB-Individual (OCB-I) distinction proposed by Williams and Anderson (1991). This framework is consistent with the work of others (e.g., Coleman and Borman, 2000; Lee and Allen, 2002), suggesting that OCBs are often highly correlated and tend to vary, in part, with respect to who benefits from the behavior (LePine et al., 2002). OCB-O encompasses behaviors that benefit the organization (for example, altruism and courtesy), whereas OCB-I encompasses behaviors that benefit individuals (for example, sportsmanship, civic virtue, and conscientiousness). Although distinguishable, these components of OCB are related. Indeed, a recent meta-analysis revealed a fairly substantial correlation between OCB-O and OCB-I ($\rho = .75$: Podsakoff et al., 2009).

OCBs are an important component of organizational life. For example, using a meta-analytic path model Podsakoff et al. (2009) found that in some cases OCBs predicted overall job performance ratings better than task performance. Additionally, they also reported that OCBs were related to overall unit performance ($\rho = .43$), subjective unit performance measures ($\rho = .47$), objective unit performance measures ($\rho = .37$), and unit efficiency ($\rho = .40$). Thus, there are compelling reasons to examine the linkage between commitment and OCBs in addition to the more traditional task performance.

COMMITMENT

Despite the thousands of articles published on commitment there remains some debate as to how it is best defined; indeed, at least eight distinct conceptualizations have guided research to date (Klein et al., 2012). The breadth of conceptualizations may be due to the complexity of the construct or perhaps the diversity of academic backgrounds guiding the perspectives of commitment researchers (Meyer, 2009). At the broadest level, some authors prefer a unidimensional model (see Chapter 2 in this volume) whereas others prefer a multidimensional model (see Chapter 3 in this volume). In this chapter we use a multidimensional model as the guiding framework; specifically, the Meyer and Allen three-component model (TCM) of organizational commitment (Allen and Meyer, 1990, 1996; Meyer and Allen, 1991).

Within the TCM there is a distinction between three underlying components of organizational commitment: affective, normative, and continuous commitment. Affective commitment (AC) is based on emotional attachment to, identification with, and involvement in the organization, whereas normative commitment (NC) is based on a perceived obligation to remain with the organization. In contrast, continuance commitment (CC) is based on the perceived costs associated with leaving the organization (Meyer et al., 2002). The three components in the TCM are not mutually exclusive and may be thought of together as comprising an employee's commitment profile (Meyer and Herscovitch, 2001). We believe this model is an effective way to guide our review because it also encompasses the unidimensional commitment framework. That is, AC has been found to correlate quite strongly with the Organizational Commitment Questionnaire (OCQ) (Mowday et al., 1979: ρ = .88; Meyer et al., 2002) and with the more recently introduced Klein target-free unidimensional measure (KUT) (r = .69, Klein et al., 2014). Consequently, findings pertaining to AC are likely to reflect those that can be expected in research using the OCQ, KUT, or related unidimensional measures.

How does commitment influence behaviors within an organization? When considering this question, the majority of theory and research has viewed each of the three commitment components as reflecting a psychological state, or mindset (Meyer and Allen, 1991: Meyer and Herscovitch, 2001). Meyer and Allen initially proposed that these mindsets might relate differently to behavior, and various theories have subsequently been proposed to explain why these differences might exist (e.g., Johnson et al., 2010; Meyer et al., 2004). More recently it has been argued that considering the commitment components in isolation might be limiting, and that it is better to consider how these components combine to form commitment profiles (Gellatly et al., 2006; Meyer and Herscovitch, 2001). Therefore, hereinafter we distinguish between the terms 'component mindset' and 'profile mindset'.

Within the TCM framework, commitment is viewed as a force that binds employees to a target and a course of action relevant to that target (Meyer and Herscovitch, 2001; Meyer et al., 2006). In the original TCM, the emphasis was on organizational commitment, and it was argued that commitment would lead to a reduction in turnover (Allen and Meyer, 1990; Meyer and Allen, 1991). Meyer and Herscovitch (2001) proposed that commitment to any particular entity would increase the likelihood of the behaviors specified within the 'terms' of that commitment (Brown, 1996). To the extent that commitments are truly binding, these behaviors become non-discretionary.

Meyer and Herscovitch (2001) noted that commitments can also have implications for more discretionary forms of behavior, and that it is with regard to these behaviors that the distinctions between the different components, or mindsets, are most important. For example, employees may be more willing to go beyond what is required for the benefit of the target entity if they are affectively or normatively committed than if their primary tie is based on CC.

For all three components of organizational commitment in the TCM, the focal consequence behavior is staying with the organization, and research has generally confirmed a negative relation with withdrawal cognition (for example, turnover intention) and turnover (Meyer et al., 2002: see Chapter 14 in this volume). In contrast, performance behaviors (task and OCB) are not focal behaviors per se (at least beyond minimum requirement for job retention). From an organizational commitment perspective, both task and citizenship behaviors can, however, be considered discretionary behaviors that occur as a consequence of the commitment. The extent to which employees choose to view certain discretionary behaviors as part of their commitment may depend on the nature of the behavior as well as both the component mindsets and the overall profile mindset underlying the commitment.

As noted previously, employees can direct their commitments to targets other than the organization, and these commitments can also have implications for task performance and OCB. The existence of multiple targets of commitment raises the potential for compatibility (Lee et al., 2000; Wallace, 1993) and conflict (Gouldner, 1957; Gordon and Ladd, 1990), and these can play out in complex ways to influence performance and OCB. The literatures pertaining to the influence of commitment to targets other than the organization, and to the interactions among these commitments, is relatively small and some of the findings are described in Chapter 4 in this volume on multiple foci, as well as in chapters pertaining to occupational (Chapter 10), social (supervisor, team, customer: Chapter 11), union (Chapter 12) and action (goals, change initiatives: Chapter 13) commitments. Therefore, we focus our review on the more well-studied relation between organizational commitment and performance. We also noted earlier that commitment and performance can be measured and related at different levels. Although important, research concerning the relation between commitment and performance at a unit or organizational level is sparse (e.g., Ostroff, 1992; Steyrer et al., 2008; Winkler et al., 2012; Wright et al., 2005). Much of this research has been conducted in the investigation of strategic human resource management (HRM) and is reviewed in Chapter 21 in this volume. Consequently, we focus our discussion on the relation between commitment and performance at the individual level.

ORGANIZATIONAL COMMITMENT AND PERFORMANCE

In order to understand the nature of commitment–outcome relations it helps to think about the terms of a commitment. Brown (1996) suggested that individuals engage in behaviors that are required to fulfill the terms of the commitment. Meyer and Herscovitch (2001) agreed, but argued that the terms of commitment vary with each component and profile mindset such that some mindsets have broader terms than others. More specifically, the nature of commitment mindsets may cause some employees to perceive the implications of their commitments broadly or narrowly. In what follows, we elaborate on the theoretical rationale for relations involving the individual component mindsets and for profile mindsets. In each case, we also provide a summary of the empirical evidence that has accumulated to date.

Component Mindsets

With respect to individual components, the implications of a mindset can be illustrated by considering CC. This component mindset focuses quite narrowly on the costs associated with leaving the organization. The terms of the commitment are correspondingly narrow and restricted to staying with the organization. That is, employees whose tie to the organization is based only on CC are likely to remain in the organization and do little more than is required to maintain their employment. In contrast, employees with strong NC remain with the organization to ensure that they are 'doing the right thing' (Meyer and Allen, 1997). Doing the right thing is arguably a somewhat broader mindset than 'having to remain', and consequently the terms of an NC might also be broader. That is, 'doing the right thing' may well include higher levels of task performance and/or OCBs. AC is a desire-based mindset characterized by identification with and attachment to the organization. Employees characterized by this type of commitment are likely to perceive the terms of their commitment to the organization very broadly, such that task performance, OCBs, and a variety of other behaviors are included. Thus, individuals with strong affective or NC will tend to engage in focal behavior (that is, staying with the organization) as well as more discretionary behaviors (for example, task performance and citizenship behaviors).

There is meta-analytic evidence supporting the hypothesized relations between component mindsets and performance (Cooper-Hakim and Viswesvaran, 2005; Meyer et al., 2002, Riketta, 2002, 2008). However, we present more recent meta-analytic estimates from Meyer et al. (2014), which is based on a greater number of studies and substantially larger overall sample size. These meta-analytic estimates were generated using the procedures outlined by Hunter and Schmidt (1990), correcting for unreliability in the predictor and criterion prior to aggregation. The analyses presented are based on studies obtained by searching PsycINFO (1983 to April 2013), ProQuest Psychology (1990 to April 2013), and ProQuest Dissertations and Theses, and the Social Science Citation Index up to April 2013.

We also summarize the results of some of the moderator analyses conducted by Meyer et al. (2014). One of these analyses was conducted to determine whether the nature of the NC measure changed as a function of the scale revisions introduced by Meyer et al. (1993). Specifically, the initial eight-item measure (Allen and Meyer, 1990) of NC was replaced with a six-item measure (Meyer et al, 1993). The earlier eight-item measure focused on socialized obligation, whereas the subsequent six-item measure focused on a more general sense of obligation to remain with the organization (see Meyer and Parfyonova, 2010). Additionally, where justified by available data, we report subgroup analyses for task and OCB performance rating source (self or supervisor): although some studies used objective indices of performance, there were not enough studies for Meyer et al. (2014) to include these in moderator analyses. Finally, Meyer et al. also conducted analyses separately for individual countries where there was a sufficient number of studies, and used cultural values (Hofstede, 2001; Schwartz, 2006) as predictors of the strength of the commitment–performance relations across countries. Although space does not permit us to report the findings of these analyses in detail, we provide a brief summary of the findings as they pertain to task performance and OCB at the end of each respective section.

Task Performance Relations for Organizational Commitment Components

Affective commitment
There was a moderate positive correlation between AC and task performance, $\rho = .25$, such that higher levels of AC were associated with higher levels of task performance. Additionally, the correlation was stronger for task performance based on self-ratings, $\rho = .26$, than supervisor ratings, $\rho = .19$.

Normative commitment
There was a weak positive correlation between NC and task performance, $\rho = .08$, such that higher levels of NC were associated with higher levels of task performance. This correlation was moderated by rating source such that the correlation was stronger for supervisor-rated performance ($\rho = .13$) than self-rated performance ($\rho = .05$). Likewise, the correlation was moderated by the NC scale such that the correlation was stronger for the six-item scale measuring generalized obligation ($\rho = .12$) than for the eight-item scale measuring socialized obligation ($\rho = .06$).

Continuance commitment
There was a negligible negative correlation between CC and task performance, $\rho = -.04$. Performance ratings were similar for self-rated ($\rho = -.04$) and supervisor-rated performance ($\rho = -.06$).

Culture as a moderator
The number of countries for which meaningful correlations between the commitment components and task performance could be computed was relatively small, but Meyer et al. (2014) noted that in all cases the 95 percent confidence interval overlapped with that of the US. Moreover, none of the cultural values used to predict the strength of the correlations across countries accounted for significant variance. Therefore, there is little evidence to suggest that the nature of the relations between task performance and AC, NC, or CC differ across those countries included in their analyses.

OCB Relations for Commitment Components

Affective commitment
There was a moderate correlation between AC and OCB, $\rho = .35$, such that high levels of AC were associated with increased OCBs. The correlation was stronger for OCBs based on self-ratings ($\rho = .41$) than for supervisor ratings ($\rho = .23$). OCB focus (OCB-I or OCB-O) had little impact on the relation ($\rho = .32$ and $\rho = .34$, respectively).

Normative commitment
There was a moderate positive correlation between NC and OCBs, $\rho = .29$, such that high levels of NC were associated with greater citizenship behaviors. This correlation was moderated by rating source such that the correlation was stronger for self-rated OCBs ($\rho = .31$) than supervisor-rated OCBs ($\rho = .16$). Likewise, the correlation was moderated by OCB focus such that the correlation was stronger for citizenship behavior directed toward the organization (OCB-O; $\rho = .32$) than individuals (OCB-I; $\rho = .23$). NC scale (six-item or eight-item) did not moderate the relation ($\rho = .29$ and $\rho = .29$, respectively).

Continuance commitment
There was a negligible positive correlation between CC and OCBs ($\rho = .05$). Relations were weak for both supervisor-rated and self-rated OCBs ($\rho = -.03$ and $\rho = .07$, respectively) and similar ($\rho = .03$ and $\rho = .03$) for OCB focus (OCB-I and OCB-O, respectively).

Culture as a moderator
Again, the number of countries for which meaningful correlations between the commitment components and OCB could be computed was relatively small. However, Meyer et al. (2014) noted that in one case, that involving the correlation between AC and OCB in South Korea, the 95 percent confidence interval around the mean ($\rho = .51$) did not overlap with that for the United States ($\rho = .34$). In addition, relative-importance analyses revealed that the positive relation between AC and OCB tended to be weaker in countries with higher scores on Hofstede's (2001) uncertainty avoidance dimension and Schwartz's (2006) egalitarianism dimension, and lower on Schwartz's mastery orientation. Thus, again, with minor exceptions, Meyer et al.'s findings suggest that the TCM components of commitment relate similarly to OCB across cultures.

Component Summary

The correlations reported by Meyer et al. (2014) regarding both task performance and OCB were generally similar to those obtained previously by Meyer et al. (2002), and consistent with predictions based on the TCM of organizational commitment. Interestingly, however, the AC–task performance correlation obtained by Meyer et al. (2014) was stronger ($\rho = .25$ versus $\rho = .16$) than that reported by Meyer et al. (2002), and is probably a better estimate given that it was based on a much larger set of studies ($K = 163$ versus $K = 25$). This stronger estimated relation is also consistent with estimates by Riketta (2002) ($\rho = .23$), and Cooper-Hakim and Viswesvaran (2005) ($\rho = .27$). One additional contribution of the Meyer et al. (2014) meta-analysis is that they were able to report a correlation ($\rho = .08$) between NC and supervisor-related task performance; whereas Meyer et al. (2002) were unable to estimate this correlation due to an insufficient number of studies.

The studies included in meta-analytic estimates were primarily cross-sectional. Consequently, although in theory commitment is a cause of task and citizenship behaviors, the analyses do not provide evidence of causality. The meta-analysis of panel studies conducted by Riketta (2008) arguably provides a better assessment of the causal influence of AC on task performance and citizenship behaviors. The correlations obtained in Riketta's analysis were weaker than the meta-analytic correlations reported by Meyer et al. (2014): $\rho = .08$ and $\rho = .25$, respectively. However, the number of studies used by Riketta to obtain those estimates was quite low: $K = 2$ and $K = 3$, respectively; consequently, the magnitude of these correlations should be interpreted with caution. The limited number of panel studies also suggests that substantially more research of this nature is needed.

In Meyer et al.'s (2014) findings, and those of Riketta (2008), correlations with task performance were considerably weaker than those obtained for citizenship behaviors. The weaker correlations for task performance may be due, in part, to an important difference between task and citizenship behaviors. That is, although both sets of behaviors are likely to be a consequence of employee intentions, task performance is likely to be more constrained by other factors (for example, employee ability or the nature of the work process; Organ and Ryan, 1995). In contrast, because OCBs are behaviors that maintain and enhance the social and psychological contexts, these behaviors are less likely to be dependent on factors such as ability or work process. They are also more likely to be included as part of the exchange process involved in the psychological contract, particularly the relational aspect, that develops between employees and the organization (see Chapter 9 in this volume). This might help to explain why OCBs relate more strongly than task performance with the AC and NC mindsets.

Profile Mindsets

The above analyses provide information about the relations involving each commitment component considered independently of the other components. As noted, however, some researchers have theorized that how an individual component relates to behavior might depend on the relative strength of the other components (e.g., Gellatly et al., 2006; Meyer and Herscovitch, 2001; Meyer et al., 2012). For example, Gellatly et al. (2006) found that NC related positively with OCB when combined with strong AC, but correlated negatively with OCB when CC was strong and AC was weak. Based on these findings, they argued that NC might be experienced differently within the context of these profiles: as a 'moral imperative' (a desire to do the right thing) in the former, and an 'indebted obligation' (a need to do what is expected) in the latter. Similarly, Meyer et al. (2012) found that strong CC was associated with more positive outcomes, including OCB, when it combined with strong AC and NC in a 'fully committed' profile than when AC and NC were weak. Thus, the zero-order correlations for any particular component may be attenuated or enhanced due to the context provided by the other components.

Although still limited, the findings of existing profile studies are generally consistent in demonstrating that OCB is greater among employees with fully committed, AC/NC-dominant, and AC-dominant profiles than for those with uncommitted (low scores on all three components) or CC-dominant profiles (e.g., Gellatly et al., 2006; Meyer et al., 2012; Wasti, 2005). Interestingly, contrary to Meyer and Herscovitch's (2001) predictions, these studies generally find that OCBs are as strong or stronger for employees with a fully committed or AC/NC-dominant profile than for those with a 'pure AC' profile. Thus, there may be some synergy associated with the combination of the components; affective (desire) and normative (obligation) commitment, in particular. Meyer and Parfyonova (2010) described this combination as reflecting a 'moral duty' that might arguably lead to continued effort in support of the commitment target even under conditions of adversity. There is some promising evidence for temporal (Kam et al., forthcoming), within-sample (e.g., Meyer et al., 2013), and cross-national (Morin et al., 2016) stability in profile structure and the pattern of relations with other variables. However, it is still too early to evaluate how well the findings of existing profile studies will generalize.

Unfortunately, relatively little research has been conducted with respect to profile mindsets and task performance. Moreover, in some cases only profiles involving AC and CC were considered. Sinclair et al. (2005) conducted one such study and found that supervisor ratings of task performance were significantly lower in a profile defined by moderate CC and low AC (that is, a cost-based mindset not buffered by AC) than other profiles. A more recent and comprehensive test of the impact of profiles on task performance was provided by Meyer et al. (2012), who used profiles based on all three commitment components. Their analyses revealed that, in contrast to their findings regarding OCB described above, task performance did not differ across the six profile groups in their study. As noted earlier, this might be due to the fact that task performance is more constrained than OCB, but it is premature to draw firm conclusions. More research is needed to determine whether meaningful patterns of task performance or OCB will emerge across studies. In the meantime, however, there is also reason to be cautious in interpreting correlations involving individual commitment components. For example, despite its weak, and sometimes negative, correlation with task performance and OCB, CC is not necessarily undesirable. When combined with strong AC and NC it might reflect the potential cost associated with discontinuing a desirable and meaningful relationship (Meyer et al., 2012).

FUTURE DIRECTIONS

Despite the impressive numbers of individual-level studies examining commitment–performance relations, more research is needed, particularly in countries outside of the Western world. Meyer et al.'s (2014) recent meta-analysis revealed that, although the number of studies being conducted outside North America is increasing, there is still a dearth of research in certain areas of the world (for example, Central America, South America, Africa, Eastern Europe, and Eurasia). Consequently, the extent to which we can generalize the findings pertaining to commitment and performance reported above to non-Western cultures remains an open question. We refer interested readers to Part VI of this volume on 'Commitment across Cultures' for more detailed discussion of the complex role that culture might play on these relations, and for summaries of some of the research that has been conducted to date in various regions of the world.

Additional research based on commitment components (particularly in the above-mentioned regions) will facilitate a more comprehensive global understanding of relations with performance outcomes. Most importantly, as the number of countries with commitment–performance research expands it becomes increasingly viable to examine cross-national effects using culture taxonomies. Indeed, Meyer et al.'s (2014) meta-analysis suggests that the AC–OCB relation may be influenced to some extent by culture. Other work has also examined the influence of culture on commitment–performance relations using meta-analysis (e.g., Jaramillo et al., 2005) and cross-national comparison studies (e.g., Felfe et al., 2008; Eisinga et al., 2010), but overall inconsistencies make it premature to draw firm conclusions about the role of culture on commitment–performance relations.

As we noted previously, individuals may be committed to a variety of targets and there is certainly reason to believe that commitments to these other targets will have a bearing on work behavior, including task performance and OCB. We refer the reader to the chapters in Part III of this volume, 'Foci of Commitment', for more detail. Although the meta-analytic analyses we report sheds some light on the implications of organizational commitment mindsets for task performance and OCB, there is a need for more research examining the independent and joint effects of commitment to other targets (see Chapter 4 in this volume).

The vast majority of the commitment–performance literature focuses on commitment at the individual level. Of course, both commitment and performance can be aggregated to higher levels such as the team, work unit, or organization. Unfortunately, the research focusing on higher levels of analysis is quite sparse and has often used a unidimensional conceptualization of commitment (e.g., Ostroff, 1992; Steyrer et al., 2008; Winkler et al., 2012; Wright et al., 2005). Relations between commitment and financial indicators (for example, return on investment and earnings growth; Steyrer et al., 2008) have been found but tend to exists only for cross-lag correlations of one year (Winkler et al., 2012). More research to investigate the relation between commitment and performance at higher levels is needed. Indeed, it might be findings at the organization level that will be most likely to convince organizations that investment in programs to bolster commitment can help to create competitive advantage (Meyer, 2009).

Moving forward, we urge all researchers using the TCM framework to provide data on both commitment components and profiles. Increasing the amount of research based on profile relations is critical for understanding commitment–performance relations. The promise of the profile approach is high, but the evidence in support of its utility is just beginning to accumulate (see Meyer and Morin, 2016). A critical consideration when conducting future component or profile research is using research designs that provide a stronger basis for causal inference (see Chapters 33, 34 and 35 in this volume).

With respect to profile research, one challenge to date has been determining which profiles are true or real, and generalize across studies. Fortunately, Morin et al. (2016) recently created a rigorous process for systematically assessing the extent to which profiles generalize across groups or time. We encourage researchers to collect multiple data sets and use this approach. Relatedly, Meyer and Morin (2016) have suggested reporting standards for profile research that may help in the synthesis of findings across studies.

Another challenge to conducting profile analyses, particularly studies that allow for cross-sample comparison, is the availability of data. One potential solution to this problem is for researchers within the commitment community to share data. This can be facilitated by making data open access (see http://www.re3data.org for options). This is not currently common practice. Indeed, a recent study found that only 38 percent of researchers will share data when requested (Vanpaemel et al., 2015). There are many possible reasons for this (see Molloy, 2011; Wicherts et al., 2011), and the notion of making data open access is admittedly controversial. However, it appears to be an emerging trend with several advantages beyond the accumulation of data for profile analyses (Asendorpf et al., 2013; Nuijten et al., 2015).

CONCLUSIONS

The meta-analytic findings we report are generally consistent with TCM predictions that organizational commitment has implications for task performance and OCBs, but that the relations will vary depending on the accompanying mindset. Relations were strongest for AC, followed by NC; CC tended to be unrelated or have a weak negative relation. These findings come with several caveats, however. First, the findings reflect cross-sectional relations. Riketta's (2008) review of the few available longitudinal studies provides stronger evidence for a causal link, but the strength of the relation is weaker than that implied in our analysis. Second, the results of recent profile studies suggest that the relations involving the individual commitment components can be misleading. Both NC (e.g., Gellatly et al., 2006) and CC (e.g., Meyer et al., 2012) have been shown to relate differently with other variables depending on the strength of the other components. Third, there is some evidence to suggest that commitment and performance are related when aggregated to higher levels (for example, unit or organization), but the number of studies is still limited. Finally, although existing evidence suggests that the relations between the TCM commitment mindsets and performance are relatively consistent across different cultures, more research, conducted within and across countries outside North America, is required to evaluate the true generalizability of the TCM.

REFERENCES

Allen, N.J., and Meyer, J.P. (1990). The measurement and antecedents of affective, continuance, and normative commitment to the organization. *Journal of Occupational Psychology, 63*, 1–18.

Allen, N.J., and Meyer, J.P. (1996). Affective, continuance, and normative commitment to the organization: an examination of construct validity. *Journal of Vocational Behavior, 49*, 252–276.

Asendorpf, J.B., Conner, M., De Fruyt, F., Houwer, J.D., Enissen, J.J.A., et al. (2013). Recommendations for increasing replicability in psychology. *European Journal of Personality, 27*, 108–119. http://doi.org/10.1002/per.1919.

Austin, J.T., and Villanova, P. (1992). The criterion problem: 1917–1992. *Journal of Applied Psychology, 77(6)*, 836.

Bernardin, H.J., and Beatty, R. (1984). *Performance appraisal: Assessing human behavior at work*. Boston, MA: Kent-PWS.

Borman, W.C., and Motowidlo, S.M. (1993). Expanding the criterion domain to include elements of contextual performance. In Schmidt, N. and Borman, W. (Eds). *Personnel Selection in Organizations*. San Francisco, CA: Jossey-Bass, 71–98.

Borman, W.C., and Motowidlo, S.J. (1997). Task performance and contextual performance: The meaning for personnel selection research. *Human Performance, 10*, 99–109.

Brown, R.B. (1996). Organizational commitment: Clarifying the concept and simplifying the existing construct typology. *Journal of Vocational Behavior, 49*, 230–251.

Campbell, J.P. (1990). Modeling the performance prediction problem in industrial and organizational psychology. In Dunnette, M. and Hough, L.M. (Eds.), *Handbook of industrial and organizational psychology* (Vol. 1, 2nd ed., pp. 687–731). Palo Alto, CA: Consulting Psychologists Press.

Coleman, V.I., and Borman, W.C. (2000). Investigating the underlying structure of the citizenship performance domain. *Human Resource Management Review, 10*, 25–44.

Cooper-Hakim, A., and Viswesvaran, C. (2005). The construct of work commitment: testing an integrative framework. *Psychological Bulletin, 131(2)*, 241.

Eisinga, R., Teelken, C., and Doorewaard, H. (2010). Assessing cross-national invariance of the three-component model of organizational commitment: A six-country study of European university faculty. *Cross-cultural Research, 44*, 341–373.

Felfe, J., Yan, W., and Six, B. (2008). The impact of individual collectivism on commitment and its influence on organizational citizenship behaviour and turnover in three countries. *International Journal of Cross Cultural Management, 8*, 211–237.

Gellatly, I.R., Meyer, J.P., and Luchak, A.A. (2006). Combined effects of the three commitment components on focal and discretionary behaviors: A test of Meyer and Herscovitch's propositions. *Journal of Vocational Behavior, 69*, 331–345.

Gordon, M.E., and Ladd, R.T. (1990). Dual allegiance: Renewal, reconsideration and recantation. *Personnel Psychology, 43*, 37–69.

Gouldner, A.W. (1957). Cosmopolitans and locals: Toward an analysis of latent social roles. *Administrative Science Quarterly, 2*, 281–306.

Hofstede, G. (2001). *Cultures consequences: Comparing values, behaviors, institutions, and organizations Across Nations* (2nd Ed.). London: Sage Publications.

Hunter, J.E., and Schmidt, F.L. (1990). *Methods of meta-analysis: Correcting for error and bias in research findings*. Newbury Park, CA: Sage.

Jaramillo, F., Mulki, J.P., and Marshall, G.W. (2005). A meta-analysis of the relationship between organizational commitment and salesperson job performance: 25 years of research. *Journal of Business Research, 58*, 705–714.

Johnson, R.E., Chang, C. and Yang, L.Q. (2010). Commitment and motivation at work: The relevance of employee identity and regulatory focus. *Academy of Management Review, 35(2)*, 226–245.

Kam, C., Morin, A.J.S., Meyer, J.P., and Topolnytsky, L. (forthcoming). Are commitment profiles stable and predictable? A latent transition analysis. *Journal of Management*. Available at http://jom.sagepub.com/content/early/2013/09/11/0149206313503010.

Katz, D. and Kahn, R.L. (1978). *The social psychology of organizations*. New York: Wiley.

Klein, H.J., Cooper, J.T., Molloy, J.C., and Swanson, J.A. (2014). The assessment of commitment: Advantages of a unidimensional, target-free approach. *Journal of Applied Psychology, 99(2)*, 222.

Klein, H.J., Molloy, J.C., and Cooper, J.T. (2012). Conceptual foundations: Construct definitions and theoretical representations of workplace commitments. In Klein, H.J., Becker, T.E., and Meyer J.P. (Eds.), *Commitment in organizations: Accumulated wisdom and new directions* (pp. 37–68). New York: Routledge.

Lee, K., and Allen, N.J. (2002). Organizational citizenship behavior and workplace deviance: the role of affect and cognitions. *Journal of Applied Psychology, 87*, 131.

Lee, K., Carswell, J.J., and Allen, N.J. (2000). A meta-analytic review of occupational commitment: Relations with person- and work-related variables. *Journal of Applied Psychology, 85*, 799–811.

LePine, J.A., Erez, A., and Johnson, D.E. (2002). The nature and dimensionality of organizational citizenship behavior: A critical review and meta-analysis. *Journal of Applied Psychology, 87*, 52–65.

Meyer, J.P. (2009). Commitment in a changing world of work. In Klein, H.J., Becker, T.E., and Meyer J.P. (Eds.), *Commitment in organizations: Accumulated wisdom and new directions* (pp. 37–68). New York: Routledge.

Meyer, J.P., and Allen, N.J. (1991). A three-component conceptualization of organizational commitment. *Human Resource Management Review, 1*, 61–89.

Meyer, J.P., and Allen, N.J. (1997). *Commitment in the workplace: theory, research, and application*. Thousand Oaks, CA: Sage.

Meyer, J.P., Allen, N.J., and Smith, C.A. (1993). Commitment to organizations and occupations: extension and test of a three-component conceptualization. *Journal of Applied Psychology, 78*, 538–551.

Meyer, J.P., Becker, T.E., and van Dick, R. (2006). Social identities and commitments at work: toward an integrative model. *Journal of Organizational Behavior, 27*, 665–683.

Meyer, J.P., Becker, T.E., and Vandenberghe, C. (2004). Employee commitment and motivation: a conceptual analysis and integrative model. *Journal of applied psychology, 89(6)*, 991.

Meyer, J.P., and Herscovitch, L. (2001). Commitment in the workplace toward a general model, *Human Resource Management Review, 11*, 299–326.

Meyer, J.P., Kam, C., Goldenberg, I., and Bremner, N.L. (2013). Organizational commitment in the military: Application of a profile approach. *Military Psychology, 25(4)*, 381.

Meyer, J.P. and Morin, A. (2016). A person-centered approach to commitment research: Theory, research, and methodology. *Journal of Organizational Behavior, 37*, 584–612.

Meyer, J.P., and Parfyonova, N.M. (2010). Normative commitment in the workplace: A theoretical analysis and re-conceptualization. *Human Resource Management Review, 20(4)*, 283–294.

Meyer, J.P., Stanley, D.J., Herscovitch, L., and Topolnytsky, L. (2002). Affective, continuance, and normative commitment to the organization: A meta-analysis of antecedents, correlates, and consequences. *Journal of Vocational Behavior*, *61*, 20–52.

Meyer, J.P., Stanley, D.J., McInnis, K., Jackson, T.A., Chris, A., and Anderson, B. (2014). Employee commitment and behaviors across cultures: A meta-analysis. In Meyer, J.P. (Chair), *Employee Commitment: An International Perspective*. Symposium presented at the 28th International Congress of Applied Psychology, Paris.

Meyer, J.P., Stanley, L.J., and Parfyonova, N.M. (2012). Employee commitment in context: The nature and implication of commitment profiles. *Journal of Vocational Behavior*, *80*, 1–16.

Molloy, J.C. (2011). The Open Knowledge Foundation: open data means better science. *PLOS Biology*, *9*, e1001195. http://doi.org/10.1371/journal.pbio.1001195.

Morin, A., Meyer, J.P., and Creusier, J., and Bietry, F. (2016). Multiple-group analysis of similarity in latent profile solutions. *Organizational Research Methods*, http://doi.org/10.1177/1094428115621148.

Morrison, E.W. (1994). Role definitions and organizational citizenship behavior: The importance of the employee's perspective. *Academy of Management Journal*, *37*, 1543–1567.

Mowday, R.T., Steers, R.M., and Porter, L.W. (1979). The measurement of organizational commitment. *Journal of Vocational Behavior*, *14*, 224–247.

Murphy, K.R. (1989). Dimensions of job performance. In Dillon, R. and Pelligrino, J. (Eds.), *Testing: Applied and theoretical perspectives* (pp. 218–247). New York: Praeger.

Nuijten, M.B., Hartgerink, C.H.J., van Assen, M.A.L.M., Epskamp, S., and Wicherts, J.M. (2015). The prevalence of statistical reporting errors in psychology (1985–2013). *Behavior Research Methods*. http://doi.org/10.3758/s13428-015-0664-2.

Organ, D.W. (1988). *Organizational citizenship behavior: The good soldier syndrome*. Chicago, IL: Lexington Books/DC Heath & Company.

Organ, D.W. (1990). The motivational basis of organizational citizenship behavior. *Research in Organizational Behavior*, *12*, 43–72.

Organ, D.W. (1997). Organizational citizenship behavior: It's construct clean-up time. *Human Performance*, *10*, 85–97.

Organ, D.W., and Ryan, K. (1995). A meta-analytic review of attitudinal and dispositional predictors of organizational citizenship behavior. *Personnel Psychology*, *48*, 775–802.

Ostroff, C. (1992). The relationship between satisfaction, attitudes, and performance: An organizational level analysis. *Journal of Applied Psychology*, *77*, 963–974.

Podsakoff, N.P., Whiting, S.W., Podsakoff, P.M., and Blume, B.D. (2009). Individual-and organizational-level consequences of organizational citizenship behaviors. *Journal of Applied Psychology*, *94*, 122–141.

Riketta, M. (2002). Attitudinal organizational commitment and job performance: a meta-analysis. *Journal of Organizational Behavior*, *23*, 257–266.

Riketta, M. (2008). The causal relation between job attitudes and performance: a meta-analysis of panel studies. *Journal of Applied Psychology*, *93*, 472–481.

Rotondo, M., and Sackett, P.R. (2002). The relative importance of task, citizenship, and counterproductive performance to global ratings of job performance: A policy-capturing approach. *Journal of Applied Psychology*, *87*, 66–80.

Schwartz, S.H. (2006). A theory of cultural value orientations: Explication and applications. *Comparative Sociology*, *5*, 137–182.

Sinclair, R.R., Tucker, J.S., Wright, C., and Cullen, J.C. (2005). Performance differences among four organizational commitment profiles. *Journal of Applied Psychology*, *90*, 1280–1287.

Smith, C.A., Organ, D.W., and Near, J.P. (1983). Organizational citizenship behavior: Its nature and antecedents. *Journal of Applied Psychology*, *68*, 653.

Steyrer, J., Schiffinger, M., and Lang, R. (2008). Organizational commitment—A missing link between leadership behavior and organizational performance? *Scandinavian Journal of Management*, *24*(4), 364–374. http://doi.org/10.1016/j.scaman.2008.04.002.

Tett, R.P., Guterman, H.A., Bleier, A., and Murphy, P.J. (2000). Development and content validation of a 'hyperdimensional' taxonomy of managerial competence. *Human Performance*, *13*, 205–251.

Van Dyne, L., Graham, J.W., and Dienesch, R.M. (1994). Organizational citizenship behavior: Construct redefinition, measurement and validation. *Academy of Management Journal*, *37*, 765–802.

Vanpaemel, W., Vermorgen, M., and Deriemaecker, L. (2015). Are we wasting a good crisis? The availability of psychological research data after the storm. *Collabra*. http://doi.org/10.1525/collabra.13.

Wallace, J.E. (1993). Professional and organizational commitment: Compatible or incompatible? *Journal of Vocational Behavior*, *42*, 333–349.

Wasti, S.A. (2005). Commitment profiles: Combinations of organizational commitment forms and job outcomes. *Journal of Vocational Behavior*, *67*, 290–308.

Wicherts, J.M., Bakker, M., and Molenaar, D. (2011). Willingness to share research data is related to the strength of the evidence and the quality of reporting of statistical results. *PloS One*, *6(11)*, e26828. http://doi.org/10.1371/journal.pone.0026828.

Williams, L.J., and Anderson, S.E. (1991). Job satisfaction and organizational commitment as predictors of organizational citizenship and in-role behaviors. *Journal of Management*, *17*, 601–617.

Winkler, S., König, C.J., and Kleinmann, M. (2012). New insights into an old debate: Investigating the temporal sequence of commitment and performance at the business unit level. *Journal of Occupational and Organizational Psychology*, *85(3)*, 503–522. http://doi.org/10.1111/j.2044-8325.2012.02054.x.

Wright, P.M., Gardner, T., Moynihan, L., and Allen, M. (2005). The HR–performance relationship: Examining causal directions. *Personnel Psychology*, *58*, 409–446.

16. Counterproductive work behaviors
Bernd Marcus

Counterproductive work behavior (CWB) is one of a growing number of umbrella terms used to summarize a range of employee behaviors generally considered undesirable or harmful. Whereas CWB can clearly be distinguished from both in-role and extra-role performance, illegitimate forms of non-attendance (for example, absenteeism, tardiness, lateness) are integral parts of the CWB construct. As attendance is the subject of a different chapter in this volume (Chapter 14), the present chapter is primarily concerned with CWBs other than non-attendance behaviors, although measurement of CWB does not always allow for precise distinctions from the latter behaviors.

Unlike both (non-)attendance and performance (see Chapter 15 in this volume), CWB has traditionally not been one of the major foci of commitment research. Broad quantitative reviews of the commitment literature (e.g., Cooper-Hakim and Viswesvaran, 2005; Meyer et al., 2002) tended to cover specifically the former two behavioral domains as outcome variables, but not CWB. Nevertheless, a considerable body of research has accumulated that links CWB with work-related commitment constructs. In the present chapter, I review empirical and theoretical aspects of this literature. I begin with an introduction to the CWB construct and its constituent elements. I then review some empirical evidence on bivariate relations between various forms of CWB and commitment. In the subsequent section, I critically review existing concepts of theoretical CWB–commitment links and develop an extended model of these links. Based on conclusions drawn from and gaps identified in previous research, the final section outlines some routes for future research on these issues.

COUNTERPRODUCTIVE WORK BEHAVIORS

In the aftermath of the seminal work by Hollinger and Clark (1983), scholars of various disciplines began to study extensively employee acts that, as opposed to a standard definition of job performance, can be considered as running counter to organizational goals. There is considerable confusion now concerning terms used to describe these behaviors, and exact boundaries and definitions of the behavioral domain (for reviews see Rotundo and Spector, 2010; Sackett and DeVore, 2001). Out of a myriad of construct labels with partially or almost totally overlapping content, probably the most inclusive and widely used terms are 'counterproductive work behavior' and 'organizational deviance', which are virtually identical in content and often used interchangeably. For the present purpose, I will focus on the term 'counterproductive work behavior' (CWB), which can be defined as any volitional behaviors by employees that potentially violate legitimate interests of, or do harm to, the organization its members (e.g., Sackett and DeVore, 2001). This definition excludes inadvertent errors due to decisions made with the best intentions, but is not restricted to acts committed with the intention to do harm. As exemplified later, harm may either be the intended outcome of CWB or simply be accepted by the actor as a side-effect of acts committed in pursuit of one's self-interest (cf. Marcus and Schuler, 2004).

A number of work groups developed structural models and scales for describing and measuring the CWB domain and related constructs. Among the most influential taxonomies of CWB facets are: (1) Bennett and Robinson's (2000) distinction between deviance directed at the organization (OD) or individual persons (ID); (2) the more fine-grained model of Spector et al. (2006), who relabeled the ID factor 'abuse' and distinguished within OD between the facets of theft, withdrawal, production deviance, and sabotage; and (3) the even narrower 11 facets specified by Gruys and Sackett (2003), which split some of the other models' components (for example, 'abuse' is split into a verbal and a physical component) and also included extensions (for example, unsafe behavior, drug and alcohol abuse) not specified in those models.

Marcus et al. (2016) recently reviewed conceptual differences between these models and presented some data addressing these differences. Their findings suggest that, contrary to some authors' assumptions, there is some evidence of a reflective general factor of CWB at the highest level of the hierarchy. This would imply that there are one or more common causes underlying all forms of CWB. Below that general level, however, Marcus et al.'s data pointed to quite a complex structure. Their findings supported a bimodal model in which each act of CWB is simultaneously described by its content or type of behavior (as specified in Gruys and Sackett's, 2003, 11 facets) and by a target mode specifying who is primarily harmed by the specific act (as in Bennett and Robinson's, 2000, ID–OD distinction, extended by primarily self-harming forms of CWB such as unsafe behavior or substance use). This would mean that, beyond common causes of general CWB, understanding deviant acts at work requires knowing what is done and to whom it is done. For example, all acts of theft load on a common content factor but differ depending on whether things are stolen from the organization or individual employees. Similarly, a common factor underlies all acts of interpersonal CWB (that is, ID) but these acts at the same time differ in content by the forms of physical or verbal aggression, theft, and so on.

EMPIRICAL RELATIONS BETWEEN CWB AND COMMITMENT

As will be discussed later, there are many theoretical conceptions of how CWB might be linked to commitment in a multivariate fashion. However, the vast majority of existing empirical studies involving CWB and commitment reported primarily bivariate relations between various operationalizations of these two constructs. It therefore may make sense to first review those empirical findings at the bivariate level and then discuss how they fit with alternative conceptions of theoretical links, which are the subject of the subsequent major section. In the present section, I first review meta-analytic estimates of CWB–commitment relations without any distinctions at the facet level of both constructs. I then turn to the empirical evidence on organizational commitment (OC), as broken down by its affective ('want to', AOC), normative ('ought to', NOC), and calculating or continuance ('have to', COC), forms, as well as on commitment foci other than the organization (for introductions to commitment forms and foci, see Chapters 3 and 4 in this volume). I conclude this section with a subsection on relations of OC to specific facets of CWB.

Meta-analyses on Broadly Defined CWB–Commitment Relations

There are currently three meta-analyses reporting estimates of bivariate true score correlations between CWB and commitment. Based on $k = 22$ independent samples, Dalal (2005) found a mean observed correlation of $r = -.28$ and a corrected value of $\rho = -.36$. More recently, but based on much fewer data points ($k = 3$), Colquitt et al. (2013) reported a slightly weaker corrected correlation of $\rho = -.24$ in their meta-analysis of the organizational justice literature. The largest database to date ($k = 46$) was collected for an unpublished doctoral dissertation (Taylor, 2012), which found an even weaker relation of $\rho = -.12$. None of these meta-analyses distinguished between different forms of either CWB or commitment. On the CWB side, all authors seem to have covered a broad set of different acts. On the side of commitment, all three meta-analyses were restricted to the organizational focus (OC). Moreover, Taylor (2012) explicitly reported only findings on AOC in her dissertation. Similarly, Gill et al. (2011), in reviewing the published meta-analysis by Dalal (2005), concluded that studies covered in that article primarily, if not exclusively, focused on AOC. Hence, a preliminary conclusion based on meta-analytic data is that there is a weak to moderate negative relationship between CWB and AOC.

Relations of CWB to Different Commitment Forms and Foci

Interest in relations between CWB and forms or foci of commitment beyond AOC began to emerge only recently. Gill et al. (2011) were among the first CWB studies employing Meyer and Allen's (1991) three-component model of OC. Whereas these authors expected to (and did) replicate the negative CWB–AOC relation observed earlier, they expected CWB to correlate positively with COC. Although they did observe a positive, albeit weak, correlation between these constructs ($r = .15$), the predictive value of COC was even lower after controlling for effects of the organizations surveyed. A number of unpublished studies (Beugré, 1996; Brock, 2010; Dawson, 1996; Lindsay, 2008; Papini, 2007; Pfaltzgraff, 1998; Villanueva, 2006) and published studies (Demir, 2011; Ménard et al., 2011) have also employed the three-component OC model in relation to CWB. Whereas correlations of CWB with the normative form of OC (NOC) tended to closely resemble those observed for AOC in these studies, virtually all observed CWB–COC relations were close to zero (that is, in the $r = -.10$ to .10 range). One notable exception to this rule is the Turkish study by Demir (2011), who reported substantial negative relations between CWB and all forms of OC (for example, $r = -.42$ for CWB–COC). Yet from the description of the CWB scale used in that study, it is not clear whether participants were surveyed about their own behavior or about perceptions of CWB by others. A few studies that used variables conceptually similar to COC, such as perceptions of alternative employment options (Gottfredson and Holland, 1990; Rusbult et al., 1988), again reported relations with CWB close to zero. Hence, a second preliminary conclusion is that whereas CWB–NOC correlations tend to parallel those observed for AOC, the bivariate linear relation between CWB and COC approximates zero.

Very few authors looked at commitment foci other than the organization. To complicate matters, those studies were conducted in a number of different countries, and results appear to vary at least as much by country as by commitment focus. In probably the most comprehensive multi-foci study, Coyne et al. (2013) compared relations of career, team, and organizational commitment to interpersonal and organizational CWB in four different countries. In general, their findings were consistent across CWB targets within each country, but no clear pattern emerged across commitment foci and subsamples. Negative CWB–commitment relations were strongest for OC in the United Kingdom, for career commitment in Turkey, and for team commitment in Greece, respectively; whereas all CWB–commitment correlations were close to zero in the Dutch sample. Moderate negative relations of commitment to one's work group, in varying operationalizations, with CWB were also observed in Singapore (Tan and Tan, 2008) and Spain (de Lara, 2008), although the latter study surprisingly found group commitment more strongly related to organizational than to interpersonal CWB. Finally, one United States study (Blau and Andersson, 2005) found some, although weak ($r = -.13$), predictive validity of occupational commitment for interpersonal CWB. Clearly, how exactly different foci of commitment relate to different forms of CWB appears to be moderated by cultural differences, which requires further clarification.

Relations of Different CWB Facets to Commitment

Drawing firm conclusions on relations of commitment to more specific facets of CWB also seems premature. Most studies reviewed for this chapter employed either Bennett and Robinson's (2000) scale of interpersonal and organizational deviance, or similarly broad measures of CWB. A number of specific forms of CWB were addressed in single studies, including theft (Boye, 1991), unsafe behaviors (DeJoy et al., 2010), and substance use (Lehman and Simpson, 1992). All these studies found weak negative relations of less than $r = -.20$ between OC and the various facets of CWB. The only specific form of CWB that has been related to commitment in multiple studies refers to employees' withholding of productive efforts while being physically present at work. This specific form of CWB has been labeled 'misuse of time and resources' by Gruys and Sackett (2003) but is also conceptually related to the absenteeism and withdrawal literature. In a number of studies, it has been investigated under various labels, including time banditry (Brock, 2010), neglect (Rusbult et al., 1988), social loafing (Şeşen et al., 2014; Tan and Tan, 2008), and work withdrawal (Cohen-Callow, 2008; Michael et al., 2005; Pfaltzgraff, 1998), and linked to (mostly affective) OC. Observed effects in these studies vary between negligibly small ($r = -.01$; Pfaltzgraff, 1998) and moderately ($r = -.33$; Michael et al., 2005) negative correlations. Overall, it seems as though observed relations between specific forms of CWB and AOC tend to be of similar, though perhaps slightly weaker, size and sign as those observed for more broadly defined CWB.

Based on this review of empirical bivariate relations between CWB and commitment, it seems justified to conclude that there is a weak to moderate correlation between various kinds of CWBs and both AOC and NOC, but that these relations do not generalize to COC. There is also considerable variation of findings across studies, which is not easily explained. Taken together, these findings appear to indicate that commitment is probably linked to CWB, but that the nature of this link is not well understood at the bivariate level and likely requires more complex theoretical explanations. I will therefore turn next to multivariate conceptual approaches to the CWB–commitment link.

THEORETICAL APPROACHES TO THE CWB–COMMITMENT LINK

Commitment as a Mediator of other CWB Predictors

In their recent meta-analysis of the justice literature, Colquitt et al. (2013) subsumed OC, together with a range of other variables, under the broader term of 'social exchange quality'. They hypothesized that dimensions of organizational justice affect employee behaviors (including CWB) in part or in total through perceptions of social exchange quality. This conceptual proposition is prototypical for the majority of models linking commitment with CWB in the empirical and theoretical literature: based on some variant of social exchange theory, commitment is conceptualized as a primarily affective state or attitude that is affected by some factor(s) in the work situation that in turn affects behavioral outcomes such as CWB. This general theme of commitment as a mediator variable appears in a multitude of models of varying complexity and with multiple variables at the origin of the causal chain, including justice (e.g., de Lara, 2008; Demir, 2011) and other antecedents of more or less related content such as leadership styles and abusive supervision (Duan et al., 2010; Mulki et al., 2006; Shamsudin et al., 2012; Tepper et al., 2008), organizational politics (DeJoy et al., 2010; Rosen and Levy, 2013; Shamsudin et al., 2012), or culture (Appelbaum et al., 2005; Ramshida and Manikandan, 2013), perceived social loafing (Şeşen et al., 2014), contract breach (Rosen and Levy, 2013), job insecurity (Tian et al., 2014), pay satisfaction (Tang and Chiu, 2003), or dissimilarity with other members of the organization (Liao et al., 2004). Most recently, the perspective of OC as a mediator has been extended to personality traits as distal antecedents (Guay et al., 2016). However, the vast majority of authors cited view CWB as the final behavioral outcome provoked by some external factor that initially leads to affective responses in terms of undesirable or uncomfortable feelings or states. This conceptual model is shown in a generalized and simplified form in the upper part (a) of Figure 16.1.

Unfortunately for the model shown in Figure 16.1a, empirical support is mixed at best. For example, based on meta-analytic structural modeling, Colquitt et al. (2013) were able to confirm their broad mediator model for task performance and organizational citizenship behavior, but not for CWB. Similar patterns of results were observed in primary studies that looked at CWB in the context of a broader range of acts including productive behaviors (de Lara, 2008; Rosen and Levy, 2013). Even if there appeared to be evidence supporting partial mediation, studies generally lacked the experimental or longitudinal design that would have permitted drawing firm conclusions on causal relationships. In addition to being weakly supported by empirical evidence for models, mediation models appear to rest on the implicit assumption that commitment acts as a state-like perceptual response to external events, which is at odds with the conception of OC as a relatively stable attachment to the organization. Hence, there may be alternative accounts for the role of commitment in causal chains leading to CWB. One such potential role is that of a moderator variable.

a) Standard Model

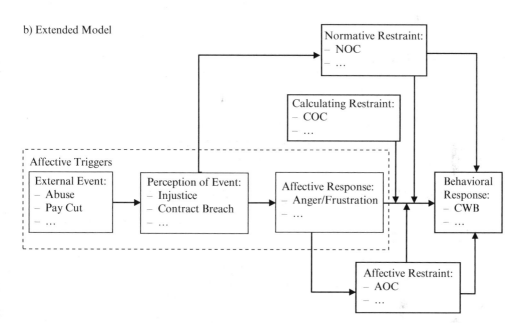

b) Extended Model

Notes:
(a) Simplified standard model in previous research based on social exchange theories; (b) extended and revised model based on affective events theory.
CWB = counterproductive work behavior; AOC = affective organizational commitment; NOC = normative organizational commitment; COC = continuance organizational commitment.

Figure 16.1   Models of how commitment is involved in non-dispositional affective processes explaining counterproductive work behaviors

Commitment as a Moderator of other CWB Predictors

As mentioned earlier, the type of model shown in Figure 16.1a belongs to a broader class of models attempting to explain CWB in terms of social exchange theory; that is, as a response to some external provocation. Among the more prominent approaches of this kind in the CWB literature are the concepts of CWB as retaliation behavior (Skarlicki and Folger, 1997), or Spector and Fox's (2002, 2005) models of emotion-centered explanations of CWB. Two early papers attempted to organize or integrate the now almost countless theoretical approaches to CWB. Martinko et al. (2002) presented an integrative causal reasoning model, in which distal situational and dispositional antecedents first lead to cognitive processes. These processes in turn cause the distinct feelings of either anger/frustration or guilt/shame. Finally, guilt/shame leads to self-destructive CWB, whereas anger/frustration causes the distinct class of retaliatory CWB. In terms of this integrative theory, social exchange theories of CWB would belong primarily to the path leading to retaliatory CWB through anger/frustration. In a simpler taxonomy of explanations of CWB, I (Marcus, 2001; see Marcus and Schuler, 2004, for a summary in English) had proposed to classify antecedents of CWB along the dimensions of person versus situation and of motivation versus control variables. In terms of this taxonomy, social exchange and emotion-centered models belong to the class of theories seeking to explain CWB primarily in terms of triggers (that is, situation–motivation variables), which are defined as external events or perceptions of such events that provoke CWB as a response. Notably, none of the major theories of CWB, or the integrative models cited, explicitly included commitment as an integral part.

Figure 16.1a visualizes the role of commitment analogous to that of anger/frustration in Martinko et al.'s (2002) theory, or to that of a (proximal) trigger in terms of my (Marcus, 2001) taxonomy. Regardless of exact specifications, (low) commitment would lead to CWB in the sense of directly causing the behavior. However, one needs to recall that OC is defined as an emotional, moral, or calculating attachment to the organization (Chapter 3 in this volume), or as a social bond between employee and employer (Chapter 2 in this volume). In terms of the general taxonomy, these definitions do not correspond to the definition of a trigger, but rather to that of an external control variable. Use of the term 'control' here was adopted from criminology, where control theories of crime (what restrains people from committing crimes) are distinguished from motivational theories (what makes people commit crimes), and should not be confused with statistical control variables. In contrast to external or internal motivators, which affect perceived benefits of CWB, control variables are held to affect behavior by changing the perception of costs for the actor associated with CWB. Employees with close ties to the organization have more to lose if their behavior is detected and punished. Unlike triggers that cause the execution of deviant acts, external (and internal) control variables cause employees to not show CWBs in the presence of temptation. This difference is easily overlooked at the bivariate level, as one would expect main effects on CWB for both triggers and external controls (though with opposite signs). However, a distinctive feature of control variables is expressed in the aforementioned addendum 'in the presence of temptation'. This feature conceptualizes control variables as moderators that buffer effects of motivational variables even when they lack main effects.

Evidence regarding commitment as a moderator of other variables' links to CWB is scarce, yet results of existing studies mostly appear promising. Two published studies report interactions of AOC with either co-worker deviance (Tepper et al., 2008) or supervisor support (Tian et al., 2014) in predicting CWB. Interestingly, both groups of authors conceptualized AOC as the independent rather than the moderator variable in their interactions. Yet exchanging independent and moderator variables in interaction terms is computationally equivalent, and these terms were consistently significant. In a paper based on student research, Gutworth (2013) reported that participants high on AOC responded with constructive behavior to situations when they experienced a conflict between personal norms and norms of the group they belong to, whereas those low on AOC tended to respond with CWB. Similarly, Brock (2010) found in her doctoral dissertation that high AOC weakened the impact of negative emotions on time banditry (that is, misuse of time). In two earlier doctoral dissertations (Drimmer, 1998; Fuentes, 1989), however, moderator effects of OC on CWBs were also hypothesized but not confirmed. Yet based on meta-analytic data, Taylor (2012) confirmed expected interactions of AOC–CWB relations with cultural dimensions of the countries in which the studies in her sample were conducted. Overall, the buffering effect of AOC on other variables' impact on CWB seems largely supported by existing evidence, but there is virtually no research on moderator effects of other forms of commitment.

An Extended Model of CWB–Commitment Relations

In lieu of more detailed empirical evidence, further extensions of the standard model presented in Figure 16.1a necessarily have to be based on theoretical rationales awaiting empirical tests. The lower part (b) of Figure 16.1 shows a preliminary extended model, which incorporates existing evidence on AOC presented above, along with more speculative considerations on different forms of OC. Furthermore, one may need to take into account foci of commitment other than the organization as well as different regulatory processes. These considerations are elaborated upon below. It needs to be emphasized that the model presented below is focused on the specific role of commitment in explaining CWB and not meant to replace more general overarching theories of CWB. Research reviewed above demonstrated that commitment may be one relevant variable, but probably not the key factor, for understanding CWB.

At the center of the extended model stands an emotion-centered causal chain in which external events (say, for example, a pay cut), through individual perceptions of this event (for example, perception of the pay cut as unjustified), lead to affective reactions (for example, anger/frustration), which in turn may lead to immediately affect-driven behavioral responses (that is, CWB as retaliation). This causal chain is essentially borrowed from Weiss and Cropanzano's (1996) affective events theory (AET). Notably, despite the emphasis of many CWB researchers on emotions, AET is not explicitly referred to in their models. A potentially important difference between AET and other influential emotion-centered theories of CWB is that AET distinguishes between immediate affect-driven ('hot') behavioral reactions and more delayed ('cold') effects on behavior (termed 'judgment-driven' in AET) that are mediated by changes in work attitudes and typically require accumulation of repeated negative experiences. In Figure 16.1b, AOC is conceptualized as such a relatively stable affective bond (considered equivalent to AET's work attitudes, for that matter) that mediates 'cold', but not 'hot', behavioral responses to external events. Some previous longitudinal research supported the existence of these two independent paths, though for the related construct of job embeddedness as a mediator (Holtom et al., 2012).

In addition to paths adopted and adapted from AET, Figure 16.1b also specifies a moderator effect of AOC on the relation between affective reactions and CWB. This proposition is based on the conceptualization of AOC as an external control variable discussed earlier. To the extent that there are intact positive emotional ties between an employee and potential targets of CWB, harmful behaviors directed at those targets should become less likely even when there are situational triggers that may provoke such reactions. In terms of the general taxonomy of antecedents (Marcus, 2001), negative external events, perceptions of these events, and affective reactions would all be considered triggers, though with varying proximity to behavioral outcomes.

So far, the discussion was restricted to the affective form of OC, as the causal chain at the center of Figure 16.1b is largely based on emotion-centered theory. Yet in this figure, the roles of normative and continuance commitment are also modeled, based on different sets of considerations. In line with some research reviewed earlier, effects of the normative form (NOC) are held to be largely analogous to AOC, except that effects of external events and perceptions on NOC are not mediated by affective reactions. For example, repeated perceptions of injustice or contract breach may weaken the normative attachment to the organization regardless of short-lived emotional states.

Whereas antecedents of AOC and NOC may partially differ, the effects of these variables on CWB should be very similar. Both of these forms of commitment are not only believed to moderate effects of other antecedents on CWB in ways described earlier, but they may also affect CWB independent of triggers. In order to understand these independent effects, the earlier-mentioned distinction between control and motivational theories of crime may prove useful. This long-standing paradigmatic distinction in criminology underlies the taxonomic distinction of motivation and control variables for explaining CWB (cf. Marcus and Schuler, 2004). Whereas motivation theorists seek the explanation of deviant behaviors in differences between situations or dispositions that lead to differential attractiveness of deviant acts, control theorists consider the motivation to commit deviant acts as more or less universal and seek to explain variance in deviance by differences in factors that prevent such acts from occurring. Applied to CWB, all variants of models based on social exchange theory or affective reactions belong to the domain of motivational theories, as CWB is assumed to occur in response to some external motivator variables. However, the exact same act of CWB may be explained without reference to differences in motivation. For example, an employee may steal money from their employer either to retaliate for perceived injustice or simply to become richer without effort. In the former case, a situational trigger motivates the act, whereas in the latter case motivation is inherent in the act and therefore does not explain why only some people steal in only some situations. In the absence of triggering events, normative and emotional ties to the target harmed may both help to explain why employees refrain from committing acts that are inherently attractive but harmful to others. In Figure 16.1b, these relations are modeled by main effects of AOC and NOC on CWB.

By contrast, the more calculating form of COC is believed to lack such direct protective effects based in personal ties with potential targets of CWB. Gill et al. (2011) even expected an opposite main effect for COC; yet, as reviewed earlier, the evidence so far appears to support neither positive nor negative main effects of COC on CWB. However, COC should moderate effects of motivational triggers in similar ways as other forms of OC, as specified in Figure 16.1b. Employees high in COC have more to lose if their CWB is detected and therefore may be more likely to resist temptations to act deviantly.

For the sake of simplicity, and also due to space limitations, a number of potentially relevant issues are not explicitly modeled in either part of Figure 16.1. Firstly, the figure does not show effects of dispositional variables. Personality traits may be of even greater relevance for explaining CWB than situational variables (e.g., Marcus and Schuler, 2004), but proposed theoretical links between personality and CWB are so diverse, including a multitude of main, mediated, and moderator effects (for a non-comprehensive review, see

Spector, 2011), that attempting to integrate them within Figure 16.1 would have probably led to a confusing degree of complexity. Nevertheless, it should be kept in mind that there is already some support for the notion that the contribution of OC to understanding CWB may also involve links with personality (Guay et al., 2016). Secondly, foci of commitment beyond the organization are not explicitly modeled in Figure 16.1. Based on considerations outlined above, it may be proposed that effects of affective and normative forms of commitment, at least in part, depend on the correspondence between commitment foci and targets of CWB. For example, commitment to one's work group should affect CWBs directed at members of this group more strongly than CWBs directed at the entire organization. This moderating effect of foci should not generalize to continuance commitment, as the latter variable's effects are believed to depend exclusively on self-serving motives regardless of who is harmed. Finally, self-destructive forms of CWB have been distinguished theoretically (Martinko et al., 2002) and empirically (Marcus et al., 2016) from both organizational and interpersonal CWB. To the extent that effects of commitment on CWB depend on correspondence between commitment foci and CWB targets, there is little reason to expect these effects to generalize to self-destructive forms of CWB.

IMPLICATIONS FOR PRACTICE AND RESEARCH

This review of the literature points to the conclusion that effects of commitment on CWB are potentially complex and probably modest in size, yet also predominantly positive in that high levels of commitment may contribute to the prevention of CWB. Therefore, practical implications for the management of CWB are relatively straightforward: Anything that fosters commitment, and especially affective and normative forms of commitment, may also aid in reducing CWB. Yet the size and scope (in terms of forms of CWB) of these effects likely depends on a multitude of other factors, only a fraction of which are currently understood.

In order to improve this situation, not just more but predominantly different kinds of research than have already accumulated are called for. The perhaps most striking issue in this regard is that, whereas most theoretical accounts of links between commitment and CWB involve dynamic processes within persons, very few of the research designs employed accounted for within-person variance in a methodologically adequate manner. Even the studies cited in the previous section explicitly modeling OC as a mediator variable employed cross-sectional or, at best, predictive designs in which proposed antecedents and outcomes were measured only once (with or without a time lag in between). Yet models based on social exchange theory, AET, or other emotion-focused models all rest on the assumption that external events, and cognitive, affective, and behavioral reactions to these events, are ordered in a particular sequence, and thus assume within-person changes. Hence, the most urgent call in this context is for more longitudinal research allowing for distinctions of within- and between-person effects. Experience-sampling designs may prove especially useful for that purpose and have already been used successfully in CWB research for supporting predictions derived from AET (Dalal et al., 2009), but this research did not involve commitment.

Furthermore, relatively little is known about commitment foci other than the organization, and about how different foci interact with targets of CWB. In this chapter, a number of propositions on such interactions are outlined, but these propositions currently await empirical tests. Similarly, the distinction between main and moderator effects proposed in the model depicted in Figure 16.1b is still based primarily on informed speculation. Unlike tests of the full causal chain, testing these propositions may not always require complex longitudinal designs, but they do require systematically matching commitment foci with commensurate CWB targets and application of analytic techniques that allow for proper modeling of mediator and moderator effects. Also, future researchers are encouraged to test alternative predictions in a relative fashion in one study rather than addressing just the absolute fit of the one model they propose. On a related note, in preparing this review it was surprising to find how often only slightly different constructs and models are presented in published papers without much reference to closely related previous research. As in many fields of organizational research, and in CWB research in particular, there appears to be a tendency to constantly reinvent the wheel.

As more research of the kind described here accumulates, it would be helpful to extend existing meta-analyses on bivariate CWB–OC correlations to the multivariate level with advanced methods such as meta-analytic structural modeling. However, to do so first requires accumulating more evidence by means of primary research. Because the outlined program of collecting such evidence (that is, beyond bivariate CWB–AOC relations) appears to still be in its infancy, such quantitative reviews are perhaps best considered a distal research goal.

REFERENCES

Appelbaum, S.H., Deguire, K.J., and Lay, M. (2005). The relationship of ethical climate to deviant workplace behavior. *Corporate Governance, 5*, 43–55.

Bennett, R.J. and Robinson, S.L. (2000). Development of a measure of workplace deviance. *Journal of Applied Psychology, 85*, 349–360.

Beugré, C.D. (1996). *Analyzing the effects of perceived fairness on organizational commitment and workplace aggression.* Doctoral dissertation. Rensselaer Polytechnic Institute, New York.

Blau, G. and Andersson, L. (2005). Testing a measure of instigated workplace incivility. *Journal of Occupational and Organizational Psychology, 78*, 595–614.

Boye, M.W. (1991). *Self-reported employee theft and counterproductivity as a function of employee turnover antecedents.* Doctoral dissertation, DePaul University, Minneapolis, IL.

Brock, M.E. (2010). *Investigating the antecedents of time banditry: climate, personality, and commitment.* Doctoral dissertation, University of Oklahoma, Norman, OK.

Cohen-Callow, A. (2008). *Factors associated with older adult volunteers' organizational withdrawal: Testing a model of volunteer behavior.* Doctoral dissertation, University of Maryland, Baltimore, MD.

Colquitt, J.A., Scott, B.A., Rodell, J.B., Long, D.M., Zapata, C.P., Conlon, D.E., and Wesson, M.J. (2013). Justice at the millennium, a decade later: A meta-analytic test of social exchange and affect-based perspectives. *Journal of Applied Psychology, 98*, 199–236.

Cooper-Hakim, A. and Viswesvaran, C. (2005). The construct of work commitment: Testing an integrative framework. *Psychological Bulletin, 131*, 241–259.

Coyne, I., Gentile, D., Born, M.P., Ersoy, N.C., and Vakola, M. (2013). The relationship between productive and counterproductive work behaviour across four European countries. *European Journal of Work and Organizational Psychology, 22*, 377–389.

Dalal, R.S. (2005). A meta-analysis of the relationship between organizational citizenship behavior and counterproductive work behavior. *Journal of Applied Psychology, 90*, 1241–1255.

Dalal, R.S., Lam, H., Weiss, H.M., Welch, E.R., and Hulin, C.L. (2009). A within-person approach to work behavior and performance: Concurrent and lagged citizenship-counterproductivity associations, and dynamic relationships with affect and overall job performance. *Academy of Management Journal, 52*, 1051–1066.

Dawson, C.L. (1996). *Dispositional and attitudinal explanations of counterproductivity in the workplace.* Doctoral dissertation, University of California, Berkeley.

DeJoy, D.M., Della, L.J., Vandenberg, R.J., and Wilson, M.G. (2010). Making work safer: Testing a model of social exchange and safety management. *Journal of Safety Research, 41*, 163–171.

De Lara, P.Z.M. (2008). Fairness, teachers' non-task behavior and alumni satisfaction. *Journal of Educational Administration, 46*, 514–538.

Demir, M. (2011). Effects of organizational justice, trust and commitment on employees' deviant behavior. *Anatolia, 22*, 204–221.

Drimmer, L.B. (1998). *Job stress: An investigation of professional and organizational commitment as moderators and relationships to organizational citizenship behavior and misbehavior.* Doctoral dissertation, Cleveland State University, Cleveland, OH.

Duan, J., Lam, W., Chen, Z., and Zhong, J. (2010). Leadership justice, negative organizational behaviors, and the mediating effect of affective commitment. *Social Behavior and Personality, 38*, 1287–1296.

Fuentes, R.R. (1989). *Employee responses to job dissatisfaction: The effects of job attitudes, worker perceptions and individual differences on withdrawal and adaptation action alternatives.* Doctoral dissertation, Texas A&M University, College Station.

Gill, H., Meyer, J.P., Lee, K., Shin, K.-H., and Yoon, C.-Y. (2011). Affective and continuance commitment and their relations with deviant workplace behaviors in Korea. *Asia Pacific Journal of Management, 28*, 595–607.

Gottfredson, G.D. and Holland, J.L. (1990). A longitudinal test of the influence of congruence: Job satisfaction, competency utilization, and counterproductive behavior. *Journal of Counseling Psychology, 37*, 389–398.

Gruys, M.L. and Sackett, P.R. (2003). Investigating the dimensionality of counterproductive work behavior. *International Journal of Selection and Assessment, 11*, 30–42.

Guay, R.P., Choi, D., Oh, I.-S., Mitchell, M.S., Mount, M.K., and Shin, K.-H. (2016). Why people harm the organization and its members: Relationships among personality, organizational commitment, and workplace deviance. *Human Performance, 29*, 1–15.

Gutworth, M. (2013). Applying the normative conflict model to organizational deviance. *TCNJ Journal of Student Scholarship, 15*(April), 1–9.

Hollinger, R.C. and Clark, J.P. (1983). *Theft by Employees.* Lexington, MA: Lexington Books.

Holtom, B.C., Burton, J.P., and Crossley, C.D. (2012). How negative affectivity moderates the relationship between shocks, embeddedness and worker behaviors. *Journal of Vocational Behavior, 80*, 434–443.

Lehman, W.E. and Simpson, D.D. (1992). Employee substance use and on-the-job behaviors. *Journal of Applied Psychology, 77*, 309–321.

Liao, H., Joshi, A., and Chuang, A. (2004). Sticking out like a sore thumb: Employee dissimilarity and deviance at work. *Personnel Psychology, 57*, 969–1000.

Lindsay, D.R. (2008). *Polychronicity and its impact on leader-member exchange and outcome behaviors.* Doctoral dissertation, Pennsylvania State University, State College.

Marcus, B. (2001). Erklärungsansätze kontraproduktiven Verhaltens im Betrieb [Approaches to the explanation of counterproductive behaviors in organizations]. In R.K. Silbereisen and M. Reitzle (eds), *Psychologie 2000* (pp. 414–425). Lengerich, Germany: Pabst.

Marcus, B. and Schuler, H. (2004). Antecedents of counterproductive behavior at work: A general perspective. *Journal of Applied Psychology, 89*, 647–660.

Marcus, B., Taylor, O.A., Hastings, S.E., Sturm, A., and Weigelt, O. (2016). The structure of counterproductive work behavior: A review, a structural meta-analysis, and a primary study. *Journal of Management, 42*, 203–233.

Martinko, M.J., Gundlach, M.J., and Douglas, S.C. (2002). Toward an integrative theory of counterproductive workplace behavior: A causal reasoning perspective. *International Journal of Selection and Assessment, 10*, 36–50.

Ménard, J., Brunet, L., and Savoie, A. (2011). Interpersonal workplace deviance: Why do offenders act out? A comparative look on personality and organisational variables. *Canadian Journal of Behavioural Science, 43*, 309–317.

Meyer, J.P. and Allen, N.J. (1991). A three-component conceptualization of organizational commitment. *Human Resource Management Review, 1*, 61–89.

Meyer, J.P., Stanley, D.J., Herscovitch, L., and Topolnytsky, L. (2002). Affective, continuance and normative commitment to the organization: A meta-analysis of antecedents, correlates, and consequences. *Journal of Vocational Behavior, 61*, 20–52.

Michael, J.H., Evans, D.D., Jansen, K.J., and Haight, J.M. (2005). Management commitment to safety as organizational support: Relationships with non-safety outcomes in wood manufacturing employees. *Journal of Safety Research, 36*, 171–179.

Mulki, J.P., Jaramillo, F., and Locander, W.B. (2006). Emotional exhaustion and organizational deviance: Can the right job and a leader's style make a difference? *Journal of Business Research, 59*, 1222–1230.

Papini, J.D.S. (2007). *Big Brother: The effect of electronic employee monitoring on electronic misbehavior, job satisfaction, and organizational commitment.* Doctoral dissertation, Alliant International University, San Francisco.

Pfaltzgraff, R.E. (1998). *Intergroup structures, systemic justice and organizational withdrawal: The development of new constructs and preliminary investigation of a model.* Doctoral dissertation, Ohio State University, Columbus.

Ramshida, A.P. and Manikandan, K. (2013). Organizational commitment as a mediator of counterproductive work behavior and organizational culture. *International Journal of Social Science and Interdisciplinary Research, 2,* 59–69.

Rosen, C.C. and Levy, P.E. (2013). Stresses, swaps, and skill: An investigation of the psychological dynamics that relate work politics to employee performance. *Human Performance, 26,* 44–65.

Rotundo, M. and Spector, P.E. (2010). Counterproductive work behavior and withdrawal. In J.L. Farr and N.T. Tippins (eds), *Handbook of Employee Selection* (pp. 489–511). New York: Routledge.

Rusbult, C.E., Farrell, D., Rogers, G., and Mainous, A.G. (1988). Impact of exchange variables on exit, voice, loyalty, and neglect: An integrative model of responses to declining job status satisfaction. *Academy of Management Journal, 31,* 599–627.

Sackett, P.R. and DeVore, C.J. (2001). Counterproductive behaviors at work. In N. Anderson, D.S. Ones, H.K. Sinangil, and C. Viswesvaran (eds), *Handbook of Industrial, Work, and Organizational Psychology,* Vol. 1 (pp. 145–164). London: Sage.

Şeşen, H., Soran, S., and Caymaz, E. (2014). Dark side of organizational citizenship behavior (OCB): Testing a model between OCB, social loafing, and organizational commitment. *International Journal of Business and Social Science, 5,* 125–135.

Shamsudin, F.M., Subramaniam, C., and Alshuaibi, A S. (2012). The effect of HR practices, leadership style on cyberdeviance: The mediating role of organizational commitment. *Journal of Marketing and Management, 3,* 22–48.

Skarlicki, D.P. and Folger, R. (1997). Retaliation in the workplace: The roles of distributive, procedural, and interactional justice. *Journal of Applied Psychology, 82,* 434–443.

Spector, P.E. (2011). The relationship of personality to counterproductive work behavior (CWB): An integration of perspectives. *Human Resource Management Review, 21,* 342–352.

Spector, P.E. and Fox, S. (2002). An emotion-centered model of voluntary work behavior. Some parallels between counterproductive work behavior and organizational citizenship behavior. *Human Resource Management Review, 12,* 269–292.

Spector, P.E. and Fox, S. (2005). The stressor-emotion model of counterproductive work behavior (CWB). In S. Fox and P.E. Spector (eds), *Counterproductive Work Behavior: Investigations of Actors and Targets* (pp. 151–174). Washington, DC: APA.

Spector, P.E., Fox, S., Penney, L.M., Bruursema, K., Goh, A., and Kessler, S. (2006). The dimensionality of counterproductivity: Are all counterproductive behaviors created equal? *Journal of Vocational Behavior, 68,* 446–460.

Tan, H.H. and Tan, M.L. (2008). Organizational citizenship behavior and social loafing: The role of personality, motives, and contextual factors. *Journal of Psychology, 142,* 89–108.

Tang, T.L.-P. and Chiu, R.K. (2003). Income, money ethic, pay satisfaction, commitment, and unethical behavior: Is the love of money the root of evil for Hong Kong employees? *Journal of Business Ethics, 46,* 13–30.

Taylor, O.A. (2012). *The relationship between culture and counterproductive workplace behaviors: A meta-analysis.* Doctoral dissertation, University of Western Ontario, Canada.

Tepper, B.J., Henle, C.A., Lambert, L.S., Giacalone, R.A., and Duffy, M.K. (2008). Abusive supervision and subordinates' organization deviance. *Journal of Applied Psychology, 93,* 721–732.

Tian, Q., Zhang, L., and Zou, W. (2014). Job insecurity and counterproductive behavior of casino dealers – the mediating role of affective commitment and moderating role of supervisor support. *International Journal of Hospitality Management, 40,* 29–36.

Villanueva, L.S. (2006). *An examination of the role of self-control in the prediction of counterproductive work behaviors: Does cognition matter?* Doctoral dissertation, University of Houston, TX.

Weiss, H.M. and Cropanzano, R. (1996). Affective events theory: A theoretical discussion of the structure, causes and consequences of affective experiences at work. *Research in Organizational Behavior, 18,* 1–74.

17. Employee commitment and well-being
Alexandra C. Chris, Elyse R. Maltin and John P. Meyer

Interest in employee commitment has traditionally been driven by its implications for an organization's ability to compete in the 'war for talent' (Michaels et al., 2001) and retain its most effective employees to achieve competitive advantage. This was true even as attention began to shift to commitments to other foci, including occupations, supervisors, teams, and clients (see Chapter 4 in this volume). Until recently, only scant attention has been paid to the implications of commitment for employees themselves (Meyer and Maltin, 2010). Our focus in this chapter is on the relevance of workplace commitments for employee well-being. We review existing evidence concerning relations between varying commitment mindsets (affective, normative, continuance; see Chapter 3 in this volume) and both physical and psychological well-being. Next, we discuss the potential moderating effects of commitment on the stressor–strain relationship. Finally, we propose a theoretical framework to explain the findings and suggest ways that they might be used to guide practice and direct future research.

COMMITMENT FORMS AND FOCI

As discussed elsewhere in this volume (Chapters 3 and 4), commitment can be experienced in different ways and be directed at different targets. For present purposes, we adapt the approach taken in the well-established three-component model (TCM) (Meyer and Allen, 1991, 1997; Meyer and Herscovitch, 2001) and view commitment as 'a force that binds an individual to a target (social or non-social) and to a course of action of relevance to that target' (Meyer et al., 2006, p. 666). This binding force can be experienced in different ways (that is, can be accompanied by different mindsets), including: an affective attachment and involvement with the target, a felt obligation to the target, and an awareness of the costs associated with discontinuing involvement with the target. In their pure forms, these mindsets are referred to as affective (AC), normative (NC), and continuance (CC) commitment, respectively. Because the vast majority of research linking commitment to well-being has focused on the organization as the target of commitment, this emphasis will also be reflected in our review. However, we discuss research pertaining to other targets of commitment where relevant.

Consistent with TCM predictions, research suggests that 'mindset matters' (Meyer et al., 2002). Although AC, NC, and CC to the organization all relate negatively to turnover intention and actual turnover, the relation is strongest for AC, followed by NC and CC, respectively. The differences are even stronger in the case of job performance and organizational citizenship behavior, where AC has the strongest positive relation, followed by NC; CC is generally unrelated or has a weak negative correlation with both (see Chapter 15 in this volume). An important question to be addressed in this chapter is whether mindset also matters for employee well-being.

THE MEANING OF WELL-BEING

According to the traditional medical model, physical well-being is conceptualized as the absence of illness. This same model has commonly been applied in defining psychological well-being (Tetrick, 2002). The notion that well-being is more than the absence of illness has its roots in ancient philosophy (Aristotle, trans. 1985) and has long been a cornerstone of the humanist tradition in psychology (e.g., Maslow, 1968; Rogers, 1961). That being said, it is only recently with the increasing popularity of the positive psychology movement (Seligman and Csikszentmihalyi, 2000) that this notion has become more widely acknowledged. There is debate among philosophers and psychologists about what the 'new' well-being is and how it should be operationalized. One of the distinctions currently being made is between hedonic and eudaimonic well-being (see Waterman, 2013a). Hedonic well-being is typically conceptualized as a state of happiness and is often operationalized using a measure of subjective well-being (Diener, 2000; Diener and Biswas-Diener, 2008): a composite of strong positive affect, weak negative affect, and life satisfaction. The concept of eudaimonic well-being derives from Aristotelean philosophy and suggests that well-being involves more than happiness. The term itself originates from the Greek *eu* (good) and *daimon* (true self) and has generally been used to reflect positive personal growth and development throughout one's life (Waterman, 2013a).

There continues to be considerable debate around the definition of eudaimonic well-being and how it should be measured. Full discussion of this debate is beyond the objectives of this chapter and interested readers are directed to an edited volume by Waterman (2013b) entitled *The Best Within Us* for a detailed discussion of the concept and its measurement. Among the many issues being debated are whether it can be measured objectively against a set of universal standards for a 'good life', or whether it is best measured as a subjective state of thriving, flourishing, or personal growth (Waterman, 2013a). There is also debate about whether eudaimonic well-being should be measured as an end state distinct from hedonic well-being (Ryan et al., 2008; Ryff and Singer, 2008), or whether both should be measured in terms of the conditions that contribute independently to an overall state of subjective well-being (Sheldon, 2013). For present purposes, we take the position that well-being is more than the absence of illness or distress and, where appropriate, make distinctions between hedonic and eudaimonic well-being.

COMMITMENT AND WELL-BEING

In this section we address the question of whether employee commitment is associated with well-being, and whether the relation varies as a function of the commitment mindset and/or measure of well-being. Maltin et al. (2015) recently attempted to address these questions as they pertain to mindsets of organizational commitment by conducting a meta-analytic review of existing studies. As we summarize these findings it is important to keep in mind that, although well-being measures are treated as outcomes of commitment, the findings are simply average correlations corrected for unreliability (ρ) and cannot be taken as evidence of causality.

Maltin et al. (2015) predicted that, regardless of the measure of well-being, AC to the organization would have the strongest positive correlation, followed by NC; CC was expected to be unrelated or negatively related. To examine the relation involving CC more fully, the researchers computed separate correlations for two subdimensions of the construct: CC based on the high sacrifice employees would have to make by leaving the organization (CC:HS), and CC based on lack of available alternatives (CC:LA). They predicted that CC:LA would be most likely to correlate negatively with well-being because it reflects the strongest level of external constraint (see the discussion below for more detail). Maltin et al. (2015) also computed correlations separately for measures reflecting physical well-being (typically operationalized with an index of health complaints), and three forms of psychological well-being: hedonic (typically operationalized by measures of ill-being, including stress, depression, anxiety, and burnout), eudaimonic, and subjective well-being. Because the notion of eudaimonic well-being is relatively recent and has yet to be the focus of systematic investigation in the commitment literature, the choice of variables to reflect eudaimonic well-being (for example, thriving, vigor, dedication, engagement) was based on their grounding in positive psychology, which shares much in common with eudaimonic philosophy (Waterman, 2013a). Finally, although subjective well-being and its components (positive affect, negative affect, and life satisfaction) are often considered synonymously with hedonic well-being, Maltin et al. (2015) treated them separately based on Sheldon's (2013) argument that they are relatively content-free measures and likely reflect varying degrees of both hedonic and eudaimonic well-being.

In this summary, all meta-analytic correlations are presented so that a positive correlation indicates that stronger commitment is associated with greater well-being (that is, correlations with negative indicators are reflected). We also report only the category correlations; for correlations with specific variables within each category see Maltin et al. (2015). As expected, AC to the organization correlated positively with physical well-being ($\rho = .22$), hedonic well-being ($\rho = .35$), eudaimonic well-being ($\rho = .53$), and subjective well-being ($\rho = .39$). The correlations for NC are in the same direction, but weaker ($\rho = .06, .26 .28$, and $.27$, respectively). The correlations for CC are weaker still, and in the reverse direction ($\rho = -.04, -.13, -.08$, and $-.05$, respectively). Although it was only possible to compute separate correlations for CC:HS and CC:LA with a few variables, the pattern of findings is interesting. For example, CC:HS correlated positively with positive affect ($\rho = .16$) and near zero with negative affect ($\rho = .01$), whereas CC:LA correlated negatively with positive affect ($\rho = -.30$) and positively with negative affect ($\rho = .27$). This suggests that the threat of losing one's job without comparable alternatives available is potentially more stressful than the associated loss of investments. Indeed, having investments to lose appears to be associated with positive affect.

Overall, this pattern of correlations is quite similar to that obtained for organization-relevant outcomes (for example, retention, performance, organizational citizenship behavior; Meyer et al., 2002) as discussed above, suggesting that mindset also matters for employee well-being. However, it appears from these findings that the nature of the well-being measure might also matter. The pattern is most obvious in the case of AC, perhaps due to the fact that the correlations are based on a larger set of studies and are therefore more reliable estimates. AC has a stronger positive correlation with psychological (hedonic, eudaimonic, and subjective) well-being than it does with physical well-being. As Maltin et al. (2015) point out, there are several reasons why this might be the case. First, measures of AC and psychological well-being reflect perceived psychological states that, although distinguishable with regard to content, are bound to overlap. Indeed, this is the basis for the theoretical explanation proposed below. Second, the correlations with the psychological measures might also be inflated to some extent due to common method bias given that the measures are often obtained from the same raters (Podsakoff et al., 2003). Although the physical health measures also generally involve self-reporting, they have a more obvious objective reference point (experienced colds, headache, sleeplessness, and so on). Finally, physical well-being is more likely than psychological well-being to be influenced by biological and environmental factors that are unrelated to commitment.

Of even greater potential interest is the finding that AC correlates more strongly with measures of eudaimonic well-being compared to hedonic psychological well-being. This finding must be interpreted with caution given that categorization of the well-being measures was subjective, and the distinction between hedonic and eudaimonic well-being continues to be debated (see Waterman, 2013b). However, one possible explanation for this finding is that employees who are highly committed to their organizations, and presumably to the people, goals, and values that define the organization, have a greater sense of purpose in their lives (eudaimonic well-being) than those who are less committed. To the extent that being committed leads individuals to exert extra effort on behalf of the organization, it might also contribute to stress and undermine hedonic well-being in some situations. At present, we can only speculate that this is the case. Verification will require more attention to the mechanisms involved in explaining these relations, an issue we address in more detail below.

There has been far less research examining the relations between commitment mindsets pertaining to other targets and employee well-being. Meyer and Maltin (2010) noted that, for the most part, the pattern of relations was similar. For example, AC to one's occupation or profession has been found to relate negatively to symptoms of stress and burnout (e.g., Cohen, 1998; Reilly, 1994; Yeh et al., 2007). Overall, therefore, the findings suggest that commitment is related to well-being and that 'mindset matters'. Before we attempt to explain why these relations exist, and why they differ across mindsets, there are a few additional issues to consider. First, in addition to examining direct relations between the commitment mindsets and well-being, there is a body of research examining its moderating effects on stressor–strain relations. Second, recent developments in commitment theory and research indicate a need to look beyond relations involving the individual commitment mindsets when considering their outcomes, including well-being. We address these issues, in turn, in the following sections.

MODERATING EFFECTS OF COMMITMENT IN THE STRESSOR–STRAIN RELATIONSHIP

A second line of research pertaining to commitment and well-being has addressed its potential moderating effects on the stressor–strain relationship. There have been two competing perspectives on this issue (Meyer and Maltin, 2010), one arguing that commitment might buffer the effects of stressors on strain (e.g., Kobassa, 1982; Lazarus and Folkman, 1984), and the other that strong commitment can increase employees' vulnerability and exacerbate the negative effects of stressors (Brockner et al., 1992; Mathieu and Zajac, 1990). For the most part, research provides more evidence for a buffering effect than an exacerbating effect. However, there are some important qualifications to this general rule. First, the evidence for a buffering effect is strongest for AC (e.g., Rivkin et al., 2015; Schmidt, 2007). There has been little research addressing potential moderating effects of NC, and the few studies that investigated CC reported either an exacerbating effect (Irving and Coleman, 2003), or no effect (King and Sethi, 1997).

Second, there are some studies that purport to have found an exacerbating effect of AC on the stressor–strain relationship (Irving and Coleman, 2003; Reilly, 1994). However, Meyer and Maltin (2010) argued that the findings reflect a 'pseudo-exacerbating effect'. That is, while it is true that the positive relations between stressors and strain were greater for those with strong as opposed to weak AC, the level of strain for the strong AC group never exceeded that of the weak AC group. The stronger relation between stressors and strain for employees with strong AC was due to the fact that they had much lower levels of strain when stressors were mild.

Finally, there may be circumstances where AC does have an exacerbating effect. Galais and Moser (2009) examined the effect of reassignment to a new client (the stressor) on psychosomatic complaints among temporary workers in an employment agency. They measured AC to both the agency and the client organization and found a buffering effect of agency AC, but an exacerbating effect of AC to the client. That is, AC to the agency helped reduce the negative impact of the reassignment, whereas AC to the client they were leaving served to increase it. In other words, if they had a strong affective attachment to the client they were leaving, the stressor–strain relationship was stronger. Furthermore, Armstrong-Stassen (2004) found that nurses with strong AC to the organization experienced fewer health problems during the early phases of a major downsizing (the stressor) than those with weak AC, presumably because they were more likely to use a control-oriented coping strategy to actively address or cognitively re-evaluate the situation (as opposed to using an avoidant strategy). However, AC was positively related to physical symptoms in the longer term, possibly due to the large investment of energy required in control-oriented coping.

In sum, research findings pertaining to the moderating effects of commitment are generally consistent with the correlational studies reviewed above in demonstrating potential benefits of strong AC for employee well-being. However, there may be situations where, as Lazarus and Folkman (1984, p. 58) pointed out, AC makes a person 'particularly vulnerable to psychological stress in the area of that commitment'. Armstrong-Stassen (2004) found that the negative effects might only emerge over time, thus illustrating the importance of longitudinal research. In contrast to AC, it appears that the implications of CC, both direct and as a moderator, are generally negative. To date, relatively little attention has been paid to the implications of NC for well-being, although this is beginning to change, as we discuss in the next section.

LOOKING BEYOND INDIVIDUAL MINDSETS

In the initial development of the TCM, Meyer and Allen (1991, p. 68) proposed that 'an employee can experience all three forms of commitment [AC, NC, and CC] to varying degrees' and that they 'might interact to influence behavior'. Allen and Meyer (1990, p. 15) argued that it might 'be possible to identify "commitment profiles" that differentiate employees who are likely to remain with the organization and to contribute positively to its effectiveness from those who are likely to remain but contribute little'. Nevertheless, most investigators, including those interested in commitment and well-being, tend to examine relations with the individual mindsets. Meyer and Herscovitch (2001) addressed the call to consider commitment profiles and developed a set of propositions concerning the nature, development, and consequences of eight distinct profiles (formed by combining high and low scores on each of the three mindsets). This stimulated a number of investigators to take a person-centered approach to the study of commitment mindsets. The person-centered approach differs from the more traditional variable-centered approach in several ways (Meyer et al., 2013; Chapter 35 in this volume; Vandenberg and Stanley, 2009). When applied to the study of commitment mindsets, the person-centered approach allows for the identification of unobserved subgroups within a population for whom the individual commitment mindsets combine differently (that is, form different profiles). By considering the mindsets in combination, individuals are treated more holistically than when individual mindsets are examined. Importantly, the person-centered approach also facilitates the detection and description of complex interactions among variables (for example, mindsets) compared to variable strategies.

One important contribution of the person-centered approach was demonstrated by Gellatly et al. (2006). They found that NC to the organization related quite differently to employees' behavior depending on whether it was accompanied by strong AC as opposed to strong CC and weak AC. Intention to stay and exert effort on behalf of the organization was greater in the first case than it was in the second. Gellatly et al. (2006) proposed that the obligation associated with NC might be experienced as a 'moral imperative' (desire to do the right thing) when combined with strong AC, but as a sense of 'indebted obligation' (need to meet others' expectations) when combined with strong CC and weak AC. Meyer et al. (2012) found that CC was associated with more positive outcomes when it was part of a fully committed (strong AC, NC, and CC) profile than when it dominated the profile (CC-dominant profile). Again, the authors proposed that the cost mindset might differ when combined with strong AC and NC than on its own. In the first case, it might reflect the perceived cost of disrupting a desirable and/or important relationship or activity; in the second case, the perceived costs might be largely economic (for example, loss of benefits, lack of alternative employment opportunities). In sum, both studies suggest that the individual mindsets can combine and reflect more complex mindsets that have potentially important implications.

The benefits of taking a person-centered approach have been demonstrated most clearly as they pertain to organization-relevant outcomes, but there have also been a few studies that addressed the implications for well-being. Meyer et al. (2012) found that physical health, subjective well-being (positive and negative affect), and eudaimonic well-being (work engagement) were greatest among employees with a fully committed (strong AC, NC, and CC) or AC/NC-dominant profile, and lowest among those with an uncommitted (weak AC, NC, and CC) or CC-dominant profile. Morin et al. (2015) reported similar findings when comparing profiles of dual organizational and occupational commitment on various measures of psychological well-being. Both of these studies demonstrate that the implications of CC for well-being may depend on the relative strength of AC and NC; the potential negative effects of CC seem to occur only when it dominates the profile. Finally, Vandenberghe et al. (2015) recently found that NC related positively to emotional exhaustion and psychological distress when combined with strong CC:LA, but was unrelated when CC:LA was weak. Although these findings do not fully undermine the relevance of the variable-centered studies, including Maltin et al.'s (2015) meta-analysis, they suggest the need for caution in the interpretation of the findings, particularly those pertaining to NC and CC.

MEDIATING MECHANISMS

Why do employees with strong AC report being physically or psychologically healthy and better able to cope with workplace stressors, and why does the reverse seem to be true for employees with strong CC? In an effort to answer these questions, Meyer and Maltin (2010) drew upon self-determination theory (SDT) (Deci and Ryan, 1985; Ryan and Deci, 2000) and earlier work linking SDT to the TCM (Meyer et al., 2004). One aspect of SDT that sets it apart from many other motivation theories is the recognition that motivation varies not only in intensity but also in quality. More specifically, the theory makes a distinction between intrinsic motivation (enjoyment of the task itself) and extrinsic motivation (desire to attain contingent outcomes). The theory also distinguishes among different forms of extrinsic motivation. When individuals engage in tasks to attain rewards or avoid punishments meted out by others, they feel controlled and are said to experience external regulation of their behavior. In contrast, when they engage in activities that are freely chosen and consistent with their values, people feel more autonomous and experience identified or integrated regulation; in the case of integrated regulation, these values are integral to their self-concept. An intermediate form of regulation (introjected regulation) is experienced when individuals internalize the external constraints and evaluate their actions accordingly, but do not fully endorse the behavior as consistent with their true values. For purposes of subsequent discussion, we refer to intrinsic motivation along with integrated and identified regulation as 'autonomous regulation'; by contrast, external and introjected regulation together are referred to as 'controlled regulation'.

Meyer et al. (2004) noted the parallels between the TCM commitment mindsets and the motivational states described in SDT. Specifically, the AC mindset (desire) was seen as similar to autonomous regulation in SDT, the NC mindset (obligation) was seen as similar to introjected regulation, and the CC mindset (cost) was compared to controlled regulation. This similarity allowed Meyer and Maltin (2010) to draw on the large SDT literature demonstrating that autonomous (compared to controlled) regulation is associated with higher levels of basic need satisfaction and greater well-being (see Ryan et al., 2008 and Ryan et al., 2013 for reviews). According to SDT, satisfaction of three basic psychological needs – autonomy, competence, and relatedness – are essential for psychological well-being, particularly eudaimonic well-being (Ryan et al., 2013). Therefore, Meyer and Maltin (2010) reasoned that need satisfaction might also help to explain the observed relations between the commitment mindsets and well-being.

Although only a few studies have examined the relations between commitment and need satisfaction, Maltin et al. (2015) computed meta-analytic correlations between organizational AC and satisfaction of the needs for autonomy ($\rho = .58$), competence ($\rho = .21$), and relatedness ($\rho = .60$). In the one study that also examined relations for NC and CC, Meyer et al. (2012) found that NC related positively with satisfaction of all three needs, whereas CC correlated negatively (although only the correlation with competence need satisfaction was significant). These investigators also compared need satisfaction levels across several commitment profiles and found that satisfaction of all three needs was greatest among those with fully committed and AC/NC-dominant profiles, and weakest among those with uncommitted and CC-dominant profiles.

Again, we emphasize that the findings reported above simply indicate that the commitment mindsets relate to self-reported levels of need satisfaction. They do not address the causal connections. There are several possible explanations for the links between commitment and need satisfaction and their mutual connection to well-being. In the next section, we offer a theoretical framework based on the foregoing discussion, and use this framework to provide an agenda for future research, including research to address causal mechanisms.

THEORETICAL FRAMEWORK AND A RESEARCH AGENDA

Based on the theory and research reviewed above, we propose the framework presented in Figure 17.1 as a guide for future research and, ultimately, management practice. The figure identifies the major variable categories discussed to this point: commitment, well-being, workplace stressors, need satisfaction, and need-supportive work conditions. Each category includes a number of important distinctions, many of which were articulated in the foregoing discussion. The entries within the workplace stressor and need-supportive conditions boxes are only examples of the myriad of variables that can be classified as such. The double-headed arrow between these boxes (path 1) indicates that variables within these categories are likely to be related, probably negatively, but this will not be a major focus of discussion here.

In the figure, we treat well-being and its subcomponents as outcome variables. As we noted earlier, research to date pertaining to the link between commitment and well-being is correlational and therefore the directional arrow (path 10) is based on theory. What we

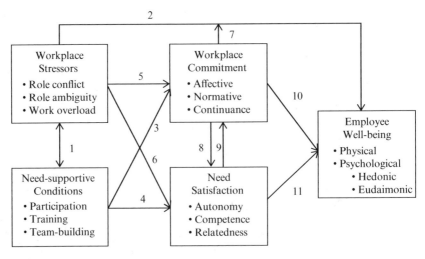

Figure 17.1　A model of employee commitment and well-being

know at this point is that AC, and to a lesser extent NC, relates positively with well-being; CC is unrelated or negatively related to well-being when considered on its own (Meyer and Maltin, 2010). These relations are qualified, however, by recent person-centered research demonstrating that NC and CC can relate differently with well-being depending on how they combine with the other components in a commitment profile (Meyer et al., 2012; Somers, 2009; Wasti, 2005). In any case, a direct causal connection has yet to be established empirically. Although it is conceivable that a commitment mindset of desire (AC) or moral imperative (AC/NC-dominant or fully committed profile) contributes directly to well-being, particularly eudaimonic well-being, there might be other possible explanations for the relationship. Similarly, strong CC might contribute directly to reduced well-being, but there could be other explanations. It was for this reason that we introduced need satisfaction into the theoretical discussion above. Need satisfaction has also been linked to well-being (path 11; Ryan et al., 2008, 2013).

There is some evidence that commitment, particularly AC alone or as part of a moral imperative profile, relates positively to need satisfaction, and that CC relates negatively (Maltin et al., 2015; Meyer et al., 2012). Again, however, the causal direction of these relations is not known (paths 8 and 9). There is a large body of research linking commitment and need satisfaction to work conditions (see Meyer et al., 2002 and Gagné and Deci, 2005, respectively). Many of these conditions, referred to as need supportive conditions in Figure 17.1 (for example, participation, training, team-building; paths 3 and 4), relate positively to need satisfaction, AC and NC, but negatively to CC. Other conditions, referred to as workplace stressors in Figure 17.1 (for example, role conflict, role ambiguity, work overload; paths 5 and 6), have the opposite relations. The fact that commitment and need satisfaction relate to one another and share common links with theoretical antecedent (work condition) and outcome (well-being) variables in our model suggests that there might be several possible explanations for the commitment–well-being relationship.

One possibility is that the correlation between commitment and well-being is spurious and reflects the fact that it relates positively with the same conditions responsible for well-being (that is, need-supportive conditions and/or need satisfaction). That is, work conditions and/or need satisfaction might be the key drivers of well-being, with commitment as another outcome with no independent causal effect on well-being. In this case, the relation between commitment and well-being (path 10) would be zero with work conditions and need satisfaction controlled.

Another possibility implied in our discussion above is that the effect of commitment on well-being is indirect through need satisfaction. In this case, commitment might mediate the effects of work conditions (stressors and/or supports) on need satisfaction or, at the very least, exert an effect on need satisfaction independent of work conditions (that is, path 8 is significant). In this case, the commitment mindset represents a meaningful psychological state that has implications for the satisfaction of one or more needs. For example, strong AC to the organization might reflect a meaningful bond that helps to satisfy the need for relatedness. It might also reflect volition in the choice of commitment target and satisfy the need for autonomy. In contrast, strong CC by itself could contribute to a sense of helplessness that thwarts the need for autonomy.

Finally, it might be that satisfaction of the basic psychological needs serves as the basis for commitment just as it does for the experience of autonomous regulation in SDT (Gagné and Deci, 2005; Ryan and Deci, 2000). This would be consistent with Meyer and Maltin's (2010) proposition that need satisfaction mediates the relations between need-supportive work conditions and commitment. If this is the case, path 9 should be significant, as should the direct path linking commitment to well-being (path 10). The links involving AC and NC should be positive, and the link with CC should be negative.

The remaining paths in Figure 17.1 (paths 2 and 7) are included to reflect theory and findings pertaining to the moderating effects of commitment on the stressor–strain relationship. As we noted earlier, AC has generally been found to buffer the effect of workplace stressors on strain, although exacerbating effects have been found in some cases, such as when severing the relationship itself is the stressor (Galais and Moser, 2009), or when efforts to cope with stressors over time contribute to strain in the long term (Armstrong-Stassen, 2004). In contrast, when it has a moderating effect, CC is most likely to exacerbate the negative effects of stressors on well-being (Irving and Coleman, 2003).

As noted above, the causal connections implied in Figure 17.1 have yet to receive much attention. The links between work conditions (stressor or need supports) and both commitment and need satisfaction are amenable to experimental or quasi-experimental studies. However, investigation of the potential direct and mediated effects of commitment on well-being that are the focus of this chapter require alternative research strategies. At a minimum, there is a need for multi-wave longitudinal research to examine how these variables relate over time (see Rivkin et al., 2015 for an example of a diary study demonstrating a buffering effect of AC on within-individual effects of daily stressors on strain). With these data available, there are a number of analytic strategies (for example, latent growth modeling) that can be used to examine how changes in commitment relate to changes in need satisfaction and/or well-being over time (see Chapter 33 in this volume). Similar, albeit more complex analyses (for example, latent growth mixture modeling) can be conducted to examine how changes in commitment profiles relate to changes in need satisfaction and well-being (see Chapter 35 in this volume).

As useful as these new analytic procedures can be in helping to establish directional relations, an important first step will be to address the debates concerning the meaning and measurement of well-being that we noted above. We suggested that commitment might have greater relevance for eudaimonic well-being than it does for hedonic well-being. However, to test this hypothesis we must be able to distinguish between the two. The categorization used by Maltin et al. (2015) in their meta-analysis seems reasonable, but this simply involved the sorting of measures included in previous research. Going forward, there will be a need for clearer definitions and the refinement or development of measures with demonstrated reliability and validity.

Finally, there is a need to look beyond organizations as the target of commitment. As noted earlier, employees can develop multiple workplace commitments (Becker, 1992; Morrow, 1983; Reichers, 1985). Based on Meyer and Maltin's (2010) earlier review, there is good reason to expect that relations between well-being and commitment to these other targets will be similar, but the mere existence of multiple targets raises other interesting and important research questions. For example, if for some reason it is not possible to establish commitment to the organization itself, will commitment to another target (for example, occupation, team, clients) serve the same purpose? What are the implications of commitments to conflicting targets (for example, organization and union) for well-being?

IMPLICATIONS FOR PRACTICE

One very important observation from our reviews is that the pattern of relations between the commitment mindsets and well-being is very similar to that observed for organization-relevant outcomes (for example, retention, job performance, organizational citizenship behavior). Therefore, organizations need not worry that efforts directed at improving employee well-being come at the cost of reduced organizational effectiveness. Efforts to foster desirable commitment mindsets or profiles should pay off for both the organization and its employees.

Of course, any definitive recommendations about the importance of commitment per se for well-being will require additional research to tease apart the causal relations and determine underlying mechanisms. However, even in the worst-case scenario described above where employee commitment contributes nothing beyond work conditions and need satisfaction to well-being, it might serve as an important 'dashboard indicator'. That is, by measuring employee commitment on a regular basis, organizations can get a general indication of whether employees are experiencing conditions conducive to their well-being (and willingness to contribute to the attainment of organizational goals). Measuring employee commitment is easier and more efficient than measuring all of the individual conditions that can contribute to employee well-being and motivation. If these measures indicate that the nature or levels of commitment are not what are desired, a more in-depth investigation of work conditions can be conducted as a follow-up.

In the likely event that research demonstrates that commitment plays a more important role than a dashboard indicator of well-being, this suggests that organizations need to take a closer look at the nature and level of commitment for their own sake. For example, if being committed contributes to well-being directly, or through the satisfaction of basic psychological needs, it might be important for organizations to find ways to foster commitment. Given the turbulent economic conditions that many organizations are confronting, it is possible that fostering strong commitment to the organization per se is neither possible nor desirable (Meyer, 2009). In that case, there are other targets of commitment that might serve the same purpose (for example, teams, supervisors, occupations, clients). As long as the goals and values of those targets are aligned with those of the organization, the resulting commitments should also have the dual benefit of improved employee well-being and organizational effectiveness.

CONCLUSION

To date, interest in employee commitment has been stimulated primarily by its implications for the target of that commitment, typically the organization. However, that is changing and more research is being conducted to examine implications for employee well-being. Evidence to date suggests that the commitment mindsets and profiles found to be associated with desirable organizational outcomes have similar relations with employee well-being. There remains a need for greater clarity in the meaning and measurement of well-being, and more research using analytic strategies better suited to establishing causal relationships. In the meantime, however, organizations can feel reasonably confident that if they foster desirable commitments to achieve their own objectives, employees will benefit as well.

REFERENCES

Allen, N.J. and Meyer, J.P. (1990). The measurement and antecedents of affective, continuance, and normative commitment to the organization. *Journal of Occupational Psychology, 63*, 1–18.

Aristotle (1985). *Nicomachean Ethics* (T. Irwin. Trans.). Indianapolis, IN: Hackett.

Armstrong-Stassen, M. (2004). The influence of prior commitment on the reactions of layoff survivors to organizational downsizing. *Journal of Occupational Health Psychology, 9*, 46–60.

Becker, T.E. (1992). Foci and bases of commitment: Are they distinctions worth making? *Academy of Management Journal, 35*, 232–244.

Brockner, J., Tyler, T.R., and Cooper-Schneider, R. (1992). The influence of prior commitment to an institution on reactions to perceived unfairness: The higher they are, the harder they fall. *Administrative Science Quarterly, 37*, 241–261.

Cohen, A. (1998). An examination of the relationship between work commitment and work outcomes among hospital nurses. *Scandinavian Journal of Management, 14*, 1–17.

Deci, E.L. and Ryan, R.M. (1985). *Intrinsic Motivation and Self-Determination in Human Behavior.* New York: Plenum.

Diener, E. (2000). Subjective well-being: The science of happiness and a proposal for a national index. *American Psychologist, 55*, 34–43.

Diener, E. and Biswas-Diener, R. (2008). *Happiness: Unlocking the Mysteries of Psychological Wealth.* Malden, MA: Blackwell.

Gagné, M. and Deci, E.L. (2005). Self-determination theory and work motivation. *Journal of Organizational Behavior, 26*, 262–331.

Galais, N. and Moser, K. (2009). Organizational commitment and the well-being of temporary agency workers: A longitudinal study. *Human Relations, 62*, 589–620.

Gellatly, I.R., Meyer, J.P., and Luchak, A.A. (2006). Combined effects of the three commitment components on focal and discretionary behaviors: A test of Meyer and Herscovitch's propositions. *Journal of Vocational Behavior, 69*, 331–345.

Irving, P.G. and Coleman, D.F. (2003). The moderating effect of different forms of commitment on role ambiguity–job tension relations. *Canadian Journal of Administrative Sciences, 20*, 97–106.

King, R.C. and Sethi, V. (1997). The moderating effect of organizational commitment on burnout in information systems professionals. *European Journal of Information Systems, 6*, 86–96.

Kobassa, S.C. (1982). Commitment and coping in stress resistance among lawyers. *Journal of Personality and Social Psychology, 42*, 707–717.

Lazarus, R.S. and Folkman, S. (1984). *Stress, Appraisal, and Coping.* New York: Springer.

Maltin, E.R., Meyer J.P., Chris, A.C., and Espinoza, J.A. (2015). Employee commitment and well-being: A meta-analysis. Manuscript, The University of Western Ontario, London, Ontario, Canada.

Maslow, A.H. (1968). *Toward a Psychology of Being* (2nd edn). Princeton, NJ: Van Nostrand.

Mathieu, J.E. and Zajac, D.M. (1990). A review and meta-analysis of the antecedents, correlates, and consequences of organizational commitment. *Psychological Bulletin, 108*, 171–194.

Meyer, J.P. (2009). Commitment in a changing world of work. In H.J. Klein, T.E. Becker and J.P. Meyer (eds), *Commitment in Organizations: Accumulated Wisdom and New Directions* (pp. 37–68). Florence, KY: Routledge/Taylor & Francis.

Meyer, J.P. and Allen, N.J. (1991). A three-component conceptualization of organizational commitment. *Human Resource Management Review, 1*, 61–89.

Meyer, J.P. and Allen, N.J. (1997). *Commitment in the Workplace: Theory, Research, and Application.* Thousand Oaks, CA: Sage Publications.

Meyer, J.P., Becker, T.E., and Van Dick, R. (2006). Social identities and commitments at work: Toward an integrative model. *Journal of Organizational Behavior, 27*, 665−683.

Meyer, J.P., Becker, T.E., and Vandenberghe, C. (2004). Employee commitment and motivation: A conceptual analysis and integrative model. *Journal of Applied Psychology, 89*, 991–1007.

Meyer, J.P. and Herscovitch, L. (2001). Commitment in the workplace: Toward a general model. *Human Resource Management Review, 11*, 299–326.

Meyer, J.P. and Maltin, E. (2010). Employee commitment and well-being: A critical review, theoretical framework and research agenda. *Journal of Vocational Behavior, 77*, 323–337.

Meyer, J.P., Stanley, D.J., Herscovitch, L., and Topolnsyky, L. (2002). Affective, continuance, and normative commitment to the organization: A meta-analysis of antecedents, correlates, and consequences. *Journal of Vocational Behavior*, *61*, 20–52.

Meyer, J.P., Stanley, L.J., and Parfyonova, N.M. (2012). Employee commitment in context: The nature and implication of commitment profiles. *Journal of Vocational Behavior*, *80*, 1–16.

Meyer, J.P., Stanley, L.J., and Vandenberg, R.J. (2013). A person-centered approach to the study of commitment. *Human Resource Management Review*, *23*, 190–202.

Michaels, E., Hadfield-Jones, H., and Axelrod, B. (2001). *The War for Talent*. Boston, MA: Harvard Business School Publishing.

Morin, A.J.S., Meyer, J.P., McInerney, D.M., Marsh, H.W., and Ganotice, F.A. (2015). Profiles of dual commitment to the occupation and organization: Relations to well-being and turnover intentions. *Asia Pacific Journal of Management*, *32*, 717–744. Electronic supplementary material available at doi:10.1007/s10490-015-9411-6.

Morrow, P.C. (1983). Concept redundancy in organizational research: The case of work commitment. *Academy of Management Review*, *8*(3), 486–500.

Podsakoff, P.M., MacKenzie, S.M., Lee, J., and Podsakoff, N.P. (2003). Common method biases in behavioral research: A critical review of the literature and recommended remedies. *Journal of Applied Psychology*, *88*, 879–903.

Reichers, A.E. (1985). A review and reconceptualization of organizational commitment. *Academy of Management Review*, *10*, 465–476.

Reilly, N.P. (1994). Exploring a paradox: Commitment as a moderator of the stressor–burnout relationship. *Journal of Applied Social Psychology*, *24*, 397–414.

Rivkin, W., Diestel, S., and Schmidt, K.-H. (2015). Affective commitment as a moderator of the adverse relationships between day-specific self-control demands and psychological well-being. *Journal of Vocational Behavior*, *88*, 185–194.

Rogers, C. (1961). *On Becoming a Person*. Boston, MA: Houghton Mifflin.

Ryan, R.M., Curren, R.R., and Deci, E.L. (2013). What humans need: Flourishing in Aristotelian philosophy and Self-Determination Theory. In A.A. Waterman (ed.), *The Best Within Us: Positive Psychology Perspectives on Eudaimonic Functioning* (pp. 57–75). Washington, DC: American Psychological Association.

Ryan, R.M. and Deci, E. (2000). Self-determination theory and the facilitation of intrinsic motivation, social development, and well-being. *American Psychologist*, *55*, 68–78.

Ryan, R.M., Huta, V., and Deci, E.L. (2008). Living well: A self-determination theory perspective on eudaimonia. *Journal of Happiness Studies*, *9*, 139–170.

Ryff, C.D. and Singer, B.H. (2008). Know thyself and become what you are: A eudaimonic approach to psychological well-being. *Journal of Happiness Studies*, *9*, 13–39.

Schmidt, K.-H. (2007). Organizational commitment: A further moderator in the relationship between work stress and strain? *International Journal of Stress Management*, *14*, 26–40.

Seligman, M.E.P. and Czikszentmihalyi, M. (2000). Positive psychology: An introduction. *American Psychologist*, *55*, 5–14.

Sheldon, K.M. (2013). Individual daimon, universal needs, and subjective well-being: Happiness as the natural consequence of a life well lived. In A.S. Waterman (Ed.), *The Best Within Us: Positive Psychology Perspectives on Eudaimonia* (pp. 119–137). American Psychological Association, Washington, DC.

Somers, M.J. (2009). The combined influence of affective, continuance and normative commitment on employee withdrawal. *Journal of Vocational Behavior*, *74*, 75–81.

Tetrick, L.E. (2002). Individual and organizational health. In P.L. Perrewé and D.C. Ganster, *Historical and Current Perspectives on Stress and Health* (pp. 117–142). Amsterdam: JAI.

Vandenberg, R.J. and Stanley, L.J. (2009). Statistical and methodological challenges for commitment researchers: Issues of invariance, change across time, and profile differences. In H.J. Klein, T.E. Becker, and J.P. Meyer (eds), *Commitment in Organizations: Accumulated Wisdom and New Directions* (pp. 383–418). New York: Routledge.

Vandenberghe, C., Mignonac, K., and Manville, C. (2015). When normative commitment leads to lower well-being and reduced performance. *Human Relations*, *68*, 843–870.

Wasti, S.A. (2005). Commitment profiles: Combinations of organizational commitment forms and job outcomes. *Journal of Vocational Behavior*, *67*, 290–308.

Waterman, A.S. (2013a). Introduction: Considering the nature of a life well-lived – Intersections of positive psychology and eudaimonist philosophy. *The Best Within Us: Positive Psychology Perspectives on Eudaimonia* (pp. 3–17). American Psychological Association, Washington, DC.

Waterman, A.S. (ed.). (2013b). *The Best Within Us: Positive Psychology Perspectives on Eudaimonia*. Washington, DC: American Psychological Association.

Yeh, Y.J.Y., Ko, J.J.R., Chang, Y.S., and Chen, C.H.V. (2007). Job stress and work attitudes between temporary and permanently employed nurses. *Stress and Health*, *23*, 111–120.

18. Affective consequences of workplace commitments
Howard J. Klein and Chad T. Brinsfield

There has been increased interest over the past decade in affect, emotion, and mood as topics of scientific investigation. Research has also begun to examine how these constructs are integrated with cognition, motivation, and neurophysiological functioning. Yet these advancements in affect-related research have not widely influenced the commitment literature. There has, for example, been little research examining the relationships between commitment and mood, distinct types of emotions, or distinct affective experiences. In this chapter, our primary focus is on the affective consequences of commitment, though we recognize that affect also plays a role in the development, maintenance, and deterioration of commitment, and that the nature of many of these relationships is likely reciprocal.

We begin by briefly reviewing the general role of affect in historical and current conceptualizations of commitment. We do so because the expected affective outcomes of commitment depend in part on how commitment is conceptualized and the extent to which commitment is viewed to contain affective elements. Specifically, we trace the evolution of commitment conceptualizations and explore the extent to which affective concepts are implicitly or explicitly included in those conceptualizations. We then review the extant literature and summarize the available theory (for example, affective events theory) and research examining the effects of commitments on emotion, moods, feelings, and other outcomes that have affective components (for example, job satisfaction, motivation, well-being). We conclude by identifying a future research agenda for better incorporating advancements in affect-related research into commitment scholarship and furthering our understanding of these relationships.

AFFECT IN COMMITMENT CONCEPTUALIZATIONS

Over the past 50 years many different conceptualizations of commitment have been developed (see Klein et al., 2009). In this section we review the role of affect (that is, emotions, moods, feelings) in these various conceptualizations and models of commitment. To organize this discussion we distinguish two general eras of commitment research. The first – prior conceptualizations – includes commitment research up to the emergence of Meyer and Allen's (1991) three-component model (TCM). The second era – current conceptualizations – includes Meyer and Allen's TCM and other recent conceptualizations of commitment.

Prior Conceptualizations

The role of affect in early investigations of commitment was sparse and/or not well explicated. Becker (1960), in the course of examining 'loyalty' to employers, sought to gain understanding of the mechanisms through which commitment to a course of action occurred. Becker described how prior choices or 'side-bets' commit a person to future actions consistent with their prior choices. Similarly, Kiesler and Sakamura (1966) examined commitment to future actions and defined commitment as 'a pledging or binding of the individual to behavioral acts' (p. 349). These early works did not focus explicitly on the role of affect, although affect-related factors (for example, self-justifications, dissonance reduction; McGee and Ford, 1987) likely play a role in the drive for behavioral consistency and favorable economic exchange.

Around this same time Etzioni (1961) developed a typology of involvement. Some have viewed Etzioni's moral and alienative involvements as two forms of affective attachment. Moral involvement is associated with positive affect (based on identification), and alienative involvement is associated with negative affect (based on lack of control). Calculative involvement, viewed as an instrumental attachment, is generally not viewed as involving affective states or processes (see Penley and Gould, 1988).

Kanter (1968) provided a typology of commitment, based on the study of social groups, that more explicitly addressed the role of affect. Kanter's typology included three different types of bonds under the umbrella of commitment: (1) a cognitive-continuance commitment, which entailed no affectivity; (2) cohesion commitment described as attachment to social relationships, which 'absorb the individuals' fund of affectivity' (p. 501) and involve affective ties between a person and their community; and (3) evaluative-control commitment, described as commitment to norms, values, and inner convictions which morally obligate an individual. This last type of bond involved positive evaluations of the demands of the social system.

Around the early 1970s, other views of commitment began to emerge with even greater emphasis on attitudes and social exchange. Notable early contributions to these perspectives include the work of Porter et al. (1974) who proposed that commitment is characterized by three factors: (1) a belief in and acceptance of the organization's goals and values; (2) a willingness to exert effort on behalf of the organization; and (3) a desire to maintain organizational membership. Although the role of affect was not explicit in their initial work, later theorizing based on this work more clearly recognized the role of affect, and this perspective became known as the attitudinal,[1] in contrast to the behavioral, perspective. Mowday et al. (1979), for example, differentiated commitment from job satisfaction by claiming that commitment reflects a general affective response to the organization as a whole, whereas job satisfaction reflects one's response to their job or certain aspects of their job. An important outcome of this work was the development of the Organizational Commitment Questionnaire (OCQ). The OCQ, however, only hints at role of affect with items such as, 'This organization really inspires the very best in me in the way of job performance'.

Similarly, Buchanan (1974) suggested identification, involvement, and loyalty as components of organizational commitment. Buchanan was more explicit about the role of affect by defining commitment as 'an affective attachment to the goals and values of an organization, to one's role in relation to goals and values, and to the organization for its own sake, apart from its purely instrumental worth' (p. 533). In testing Becker's (1960) side-bet model of commitment, Meyer and Allen (1984) further clarified the distinction between commitment based on investments, and commitment based on emotional attachment. In fact, they found that scales previously developed to assess commitment based on side-bets (e.g., Hrebiniak and Alutto, 1972) were more strongly associated with affective commitment (that is, based on emotional attachment) than to continuance commitment (that is, based on side-bets or prior investments).

O'Reilly and Chatman (1986), drawing from Kelman's (1958) bases for attitude change, examined compliance, identification, and internalization as distinct bases for and dimensions of commitment. Compliance occurs to gain specific rewards or to avoid negative consequences. Identification involves the psychological merging of one's sense of self with the target. Internalization is predicated on congruence between individual and organizational values. Although not explicit in this work, some retrospective theorizing indicates the general role of affect in these bases of commitment. At a very basic level, compliance is likely driven by approach–avoidance motivation (that is, the desire to seek pleasant outcomes and avoid painful ones; see Elliot, 2006). Similarly, the drive for self-enhancement and the associated positive affect partly underpins the process of identification (see Fiske, 2004). Internalization, which involves value congruence, also involves affective forces in that congruency between one's values and those of the organization or related foci (for example, supervisor) may contribute to positive affect (see Meglino and Ravlin, 1998).

Despite this gradual emergence of the role of affect in these prior conceptualizations of organizational commitment, the nature and role of affect in these models was not well developed. Moreover, as Jaros et al. (1993) point out, many studies during this period, although seeking to address the domain of affective commitment, actually conceptualized and measured concepts well beyond emotional attachment (for example, value alignment, desire to stay, willingness to exert effort; Angle and Perry, 1983; Bateman and Strasser, 1984). In addition, the organization was the primary commitment target for the conceptualizations noted above, but researchers have long acknowledged that commitment can be directed at multiple foci or targets, and that individuals hold multiple commitments. Other targets were researched during this time period (for example, careers, goals, professions, unions; Blau, 1985; Gouldner, 1958; Gordon et al., 1984; Locke et al., 1988) but the role of affect was rarely, if ever, explicit in these conceptualizations. We next turn to more current conceptualizations of commitment, wherein the role of affect has become further, but not fully, explicated.

Current Conceptualizations

Meyer and Allen's (Allen and Meyer, 1990; Meyer and Allen, 1991, 1997) TCM has a singular core essence of commitment experienced as one or more multiple mindsets: affective ('want to' or desire), normative ('ought to' or obligation), and continuance ('have to' or cost). Of these, the affective mindset has generated the most research attention. Correlates of the affective mindset have been widely examined, but the nature of the 'affect' in this mindset is less clear. Meyer and Allen (1991) defined the affective mindset as an 'employee's emotional attachment to, identification with, and involvement in the organization' (p. 67). Some (but not all) more recent definitions of this mindset recognize that identification and commitment are distinct, and therefore simply describe affective commitment as reflecting 'desire' or 'emotional attachment' or other similar terms (e.g., Bergman et al., 2009; Meyer et al., 2012). Even here, however, it is unclear exactly what emotional attachment means. Are specific emotions involved in this process, or is it simply general feelings of positive affect toward a commitment target? The latter seems to be implied in most of the related literature, but other affective processes (for example, discrete emotions, negative valence, arousal, moods) may be involved. It is also unclear whether these affective elements and processes should be viewed as part of, versus separate from (for example, antecedent or resulting), the commitment construct.

Klein et al. (2012) present an alternative, unidimensional definition and model of commitment (see also Chapter 2 in this volume). Klein et al.'s (2012) process model holds that four basic perceptual processes (that is, salience of, affect toward, trust in, and control over the target) are the most proximal antecedents of commitment to a given target. According to Klein et al., affect is critical for the formation of commitment because people are much more likely to dedicate themselves to, and accept responsibility for, a positively evaluated target than a negatively evaluated target. The Klein et al. model proposes two direct outcomes of commitment – continuation and motivation – which can influence affect and related outcomes, as well as cycle back to subsequently influence commitment. Next, we shift our discussion from the role of affect in conceptualizations of commitment to outcomes of commitment that are affective in nature, and/or which impact people's affective experiences.

AFFECTIVE CONSEQUENCES OF COMMITMENT

A substantial amount of research has demonstrated a consistent relationship between commitment and many important outcomes (see Cooper-Hakim and Viswesvaran, 2005; Meyer et al., 2002). Across conceptualizations and targets, commitment appears to have three general types of outcomes: (1) a reluctance to withdraw from a target; (2) a willingness to put forth effort on behalf of the target; and (3) affectivity toward the target. Of these, affective outcomes have probably been the least examined (Becker et al., 2009). In this section we review the research on the most widely examined affect-related outcomes of commitment and then examine other affective outcomes that have received less research attention, but appear to be important for theory and practice. In addition to reviewing prior research, throughout this section we also discuss how existing commitment models explain the processes by which commitment impacts these affective outcomes.

More Widely Examined Affective Consequences

Job satisfaction
Over the last five decades job satisfaction has been one of the most frequently researched employee attitudes. Although job satisfaction was originally defined as job-related affect (see Locke, 1969), Weiss and Cropanzano's (1996) affective events theory (AET) articulated that job satisfaction is an attitude rather than an emotional experience, and that the evaluation of one's job is not entirely affective, but also has a cognitive component.

Weiss (2002) further argued that job satisfaction comes from three distinct factors: affective experiences, evaluative judgments, and beliefs about one's job.

The relationship between job satisfaction and commitment has been of great interest to scholars. Meta-analytic investigations have found positive correlations between job satisfaction and both the affective and normative TCM commitment mindsets (average effect sizes of .65 and .31, respectively; Meyer et al., 2002). Commitment to work-related targets other than the organization have also been found to be related to satisfaction. For instance, studies have shown a consistent positive relationship between goal commitment and job and task satisfaction (e.g., Chang et al., 2010; Roberson, 1990). Team commitment has been found to be positively related to satisfaction with co-workers and supervision (Bishop and Scott, 2000). Kelloway et al. (1992) found positive correlations between satisfaction with the union and union commitment. As a final example, Busch (1998) found that employees with higher levels of commitment to their goals had more positive attitudes toward the management-by-objectives system that produced those goals.

The causal ordering of the relationship between job satisfaction and organizational commitment has been a debated issue in the literature. Authors have concluded that satisfaction causes commitment (e.g., Brown and Peterson, 1993), commitment causes satisfaction (e.g., Bateman and Strasser, 1984; Vandenberg and Lance, 1992), and that the two constructs are both caused by other determinants (e.g., Tett and Meyer, 1993). Still others have found a reciprocal relationship (e.g., Farkas and Tetrick, 1989). It should be emphasized that the posited causality for most of this research is based on statistical or theoretical inference, with definitive conclusions regarding causal ordering hindered by research design limitations.

Based on the Klein et al. (2012) model, we view the relationship between commitment and satisfaction as largely reciprocal, such that any of the aforementioned may be observed depending on the situation. Specifically, commitment likely impacts satisfaction through continuation, motivation, and action: the direct outcomes of commitment. For example, research has shown that higher performance, a possible indirect commitment outcome, enhances job satisfaction (see Judge et al., 2001). Moreover, Salancik and Pfeffer (1978) suggested that commitment might initiate a rationalizing process through which individuals develop attitudes consistent with their commitment.

Well-being

Well-being is a broad concept with some debate among researchers about the specific constructs that should be included under this umbrella term. Common to most conceptualizations of well-being are affective elements including the experience of high positive affect and low negative affect (Tetrick, 2002). Research has demonstrated that commitment is linked to many outcomes related to employee well-being, relationships that are thoroughly explored elsewhere in this volume (see Chapter 17). For example, affective commitment has been found to negatively relate to anxiety and depression (Tucker et al., 2005), job-related tension (Irving and Coleman, 2003), burnout (Cropanzano et al., 2003), physical health complaints (Wegge et al., 2006), and psychosomatic symptoms (Richardson et al., 2006). The reciprocal influences of commitment outcomes on perceptions of affect, trust, and control relative to the target and environment (see Klein et al., 2012) also have implications for personal well-being, as all four of these commitment antecedents have been linked to well-being.

Despite the evidence that commitment is generally positively associated with well-being, competing commitments or overcommitment may threaten a person's sense of well-being. Commitments that are in direct conflict or in competition for an individual's limited emotional and attentional resources (Kanfer and Ackerman, 1989) and/or time and effort (Naylor et al., 1980) can be expected to lead to feelings of ambivalence or stress. Similarly, overcommitment – when the strength of a particular commitment results in an individual expending levels of time and effort on behalf of a target that are not sustainable – will likely result in high levels of stress and burnout. Negative effects on well-being have also been demonstrated for the TCM continuance mindset. These bonds, characterized by a lack of alternatives or sunk costs, have been found to be negatively related to life satisfaction (Zickar et al., 2004), and positively associated with job-related tension (Irving and Coleman, 2003) and emotional exhaustion (Bakker et al., 2003; Wasti, 2005). Relationships between the normative commitment mindset and well-being have generally been non-significant (e.g., Somers, 2009), with the exception of a study of Chinese employees where normative commitment was positively related to emotional exhaustion (Tan and Akhtar, 1998). These authors speculated that the normative mindset in the Chinese culture reflects an internalization of normative pressures for loyalty.

Although most of the research examining commitment and employee well-being is based on commitment to the employing organization, some research has examined well-being and commitment to other work-related targets. For example, Cohen (1998) found a negative relationship between occupational commitment and job-induced tension. Similarly, Miller et al. (1990) found a negative relationship between occupational commitment and role stress, depersonalization, and emotional exhaustion in care-givers at a psychiatric hospital. These types of findings also extend to commitment to goals. Commitment to a set of goals may provide a sense of personal agency, structure, and meaning to life. Commitment to goals may help people to cope with daily problems and hence maintain personal as well as social well-being in times of adversity (Diener et al., 1999).

Motivation

Motivation is often defined as involving a set of internal and external forces that energize, activate, and direct behavior (Pinder, 1998). Although there have been a myriad of different views on the relationship between affect and motivation, many researchers view motivation as inexorably linked to affective or emotional processes (e.g., Carver and White, 1994; Higgins, 1997). The relationship between commitment and motivation has also been of interest to scholars for several decades (e.g., Klein et al., 2012; Meyer et al., 2004; Wiener, 1982). Some view commitment as a motivational phenomenon or as a component of motivation (e.g., Meyer et al., 2004; Wiener, 1982). Others view motivation as a direct outcome of commitment with the potential to reciprocally affect commitment (e.g., Klein et al., 2012). The nature of the relationship between commitment and motivation thus depends on the conceptual definitions used.

Meyer et al. (2004) provided a model of the relationship between commitment (defined in terms of the affective, normative, and continuance mindsets) and motivation (defined in terms of regulatory focus and self-determination theory; see Higgins, 1997; Ryan and Deci, 2000). They propose that an affective mindset is more likely associated with intrinsic motivation and a promotion focus, whereas a continuance mindset is more likely associated with extrinsic motivation and a prevention focus. A normative mindset was proposed to fall somewhere in between the other two mindsets relative to these different forms of motivation. In the Meyer et al. model, commitment to social foci (for example, organization, supervisor, team) based on the three commitment mindsets differentially impacts goal regulation (that is, locus of causality and perceived purpose; see Higgins, 1997; Ryan and Deci, 2000) and goal commitment. Goal regulation subsequently impacts goal choice (difficulty, specificity), which leads to motivation. Goal commitment moderates the relationship between goal choice and motivation. Behavior, which follows from motivation, can cycle back to influence both commitment and goal regulation depending on how one feels about the resultant behavior.

Klein et al. (2012) also propose a relationship between commitment and motivation. Specifically, Klein et al.'s process model depicts motivation as one of the two direct outcomes of commitment (the other being continuation with the target). These outcomes can then lead to more distal affective, cognitive, and behavioral outcomes. As with the Meyer et al. (2004) model (and others: for example, Mathieu, 1991; Morrow, 1983), the outcomes of commitment may influence the ensuing commitment. The Klein et al. model differs from the Meyer et al. model as it depicts commitment and motivation as distinct constructs, rather than commitment as a facet of motivation. These differing views stem from the way commitment is conceptualized in each of the respective models (see Klein et al., 2009; Chapter 2 in this volume).

Klein et al.'s (2012) conceptualization of commitment has implications for the form of motivation and associated affect that may result. Klein et al. propose that commitment bonds are more likely associated with intrinsic and promotion-oriented motivational forces. In contrast, bonds based on instrumental concerns or lack of alternatives are likely associated with extrinsic and prevention forces (see Higgins, 1997; Meyer et al., 2004; Ryan and Deci, 2000). Therefore, one can surmise that commitment, as conceptualized by Klein et al., may facilitate positive affect because of its influence on motivation. This is based on a wide range of research that indicates that intrinsic, autonomous, and promotion-oriented motivational processes are more likely associated with positive, rather than negative, affective experiences (e.g., Deci and Ryan, 1987).

Less Frequently Examined Affective Consequences

Negative affect

Although most of the research suggests that commitment generally results in positive affect, under certain circumstance commitment can contribute to negative affect. In addition to the negative effects commitment can have on well-being and related affect discussed earlier, commitment may be an important precondition for cognitive dissonance (Festinger, 1957). In fact, dissonance theorists have long been interested in commitment as an important independent variable (e.g., Wicklund and Frey, 1981). Dissonance involves negative affect when there is inconsistency between one's behaviors, goals, attitudes, or beliefs (see Harmon-Jones, 2000). The stronger the commitment to the target (for example, decision, program, person, organization) involved in creating the dissonance, the greater the possible magnitude of that dissonance (see Brickman, 1987) and the resulting negative affect. Moreover, when commitment to the relevant behavior, goal, attitude, or belief that is causing the dissonance is low, feelings of dissonance can easily be resolved by changing the behavior, goal, attitude, or belief. In addition, researchers have found that thwarted commitments may lead to rumination, counterfactual thinking, and negative affect (Lazarus, 1991; Schultheiss et al., 2008).

Emotional contagion

Another affective consequence of commitment may be its influence on emotional contagion. Emotional contagion is a process in which a person or group influences the moods and/or emotions of another person or group through the conscious or unconscious induction of affective states (e.g., Schoenewolf, 1990). For example, Totterdell et al. (1998) conjectured that people who are more committed to their teams would be more likely to experience moods that are synchronized with those of other team members. They based this reasoning, in part, on discoveries of shared affect in organizational climate and team cohesiveness research (e.g., Piper et al., 1983). And indeed, in a study of nursing teams they found that mood convergence among team members was stronger for those reporting greater commitment to their teams. It is not clear from this research, however, whether team commitment contributed to mood convergence, or whether mood convergence contributed to team commitment.

In a study related to emotional contagion, McCulloch et al. (2011) found evidence for vicarious goal satiation, a phenomenon wherein individuals experience a reduction in their goal strength as a result of observing another person pursue and complete that same goal. They found that this effect was stronger when the person observed completing the goal was perceived to be more committed to the goal. The authors reason that witnessing another's strong commitment to a goal creates a stronger goal-priming effect (Dik and Aarts, 2007). More research is needed to examine the mechanisms through which these effects can occur, and whether witnessing others' commitment (or lack thereof) can facilitate vicarious effects in other psychological phenomenon (for example, cognitive dissonance, ego depletion, ostracism; Ackerman et al., 2009; Norton et al., 2003; Wesselmann et al., 2009).

Quondam commitment

In a recent study, Klein et al. (in press) examined the commitments employees used to have, but no longer hold; a phenomenon they termed 'quondam commitment'. Like commitment, quondam commitments appear to have affect-related consequences (and causes). Those affective consequences may be positive or negative, depending on the reason why someone is no longer committed and whether the ending of that commitment was expected or desired. Klein et al. (in press) identified 11 categories of the reasons employees reported for no longer being committed to work-related targets. Some of these reasons appear to have strong affective components. For example, in nearly five percent of cases respondents reported some type of negative psychological or physiological consequence of their commitment as a reason for quondam commitment. Many of these responses included statements about it being depressing to maintain the commitment, or suggested burnout (for example, 'It wore me down'). Although, as discussed earlier, commitment can sometimes have negative effects on well-being, this is the first time that these affective consequences of commitment have been identified as contributing to the ending of commitment.

UNANSWERED QUESTIONS

This review of research on the affective consequences of commitment documents substantial progress but also highlights numerous questions that remain unanswered. On a conceptual level, more recent theorizing better distinguishes commitment itself from affect as an antecedent or outcome of commitment. These advancements notwithstanding, the exact processes by which commitment influences affect, and related outcomes, is a fruitful area for future research.

Additional research is needed examining the extent to which, and under what circumstances, being committed to a target results in that target being more positively evaluated. Research is also needed examining the effects of commitment on positive and negative mood. Similarly, research is needed on the effects of commitment on distinct types of emotions rather than general work-related affect (for example, job satisfaction). Different affective reactions have distinct phenomenological structures and thus might differentially result from workplace commitments, and in turn have different psychological and behavioral outcomes. Similarly, future research is also needed to determine whether certain types of emotions (for example, guilt, empathy) are differentially associated with commitment to different targets. For example, social emotions may be more relevant for commitment to social targets (for example, individuals, groups) than for non-social targets (for example, decisions, goals).

Another research need is to better understand the processes through which commitment relates to emotions, moods, and well-being. Potential differences in those mechanisms for different commitment targets (for example, social versus personal targets) also need to be examined. A better understanding is needed of the conditions under which commitment has positive or negative affective consequences. Uncovering the mechanisms, as noted above, along with key contextual moderators will be important in this effort. In general, research has tended to overlook the potential dark side of commitment. Additional research is needed on the affective consequences of escalation of commitment, overcommitment, conflicting commitments, and quondam commitments, and the factors (for example, resiliency) that may moderate those relationships.

Research is also needed to better understand the interrelationships among the affective and other outcomes of commitment (that is, continuation, performance). For example, does commitment facilitate positive affect through its influence on motivation? Alternatively, do specific moods or emotions moderate the effects of commitment on other outcomes such as citizenship behaviors? A final issue needing future research is the presumed reciprocal relationship between affect and commitment. Specifically, studies are needed to either confirm or refute this assumption, and if confirmed, determine whether the relationship is stronger in one direction versus the other.

Across all of the aforementioned required future research is the need to better determine the causal nature of the examined relationships and to provide richer theoretical integration and development. Within-person longitudinal research could help to tease apart and verify the relative strength and ordering of these relationships. Current models could be expanded, using outside theories (for example, affective events theory) to inform the expected relationships with affect and to build more robust theoretical foundations. An alternative or complementary approach would be to use a grounded theory-building approach that could co-evolve with the findings of future research.

CONCLUSION

Previous research on commitment, work attitudes, well-being, and affect has yielded many significant insights concerning the nature, interrelatedness, and implications of these important workplace phenomena. However, there is still much that we do not know. Recent developments regarding the nature of the commitment construct may be an important catalyst for bringing synergy to the existing body of commitment research. These developments could also further advance our understanding of how this type of workplace bond relates to other important psychological and behavioral factors in the workplace. Moreover, considering the dynamic and interactive nature of commitment with the target and environment, further examination of how commitment relates to job attitudes, well-being, and distinct forms of affect as commitment begins, strengthens, and dissipates over time will be insightful. We hope that the ideas presented in this chapter serve to stimulate research and a better understanding of the effects commitment can have on affect and related outcomes.

NOTE

1. Although there was considerable disagreement about the precise nature of attitudes during this time, most definitions of attitude involved some combination of affect and cognition (see Fishbein and Ajzen, 1972).

REFERENCES

Ackerman, J.A., Goldstein, N.J., Shapiro, J.R., and Bargh, J.A. (2009). You wear me out: The vicarious depletion of self-control. *Psychological Science, 20,* 326–332.

Allen, N.J. and Meyer, J.P. (1990). The measurement and antecedents of affective, continuance and normative commitment to the organization. *Journal of Occupational Psychology, 63,* 1–18.

Angle, H.L. and Perry, J.L. (1983). Organizational Commitment. *Work and Occupations, 10,* 123–146.

Bakker, A.B., Demerouti, E., de Boer, E., and Shaufeli, W.B. (2003). Job demands and job resources as predictors of absence duration and frequency. *Journal of Vocational Behavior, 62,* 341–356.

Bateman, T.S. and Strasser, S. (1984). A longitudinal analysis of the antecedents of organizational commitment. *Academy of Management Journal, 27,* 95–112.

Becker, H.S. (1960). Notes on the concept of commitment. *American Journal of Sociology, 66,* 32–40.

Becker, T.E., Klein, H.J., and Meyer, J.P. (2009). Commitment in organizations: Accumulated wisdom and new directions. In H.J. Klein, T. Becker and J.P. Meyer (eds), *Commitment in Organizations: Accumulated Wisdom and New Directions* (pp. 417–450). New York: Routledge/Taylor & Francis.

Bergman, M.E., Benzer, J.K., and Henning, J.B. (2009). The role of individual differences as contributors to the development of commitment. In H.J. Klein, T. Becker and J.P. Meyer (Eds), *Commitment in Organizations: Accumulated Wisdom and New Directions* (pp. 217–252). New York: Routledge/Taylor & Francis.

Bishop, J.W. and Scott, K.D. (2000). An examination of organizational and team commitment in a self-directed team environment. *Journal of Applied Psychology, 85,* 439–450.

Blau, G.J. (1985). The measurement and prediction of career commitment. *Journal of Occupational Psychology, 58,* 277–288.

Brickman, P. (1987). *Commitment, Conflict, and Caring.* Englewood Cliffs, NJ: Prentice Hall.

Brown, S.P. and Peterson, R.A. (1993). Antecedents and consequences of salesperson job satisfaction: Meta-analysis and assessment of causal effects. *Journal of Marketing Research, 30,* 63–77.

Buchanan, B. (1974). Building organizational commitment: The socialization of managers in work organizations. *Administrative Science Quarterly, 19,* 533–546.

Busch, T. (1998). Attitudes towards management by objectives: An empirical investigation of self-efficacy and goal commitment. *Scandinavian Journal of Management, 14,* 289–299.

Carver, C.S. and White, T.L. (1994). Behavioral inhibition, behavioral activation, and affective responses to impending reward and punishment: The BIS/BAS Scales. *Journal of Personality and Social Psychology, 67,* 319–333.

Chang, C., Johnson, R.E., and Lord, R.G. (2010). Moving beyond discrepancies: The importance of velocity as a predictor of satisfaction and motivation. *Human Performance, 23,* 58–80.

Cohen, A. (1998). An examination of the relationship between work commitment and work outcomes among hospital nurses. *Scandinavian Journal of Management, 14,* 1–17.

Cooper-Hakim, A. and Viswesvaran, C. (2005). The construct of work commitment: Testing an integrative framework. *Psychological Bulletin, 131,* 241–259.

Cropanzano, R., Rupp, D.E., and Byrne, Z. S. (2003). The relationship of emotional exhaustion to work attitudes, job performance, and organizational citizenship behaviors. *Journal of Applied Psychology, 88,* 160–169.

Deci, E.L. and Ryan, R.M. (1987). The support of autonomy and the control of behavior. *Journal of Personality and Social Psychology, 53,* 1024–1037.

Diener, E., Suh, E.M., Lucas, R.E., and Smith, H.L. (1999). Subjective well-being: Three decades of progress. *Psychological Bulletin, 125,* 276–302.

Dik, G. and Aarts, H. (2007). Behavioral cues to others' motivation and goal pursuits: The perception of effort facilitates goal inference and contagion. *Journal of Experimental Social Psychology, 43,* 727–737.

Elliot, A.J. (2006). The hierarchical model of approach–avoidance motivation. *Motivation and Emotion, 30,* 111–116.

Etzioni, A. (1961). *A Comparative Analysis of Complex Organizations.* New York: Free Press.

Farkas, A.J. and Tetrick, L.E. (1989). A three-wave longitudinal analysis of the causal ordering of satisfaction and commitment on turnover decisions. *Journal of Applied Psychology, 74,* 855–868.

Festinger, L. (1957). *A Theory of Cognitive Dissonance.* Stanford, CA: Stanford University Press.

Fishbein, M. and Ajzen, I. (1972). Attitudes and opinions. *Annual Review of Psychology, 23,* 487–544.

Fiske, S.T. (2004). *Social Beings: A Core Motives Approach to Social Psychology.* Danvers, MA: Wiley.

Gordon, M.E., Beauvais, L.L., and Ladd, R.T. (1984). The job satisfaction and union commitment of unionized engineers. *Industrial and Labor Relations Review, 37,* 359–370.

Gouldner, A.W. (1958). Cosmopolitans and locals: Toward an analysis of latent social roles. Part II. *Administrative Science Quarterly, 2,* 444–480.

Harmon-Jones, E. (2000). An update on cognitive dissonance theory, with a focus on the self. In A. Tesser and R.B. Felson and J.M. Suls (eds), *Psychological Perspectives on Self and Identity* (pp. 119–144). Hillside, NJ: Erlbaum.

Higgins, E.T. (1997). Beyond pleasure and pain. *American Psychologist, 52,* 1280–1300.

Hrebiniak, L.G. and Alutto, J.A. (1972). Personal and role-related factors in the development of organizational commitment. *Administrative Science Quarterly, 17,* 555–572.

Irving, P.G. and Coleman, D.F. (2003). The moderating effect of different forms of commitment on role-ambiguity–job tension relations. *Canadian Journal of Administrative Sciences, 20,* 97–106.

Jaros, S.J., Jermier, J.M., Koehler, J.W., and Sincich, T. (1993). Effects of continuance, affective, and moral commitment on the withdrawal process: An evaluation of eight structural equation models. *Academy of Management Journal, 36,* 951–994.

Judge, T.A., Thoresen, C.J., Bono, J.E., and Patton, G.K. (2001). The job satisfaction–job performance relationship: A qualitative and quantitative review. *Psychological Bulletin, 127,* 376–407.

Kanfer, R. and Ackerman, P.L. (1989). Motivation and cognitive abilities: An integrative/aptitude–treatment interaction approach to skill acquisition. *Journal of Applied Psychology, 74,* 657–690.

Kanter, R.M. (1968). Commitment and social organization: A study of commitment mechanisms in utopian communities. *American Sociological Review, 33,* 499–517.

Kelloway, E.K., Catano, V.M., and Southwell, R.R. (1992). The construct validity of union commitment: Development and dimensionality of a shorter scale. *Journal of Occupational and Organizational Psychology, 65,* 197–211.

Kelman, H.C. (1958). Compliance, identification, and internalization: Three processes of attitude change. *Journal of Conflict Resolution, 2,* 51–60.

Kiesler, C.A. and Sakumura, J. (1966). A test of a model for commitment. *Journal of Personality and Social Psychology, 3,* 349–353.

Klein, H.J., Brinsfield, C.T., Cooper, J.T., and Molloy, J.C. (in press). Quondam commitments: An examination of commitments employees no longer have. *Academy of Management Discoveries.*

Klein, H.J., Molloy, J.C., and Brinsfield, C.T. (2012). Reconceptualizing workplace commitment to redress a stretched construct: Revisiting assumptions and removing confounds. *Academy of Management Review, 37,* 130–151.

Klein, H.J., Molloy, J.C., and Cooper, J.T. (2009). Conceptual foundations: Construct definitions and theoretical representations of workplace commitments. In H.J. Klein, T.E. Becker, and J.P. Meyer (eds), *Commitment in Organizations: Accumulated Wisdom and New Directions* (pp. 3–36). New York: Routledge/Taylor & Francis.

Lazarus, R.S. (1991). *Emotion and Adaptation*. New York: Oxford University Press.

Locke, E.A. (1969). What is job satisfaction? *Organizational Behavior and Human Performance*, *4*, 309–336.

Locke, E.A., Latham, G.P., and Erez, M. (1988). The determinants of goal commitment. *Academy of Management Review*, *13*, 23–39.

Mathieu, J.E. (1991). A cross-level nonrecursive model of the antecedents of organizational commitment and satisfaction. *Journal of Applied Psychology*, *76*, 607–618.

McCulloch, K.C., Fitzsimons, G.M., Chua, S.N., and Albarracín, D. (2011). Vicarious goal satiation. *Journal of Experimental Social Psychology*, *47*, 685–688.

McGee, G.W. and Ford, R.C. (1987). Two (or more?) dimensions of organizational commitment: Reexamination of the affective and continuance commitment scales. *Journal of Applied Psychology*, *72*, 638–641.

Meglino, B.M. and Ravlin, E.C. (1998). Individual values in organizations: Concepts, controversies, and research. *Journal of Management*, *24*, 351–389.

Meyer, J.P. and Allen, N.J. (1984). Testing the "side-bet theory" of organizational commitment: Some methodological considerations. *Journal of Applied Psychology*, *69*, 372–378.

Meyer, J.P. and Allen, N.J. (1991). A three-component conceptualization of organizational commitment. *Human Resource Management Review*, *1*, 61–89.

Meyer, J.P. and Allen, N.J. (1997). *Commitment in the Workplace: Theory, Research, and Application*. Thousand Oaks, CA: Sage.

Meyer, J.P., Becker, T.E., and Vandenberghe, C. (2004). Employee commitment and motivation: A conceptual analysis and integrative model. *Journal of Applied Psychology*, *89*, 991–1007.

Meyer, J.P., Stanley, D.J., Herscovitch, L., and Topolnytsky, L. (2002). Affective, continuance, and normative commitment to the organization: A meta-analysis of antecedents, correlates, and consequences. *Journal of Vocational Behavior*, *61*, 20–52.

Meyer, J.P., Stanley, L.J., and Parfyonova, N.M. (2012). Employee commitment in context: The nature and implication of commitment profiles. *Journal of Vocational Behavior*, *80*, 1–16.

Miller, K.I., Ellis, B.H., Zook, E.G., and Lyles, J.S. (1990). An integrated model of communication, stress, and burnout in the workplace. *Communication Research*, *17*, 300–326.

Morrow, P.C. (1983). Concept redundancy in organizational research: The case of work commitment. *Academy of Management Review*, *8*, 486–500.

Mowday, R.T., Steers, R.M., and Porter, L.W. (1979). The measurement of organizational commitment. *Journal of Vocational Behavior*, *14*, 224–247.

Naylor, J.C., Pritchard, R.D., and Ilgen, D.R. (1980). *A Theory of Behavior in Organizations*. New York: Academic Press.

Norton, M.I., Monin, B., Cooper, J., and Hogg, M.A. (2003). Vicarious dissonance: Attitude change from the inconsistency of others. *Journal of Personality and Social Psychology*, *85*, 47–62.

O'Reilly, C. and Chatman, J. (1986). Organizational commitment and psychological attachment: The effects of compliance, identification, and internalization on prosocial behavior. *Journal of Applied Psychology*, *71*, 492–499.

Penley, L.E. and Gould, S. (1988). Etzioni's model of organizational involvement: A perspective for understanding commitment to organizations. *Journal of Organizational Behavior*, *9*, 43–59.

Pinder, C.C. (1998). *Motivation in Work Organizations*. Upper Saddle River, NJ: Prentice Hall.

Piper, W.E., Marrache, M., Lacroix, R., Richardsen, A.M., and Jones, B.D. (1983). Cohesion as a basic bond in groups. *Human Relations*, *36*, 93–108.

Porter, L.W., Steers, R.M., Mowday, R.T., and Boulian, P.V. (1974). Organizational commitment, job satisfaction, and turnover among psychiatric technicians. *Journal of Applied Psychology*, *59*, 603–609.

Richardson, A.S., Burke, R.J., and Martinussen, M. (2006). Work and health outcomes among police officers: The mediating role of police cynicism and engagement. *International Journal of Stress Management*, *13*, 555–574.

Roberson, L. (1990). Prediction of job satisfaction from characteristics of personal work goals. *Journal of Organizational Behavior*, *11*, 29–41.

Ryan, R.M. and Deci, E.L. (2000). Self-determination theory and the facilitation of intrinsic motivation, social development, and well-being. *American Psychologist*, *55*, 68–78.

Salancik, G.R. and Pfeffer, J. (1978). A social information processing approach to job attitudes and task design. *Administrative Science Quarterly*, *23*, 224–253.

Schoenewolf, G. (1990). Emotional contagion: Behavioral induction in individuals and groups. *Modern Psychoanalysis*, *15*, 49–61.

Schultheiss, O.C., Jones, N.M., Davis, A.Q., and Kley, C. (2008). The role of implicit motivation in hot and cold goal pursuit: Effects on goal progress, goal rumination, and emotional well-being. *Journal of Research in Personality*, *42*, 971–987.

Somers, M.J. (2009). The combined influence of affective, continuance, and normative commitment on employee withdrawal. *Journal of Vocational Behavior*, *74*, 75–81.

Tan, D.S.K. and Akhtar, S. (1998). Organizational commitment and experienced burnout: An exploratory study from a Chinese cultural perspective. *International Journal of Organizational Analysis*, *6*, 310–333.

Tetrick, L.E. (2002). Individual and organizational health. In P.L. Perrewé and D.C. Ganster (eds), *Historical and Current Perspectives on Stress and Health* (pp. 117–142). Amsterdam: JAI Press.

Tett, R.P. and Meyer, J.P. (1993). Job satisfaction, organizational commitment, turnover intention, and turnover: Path analyses based on meta-analytic findings. *Personnel Psychology*, *46*, 259–293.

Totterdell, P., Kellett, S., Teuchmann, K., and Briner, R.B. (1998). Evidence of mood linkage in work groups. *Journal of Personality and Social Psychology*, *74*, 1504–1515.

Tucker, J.S., Sinclair, R.R., and Thomas, J.L. (2005). The multilevel effects of occupational stressors on soldiers' well-being, organizational attachment, and readiness. *Journal of Occupational Health Psychology*, *10*, 276–299.

Vandenberg, R.J. and Lance, C.E. (1992). Examining the causal order of job satisfaction and organizational commitment. *Journal of Management*, *18*, 153–167.

Wasti, S.A. (2005). Commitment profiles: Combinations of organizational commitment forms and job outcomes. *Journal of Vocational Behavior*, *67*, 290–308.

Wegge, J., van Dick, R., Fisher, G.K., West, M.A., and Dawson, J.F. (2006). A test of basic assumptions of affective events theory (AET) in call centre work. *British Journal of Management*, *17*, 237–254.

Weiss, H.M. (2002). Deconstructing job satisfaction: Separating evaluations, beliefs and affective experiences. *Human Resource Management Review*, *12*, 173–194.

Weiss, H.M. and Cropanzano, R. (1996). Affective events theory: A theoretical discussion of the structure, causes and consequences of affective experiences at work. In B.M. Staw and L.L. Cummings (eds), *Research in organizational behavior: An Annual Series of Analytical Essays and Critical Reviews*, Vol. 18. (pp. 1–74). Greenwich, CT: JAI Press.

Wesselmann, E.D., Bagg, D., and Williams, K.D. (2009). 'I feel your pain': The effects of observing ostracism on the ostracism detection system. *Journal of Experimental Social Psychology*, *45*, 1308–1311.

Wicklund, R.A. and Frey, D. (1981). Cognitive consistency: Motivational vs non-motivational perspectives. In J.P. Forgas (ed.), *Social Cognition: Perspectives on Everyday Understanding* (pp. 141–163). London: Academic Press.

Wiener, Y. (1982). Commitment in organizations: A normative view. *Academy of Management Review*, *7*, 418–428.

Zickar, M.J., Gibby, R.E., and Jenny, T. (2004). Job attitudes of workers with two jobs. *Journal of Vocational Behavior*, *64*, 222–235.

PART V

DRIVERS OF COMMITMENT

19. Individual differences as causes of the development of commitment
Mindy E. Bergman and Vanessa A. Jean

This chapter focuses on how individual differences (IDs) are relevant to the development of commitment. IDs are the relatively stable traits – such as personality and abilities – that are present in all people and upon which people vary (Chernyshenko et al., 2011). Although individual studies have explained why particular IDs should be related to particular commitment mindsets (e.g., Brimeyer et al., 2010; Coleman et al., 1999; Wasti, 2003), a general framework for how IDs influence the development of commitment (that is, how IDs cause commitment and contribute to stability and/or change in commitment over time) has not been articulated. Thus, the goal of this chapter is to articulate this general framework.

In this chapter, we first review two general approaches to theoretical perspectives on the development of commitment from IDs. We also review two specific IDs (goal orientation and attachment cognitions) as examples. Then, we review a specific theory of IDs as contributors to the development of commitment (Bergman et al., 2013) and expand it by using the self-concept to explain how multiple IDs together contribute to commitment development. We conclude with a discussion of interesting research questions as well as some practical implications from our review.

COMMITMENT AND ITS CAUSES

In this chapter, we focus more on general commitment development rather than specific hypotheses associated with a particular conceptualization of commitment. However, where we do describe specific hypothesized relationships, we use the three-mindset model of commitment, which includes: (1) affective commitment (AC), a positive, emotional desire to identify and remain with the organization; (2) continuance commitment (CC), a calculated understanding that there are costs associated with organizational membership and the loss thereof; and (3) normative commitment (NC), a sense of obligation to the organization (see Chapter 3 in this volume for a review). Of course, other conceptualizations of commitment exist (see Chapter 2 in this volume, for example) and our chapter is applicable to those as well. Further, we use commitment to the organization as our exemplar, but like Meyer and Herscovitch (2001), we believe commitment is a process relevant to a variety of targets (that is, foci; see Chapter 4 in this volume).

Most research on the 'causes' of commitment have examined either antecedents or bases of commitment, but not how commitment develops (that is, changes over time and the causes of those changes; Beck and Wilson, 2001). Antecedents of commitment are variables that correlate with and theoretically precede commitment. These antecedents commonly include demographic variables (for example, age, sex), work-related person variables (for example, tenure), and positive workplace experiences (for example, organizational support, justice, or low role conflict). Bases are processes that link commitment to various workplace experiences. These processes include identification, internalization, compliance, and socialization (Meyer et al., 2004; Meyer et al., 2006; O'Reilly and Chatman, 1986).

HOW ARE IDs PORTRAYED AS CAUSES OF COMMITMENT?

There are two general ways that IDs as causes of commitment are described. Borrowing from the leadership literature (Barling et al., 2011), we term these the 'trait approach' and the 'contingency approach'.[1]

Trait Approach

The trait approach argues that individual difference X is correlated with and, ostensibly, a direct cause of commitment Y. For example, meta-analytic evidence demonstrates that self-efficacy and internal locus of control are positively correlated with AC (Meyer et al., 2002). Erdheim et al. (2006) found that conscientiousness and neuroticism predict CC and that extraversion is positively related to AC and NC but negatively related to CC. Choi et al. (2015) show that all five factor model traits (that is, extraversion, conscientiousness, agreeableness, openness, emotional stability) are positively related to AC and NC, whereas CC is negatively related to extraversion, openness, and emotional stability.

The primary criticism of the trait approach is that it can only account for between-person differences in commitment, with no ability to explain within-person commitment development. This is because there is essentially no variability within persons on IDs but there is variability between persons. Additionally, there is theoretically little variability in commitment within persons once it is developed (Meyer and Allen, 1997; Meyer and Herscovitch, 2001), although the empirical evidence is as yet unclear (Kam et al., forthcoming). This further contributes to the trait approach only accounting for between-persons differences in commitment. Relatedly, these factors are probably the primary reasons that research on IDs and commitment are cross-sectional correlational designs, as: (1) they are between-person designs; and (2) both commitment and the IDs are presumed to be stable.

Contingency Approach

The contingency approach argues that some IDs lead to commitment under some circumstances or situations rather than via a direct causal route. Essentially, the contingency approach argues that it is not the presence of any particular disposition but rather how the disposition fits into the workplace that determines commitment. This implies that there is no one 'right kind' of employee in order for organizations to have a committed workforce; instead, it is the person-in-situation that leads to commitment. Thus, the contingency approach can be viewed through a lens of person–environment fit (Kristof-Brown and Guay, 2011; see Chapter 20 in this volume for a review).

The contingency approach can account – if the right methods are used – for any or all of: (1) between-persons; (2) between-situations; and (3) within-person perspectives on commitment. Between-persons effects are seen when the situation is held constant; to the extent that two people differ on an ID, they should also differ in the extent to which they fit the situation. These between-persons effects are much like the trait approach's between-persons effects, with the caveat that the contingency approach focuses on commitment caused by fit at this particular situation rather than the effect of a particular trait that is hypothesized to be a contributor to commitment across all situations. Between-situations effects are essentially the reverse: when an ID is held constant but the situations vary. This could be observed with the same person in two different situations (for example, changing organizations and the person is more committed at Organization ABC than at Organization XYZ) or two people with the same ID level in two situations. Again, the assumption is that particular kinds of people will fit, rather than that there is a single right way for all organizations to engender commitment. Finally, the contingency approach can account for within-persons changes in commitment. Assuming that either the person or the situation change at some point in time, fit between the person and the situation will change over time, resulting in a change in commitment. Notably, this is about not just the initial development of commitment but also the stability (or not) of commitment once it develops. In the contingency approach perspective, the apparent stability of commitment over time (e.g., Kam et al., forthcoming) is due in large part to the relative stability of IDs (Chernyshenko et al., 2011) and of workplace features over time.

As an example, goal orientation is an ID regarding how people approach and frame achievement situations and their sense of competence (Dweck, 1986; VandeWalle, 1997). There are at least three kinds of goal orientation: learning (that is, competence is experienced via mastery), performance-prove (that is, competence is experienced via favorable appraisal of performance), and performance-avoid (that is, competence is experienced via avoidance of negative appraisal of performance; Dweck, 1986; VandeWalle, 1997). The contingency approach to commitment suggests that there is no one right goal orientation that will engender commitment; instead, when people are in organizations and jobs that match their goal orientations, they will be more successful and perceive greater fit, which should cause commitment. Further, the contingency approach suggests that if a workplace were to change its goal expectations and framing (for example, from learning goals to performance-prove goals), commitment should also change.

The modest ID–commitment relationships reviewed above in the trait approach section (e.g., Choi et al., 2015; Meyer et al., 2002) are the effects that would be expected via the contingency approach. Although the contingency approach proposes that that commitment is not engendered by a specific set of IDs across all situations, work organizations do have a number of features in common and these common workplace features help to explain why there is a modest effect of some IDs on commitment across organizations. For example, workers who are more reliable in terms of attendance and performance (that is, more conscientious) and who get along better with others (that is, more agreeable) are likely to experience greater fit to a greater number of workplaces, resulting in commitment across workplaces.

Further, there are some IDs that should have near-universal effects on commitment because they develop and maintain relationships. For example, attachment theory proposes that people develop schemas of: (1) the reliability of others as sources of care and comfort (that is, model of others); and (2) their own worthiness of care and comfort from others (that is, model of self; Ainsworth, 1989; Bowlby, 1988; Fraley and Waller, 1998). When both of these models are positive, the person has achieved a 'secure base'; otherwise, the person tends toward insecure attachments of various prototypes (for example, anxious, avoidant). The secure base is a source of comfort and confidence that allows a person to feel psychologically safe in a world that involves exploration and risk (Ainsworth, 1989; Bowlby, 1988). It seems likely that most organizations and jobs provide events that activate attachment cognitions because organizations are social entities, made up of people who have to interact in order to complete the organization's work. It is difficult to imagine an organization that does not benefit from having members with secure bases rather than other kinds of attachment schemas.

BERGMAN ET AL.'S CONTINGENCY APPROACH TO THE DEVELOPMENT OF COMMITMENT

Bergman et al. (2013) proposed a contingency approach to the development of commitment that focused on micro-events in the workplace and how these events – and people's reactions to them – shaped commitment over time. Bergman et al. (2013) began with the notion that commitment is a motivated bond to a focus or target (Meyer and Herscovitch, 2001); therefore, the maintenance of the relationship and acting on behalf of the target must have a purpose (that is, a motive) for the person. They argued that two processes – trait activation and person–environment fit – were essential to understanding the development of commitment from IDs because together they explained how a person evaluates the utility of a relationship, which is what leads to the development and maintenance (or not) of commitment. The person–environment fit literature argues that positive outcomes occur when people fit to situations (Kristof-Brown and Guay, 2011), in part because fit is an inherently positive (that is, satisfying) experience, but also because the level of fit is information about the utility of the person–situation combination (Bergman et al., 2013; Kristof-Brown and Guay, 2011). Trait activation theory argues that people have a variety of characteristics, but only some of these characteristics are relevant to any situation (Tett and Burnett, 2003; Tett and Guterman, 2000). When situations call upon a particular trait, that trait is marshaled into use. Sometimes the person has a sufficient level of the trait to be successful in the situation, but in other situations the trait level is deficient and there is no success.

Drawing on these perspectives, Bergman et al. (2013) argued that organizational events (Weiss and Cropanzano, 1996) activate some of a person's values.[2] Next, the outcomes of events satisfy those values to some extent, which provides information about the fit between the person and the focus. Satisfaction of values should be positively related to commitment because satisfaction indicates the utility of the relationship with the commitment focus, relative to the person's values. As satisfaction increases, so should the person's motivation to maintain the relationship and to act in ways that satisfy the conditions of the relationship (that is, commitment; Meyer and Herscovitch, 2001).

Bergman et al. (2013) noted that multiple values could be activated by a single event, which means that events could cause both fit and misfit, so that the relationship is both useful and not useful for the person. As an example, consider the practice in universities of shielding assistant professors from taxing service work while they are pre-tenure.

Such a practice could activate two distinct values: support and inclusion. Minimizing demanding service assignments could send the message to the assistant professor that they are supported by the department as they focus on creating the research record to earn tenure and promotion; this would satisfy their need for support. At the same time, being excluded from engaging in some of the serious work of departmental life could send the message that the assistant professor's voice is not valued and that they are not a full member of the department; this would result in misfit for inclusion. This example illustrates how a single event (or practice in this case, as there will be multiple events) can cause both fit and misfit.

The ability of a single event to activate multiple values leads to the question: what happens when there is both fit and misfit from events? Bergman et al. (2013) resolved this problem by considering the value hierarchy (Kluger and DeNisi, 1996; Locke, 1991; Vallacher and Wegner, 1987), proposing that the fit or misfit to values higher in the hierarchy are weighted more in the determination of commitment (Bergman et al., 2013). Returning to the example, a person who values support more than inclusion (that is, the fitted value over the misfitted value) should develop higher commitment than a person who values inclusion over support (that is, the misfitted value over the fitted value).

Finally, Bergman et al. (2013) described how their contingency approach explained the development of commitment, and not just for newcomers. Bergman et al. argued that – assuming stability of values – the accumulation of events over time created commitment, its stability, and/or its changes. As people encounter events that indicated fit (and misfit) with their values, then commitment accrued (or not). As more events accumulate, each event should have less total impact on commitment because: (1) events early in the relationship are particularly informative relative to the total amount of information about the relationship; and (2) people seek out confirming information and events that indicate fit, so earlier fit information helps to drive the accumulation of later fit information. However, Bergman et al. (2013) did not assume that organizations (and their events) or individuals' values never change. Even though later events were proposed to have less impact on commitment than do earlier events, if the trend of events were to change (for example, a corporate reorganization, causing a person to experience misfit continually), then commitment would change. Additionally, individual needs are likely to change, sometimes slowly (for example, feeling less challenged by work over time) and sometimes rapidly (for example, the unexpected illness of a parent, leading the employee to value a different work–life balance); these changes to the individuals' values would also cause changes in fit and misfit, leading to changes in experienced commitment.

The Self-Concept as an Organizing Structure in the Development of Commitment from IDs

A limitation of Bergman et al.'s (2013) work is the exclusive focus on values and the value hierarchy. Here, we address this limitation and expand Bergman et al.'s theory to include other IDs. First, Bergman et al.'s argument about events activating values (that is, trait activation theory; Tett and Burnett, 2003; Tett and Guterman, 2000) can be straightforwardly applied to other IDs, such that events activate some traits and not others. Second, Bergman et al.'s perspective that the fit of events to the person's values as indicating the utility of the relationship – and thus, driving commitment – can again be applied straightforwardly to other IDs. The final major piece of Bergman et al.'s (2013) work is the organizing effect of the value hierarchy when considering the activation of multiple values. The self-concept is a good candidate for understanding how IDs more broadly – not just values – combine in the development of commitment.

McCrae and Costa (1996; see also McAdams and Pals, 2006) state that the self-concept explains how IDs are organized and why they are motivational. The self-concept is comprised of self-referential knowledge, skills, attitudes, schemas, and beliefs that define the individual's sense of self and meaning in life (McCrae and Costa, 1996; Skaalvik and Bong, 2003). The self-concept is active, meaning that people use their self-concepts to determine which experiences to seek out, and to evaluate and understand their experiences relative to their sense of self (Markus and Wurf, 1987; McAdams and Pals, 2006). The self-concept allows people to organize their experiences and understand them as a coherent life story (Leary and Tangney, 2012; McAdams and Pals, 2006). Although the exact structure of the self-concept is a long-debated topic (Markus and Wurf, 1987), several factors are clearly relevant here. First, the self-concept is multifaceted and differentiated (Marsh, 1990; Prebble et al., 2013), containing a wide variety of characteristics, some of which are more relevant to some situations than others (Hattie, 1992/2014; Markus and Wurf, 1987). Second, some components of the self-concept are more central or more important to self-definition (Markus and Wurf, 1987; Stryker, 1986). Finally, the self-concept is motivational and self-regulatory (Markus and Wurf, 1987).

To expand Bergman et al.'s (2013) view from a narrow focus on values to IDs more generally, the self-concept can replace the value hierarchy. The self-concept influences the effect of IDs (via their activation by workplace events) on commitment in the same way that the value hierarchy influences the effect of values on commitment. Because the self-concept is motivational, self-regulatory, and active, people select and evaluate the success of actions relative to their sense of self. Thus, people will purposefully seek out some situations because the situations align with the person's self-concept. The resulting fit (or misfit) that arises from the success (or failure) will demonstrate the utility of maintaining the relationship (Kristof-Brown and Guay, 2011; Chapter 20 in this volume). Further, the integration of the self-concept into this expanded theory can resolve the problem that events can activate multiple IDs simultaneously, just as events can activate multiple values simultaneously. Like the value hierarchy, the self-concept identifies which IDs are most self-definitional. Self-representations that are more central or more organizing, or higher in the self-concept hierarchy, should carry more weight in the determination of fit to the organization.

In sum, Bergman et al.'s (2013) framework can be expanded to include all IDs by considering the role of the self-concept as a way of organizing, prioritizing, and sense-making individuals' experiences. The self-concept provides content when a person is assessing the utility of some relationship, resulting in higher commitment when utility is higher. The self-concept also explains how fit and misfit information arising from the same event can be resolved, as some components of the self-concept are more central than others.

FUTURE DIRECTIONS FOR RESEARCH ON IDs AND COMMITMENT

In this section, we briefly describe three future directions for research on IDs and commitment: person-centered approaches to commitment and IDs; the usefulness of IDs in the prediction of the stability and change of commitment; and how IDs interface with nested and/or interrelated commitments.

Person-Centered Approach to Commitment and IDs

Our review focused on the variable-centered approach (that is, the traditional view of linear relationships between variables) to commitment. However, Meyer and Allen's (1997) conceptualization of commitment suggests intra-individual interactive effects among commitment mindsets, such that people experience a general bond to commitment foci accompanied by various mindsets (that is, AC, CC, NC). Meyer and Herscovitch (2001) further refined this view, arguing for distinctly different outcomes depending on the mindset combination (see also Meyer and Parfyonova, 2010; Meyer et al., 2012). This intra-individual perspective evolved into what is now called the person-centered or profile approach. The person-centered approach assumes that there are qualitative differences across the various combinations of mindsets and these qualitative differences have non-trivial effects on outcomes (Meyer et al., 2013; Vandenberg and Stanley, 2009). In the person-centered approach, people can be grouped into classes based on the similarity of the combination of their commitment mindsets (often called profiles). The profiles literature is relatively young compared to the variable-centered commitment literature and therefore has considerably less empirical evidence. Like the early days of the variable-centered commitment literature, the person-centered commitment literature has focused more on the outcomes of commitment profiles rather than the antecedents of commitment profiles (Kabins et al., 2016). Thus, the time is ripe to begin studying the ID causes of commitment profiles.

Like commitment, personality is typically described via a variable-centered approach (Choi et al., 2015; McCrae and Costa, 1996), but also like commitment, personality has intra-individual effects and can be viewed from a person-centered perspective, which has recently gained attention (e.g., Claes et al., 2006; Meeus et al., 2011; Merz and Roesch, 2011). To conjointly examine IDs and commitment from the person-centered approach, theory would be needed to explain the set of profiles in the commitment domain and the set of profiles in the personality domain. This is in progress in the commitment literature (Meyer et al., 2012; Meyer et al., 2013; Morin et al., 2015) and is starting to happen in the personality literature (e.g., Claes et al., 2006; Meeus et al., 2011; Merz and Roesch, 2011). Theory would also be needed to explain the conjoint profiles, or why membership in personality profile A is associated with membership in commitment profile Q. Importantly, such theorizing also needs to be more than the sum of variable-centered approaches; that is, it needs to be more than 'individual difference A is linked to commitment B whereas individual difference C is linked to commitment D, therefore individual difference profile AC will be linked to commitment profile BD'.

One interesting issue to resolve in this area is whether there are some IDs that predispose people to have any commitment bond, and whether other IDs predispose people to have particular commitment profiles. Kabins et al. (2016) argue that a commitment only exists if at least one of the three mindsets is high,[3] so theoretically any of the three mindsets could be high enough to create a commitment bond. Some IDs might determine the propensity to form any commitment bond. For example, conscientiousness – as an indicator of the sensitivity to responsibility and achievement cues – might be particularly adept at precipitating any commitment. Attachment cognitions – as indicators of receptiveness to relationship development and maintenance – might also precipitate any commitment. In contrast, there could be some IDs (and, especially, combinations of IDs; Kabins et al., 2016) that could be linked to the development of particular profiles. As an example, Kabins et al. (2016) argue that low levels of job mobility indicators might be linked to the development of exchange-based commitments (Meyer et al., 2006), whereas high levels of job mobility indicators might be linked to the development of both value-based (Meyer et al., 2006) and weak (Kabins et al., 2016) commitments.

Do IDs Predict the Stability of Commitment?

Most commitment research explicitly or implicitly assumes that commitment is relatively stable (for an exception, see Solinger et al., 2015) and there is some evidence in favor of this stability over relatively long periods of time (Kam et al., forthcoming). But most commitment research also implicitly or explicitly states that commitment is not fixed after its initial development, as individuals and organizations both change. As more research into the developmental trajectories of commitment occurs, there is likely to be interest in whether and why individuals differ in their commitment stability, which refers to the extent to which there are fluctuations in mean commitment levels (in the variable-centered approach) or transitions to other commitment profiles (in the person-centered approach).

IDs might play a role in the stability of commitment. Conscientiousness, for example, might be related to within-person commitment stability, such that regardless of the particular profile or mean levels of commitment that a person possesses, conscientiousness (between persons) will be positively related to stability of commitment within persons. This might occur because one of the markers of conscientiousness is stability. Emotional stability might also be linked to commitment stability, as its opposite pole (neuroticism) is linked to experiencing a greater variety of emotional states or being on an 'emotional roller-coaster'. This could lead to greater variety in the interpretation of ID–event fit, creating more volatility in commitment. These are just two examples of how IDs could influence the variability of commitment states beyond the development of commitment.

How are IDs Related to Nested and/or Interrelated Commitments?

People are not committed to only one focus at a time and it is possible – if not likely – that these commitments affect each other. Nested commitments occur when lower-level foci are subsumed in higher-level foci (for example, co-workers, department, organization). Interrelated commitments are not nested but have other dependencies. For example, people might experience commitment to their work because of their commitment to their families. Some theories suggest that commitments to nested foci should be the same (Lawler, 1992; Reichers, 1985), whereas others suggest that people can hold very different commitments toward nested foci despite the structural dependencies among them (Meyer and Allen, 1997); interrelated commitments are more likely to be theorized like the latter than the former (Meyer and Allen, 1997).

It is possible that IDs influence the alignment of nested commitments and the inter-relatedness of commitments. First, some people are more likely to segment relationships or aspects of their lives, making them less likely to perceive connections among foci. For example, in the work–family literature, the role segmentation–role integration ID describes an individual's preference for either separating or intermingling their work and non-work time, tasks, and responsibilities (Nippert-Eng, 1995). These IDs could be used in the commitment literature to examine whether and why some people are more likely to perceive interrelated commitments than others. Second, different foci might tap into different parts of the self-concept. Because the self-concept is multifaceted, it may be the case that even though some foci have structural relationships, the corresponding intra-individual identity components are not very related, resulting in the person seeing little connection among the commitments to these foci. As an example, a conscripted soldier might not feel committed to the armed services because the soldier does not deeply iden-tify as a soldier, but might feel very committed to the comrades in their unit; the depend-encies among the comrades and the armed services would seem to require commitments to both, but that might not be the case because of the identity factors in the self-concept. Finally, the dependencies among commitment foci can create duties-to-others foci (for example, commitment to your spouse can create a duty to your in-laws). There might be IDs that explain how these subordinate commitments are experienced. For example, allocentrism and idiocentrism (the ID constructs that are parallel to the cultural dimen-sions of collectivism and individualism, respectively) could influence the extent to which individuals perceive commitments as interrelated and whether the subordinate commit-ments are resented or appreciated (Berg et al., 2001; Janoff-Bulman and Leggatt, 2002).

PRACTICAL IMPLICATIONS

Although previous researchers have cautioned against the use of person–organization fit as a selection measure due to its weak relationship with job performance, it could be used for other work-related purposes (Arthur et al., 2006). Meta-analytic estimates show a weak relationship between PO fit and overall job performance ($\rho = .15$), but a much stronger relationship between PO fit and organizational commitment ($\rho = .31$; Arthur et al., 2006). Given these estimates, it may be best for practitioners to focus on how organ-izations can strengthen this fit–commitment relationship post-hire.

Based on this chapter, there are several ways that practitioners can assist in the devel-opment of organizational commitment. First, organizations can determine not only what IDs a person has but also how central those IDs are. Organizations that select people who are high on IDs that are linked to job performance should find that organizational out-comes are enhanced through commitment as well when those performance-related IDs are also central to the person's self-concept. Further, organizations can assess employ-ees' IDs and then alter aspects of the organization to fit with employees (for example, providing benefits, allowing for different work styles, placing in different career path), which should engender commitment (House, 1996). Lastly, organizations can provide an abundance of POS (Chapter 24 in this volume) such that employees who fit less well with the organization will still feel valued and, in return, committed to the organization.

CONCLUSION

This chapter has reviewed the two general approaches that account for IDs as causes of commitment: the trait approach and the contingency approach. The review indicated the strength and flexibility of the contingency approach over the trait approach and recast trait approach research into contingency approach terms. One theory within the contingency approach (Bergman et al., 2013) was reviewed and expanded by invoking the self-concept as an important organizing component to reconcile different experiences related to different IDs. Future research should examine person-centered approaches to commitment and IDs, as well as the role that IDs play in the stability of commitment and the alignment of commitments across foci. We hope that this chapter contributes to the development of a vibrant literature on the relationship between IDs and commitment.

NOTES

1. There are also situational approaches to the causes of commitment, which do not focus on IDs.
2. Bergman et al. (2013) used the term 'values' for both values and goals. They acknowledged that values (that is, attitude or belief statements that indicate preferences for objects or activities that could fulfill needs) and goals (that is, statements of how to achieve valued outcomes within situations) were different, but used the term 'values' because goals reflect what is valued by the individual within a context (Locke, 1991; Vallacher and Wegner, 1987). According to Locke (1991), values link needs (that is, innate or deeply ingrained drives that must be satisfied for psychological or physical health) and actions (that is, behaviors that satisfy those needs) by explicating a preferred manner of need satisfaction; goals are applied value statements, indicating what outcomes are desired in a particular situation (Locke, 1991; Vallacher and Wegner, 1987).
3. Kabins et al. (2016) refer to profiles with no high mindset elements as 'weak' profiles. This reinforces the idea that commitment is not a sum of the different mindsets, but rather a general bond that is phenomenologically experienced via the different mindsets (Meyer and Allen, 1997; Meyer and Herscovitch, 2001). As an example, a person who is moderate on AC, NC, and CC might score 3 on each 1–5 scale, for a 'total' score (not typically calculated in the commitment literature) of 9. A person with a CC-dominant profile might score 5 on CC and 1 on each of AC and NC on a 1–5 scale, with a 'total' score of 7. Despite these 'total' scores, a person would have strong commitment via the CC-dominant profile, not the moderate profile (Kabins et al., 2016).

REFERENCES

Ainsworth, M.D.S. (1989). Attachments beyond infancy. *American Psychologist, 44*, 709–716.
Arthur, W., Jr., Bell, S.T., Villado, A.J., and Doverspike, D. (2006). The use of person–organization fit in employment decision making: An assessment of its criterion-related validity. *Journal of Applied Psychology, 91*, 786–801.
Barling, J., Christie, A., and Hoption, C. (2011). Leadership. In S. Zedeck (ed.), *APA Handbook of Industrial and Organizational Psychology, Volume I* (pp. 183–240). Washington, DC: American Psychological Association.
Beck, K. and Wilson, C. (2001). Have we studied, should we study, and can we study the development of commitment? Methodological issues and the developmental study of work-related commitment. *Human Resource Management Review, 11*, 257–278.
Berg, M.R., Janoff-Bulman, R., and Cotter, J. (2001). Perceiving value in obligations and goals: Wanting to do what should be done. *Personality and Social Psychology Bulletin, 27*, 982–995.

Bergman, M.E., Benzer, J.K., Kabins, A.H., Bhupatkar, A., and Panina, D. (2013). An event-based perspective on the development of commitment. *Human Resource Management Review, 23*, 148–160. http://dx.doi.org/10.1016/j.hrmr.2012.07.005.

Bowlby, J. (1988). *A Secure Base: Parent–Child Attachment and Healthy Human Development.* New York: Basic Books.

Brimeyer, T.M., Perrucci, R., and Wadsworth, S.M. (2010). Age, tenure, resources for control, and organizational commitment. *Social Science Quarterly, 91*, 511–530.

Chernyshenko, O.S., Stark, S., Drasgow, F. (2011). Individual differences: Their measurement and validity. In S. Zedeck (ed.), *APA Handbook of Industrial and Organizational Psychology*, Volume III (pp. 117–151). Washington, DC: American Psychological Association.

Choi, D., Oh, I.S., and Colbert, A.E. (2015). Understanding organizational commitment: A meta-analytic examination of the roles of the Five-Factor Model of personality and culture. *Journal of Applied Psychology, 100*, 1542–1567.

Claes, L., Vandereycken, W., Luyten, P., Soenens, B., Pieters, G., and Vertommen, H. (2006). Personality prototypes in eating disorders based on the big five model. *Journal of Personality Disorders, 20*, 401–416.

Coleman, D.F., Irving, G.P., and Cooper, C.L. (1999). Another look at the locus of control–organizational commitment relationship: It depends on the form of commitment. *Journal of Organizational Behavior, 20*, 995–1001.

Dweck, C.S. (1986). Motivational processes affecting learning. *American Psychologist, 41*, 1040–1048.

Erdhiem, J., Wang, M., and Zickar, M.J. (2006). Linking the Big Five personality constructs to organizational commitment. *Personality and Individual Differences, 41*, 959–970.

Fraley, R.C. and Waller, N.G. (1998). Adult attachment patterns: A test of the typological model. In J.A. Simpson and W.S. Rholes (eds), *Attachment Theory and Close Relationships* (p. 77–114). New York: Guilford.

Hattie, J. (1992/2014). *Self-concept.* New York: Lawrence Earlbaum.

House, R.J. (1996). Path–goal theory of leadership: Lessons, legacy, and a reformulated theory. *Leadership Quarterly, 7*, 323–352.

Janoff-Bulman, R. and Leggatt, H.K. (2002). Culture and social obligation: When 'shoulds' are perceived as 'wants'. *Journal of Research in Personality, 36*, 260–270.

Kabins, A.H., Xu, X., Bergman, M.E., Berry, C.M., and Willson, V.L. (2016). A profile of profiles: A meta-analysis of the nomological net of commitment profiles. *Journal of Applied Psychology, 101*, 881–904. http://dx.doi.org/10.1037/apl0000091.

Kam, C., Morin, A.J.S., Meyer, J.P., and Topolnytsky, L. (forthcoming). Are commitment profiles stable and predictable? A latent transition analysis. *Journal of Management.*

Kluger, A.N. and DeNisi, A. (1996). The effects of feedback interventions on performance: A historical review, a meta-analysis, and a preliminary feedback intervention theory. *Psychological Bulletin, 119*, 254–284.

Kristof-Brown, A.L. and Guay, R.P. (2011). Person–environment fit. In S. Zedeck (ed.), *APA Handbook of Industrial and Organizational Psychology*, Volume III (pp. 3–50). Washington, DC: American Psychological Association.

Lawler, E.J. (1992). Affective attachment to nested groups: A choice-process theory. *American Sociological Review, 57*, 327–339.

Leary, M.R. and Tangney, J.P. (2012). The self as an organizing construct in the behavioral and social sciences. In M.R. Leary and J.P. Tangney (eds), *Handbook of Self and Identity*, 2nd edn (pp. 1–18). New York: Guilford Press.

Locke, E.A. (1991). The motivation sequence, the motivation hub, and the motivation core. *Organizational Behavior and Human Decision Processes, 50*, 288–299.

Markus, H. and Wurf, E. (1987). The dynamic self-concept: A social psychological perspective. *Annual Review of Psychology, 38*, 299–337.

Marsh, H.W. (1990). A multidimensional, hierarchical model of self-concept: Theoretical and empirical justification. *Educational Psychology Review, 2*, 77–172.

McAdams, D.P., and Pals, J.L. (2006). A new big five: Fundamental principles for an integrative science of personality. *American Psychologist, 61*, 204–217.

McCrae, R.R. and Costa, P.T. (1996). Toward a new generation of personality theories: Theoretical contexts for the five-factor model. In J.S. Wiggins (ed.), *The Five-Factor Model of Personality* (pp. 51–87). New York: Guilford.

Meeus, W., Van de Schoot, R., Klimstra, T., and Branje, S. (2011). Personality types in adolescence: Change and stability and links with adjustment and relationships: A five-wave longitudinal study. *Developmental Psychology, 47*, 1181–1195.

Merz, E.L. and Roesch, S.C. (2011). A latent profile analysis of the five factor model of personality: Modeling trait interactions. *Personality and Individual Differences, 51*, 915–919.

Meyer, J.P. and Allen, N.J. (1997). *Commitment in the Workplace.* Thousand Oaks, CA: Sage.

Meyer, J.P., Becker, T.E., and Vandenberghe, C. (2004). Employee commitment and motivation: A conceptual analysis and integrative model. *Journal of Applied Psychology*, *89*, 991–1007.

Meyer, J.P., Becker, T.E., and van Dick, R. (2006). Social identities and commitments at work: Toward an integrative model. *Journal of Organizational Behavior*, *27*, 665–683.

Meyer, J.P. and Herscovitch, L. (2001). Commitment in the workplace: Toward a general model. *Human Resource Management Review*, *11*, 299–326.

Meyer, J.P. and Parfyonova, N.M. (2010). Normative commitment in the workplace: A theoretical analysis and re-conceptualization. *Human Resource Management Review*, *20*, 283–294.

Meyer, J.P., Stanley, D.J., Hercovitch, L., and Topolnytsky, L. (2002). Affective, continuance, and normative commitment to the organization: A meta-analysis of antecedents, correlates, and consequences. *Journal of Vocational Behavior*, *61*, 20–52.

Meyer, J.P., Stanley, L.J., and Parfyonova, N.M. (2012). Employee commitment in context: The nature and implication of commitment profiles. *Journal of Vocational Behavior*, *80*, 1–16.

Meyer, J.P., Stanley, L.J., and Vandenberg, R. (2013). A person-centered approach to the study of commitment. *Human Resource Management Review*, *23*, 190–202.

Morin, A.J.S., Meyer, J.P., McInerney, D.M., Marsh, H.W., and Ganotice, F.A., Jr. (2015). Profiles of dual commitment to the occupation and organization: Relations to well-being and turnover intentions. *Asia Pacific Journal of Management*, *32*, 717–744.

Nippert-Eng, C.E. (1995). *Home and Work: Negotiating Boundaries through Everyday Life*. Chicago, IL: University of Chicago Press.

O'Reilly, C.A., III. and Chatman, J. (1986). Organizational commitment and psychological attachment: The effects of compliance, identification, and internalization on prosocial behavior. *Journal of Applied Psychology*, *71*, 492–499.

Prebble, S.C., Addis, D.R., and Tippett, L.J. (2013). Autobiographical memory and sense of self. *Psychological Bulletin*, *139*, 815–840.

Reichers, A.E. (1985). A review and reconceptualization of organizational commitment. *Academy of Management Review*, *10*, 465–476.

Skaalvik, E.M. and Bong, M. (2003). Self-concept and self-efficacy revisited. In H.W. Marsh, R.G. Craven, and D.M. McInerney (eds), *International Advances in Self-Research* (Vol. 1, 67–89). Charlotte, NC: Information Age Publishing.

Solinger, O.N., Hofmans, J., and van Olffen, W. (2015). The dynamic microstructure of organizational commitment. *Journal of Occupational and Organizational Psychology*, *88*, 773–796.

Stryker, S. (1986). Identity theory: Developments and extensions. In K. Yardley and T. Honess (eds), *Self and Identity* (pp. 89–103). New York: Wiley.

Tett, R.P. and Burnett, D.D. (2003). A personality trait-based interactionist model of job performance. *Journal of Applied Psychology*, *88*, 500–517.

Tett, R.P. and Guterman, H.A. (2000). Situation trait relevance, trait expression, and cross-situational consistency: Testing a principle of trait activation. *Journal of Research in Personality*, *34*, 397–423.

Vallacher, R.R. and Wegner, D.M. (1987). What do people think they're doing? Action identification and human behavior. *Psychological Review*, *94*, 3–15.

Vandenberg, R.J. and Stanley, L.J. (2009). Statistical and methodological challenges for commitment researchers: Issues of invariance, change across time, and profile differences. In H.J. Klein, T.E. Becker, and J.P. Meyer (eds), *Commitment in Organizations: Accumulated Wisdom and New Directions* (pp. 383–416). New York: Taylor & Francis.

VandeWalle, D. (1997). Development and validation of a work domain goal orientation instrument. *Educational and Psychological Measurement*, *8*, 995–1015.

Wasti, S.A. (2003). Organizational commitment, turnover intentions, and the influence of cultural values. *Journal of Occupational and Organizational Psychology*, *76*, 303–321.

Weiss, H.M. and Cropanzano, R. (1996). Affective events theory: A theoretical discussion of the structure, causes and consequences of affective experiences at work. *Research in Organizational Behavior*, *18*, 1–74.

20. Person–environment fits as drivers of commitment

Annelies E.M. van Vianen, Melvyn R.W. Hamstra and Jessie Koen

Employees' work-related commitments are highly influenced by how employees connect to specific features of their work (for example, job, peers, supervisor, and organization). Person–environment (PE) fit theories postulate that individuals: (1) have a basic need to fit their environments; (2) seek out environments that match their own characteristics; and (3) are satisfied with and committed to their environment to the extent that they experience a good fit (Van Vianen et al., 2013).

Several seminal theories in organizational psychology share these basic assumptions, such as PE fit models of stress (Edwards and Cooper, 1990), the theory of work adjustment (Dawis and Lofquist, 1984), the model of vocational personality types (Holland, 1985), and the attraction–selection–attrition (ASA) framework (Schneider, 1987). Furthermore, these theories emphasize that the interaction between individuals and environments affects individual and organizational outcomes. However, contrary to interaction models in which relationships between predictor and outcome variables are moderated by individual or contextual characteristics, PE fit theories claim that outcomes are optimal when persons and environments are identical, whereas they become suboptimal to the extent that individual characteristics exceed or fall short of contextual characteristics.

The purpose of this chapter is to show that employees' fit experiences are among the strongest predictors of employees' affective reactions and are thus important drivers of commitment. Employees experience multiple fits and multiple commitments because the work environment comprises varying domains to which they may connect, such as the job, the supervisor, the work team, and the organization as a whole. We describe how fits and commitments are related in these different domains.

Fit–commitment relationships are generally strong, but their precise strength depends on how fit is assessed (Van Vianen et al., 2013). Individuals tend to form holistic perceptions about their fit with the environment (that is, an overall feeling of the amount of fit). Because these holistic fit perceptions affect their commitments most strongly, we further explore how these holistic perceptions emerge and how they can be influenced by organizational practices. In addition, we argue that employees' holistic fit perceptions and commitment are informed by two sources: the experienced fit on the needs, preferences, and values that they share with all other people (universal fits); and the experienced fit on the needs, preferences, and values that they do not necessarily share with others (distinctive fits). Finally, we propose that fit research and organizational practice could benefit from a person-centered approach that distinguishes groups of individuals with similar fit and commitment profiles.

In the next section, we first describe different domain-specific fits that employees develop in their work. The purpose is to show that these different fit sources relate to commensurate commitments and involve various processes connecting fits to commitments.

MULTIPLE FITS

Employees make fit assessments regarding their job, organization, supervisor, and team (e.g., Edwards and Billsberry, 2010). Person–job fit comprises two types of fit: demands–abilities fit and needs–supplies fit. Demands–abilities fit exists when employees' abilities, knowledge, and skills match with the job requirements. Needs–supplies fit exists when an employee has specific needs, desires, or preferences (for example, a strong desire for structure) that are fulfilled by the work context (for example, clear instructions from the supervisor).

Person–organization fit concerns the match between a person's values and those of the organization (e.g., Kristof-Brown et al., 2005b). Values are fundamental for both individuals and organizations. At the individual level, values represent preferences, interests, and motives which are central to a person's self-identity (Chatman, 1991). It is for this reason that people desire that their values are recognized by their work environment. At the organizational level, values are the basic assumptions that are central to an organization's culture (Schein, 2004).

Person–supervisor fit concerns the match between employees' characteristics and those of their supervisor (for example, values, personality). Schein (2004) argues that supervisors are important for employees' environmental experiences because supervisors shape these experiences through their own values and actions, and they transmit organizational values to the daily work environment. Furthermore, organizational leaders are supposed to voice and confirm an organization's culture because they are promoted to higher job levels due to their excellent match with this culture (e.g., Giberson et al., 2005). Sluss et al. (2012) have shown that identification with the supervisor increases the influence the supervisor has on employees' opinions about the organization and promotes behaviors that are aligned with the goals of the organization, particularly when a supervisor endorses the organization's values. Moreover, other research found that leaders affect follower perceptions of person–supervisor and person–organization fit through their (transformational) leadership behaviors (Hoffman et al., 2011). Hence, employees may experience fit with their supervisor as similar to fit with their organization.

However, person–organization and person–supervisor fits are conceptually distinct as the organization and the supervisor refer to different contents (cultural values versus individual characteristics) and levels of comparison (organizational versus individual). An organization's culture originates not only from its basic norms and values but also from its strategic position and business environment (Joyce and Slocum, 1990). Moreover, an organization's culture represents the more distal work environment, whereas supervisors' behaviors represent employees' proximal work context. Hence, organization-focused fit perceptions originate in characteristics that are different from supervisor-related ones. Indeed, research has shown that person–organization and person–supervisor fit measures are differently related to organizational outcomes (Jansen and Kristof-Brown, 2006; Van Vianen et al., 2011).

Person–team or person–group fit concerns the compatibility between employees and their work group (Kristof-Brown et al., 2005b). Person–team fit refers to surface-level characteristics such as team members' demographics (e.g., Martins and Shalley, 2011; Thatcher and Patel, 2011), or deep-level characteristics such as team members' goals, values, personality, abilities, and preferences (Dragoni and Kuenzi, 2012). Riketta and

Van Dick (2005) evidenced that the team is a salient environment with which employees compare themselves.

Employees' fits are strongly associated with positive individual and organizational outcomes (Kristof-Brown et al., 2005a). Next, we will address relationships between domain-specific fits and commensurate commitments. Furthermore, we will elaborate on the processes underlying these relationships.

HOW FITS RELATE TO COMMITMENTS

Domain-specific fits have mostly been associated with employees' commitment to the organization. However, commitment is a multifaceted construct that can be directed toward different foci in the organization (see Chapter 4 in this volume). Although sparsely researched, domain-specific fit conceptualizations are strongly associated with their commensurate commitments. That is, person–team fit relates positively to commitment to the team (Glew, 2012), person–organization fit is a strong predictor of organizational commitment (e.g., Boon et al., 2011; Cooper-Thomas and Poutasi, 2011), and organizational identification (the psychological merging of self and organization; Van Knippenberg and Sleebos, 2006), and person–supervisor fits link to commitment to the supervisor (Van Vianen et al., 2011).

The literature distinguishes two main processes through which these fits and commitments are related: complementarity or similarity of persons and environments. Self-determination theory (Deci and Ryan, 2000) argues that individuals are committed to the extent that the environment complements their needs. The basic premise of this theory is that individuals strive to satisfy three universal psychological needs: the need for autonomy (that is, the need to feel in control of one's actions, to experience a sense of volition), competence (that is, the need to gain mastery of tasks and to feel effective), and relatedness (that is, the need to feel connected to others, to love and care for others, and to be loved and cared for by others). The satisfaction of these needs leads to favorable outcomes such as job satisfaction, commitment, and well-being. Greguras and Diefendorff (2009) found that demands–abilities fit and person–group fit were positively related to competence-need satisfaction and relatedness-need satisfaction, respectively; whereas person–organization fit was associated to the satisfaction of all three needs. The satisfaction of the three needs was, in turn, related to affective organizational commitment. In addition, demands–abilities and person–organization fit contributed to organizational commitment directly, whereas person–supervisor fit influenced organizational commitment indirectly through the satisfaction of relatedness needs. Although Greguras and Diedendorff's study included organizational commitment instead of domain-specific commitments, their findings suggest that the fulfillment of specific needs is a likely mechanism through which different fits lead to their corresponding commitments.

Other person–environment fit theories (e.g., Schneider, 1987) argue that individuals are committed to the extent that their characteristics are similar to those of the environment. These theories stress psychological processes of experienced similarity (rather than complementarity) between individuals and environments, and mutual attraction (Cable and Edwards, 2004). People feel attracted to similar environments (for example, other people) because these environments validate their opinions, affirm the consistency in their belief system, and generate more certainty about their social world (e.g., Hogg, 2000). Moreover, similarity with other people strengthens interpersonal relationships (Byrne et al., 1986; Shaikh and Kanekar, 1994) and induces prosocial behaviors (O'Reilly and Chatman, 1986) and reciprocal relationships, and thus better cooperation (Lusk et al., 1998) and mutual trust (Glew, 2012). Furthermore, employees' perception of value similarity with the organization promotes feelings of trust in the organization (the belief that they will not be harmed by the organization; Edwards and Cable, 2009) which, in turn, impact employees' feelings of organizational commitment (e.g., Cha et al., 2014; Meyer et al., 2010) and identification (Edwards and Cable, 2009). Value similarity promotes trust directly and indirectly through fostering open communication, perceptions of predictability (behaviors are viewed as consistent and reliable), and positive feelings toward others. In a similar vein, employees who experience similarity with their supervisor feel attracted to the supervisor and report a high quality of leader–member exchange (Van Vianen et al., 2011). These employees tend to view their exchange relationship as reciprocal and based on mutual trust and respect, which fosters commitment to the supervisor (Law et al., 2000; Vandenberghe et al., 2004).

Although numerous studies have shown substantial relationships between fits, commitments, and their mediating processes, several factors appear to affect the strength of these relationships. For example, the relationship between person–organization fit and commitment is weaker for employees who have few job alternatives (Da Silva et al., 2010), who have a cynical attitude toward social environments in general (Deng et al., 2011), or who have a more independent self-construal (that is, who deem themselves as unique and distinctive from others; Guan et al., 2011). Furthermore, the relationship between fit and commitment is moderated by cultural context. A recent meta-analysis (Oh et al., 2014) found that relationships between overall fit (with the job, the organization, the team, and the supervisor) and organizational commitment are stronger in North America ($R^2 = .71$) than in East Asia ($R^2 = .49$). Specifically, person–organization and person–job fits are relatively more strongly related to organizational commitment in North America and, to a lesser extent, Europe than in East Asia, whereas person–team and person–supervisor fits are (relatively) more strongly related to organizational commitment in the collectivistic, relationship-oriented, and hierarchical culture present in East Asia.

All in all, the precise strength of the relationship between fit and commitment depends on factors at the personal, organizational, and national level. In the next section we will show that this relationship also depends on the fit measures that researchers use in their studies, and we will discuss why these measures produce different outcomes.

FIT MEASUREMENTS AND COMMITMENT

Person–environment fit researchers have used various operationalizations and methods to establish fit (e.g., Edwards et al., 2006). Person–environment fit can be measured by asking people directly about their overall perceptions of fit (that is, holistic fit) or, more indirectly, by asking individuals to assess their own characteristics and to compare them with those of the environment, either assessed by the individual or derived from other sources (other individuals or objective data). For example, researchers have distinguished various organizational values (for example, service, innovation, regulation) and measured employees' preferences and perceptions with regard to these values for estimating the relationship between their person–organization fit and affective commitment (e.g., Meyer et al., 2010; O'Reilly et al., 1991). In these studies, culture preferences and perceptions were derived from the same source (the employees themselves) or from different sources (an employee and other group members, respectively).

While directly measured holistic fit perceptions may arise from an idiosyncratic weighting of various pieces of (person and environment) information as assessed in the minds of respondents, indirect fit measures are based on uniform calculations with a selected set of attributes as chosen by researchers. Not surprisingly, direct holistic fit measures are only moderately related to calculated indirect fit indices (Kristof-Brown and Guay, 2010). Moreover, because people's fit perceptions are most likely based on attributes they find important, direct holistic fit measures are more strongly related to commitment than indirect fit indices that may include attributes that are trivial. Meta-analytic results (Kristof-Brown et al., 2005b) show true score correlations between person–organization fit and organizational commitment of .77 and .32 for direct and indirect measures of person–organization fit, respectively.

Because direct holistic perceptions of fit are more influential than indirect measures of fit, we will further elaborate on how individuals establish and combine their holistic fit perceptions. In the next section, we first address the question of whether individuals aggregate different attributes (for example, values) or whether they focus on a specific set of attributes when establishing their domain-related fit. Second, we discuss whether and how individuals combine their domain-related fits. If more is known about the content and combination of fit perceptions, researchers may be better able to disentangle the processes through which these perceptions affect employee commitments.

DEVELOPMENT OF FIT PERCEPTIONS

Employees start to develop their fit impressions immediately after joining an organization. Generally, employees need three to six months to learn about an organization's culture and to know whether they fit in (e.g., Cooper-Thomas et al., 2004). To date, little is known about how individuals assess their fit and whether they vary in this assessment. Individuals may either establish their fit on different attributes (for example, values, needs) and aggregate these attribute-based fits into a holistic fit perception, or they may first form a holistic fit impression and then evaluate specific attributes to align with this impression. The former strategy suggests the use of a rational approach, whereas the latter reflects a more intuitive and holistic process in which fit is a multidimensional construct consisting of a coherent set of attribute-based fits. Theories on human rationality and decision-making (e.g., Kahneman, 2011) suggest that individuals are barely able to combine complex information into a rational decision and, rather, tend to seek consistency in their experiences and to form coherent wholes (Cable and Edwards, 2004; Edwards et al., 2006). Seong and Kristof-Brown (2012) tested rational and holistic models of person–group fit and indeed found support for a holistic superordinate fit concept.

Evidence that individuals generally form holistic fit perceptions does not preclude the possibility that some attributes carry more weight than others. It has been argued that values that are most representative of a person's core self will contribute most to their overall perceptions of fit (e.g., Bergman et al., 2013; Chapter 19 in this volume). In addition, individuals may further narrow their focus to a specific subset of these important values, depending on the situation in which they assess their fit. For example, individuals who search for a job tend to base their person–organization fit perceptions (regarding organizations that they may apply to) mainly on organizational information about attributes they find attractive and wish to attain, and to a lesser extent on information about attributes they find unattractive and wish to avoid (De Goede et al., 2013). This implies that employees' commitment to the organization in the first few months after entry is based primarily on the presence of attractive organizational attributes rather than on the absence of unattractive organizational attributes. Over time, however, this perspective may change as employees' experiences expand.

The question of how employees balance their fit with organizational features they find attractive and unattractive deserves further elaboration because answering this question is important for the nature and development of employees' commitment. For example, if the organization does not provide the attributes an employee seeks, this employee may initially be motivated to engage in activities that could increase attainment of these attractive attributes (for example, opportunities for growth and development). By doing so, they put effort into finding resources in the work environment and – if successful – may increase their commitment over time. However, what happens if the organization emphasizes attributes an employee wishes to avoid? Adapting to or removing unattractive environmental attributes (for example, a highly demanding or competitive work climate) will be difficult. In that case, employees may stay only if no other job options are available (continuous commitment) and they may psychologically detach from the organization. We speculate that an organization's effort to promote new employees' person–organization (PO) fit perceptions and commitment is more likely doomed to fail when perceptions of misfit are primarily caused by the presence of attributes employees find unattractive, rather than by the absence of attributes they find attractive.

This brings us to the question of whether organizations affect employees' fit perceptions at all. If fit perceptions exclusively emerge from a unique constellation of an individual's core attributes, then how could organizations impact these perceptions?

The Malleability of Fit Perceptions

Organizations are able to raise newcomers' fit experiences and thereby their commitment by providing social support from supervisors and co-workers. A supportive social environment helps newcomers to develop social ties with other organizational members and signals organizational values, such as cooperativeness and care for others, that people in general tend to prefer (Van Vianen and De Pater, 2012). Research shows that social support in the first stage after entry positively affects organizational commitment over time (Kammeyer-Mueller et al., 2013). Early support enhances newcomers' proactive socialization behaviors (that is, volitional activities to foster adaptation to the workplace) that, in turn, boost task mastery, role clarity, and social integration, which are indicators of demands–abilities fit and PO fit (Chan and Schmitt, 2000; Kammeyer-Mueller and Wanberg, 2003).

An organization also positively impacts newcomers' fit experiences and organizational commitment by means of 'high-performance' human resource (HR) practices (see Chapter 21 in this volume). High-performance HR practices communicate universally attractive values such as employee participation, autonomy, development, reward, and work–life balance (e.g., Ramsay et al., 2000). Research shows that these HR practices promote organizational commitment directly as well as indirectly through enhancing employees' person–organization fit perceptions (Boon et al., 2011).

Altogether, organizations that provide early social support and high-performance HR practices facilitate the development of affective commitment through improving experiences of person–organization fit. In addition, person–organization fit promotes positive perceptions of the psychological contract (the unwritten agreement about mutual obligations; see Chapter 9 in this volume) and social exchange (the mutual transfer of socio-emotional resources such as caring and approval; Kim et al., 2013) that employees experience with their employer, which facilitate the development of normative commitment[1] (Amos and Weathington, 2008; Meyer et al., 2004).

Two Routes to Fits and Commitments

The research described above suggests that the development of fits and commitments involves two routes. The first route is through experiencing a match pertaining to preferences, values, and needs that are unique for individuals (for example, the specific environmental features an individual wants to attain or avoid). This route creates perceptions of fit when the environment is complementary or similar to an employee's unique characteristics (distinctive fit). The second route is through experiencing a match pertaining to preferences, values, and needs that are universally cherished (or disapproved). This route creates perceptions of fit when the environment is complementary or similar to the characteristics that all workers share (universal fit).

Direct holistic measures of employees' fit perceptions comprise both these distinctive and universal fits. They are therefore stronger predictors of organizational commitment than indirect fit measures that mostly tap into the distinctive part of the fit experience. Studies using holistic person–organization fit perceptions do not reveal what part of the association between person–organization fit, psychological processes, and commitment is due to experiences of distinctive fit. The findings might instead be due to experiencing universal fit, such as when employees experience organizational values (for example, through HR practices) that are universally appreciated (or disapproved).

Distinctive and universal fit perceptions concern not only person–organization fit, but also other domain-related fits. For example, employees may experience person–job fit when the job includes attributes that they distinctively prefer (for example, responsibility, social power) and those that are universally appreciated (for example, skill variety, task identity, feedback). In a similar vein, employees may experience person–supervisor fit when the supervisor has similar personality traits (distinctive fit) and when the supervisor is honest and fair (universal fit). In the next section, we will discuss how employees combine their domain-related fit perceptions.

COMBINING DOMAIN-RELATED FITS

The different domain-related fits may add to each other or they may interact in predicting organizational commitment (Guan et al., 2011; Piasentin and Chapman, 2007; Van Vianen et al., 2011). If fits add to each other, this means that a lower fit in one domain will negatively affect an individual's commitment. If multiple fits interact, a lower fit in one domain will impact an individual's commitment less because it is buffered by positive fit experiences in other domains (Jansen and Kristof-Brown, 2006). The studies that examined the additive or interactive effects of domain-related fits revealed more support for the additive effects (Kristof-Brown et al., 2002; Resick et al., 2007; Van Vianen et al., 2011), but interactions appeared as well. Some studies found interactions of person–organization and person–job fits (Resick et al., 2007) and person–team and person–job fits, but not of person–group and person–organization fits (Vogel and Feldman, 2009). Apparently, interactions concerned person–job fit with person–organization or person–group fit. This could mean that fits that are primarily based on processes of complementarity (for example, demands–abilities and need–supplies fits) interact with fits that are primarily based on processes of similarity (the person and the social environment are similar), whereas fits that belong to one specific (complementarity-based or similarity-based) fit category may add to each other.

Conversely, individuals may differ in how they combine their multiple fits. In other words, individuals' holistic fit perceptions may be based on a unique constellation of domain-related fits. If so, fit researchers could try to identify subgroups of individuals with similar combinations of domain-related fits and examine how these subgroups relate to their work environment.

A Person-Centered Approach to Fit

Above we have argued that the relationship between fits, commitments, and their mediating processes depend on situational factors (for example, the labor market, national culture) and personality characteristics (for example, dependent or independent self-construal).

Hence, employees may vary in how they weigh their different fits. For example, employees who prefer being unique and distinctive from others (high independent self-construal) may find similarity with others in the social environment (peers and supervisors) less important than having a good demands–abilities fit (which enables them to excel). The holistic fit perception (and commitment) of these employees may be relatively less informed by similarity-based fits (for example, person–team, person–supervisor) than the holistic fit perception of colleagues who prefer having close relationships at work.

To date, there is no research that has examined specific configurations of domain-related fits within individuals that lead to experiences of holistic fit and commitment. Person-centered approaches in commitment research (Chapter 35 in this volume) provide some good examples of how the existence of fit profiles could be examined. Moreover, if fit profiles are detected they could be related to the commitment profiles that were found in person-centered commitment research (e.g., Morin et al., 2011). For example, employees who are highly committed to the supervisor and moderately committed to other domains may show a fit profile of high experienced person–supervisor fit and reasonable levels of experienced person–team and person–organization fits. In this case, the 'experienced fit profile' impacts the commitment profile.

However, it is also possible that commitment profiles affect the weighing of domain-related fits and thus the emergence of 'preferred fit profiles'. For example, career-committed individuals (who are highly committed to their career and moderately committed to other domains) may be mostly focused on whether the organization meets their career aspirations (person–job fit), and to a lesser extent on their similarities with the social work environment. In this case, employees' commitment profile will impact their preferred fit profile.

We believe that person–environment fit research could benefit from adopting a person-centered strategy. First, researchers could establish preferred fit profiles that reflect how individuals weigh their domain-related fits (that is, their relative importance). This may help job seekers to select a job that meets their fit profile (for example, there is fit in the salient domain despite lower fits in other domains) and this may help recruiters to select suitable applicants, that is, applicants who fit the organization regarding their salient fit domain.

Second, by associating employees' preferred fit profiles to their experienced fit profiles and subsequent commitments, researchers could investigate the predictive validity of preferred fit profiles. This research could reveal whether domain-related fit needs should be met depending on an individual's preferred fit profile. For example, individuals who believe that they value career fit relatively more than other domain-related fits may indeed experience holistic fit and organizational commitment as long as they experience career fit, irrespective of the level of other domain-related fits. Alternatively, despite their career fit these individuals could experience low holistic fit and commitment because of misfit in domains they initially considered as relatively less relevant.

Third, employees' preferred and experienced fit profiles could be linked to personality variables. In keeping with our earlier example of employees with a high independent self-construal, these employees may have a preferred and /or experienced fit profile including relatively low similarity-based fits (for example, person–team fit), while employees with a high dependent self-construal may have a fit profile that includes relatively high similarity-based fits. Hence, researchers could investigate whether personality variables affect the emergence of preferred and experienced fit profiles.

Finally, preferred and experienced fit profiles could also be linked to situational variables such as labor market conditions and situations of organizational change. Labor market conditions may affect preferred fit profiles whereby job seekers may attach more weight to, for example, person–organization fit if the chance of finding a job that matches one's abilities (demands–abilities fit) is low. The organization will affect employees' experienced fit profiles when, for example, functional (job demands) or structural (teams, organizational culture) changes occur. It would be worthwhile to study how experienced fit profiles change and whether these changes facilitate or hinder the adaptation process.

SUMMARY AND FUTURE DIRECTIONS

Person–environment fit is a significant driver of commitment. Individuals have a basic need to fit their work environment and when they experience fit they feel attached to salient domains, such as the job, the supervisor, the team members, and the organization as a whole. Individuals tend to form a holistic perception of their fit, which fosters experiences of fair social exchange, trust, certainty, and predictability. This explains why individuals' holistic fit perceptions are strongly associated with their commitment.

Person–environment fit theories propose that fit perceptions originate in the unique match of personal and environmental attributes as individuals strive to experience complementarity (need satisfaction) and similarity with their environment. However, fit perceptions are also receptive to an organization's socialization and human resource practices. In this chapter, we have argued that individuals' holistic fit perceptions (and commitments) comprise two types of fit: fit pertaining to an individual's distinctive attributes (distinctive fit), and fit pertaining to attributes that are universally shared (universal fit). Since holistic fit perceptions are the strongest predictors of commitment, future research should disentangle distinctive and universal fits in order to extend our knowledge about the malleability of fits and commitments.

In addition, distinctive fit perceptions emerge from the attributes that people attend to in a specific situation. Job seekers focus on attributes that they find attractive and wish to attain rather than on attributes that they find unattractive and wish to avoid. We have proposed that job seekers may shift their focus to the second type of attributes once they have entered the organization. Future research could test this proposition.

Individuals experience multiple domain-related fits that may add to or interact with each other, resulting in an overall experience of fit and commitment at work. Furthermore, individuals will vary in the importance they attach to specific domain-related fits. In line with the person-centered approach in commitment research, we have proposed that individuals can be grouped according to fit profiles that consist of varying levels of domain-related fits they wish to attain (preferred fit profile) or experience (experienced fit profile) at work. A person-centered approach in fit research could advance our understanding of how job seekers (could) select a job and recruiters (could) select applicants, how the predictive validity of fit assessments could be improved, and how fit profiles relate to personal and situational variables.

Finally, because fit is a dynamic rather than static phenomenon (Shipp and Jansen, 2011), more research attention could be paid to the antecedents, processes, and outcomes of changes in individuals' fits and related commitments. These changes could be studied with a within-person design that captures individuals' fit profiles over time (see Chapter 34 in this volume).

Practical Implications

Fit perceptions are one of the strongest drivers of commitment. It is, therefore, important for organizations to know what they can do to promote these perceptions. In this chapter, we have distinguished two routes that lead to individuals' holistic fit perceptions. The first route involves the experience of what we have called universal fit. This route refers to organizational practices that fulfill employees' basic human needs for autonomy, competence, and relatedness. Organizations promote experiences of universal fit among their employees if they allow them to have discretion over their tasks and actions, provide them with constructive feedback and rewards, and care for their welfare. These positive organizational practices generate experiences of universal fit and, through this, commitment among employees. Especially, experiences of universal fit tap into employee mindsets of reciprocity and obligation (Kam et al., forthcoming; Meyer and Parfyonova, 2010) as this fit exemplifies that the organization adheres to the psychological contract employees have with their organization. As such, positive organizational practices may particularly evoke normative commitment among employees.

A second route to the formation of holistic fit perceptions concerns experiences of distinctive fit. Employees experience distinctive fit if their unique attributes (personality, values, interests) are similar to those of important others in the organization (team members, supervisor) and match with the organization's core values and goals. Distinctive fit evokes deep affective responses to the organization (that is, affective commitment) and supports processes of organizational identification.

Obviously, employees who experience both universal and distinctive fits will develop stronger normative and affective commitments than those who experience only universal fit. Hence, besides promoting fit and commitment through good organizational practices, organizations could develop recruitment and selection methods aimed at establishing distinctive fit. Research has shown that recruiters use their impression of applicants' PO fit for making selection decisions (e.g., Sekiguchi and Huber, 2011). However, it is questionable whether these impressions are sufficiently predictive for an applicant's future commitment and functioning. We encourage organizations to develop methods that, for example, measure applicants' important values, and the types of values and supplies they wish to find in an organization and those they wish to avoid. Recruiters can use this information to assess whether an applicant's preferences and expectations will be met in the job.

In addition, organizations could put effort in collecting information about why newcomers leave the organization prematurely. It is possible, for example, that employees leave early because they experience job and/or organizational attributes that they dislike but did not consider when applying for the job. Information about the reasons causing turnover could help organizations to develop strategies and methods for attracting and selecting employees who fit the organization better.

Because individuals will vary in the weight they put on different domain-related fits, organizations could assess applicants' preferred fit profile. First, many if not most employees will experience optimal fit in some but not all work domains. If so, it would be good to know which fits really matter to individuals and to discern if fit in an applicant's salient domain is tenable. Second, several authors have noted that the attraction–selection–attrition process (people are attracted to and selected by an organization based on their fit, and leave the organization if there is a misfit) may lead to homogeneity of people in the organization, which may hinder an organization's innovativeness and capacity to change (e.g., Schneider et al., 1995). In order to induce organizational changes, organizations may wish to attract individuals who do not have an optimal fit with, for example, the existing culture. However, in this case it is also vital to detect which fits (other than PO fit) matter to these individuals and whether they will experience sufficient fit to function effectively.

Finally, employees may be better able to adapt to organizational changes if organizations pay attention to the domain-related fits that are important to individual employees. For example, an employee may more easily adjust to specific changes (for example, initially causing lower job fit) as long as they can stay in their team, their dominant fit domain. All in all, the person-centered approach of fit profiling might help organizations to create flexibility while preserving fit and commitment among their employees.

NOTE

1. See Chapter 3 in this volume for the distinction between affective and normative commitment.

REFERENCES

Amos, E.A. and Weathington, B.L. (2008). An analysis of the relation between employee–organization value congruence and employee attitudes. *Journal of Psychology: Interdisciplinary and Applied*, *142*, 615–632.

Bergman, M.E., Benzer, J.K., Kabins, A.H., Bhupatkar, A., and Panina, D. (2013). An event-based perspective on the development of commitment. *Human Resource Management Review*, *23*, 148–160.

Boon, C., Den Hartog, D.N., Boselie, P., and Paauwe, J. (2011). The relationship between perceptions of HR practices and employee outcomes: examining the role of person–organisation and person–job fit. *International Journal of Human Resource Management*, *22*, 138–162.

Byrne, D., Clore, G.L., and Smeaton, G. (1986). The attraction hypothesis: Do similar attitudes affect anything? *Journal of Personality and Social Psychology*, *5*, 1167–1170.

Cable, D.M. and Edwards, J.R. (2004). Complementary and supplementary fit: a theoretical and empirical integration. *Journal of Applied Psychology*, *89*, 822–834.

Cha, J., Chang, Y.K., and Kim, T.Y. (2014). Person–organization fit on prosocial identity: Implications on employee outcomes. *Journal of Business Ethics*, *123*, 57–69.

Chan, D. and Schmitt, N. (2000). Interindividual differences in intraindividual changes in proactivity during organizational entry: A latent growth modeling approach to understanding newcomer adaptation. *Journal of Applied Psychology*, *85*, 190–210.

Chatman, J.A. (1991). Matching people and organizations: Selection and socialization in public accounting firms. *Administrative Science Quarterly*, *36*, 459–484.

Cooper-Thomas, H.D. and Poutasi, C. (2011). Attitudinal variables predicting intent to quit among Pacific healthcare workers. *Asia Pacific Journal of Human Resources*, *49*, 180–192.

Cooper-Thomas, H.D., Van Vianen, A.E.M., and Anderson, N. (2004). Changes in person–organization fit: The impact of socialization tactics on perceived and actual P–O fit. *European Journal of Work and Organizational Psychology*, *13*, 52–78.

Da Silva, N., Hutcheson, J., and Wahl, G.D. (2010). Organizational strategy and employee outcomes: A person–organization fit perspective. *Journal of Psychology*, *144*, 145–161.

Dawis, R.V. and Lofquist, L.H. (1984). *A Psychological Theory of Work Adjustment*. Minneapolis, MN: University of Minnesota Press.

Deci, E.L. and Ryan, R.M. (2000). The 'what' and 'why' of goal pursuits: Human needs and the self-determination of behavior. *Psychological Inquiry*, *11*, 227–268.

De Goede, M.E.E., Van Vianen, A.E.M., and Klehe, U.C. (2013). A tailored policy-capturing Study on PO Fit Perceptions: The ascendancy of attractive over aversive fit. *International Journal of Selection and Assessment*, *21*, 85–98.

Deng, H., Guan, Y., Bond, M.H., Zhang, Z., and Hu, T. (2011). The interplay between social cynicism beliefs and person–organization fit on work-related attitudes among Chinese employees. *Journal of Applied Social Psychology*, *41*, 160–178.

Dragoni, L., and Kuenzi, M. (2012). Better understanding work unit goal orientation: Its emergence and impact under different types of work unit structure. *Journal of Applied Psychology*, *97*, 1032–1048.

Edwards, J.A. and Billsberry, J. (2010). Testing a multidimensional theory of person–environment fit. *Journal of Managerial Issues*, *22*, 476–493.

Edwards, J.R. and Cable, D.M. (2009). The value of value congruence. *Journal of Applied Psychology*, *94*, 654–677.

Edwards, J.R., Cable, D.M., Williamson, I.O., Lambert, L.S., and Shipp, A.J. (2006). The phenomenology of fit: Linking the person and environment to the subjective experience of person–environment fit. *Journal of Applied Psychology*, *91*, 802–827.

Edwards, J.R. and Cooper, C.L. (1990). The person–environment fit approach to stress: recurring problems and some suggested solutions. *Journal of Organizational Behavior*, *11*, 293–307.

Giberson, T.R., Resick, C.J., and Dickson, M.W. (2005). Embedding leader characteristics: an examination of homogeneity of personality and values in organizations. *Journal of Applied Psychology*, 90, 1002–1010.

Glew, D.J. (2012). Effects of interdependence and social interaction-based person–team fit. *Administrative Sciences*, 2, 26–46.

Greguras, G.J. and Diefendorff, J.M. (2009). Different fits satisfy different needs: linking person–environment fit to employee commitment and performance using self-determination theory. *Journal of Applied Psychology*, 94, 465–477.

Guan, Y., Deng, H., Risavy, S.D., Bond, M.H., and Li, F. (2011). Supplementary fit, complementary fit, and work-related outcomes: The role of self-construal. *Applied Psychology*, 60, 286–310.

Hoffman, B.J., Bynum, B.H., Piccolo, R.F., and Sutton, A.W. (2011). Person–organization value congruence: How transformational leaders influence work group effectiveness. *Academy of Management Journal*, 54, 779–796.

Hogg, M.A. (2000). Subjective uncertainty reduction through self-categorization: A motivational theory of social identity processes. *European Review of Social Psychology*, 11, 223–255.

Holland, J.L. (1985). *Making Vocational Choices: A Theory of Vocational Personalities and Work Environments*. Englewood Cliffs, NJ: Prentice Hall.

Jansen, K.J. and Kristof-Brown, A. (2006). Toward a multidimensional theory of person–environment fit. *Journal of Managerial Issues*, 8(2), 193–212.

Joyce, W.F. and Slocum, J.W. (1990). Strategic context and organizational climate. In B. Schneider (ed.), *Organizational Climate and Culture* (pp. 130–150). San Francisco, CA: Jossey-Bass.

Kahneman, D. (2011). *Thinking, Fast and Slow*. New York: Farrar, Straus & Giroux.

Kam, C., Morin, A.J.S., Meyer, J.P. and Topolnytsky, L. (forthcoming). Are commitment profiles stable and predictable? A latent transition analysis. *Journal of Management*.

Kammeyer-Mueller, J.D. and Wanberg, C.R. (2003). Unwrapping the organizational entry process: disentangling multiple antecedents and their pathways to adjustment. *Journal of Applied Psychology*, 88, 779–794.

Kammeyer-Mueller, J.D., Wanberg, C., Rubenstein, A., and Song, Z. (2013). Support, undermining, and newcomer socialization: Fitting in during the first 90 days. *Academy of Management Journal*, 56, 1104–1124.

Kim, T.Y., Aryee, S., Loi, R., and Kim, S.P. (2013). Person–organization fit and employee outcomes: test of a social exchange model. *International Journal of Human Resource Management*, 24, 3719–3737.

Kristof-Brown, A., Barrick, M.R., and Kay Stevens, C. (2005a). When opposites attract: A multi-sample demonstration of complementary person–team fit on extraversion. *Journal of Personality*, 73, 935–958.

Kristof-Brown, A.L. and Guay, R. (2010). Person–environment fit. In S. Zedeck (ed.), *APA Handbook of Industrial and Organizational Psychology* (pp. 3–50). Washington, DC: American Psychological Association.

Kristof-Brown, A.L., Jansen, K.J., and Colbert, A.E. (2002). A policy-capturing study of the simultaneous effects of fit with jobs, groups, and organizations. *Journal of Applied Psychology*, 87, 985–993.

Kristof-Brown, A.L., Zimmerman, R.D., and Johnson, E.C. (2005b). Consequences of individuals' fit at work: A meta-analysis of person–job, person–organization, person–group, and person–supervisor fit. *Personnel Psychology*, 58, 281–342.

Law, K.S., Wong, C.S., Wang, D., and Wang, L. (2000). Effect of supervisor–subordinate guanxi on supervisory decisions in China: An empirical investigation. *International Journal of Human Resource Management*, 11, 751–765.

Lusk, J., MacDonald, K., and Newman, J.R. (1998). Resource appraisals among self, friend and leader: Implications for an evolutionary perspective on individual differences. *Personality and Individual Differences*, 24, 685–700.

Martins, L.L. and Shalley, C.E. (2011). Creativity in virtual work: Effects of demographic differences. *Small Group Research*, 42, 536–561.

Meyer, J.P., Becker, T.E., and Vandenberghe, C. (2004). Employee commitment and motivation: A conceptual analysis and integrative model. *Journal of Applied Psychology*, 89, 991–1007.

Meyer, J.P., Hecht, T.D., Gill, H., and Toplonytsky, L. (2010). Person–organization (culture) fit and employee commitment under conditions of organizational change: A longitudinal study. *Journal of Vocational Behavior*, 76, 458–473.

Meyer, J.P. and Parfyonova, N.M. (2010). Normative commitment in the workplace: A theoretical analysis and re-conceptualization. *Human Resource Management Review*, 20, 283–294.

Morin, A.J., Morizot, J., Boudrias, J.S., and Madore, I. (2011). A multifoci person-centered perspective on workplace affective commitment: A latent profile/factor mixture analysis. *Organizational Research Methods*, 14, 58–90.

Oh, I.S., Guay, R.P., Kim, K., Harold, C.M., Lee, J.H., Heo, C.G., and Shin, K.H. (2014). Fit happens globally: A meta-analytic comparison of the relationships of person–environment fit dimensions with work attitudes and performance across East Asia, Europe, and North America. *Personnel Psychology*, 67, 99–152.

O'Reilly, C.A. and Chatman, J. (1986). Organizational commitment and psychological attachment: The effects of compliance, identification, and internalization on prosocial behavior. *Journal of Applied Psychology, 71*, 492–499.

O'Reilly, C.A., Chatman, J., and Caldwell, D.F. (1991). People and organizational culture: A profile comparison approach to assessing person–organization fit. *Academy of Management Journal, 34*, 487–516.

Piasentin, K.A. and Chapman, D.S. (2007). Perceived similarity and complementarity as predictors of subjective person–organization fit. *Journal of Occupational and Organizational Psychology, 80*, 341–354.

Ramsay, H., Scholarios, D., and Harley, B. (2000). Employees and high-performance work systems: Testing inside the black box. *British Journal of Industrial Relations, 38*, 501–531.

Resick, C.J., Baltes, B.B., and Shantz, C.W. (2007). Person–organization fit and work-related attitudes and decisions: Examining interactive effects with job fit and conscientiousness. *Journal of Applied Psychology, 92*, 1446–1455.

Riketta, M. and Van Dick, R. (2005). Foci of attachment in organizations: A meta-analytic comparison of the strength and correlates of workgroup versus organizational identification and commitment. *Journal of Vocational Behavior, 67*, 490–510.

Schein, E.H. (2004). *Organizational culture and leadership.* San Francisco, CA: John Wiley & Sons.

Schneider, B. (1987). The people make the place. *Personnel Psychology, 40*, 437–453.

Schneider, B., Goldstein H.W., and Smith, D.B. (1995). The ASA framework: An update. *Personnel Psychology, 48*, 747–779.

Sekiguchi, T. and Huber, V.L. (2011). The use of person–organization fit and person–job fit information in making selection decisions. *Organizational Behavioral and Human Decision Processes, 116*, 203–216.

Seong, J.Y. and Kristof-Brown, A.L. (2012). Testing multidimensional models of person–group fit. *Journal of Managerial Psychology, 27*, 536–556.

Shaikh, T. and Kanekar, S. (1994). Attitudinal similarity and affiliation need as determinants of interpersonal attraction. *Journal of Social Psychology, 134*, 257–259.

Shipp, A.J. and Jansen, K.J. (2011). Reinterpreting time in fit theory: Crafting and recrafting narratives of fit in medias res. *Academy of Management Review, 36*, 76–101.

Sluss, D.M., Ployhart, R.E., Cobb, M.G., and Ashforth, B.E. (2012). Generalizing newcomers' relational and organizational identifications: Processes and prototypicality. *Academy of Management Journal, 55*, 949–975.

Thatcher, S. and Patel, P.C. (2011). Demographic faultlines: A meta-analysis of the literature. *Journal of Applied Psychology, 96*, 1119–1139.

Vandenberghe, C., Bentein, K., and Stinglhamber, F. (2004). Affective commitment to the organization, supervisor, and work group: Antecedents and outcomes. *Journal of Vocational Behavior, 64*, 47–71.

Van Knippenberg, D., and Sleebos, E. (2006). Organizational identification versus organizational commitment: Self-definition, social exchange, and job attitudes. *Journal of Organizational Behavior, 27*, 571–584.

Van Vianen, A.E.M. and De Pater, I.E. (2012). Content and development of newcomer person–organization fit: An agenda for future research. In C.R. Wanberg (ed.), *The Oxford Handbook of Socialization* (pp. 139–157). Oxford: Oxford University Press.

Van Vianen, A.E.M., Shen, C.T., and Chuang, A. (2011). Person–organization and person–supervisor fits: Employee commitments in a Chinese context. *Journal of Organizational Behavior, 32*, 906–926.

Van Vianen, A.E.M, Stoelhorst, J., and De Goede, M.E.E. (2013). The construal of person–organization fit during the ASA Stages: Content, source, and focus of comparison. In A.L. Kristof-Brown and J. Billsberry (eds), *Key Issues and New Directions in Organizational Fit* (pp. 145–169). Chichester: Wiley-Blackwell.

Vogel, R.M. and Feldman, D.C. (2009). Integrating the levels of person–environment fit: The roles of vocational fit and group fit. *Journal of Vocational Behavior, 75*, 68–81.

21. Strategic human resource management and organizational commitment
Kaifeng Jiang

Strategic human resource management (HRM) has attracted the attention of researchers and practitioners for three decades (Jackson et al., 2014). Wright and McMahan (1992) defined strategic HRM as a research field focusing on 'the pattern of planned human resource deployments and activities intended to enable an organization to achieve its goals' (p. 298). This definition distinguishes strategic HRM research, which is a relatively young research field, from traditional HRM research in two primary respects (Wright and Boswell, 2002). First, strategic HRM focuses on the influence of bundles or systems of HRM practices rather than that of single HRM practices on variables of interest. This systems perspective suggests that multiple practices within an organization work together to affect employee and organizational outcomes and, thus, should be studied as a system rather than as isolated practices (Delery, 1998; Jiang et al., 2012a; Lepak et al., 2006). Second, strategic HRM research examines HRM practices or systems at the organizational level of analysis (for example, firm, business units, and organizations), rather than at the individual level. This macro approach emphasizes the differences in the use of HRM practices between organizations, as well as the impact on outcomes associated with those differences. In line with the two features of strategic HRM research, scholars have conducted numerous studies to examine the influence of organizational-level HRM systems on important outcomes, including organizational commitment, at both the individual and organizational levels (Combs et al., 2006; Jiang et al., 2012b; Rabl et al., 2014; Subramony, 2009).

The purpose of this chapter is to provide a qualitative review of empirical research on the relationship between HRM systems and organizational commitment. In accordance with the definition of strategic HRM, this chapter focuses on studies examining organizational-level HRM systems as an antecedent of organizational commitment. Readers who are interested in understanding the influence of individual HRM practices on organizational commitment may refer to other review articles (e.g., Kooij et al., 2010). Moreover, this chapter is not intended to provide a comprehensive review including all studies related to the HRM systems–organizational commitment relationship. Instead, it is intended as a primer for those interested in learning what we know and do not know about this relationship.

In the following, I first introduce the primary theoretical perspectives for the linkage between HRM systems and organizational commitment. Then I review empirical studies examining the influence of HRM systems on both individual-level and aggregate organizational commitment, as well as those examining the moderators of the relationship between HRM systems and organizational commitment. Finally, I shift my attention to discuss practical implications regarding how to utilize HRM systems to build organizational commitment as well as future direction of research on the relationship between HRM systems and organizational commitment.

THEORETICAL PERSPECTIVES OF THE HRM SYSTEMS–ORGANIZATIONAL COMMITMENT RELATIONSHIP

Organizational commitment has been examined as one of the most important employee outcomes in the field of organizational behavior and human resource management. Even though researchers may still have different opinions about the concept and structure of this construct (for example, see Chapters 3 and 4 in this volume), organizational commitment has commonly been studied as a multidimensional construct in the literature of strategic HRM, including affective commitment, continuance commitment, and normative commitment (Allen and Meyer, 1990; Meyer et al., 1993). In particular, as shown later in this chapter, affective commitment, which reflects an emotional attachment to organizations, has been most frequently studied in the literature on strategic HRM. Before I provide more details about the empirical findings of the relationship between HRM systems and organizational commitment, I first introduce several theoretical perspectives that can help to explain this relationship.

Behavioral Perspective

The behavioral perspective is one of the primary theoretical perspectives that can explain how HRM systems influence organizational outcomes (Schuler and Jackson, 1987). This perspective suggests that organizations do not perform by themselves and, instead, use HRM systems as a means to manage and control desired attitudes and behaviors of employees that can further lead to positive organizational outcomes. Affective commitment can serve as a desired attitudinal outcome due to its positive relationships with important behavioral outcomes (Meyer et al., 2002). In order to elicit and sustain employees' positive behaviors, organizations can design HRM systems to enhance employees' commitment to organizations.

Ability–Motivation–Opportunity (AMO) Model

As a variant of the behavioral perspective, the AMO model states that employee performance is a function of three elements: abilities, motivation, and opportunities to perform the work (Appelbaum et al., 2000; Gerhart, 2007). Accordingly, HRM practices can be categorized into three components that are intended to enhance the three elements of employee performance, including skill-enhancing, motivation-enhancing, and opportunity-enhancing practices (Gardner et al., 2011; Jiang et al., 2012a; Jiang et al., 2012b; Lepak et al., 2006). As affective commitment reflects employees' emotional attachment to their organizations, it has often been considered as a representative construct of employee motivation that can be affected by HRM systems.

Employee–Organization Relationship

Another theoretical framework that can explain the influence of HRM systems on employee outcomes is the employee–organization relationship (Tsui et al., 1995; Tsui et al., 1997). This framework suggests that HRM systems reflect organizations' investments in their employees and expectations of their employees and, thus, can be divided into two categories: practices focusing on inducements and investments towards employees (for example, training, job security, and benefits), and those focusing on contributions from employees (for example, performance appraisal and performance-based compensation). Based on these two dimensions, organizations may establish four different types of exchange relationships with employees – overinvestment, mutual investment, quasi-spot-contract, and underinvestment (Tsui et al., 1997) – which may determine how likely it is that employees may commit themselves to their organizations.

Organizational Climate Perspective

Researchers have also adopted an organizational climate perspective to explain the relationship between HRM systems and performance outcomes. This perspective suggests that HRM systems can communicate messages to employees to guide their attitudes and behaviors in the workplace (Bowen and Ostroff, 2004). A strong HRM system can, therefore, lead to a shared climate among employees about what attitudes and behaviors are expected and rewarded in organizations; for example, climate for service (Chuang and Liao, 2010; Jiang et al., 2015), climate for safety (Zacharatos et al., 2005), justice climate (Walumbwa et al., 2010), and concern for employees climate (Takeuchi et al., 2009). These climates can further affect employees' work attitudes and behaviors.

Social Exchange Theory

In addition to the theoretical perspectives that explain the general influence of HRM systems on employee outcomes, two other theoretical perspectives have been used to specifically explain why HRM systems have an impact on organizational commitment: social exchange theory and self-determination theory. Social exchange theory is based on Gouldner's (1960) norm of reciprocity and Blau's (1964) work on social exchange relationships, and suggests that individuals who receive benefits from one party tend to respond in kind. Applying this logic to strategic HRM research, HRM systems intended to enhance employees' benefits can be considered as the organizations' investment in employees; in order to maintain the exchange relationship, employees may reciprocate by holding positive attitudes towards organizations such as affective commitment (Messersmith et al., 2011).

Self-Determination Theory

Self-determination theory focuses on three psychological needs of individuals: the needs for autonomy, competence, and relatedness (Deci and Ryan, 1985). The factors that can satisfy the three needs can provide intrinsic motivation to employees and lead them to have positive attitudes toward work and organizations. More specifically, researchers have suggested that satisfaction of the three psychological needs is related to the psychological processes that drive affective commitment (Meyer and Allen, 1997; Meyer and Herscovitch, 2001). For example, HRM systems may enhance affective commitment by providing employees with autonomy, competence, and relatedness (Gardner et al., 2011).

EMPIRICAL FINDINGS OF THE HRM SYSTEMS–ORGANIZATIONAL COMMITMENT RELATIONSHIP

Strategic HRM scholars have examined the relationship between HRM systems and organizational commitment at different levels of analyses. I searched for empirical studies published by the year 2015 by using Google Scholar with different combinations of the keywords of HRM systems (for example, 'high-performance' and 'high-commitment') and the keywords of organizational commitment (for example, 'organizational commitment', 'affective commitment', 'continuance commitment', and 'normative commitment'). As strategic HRM research focuses on the use and the impact of HRM systems at the unit level according to Wright and Boswell's (2002) framework, I included all studies examining HRM systems at the unit level no matter whether commitment was examined at the unit level or the individual level. As researchers have become increasingly interested in understanding employees' perceptions of HRM systems in the past few years, I also included some examples of studies examining the HRM systems and organizational commitment relationship purely at the individual level. As shown in Table 21.1, I categorize the studies into unit-level analysis, cross-level analysis, and individual-level analysis.

Most of those studies examined the influence on organizational commitment of a specific type of HRM systems, which is called high-performance work systems (HPWSs). HPWSs refer to a bundle of HRM practices that 'can improve the knowledge, skills, and abilities of a firm's current and potential employees, increase their motivation, reduce shirking, and enhance retention of quality employees while encouraging non-performers to leave the firm' (Huselid, 1995, p. 635). Typical HRM practices included in HPWSs are comprehensive recruitment, rigorous selection, extensive training, developmental performance management, performance-based compensative, extensive benefits, internal promotion and career development, job security, flexible job design, work teams, employee involvement, and information-sharing (Lepak et al., 2006; Posthuma et al., 2013). Researchers have also labeled the same type of HRM systems as high-commitment, high-involvement, and high-investment HRM systems. Even though those labels are expected to reflect different objectives of HRM systems, Posthuma et al. (2013) found significant overlap among practices included in HRM systems with different names. Also, I found that some authors provided no specific name for the HRM systems examined in their studies, but the practices of those systems were similar to those included in HPWSs.

Unit-Level Analysis

I identified ten articles examining the relationship between HRM systems and organizational commitment at the unit level of analysis. In general, those studies found a significantly positive relationship between the two variables. Most of these studies examined affective commitment as a mediator of the influence of HRM systems on other outcomes (for example, collective organizational citizenship behavior, task performance, turnover, and unit performance). For example, based on a sample of 119 service departments, Messersmith et al. (2011) found that HPWSs first affected employee attitudes as represented by affective commitment which further led to organizational citizenship behaviors and department performance. Similarly, with a sample of 50 autonomous business units,

Table 21.1 Empirical studies examining the influence of HRM systems on organizational commitment

Articles	Type of HRM systems	Level of HRM systems	Type of commitment	Level of commitment	Role of commitment	Other key variables
Gardner et al. (2011)	Skill-enhancing, motivation-enhancing, and empowerment-enhancing practices	Unit	Affective	Unit	Mediator	Turnover as a dependent variable
Gong et al. (2010)	High-performance work systems	Unit	Affective	Unit	Mediator	Collective organizational citizenship behavior as a dependent variable
Gong et al. (2009)	Maintenance-oriented and performance-oriented HRM practices	Unit	Affective and continuance	Unit	Mediator	Firm performance as a dependent variable
Hoque (1999)	Unspecified HRM systems	Unit	Affective	Unit	Outcome	Job satisfaction, quality of work, and absenteeism as parallel dependent variables
Katou et al. (2014)	Unspecified HRM systems	Unit	Affective	Unit	Mediator	Organizational performance as a dependent variable; HR practices features as a moderator
Messersmith et al. (2011)	High-performance work systems	Unit	Affective	Unit	Mediator	Job satisfaction and psychological empowerment as parallel mediators, and organizational citizenship behavior and department performance as dependent variables
Ramsay et al. (2000)	High-performance work systems	Unit	Affective	Unit	Mediator	Job discretion and job strain as parallel mediators, and workplace performance as a dependent variable

Table 21.1 (continued)

Articles	Type of HRM systems	Level of HRM systems	Type of commitment	Level of commitment	Role of commitment	Other key variables
Veld et al. (2010)	Unspecified HRM systems	Unit	Affective	Unit	Outcome	Climate for quality and climate for safety as mediators
Wright et al. (2003)	Unspecified HRM systems	Unit	Affective	Unit	Mediator	Operational performance and profits as dependent variables
Zheng et al. (2006)	Unspecified HRM systems	Unit	Overall commitment	Unit	Mediator	Enterprise performance as a dependent variable
Bal et al. (2013)	Developmental and Accommodative HRM systems	Unit	Affective	Individual	Outcome	Psychological contract as a mediator; selection and compensation as moderators
Chang and Chen (2011)	High-performance work systems	Unit	Affective	Individual	Mediator	Job performance as a dependent variable; human capital as a parallel mediator
Kehoe and Wright (2013)	High-performance work systems	Unit	Affective	Individual	Mediator	Organizational citizenship behavior, intention to remain, and absenteeism as the dependent variables
Takeuchi et al. (2009)	High-performance work systems	Unit	Affective	Individual	Outcome	Concern for employees climate as a mediator
Van De Voorde and Beijer (2015)	High-performance work systems	Unit	Affective	Individual	Outcome	HR attribution as a mediator

		Unit				
Wu and Chaturvedi (2009)	High-performance work systems	Unit	Affective	Individual	Outcome	Procedural justice as a mediator; organizational power distance as a moderator
Boon et al. (2011)	Unspecified HRM systems	Individual	Affective	Individual	Outcome	Person–organization fit and person–job fit as mediators and moderators
Boxall et al. (2011)	Espoused HR practices	Individual	Affective	Individual	Outcome	Empowerment as a mediator
Butts et al. (2009)	High-involvement work processes	Individual	Affective	Individual	Outcome	Empowerment as a mediator
Kuvaas (2008)	Developmental HRM practices	Individual	Affective	Individual	Moderator	Individual work performance as a dependent variable
Macky and Boxall (2007)	High-performance work systems	Individual	Affective	Individual	Outcome	Job satisfaction and trust in management as mediators
Sanders and Yang (2016)	High-commitment HRM systems	Individual	Affective	Individual	Outcome	HR attributions as a moderator

Wright et al. (2003) found that affective commitment mediated the influence of HRM systems on operational performance (for example, quality and productivity), which was further related to financial performance (for example, expenses and profits). Those findings were consistent with the behavioral perspective that considers employees' attitudes and behaviors as mediating mechanisms of the relationship between HRM systems and more distal performance outcomes. Among the few studies that considered affective commitment as a unit-level outcome, Veld et al. (2010) found that climate for quality (emphasis on providing good-quality care) partially mediates the relationship between HRM systems and affective commitment in healthcare organizations.

Differently from most studies that focused exclusively on affective commitment, Gong et al. (2009) provided one of the first investigations on the influence of HRM systems on both affective and continuance commitment. Consistent with the employee–organization relationship framework, those scholars divided HRM systems into two subsystems, with maintenance-oriented HRM practices focusing on employee protection, and equality and performance-oriented HRM practices focusing on employee motivation and empowerment. They found that performance-oriented HRM practices were significantly related only to affective commitment, but not to continuance commitment; and in contrast, maintenance-oriented HRM practices were positively associated only with continuance commitment, but not affective commitment. Furthermore, they found that affective commitment was the only commitment that was positively related to firm performance. Gong et al.'s (2009) study suggests that the components of HRM systems may have differential effects on different types of commitment. Along these lines, Gardner et al. (2011) drew upon the AMO model and self-determination theory to examine the influence of skill-enhancing, motivation-enhancing, and empowerment-enhancing HRM practices on collective affective commitment and turnover, and found that collective affective commitment mediated the influence of only motivation-enhancing and empowerment-enhancing HRM practices but not that of skill-enhancing HRM practices on turnover. Gardner et al. (2011) further suggested that the motivation and empowerment components may rely more on psychological processes, but the skill component may rely on labor market processes and, thus, have different effects on affective commitment.

Cross-Level Analysis

With the development of multilevel theory and methodology, strategic HRM scholars have also started to examine the cross-level influence of HRM systems on organizational commitment. All of the six studies I found focused on affective commitment and most of the studies treated commitment as a dependent variable and explored the mediating process through which HRM systems can be related to affective commitment. Focusing on unit-level mediators, Takeuchi et al.'s (2009) study was among the first to integrate micro and macro views of HRM to understand the underlying process of the influence of HRM systems on individual work attitudes. Takeuchi et al. (2009) found that a concern-for-employees climate serves as an important mediator that translates the cross-level influence of HPWSs on affective commitment. Their findings indicate that HRM practices may not directly affect individual attitudes; instead, a concern-for-employees climate may help employees to interpret HRM practices and, thus, play an important role in eliciting employees' affective commitment.

Researchers have also examined individual-level mediators of the cross-level relationship between HRM systems and affective commitment. For example, Wu and Chaturvedi (2009) examined the role of procedural justice in the relationship between HPWSs and affective commitment and found that HPWSs can enhance individual employees' perceived fairness of the means used to make decisions (that is, procedural justice), which may further make employees more likely to reciprocate with high affective commitment. As another example, Bal et al. (2013) examined the mediating role of psychological contract, which refers to employees' perceptions about the nature of their relationship with their organizations (Rousseau, 1995: see Chapter 9 in this volume), and found that developmental HRM practices, including training, internal promotion, job enrichment, lateral job movement, and second career, can be related to affective commitment by reducing the transactional contract and enhancing the relational contract. In a recent study, Van De Voorde and Beijer (2015) identified another mediator, HR attributions. They followed Nishii et al.'s (2008) work to argue that employees have two types of attributions for the use of HRM systems in organizations, with one attributing HRM practices to enhancing employees' well-being and the other attributing HRM practices to maximizing employee performance. They found that even though the use of HPWSs is positively related to both well-being attribution and performance attribution, only well-being attribution mediates the influence of HRM systems on affective commitment. In general, these studies suggest that other psychological factors, reviewed in other chapters of this book (for example, Chapter 25 on organizational justice, Chapter 23 on empowerment, and Chapter 24 on perceived organizational support), may help to explain how HRM systems can influence affective commitment.

Two other studies also examined affective commitment as an individual-level mediator that translates the influence of HRM systems on consequence variables. Chang and Chen (2011) found that affective commitment mediates the positive influence of HPWSs on job performance. Kehoe and Wright (2013) also found a role of affective commitment in mediating the influence of HPWSs on intention to remain and organizational citizenship behaviors, but not on absenteeism. These findings suggest that affective commitment is an intermediate variable that links HRM systems and more distal behavioral outcomes, that are reviewed in other chapters of this book (for example, Chapter 14 on retention and attendance, Chapter 15 on in-role and extra-role performance, and Chapter 16 on counterproductive work behavior).

Individual-Level Analysis

Even though HRM systems have traditionally been measured by asking managers to report the use of HRM practices at the unit level (for example, the proportion of the workforce covered by an HR practice), some scholars have recently started to emphasize the importance of employees' perceptions of HRM systems. For example, Nishii and Wright (2008) argue that the intended HRM practices are different from what are implemented in organizations, which are also different from what are perceived by employees. To support this argument, Liao et al. (2009) found weak relationships between manager-perceived HRM practices and employee-perceived HRM practices, and suggest that it is important to examine HRM systems from both employees' and managers' perspectives. In particular, when examining the influence of HRM systems on individual outcomes, researchers need to consider how employees perceive and interpret HRM systems because it is arguably employees' perceptions, rather than intended or actual HRM systems, that affect employees' attitudes and behaviors. Therefore, I also include six sample studies that examine the influence of perceived HRM systems on organizational commitment.

Similar to the above-reviewed cross-level studies, all individual-level studies focused on affective commitment rather than other forms of commitment. Most of those studies explored the mediating processes through which perceived HRM systems are related to affective commitment. For example, Boxall et al. (2011) and Butts et al. (2009) demonstrated that psychological empowerment is a more proximal outcome of HRM systems that can enhance employees' affective commitment, because employees generally value enhanced autonomy in their work. Macky and Boxall (2007) also found that job satisfaction and trust in management are two mediating mechanisms through which HPWSs can be related to affective commitment. From the person–environment fit perspective, Boon et al. (2011) theorized and found that person–organization fit mediates the relationship between HRM systems and affective commitment.

In addition to the studies on the mediating processes between HRM systems and affective commitment, individual-level research also examined potential moderators of the HRM–commitment relationship. Sanders and Yang (2016) found that employees' interpretation of HRM systems may moderate the relationship between high-commitment HRM systems and affective commitment. More specifically, they found that the perceived high-commitment HRM systems are more likely to be associated with affective commitment when HRM systems are high in distinctiveness, consistency, and consensus. This is because distinctiveness, consistency, and consensus of HRM systems can help employees to make confident attributions about the use of HRM practices and help them have a better understanding of behaviors that are expected, encouraged, and rewarded by organizations.

Taken together, the individual-level research emphasizes the influence of the perceived HRM systems rather than actual or intended HRM practices on affective commitment. The findings shed light on the psychological mechanisms through which HRM systems affect affective commitment. The research also provides some preliminary information about the boundary conditions of the relationship between HRM systems and affective commitment.

DISCUSSION AND FUTURE DIRECTION

HRM systems have been examined as an important antecedent of organizational commitment in the strategic HRM literature. Previous research has demonstrated the positive relationship between HPWSs and affective commitment using unit-level, individual-level, and cross-level analyses. Researchers have also examined the mediating effect of affective commitment on distal performance outcomes, psychological processes translating HRM systems' influence on affective commitment, as well as boundary conditions for the HRM–commitment relationship. These studies have made important contributions to both the commitment and strategic HRM literatures by helping us to understand how, why, and when HRM systems can impact affective commitment. The accumulated knowledge about the HRM–commitment relationship has also offered managerial implications for firms to build organizational commitment, and has suggested several avenues that might be pursued in future research to give a more comprehensive understanding of the relationship between HRM systems and organizational commitment.

Practical Implications

The findings of the HRM systems–organizational commitment relationship offer important implications for organizations aimed at enhancing employees' organizational commitment. In order to foster affective commitment, organizations can invest in training and development programs and provide employees with clear career paths, which may make employees feel that organizations care about their personal growth and development. Moreover, organizations can accurately evaluate employees' performance and compensate them based on performance, which may make employees feel that the organizations recognize and value their contributions. In addition, organizations can empower employees to make work decisions and share work-related information with them in a timely manner, which may enhance job autonomy and the feeling of belongingness. All those practices together can help to strengthen employees' emotional bonds with organizations. Furthermore, other organizational HRM practices might be likely to enhance continuance commitment. For example, organizations can provide more job security and develop firm-specific skills that cannot be easily transferred to other organizations.

Future Directions

Components and types of HRM systems
Most of the existing studies focus on the influence of whole HRM systems on organizational commitment. This systems approach is useful for us to understand the overall relationship between HRM systems and organizational commitment, but may overlook the possibility that different components of HRM systems may affect organizational commitment in different ways. For example, Gong et al. (2009) and Gardner et al. (2011) have shown that not all dimensions of HRM systems have the same relationship with organizational commitment, and thus suggest that researchers investigate what components of HRM systems are most important to influence employees' commitment to their organizations. Relatedly, previous research has primarily focused on the influence of HPWSs on organizational commitment rather than other types of HRM systems. However, scholars have found that there are multiple configurations of HRM practices (Arthur, 1992; Toh et al., 2008). Future research can explore how other types of HRM systems influence organizational commitment and whether we can identify certain types of HRM systems that can reduce employees' commitment to their organizations.

Forms and foci of commitment
Another issue that needs more research attention is to examine how HRM systems influence other types of commitment. Almost all empirical studies have focused on HRM's influence on affective commitment, except for Gong et al. (2009) who found that managers' affective commitment and continuance commitment are driven by different subsystems of HRM systems. Given the fact that all forms of organizational commitment (that is, affective, continuance, and normative commitment) are negatively

related to turnover outcomes and have differential relationships with performance outcomes (Meyer et al., 2002), it is important to understand how HRM systems, or different components of HRM systems, may affect behavioral outcomes through different forms of organizational commitment. In addition, organizational commitment is just one of the multiple foci of employee commitment (see Chapter 4 as well as the chapters in Part III, 'Foci of Commitment', in this volume). In future, researchers may also examine whether and how HRM systems may influence other foci of employee commitment in addition to organizational commitment. For example, it is possible that HRM systems that select individuals based on person–organization fit and provide training and career development opportunities may also enhance employees' commitment to their occupation or profession. Also, how organizations treat employees by using HRM practices may also affect their commitment to outside organizations (for example, union commitment).

Moderators of the HRM–commitment relationship
Strategic HRM research has examined HRM systems as the most primary antecedent of employee attitudes and behaviors including organizational commitment. Therefore, there is a dearth of studies examining how HRM systems may work with other antecedents to affect organizational commitment. For example, Chapter 22 in this volume reviews studies focusing on leadership as one of the drivers of commitment. If both HRM systems and leadership can affect organizational commitment, examining only one of them may lead to an incomplete understanding of how to promote employees' organizational commitment in a more effective way. Several recent studies have suggested that HRM systems and leadership may serve as substitutes for one another to affect employee outcomes in small work units. For example, Chuang et al. (2016) found that the relationship between HRM systems for knowledge-intensive teamwork was more positively related to team knowledge acquisition and sharing when empowering leadership was low than when it was high. Jiang et al. (2015) also found that service leadership substitutes for the effect of service-oriented HPWSs on customer knowledge and service climate. These findings suggest that leaders who work closely with employees may have a substantial impact on employees' organizational commitment and, thus, substitute for the influence of HRM systems on commitment. However, it is also possible that HRM systems and leadership may work in a synergistic way to affect organizational commitment, which means that when both are present, employees are more likely to experience the highest level of organizational commitment, and the absence of either may weaken the positive effect of the other. In order to understand the nature of these relationships, both theoretical developments and empirical evidences are needed in the future.

In addition to leadership, researchers can study other boundary conditions of the relationship between HRM systems and organizational commitment. This is consistent with the vertical-fit argument of the strategic HRM literature, which suggests that HRM systems are more likely to achieve desirable outcomes when the systems fit with the internal and external environments (Jackson and Schuler, 1995; Jackson et al., 2014). Previous research has examined the moderating effects of some internal and external factors on the influence of HRM systems on performance outcomes. For example, Youndt et al. (1996) found that business strategy focusing on quality can magnify the influence of human capital-enhancing HRM systems on employee productivity. Datta et al. (2005)

also found that industrial characteristics (for example, industry capital intensity, growth, and differentiation) can moderate the relationship between HRM systems and employee productivity. Future research may follow these studies to better understand when HRM systems are more or less likely to improve employees' organizational commitment.

Another set of potential moderators includes individual characteristics. As suggested by several scholars (e.g., Lepak et al., 2012; Nishii and Wright, 2008), individuals may respond to HRM practices in different ways depending on their personal characteristics (for example, needs, experiences, and personality traits). For example, those with high exchange orientation may be more likely to reciprocate organizations that invest in HPWSs than those with low exchange orientation. Future research examining the moderating effects of such individual characteristics can help researchers to better understand the variation of the influence of HRM systems on individuals' organizational commitment, and facilitate practitioners to design and implement HRM systems that can better address employees' needs and preferences.

Team-level analysis
The empirical studies reviewed in this chapter have primarily examined the relationship between HRM systems and organizational commitment at either the individual or unit level, with a lack of research on this relationship at the team level of analysis. Both the strategic HRM literature (Jiang et al., 2013) and the commitment literature (e.g., Porter, 2005) have emphasized the importance of team-level research. Future research may study the variance in collective commitment among teams or subunits within the same organization, and examine how HRM systems may help to understand why different groups or teams of employees within the same organization have different levels of collective commitment. Researchers can also examine how team-level factors may affect cross-level influence of HRM systems on individual-level organizational commitment. For example, Chang et al. (2014) found that team cohesion and task complexity at the team level enhance the influence of high-commitment work systems on individual-level creativity, thus suggesting that team characteristics may influence how HRM systems at the organizational level influence the organizational commitment of individual employees. Future studies along these lines may shed more insight on the HRM systems–commitment relationship by integrating the individual level, team level, and unit level of analysis.

CONCLUSION

The primary objective of this chapter is to summarize primary theoretical perspectives and key empirical findings of the relationship between HRM systems and organizational commitment. This chapter also explores the potential directions for future research to delve into this important relationship in both commitment and strategic HRM literatures. The hope is that future research on this relationship will offer more insights into why, how, and when different types of HRM systems can affect multiple types of employee commitment at different levels of analysis, and help organizations to better manage employee commitment in order to realize their strategic objectives.

REFERENCES

Allen, N.J., and Meyer, J.P. (1990). The measurement and antecedents of affective, continuance and normative commitment to the organization, *Journal of Occupational Psychology*, *63(1)*, 1–18.

Appelbaum, E., Bailey, T., Berg, P., and Kalleberg, A.L. (2000). *Manufacturing Advantage: Why High-Performance Work Systems Pay Off*. Ithaca, NY: Cornell University Press.

Arthur, J.B. (1992). The link between business strategy and industrial relations systems in American steel mini-mills, *Industrial and Labor Relations Review*, *45(3)*, 488–506.

Bal, P.M., Kooij, D.T., and De Jong, S.B. (2013). How do developmental and accommodative HRM enhance employee engagement and commitment? The role of psychological contract and SOC strategies, *Journal of Management Studies*, *50(4)*, 545–572.

Blau, P.M. (1964). *Exchange and Power in Social Life*. New Brunswick, NJ: Transaction Publishers.

Boon, C., Den Hartog, D.N., Boselie, P., and Paauwe, J. (2011). The relationship between perceptions of HR practices and employee outcomes: examining the role of person–organisation and person–job fit, *International Journal of Human Resource Management*, *22(1)*, 138–162.

Bowen, D.E., and Ostroff, C. (2004). Understanding HRM–firm performance linkages: The role of the 'strength' of the HRM system, *Academy of Management Review*, *29(2)*, 203–221.

Boxall, P., Ang, S.H., and Bartram, T. (2011). Analysing the black box of HRM: Uncovering HR goals, mediators, and outcomes in a standardized service environment, *Journal of Management Studies*, *48(7)*, 1504–1532.

Butts, M.M., Vandenberg, R.J., DeJoy, D.M., Schaffer, B.S., and Wilson, M.G. (2009). Individual reactions to high involvement work processes: investigating the role of empowerment and perceived organizational support, *Journal of Occupational Health Psychology*, *14(2)*, 122–136.

Chang, P.C., and Chen, S.J. (2011). Crossing the level of employees performance: HPWS, affective commitment, human capital, and employee job performance in professional service organizations, *International Journal of Human Resource Management*, *22(4)*, 883–901.

Chang, S., Jia, L., Takeuchi, R., and Cai, Y. (2014). Do high-commitment work systems affect creativity? A multilevel combinational approach to employee creativity, *Journal of Applied Psychology*, *99(4)*, 665–680.

Chuang, C., and Liao, H. (2010). Strategic human resource management in service context: Taking care of business by taking care of employees and customers, *Personnel Psychology*, *63(1)*, 153–196.

Chuang, C.H., Jackson, S.E., and Jiang, Y. (2016). Can knowledge-intensive teamwork be managed? Examining the roles of HRM systems, leadership, and tacit knowledge, *Journal of Management*, *42(2)*, 524–554.

Combs, J., Liu, Y., Hall, A., and Ketchen, D. (2006). How much do high-performance work practices matter? A meta-analysis of their effects on organizational performance, *Personnel Psychology*, *59(3)*, 501–528.

Datta, D.K., Guthrie, J.P., and Wright, P.M. (2005). Human resource management and labor productivity: does industry matter? *Academy of Management Journal*, *48(1)*, 135–145.

Deci, E.L., and Ryan, R.M. (1985). *Intrinsic motivation and self-determination in human behavior*. New York: Springer Science and Business Media.

Delery, J.E. (1998). Issues of fit in strategic human resource management: Implications for research, *Human Resource Management Review*, *8(3)*, 289–309.

Gardner, T.M., Wright, P.M., and Moynihan, L.M. (2011). The impact of motivation, empowerment, and skill-enhancing practices on aggregate voluntary turnover: the mediating effect of collective affective commitment, *Personnel Psychology*, *64(2)*, 315–350.

Gerhart, B. (2007). Horizontal and vertical fit in human resource systems. In C. Ostroff and T.A. Judge (eds), *Perspectives on Organizational Fit*. New York: Psychology Press, pp. 317–348.

Gong, Y., Chang, S., and Cheung, S.Y. (2010). High performance work system and collective OCB: A collective social exchange perspective. *Human Resource Management Journal*, *20(2)*, 119–137.

Gong, Y., Law, K.S., Chang, S., and Xin, K.R. (2009). Human resources management and firm performance: The differential role of managerial affective and continuance commitment, *Journal of Applied Psychology*, *94(1)*, 263–275.

Gouldner, A.W. (1960). The norm of reciprocity: A preliminary statement, *American Sociological Review*, *25(2)*, 161–178.

Hoque, K. (1999). Human resource management and performance in the UK hotel industry. *British Journal of Industrial Relations*, *37(3)*, 419–443.

Huselid, M.A. (1995). The impact of human resource management practices on turnover, productivity, and corporate financial performance, *Academy of Management Journal*, *38(3)*, 635–672.

Jackson, S.E., and Schuler, R.S. (1995). Understanding human resource management in the context of organizations and their environments. In J.T. Spence, J.M. Darley, and D.J. Foss (eds), *Annual Review of Psychology*, Palo Alto, CA: Annual Reviews, pp. 237–264.

Jackson, S.E., Schuler, R.S., and Jiang, K. (2014). An aspirational framework for strategic human resource management, *Academy of Management Annals*, *8(1)*, 1–56.

Jiang, K., Lepak, D.P., Han, K., Hong, Y., Kim, A., and Winkler, A.L. (2012a). Clarifying the construct of human resource systems: Relating human resource management to employee performance, *Human Resource Management Review*, *22(2)*, 73–85.

Jiang, K., Chuang, C.H., and Chiao, Y.C. (2015). Developing collective customer knowledge and service climate: The interaction between service-oriented high-performance work systems and service leadership, *Journal of Applied Psychology*, *100(4)*, 1089–1106.

Jiang, K., Lepak, D., Hu, J., and Baer, J. (2012b). How does human resource management influence organizational outcomes? A meta-analytic investigation of mediating mechanisms, *Academy of Management Journal*, *55(6)*, 1264–1294.

Jiang, K., Takeuchi, R., and Lepak, D.P. (2013). Where do we go from here? New perspectives on the black box in strategic human resource management research, *Journal of Management Studies*, *50(8)*, 1448–1480.

Katou, A.A., Budhwar, P.S., and Patel, C. (2014). Content vs. process in the HRM-performance relationship: An empirical examination. *Human Resource Management*, *53(4)*, 527–544.

Kehoe, R.R., and Wright, P.M. (2013). The impact of high-performance human resource practices on employees' attitudes and behaviors, *Journal of Management*, *39(2)*, 366–391.

Kooij, D.T., Jansen, P.G., Dikkers, J.S., and De Lange, A.H. (2010). The influence of age on the associations between HR practices and both affective commitment and job satisfaction: A meta-analysis, *Journal of Organizational Behavior*, *31(8)*, 1111–1136.

Kuvaas, B. (2008). An exploration of how the employee–organization relationship affects the linkage between perception of developmental human resource practices and employee outcomes. *Journal of Management Studies*, *45(1)*, 1–25.

Lepak, D.P., Jiang, K., Han, K., Castellano, W.G., and Hu, J. (2012). Strategic HRM moving forward: what can we learn from micro perspectives? In G. Hodgkinson and J.K. Ford (eds), *International Review of Industrial and Organizational Psychology*. Chichester: John Wiley and Sons, pp. 231–259.

Lepak, D.P., Liao, H., Chung, Y., and Harden, E.E. (2006). A conceptual review of human resource management systems in strategic human resource management research, In J.J. Martocchio (ed.), *Research in Personnel and Human Resource Management*, Vol. 25. Greenwich, CT: JAI, pp. 217–271.

Liao, H., Toya, K., Lepak, D.P., and Hong, Y. (2009). Do they see eye to eye? Management and employee perspectives of high-performance work systems and influence processes on service quality. *Journal of Applied Psychology*, *94(2)*, 371–391.

Macky, K., and Boxall, P. (2007). The relationship between high-performance work practices and employee attitudes: an investigation of additive and interaction effect. *International Journal of Human Resource Management*, *18(4)*, 537–567.

Messersmith, J.G., Patel, P.C., Lepak, D.P., and Gould-Williams, J.S. (2011). Unlocking the black box: exploring the link between high-performance work systems and performance, *Journal of Applied Psychology*, *96(6)*, 1105–1118.

Meyer, J.P. and Allen, N.J. (1997). *Commitment in the Workplace: Theory, Research, and Application*. Thousand Oaks, CA: Sage.

Meyer, J.P., Allen, N.J., and Smith, C.A. (1993). Commitment to organizations and occupations: Extension and test of a three-component conceptualization. *Journal of Applied Psychology*, *78(4)*, 538–551.

Meyer, J.P. and Herscovitch, L. (2001). Commitment in the workplace: Toward a general model. *Human Resource Management Review*, *11(3)*, 299–326.

Meyer, J.P., Stanley, D.J., Herscovitch, L., and Topolnytsky, L. (2002). Affective, continuance, and normative commitment to the organization: A meta-analysis of antecedents, correlates, and consequences. *Journal of Vocational Behavior*, *61(1)*, 20–52.

Nishii, L.H., Lepak, D.P., and Schneider, B. (2008). Employee attributions of the 'why' of HR practices: Their effects on employee attitudes and behaviors, and customer satisfaction. *Personnel Psychology*, *61(3)*, 503–545.

Nishii, L.H. and Wright, P.M. (2008). Variability within organizations: Implications for strategic human resources management. In D.B. Smith (ed.), *The People Make the Place: Dynamic Linkages between Individuals and Organizations*. New York: Lawrence Erlbaum Associates, pp. 225–248.

Porter, C.O. (2005). Goal orientation: effects on backing up behavior, performance, efficacy, and commitment in teams. *Journal of Applied Psychology*, *90(4)*, 811–818.

Posthuma, R., Campion, M.C., Masimova, M., and Campion, M.A. (2013). A high performance work practices taxonomy integrating the literature and directing future research. *Journal of Management*, *39(5)*, 1184–1220.

Rabl, T., Jayasinghe, M., Gerhart, B., and Kühlmann, T.M. (2014). A meta-analysis of country differences in the high-performance work system–business performance relationship: The roles of national culture and managerial discretion. *Journal of Applied Psychology*, *99(6)*, 1011–1141.

Ramsay, H., Scholarios, D., and Harley, B. (2000). Employees and high-performance work systems: testing inside the black box. *British Journal of Industrial Relations, 38(4)*, 501–531.

Rousseau, D. (1995). *Psychological Contracts in Organizations: Understanding Written and Unwritten Agreements*. Thousand Oaks, CA: Sage.

Sanders, K., and Yang, H. (2016). The HRM process approach: The influence of employees attribution to explain the HRM–performance relationship. *Human Resource Management, 55(2)*, 201–217.

Schuler, R.S., and Jackson, S.E. (1987). Linking competitive strategies with human resource management practices. *Academy of Management Executive, 1(3)*, 207–219.

Subramony, M. (2009). A meta-analytic investigation of the relationship between HRM bundles and firm performance. *Human Resource Management, 48(5)*, 745–768.

Takeuchi, R., Chen, G., and Lepak, D.P. (2009). Through the looking glass of a social system: cross-level effects of high-performance work systems on employees attitudes. *Personnel Psychology, 62(1)*, 1–29.

Toh, S.M., Morgeson, F.P., and Campion, M.A. (2008). Human resource configurations: investigating fit with the organizational context. *Journal of Applied Psychology, 93(4)*, 864–882.

Tsui, A.S., Pearce, J.L., Porter, L.W., and Hite, J.P. (1995). Choice of employee–organization relationship: Influence of external and internal organizational factors. In G.R. Ferris (ed.), *Research in Personnel and Human Resource Management*, Vol. 13. Greenwich, CT: JAI, pp. 117–151.

Tsui, A.S., Pearce, J.L., Porter, L.W., and Tripoli, A.M. (1997). Alternative approaches to the employee–organization relationship: does investment in employees pay off? *Academy of Management Journal, 40(5)*, 1089–1121.

Van De Voorde, K., and Beijer, S. (2015). The role of employee HR attributions in the relationship between high-performance work systems and employee outcomes, *Human Resource Management Journal, 25(1)*, 62–78.

Veld, M., Paauwe, J., and Boselie, P. (2010). HRM and strategic climates in hospitals: does the message come across at the ward level?. *Human Resource Management Journal, 20(4)*, 339–356.

Walumbwa, F.O., Hartnell, C.A., and Oke, A. (2010). Servant leadership, procedural justice climate, service climate, employee attitudes, and organizational citizenship behavior: a cross-level investigation. *Journal of Applied Psychology, 95(3)*, 517–529.

Wright, P.M., and Boswell, W.R. (2002). Desegregating HRM: A review and synthesis of micro and macro human resource management research. *Journal of Management, 28(3)*, 247–276.

Wright, P.M., Gardner, T.M., and Moynihan, L.M. (2003). The impact of HR practices on the performance of business units. *Human Resource Management Journal, 13(3)*, 21–36.

Wright, P.M., and McMahan, G.C. (1992). Theoretical perspectives for strategic human resource management. *Journal of Management, 18(2)*, 295–320.

Wu, P.C. and Chaturvedi, S. (2009). The role of procedural justice and power distance in the relationship between high-performance work systems and employee attitudes: A multilevel perspective. *Journal of Management, 35(5)*, 1228–1247.

Youndt, M.A., Snell, S.A., Dean, J.W., and Lepak, D.P. (1996). Human resource management, manufacturing strategy, and firm performance. *Academy of Management Journal, 39(4)*, 836–866.

Zacharatos, A., Barling, J., and Iverson, R.D. (2005). High-performance work systems and occupational safety. *Journal of Applied Psychology, 90(1)*, 77–93.

Zheng, C., Morrison, M., and O'Neill, G. (2006). An empirical study of high performance HRM practices in Chinese SMEs. *International Journal of Human Resource Management, 17(10)*, 1772–1803.

22. Organizational leadership and employee commitment
Melissa Trivisonno and Julian Barling

Organizational leadership has been the subject of systematic theoretical and empirical research ever since World War II, with hundreds of new studies now appearing annually (Barling, 2014). Most of this research has focused on the outcomes of leadership, and the possible effects of organizational leadership on employee commitment have not escaped attention, both in itself, and in terms of the extent to which any proximal effects on commitment help us to understand why leadership has such widespread and distal consequences.

Our goal in this chapter is to explain how different types of leadership influence different facets of employee commitment. To do so, we first review what is known about the effects of positive leadership on employee commitment. Second, we review the possible influence of negative forms of leadership on employee commitment. Third, we investigate the outcomes of high-quality leadership in alternative organizations, specifically labor organizations. Finally, we offer some research questions that will help advance our understanding of the nature and effects of the construct of commitment, before drawing conclusions.

POSITIVE LEADERSHIP AND EMPLOYEE COMMITMENT TO THE ORGANIZATION

As is apparent throughout this *Handbook*, it is widely accepted that there are meaningfully different forms of organizational commitment (that is, affective, normative, continuance). Similarly, a reading of the leadership literature shows that a range of differing leadership theories have been the focus of empirical investigation. In this section, we discuss what has been learned from research about the relationship between various positive leadership theories (namely, transformational, charismatic, ethical, leader–member exchange, servant, and authentic leadership) and the different facets of organizational commitment.

Transformational Leadership

As the most frequently studied leadership theory (Barling, 2014), transformational leadership posits that leaders exhibit four separate behaviors (Bass and Riggio, 2006). First, idealized influence reflects the ethical component of transformational leadership. Leaders high in idealized influence go beyond self-interest; they are guided by their moral commitments and responsibilities and want what is best for the organization and its members. These leaders serve as role models, act with integrity and humility, and show a deep respect for others. Second, inspirational motivation involves behaviors that encourage and inspire others to achieve their goals. Leaders high in inspirational motivation set high but realistic standards through interpersonal interactions, and help others believe that they can overcome obstacles or psychological setbacks, thereby enhancing follower self-efficacy. Third, intellectual stimulation reflects behaviors that encourage followers to think for themselves, question their commonly held ideas and beliefs, restructure the way they think about and approach problems, and foster creativity. Finally, individualized consideration involves behaviors that recognize and respond to followers' needs and capabilities; the compassion, care, and empathy involved promote follower well-being and development. Through individualized consideration, high-quality leader–follower relationships reflected in mutual trust are established (Bass and Riggio, 2006).

Despite the conceptually distinct nature of the four aspects of transformational leadership, research has failed to adequately document their construct validity (e.g., Bycio et al., 1995). As a result, transformational leadership is most frequently investigated as a unidimensional construct; and we follow that tradition in our discussion of transformational leadership and employee commitment to the organization.

While the effects of transformational leadership on employees' organizational commitment are well documented (Walumbwa et al., 2005), the direction of this association differs across the components of commitment. For example, Jackson et al.'s (2013) recent meta-analysis showed that transformational leadership was positively associated with affective and normative commitment. Importantly, these relationships held true outside of the North American and European contexts; for example, transformational leadership predicted affective and normative commitment in the Malaysian manufacturing industry (Lo et al., 2010), while in China, pride in being a follower of the leader mediated the relationship between transformational leadership and affective and normative commitment (Chan and Mak, 2014).

In contrast, mixed findings have emerged regarding transformational leadership and continuance commitment. Some studies established positive relationships (Bučiūnienė and Škudienė, 2008; Felfe et al., 2008) while others reported negative correlations (Mendelson et al., 2011; Rafferty and Griffin, 2004). One possible reason for these inconsistent findings is the lack of clarity or consistency in the way continuance commitment is conceptualized and operationalized (Viator, 2001). While there is some support for the notion that there are two components to continuance commitment (namely, personal sacrifice associated with leaving the organization, and lack of employment alternatives; McGee and Ford, 1987), most research has used a unidimensional measure of continuance commitment. Yet when the relationship between transformational leadership and the components of commitment were examined separately, Gillet and Vandenberghe (2014) showed that transformational leadership was positively associated with perceived sacrifice commitment, and negatively associated with commitment based on the perceived lack of employment alternatives.

The effects of transformational leadership on employees' commitment to the organization are not always direct; and the indirect effects of transformational leadership on employees' organizational commitment have been investigated. Followers' compliance with their leader's power (Pierro et al., 2013), trust (Goodwin et al., 2011), psychological empowerment (Castro et al., 2008), and collective efficacy (Walumbwa et al., 2004) all mediate the link between transformational leadership and affective commitment. These findings are strengthened as the indirect effects of transformational leadership on organizational commitment (through procedural justice; Pillai et al., 1999; and job satisfaction; Nguni et al., 2006) emerge across different measures (for example, the Organizational Commitment Questionnaire; Mowday et al., 1979) of organizational commitment.

Charismatic Leadership

The two most prominent interpretations of charismatic leadership theory suggest that charismatic leadership emphasizes either the behavior and personality of the individual leader (House, 1977), or attributions that followers make about the leader (Conger and Kanungo, 1998). The behavioral approach suggests that charismatic leaders behave in ways that support and reinforce their belief that followers can accomplish and surpass performance expectations, highlight ideological aspects of work, display self-confidence, and emphasize a collective identity (House and Howell, 1992). Moving away from leadership behaviors, the attributional approach suggests that charisma is more a function of followers' attributions about their leaders' behaviors; in this sense, charisma rests 'in the eye of the beholder' (Conger and Kanungo, 1998).

Based on the attributional approach, one study of 235 employees showed that charismatic leadership was positively related to organizational commitment (Rowden, 2000). Furthermore, Michaelis et al. (2009) examined whether affective commitment – specifically, affective commitment to change – mediated the relationship between charismatic leadership and followers' innovation implementation behavior. Data from 194 employees in research and development (R&D) teams of a multinational automotive company demonstrated that charismatic leadership positively associated to subordinates' affective commitment to change; in turn, affective commitment to change positively related to innovation implementation behavior. This study gains in importance as it shows that affective commitment to change can be an end in itself, but also accounts for subsequent employee behaviors.

Despite these findings, the relative lack of research on charismatic leadership and employees' organizational commitment is curious, given that charismatic leadership is the second most frequently researched leadership theory (Barling, 2014). Clearly more research is needed, and because both studies discussed took an attributional approach, any such research should differentiate between behavioral and attributional conceptualizations, and investigate other conceptualizations of charismatic leadership (that is personalized versus socialized; Howell, 1988).

Ethical Leadership

Recent government corruption and corporate scandals have exacted enormous organizational and societal costs. Anecdotally at least, much blame for these ethical lapses has been attributed to the leaders of these organizations (for example, Enron and Tyco; Hansen et al., 2013). Perhaps not surprisingly, there has been a marked increase in research on ethical leadership.

Although many different approaches to understanding ethical leadership exist (for example, moral reasoning; Turner et al., 2002; and ethic of care; Simola et al., 2010), Brown et al. (2005) provide an overall encompassing definition: 'the demonstration of normatively appropriate conduct through personal actions and interpersonal relationships, and the promotion of such conduct to followers through two-way communication, reinforcement, and decision-making' (p. 120). To date, this would appear to be the framework within which most ethical leadership is conceptualized in research, and the one we follow in this discussion.

Using a longitudinal design, data from 108 employees in an Israeli regional council showed that perceived ethical leadership predicted later organizational commitment (Beeri et al., 2013). Neubert et al. (2009) help to explain why this effect emerges. Based on survey data from 250 employees, their results demonstrated an indirect relationship between ethical leadership and affective commitment, and ethical climate served as the mediator. Because these studies used different scales to measure organizational commitment, the conclusion is that the ethical leadership–commitment link exists irrespective of commitment scales used.

However, the information provided by these studies remains somewhat limited as they assumed a unidimensional approach to commitment. Studying ethical leadership at different levels of management, Hansen et al. (2013) examined the relationship between ethical leadership and multiple foci of employee commitment. Based on data from 201 employees from a large waste management corporation in the United States (US), followers' relationships with their organizations partially mediated the relationship between organizational ethical leadership and employees' affective commitment to the organization. Followers' relationship with their supervisor also partially mediated the link between supervisory ethical leadership and employee affective commitment to the supervisor (Hansen et al., 2013). These findings suggest that all levels of management can benefit from behaving ethically; senior organizational leaders and supervisors must recognize that building positive relationships with their followers is crucial for employee commitment to the organization and supervisor, respectively.

To shed more light on how ethical leadership fosters employee commitment, Kottke and Pelletier (2013) extended the focus on the effects of top managers' and immediate supervisors' ethical leadership to include normative and continuance commitment. Data obtained from 371 employees revealed that perceptions of both top managers' and supervisors' ethical leadership predicted subordinates' affective and normative commitment to the organization. In contrast, irrespective of the level at which it was enacted, ethical leadership did not predict continuous commitment (Kottke and Pelletier, 2013). These findings show that the benefits of ethical leadership extend to both affective and normative commitment, and are informative as the antecedents of employees' normative commitment generally receive less attention.

Leader–Member Exchange

While transformational, charismatic, and ethical leadership focus primarily on the behavior of the leader, leader–member exchange (LMX) theory takes a relational perspective to leadership and emphasizes the quality of the leader–member dyad. LMX theory posits that leaders develop different-quality relationships with each of their followers, and that mutual influence occurs within each dyadic relationship (Graen and Cashman, 1975). Thus, rather than assume a unidirectional and downward influence from leader to follower as is the case in most other leadership theories, LMX highlights the reciprocal nature of leader–follower relationships, and that higher-quality relationships yield more positive organizational outcomes than lower-quality relationships. High-quality LMX relationships are defined by autonomy, understanding, support, trust, opportunities for involvement in decision-making, provision of information, and role latitude. In contrast, poor-quality LMX relationships are characterized by aspects such as contractual obligations, one-way communication and downward influence, role distinctions, formal transactions based on distrust, and social distance (Schriesheim et al., 1999).

Numerous studies have also been conducted on the relationship between LMX and organizational commitment. One typical field investigation of 337 employees showed that LMX was positively related to affective commitment (Liden et al., 2000). Similarly, using a sample of 220 R&D employees from Singapore, Lee (2005) demonstrated that LMX predicted followers' affective and normative commitment. Moving beyond direct relationships, Cheung and Wu (2012) demonstrated that LMX indirectly predicted employees' organizational commitment through employees' job satisfaction among 196 Chinese employees in the manufacturing industry. Data collected from 1283 nurses in Australia showed that employees' psychological empowerment mediated the association between LMX and employees' affective commitment to the organization (Brunetto et al., 2012). These findings are notable in that they are drawn from several different countries (Australia, China, Singapore, and the US), pointing to the cross-national validity of the link between LMX and employee commitment to the organization.

Examining LMX as a moderator, Hung et al. (2004) investigated the association between fairness perceptions of human resource management practices and affective commitment among 224 managers in nine Malaysian manufacturing companies. As predicted, LMX moderated the relationship such that members who perceived their employee relations and compensation as fair were more likely to demonstrate affective commitment when LMX was high (Hung et al., 2004). Similarly, based on data from 162 Chinese employees, perceived organizational support was more likely to influence employees' affective commitment with higher LMX (Liu and Ipe, 2010). By treating LMX as a moderator, these findings indicate not just whether LMX predicts organizational commitment, but when or under what conditions affective commitment may be enhanced.

Servant Leadership

First described by Robert Greenleaf in the 1970s (Greenleaf, 1970), current research would suggest that servant leadership is best viewed as comprising seven separate but related dimensions: putting subordinates first, empowering, conceptual skills, behaving ethically, helping subordinates to grow and succeed, emotional healing, and creating value for the community (Liden et al., 2008). Although servant leadership may seem similar to behaviors included in other leadership theories (for example, transformational, LMX), proponents of servant leadership highlight two critical differences. First, servant leadership emphasizes employee development not just for the sake of the organization but also for personal growth and advancement, and the good of the community. Second, servant leadership may be most appropriate for contexts that are stable and include an abundance of resources (Schaubroeck et al., 2011).

To test these differences, Schneider and George (2011) diverged from most research on organizational leadership and employee commitment, which has invariably focused only on a single leadership theory within each study, by directly comparing the effects of servant and transformational leadership on organizational commitment. Based on 110 participants in a US national voluntary service organization, servant leadership predicted organizational commitment through followers' empowerment. Surprisingly, no significant relationship was found between transformational leadership and organizational commitment after taking the effects of servant leadership into account. Although this seems to contradict research showing a link between transformational leadership and employee commitment that was discussed earlier in this chapter, one reason for these findings could be the study context: Schneider and George's research was conducted within voluntary organizations, which we have already seen may be uniquely suited for the effects of servant leadership. Nevertheless, these results provide empirical support for the influence of servant leadership on employee commitment; and begin to raise the question of the relative importance of the different leadership theories in explaining employee commitment.

To further compare the effects of servant and transformational leadership, van Dierendonck et al. (2014) examined two mechanisms through which servant and transformational leadership might differentially influence organizational commitment. Across two experimental studies and one field study, both servant and transformational leadership predicted organizational commitment. Importantly, however, the way in which they influenced organizational commitment differed. Servant leadership functioned mainly through follower need satisfaction, whereas transformational leadership functioned primarily through perceived leadership effectiveness (van Dierendonck et al., 2014). These findings provide some understanding of different processes that may underlie servant and transformational leadership; future research should now contrast the processes through which servant and transformational leadership affect the three components of employee commitment differently.

One remaining question is whether the different aspects of servant leadership differentially predict the three components of employee commitment (Bobbio et al., 2012). Bobbio et al.'s study in a sample of over 800 employees in profit and non-profit organizations in Italy showed that empowerment, accountability, standing back, and stewardship enhanced affective commitment; and that empowerment, standing back, courage, and stewardship improved normative commitment. In contrast, both humility and forgiveness were negatively associated with normative commitment. Last, authenticity positively related with continuance commitment, and empowerment negatively correlated with continuance commitment (Bobbio et al., 2012).

While this study sheds light on how servant leadership influences the different facets of employee commitment, the puzzling nature of the latter two findings warrants discussion. One explanation may be the use of different conceptualizations and operationalizations of servant leadership and organizational commitment. For example, as discussed previously, different results were found when the components of continuance commitment were examined separately (Gillet and Vandenberghe, 2014). Furthermore, like the other research we have discussed linking servant leadership and employee commitment, Bobbio et al. used a cross-sectional design; and the potential effects of servant leadership on employee commitment remain to be investigated.

Authentic Leadership

Authentic leadership is the most recent leadership theory subjected to a reasonable level of empirical scrutiny (Avolio and Luthans, 2006), and includes four components: self-awareness, unbiased processing of external information, relational transparency, and an internalized moral perspective.

Early findings already point to a link between authentic leadership and organizational commitment. Based on survey data from 157 employees, Peus et al. (2012) showed that perceived predictability of the leader, a facet of trust, partially mediated the relationship between authentic leadership and subordinates' affective commitment. Similarly, Leroy et al. (2012) showed an indirect effect of authentic leadership on organizational commitment through behavioral integrity ('practice what you preach'; Simons, 2002) using a sample of 49 teams in the service industry. Leaders who were perceived as authentic were more likely to be perceived as aligning their thoughts and actions, and in turn influenced followers to be more affectively committed to the organization. Not surprisingly, given its relative recency, these would appear to be the only two studies investigating authentic leadership and employee commitment. More research is needed to extend this focus by investigating whether and how authentic leadership relates to normative and continuance commitment.

Taken together, a review of the positive leadership literature demonstrates the beneficial consequences on employees' organizational commitment. Specifically, there is widespread agreement among the leadership theories showing a positive relationship with affective commitment; positive leadership is also consistently related to normative commitment, although there is less research focusing on this commitment facet. In contrast, the evidence is mixed regarding continuance commitment: both positive and negative relationships between positive leadership and continuance commitment have emerged.

NEGATIVE LEADERSHIP AND EMPLOYEE COMMITMENT TO THE ORGANIZATION

So far, our discussion has focused on the links between positive, or high-quality, leadership and organizational commitment. Missing from this discussion is any concern for the role of negative, or poor-quality, leadership on employee commitment. In this section, we review what has been learned from research about the role of negative leadership (abusive supervision and laissez-faire leadership) on employees' commitment to the organization. In the discussion that follows, we address how abusive supervision and laissez-faire leadership are associated with different components of organizational commitment.

Abusive Supervision

As one of the most widely studied approaches to negative leadership (Martinko et al., 2013), abusive supervision is defined as 'subordinates' perceptions of the extent to which supervisors engage in the sustained display of hostile verbal and nonverbal behaviors, excluding physical contact' (Tepper, 2000, p. 178). Examples of behaviors include yelling at, lying to, and belittling subordinates; criticizing subordinates in front of others; and unjustifiably blaming subordinates for mistakes. While studies show that abusive supervision results in a multitude of negative outcomes, including turnover, diminished psychological health, follower deviance, poor performance, and lower work–family functioning (for a review, see Tepper, 2007), our question is whether abusive supervision has any meaningful negative effects on organizational commitment.

Tepper et al. (2008) developed and tested a model of the relationships between abusive supervision, affective commitment, and organizational deviance. They hypothesized that affective commitment would mediate the relationship between abusive supervision and organizational deviance. Across two studies, targets of abusive supervision experienced lower levels of affective commitment, which led to greater deviance toward the organization (Tepper et al., 2008). These findings draw attention to the critical role that abusive supervisors play in influencing subordinates' organizational detachment, which could result in potentially detrimental and costly organizational behaviors.

Examining how abusive supervision influences the different facets of commitment, Tepper (2000) demonstrated that abusive supervision was negatively related to affective and normative commitment, and positively related to continuance commitment. Tepper's research went further, however, showing that these relationships were mediated by overall perceptions of organizational justice. Building on these results, Aryee et al. (2007) examined the separate mediating roles of interactional and procedural justice on the link between abusive supervision and affective commitment. Their data from leader–member dyads in a Chinese telecommunication company revealed that subordinates' perceptions of interactional but not procedural justice mediated the abusive supervision–affective organizational commitment relationship. In other words, abusive supervision resulted in lower interactional justice which, in turn, reduced subordinates' affective commitment to the organization (Aryee et al., 2007). Extending these findings, Gabler et al. (2014) showed that perceptions of sales managers' abusive supervision negatively associated to employees' affective commitment through employees' job satisfaction.

The effects of abusive supervision on organizational commitment have also received attention at the team level. Rousseau and Aubé (2014) investigated the moderating role of abusive supervision on the relationship between team-based reward leadership (conceptualized as administering positive reinforcements in the form of acknowledgements, commendation, and praise, contingent on fulfilling requirements delivered by the group as a whole) and team commitment. Data collected from 101 work teams in a public safety organization showed that abusive supervision weakened the relationship between team-based reward leadership and team commitment when abusive supervision was high (Rousseau and Aubé, 2014).

Taken together, we conclude that abusive supervision compromises employees' commitment to the organization. However, because most of the studies were cross-sectional in nature, future research should examine whether abusive supervision has long-term consequences on organizational commitment. Furthermore, affective commitment was the most commonly studied outcome of abusive supervision. More research is necessary to investigate how abusive supervision relates to normative and continuance commitment.

Laissez-Faire Leadership

Reflecting the absence of leadership, laissez-faire behaviors include the failure to provide direction, avoiding and denying responsibility, and neglecting to intervene even in dire situations (Bass and Riggio, 2006). Laissez-faire leadership has received little empirical attention in general (Barling, 2014), and this is true of the link between laissez-faire leadership and employee commitment. In one of the few studies on this topic, Nguni et al. (2006) found a negative association between laissez-faire leadership and organizational commitment in a sample of 545 Tanzanian elementary school teachers. In a separate study, Bučiūnienė and Škudienė (2008) showed that laissez-faire leadership negatively correlated with affective and normative commitment among 191 middle-level managers from five Lithuanian manufacturing companies. Findings from both studies provide initial evidence for the negative effects of laissez-faire leadership on employee commitment, and also suggest that these effects generalize across countries. Additionally, meta-analytic results by Jackson et al. (2013) demonstrated a negative correlation between laissez-faire leadership and affective and normative commitment. In contrast, laissez-faire leadership positively associated to continuance commitment (Jackson et al., 2013).

The indirect effects of laissez-faire on employees' commitment to the organization have also been investigated. Bernhard and O'Driscoll (2011) showed that psychological ownership of the organization mediated the relationship between laissez-faire leadership and affective commitment, using data obtained from 229 non-family employees from 52 small family-owned German businesses. These findings suggest that employees are less likely to connect with their organizations in the absence of leadership. Taken together with findings regarding positive or high-quality leadership, we infer that it is through high-quality relationships with their leaders that employees experience commitment to their employing organizations.

In summary, a review of the limited literature available shows that poor-quality leadership is negatively associated with employees' organizational commitment. Still, more research is needed to examine how other negative forms of leadership (for example, unethical leadership) affect the different facets of employees' commitment to the organization.

LEADERSHIP AND UNION COMMITMENT

While our discussion thus far has focused on leadership and employee commitment in traditional work settings, context matters, and leadership is also central within other types of organizations. One particular context is labor unions. Unions are 'fascinating organizations' (Klandermans, 1986, p. 199). Unlike traditional organizations, union leaders are elected based on votes from those they will represent, and exercise very little formal authority or power. Moreover, contrary to popular stereotypes, people are more likely to become union leaders out of a sense of obligation to the organization than any underlying ideological beliefs (Barling, 2014). In this section, we discuss the link between union leadership and members' commitment to the union, defined as an attitude of loyalty and feeling of responsibility toward the union, a willingness to exert effort on behalf of the union, as well as a belief in union goals (Fullagar and Barling, 1987).

Kelloway and Barling (1993) investigated the influence of shop stewards' transformational leadership on union members' commitment and voluntary participation in union-related activities. Data were obtained from two different samples in a large government union in Canada; the first consisted of 202 clerical and maintenance employees, and the second comprised of 147 guards and rehabilitation staff in a correctional institution. Perceptions of shop stewards' transformational leadership predicted different aspects of union commitment – namely, loyalty and responsibility to the union, and a willingness to work for the union – which in turn influenced members' union participation (Kelloway and Barling, 1993). Similarly, Fullagar et al. (1992) found that two components of union leaders' transformational leadership – namely, intellectual stimulation and individualized consideration – positively related to members' attitudes toward the union and, in turn, positively associated to members' loyalty toward the union.

Focusing on union presidents, Hammer et al. (2009) examined the effects of internal leadership (for example, solving problems for, consulting with, and informing union members) and external leadership (for example, developing external political support for teachers and education) on members' commitment. Based on data from 3871 union members in 248 local teachers' unions, perceptions of union instrumentality and justice partially mediated the link between union presidents' internal leadership and members' loyalty and willingness to work for the union. Furthermore, perceptions of union instrumentality and justice fully mediated the association between union presidents' external leadership and union loyalty (Hammer et al., 2009). Thus, taking the literature on union leadership and commitment as one example, we suggest that the effects of leadership on commitment extend beyond traditional work organizations.

FUTURE DIRECTIONS

To end our discussion, we propose various opportunities to help further our understanding of the relationship between organizational leadership and employee commitment. In particular, we suggest that future research might focus on: (1) project teams; (2) leaders' rather than employees' commitment; and (3) methodological refinements that will allow for sturdier inferences to be made from the findings of the many studies that are conducted on the topic of leadership and commitment each year.

First, greater exploration of the effects of leadership on employee commitment other than to their employing organization is warranted, and we suggest that one such opportunity exists in exploring commitment in project teams. Being a member of a team, and a project team in particular, may sometimes be more relevant than being a member of an organization; project teams have specific characteristics that distinguish them from traditional work groups, such as their need to clarify goals and produce unique products, and function in complex organizational contexts, their greater levels of diversity, and their temporal nature, thus providing unique opportunities to study leadership in alternative settings (Byrne and Barling, 2015).

Keegan and Den Hartog's (2004) research on government employees showed that while subordinates did not perceive project and line managers' transformational leadership differently, only line managers' transformational leadership predicted line members' affective commitment. Refining this finding, de Poel et al. (2014) found that private sector project leaders' transformational leadership positively influenced team members' organizational commitment when organizational tenure diversity was high. These contradictory findings suggest that the characteristics unique to project teams may limit or enhance the effectiveness of project managers' leadership on employees' commitment, and more research is necessary to understand commitment within this context.

Second, while we have suggested throughout this chapter that more research is needed to examine how leadership influences the different facets of commitment, we also encourage scholars to shift their focus to leaders' organizational commitment. For example, while leadership seems to influence employee commitment, might leaders' own organizational commitment predict better-quality leadership? Following findings on employee commitment (e.g., Meyer et al., 1989), might leaders' affective and normative commitment translate into more positive leadership performance? And could continuance commitment predict negative leadership performance?

Finally, methodological and statistical improvements will place inferences about the causal effects of organizational leadership on employee commitment on more solid ground. There is considerable room in future research for greater reliance on longitudinal designs and multisource and/or mixed-methods approaches (Hunter et al., 2007). Similarly, causal inferences will be enhanced from laboratory studies using experimental designs. For example, an experimental field study by Barling et al. (1996) showed that transformational leadership training positively affected employees' organizational commitment.

CONCLUSION

Organizational scholars have long been interested in the nature and effects of organizational leadership; and interest in the nature, antecedents and consequences of organizational commitment can be traced back at least to the emergence of Meyer and Allen's three-component model of organizational commitment (e.g., Allen and Meyer, 1990). What we have learnt since then is that leadership quality remains one of the major antecedents of organizational commitment. Leaders serve as representatives of their organizations to their employees; faced with positive leadership, employees reciprocate with their affective, normative, and some aspects of continuance commitment to the organization. In contrast, exposed to negative leadership, employees are likely to withhold any commitment to their organizations.

REFERENCES

Allen, N.J. and Meyer, J.P. (1990). The measurement and antecedents of affective, continuance and normative commitment to the organization. *Journal of Occupational Psychology*, 63, 1–18.

Aryee, S., Chen, Z.X., Sun, L.Y., and Debrah, Y.A. (2007). Antecedents and outcomes of abusive supervision: test of a trickle-down model. *Journal of Applied Psychology*, 92, 191.

Avolio, B.J. and Luthans, F.W. (2006). *The High Impact Leader: Authentic, Resilient Leadership that Gets Results and Sustains Growth*. New York: McGraw Hill.

Barling, J. (2014). *The Science of Leadership: Lessons from Research for Organizational Leaders.* New York: Oxford University Press.

Barling, J., Weber, T., and Kelloway, E.K. (1996). Effects of transformational leadership training on attitudinal and financial outcomes: A field experiment. *Journal of Applied Psychology*, *81*, 827–832.

Bass, B.M. and Riggio, R.E. (2006). *Transformational Leadership* (2nd edn). Mahwah, NJ: Lawrence Erlbaum.

Beeri, I., Dayan, R., Vigoda-Gadot, E., and Werner, S.B. (2013). Advancing ethics in public organizations: The impact of an ethics program on employees' perceptions and behaviors in a regional council. *Journal of Business Ethics*, *112*, 59–78.

Bernhard, F. and O'Driscoll, M.P. (2011). Psychological ownership in small family-owned businesses: Leadership style and nonfamily-employees' work attitudes and behaviors. *Group and Organization Management*, *36*, 345–384.

Bobbio, A., Van Dierendonck, D., and Manganelli, A.M. (2012). Servant leadership in Italy and its relation to organizational variables. *Leadership*, *8*, 229–243.

Brown, M.E., Treviño, L.K., and Harrison, D.A. (2005). Ethical leadership: A social learning perspective for construct development and testing. *Organizational Behavior and Human Decision Processes*, *97*, 117–134.

Brunetto, Y., Shacklock, K., Bartram, T., Leggat, S.G., Farr-Wharton, R., Stanton, P., and Casimir, G. (2012). Comparing the impact of leader–member exchange, psychological empowerment and affective commitment upon Australian public and private sector nurses: Implications for retention. *International Journal of Human Resource Management*, *23*, 2238–2255.

Bučiūnienė, I. and Škudienė, V. (2008). Impact of leadership styles on employees' organizational commitment in Lithuanian manufacturing companies. *South East European Journal of Economics and Business*, *3*, 57–66.

Bycio, P., Hackett, R.D., and Allen, J.S. (1995). Further assessments of Bass's (1985) conceptualization of transactional and transformational leadership. *Journal of Applied Psychology*, *80*, 468–478.

Byrne, A. and Barling, J. (2015). Leadership and project management teams. In F. Chiocchi, E.K. Kelloway, and B. Hobbs (eds), *The Psychology of Project Teams: An Interdisciplinary Perspective* (pp. 137–163). New York: Oxford University Press.

Castro, C.B., Periñan, M.M., and Bueno, J.C. (2008). Transformational leadership and followers' attitudes: The mediating role of psychological empowerment. *International Journal of Human Resource Management*, *19*, 1842–1863.

Chan, S. and Mak, W.M. (2014). Transformational leadership, pride in being a follower of the leader and organizational commitment. *Leadership and Organization Development Journal*, *35*, 674–690.

Cheung, M.F. and Wu, W.P. (2012). Leader–member exchange and employee work outcomes in Chinese firms: The mediating role of job satisfaction. *Asia Pacific Business Review*, *18*, 65–81.

Conger, J.A. and Kanungo, R.N. (1998). *Charismatic Leadership in Organizations.* Thousand Oaks, CA: Sage Publications.

de Poel, F.M., Stoker, J.I., and Van der Zee, K.I. (2014). Leadership and organizational tenure diversity as determinants of project team effectiveness. *Group and Organization Management*, *39*, 532–560.

Felfe, J., Yan, W., and Six, B. (2008). The impact of individual collectivism on commitment and its influence on organizational citizenship behaviour and turnover in three countries. *International Journal of Cross Cultural Management*, *8*, 211–237.

Fullagar, C. and Barling, J. (1987). Toward a model of union commitment. In D. Lewin, D.B. Lipsby and D. Sockell (eds), *Advances in Industrial and Labor Relations* (pp. 43–78). Greenwich, CT: JAI Press.

Fullagar, C., McCoy, D., and Shull, C. (1992). The socialization of union loyalty. *Journal of Organizational Behavior*, *13*, 13–26.

Gabler, C.B., Nagy, K.R., and Hill, R.P. (2014). Causes and consequences of abusive supervision in sales management: A tale of two perspectives. *Psychology and Marketing*, *31*, 278–293.

Gillet, N. and Vandenberghe, C. (2014). Transformational leadership and organizational commitment: The mediating role of job characteristics. *Human Resource Development Quarterly*, *25*, 321–347.

Goodwin, V.L., Whittington, J.L., Murray, B., and Nichols, T. (2011). Moderator or mediator? Examining the role of trust in the transformational leadership paradigm. *Journal of Managerial Issues*, *23*(4), 409–425.

Graen, G.B. and Cashman, J. (1975). A role-making model of leadership in formal organizations: A developmental approach. In J.G. Hunt and L.L. Larson (eds), *Leadership Frontiers* (pp. 143–166). Kent, OH: Kent State University Press.

Greenleaf, R.K. (1970). *The Servant as Leader.* Newton Centre, MA: Robert K. Greenleaf Center.

Hammer, T.H., Bayazit, M., and Wazeter, D.L. (2009). Union leadership and member attitudes: A multi-level analysis. *Journal of Applied Psychology*, *94*, 392–410.

Hansen, S.D., Alge, B.J., Brown, M.E., Jackson, C.L., and Dunford, B.B. (2013). Ethical leadership: Assessing the value of a multifoci social exchange perspective. *Journal of Business Ethics*, *115*, 435–449.

House, R.J. (1977). A 1976 theory of charismatic leadership. In J.G. Hunt and L.L. Larsen (eds), *Leadership: The Cutting Edge* (pp. 189–207). Carbondale, IL: Southern Illinois University Press.

House, R.J. and Howell, J.M. (1992). Personality and charismatic leadership. *Leadership Quarterly*, *3*, 81–108.

Howell, J.M. (1988). Two faces of charisma: Socialized and personalized leadership in organizations. In J.A. Conger and R.N. Kanungo (eds), *Charismatic Leadership* (pp. 213–236). San Francisco, CA: Jossey Bass.

Hung, D.K.M., Ansari, M.A., and Aafaqi, R. (2004). Fairness of human resource management practices, leader–member exchange and organizational commitment. *Asian Academy of Management Journal*, *9*, 99–120.

Hunter, S.T., Bedell-Avers, K.E., and Mumford, M.D. (2007). The typical leadership study: Assumptions, implications, and potential remedies. *Leadership Quarterly*, *18*, 435–446.

Jackson, T., Meyer, J., and Wang, X. (2013). Leadership, commitment, and culture: A meta-analysis. *Journal of Leadership and Organizational Studies*, *20*, 84–106.

Keegan, A. and Den Hartog, D.N. (2004). Transformational leadership in a project-based environment: A comparative study of the leadership styles of project managers and line managers. *International Journal of Project Management*, *22*, 609–617.

Kelloway, E.K. and Barling, J. (1993). Members' participation in local union activities: Measurement, prediction, and replication. *Journal of Applied Psychology*, *78*, 262–279.

Klandermans, B. (1986). Psychology and trade union participation: Joining, acting, quitting. *Journal of Occupational Psychology*, *59*, 189–204.

Kottke, J.L., and Pelletier, K.L. (2013). Measuring and differentiating perceptions of supervisor and top leader ethics. *Journal of Business Ethics*, *113*, 415–428.

Lee, J. (2005). Effects of leadership and leader–member exchange on commitment. *Leadership and Organization Development Journal*, *26*, 655–672.

Leroy, H., Palanski, M.E., and Simons, T. (2012). Authentic leadership and behavioral integrity as drivers of follower commitment and performance. *Journal of Business Ethics*, *107*, 255–264.

Liden, R.C., Wayne, S.J., and Sparrowe, R.T. (2000). An examination of the mediating role of psychological empowerment on the relations between the job, interpersonal relationships, and work outcomes. *Journal of Applied Psychology*, *85*, 407–416.

Liden, R.C., Wayne, S.J., Zhao, H., and Henderson, D. (2008). Servant leadership: Development of a multidimensional measure and multi-level assessment. *Leadership Quarterly*, *19*, 161–177.

Liu, Y. and Ipe, M. (2010). The impact of organizational and leader–member support on expatriate commitment. *International Journal of Human Resource Management*, *21*, 1035–1048.

Lo, M.C., Ramayah, T., Min, H.W., and Songan, P. (2010). The relationship between leadership styles and organizational commitment in Malaysia: Role of leader–member exchange. *Asia Pacific Business Review*, *16*, 79–103.

Martinko, M.J., Harvey, P., Brees, J.R., and Mackey, J. (2013). A review of abusive supervision research. *Journal of Organizational Behavior*, *34*, 120–137.

McGee, G.W. and Ford, R.C. (1987). Two (or more?) dimensions of organizational commitment: Reexamination of the affective and continuance commitment scales. *Journal of Applied Psychology*, *72*, 638–641.

Mendelson, M.B., Turner, N., and Barling, J. (2011). Perceptions of the presence and effectiveness of high involvement work systems and their relationship to employee attitudes: A test of competing models. *Personnel Review*, *40*, 45–69.

Meyer, J.P., Paunonen, S.V., Gellatly, I.R., Goffin, R.D., and Jackson, D.N. (1989). Organizational commitment and job performance: It's the nature of the commitment that counts. *Journal of Applied Psychology*, *74*, 152–156.

Michaelis, B., Stegmaier, R., and Sonntag, K. (2009). Affective commitment to change and innovation implementation behavior: The role of charismatic leadership and employees' trust in top management. *Journal of Change Management*, *9*, 399–417.

Mowday, R.T., Steers, R.M., and Porter, L.W. (1979). The measurement of organizational commitment. *Journal of Vocational Behavior*, *14*, 224–247.

Neubert, M.J., Carlson, D.S., Kacmar, K.M., Roberts, J.A., and Chonko, L.B. (2009). The virtuous influence of ethical leadership behavior: Evidence from the field. *Journal of Business Ethics*, *90*, 157–170.

Nguni, S., Sleegers, P., and Denessen, E. (2006). Transformational and transactional leadership effects on teachers' job satisfaction, organizational commitment, and organizational citizenship behavior in primary schools: The Tanzanian case. *School Effectiveness and School Improvement*, *17*, 145–177.

Peus, C., Wesche, J.S., Streicher, B., Braun, S., and Frey, D. (2012). Authentic leadership: An empirical test of its antecedents, consequences, and mediating mechanisms. *Journal of Business Ethics*, *107*, 331–348.

Pierro, A., Raven, B.H., Amato, C., and Bélanger, J.J. (2013). Bases of social power, leadership styles, and organizational commitment. *International Journal of Psychology*, *48*, 1122–1134.

Pillai, R., Schriesheim, C.A., and Williams, E.S. (1999). Fairness perceptions and trust as mediators for transformational and transactional leadership: A two-sample study. *Journal of Management*, *25*, 897–933.

Rafferty, A.E. and Griffin, M.A. (2004). Dimensions of transformational leadership: Conceptual and empirical extensions. *Leadership Quarterly*, *15*, 329–354.

Rousseau, V. and Aubé, C. (2014). The reward–performance relationship in work teams: The role of leader behaviors and team commitment. *Group Processes and Intergroup Relations*, *17*, 645–662.

Rowden, R.W. (2000). The relationship between charismatic leadership behaviors and organizational commitment. *Leadership and Organization Development Journal*, *21*, 30–35.

Schaubroeck, J., Lam, S.S., and Peng, A.C. (2011). Cognition-based and affect-based trust as mediators of leader behavior influences on team performance. *Journal of Applied Psychology*, *96*, 863–871.

Schneider, S.K. and George, W.M. (2011). Servant leadership versus transformational leadership in voluntary service organizations. *Leadership and Organization Development Journal*, *32*, 60–77.

Schriesheim, C.A., Castro, S.L., and Cogliser, C.C. (1999). Leader–member exchange (LMX) research: A comprehensive review of theory, measurement, and data-analytic practices. *Leadership Quarterly*, *10*, 63–113.

Simola, S.K., Barling, J., and Turner, N. (2010). Transformational leadership and leader moral orientation: Contrasting an ethic of justice and an ethic of care. *Leadership Quarterly*, *21*, 179–188.

Simons, T.L. (2002). Behavioral integrity: The perceived alignment between managers' words and deeds as a research focus. *Organization Science*, *13*, 18–35.

Tepper, B. (2000). Consequences of abusive supervision. *Academy of Management Journal*, *43*, 178–190.

Tepper, B.J. (2007). Abusive supervision in work organizations: Review, synthesis, and research agenda. *Journal of Management*, *33*, 261–289.

Tepper, B., Henle, C.A., Lambert, L.S., Giacalone, R.A., and Duffy, M.K. (2008). Abusive supervision and subordinates' organization deviance. *Journal of Applied Psychology*, *93*, 721–732.

Turner, N., Barling, J., Epitropaki, O., Butcher, V., and Milner, C. (2002). Transformational leadership and moral reasoning. *Journal of Applied Psychology*, *87*, 304–311.

van Dierendonck, D., Stam, D., Boersma, P., de Windt, N., and Alkema, J. (2014). Same difference? Exploring the differential mechanisms linking servant leadership and transformational leadership to follower outcomes. *Leadership Quarterly*, *25*, 544–562.

Viator, R.E. (2001). The relevance of transformational leadership to nontraditional accounting services: Information systems assurance and business consulting. *Journal of Information Systems*, *15*, 99–125.

Walumbwa, F.O., Orwa, B., Wang, P., and Lawler, J.J. (2005). Transformational leadership, organizational commitment, and job satisfaction: A comparative study of Kenyan and US financial firms. *Human Resource Development Quarterly*, *16*, 235–256.

Walumbwa, F.O., Wang, P., Lawler, J.J., and Shi, K. (2004). The role of collective efficacy in the relations between transformational leadership and work outcomes. *Journal of Occupational and Organizational Psychology*, *77*, 515–530.

23. Employee empowerment and organizational commitment
Heather K. Laschinger, Emily Read and Junhong Zhu

Structural and psychological empowerment are related forms of empowerment that have both been recognized as important drivers of employee commitment across a range of industries, including the public sector, hospitality services, and healthcare (Ahmad and Oranye, 2010; Joo and Shim, 2010; Laschinger et al., 2009a; Namasivayam et al., 2014; Raub and Robert, 2013; Spreitzer, 1995). Structural empowerment refers to socio-cultural conditions in the workplace that enable employees to accomplish their work in meaningful ways (Kanter, 1977). Psychological empowerment, on the other hand, refers to employees' cognitive responses to working in environments structured in this way (Kraimer et al., 1999). Thus, managers wishing to create a psychologically empowered workforce can use structurally empowering management practices to achieve this goal. Research has supported the proposition that structural empowerment is an important contextual antecedent of psychological empowerment (Faulkner and Laschinger, 2008; Laschinger et al., 2001; Stewart et al., 2010) and that both forms of empowerment are associated with higher employee commitment to their organization (Cho et al., 2006; DeCicco et al., 2006; Laschinger et al., 2001; Najafi et al., 2011). Although both forms of empowerment are important, most of the studies linking structural empowerment to commitment have been conducted within the realm of healthcare, and nursing in particular. Therefore, this chapter will focus on summarizing research linking workplace empowerment and organizational commitment in nursing and healthcare settings.

EMPOWERMENT AND COMMITMENT IN HEALTHCARE

Healthcare delivery systems depend on a healthy committed workforce to ensure high-quality patient care. Nurses represent the largest occupational group in the healthcare workforce and understanding factors that contribute to their work effectiveness and workplace well-being are important to sustaining stable healthcare delivery systems around the world. Workplaces that empower nurses to practise according to their professional standards have been shown to be important for nurses' responses to their work (Laschinger et al., 2004). Nurses' sense of empowerment in their workplace is related to job satisfaction and organizational commitment (Laschinger et al., 2009a), which in turn discourage organizational turnover. Nursing turnover is costly for healthcare organizations, both financially and in terms of poor patient outcomes (Hayes et al., 2006). Therefore, it behoves nursing management to make every effort to create empowering nursing work environments that foster higher levels of organizational commitment among nurses in order to sustain stable work environments that support high-quality care.

THEORETICAL FOUNDATIONS

Organizational Commitment

Meyer and Allen (1991) described a model of employee organizational commitment consisting of three interrelated aspects of employees' mindsets about their relationship with their workplace: affective, normative, and continuance commitment. These components are described in detail elsewhere (see Chapter 3 in this volume).

Research has shown that each of the three components of commitment are correlated with one another. In their meta-analysis, Meyer et al. (2002) found that affective and normative commitment tended to be highly correlated, whereas continuance commitment was only weakly correlated with the other commitment components. They suggest that affective and normative commitment may reflect internal motivational processes (sense of belonging, enjoying one's work, and a desire to be loyal), whereas continuance commitment may reflect external motivational processes (avoiding punishments or seeking rewards such as financial gain) (Meyer et al., 2004). Employees are thought to have differential combinations of the three components of commitment which influences their work attitudes and behaviours. Recent work has shown that different profiles of employee commitment result in different organizational outcomes, such as need satisfaction and work engagement (Meyer et al., 2013). In nursing, affective-dominant commitment profiles are associated with more positive work unit relationships and lower turnover than continuance-dominant profiles (Gellatly et al., 2014).

Research has shown that positive workplace conditions play an important role in employee commitment to their place of employment (Meyer et al., 2002). For instance, transformational leadership behaviours, organizational justice, and organizational support were the strongest predictors of organizational commitment in Meyer et al.'s (2002) meta-analysis of 155 independent samples. These workplace characteristics have also been associated with both structural and psychological empowerment (Kanter, 1977; Spreitzer, 1995). It is reasonable to expect that work environments that enable employees to accomplish their work in meaningful ways (structural empowerment) and the subsequent positive motivational response to these conditions (psychological empowerment) are likely to result in strong feelings of accomplishment and satisfaction and, ultimately, higher levels of positive commitment. In other words, workplace empowerment is a logical driving force behind employee commitment.

Workplace Empowerment Theory

The notion of organizational empowerment addresses employees' sense of power and agency within their organization (Laschinger et al., 2001). There are two theoretical approaches to empowerment in the organizational literature. The structural approach (Kanter, 1977, 1993) describes organizational conditions within work settings that facilitate employees' ability to accomplish their work, such as access to information, support, resources, and development opportunities to be effective (Kanter, 1979). The other approach, psychological empowerment, focuses on employees' internal motivational orientations to their work as reflected by four key cognitions: meaning, competence, self-determination, and impact (Conger and Kanungo, 1988; Spreitzer, 1995).

Kanter (1977) was the first theorist to propose the notion of empowerment in the organizational literature (Seibert et al., 2011). Kanter's (1977, 1993) theory of structural empowerment describes how workplace conditions influence employees' ability to accomplish their work in meaningful ways. These conditions include having access to social structures in the workplace that provide information, support, resources required to do the job, and opportunities for learning and development. Access to these empowerment structures is facilitated by formal and informal systems within the work environment. For example, formal power may arise from jobs that are intentionally designed to be visible and central to the organization's goals and allow flexibility, while informal power comes from job characteristics such as positive relationships with leaders and co-workers which are not typically mandated by the organization. According to Kanter, structural empowerment is amenable to management practices targeted at increasing employees' level of power to accomplish work goals.

Although originally developed in the general management literature, most of the empirical research related to Kanter's empowerment model has been in nursing and healthcare (Laschinger et al., 2001). Structural empowerment has been significantly associated with numerous organizational outcomes, such as job performance (Wong and Laschinger, 2013), satisfaction (Laschinger et al., 2004), organizational commitment (Laschinger et al., 2009a), and turnover (Laschinger et al., 2004). It has also been linked to health outcomes in numerous studies, such as lower burnout and better health (Laschinger et al., 2009b; Laschinger and Grau, 2012a; Laschinger et al., 2013). Positive leadership practices have been a consistent predictor of nurses' perceptions of structurally empowering work environments (Lucas et al., 2008; Young-Ritchie et al., 2009) and subsequent outcomes, including job satisfaction (Wong and Laschinger, 2013), organizational commitment (Laschinger et al., 2009a), and patient care quality (Laschinger and Fida, 2015).

From this theoretical perspective, structural empowerment of employees is manifested by their perceived access to these social empowerment structures in their work settings. Thus, structural empowerment was regarded as an indicator of employee empowerment in general (Seibert et al., 2011). More recently, structural empowerment has come to be seen as a contextual antecedent to employees' feelings of being empowered to be effective in their jobs (Laschinger et al., 2004; Morgeson and Campion, 2003; Spreitzer, 2008).

Thomas and Velthouse (1990) were the first to propose the concept of psychological empowerment to explain employees' sense of agency in the workplace. Psychological empowerment refers to a set of four intrinsically motivating cognitions that reflect an employee's active orientation to the work role (Thomas and Velthouse, 1990; Spreitzer, 1995). The dimensions of psychological empowerment are: (1) meaning (congruence between work goals and an employee's beliefs, values, and behaviors); (2) competence (confidence in one's ability to perform their job well); (3) self-determination (feelings of control and autonomy regarding one's work); and (4) impact (a sense of being able to influence important outcomes within the organization) (Spreitzer, 1995). Employees who are psychologically empowered feel that they can and want to help craft their work role and context.

Psychological empowerment has been linked to work engagement (Macsinga et al., 2015), employee performance (Maynard et al., 2014), organizational citizenship behaviours (Auh et al., 2014), organizational commitment (Raub and Robert, 2013), and better

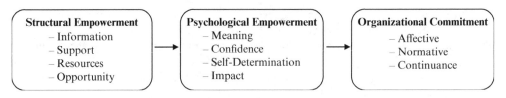

Figure 23.1   Organizing theoretical framework

mental health (Srivastava and Singh, 2013). In nursing, psychological empowerment is related to lower job strain and higher job satisfaction (Laschinger et al., 2004; Laschinger et al., 2009a; Laschinger et al., 2009b; Manojlovich and Laschinger, 2002), lower burnout (Boudrias et al., 2012), and higher ratings of patient care quality (Purdy et al., 2010).

Current theoretical conceptualizations of workplace empowerment have incorporated both forms of empowerment into explanations of how empowerment influences employee experiences at work (Seibert et al., 2011; Spreitzer, 2008). That is, psychological empowerment is viewed as the mechanism by which structural empowerment influences outcomes (Seibert et al., 2011; Spreitzer, 2008). Psychological empowerment is a logical outcome of structural empowerment (Laschinger et al., 2001; Spreitzer, 2008). Working conditions that provide employees with power to accomplish their work in meaningful ways understandably lead to a greater sense of meaning, self-determination, and impact at work. This association between structural and psychological empowerment has been supported in several nursing studies (DeCicco et al., 2006; Laschinger et al., 2001; Manojlovich and Laschinger, 2002; Wagner et al., 2010). Psychological empowerment is considered the mediating mechanism whereby structural empowerment influences organizational outcomes (Laschinger et al., 2001; Morgeson and Campion, 2003; Spreitzer, 2008). This broader theoretical perspective of empowerment was used to review studies linking organizational commitment to workplace empowerment. Figure 23.1 illustrates the theoretical framework guiding our review of empowerment and commitment in healthcare.

EMPIRICAL FINDINGS

In healthcare and nursing, structural and psychological empowerment have been linked to all three types of organizational commitment. Studies have mostly focused on affective commitment, less often on normative commitment, and rarely on continuance commitment. This may be because of the large body of work demonstrating the value of affective organizational commitment and, possibly, the perception that continuance commitment is the least amenable to change.

The link between empowerment and affective organizational commitment has been examined in numerous studies in healthcare settings. Overall, these studies have shown that nurses and other healthcare workers have moderate levels of affective commitment, with average scores of 4.07 (3.14–4.89) on a seven-point scale (Brunetto et al., 2012; Caykoylu et al., 2011; Cho et al., 2006; Farr-Wharton et al., 2012; DeCicco et al., 2006; Laschinger et al., 2001; Laschinger et al., 2009a; Laschinger et al., 2000; Laschinger et al., 2009b; McDermott et al., 1996; Smith et al., 2010; Wilson and Laschinger, 1994; Yang et al., 2014; Young-Ritchie et al., 2009). Affective commitment levels of nurses appear to be similar across cultures. These levels are somewhat higher than in other occupations (average of 3.86 on a seven-point scale) (Ackfeldt and Malhotra, 2013; Bordin et al., 2007; Chen et al., 2011; Daily and Bishop, 2003; Fisher, 2014; Gohar et al., 2015; Jha, 2011; Kazlauskaite et al., 2012; Raub and Robert, 2013; Sawalha et al., 2012). This may reflect differences between healthcare professionals and other occupations studied in the general management literature.

Past studies consistently revealed moderately strong positive relationships between structural empowerment and affective commitment (Ackfeldt and Malhotra, 2013; Bordin et al., 2007; Daily and Bishop, 2003; Fisher, 2014; Jha, 2011; Kazlauskaite et al., 2012; Sawalha et al., 2012) (average $r = .52$; range .40 to .77). Of the four sources of structural empowerment described by Kanter (1977, 1993), support was most strongly correlated to nurses' affective commitment in the studies we reviewed (average $r = .43$), followed by information ($r = .37$), resources ($r = .33$), and opportunity ($r = .32$). Similar associations have been reported in non-healthcare settings (average $r = .50$ across seven studies; range .23–.71) (Ackfeldt and Malhotra, 2013; Bordin et al., 2007; Daily and Bishop, 2003; Fisher, 2014; Jha, 2011; Kazlauskaite et al., 2012; Sawalha et al., 2012). This suggests that regardless of occupation, structural empowerment, particularly access to support, is important to employees' feelings of belonging in their workplaces and willingness to be involved in organizational life (organizational commitment). These findings are important because they imply that employee commitment may be influenced by management strategies targeted at increasing structural empowerment.

Similarly, affective commitment has been positively correlated to psychological empowerment in six healthcare studies (average $r = .42$) (Brunetto et al., 2012; Dahinten et al., 2014; DeCicco et al., 2006; Farr-Wharton et al., 2012; Laschinger et al., 2009a; Smith et al., 2010), and three studies of workers in other occupations (average $r = .55$) (Chen et al., 2011; Gohar et al., 2015; Kazlauskaite et al., 2012). The magnitude of these relationships is similar to those with structural empowerment. These findings may reflect overlap between structural and psychological empowerment. We could find no study that included both in the same analysis. On the other hand, the findings may suggest that fostering both types of empowerment in organizations may be a way of building and sustaining affective commitment. Given research supporting the importance of structural empowerment in creating a sense of psychological empowerment among employees, managerial strategies to foster structural empowerment are a logical first step to increasing psychological empowerment and, ultimately, affective commitment. Further research is needed to tease out the roles played by structural and psychological empowerment in building affective commitment.

Normative commitment has not been widely studied in nursing and healthcare. We located one study by Yang et al. (2014), who found that normative commitment was strongly positively correlated to structural empowerment ($r = .51$). The magnitude of this relationship is similar to those found between empowerment and affective commitment. This makes sense given that affective commitment and normative commitment are highly correlated (Meyer et al., 2002). Outside of nursing, Jha (2011) found that psychological empowerment was significantly related to normative commitment ($r = .34$), similar in magnitude to the correlation found between structural empowerment and affective commitment. The consistency is not surprising given the strong association between structural and psychological empowerment (Wagner et al., 2010). This suggests that management strategies to increase both structural and psychological empowerment are likely to result in higher normative commitment.

Continuance commitment also has been less frequently studied in relation to empowerment. We found only two studies in healthcare and one in non-healthcare settings examining this relationship. These studies had mixed results. For example, Laschinger et al. (2000) found that empowerment was weakly and negatively related to continuance commitment ($r = -.13$). On the other hand, Yang et al. (2014), using a different measure of continuance commitment, found a positive correlation ($r = .33$). Moderately high levels of continuance commitment (4.4 out of 7) were reported in the nursing studies (Laschinger et al., 2000; Laschinger et al., 2001). These levels may reflect the tight job market in nursing settings and the relative lack of alternative nursing employment opportunities in financially constrained healthcare settings. Outside of nursing, Jha (2011) found a weak negative correlation between psychological empowerment and continuance commitment ($r = -.13$). The positive relationship between empowerment and continuance commitment is perplexing, given Meyer et al.'s (2002) findings that continuance commitment tended to be negatively associated with positive outcomes, such as overall job satisfaction, satisfaction with co-workers and supervisor, and job performance. Further research is needed to explore this phenomenon more fully.

In summary, the relationships between affective commitment and empowerment are well established. Less is known about the relationships between empowerment and normative and continuance commitment. Too little research is available to draw conclusions about the relationships of empowerment to these latter forms of organizational commitment.

EMPOWERMENT AS A PREDICTOR OF COMMITMENT

Several studies have shown that empowerment is a mechanism through which organizational factors influence commitment. For instance, considerable evidence exists to suggest that leadership is important to building organizational commitment (Meyer et al., 2004: see Chapter 22 in this volume). Leaders shape qualities of the work environment that influence how well employees are able to accomplish their work (Cummings et al., 2010; Laschinger et al., 1999). Assuming most workers are motivated to do their best in their jobs, working in settings that promote work effectiveness is likely to result in higher job satisfaction and greater commitment to the organization. Leadership has been linked to both structural and psychological empowerment in numerous studies (Amundsen and Martinsen, 2015; Chen et al., 2011; Fong and Snape, 2015; Laschinger and Fida, 2015; Laschinger et al., 2009a; Laschinger et al., 2013). Leaders who are empowering are thought to share power with employees by involving them in decisions, providing them with autonomy in their work, and encouraging accountability and trust, resulting in positive responses to the workplace (Kirkman and Rosen, 1999).

Several studies have shown that leaders influence employee commitment through their effect on workplace empowerment (both structural and psychological). Young-Ritchie et al. (2009) found that emotionally intelligent nurse manager behaviours influenced emergency nurses' affective commitment through their effects on structural empowerment.

They argued that emotionally intelligent leaders were likely to be sensitive to what nurses need to provide high-quality care and therefore ensured that empowering working conditions were in place. As a result, nurses felt more committed to their organization. Similarly, Laschinger et al. (2009a) found that unit-level leader–follower relationship quality influenced individual nurses' affective commitment through its effect on unit-level structural empowerment and individual nurses' feelings of psychological empowerment. This study demonstrated how the organizational context created by leaders (unit empowerment) influenced individual team members' sense of empowerment, which in turn influenced affective organizational commitment. This finding is similar to those of Farr-Wharton et al. (2012) and Brunetto et al. (2012) who linked leader–follower relationship quality to commitment through nurses' psychological empowerment.

Chen et al. (2011) further corroborated these relationships in a controlled study demonstrating that empowering leadership practices had a strong positive effect on both psychological empowerment and affective commitment, which in turn resulted in greater teamwork and lower turnover intentions. Both structural and psychological empowerment were significantly related to affective commitment in this study. Daily and Bishop (2003) found similar effects of empowering management practices in a quality improvement study. Empowerment strategies such as managerial support, training, rewards, and teamwork resulted in greater feelings of psychological empowerment, and subsequently, higher levels of organizational commitment. These studies suggest that leaders play an important role in influencing employees' affective commitment by creating work environments that promote both structural and psychological empowerment of employees, and support the proposition that workplace empowerment is an important mediator of the influence of leadership practices on employee commitment.

Workplace empowerment in hospital settings has been found to influence healthcare workers' affective organizational commitment through its effect on aspects of work satisfaction (Caykoylu et al., 2011). Caykoylu et al. reasoned that structural empowerment signals to employees that they are trusted by management to make decisions regarding how their work is performed, leading them to feel satisfied with their work. Logically, employees who are satisfied with their work are more likely to feel a sense of affective commitment to their organization, although there is no consensus about the causal direction of this relationship (Meyer et al., 2002). Structural empowerment was found to have a direct positive effect on hospital employees' career advancement satisfaction and satisfaction with their supervisor, which in turn positively influenced affective commitment. Meyer et al.'s study provides further support for the role of empowerment in shaping specific facets of job satisfaction that result in greater affective commitment. The authors recommend empowerment as an important motivational strategy for management.

The influence of individual difference factors on empowerment and commitment has received less attention in the literature. In a study testing the relative effects of personal and organizational factors on employee commitment, Laschinger et al. (2009a) found that psychological empowerment mediated the effect of core self-evaluation (CSE) – an intrapersonal resource consisting of self-esteem, locus of control, emotional stability, and self-efficacy – on staff nurses' affective commitment. This study showed that both individual difference variables (CSE) and a situational variable (structural empowerment) influenced organizational commitment through psychological empowerment, although the indirect effect of structural empowerment on commitment was stronger than that of

CSE. Macsinga et al. (2015) also found that psychological empowerment was a significant predictor of affective organizational commitment above and beyond age and personality characteristics, such as extraversion and conscientiousness. However, the effect of psychological empowerment was stronger than that of individual difference variables. In other words, regardless of age and personality, employees' psychological responses to their work (psychological empowerment) are critical to generating affective organizational commitment.

Finally, there is some evidence that there are generational differences in the effect of empowerment on commitment. In a cross-sectional study, Farr-Wharton et al. (2012) found that younger nurses (Generation Y, born 1980–2000) had lower levels of both psychological empowerment and affective commitment than older nurses (Generation X, born 1962–1979; and Baby Boomers, born 1946–1961). The relationship between psychological empowerment and affective commitment was also weaker for younger nurses than their older counterparts. These findings suggest that nurses in different generational cohorts may view and value work in different ways, which may influence their perceptions of psychological empowerment and their commitment to their organization. However, it may also be the case that years of experience, rather than generation, are the driving factor of commitment. Therefore, further research is needed to explore these relationships more fully.

In summary, empowerment appears to be an important driver of commitment, both directly and indirectly. Structural empowerment is a leadership strategy that can influence psychological empowerment and ultimately organizational commitment. By building high-quality relationships with employees and creating positive, empowering working conditions characterized by access to the resources, support, and information needed to accomplish one's work (structural empowerment), leaders can foster psychological empowerment, which in turn appears to result in employees feeling committed to their job and organization. Although personal characteristics have been found to influence empowerment and commitment, more research is needed to understand the nature of these effects.

IMPLICATIONS FOR MANAGEMENT

A key aspect of healthcare managers' role is to create work environment conditions that empower nurses to provide the best possible care for their clients or patients according to their professional standards (Laschinger, 2008). The strong relationship between empowerment and commitment found in studies reviewed in this chapter suggests that managers can employ structural empowerment strategies to increase commitment among nurses. Structural empowerment has been shown to be positively related to two dimensions of organizational commitment – affective commitment and normative commitment – but negatively related to the third dimension, continuance commitment. Thus, strategies to increase access to the different components of Kanter's structural empowerment model provide a practical approach for nursing managers to empower nurses and enhance their organizational commitment in healthcare settings.

Laschinger and Grau (2012b) describe ways in which management can create empowering work environments based on Kanter's workplace empowerment theory. Given the strong relationships between structural empowerment and psychological empowerment demonstrated in the literature, it is reasonable to expect that strategies to increase structural empowerment are likely to increase psychological empowerment and ultimately organizational commitment. The evidence suggests that affective organizational commitment may be the most important focus for managers. While normative and continuance commitment are still important, studies have shown that, regardless of normative and continuance commitment levels, when affective commitment is low, employees tend to be dissatisfied with their job and have high job turnover intentions. On the other hand, when affective commitment is high, employees tend to be more satisfied with their job and have low intentions to leave (Gellatly et al., 2014; Meyer et al., 2013). Moreover, of the three types of commitment, affective commitment is most likely to be influenced by empowerment. Therefore, the following strategies will focus primarily on structural empowerment strategies that managers can use to promote affective organizational commitment among employees.

Access to Information

One empowerment strategy involves providing nurses with timely and transparent information. It is essential for management to clearly and effectively communicate organizational goals so that staff will understand the current status of the organization and the vision for the future. Additionally, providing open access to technical knowledge will help nurses perform their job more effectively. To accomplish the goal of open access to information, it is advisable for leaders to use multiple methods of communication with staff (for example, staff meetings, 'huddles', emails, and newsletters). In addition, building positive relationships with staff through relational (versus merely transactional) leadership styles may help leaders to communicate more effectively with employees, leading to greater feelings of emotional attachment to their job and organization (Gellatly et al., 2014).

Access to Support

Another empowerment strategy is to provide nurses with ongoing support in the work environment. In day-to-day operations, nurse managers should make themselves visible on their units and be available to meet with employees, providing them with opportunities to discuss concerns. Nurses should also be provided with recognition and applauded for their achievements in a timely manner. In addition, it is important for managers to encourage collaboration and collegiality among staff and provide access to helpful people when needed. By providing formal and informal support in these ways, managers help employees accomplish their work and help meet their emotional and social needs, which are likely to fortify positive feelings about their job and organization (affective commitment). Nurses at various career stages can benefit from different kinds of support that enhance their performance and job satisfaction. For example, comprehensive orientation programmes for new graduate nurses as well as mentorship opportunities throughout their development to ease the transition to professional practice. Similarly, more experienced nurses transitioning to a new job or clinical area may benefit from orientation and mentoring tailored to their individual needs. As nurses become more experienced, greater autonomy and decision-making should be encouraged. Leaders can also offer support by discussing internal career advancement opportunities and supporting staff in their pursuit of personal and professional goals. These supports are likely to provide a greater sense of belonging in the workforce and go a long way towards increasing their commitment to the organization.

Access to Resources

Providing adequate resources is vital to ensure that nurses are able to perform their jobs effectively. These resources involve adequate unit staffing, including any necessary support staff. During this time of growing budgetary constraints, facilitating access to resources may be difficult. However, managers can encourage nurses to interpret workload data as a necessary part of decision-making and involve nurses in resource decision-making and evaluation of supplies to assure quality.

Access to Opportunities to Learn and Grow

It is important for leaders to encourage and facilitate advanced education and lifelong learning for staff, and to support professional training and development opportunities that meet employees' needs for fulfillment and growth. These development-oriented management practices empower employees by promoting increased autonomy and competence, leading to greater feelings of control, meaning, and impact, and enhancing feelings of commitment. Additionally, by practising relational-focused leadership and getting to know employees' career goals and plans, managers can help meet the needs of both employees and organizations through leadership development and succession planning (Gellatly et al., 2014).

Theoretically, these empowering workplace strategies derived from Kanter's theory should result in greater psychological empowerment characterized by higher levels of job meaningfulness, competence, self-determination, and sense of being able to make an impact among employees. In other words, by creating environments that are both structurally and psychologically empowering, healthcare managers contribute to employee well-being and, ultimately, higher levels of organizational commitment.

From a practical standpoint, the Conditions of Work Effectiveness Questionnaire-II (Laschinger et al., 2001) provides a valid and reliable self-report questionnaire that organizations could use to assess employees' perceptions of structural empowerment at work. These results could be used to help managers understand employees' needs and improve access to information, support, resources, and opportunities for professional growth that they value and need to accomplish their work. Similarly, Spreitzer's Psychological Empowerment Scale (Spreitzer, 1995) can be used to assess and monitor psychological empowerment. Both measures have been shown to have strong reliability and validity (Kraimer et al., 1999; Laschinger et al., 2001; Spreitzer, 1995). Moreover, empowerment could be measured periodically, allowing managers to monitor changes in empowerment over time. This may be especially important during times of institutional change or restructuring.

DIRECTIONS FOR FUTURE RESEARCH

Despite considerable evidence linking workplace empowerment, particularly structural empowerment, to employee commitment in healthcare, less is known about the nature of this relationship in other industries. Therefore, future research examining this link in other occupations would add to our current knowledge about workplace empowerment and commitment. Seibert et al. (2011) called for research that incorporates both structural and psychological forms of empowerment to examine more fully how empowerment influences organizational outcomes, such as commitment. This review has uncovered promising evidence for the link between empowerment and organizational commitment. Further research using more robust research designs (longitudinal and experimental) is needed to provide evidence-based direction for management seeking to create an empowered and committed workforce.

CONCLUSION

Employee empowerment appears to play an important role in increasing positive organizational commitment in healthcare settings. Retaining high-quality employees and reducing costly turnover is an important priority for healthcare organizations as demands for high-quality care increase in a climate of financial constraint. Focusing on creating empowering work environments that promote positive organizational commitment is one way that healthcare leaders can have a positive impact on retaining valuable health human resources and ensure high-quality care in resource-challenged healthcare systems.

REFERENCES

Ackfeldt, A.L. and Malhotra, N. (2013). Revisiting the role stress–commitment relationship. *European Journal of Marketing*, 47(3–4), 353–374.

Ahmad, N. and Oranye, N.O. (2010). Empowerment, job satisfaction and organizational commitment: a comparative analysis of nurses working in Malaysia and England. *Journal of Nursing Management*, 18(5), 582–591.

Amundsen, S. and Martinsen, Ø.L. (2015). Linking empowering leadership to job satisfaction, work effort, and creativity: the role of self-leadership and psychological empowerment. *Journal of Leadership and Organizational Studies*, 22(3), 304–232.

Auh, S., Menguc, B., and Jung, Y.S. (2014). Unpacking the relationship between empowering leadership and service-oriented citizenship behaviors: A multilevel approach. *Journal of the Academy of Marketing Science*, 42(5), 558–579.

Bordin, C., Bartram, T., and Casimir, G. (2007). The antecedents and consequences of psychological empowerment among Singaporean IT employees. *Management Research News*, 30(1), 34–46.

Boudrias, J., Morin, A.J.S., and Brodeur, M. (2012), Role of psychological empowerment in the reduction of burnout in Canadian healthcare workers. *Nursing and Health Sciences*, 14(1), 8–17.

Brunetto, Y., Shacklock, K., Bartram, T., Leggat, S.G., Farr-Wharton, R., et al. (2012). Comparing the impact of leader–member exchange, psychological empowerment and affective commitment upon Australian public and private sector nurses: implications for retention. *International Journal of Human Resource Management*, 23(11), 2238–2255.

Caykoylu, S., Egri, C.P., Havlovic, S., and Bradley, C. (2011). Key organizational commitment antecedents for nurses, paramedical professionals and non-clinical staff. *Journal of Health Organization and Management*, 25(1), 7–33.

Chen, G., Sharma, P.N. Edinger, S.K., D.L. Shapiro, and Farh, J.L. (2011). Motivating and demotivating forces in teams: Cross-level influences of empowering leadership and relationship conflict. *Journal of Applied Psychology*, 96(3), 541–557.

Cho, J., Laschinger, H.K.S., and Wong, C.A. (2006). Workplace empowerment, work engagement and organizational commitment of new graduate nurses. *Nursing Leadership*, 19(3), 43–60.

Conger, J.A. and Kanungo, R.N. (1988). The empowerment process: Integrating theory and practice. *Academy of Management Review*, 13(3), 471–482.

Cummings, G.G., MacGregor, T., Davey, M., Lee, H., Wong, C.A., et al. (2010). Leadership styles and outcome patterns for the nursing workforce and work environment: a systematic review. *International Journal of Nursing Studies*, 47(3), 363–385.

Dahinten, V.S., MacPhee, M., Hejazi, S., Laschinger, H., Kazanjian, M., et al. (2014). Testing the effects of an empowerment-based leadership development programme: part 2–staff outcomes. *Journal of Nursing Management*, 22(1), 16–28.

Daily, B.F. and Bishop, J.W. (2003). TQM workforce factors and employee involvement: the pivotal role of teamwork. *Journal of Management Issues*, 15(4), 393–412.

DeCicco, J., Laschinger, H.K.S., and Kerr, M. (2006). Perceptions of empowerment and respect: effect on nurses' organizational commitment in nursing homes. *Journal of Gerontological Nursing*, 32(5), 49–56.

Farr-Wharton, R., Brunetto, Y., and Shacklock, K. (2012). The impact of intuition and supervisor–nurse relationships on empowerment and affective commitment by generation. *Journal of Advanced Nursing*, 68(6), 1391–1401.

Faulkner, J., and Laschinger, H. (2008). The effects of structural and psychological empowerment on perceived respect in acute care nurses. *Journal of Nursing Management*, 16(2), 214–221.

Fisher, D.M. (2014). A multilevel cross-cultural examination of role overload and organizational commitment: Investigating the interactive effects of context. *Journal Applied Psychology*, 99(4), 723–736.

Fong, K.H. and Snape, E. (2015). Empowering leadership, psychological empowerment and employee outcomes: Testing a multi-level mediating model. *British Journal of Management*, 26(1), 126–138.

Gellatly, I.R., Cowden, T.L., and Cummings, G.G. (2014). Staff nurse commitment, work relationships, and turnover intentions. *Nursing Research*, 63(3), 170–181.

Gohar, F.R., Bashir, M., Abrar, M., and Asghar, F. (2015). Effect of psychological empowerment, distributive justice and job autonomy on organizational commitment. *International Journal of Information, Business and Management*, 7(1), 144–173.

Hayes, L.J., O'Brien-Pallas, L., Duffield, C., Shamian, J., Buchan, J., et al. (2006). Nurse turnover: A literature review. *International Journal of Nursing Studies*, 43(2), 237–263.

Jha, S. (2011). Influence of psychological empowerment on affective, normative and continuance commitment. *Journal of Indian Business Research*, 3(4), 263–282.

Joo, B.K. and Shim, J.H. (2010). Psychological empowerment and organizational commitment: the moderating effect of organizational learning culture. *Human Resource Development International*, 13(4), 425–441.

Kanter, R.M. (1977). *Men and Women of the Corporation*. New York: Basic Books.

Kanter, R.M. (1979). Power failure in management circuits. *Harvard Business Review*, 57(4), 65–75.

Kanter, R.M. (1993). *Men and Women of the Corporation*. (2nd ed.). New York: Basic Books.

Kazlauskaite, R., Buciuniene, I. and Turauskas, L. (2012). Organisational and psychological empowerment in the HRM–performance linkage. *Employment Relations*, 34(2), 138–158.

Kirkman, B.L. and Rosen, B. (1999). Beyond self-management: Antecedents and consequences of team empowerment. *Academy of Management Journal*, 42, 58–74.

Kraimer, M.L., Seibert, S.E., and Liden, R.C. (1999). Psychological empowerment as a multidimensional construct: A test of construct validity. *Educational and Psychological Measurement*, 59(1), 127–142.

Laschinger, H.K.S. (2008). Effect of empowerment on professional practice environments, work satisfaction, and patient care quality: Further testing the nursing worklife model. *Journal of Nursing Care Quality*, 23(4), 322–330.

Laschinger, H.K.S. and Fida, R. (2015). Linking nurses' perceptions of patient care quality to job satisfaction: The role of leadership and empowering professional practice environments. *Journal of Nursing Administration*, 45(5), 276–283.

Laschinger, H.K.S., Finegan, J., Shamian, J. and Casier, S. (2000). Organizational trust and empowerment in restructured healthcare settings: effects on staff nurse commitment. *Journal of Nursing Administration*, 30(9), 413–425.

Laschinger, H.K.S., Finegan, J., Shamian, J., and Wilk, P. (2001). Impact of structural and psychological empowerment on job strain in nursing work settings: expanding Kanter's model. *Journal of Nursing Administration*, 31(5), 260–272.

Laschinger, H.K.S., Finegan, J.E., Shamian, J., and Wilk, P. (2004). A longitudinal analysis of the impact of workplace empowerment on work satisfaction. *Journal of Organizational Behavior*, 25(4), 527–545.

Laschinger, H.K.S., Finegan, J., and Wilk, P. (2009a). Context matters: The impact of unit leadership and empowerment on nurses' organizational commitment. *Journal of Nursing Administration*, 39(5), 228–235.

Laschinger, H.K.S. and Grau, A. L. (2012a). The influence of personal dispositional factors and organizational resources on workplace violence, burnout, and health outcomes in new graduate nurses: A cross-sectional study. *International Journal of Nursing Studies*, *49*(3), 282–291.

Laschinger, H.K.S. and Grau, A. (2012b). Creating empowerment work environments to promote professional nursing practice. In J.I. Erickson, D.A. Jones, and M. Ditomassi (eds), *Fostering Nurse-led care: Professional Practice for the Bedside Leader from Massachusetts General Hospital* (pp. 39–63). Indianapolis, IN: Sigma Theta Tau International.

Laschinger, H.K.S., Leiter, M., Day, A., and Gilin, D. (2009b). Workplace empowerment, incivility, and burnout: Impact on staff nurse recruitment and retention outcomes. *Journal of Nursing Management*, *17*(3), 302–311.

Laschinger, H.K.S., Wong, C.A., and Grau, A.L. (2013). Authentic leadership, empowerment and burnout: a comparison in new graduates and experienced nurses. *Journal of Nursing Management*, *21*(3), 541–552.

Laschinger, H.K.S., Wong, C., McMahon, L., and Kaufmann, C. (1999). Leader behavior impact on staff nurse empowerment, job tension, and work effectiveness. *Journal of Nursing Administration*, *29*(5), 28–39.

Lucas, V., Laschinger, H.K.S., and Wong, C.A. (2008). The impact of emotional intelligent leadership on staff nurse empowerment: the moderating effect of span of control. *Journal of Nursing Management*, *16*(8), 964–973.

Macsinga, I., Sulea, C., Sârbescu, P., Fischmann, G., and Dumitru, C. (2015). Engaged, committed and helpful employees: the role of psychological empowerment. *Journal of Psychology: Interdisciplinary and Applied*, *149*(3), 263–276.

Manojlovich, M. and Laschinger, H.K.S. (2002). The relationship of empowerment and selected personality characteristics to nursing job satisfaction. *Journal of Nursing Administration*, *32*(11), 586–595.

Maynard, M.T., Luciano, M.M., D'Innocenzo, L., Mathieu, J.E., and Dean, M.D. (2014). Modeling time-lagged reciprocal psychological empowerment–performance relationships. *Journal of Applied Psychology*, *99*(6), 1244.

McDermott, K., Laschinger, H.K.S. and Shamian, J. (1996). Work empowerment and organizational commitment. *Nursing Management*, *27*(5), 44–47.

Meyer, J.P. and Allen, N.J. (1991). A three-component conceptualization of organizational commitment. *Human Resource Management Review*, *1*(1), 61–89.

Meyer, J.P., Becker, T.E., and Vandenberghe, C. (2004). Employee commitment and motivation: a conceptual analysis and integrative model. *Journal of Applied Psychology*, *89*(6), 991.

Meyer, J.P., Kam, C., Goldenberg, I., and Bremner, N.L. (2013). Organizational commitment in the military: Application of a profile approach. *Military Psychology*, *25*(4), 381.

Meyer, J.P., Stanley, D.J., Herscovitch, L. and Topolnytsky, L. (2002). Affective, continuance, and normative commitment to the organization: A meta-analysis of antecedents, correlates, and consequences. *Journal of Vocational Behavior*, *61*(1), 20–52.

Morgeson, F.P. and Campion, M.A. (2003). Work Design. In W. Borman, D. Ilgen, and R. Klimoski (eds). *Handbook of Psychology: Industrial and Organizational Psychology* (Vol. 12, pp. 423–452). Hoboken, NJ: Wiley.

Najafi, S., Noruzy, A., Azar, H.K., Nazari-Shirkouhi, S., and Dalvand, M.R. (2011). Investigating the relationship between organizational justice, psychological empowerment, job satisfaction, organizational commitment and organizational citizenship behavior: An empirical model. *African Journal of Business Management*, *5*(13), 5241–5248.

Namasivayam, K., Guchait, P., and Lei, P. (2014). The influence of leader empowering behaviors and employee psychological empowerment on customer satisfaction. *International Journal of Contemporary Hospitality Management*, *26*(1), 69–84.

Purdy, N., Laschinger, H.K.S., Finegan, J., Kerr, M., and Olivera, F. (2010). Effects of work environments on nurse and patient outcomes. *Journal of Nursing Management*, *18*(8), 901–913.

Raub, S., and Robert, C. (2013). Empowerment, organizational commitment, and voice: behavior in the hospitality industry evidence from a multinational sample. *Cornell Hospitality Quarterly*, *54*(2), 136–148.

Sawalha, N., Zaitouni, M., and ElSharif, A. (2012). Corporate culture dimensions associated with organizational commitment: an empirical study. *Journal of Applied Business Research*, *28*(5), 957–975.

Seibert, S.E., Wang, G., and Courtright, S.H. (2011). Antecedents and consequences of psychological and team empowerment in organizations: a meta-analytic review. *Journal of Applied Psychology*, *96*(5), 981.

Smith, L.M., Andrusyszyn, M.A., and Laschinger, H.K.S. (2010). Effects of workplace incivility and empowerment on newly-graduated nurses' organizational commitment. *Journal of Nursing Management*, *18*(8), 1004–1015.

Spreitzer, G.M. (1995). Psychological empowerment in the workplace: Dimensions, measurement, and validation. *Academy of Management Journal*, *38*(5), 1442–1465.

Spreitzer, G.M. (2008). Taking stock: A review of more than twenty years of research on empowerment at work. In J. Barling and C.L. Cooper (eds) *The Sage Handbook of Organizational Behaviour* (pp. 55–72). Trowbridge, UK: Cromwell Press.

Srivastava, U.R. and Singh, M. (2013). Linking job characteristics and mental health among middle level Indian managers: Testing the mediating role of psychological empowerment. *Psychological Studies, 58*(2), 188–200.

Stewart, J.G., McNulty, R., Griffin, M.T.Q., and Fitzpatrick, J.J. (2010). Psychological empowerment and structural empowerment among nurse practitioners. *Journal of the American Academy of Nurse Practitioners, 22*(1), 27–34.

Thomas, K.W. and Velthouse, B.A. (1990). Cognitive elements of empowerment: An 'interpretive' model of intrinsic task motivation. *Academy of Management Review, 15*(4), 666–681.

Wagner, J.I., Cummings, G., Smith, D.L., Olson, J., Anderson, L., and Warren, S. (2010). The relationship between structural empowerment and psychological empowerment for nurses: a systematic review. *Journal of Nursing Management, 18*(4), 448–462.

Wilson, B. and Laschinger, H.K.S. (1994). Staff nurse perception of job empowerment and organizational commitment: A test of Kanter's theory of structural power in organizations. *Journal of Nursing Administration, 24*(4S), 39–47.

Wong, C.A. and Laschinger, H.K.S. (2013). Authentic leadership, performance, and job satisfaction: the mediating role of empowerment. *Journal of Advanced Nursing, 69*(4), 947–959.

Yang, J., Liu, Y., Chen, Y., and Pan, X. (2014). The effect of structural empowerment and organizational commitment on Chinese nurses' job satisfaction. *Applied Nursing Research, 27*(3), 186–191.

Young-Ritchie, C., Laschinger, H.K.S., and Wong, C. (2009). The effects of emotionally intelligent leadership behaviour on emergency staff nurses' workplace empowerment and organizational commitment. *Nursing Leadership, 22*(1), 70–85.

24. Perceived organizational support

Florence Stinglhamber, Gaëtane Caesens, Laura Clark and Robert Eisenberger

Research on perceived organizational support began with the realization that organizational commitment may be a two-way street. In 1986, Eisenberger and his colleagues (Eisenberger et al., 1986) indeed proposed that, if many organizations are concerned with employees' commitment, employees are more interested in the organization's regard for them. They called these employees' inferences concerning the organization's regard for them 'perceived organizational support' (POS), which is defined as employees' perceptions concerning the extent to which the organization values their contributions and cares about their well-being (Eisenberger et al., 1986). According to organizational support theory (Rhoades and Eisenberger, 2002; Eisenberger and Stinglhamber, 2011), the formation of POS is promoted by employees' view of the organization as a powerful life-like being whose positive or negative orientation toward them influences how it treats them (Levinson, 1965).

Organizational support theory (Eisenberger et al., 1986; Eisenberger and Stinglhamber, 2011; Shore and Shore, 1995) considers the antecedents and consequences of POS. Concerning its antecedents, research has consistently shown that POS develops based on the receipt of favorable job conditions and rewards, the experience of personally relevant organizational policies, the experience of fair treatment, and the interactions with agents or representatives of the organization (for reviews, see Eisenberger and Stinglhamber, 2011; Kurtessis et al., 2015). Regardless of the type of the favorable treatment, organizational support theory holds that favorable treatment contributes more substantially to POS if employees perceive that the organization has provided such treatment voluntarily rather than as a result of external constraints (for example, union contracts, government regulations; Eisenberger et al., 1997; Stinglhamber and Vandenberghe, 2004). In the view of the employee, such voluntary treatment provides a clearer indication of the organization's valuation and caring (Gouldner, 1960).

Concerning the outcomes of POS, a considerable body of evidence indicates that POS enhances employees' subjective well-being (for example, higher job satisfaction and reduced job stress), positive orientation to the organization and work (for example, higher affective organizational commitment and work engagement), and beneficial behaviors directed toward the organization (for example, higher performance and less absenteeism; for a review, see Eisenberger and Stinglhamber, 2011). Of greatest interest for this chapter is the relationship between POS and various forms of commitment. Much empirical evidence indicates that POS is related to organizational commitment. In particular, Meyer et al.'s meta-analysis found that POS was the strongest driver of affective commitment (Meyer et al., 2002).

In this chapter, we will first review the literature linking POS to the three forms of commitment delineated by Meyer and Allen (1991), with special emphasis on affective organizational commitment because it is the most studied form in relationship with POS. Second, we will extend our review to other sources of perceived support and other foci of commitment. Consistent with extensions of commitment theory to other foci besides the whole organization (for details on the multi-foci approach of commitment, see Chapter 4 in this volume), organizational support theory encompasses perceptions of support from any workplace entity that is an important source of informational, socio-emotional, and tangible support (for example, the supervisor). Therefore, we will consider how perceptions of support from these other sources combine with commitments to multiple foci. Third, we will consider new suggestions for future research on support and commitment. Finally, we will conclude with a discussion of practical implications of support–commitment relationships.

RELATIONSHIPS BETWEEN POS AND ORGANIZATIONAL COMMITMENT

Among the three dimensions of organizational commitment proposed by Meyer and Allen (1991; see Chapter 3 in this volume), most attention has been given to the link between POS and affective commitment, with some 240 studies on the topic (Kurtessis et al., 2015). Although there has been less attention paid to the relationships of POS with normative and continuance commitments, these associations are of substantial theoretical and practical interest and are considered here as well.

POS and Affective Commitment

POS and affective commitment are strongly associated, yet empirically distinct, constructs (e.g., Bishop et al., 2005; Eisenberger et al., 1990; Rhoades and Eisenberger, 2002; Shore and Wayne, 1993). Considerable research indicates that the more employees feel supported by the organization, the more they feel emotionally attached to it. Most of this research, however, is based on cross-sectional designs, leaving unclear the direction of causality between the two constructs. Filling this gap in the literature, Rhoades et al. (2001) found, using a cross-lagged panel design, that POS was positively related to changes in affective commitment over time, providing evidence that POS leads to and is thus an antecedent of affective commitment.

Consistent with a causal relationship between POS and affective commitment, empirical evidence has also shown that POS mediates the relationships between major antecedents of POS (that is, organizational justice, supportive supervision, and favorable job conditions) and affective commitment (e.g., Rhoades et al., 2001; Shore and Shore, 1995; Stinglhamber and Vandenberghe, 2003; Wayne et al., 1997; Wayne et al., 2002). Further, affective commitment has been found to mediate the relationship between POS and some of its major consequences (for example, employee performance and turnover; e.g., Bishop et al., 2000; Maertz et al., 2007; Rhoades et al., 2001).

Organizational support theory explains the relationship between POS and affective commitment both in terms of social exchange and reciprocity, and on the basis of self-enhancement and self-definition (Eisenberger and Stinglhamber, 2011; Rhoades and Eisenberger, 2002). Social exchange theory (Blau, 1964) emphasizes the norm of reciprocity (Gouldner, 1960), according to which the receipt of favorable treatment calls for the return of favorable treatment. In contrast with economic exchanges which involve financial and tangible aspects, social exchanges include socio-emotional aspects of relationships (for example, expressions of affection and esteem) and are mainly based on trust (Shore et al., 2006). In line with this view, organizational support theory holds that POS encourages employees to reciprocate the organization's valuation and caring by developing an emotional attachment to the organization. Specifically, POS would increase affective commitment by creating a felt obligation to care about the organization's welfare and to help it to reach its goals (Eisenberger et al., 2001). Consistent with this view, felt obligation was found to partially mediate the relationship between POS and affective commitment (Coyle-Shapiro et al., 2006; Eisenberger et al., 2001; Lew, 2009). Further supporting this explanation in terms of reciprocity, the relationship between POS and felt obligation was found to be stronger among those who strongly endorse the reciprocity norm as applied to work (Eisenberger et al., 2001).

Concerning the explanation of the POS–affective commitment relationship on the basis of self-enhancement and self-definition, research has referred to the theoretical and empirical work relying on social identity theory. Social identity theory (Tajfel and Turner, 1985; Turner, 1985) holds that individuals categorize themselves and others into different social categories in order to define and locate themselves in a given environment. The principal motivation underlying social identity processes is self-enhancement, reflected in the pursuit of a positive self-evaluation grounded in the identification with groups perceived positively. In line with this view, organizational support theory holds that, in meeting socio-emotional needs (that is, needs for approval, esteem, affiliation, and emotional support), POS enhances the attractiveness of the organization and therefore increases the likelihood of employees' organizational identification (e.g., Eisenberger and Stinglhamber, 2011; Sluss et al., 2008). In the same vein, Meyer and Allen (1997) proposed that work experiences increase individuals' affective commitment by fulfilling their need to feel that they are worthwhile persons. POS should thus lead to organizational identification which, in turn, may contribute to affective commitment (Meyer et al., 2006) (for more details on organizational identification and its links with organizational commitment, see Chapter 8 in this volume). Consistent with this view, organizational identification was found to mediate the relationship between POS and affective commitment (Marique et al., 2013; Ngo et al., 2013; Stinglhamber et al., 2015).

Caesens et al. (2014) integrated both the social exchange and the social identity theories in their research on the relationship between POS and affective commitment. They found across two samples that the two constructs capturing these frameworks – felt obligation and organizational identification – partially mediated the POS–affective commitment relationship. Their findings indicate that the POS–affective commitment relationship should be understood both in terms of social exchange and reciprocity and in terms of self-enhancement and self-definition. The two routes indeed play a concomitant role in the relationship between POS and affective commitment.

POS and Normative Commitment

Approximately 50 studies have been carried out on the relationship between POS and normative commitment, with a strong positive relationship between the two (Kurtessis et al., 2015). According to Meyer and colleagues (Meyer and Allen, 1997; Meyer and Herscovitch, 2001; Meyer and Parfyonova, 2010), normative commitment develops through: (1) individuals' internalization of norms and appropriate behaviors to remain loyal to their employer; or (2) the benefits and favorable treatment received by the organization that creates a need to reciprocate among individuals. Within the organizational support literature (e.g., Aubé et al., 2007; Eisenberger et al., 1986), the positive relationship between POS and normative commitment has mainly been explained through social exchange theory (Blau, 1964) involving the norm of reciprocity (Gouldner, 1960).

After the early conceptualization of normative commitment by Meyer et al. (1993), normative commitment was reformulated by Meyer and Herscovitch (2001) as 'the mindset that one has an obligation to pursue a course of action of relevance to a particular target' (p. 316). As a result of this important redefinition, normative commitment now represents a more general obligation to help the organization, rather than only the obligation to remain within the organization (Eisenberger and Stinglhamber, 2011; Wayne et al., 2009). Therefore, normative commitment is now closely related to the concept of employees' felt obligation as described in the organizational support literature (that is, a felt obligation to care about the organization's welfare and to help it to reach its goals – see above; Eisenberger et al., 2001) (Wayne et al., 2009). As stated by Eisenberger and Stinglhamber (2011), 'findings of a positive relationship between POS and normative commitment are similar to findings relating POS to felt obligation' (p. 167). There is thus a convergence of both conceptualizations and findings: POS is positively associated with normative commitment or felt obligation (Kurtessis et al., 2015). Whether the construct is stated as normative commitment or felt obligation, research findings suggest that POS is strongly related to a desire to be helpful in meeting the organization's goals and objectives.

POS and Continuance Commitment

POS might reduce employees' feelings of entrapment in their organization, involving their belief that they have no other option than to continue working for their current organization because of the high costs associated with leaving (Aubé et al., 2007; Rhoades and Eisenberger, 2002; Shore and Tetrick, 1991). Hence, POS should be negatively related to continuance commitment. This suggestion, however, has received mixed support in the empirical literature. Some research reported a modest negative relationship between POS and continuance commitment (e.g., Armstrong-Stassen, 1997; Casper et al., 2002; Fu et al., 2009; O'Driscoll and Randall, 1999), whereas other studies found a null relationship between these two constructs (e.g., Aubé et al., 2007; Gakovic and Tetrick, 2003; Meyer and Smith, 2000; Shore and Wayne, 1993). Overall, the meta-analytic review of Rhoades and Eisenberger (2002) indicated a small negative correlation between POS and continuance commitment.

The heterogeneity in the results regarding the POS–continuance commitment relationship (Rhoades and Eisenberger, 2002) may be explained by the weight that employees give to the two subdimensions of the continuance commitment construct. McGee and Ford (1987) identified two distinguishable aspects within continuance commitment, one reflecting 'the role of available alternatives in the decision to remain on one's job' ('lack of alternatives') and the other referring to the 'personal sacrifice that would result from leaving the organization' ('high sacrifice') (p. 639). According to Panaccio and Vandenberghe (2009), the negative correlation between POS and continuance commitment found in some prior studies is due to the 'lack of alternatives' subdimension. They argued that POS should reduce this subdimension of continuance commitment because POS enhances employees' feeling of self-worth that should make them feel attractive to potential employers. In contrast, POS might be positively related to the 'high sacrifice' subdimension, because it 'represents in and of itself a valued advantage one would lose upon termination of the employment relationship' (Panaccio and Vandenberghe, 2009, p. 226). Supporting this view, Pannaccio and Vandenberghe (2009) and Vandenberghe et al. (2007) found that POS was negatively related to the 'lack of alternatives' subdimension and positively related to the 'high sacrifice' subdimension of the continuance commitment construct.

Furthermore, Gellatly et al.'s (2007) study suggests that the relationship between POS and continuance commitment may not be understood in isolation to affective and normative commitment. Gellatly et al. examined the influence of POS on employees' 'commitment profiles' reflecting how the three dimensions (that is, affective, normative, and continuance) of organizational commitment combine in naturally occurring groups of employees. Their results indicated that POS was positively related to the fully committed profile (that is, strong affective, normative, and continuance commitment). In contrast, POS was strongly negatively linked to the uncommitted profile (that is, weak affective, normative, and continuance commitment). According to Wayne et al. (2009), employees' continuance commitment might be experienced positively in a context of high affective attachment and normative commitment. For these employees, 'POS might enhance perceived entitlements and opportunities specific to the organization that would be difficult to duplicate elsewhere' (Wayne et al., 2009, p. 267). In contrast, in the absence of a high affective and normative commitment context, continuance commitment might be experienced in a negative way (see Meyer et al., 2012, for more empirical evidence) and linked to feelings of entrapment in the organization that might be reduced by POS (Wayne et al., 2009).

MULTIPLE SOURCES OF SUPPORT AND FOCI OF COMMITMENT

Organizational support theory suggests that just as employees develop perceptions of support emanating from the organization, they also evaluate the extent to which other workplace entities value their contributions and care about their well-being (Eisenberger and Stinglhamber, 2011). The literature has mainly identified supervisors, co-workers, and unions as important sources of support. As representatives of the organization who direct and evaluate performance and provide coaching and training, supervisors are sources of instrumental resources such as access to information and opportunities for advancement, and socio-emotional resources such as encouragement and emotional support (Stinglhamber and Vandenberghe, 2003). Additionally, the flattening of organizational power structures, characterized by greater employee interdependence, has enhanced the value of support from teams, work groups, or co-workers (Ashforth and Johnson, 2001; Chiaburu and Harrison, 2008; Hayton et al., 2012). Finally, in organizations where unions exist, employees can form perceptions of their unions' support involving the degree to which unions are perceived as being committed to their members (Shore et al., 1994).

Employees thus conceptualize their work experiences in a multifaceted way, differentiating between sources of support, just as they commit themselves to other workplace foci than the organization as a whole (for details on the multi-foci approach of commitment, see Chapter 4 in this volume). Grounded in this multi-foci literature, Lavelle and colleagues' target-similarity model proposes that the support from a particular workplace entity should produce greater commitment to that entity than to other entities (Lavelle et al., 2007). Consistent with this view, Vandenberghe et al. (2004) found that POS was a stronger predictor of organizational commitment than were work group and supervisor support. Further, Stinglhamber and Vandenberghe (2003) found that POS was positively related to commitment to the organization but not to supervisors, while perceived supervisor support was positively related to commitment to the supervisor and not to the organization. In the same vein, research suggests that perceived team support is a stronger contributor to team commitment than to organizational commitment (Bishop et al., 2005), and that perceived team support has more influence than POS on team commitment (Howes et al., 2000).

Even though the target-similarity model emphasizes stronger relationships among variables referring to the same workplace entity or focus, the model does not exclude cross-foci effects. Lavelle et al. (2007) considered the possibility of weaker relationships or 'spillover' effects among entities that are nested within each other. Their model proposes, for instance, that POS might lead to a greater commitment to the supervisor, while perceived supervisor support might foster organizational commitment. Organizational support theory similarly holds that employees perceive workplace entities as partially reflective of the entire organization. Employees would therefore generalize, to some degree, the support they receive from their supervisor and work group to the entire organization. Accordingly, research shows that perceived supervisor support and perceived co-worker support contribute to POS, which in turn influences employees' organizational commitment (Ng and Sorensen, 2008; Rhoades et al., 2001).

Further, organizational support theory holds that the degree to which employees generalize support from organizational entities to the overall organization depends on the extent of employees' identification of these entities with the organization ('organizational embodiment'). Consistent with this view, Eisenberger et al. (2010) found that the relationship between leader–member exchange and affective organizational commitment was stronger among employees experiencing a high 'supervisor's organizational embodiment', defined as a perception concerning the extent to which the supervisor shares the organization's identity. When employees identified their supervisor with the organization, viewing them as highly representative of the organization, their favorable exchange relationship with their supervisor generalized to the organization, resulting in greater affective organizational commitment. Similarly, Eisenberger et al. (2011) found that the positive relationship between perceived supervisor support and POS was strengthened when supervisors were perceived as strongly embodying the organization. Taken together, these findings suggest that although employees develop commitment most strongly to entities providing support, such support can lead to commitment to other entities that share identity with the source of support.

DIRECTIONS FOR FUTURE RESEARCH

As we have seen above, much research linking support and commitment has been carried out so far on the relationship between POS and affective organizational commitment. In contrast, much remains to be done both at the theoretical and empirical level regarding the relationship of POS with normative and continuance commitment, including commitment profiles. As we have noted earlier, felt obligation appears to be essentially the same construct as normative commitment. Consistent with social exchange theory, POS has been found to lead to felt obligation or normative commitment to the organization. Although several studies have reported that felt obligation mediated the relationship between POS and affective commitment (Caesens et al., 2014; Coyle-Shapiro et al., 2006; Eisenberger et al., 2001), the variables were measured simultaneously. Thus, evidence is needed concerning the causal directions of these relationships. Regarding continuance commitment, organizational support theory does not shed much light so far on its possible relationship with POS (Wayne et al., 2009). A solid conceptual analysis of the conditions under which the relationship would be negative versus null would be very useful, as previously discussed. Finally, research has only just begun on how POS influences commitment profiles involving combinations of various degrees of affective, normative, and continuance commitment (e.g., Meyer et al., 2012). More research on this important issue is certainly warranted.

Besides the work that has to be done regarding the relationship between POS and normative and continuance commitment, we identify in the present section a few perspectives for future research that would help to develop our understanding of the support–commitment relationship in general. Specifically, we suggest that the literature would benefit from more research concerning the processes responsible for the relationships between support and commitment as well as the factors that influence the strength of these relationships. Regarding the processes, there is some room to improve our understanding and develop a more refined and complete picture of the mechanisms intervening in the support–commitment relationship. For example, several studies have found that trust in management or the organization mediates the positive relationship between POS and affective commitment (e.g., Albrecht and Travaglione, 2003; Chen et al., 2005; Whitener, 2001). Shore et al. (2006) maintained that trust, investment of increased time and effort, and a long-term outlook distinguished employees' social exchange relationships with organizations from economic exchange in which a defined level of effort is traded for explicit incentives. In contrast with economic exchange, trust therefore lies at the core of social exchange relationships (Shore et al., 2006). Rousseau defines trust as a willingness to make oneself vulnerable to the actions of another based on the expectation that the other will act in one's best interest (Rousseau et al., 1998). Trust may be distinguished from trustworthiness involving characteristics of another individual, leading to trust, which Mayer et al. (1995) suggested involve ability, benevolence, and integrity. Yet, the scales used to assess trust in the studies showing the mediating role of trust in the POS–affective commitment relationship did not often distinguish between trust and trustworthiness. Clearly, more theoretical and empirical work needs to be done concerning the role of trust in the support–commitment relationship.

Regarding the factors that may strengthen or attenuate the relationships between support and commitment, researchers may first be interested in clarifying the role of employees' socio-emotional needs. A central tenet of organizational support theory (Eisenberger and Stinglhamber, 2011) is that POS meets employees' socio-emotional needs, such as needs for approval, esteem, affiliation, and emotional support. More precisely, the theory proposes that these socio-emotional needs contribute to the relationship between POS and affective commitment by both social exchange and reciprocity, and self-enhancement and self-definition processes (see above for a description of these two routes). On the one hand, because POS would be more valued by employees having high socio-emotional needs, these employees would experience a greater obligation to reciprocate with a higher affective commitment (Armeli et al., 1998). On the other hand, the fulfillment of socio-emotional needs induced by POS should facilitate the incorporation of employees' organizational membership into their social identity (that is, organizational identification), with positive effects on their affective commitment (Rhoades et al., 2001). Theoretically, employees with high socio-emotional needs should thus show a stronger relationship between POS and affective commitment via both routes. Empirical evidence, however, is needed to test whether socio-emotional needs moderated both routes as predicted by organizational support theory, or whether they are more relevant for one route than for the other (Caesens et al., 2014).

Second, the literature would also strongly benefit from the examination of other dispositional differences, besides socio-emotional needs, that may play an important role in the strength of the relationships between POS and commitment. Eisenberger et al. (2009) examined the extent to which the association between POS and affective commitment depended on the employee's collectivist personal orientation (Triandis, 1995). These authors argued that the positive valuation signified by POS should be especially important to individuals with high collectivism because of their strong desire for acceptance, approval, and esteem by salient collectives to which they belong (Oyserman et al., 2002). Accordingly, employees with high collectivism showed an increased positive relationship between POS and affective commitment. Beyond differing among individuals within a culture, collectivism also varies in strength from one culture to another (Hofstede et al., 2010; Triandis, 1995). Just as collectivism as an individual propensity moderates the relationship between POS and affective commitment, this relationship may thus also vary from one nation to another based on cross-cultural differences. In line with the recent work of Chiaburu et al. (2015), cross-cultural studies on the effects of POS on the major commitment mindsets would therefore be very helpful.

Finally, more research is needed regarding the relationships between support and commitment across foci. As previously explained, relying on the recent research on supervisor organizational embodiment (e.g., Eisenberger et al., 2010) helps to understand when support from supervisors may spill over to commitment to the organization above and beyond its impact on commitment to the supervisor. Although such organizational embodiment was originally developed with regard to the supervisor (Eisenberger et al., 2010), it would likely apply to other embedded organizational entities besides the employee's supervisor. Overall, this concept suggests how individuals generalize treatment from embedded workplace entities to more encompassing entities. For example, work group support may generalize to the organization, depending on the extent to which the work group is identified with the overall organization, with positive consequences for affective organizational commitment. The organizational embodiment construct suggests very promising avenues for future research on support–commitment effects across foci that are embedded within each other.

PRACTICAL CONSIDERATIONS

This chapter shows that POS has strong relationships with affective and normative commitment. Yet, scientific literature has consistently shown that affective and normative commitment are in turn correlated with outcomes that are crucial for both organizations and employees (see Part IV, 'Consequences of Commitment', in this volume for more information). Regarding organization-relevant outcomes, both forms of commitment are negatively related to withdrawal cognitions and actual turnover. Further, affective commitment has the strongest positive correlation with job attendance, job performance, and organizational citizenship behaviors, followed by normative commitment (Meyer et al., 2002). Concerning employee-relevant outcomes, affective commitment was found to correlate positively with indicators of employee well-being (for example, mental health and positive affect) and negatively with indices of strain (for example, physical health complaints and burnout), whereas normative commitment generally yields non-significant relations with these outcomes (Meyer and Maltin, 2010; Meyer et al., 2002) (for more information on the consequences of commitment in terms of employee well-being, see Chapter 17 in this volume). Because of these important consequences of affective and normative commitment, identifying day-to-day practices and organizational policies that enhance POS is thus of utmost importance for organizations.

Research findings provide a menu of practical approaches for enhancing POS in order to finally increase affective and normative commitment (Eisenberger and Stinglhamber, 2011, see pp. 211–238). We will consider here two of the major approaches. First, to increase the POS of their subordinates and their subsequent affective and normative commitment to the organization, managers can engage in supportive behaviors. Because of the important role of managers in representing the organization to subordinates, employees generally view such support from managers as partly attributable to the organization as a whole, leading to greater POS. Managers can, for example, provide employees with autonomy in fulfilling their job responsibilities, resolve their conflicting job responsibilities, and provide them with the needed resources to perform their jobs effectively (Eisenberger and Stinglhamber, 2011). If managers do not spontaneously display this supportive treatment toward their subordinates, organizations can train managers to be more supportive in their role of directing, coaching, and evaluating employees. Organizations can also contribute to this process by treating managers more supportively, who in turn pass the support down to subordinates who, in turn, demonstrate higher POS (Shanock and Eisenberger, 2006).

Second, organizations can promote HR practices and policies that foster POS and thus facilitate affective and normative commitment to the organization. Promoting fairness in the way policies and rewards are administered, maintaining open channels of communication, treating applicants respectfully and fairly, providing meaningful training and developmental programs that promote personal growth, and allowing flexible work time, represent very concrete ways that create a supportive organizational culture (Eisenberger and Stinglhamber, 2011).

Whichever approach managers and organizations adopt to enhance their employees' POS and subsequent commitment, it is important that managers and organizations communicate on the voluntary nature of their favorable actions. Favorable treatment from managers or the whole organization contributes much more substantially to affective and normative commitment via POS if it is considered to be a discretionary act, as opposed to the result of external pressure (Eisenberger et al., 1997; Stinglhamber and Vandenberghe, 2004). The influence of employer initiatives undertaken freely, as opposed to those caused by government regulations, union contracts, and so on, on POS is indeed more than six times greater (Eisenberger et al., 1997). As employees may not understand that such initiatives are voluntary and in the employees' best interest, communicating on such initiatives and their benefits for employees is often needed to obtain a substantial increase in POS.

CONCLUSION

The view of organizational commitment as a two-way street, which inspired the development of the POS construct and organizational support theory, has been borne out. Employees are quite concerned with the organization's valuation of them in terms of the contribution they make and their well-being. They respond to high POS very strongly by developing affective and normative commitment. Research has now turned to better understand why and when POS leads to commitment. Moreover, new research is being carried out on perceived support–commitment relationships involving entities embedded in the overall organization (for example, the supervisor and the work group). As research topics have grown more refined, the value of viewing commitment from the employee's viewpoint remains undiminished.

REFERENCES

Albrecht, S., and Travaglione, A. (2003). Trust in public-sector senior management. *International Journal of Human Resource Management*, *14*, 76–92.
Armeli, S., Eisenberger, R., Fasolo, P., and Lynch, P. (1998). Perceived organizational support and police performance: The moderating influence of socioemotional needs. *Journal of Applied Psychology*, *83*, 288–297.
Armstrong-Stassen, M. (1997). The effect of repeated management downsizing and surplus designation on remaining managers: An exploratory study. *Anxiety Stress and Coping*, *10*, 377–384.
Ashforth, B.E., and Johnson, S.A. (2001). Which hat to wear? The relative salience of multiple identities in organizational contexts. In M.A. Hogg and D.J. Terry (eds), *Social Identity Processes in Organizational Contexts* (pp. 31–48). Hove, UK: Psychology Press.
Aubé, C., Rousseau, V., and Morin, E.M. (2007). Perceived organizational support and organizational commitment. *Journal of Managerial Psychology*, *22*, 479–495.
Bishop, J.W., Scott, K.D., and Burroughs, S.M. (2000). Support, commitment, and employee outcomes in a team environment. *Journal of Management*, *26*, 1113–1132.
Bishop, J.W., Scott, K.D., Goldsby, M.G., and Cropanzano, R. (2005). A construct validity study of commitment and perceived support variables: A multifoci approach across different team environments. *Group and Organization Management*, *30*, 153–180.
Blau, P.M. (1964). *Exchange and Power in Social Life.* New York: Wiley.
Caesens, G., Marique, G., and Stinglhamber, F. (2014). The relationship between perceived organizational support and affective commitment: More than reciprocity, it is also a question of organizational identification. *Journal of Personnel Psychology*, *13*, 167–173.
Casper, W., Martin, J., Buffardi, L., and Erdwins, C. (2002). Work–family conflict, perceived organizational

support, and organizational commitment among employed mothers. *Journal of Occupational Health Psychology*, 7, 99–108.

Chen, Z.X., Aryee, S., and Lee, C. (2005). Test of a mediation model of perceived organizational support. *Journal of Vocational Behavior*, 66, 457–470.

Chiaburu, D.S., Chakrabarty, S., Wang, J., and Li, N. (2015). Organizational support and citizenship behaviors: A comparative cross-cultural meta-analysis. *Management International Review*, 55, 707–736.

Chiaburu, D.S., and Harrison, D.A. (2008). Do peers make the place? Conceptual synthesis and meta-analysis of coworker effects on perceptions, attitudes, OCBs, and performance. *Journal of Applied Psychology*, 93, 1082–1103.

Coyle-Shapiro, J.A.M., Morrow, P.C., and Kessler, I. (2006). Serving two organizations: Exploring the employment relationship of contracted employees. *Human Resource Management*, 45, 561–583.

Eisenberger, R., Armeli, S., Rexwinkel, B., Lynch, P.D., and Rhoades, L. (2001). Reciprocation of perceived organizational support. *Journal of Applied Psychology*, 86, 42–51.

Eisenberger, R., Cummings, J., Armeli, S., and Lynch, P. (1997). Perceived organizational support, discretionary treatment, and job satisfaction. *Journal of Applied Psychology*, 82, 812–820.

Eisenberger, R., Fasolo, P., and Davis-LaMastro, V. (1990). Perceived organizational support and employee diligence, commitment, and innovation. *Journal of Applied Psychology*, 75, 51–59.

Eisenberger, R., Huntington, R., Hutchison, S., and Sowa, D. (1986). Perceived organizational support. *Journal of Applied Psychology*, 71, 500–507.

Eisenberger, R., Karagonlar, G., Stinglhamber, F., Neves, P., Becker, T.E., et al. (2010). Leader–member exchange and affective organizational commitment: The contribution of supervisor's organizational embodiment. *Journal of Applied Psychology*, 95, 1085–1103.

Eisenberger, R., and Stinglhamber, F. (2011). *Perceived Organizational Support: Fostering Enthusiastic and Productive Employees*. Washington, DC: APA Books.

Eisenberger, R., Stinglhamber, F., and Becker, T.E. (2011). Perceived organizational support: The role of supervisor's organizational embodiment. Academy of Management, San Antonio, August.

Eisenberger, R., Stinglhamber, F., Shanock, L.R., Jones, J.R., and Aselage, J. (2009). Extending the social exchange perspective of perceived organizational support: Influences of collectivism and competitiveness. Unpublished manuscript, University of Delaware.

Fu, F.Q., Bolander, W., and Jones, E. (2009). Managing the drivers of organizational commitment and salesperson effort: An application of Meyer and Allen's three-component model. *Journal of Marketing Theory and Practice*, 17, 335–350.

Gakovic, A., and Tetrick, L.E. (2003). Perceived organizational support and work status: A comparison of the employment relationships of part-time and full-time employees attending university classes. *Journal of Organizational Behavior*, 24, 649–666.

Gellalty, I.R., Hunter, K.H., Luchak, A.A., and Meyer, J.P. (2007). Predicting commitment profile membership: The role of perceived organizational support and autonomy. Paper presented at 22nd annual meeting of the Society for Industrial and Organizational Psychology, New York, April.

Gouldner, A.W. (1960). The norm of reciprocity: A preliminary statement. *American Sociological Review*, 25, 161–178.

Hayton, J.C., Carnabuci, G., and Eisenberger, R. (2012). With a little help from my colleagues: A social embeddedness approach to perceived organizational support. *Journal of Organizational Behavior*, 33, 235–249.

Hofstede, G., Hofstede, G.J., and Minkov, M. (2010). *Cultures and Organizations: Software of the Mind* (3rd edn). New York: McGraw-Hill.

Howes, J.C., Cropanzano, R., Grandey, A.A., and Mohler, C.J. (2000). Who is supporting whom? Quality team effectiveness and perceived organizational support. *Journal of Quality Management*, 5, 207–223.

Kurtessis, J., Eisenberger, R., Ford, M.T., Buffardi, L.C., Stewart, K.A., and Adis, C.S. (2015). Perceived organizational support: A meta-analytic evaluation of organizational support theory. *Journal of Management*. Advance online publication. doi: 10.1177/0149206315575554.

Lavelle, J.J., Rupp, D.E., and Brockner, J. (2007). Taking a multifoci approach to the study of justice, social exchange, and citizenship behavior: The target similarity model. *Journal of Management*, 33, 841–866.

Levinson, H. (1965). Reciprocation: The relationship between man and organization. *Administrative Science Quarterly*, 9, 370–390.

Lew, T.Y. (2009). The relationships between perceived organizational support, felt obligation, affective organizational commitment and turnover intention of academics working with private higher educational institutions in Malaysia. *European Journal of Social Sciences*, 9, 72–87.

Maertz, C.P., Griffeth, R.W., Campbell, N.S., and Allen, D.G. (2007). The effects of perceived organizational support and perceived supervisor support on employee turnover. *Journal of Organizational Behavior*, 28, 1059–1075.

Marique, G., Stinglhamber, F., Desmette, D., Caesens, G., and De Zanet, F. (2013). The relationship between perceived organizational support and affective commitment: A social identity perspective. *Group and Organization Management*, *38*, 68–100.

Mayer, R.C., Davis, J.H., and Schoorman, F.D. (1995). An integrative model of organizational trust. *Academy of Management Review*, *20*, 709–734.

McGee, G.W., and Ford, R.C. (1987). Two (or more?) dimensions of organizational commitment: Reexamination of the affective and continuance commitment scales. *Journal of Applied Psychology*, *72*, 638–642.

Meyer, J.P., and Allen, N.J. (1991). A three-component conceptualization of organizational commitment. *Human Resource Management Review*, *1*, 61–89.

Meyer, J.P., and Allen, N.J. (eds) (1997). *Commitment in the Workplace: Theory, Research and Application*. Thousand Oaks, CA: Sage Publications.

Meyer, J.P., Allen N.J., and Smith, C.A. (1993). Commitment to organizations and occupations: Extension and test of a three-component conceptualization. *Journal of Applied Psychology*, *78*, 538–551.

Meyer, J.P., Becker, T.E., and Van Dick, R. (2006). Social identities and commitments at work: Toward an integrative model. *Journal of Organizational Behavior*, *27*, 665–683.

Meyer, J.P., and Herscovitch, L. (2001). Commitment in the workplace: Toward a general model. *Human Resource Management Review*, *11*, 299–326.

Meyer, J.P., and Maltin, E.R. (2010). Employee commitment and well-being: A critical review, theoretical framework and research agenda. *Journal of Vocational Behavior*, *77*, 323–337.

Meyer, J.P., and Parfyonova, N.M. (2010). Normative commitment in the workplace: A theoretical analysis and re-conceptualization. *Human Resource Management Review*, *20*, 283–294.

Meyer, J.P., and Smith, C.A. (2000). HRM practices and organizational commitment: Test of a mediation model. *Canadian Journal of Administrative Sciences*, *17*, 319–331.

Meyer, J.P., Stanley, D.J., Herscovitch, L., and Tonolnytsky, L. (2002). Affective, continuance, and normative commitment to the organization: A meta-analysis of antecedents, correlates, and consequences. *Journal of Vocational Behavior*, *61*, 20–52.

Meyer, J.P., Stanley, L.J., and Parfyonova, N.M. (2012). Employee commitment in context: The nature and implication of commitment profiles. *Journal of Vocational Behavior*, *80*, 1–16.

Ng, T.W. and Sorensen, K.L. (2008). Toward a further understanding of the relationships between perceptions of support and work attitudes: a meta-analysis. *Group and Organization Management*, *33*, 243–268.

Ngo, H., Loi, R., Foley, S., Zheng, X., and Zhang, L. (2013). Perceptions of organizational context and job attitudes: The mediating effect of organizational identification. *Asia Pacific Journal of Management*, *30*, 149–168.

O'Driscoll, M.P., and Randall, D.M. (1999). Perceived organisational support, satisfaction with rewards, and employee job involvement and organisational commitment. *Applied Psychology: An international Review*, *48*, 197–209.

Oyserman, D., Coon, H.M., and Kemmelmeier, M. (2002). Rethinking individualism and collectivism: Evaluation of theoretical assumptions and meta-analyses. *Psychological Bulletin*, *128*, 3–72.

Panaccio, A., and Vandenberghe, C. (2009). Perceived organizational support, organizational commitment and psychological well-being: A longitudinal study. *Journal of Vocational Behavior*, *75*, 224.

Rhoades, L., and Eisenberger, R. (2002). Perceived organizational support: A review of the literature. *Journal of Applied Psychology*, *87*, 698–714.

Rhoades, L., Eisenberger, R., and Armeli, S. (2001). Affective commitment to the organization: The contribution of perceived organizational support. *Journal of Applied Psychology*, *86*, 825–836.

Rousseau, D.M., Sitkin, S.B., Burt, R.S., and Camerer, C. (1998). Not so different after all: A cross-discipline view of trust. *Academy of Management Review*, *23*, 393–404.

Shanock, L.R. and Eisenberger, R. (2006). When supervisors feel supported: relationships with subordinates' perceived supervisor support, perceived organizational support, and performance. *Journal of Applied Psychology*, *91*, 689–695.

Shore, L.M. and Shore, T.H. (1995). Perceived organizational support and organizational justice. In R.S. Cropanzano and K.M. Kacmar (eds), *Organizational Politics, Justice, and Support: Managing the Social Climate of the Workplace* (pp. 149–164). Westport, CT: Quorum.

Shore, L.M., and Tetrick, L.E. (1991). A construct-validity study of the Survey of Perceived Organizational Support. *Journal of Applied Psychology*, *76*, 637–643.

Shore, L.M., Tetrick, L.E., Lynch, P., and Barksdale, K. (2006). Social and economic exchange: Construct development and validation. *Journal of Applied Social Psychology*, *36*, 837–867.

Shore, L.M., Tetrick, L.E., Sinclair, R.R., and Newton, L.A. (1994). Validation of a measure of perceived union support. *Journal of Applied Psychology*, *79*, 971–977.

Shore, L.M., and Wayne, S.J. (1993). Commitment and employee behavior: Comparison of affective commitment and continuance commitment with perceived organizational support. *Journal of Applied Psychology*, *78*, 774–780.

Sluss, D.M., Klimchak, M., and Holmes, J.J. (2008). Perceived organizational support as a mediator between relational exchange and organizational identification. *Journal of Vocational Behavior*, *73*, 457–464.

Stinglhamber, F., and Vandenberghe, C. (2003). Organizations and supervisors as sources of support and targets of commitment: A longitudinal study. *Journal of Organizational Behavior*, *24*, 251–270.

Stinglhamber, F., and Vandenberghe, C. (2004). Favorable job conditions and perceived support: The role of organizations and supervisors. *Journal of Applied Social Psychology*, *34*, 1470–1493.

Stinglhamber, F., Marique, G., Caesens, G., Desmette, D., Hansez, I., Hanin, D., and Bertrand, F. (2015). Employees' organizational identification and affective organizational commitment: An integrative approach. *PLOS One*, *10*, e0123955.

Tajfel, H., and Turner, J.C. (1985). The social identity theory of intergroup behavior. In S. Worchel and W.G. Austin (eds), *Psychology of Intergroup Relations* (2nd edn, pp. 7–24). Chicago, IL: Nelson-Hall.

Triandis, H.C. (1995). *Individualism and Collectivism*. Boulder, CO: Westview.

Turner, J.C. (1985). Social categorization and the self-concept: A social cognitive theory of group behavior. In E.J. Lawler (ed.), *Advances in Group Processes* (Vol. 2, pp. 77–122). Greenwich, CT: JAI Press.

Vandenberghe, C., Bentein, K., Michon, R., Chebat, J.C., Tremblay, M., and Fils, J.F. (2007). An examination of the role of perceived support and employee commitment in employee–customer encounters. *Journal of Applied Psychology*, *92*, 1177–1187.

Vandenberghe, C., Bentein, K., and Stinglhamber, F. (2004). Affective commitment to the organization, supervisor, and work group: Antecedents and outcomes. *Journal of Vocational Behavior*, *64*, 47–71.

Wayne, S.J., Coyle-Shapiro, J.A.-M., Eisenberger, R., Liden, R.C., Rousseau, D.M., and Shore, L.M. (2009). Social influences. In H.J. Klein, T.E. Becker, and J.P. Meyer (eds), *Commitment in Organizations: Accumulated Wisdom and New Directions* (pp. 253–284). New York: Routledge.

Wayne, S.J., Shore, L.M., Bommer, W.H., and Tetrick, L.E. (2002). The role of fair treatment and rewards in perceptions of organizational support and leader–member exchange. *Journal of Applied Psychology*, *87*, 590–598.

Wayne, S.J., Shore, L.M., and Liden, R.C. (1997). Perceived organizational support and leader–member exchange: A social exchange perspective. *Academy of Management Journal*, *40*, 82–111.

Whitener, E.M. (2001). Do 'high commitment' human resource practices affect employee commitment? A cross-level analysis using hierarchical linear modeling. *Journal of Management*, *27*, 515–535.

25. Organizational justice and employee commitment: a review of contemporary research

D. Ramona Bobocel and Frank Mu*

The literature on organizational justice is concerned with understanding the relation between people's perceptions of fairness and their attitudes and behaviors at work. Commitment has long been an outcome of interest in the study of organizational justice (e.g., Folger and Konovsky, 1989; Lind and Tyler, 1988). Thus, it is not surprising that numerous studies beginning in the 1980s have demonstrated a robust relation between justice perceptions and organizational commitment.

Much of the early research conducted between 1980 and 2000 was guided by two conceptual paradigms. In one stream of research, which we refer to as the 'differential effects paradigm', researchers focused on examining the unique effects of distributive, procedural, and interactional justice perceptions in predicting commitment and other work outcomes. Distributive justice perceptions (e.g., Adams, 1965) refer to people's perceptions of the fairness of outcomes that they receive from the organization, such as their pay. Procedural justice perceptions (e.g., Leventhal, 1980; Lind and Tyler, 1988; Thibaut and Walker, 1975) refer to people's perceptions of the fairness of the procedures by which decisions are made. Interactional justice (e.g., Bies and Moag, 1986) comprises people's perceptions of the quality of information and interpersonal treatment that they receive from agents who make decisions.[1] The differential effects research was summarized in several meta-analyses published in 2001–2002 (e.g., Cohen-Charash and Spector, 2001; Colquitt et al., 2001; Viswesvaran and Ones, 2002). Overall, the findings indicated that distributive, procedural, and interactional justice perceptions are each significantly related to employee commitment, although typically procedural justice is most strongly associated with organizational commitment (also see Meyer et al., 2002).

In the other stream of research, investigators were guided by the 'interaction effects paradigm', in which researchers examined the combined effects of information regarding outcomes and information regarding decision processes (with procedural and interactional justice sometimes combined) on employees' support for decisions, authorities, and the organization.[2] The results of an early meta-analysis (Brockner and Weisenfeld, 1996) indicated that outcome and process information have joint effects, such that fair process mitigates the otherwise adverse effect of receiving unfair or unfavorable outcomes on employee support and commitment. These findings had important practical implications because they suggested that organizations could garner support for unfavorable decisions and maintain employee commitment to the extent that they used fair procedures, explained decision processes, and treated people respectfully: the hallmarks of process fairness.

Between 2001 and 2015, research on justice and commitment has continued to flourish. Many studies have examined separate predictive effects of distributive, procedural, and interactional justice on commitment. For example, researchers have examined the degree to which there is cross-cultural generalizability of the differential justice–commitment relations (see Li and Cropanzano, 2009, for a meta-analytic review). Similarly, studies continue to examine the process–outcome interaction, identifying factors that heighten, attenuate, or even reverse the beneficial effect of process fairness for assuaging negative reactions to unfavorable outcomes (Bianchi et al., 2015; see Brockner, 2010, for a review). Collectively, we continue to glean many insights regarding employee commitment from both of these lines of research.

Of course, from 2001 onwards, researchers have developed new conceptual paradigms to guide research on justice and commitment. The primary purpose of our chapter is to review three such emergent paradigms, and to summarize their novel contributions to our understanding of the connection between justice and employee commitment.[3] In this context, we also discuss the mechanisms by which justice has been theorized to promote commitment. Finally, we consider practical implications that stem from our review. As with the early research, the vast majority of studies conducted after 2001 have focused on predicting affective commitment (Meyer and Allen, 1991; Allen and Meyer, 1990), thus, we confine our review to this form of commitment.[4]

EMERGENT PARADIGMS IN THE STUDY OF JUSTICE AND COMMITMENT

Entity versus Event Justice

As already noted, organizational justice research traditionally focused on examining the unique contributions of distributive, procedural, and interactional justice perceptions in predicting commitment, as well as their joint effects. In addition, for the most part in this research, the outcomes, procedures, and interpersonal treatment pertained to specific events, such as a performance appraisal, a selection or promotion decision, a pay cut, or a lay-off. Around the turn of the millennium, a number of organizational justice researchers began to acknowledge that the focus on the separate effects of distributive, procedural, and interactional justice may not adequately capture employees' experiences of justice. In particular, the traditional approach failed to consider the role of employees' holistic, or global, impressions of justice.

For example, Cropanzano et al. (2001) argued that employees aggregate their perceptions of the fairness of specific organizational 'events' (for example, a pay cut) to form global judgments of the overall fairness of 'social entities' such as the organization and decision-makers. Thus, Cropanzano et al. differentiated between two objects of employees' justice perceptions: 'specific events' that are evaluated in terms of distributive, procedural, and interactional justice; and 'social entities' who are held accountable for those events, especially managers or supervisors who are viewed as agents of the organization, and the organization itself. Similarly, in their fairness heuristic theory, Lind (2001) and Van den Bos (2001) argued that people are motivated to form overall justice perceptions quickly within their social interactions in an effort to determine whether their interaction partner can be trusted not to exploit or exclude them. To do so, Lind and Van den Bos suggested that people use whatever fairness information is available, whether pertaining to outcomes, procedures, or interpersonal treatment (e.g., Van den Bos et al., 2001).

In line with these ideas, Ambrose and Schminke (2009) validated a six-item measure by which to assess employees' perceptions of overall justice (for example, 'Overall, I'm treated fairly by my organization', 'In general, I can count on my supervisor to be fair').

Since then, growing evidence suggests that examining employees' holistic justice perceptions contributes added value to understanding employee commitment and other work outcomes. For example, several studies have demonstrated that perceptions of overall organizational justice mediate the effects of event distributive, procedural, and interactional justice on employee commitment (e.g., Jones and Martens, 2009; Ambrose and Schminke, 2009; Marzucco et al., 2014). Indeed, a recent justice meta-analysis indicated that entity judgments were a stronger predictor of employee commitment than distributive, procedural, and interactional justice perceptions (Rupp et al., 2014).

Interestingly, researchers also have begun to examine the joint effects of event and entity justice perceptions on commitment. For example, Choi (2008) predicted that employees' entity justice perceptions would moderate event justice perceptions, such that event perceptions would be a stronger predictor of distal work attitudes (commitment) and behaviors (citizenship) when entity justice perceptions are relatively lower. He reasoned that when entity justice perceptions are higher (for example, employees perceive the organization as generally fair), employees would be less sensitive to fairness of specific events. In contrast, when employees have developed low entity justice perceptions (for example, as when they perceive the organization as generally unfair), then they will be more sensitive to the perceived fairness of specific events, and therefore event justice perceptions should be more strongly related to work outcomes.

Choi tested this idea in a study of employee–supervisor dyads in which he assessed employees' perceptions of distributive, procedural, informational, and interpersonal justice in relation to a recent performance appraisal, as well as their perceptions of overall fairness of their supervisor and the organization. He examined the relations of these measures to employee commitment, supervisor trust, and citizenship behavior. In line with the meta-analytic finding noted above, Choi found that employees' perceptions of the organization and of the supervisor as fair entities were stronger predictors of commitment, trust, and citizenship behavior than were event justice perceptions. Moreover, as predicted, entity perceptions moderated event justice perceptions such that event justice perceptions were a weaker predictor of employee support when entity justice perceptions were higher rather than lower. For example, organizational commitment was higher when employees believed that the organization was fair overall, regardless of their perceptions of the procedural justice of the performance appraisal.

In summary, Choi's results suggest that employee commitment is shaped not only by the distributive, procedural, and interactional justice of specific events, but also by employees' global judgments of the fairness of relevant social entities. Consequently, to the extent that employees hold the view that their organization is generally fair, they may be more willing to discount incidents when they feel unfairly treated. In this situation, then, overall fairness may buffer declines in affective commitment, which might otherwise occur.

It is worth noting a conceptual parallel between Choi's findings and the early process–outcome interaction effect (Brockner and Wiesenfeld, 1996). As noted in the introduction, the shape of the traditional process–outcome interaction reveals that employees are more accepting of unfair or unfavorable outcomes to the extent that they perceive those outcomes to have been allocated via fair processes (procedural and/or interactional justice). Here, we see that employees are more supportive of the organization in the face of a procedurally unfair performance appraisal, the more they perceive the organization to be fair overall (also see Bobocel, 2013, for similar findings on proximal reactions to unfair events).

The concept of overall justice raises other interesting questions for future research. For example, what is the process by which employees update or revise their holistic impressions? Fairness heuristic theory suggests that people ordinarily will use their overall justice perceptions to guide their actions, but it also recognizes that people will revise or update their overall justice perceptions as necessary based on new justice-related experiences (Lind, 2001). Lind suggested that reappraisal will be induced by events that raise fears of exploitation or social exclusion, such as when relationships are new or during times of salient change and uncertainty. Of note, research has demonstrated that there is significant within-person variability in overall justice perceptions over time (Holtz and Harold, 2009), but future research is needed to systematically examine the causes of revision.

Some researchers have begun to examine the possible consequences of changes in employees' justice perceptions over time (e.g., Loi et al., 2009; Hausknecht et al., 2011). Especially relevant for the present purposes, Hausknecht et al. (2011) surveyed employees four times over a year and found that trends in justice perceptions explained additional variance in employee commitment over and above end-state justice perceptions.[5] More specifically, previous improvements in justice perceptions (for example, positive trends) were associated with greater current commitment beyond justice perceptions assessed concurrently. Similarly, previous declines in justice perceptions (for example, negative trends) were associated with lower commitment. These results illustrate that employee commitment is shaped not only by current justice perceptions but also by changes in justice perceptions over time. It will be important for future research to continue to incorporate time into the study of justice and commitment.

Justice Source versus Justice Type

Building on the idea of entity justice, researchers also began to point out that the scales used in research to assess justice perceptions confounded the 'source' of justice with the 'element' of evaluation (e.g., Byrne, 1999; Masterson et al., 2000). For example, procedural justice perceptions typically were measured in reference to the organization, whereas interactional justice perceptions were measured in reference to supervisors. This led some justice researchers to wonder whether the important distinctions in predicting employees' reactions to justice and injustice are the 'sources' rather than the 'types' of justice.

From this recognition grew the 'multi-foci' model of justice, which recognized explicitly that different social entities each have the capacity to deliver outcomes, procedures, and interpersonal treatment, and therefore that each entity can be evaluated in terms of any justice-related information (Rupp and Cropanzano, 2002). Moreover, building on this idea, researchers suggested that employees reciprocate responses toward the particular entity to whom (in)justice is attributed due to social exchange relationships that develop between themselves and the particular entity (for review, see Lavelle et al., 2007).

Rupp and Cropanzano (2002) provided an early test of these ideas in a survey of employee–supervisor dyads. As predicted, they found that organization-emanating justice (procedural and interactional justice attributed to the organization) was significantly related to organization-directed variables (for example, job performance, citizenship behavior directed toward the organization). In contrast, supervisor-emanating justice (procedural and interactional justice attributed to the supervisors) was significantly related to supervisor-directed variables (for example, citizenship behavior directed toward the supervisor). Moreover, in line with their social exchange framework, the researchers demonstrated that these effects were mediated, respectively, by organization-focused relational exchange and supervisory-focused relational exchange.

Of note, Rupp and Cropanzano argued for an interesting 'cross-foci' effect in which supervisor-emanating justice would predict organization-directed outcomes. In brief, because supervisors generally are perceived as agents of the organization, supervisor-emanating justice may affect organization-directed variables as well as supervisor-directed variables, albeit less strongly. As predicted, the results showed a cross-foci effect for supervisor-emanating justice but not for organization-emanating justice.[6]

Building on this line of research, Rupp et al. (2014) recently argued that the focus in the literature on the role of the separate justice dimensions (distributive, procedural, interactional) as predictors of work outcomes has led to an underappreciation of the role of the source of justice in reactions. As they point out, between 2000 and 2014, researchers have tended to operationalize justice perceptions as employees' assessments of the extent to which normative rules (distributive, procedural, informational, interpersonal justice criteria) have been upheld or violated, and have examined the effects of such judgments on attitudes and behaviors. In contrast, they argue that researchers have often neglected the related, but separate, role of accountability judgments; that is, how specific parties or entities such as the organization, supervisors, or co-workers are seen as upholding or violating the normative rules, and the effects of such accountability judgments on attitudes and behaviors.

Rupp et al. (2014) conducted a meta-analysis to compare the predictive validities of type-based justice perceptions (distributive, procedural, interactional) and source-based justice perceptions (supervisor, organization) on several work attitudes and behaviors. Most relevant for our purpose, their results demonstrated that organization-based justice is a better predictor of organizational commitment than are the three justice types (distributive, procedural, interactional). Similarly, supervisor-based justice is a stronger predictor of supervisor commitment than are the three justice types.

Moreover, Rupp et al. (2014) found that justice–outcome relations are stronger when the source of justice aligns with the target of reaction. In other words, organization-based justice is more strongly related to organization-focused commitment than is supervisor-based justice. In contrast, supervisor-based justice is more strongly related to supervisor-focused commitment than is organization-based justice. However, similar to Rupp and Cropanzano (2002), they also predicted and found evidence for cross-foci effects, in which supervisor-based justice predicts organization-focused commitment in addition to supervisor-focused commitment (albeit more weakly), but organization-based justice does not have the same influence across foci (see also Colquitt et al., 2013).

In summary, Rupp et al.'s (2014) findings demonstrate that investigators can understand more about the relation between justice and employee commitment (and other outcomes) by considering not only employees' perceptions of whether normative rules (distributive, procedural, informational, interpersonal justice criteria) have been upheld or violated, but also the identifiable parties whom employees hold accountable for upholding or violating those normative rules. In addition, their data suggest that: (1) employees direct their positive responses to the entity to whom they attribute fair treatment (cf. Colquitt et al., 2013); and (2) supervisor entity justice has an important role in shaping reactions directed toward multiple sources. It is interesting to note that source-matching effects have been shown to be stronger in national cultures that emphasize individuality, femininity, uncertainty avoidance, and low power distance (Shao et al., 2013).

Group-Level versus Individual-Level Justice

Thus far, we have discussed the role of individuals' perceptions of justice in shaping their commitment. Around the turn of the millennium, justice researchers also began to examine the effect of group-level justice (typically operationalized as the aggregate of individual-level justice[7]) perceptions on employee commitment. Naumann and Bennett (2000; also see Mossholder et al., 1998, p. 882) used the term 'justice climate' to refer to 'a group-level cognition about how a work group as a whole is treated' (for a review and alternative definitions, see Li and Cropanzano, 2009). Similarly to individual-level justice perceptions, researchers have demonstrated a positive relation between justice climate and individuals' affective commitment using cross-level analyses.

For example, in an early study involving 4539 employees in 783 departments and 97 hotel properties, Simons and Roberson (2003) found unique paths between justice and commitment at both the individual and department levels of analysis. Roberson and Colquitt (2005) developed a model describing how shared perceptions of justice emerge in teams, and how such shared perceptions influence attachment to the team and team effectiveness. Liao and Rupp (2005) examined the associations between four justice climates and individual-level commitment (as well as satisfaction and citizenship behavior) after controlling for corresponding individual-level justice perceptions. More recently, Ohana (2014) examined the effects of justice climate using a data set from 1496 companies included in the 2004 Workplace Employment Relationships Survey. The results demonstrated that justice climate (procedural, interpersonal, and informational) explains additional variance in individual employee commitment beyond individual-level justice perceptions, providing further support for group-level effects.

Researchers have also examined the cross-level interaction of justice climate and individual-level justice perceptions in the prediction of employee commitment. Mayer et al. (2007) argued that climate may serve as a boundary for individual-level justice perceptions, in that group-level justice perceptions should attenuate the relation between individual-level justice and employee commitment. When employees are members of a group that perceives an unfair climate, reactions to individual experiences should be unfavorable regardless of how employees are treated individually. For example, if employees experience fair treatment personally, they conclude that people are not treated equally and there is a potential for unfairness in the future; if they experience unfairness personally, they externalize the experience as the (negative) norm. In contrast, within a group that perceives a fair climate, individuals' commitment should be more strongly related to their personal experiences. For example, if they experience fair treatment personally, this should increase commitment because both the group and the individual are treated fairly; if they are treated unfairly, this should be particularly detrimental because it suggests that they could have been treated better and are valued relatively less than others. As predicted, Mayer et al. (2007) found that justice climate (procedural, interpersonal, and informational) moderated the effect of individual-level justice perceptions in predicting commitment, such that the relations between individual-level justice perceptions and commitment were stronger for employees within groups who perceived the climate to be fair.

In summary, research on justice climate demonstrates that employee commitment is developed not solely as a function of individual's personal experiences, but also as a function of the group context in which these experiences are embedded. Indeed, employees' personal experiences may have little impact on commitment within an unfair climate.

Summary

We have reviewed three paradigms that have emerged in justice research between 2001 and 2015, which provide novel insights into the relation between justice and employee commitment. In particular, the research on entity and multi-foci justice reveals that, in addition to evaluating the fairness of events, employees also form holistic impressions of the fairness of important social entities (for example, managers, organization as a whole) and these impressions have independent explanatory power beyond event perceptions. In fact, positive global impressions of fairness may offset declines in commitment that might otherwise occur when employees experience an unfair event. The research on entity and multi-foci justice is also important because it helps to explain how employees may become committed to different parties with whom they interact. Similarly, research on justice climate reveals the added value of considering group-level justice perceptions in the prediction of individual-level commitment. Indeed, individual-level perceptions of fairness may have little impact on employee commitment when, as a group, employees generally feel unfairly treated.

WHY DOES JUSTICE FOSTER COMMITMENT?

Two theoretical frameworks are frequently utilized to explain why fair treatment fosters employee commitment. In this section, we briefly review the history and main tenets of each framework, and highlight some of the relevant research.

Relational and Identity-Based Explanation

Lind and Tyler (1988) were among the first to theorize about the connection between justice and organizational commitment in their group-value model of procedural justice, and later in the relational model of authority (Tyler and Lind, 1992). Prior to this time, distributive and procedural justice research (Adams, 1965; Leventhal, 1980; Thibaut and Walker, 1975) was rooted in a view of people as self-interested and primarily concerned with maximizing material outcomes in their interactions with others. Under this view, people desire fair distributions and procedures because fairness has instrumental value for obtaining favorable outcomes in the long term (for a review, see Bobocel and Gosse, 2015).

In contrast, Lind and Tyler argued that people care about procedures not only for their instrumental value vis-à-vis material outcomes but also (and often more so) because fair procedures convey information about whether people are valued members of the group. Drawing on social identity theory (e.g., Tajfel and Turner, 1979), Lind and Tyler argued that people's views of the self are shaped by their experiences in the groups to which they belong. Similarly, the relational model argued that procedures are interpreted as reflecting basic values of the group; thus procedures convey information regarding people's relationship with the group and the authority enacting the procedure. Therefore, common to these approaches – broadly referred to as relational models – is the idea that employees become attached to groups which treat them fairly, because fair treatment communicates that they are valued and worthy group members.[8]

In recent years, Tyler and Blader advanced another relational framework, the group engagement model, to explain cooperation in groups (Tyler and Blader, 2003). The group engagement model is broader in scope and elaborates on the process by which procedural justice leads to psychological engagement with the group and to cooperative behavior. In brief, the model suggests that procedural fairness shapes key identity-related judgments. Namely, it signals whether the group has high status (which leads to feelings of pride) and whether one has high status within the group (which leads to feelings of respect). Pride and respect promote merging of the self with the group (that is, identification), which in turn affects whether individuals develop supportive attitudes and engage in cooperative behaviors (Tyler and Blader, 2003).

Of note is that, as with the earlier models, the group engagement model recognizes that outcome favorability and distributive justice perceptions can also shape people's attitudes and behaviors toward the group. The model contends, however, that judgments about material resources have an indirect effect on attitudes and behaviors via their influence on social identity assessments. As the authors state: 'to the extent that having more resources in a group leads people to feel better about their identity with the group, they will engage themselves more in that group' (Tyler and Blader, 2003, p. 355).

Historically, the relational models of procedural justice have stimulated a vast amount of research linking justice to organizational commitment. Indeed, one of the first studies to demonstrate the differential effects of procedural and distributive justice on employee commitment was theoretically grounded in the group-value model (Folger and Konovsky, 1989). Lind and Tyler (1988) argued that procedural justice perceptions should be most relevant in the formation of people's general attitudes (such as commitment and trust) toward groups, whereas distributive justice perceptions should be a more relevant predictor of people's reactions to specific outcomes (such as satisfaction with one's pay). As noted earlier, the differential effects paradigm guided research for many years between the 1980s and 2000, and indeed continues to do so (e.g., Camerman et al., 2007; Hausknecht et al., 2011).

After 2000, many studies offered support for relational models by testing theoretically derived moderation effects. For example, Brockner et al. (2005) demonstrated that the positive effect of procedural justice on cooperation and on positive affect is strengthened among people for whom social identity is especially important (stronger interdependent self-construal), a prediction that follows from the relational models. Similarly, Johnson and Chang (2008) found that procedural justice is more strongly associated with organizational commitment among people who more highly identify with the organization.

More recent research has focused on examining the mediating role of social identity in the relation between procedural justice and group-related attitudes and behaviors (e.g., Blader and Tyler, 2009; De Cremer et al., 2005). For example, Michel et al. (2010) drew on the group engagement model to predict that procedural justice during an organizational change would enhance commitment to the change via increased organizational identification. The authors conducted a longitudinal study of academic staff at a German university undergoing major restructuring. As expected, they found that procedural justice perceptions predicted employees' affective commitment to the change initially and six months later via enhanced identification with the organization.

Social Exchange-Based Explanation

The connection between justice and employee reactions is also often interpreted from the perspective of social exchange theory. Although there are important nuances to social exchange theory as a conceptual framework, in general it describes how relationships develop based on the exchange of resources (for a review, see Cropanzano and Mitchell, 2005). Blau (1964) distinguished two types of exchange relationships. Economic exchange relationships are those in which the parties specify precisely the benefits offered by one party and the obligations to be borne by the other party, usually within an explicit time frame. Such agreements can be enforced by a contract and therefore do not depend on trust between parties.

In contrast, social exchange relationships are those in which benefits and obligations are diffuse and unspecified, and which therefore depend on trust and long-term commitment between the parties involved. Trust and commitment from both parties are needed to ensure that reciprocation of benefits will occur in the long term. According to the social exchange perspective, then, employees reciprocate fair treatment with commitment and other responses that benefit the organization because of a social exchange relationship that develops between employees and the organization.

Organ (1988) was among the first to draw on the social exchange perspective to interpret the relation between justice and citizenship behavior; therefore much of the early research in this vein was conducted in this context (e.g., Organ and Konovsky, 1989; Moorman, 1991). However, as noted in the previous section, around 2000, justice researchers turned to social exchange theory to explain multi-foci justice effects on employee attitudes and behaviors more broadly (see Masterson et al., 2000; Rupp and Cropanzano, 2002). As noted earlier, researchers suggested that employees reciprocate fair treatment which they attribute to different entities (for example, supervisors, co-workers, organization) with responses that are targeted toward the entity via multi-foci social exchange relationships (Rupp and Cropanzano, 2002).

Since this time, many studies have examined the idea that justice induces a high-quality social exchange relationship with the source of justice, which in turn predicts affective commitment. Researchers have operationalized the social exchange relationship in different ways (for reviews, see Colquitt et al., 2014; Cropanzano and Byrne, 2000). Most often, perceptions of organizational support (POS) (Eisenberger et al., 1986) and organizational trust are used as indicators of social exchange quality when the source of justice is the organization. Leader–member exchange (LMX) (Gerstner and Day, 1997) and supervisor trust are used as indicators when the source of justice is the organization.

For example, in a study of commitment among contingent workers, Liden et al. (2003) argued that employees form social exchange relationships with both the temporary organization and their employment agency. Thus, they predicted (and found) that foci-specific POS mediated the relations between foci-specific procedural justice perceptions and foci-specific commitments. Similarly, in a sample of temporary workers in Belgium, Camerman et al. (2007) found that POS mediated the relation between procedural justice and affective commitment to employees' current organization, whereas trust in one's staffing agent mediated the relation between informational justice and affective commitment to the staffing agency (also see Rhee et al., 2011). In related research, Arshad and Sparrow (2010) found among downsizing survivors in Malaysia that procedural unfairness had an adverse effect on affective commitment because employees perceived that the organization had failed to meet their obligations.

In other studies, affective commitment is itself conceptualized as the indicator of the quality of social exchange relationship; thus, researchers have examined the role of affective commitment in mediating the relation between justice and other work outcomes, such as job performance and citizenship behaviors. The results of two recent justice meta-analyses support the idea that affective commitment plays a mediating role in justice–work outcome relations, therefore supporting the potency of the social exchange framework more generally (Colquitt et al., 2013; Rupp et al., 2014).

Summary

We have reviewed two theoretical frameworks that are typically used to explain the relation between justice and commitment. The identity-based explanation argues that employees become committed to groups and authorities that treat them fairly because fairness (especially process fairness) communicates that they are valued members of the group, which leads to identification with the source of justice. The social exchange-based explanation argues that employees become committed to organizations in which they are treated fairly because of a positive social exchange relationship that develops between employees and the organization. Under this account, fairness is perceived as a benefit, which employees feel obliged to repay, and which they expect to continue receiving in the future. Although these explanations are often conceptualized as separate processes connecting justice to work outcomes (e.g., Moorman and Byrne, 2005; Tyler and Blader, 2003), in general little research has sought to distinguish them empirically. Thus, consensus is lacking as to whether they represent separate processes that both occur, or are alternative interpretations of the relation between justice and commitment.

PRACTICAL IMPLICATIONS AND CONCLUSION

Altogether, a large volume of research has accumulated between 1980 and 2015, which indicates that organizational justice is an important driver of employee commitment. This research has many practical implications. A key implication of the early research within the differential effects paradigm is that, to enact fairness and promote affective commitment, organizations should strive to distribute outcomes fairly, make decisions using fair procedures, explain decision procedures, and treat recipients with sensitivity and respect. Moreover, the early research on the process–outcome interaction implies that, even when a decision outcome is unfavorable or unfair, organizations can maintain employee commitment by ensuring that employees perceive procedural and interactional justice. Indeed, between 2000–2015, many studies have demonstrated the efficacy of process fairness for maintaining employee commitment in the context of organizational downsizing (see Van Dierendonck and Jacobs, 2012, for a meta-analytic review), and organization change more generally (e.g., Marzucco et al., 2014; Michel et al., 2010).

These recommendations remain applicable today but, unsurprisingly, the more recent research indicates that there is more to the story. For example, as noted earlier, recent research indicates that in addition to judging the distributive, procedural, and interactional justice of events, employees are forming holistic impressions of the fairness of their supervisors and the organization as a whole, and these global judgments are influential over and above event fairness perceptions. Thus, although employees are clearly motivated to assess the fairness of events, they are also motivated to judge the fairness of those who are deemed to be responsible for those events; assessments that have independent downstream consequences. Given the importance of these latter justice judgments for predicting employee commitment, supervisors and organizations thus should strive to ensure that they are viewed as fair entities in the eyes of employees.

Interestingly, scholars have long argued that being fair is not necessarily sufficient for appearing fair, and that organizations should both enact fairness and proactively promote an image of fairness (Greenberg, 1990). For example, organizations could highlight past successful fair actions and policies (for example, successful organizational restructuring, employee performance awards) in internal employee communications, press releases, and advertising to promote an image of fairness. Managers could similarly highlight past efforts undertaken to uphold event fairness (for example, performance evaluation or resource allocation decisions) in discussions with employees or in company newsletters. These mechanisms could also be used to proactively communicate managers' fairness values, intentions, and goals. For example, organizational agents could use the success of past fairness-related events to garner support for new decisions. Note that these actions may simultaneously foster a climate of fairness. As reviewed earlier, the relation between the event fairness perceptions and employee commitment is stronger in the context of a workgroup in which everyone feels fairly treated.

Clearly, such efforts must be supplementary to actually enacting fairness. Nevertheless, given the importance of holistic perceptions of justice in the prediction of employee commitment, it seems important for managers and organizations to both enact fairness (by upholding normative justice rules when making decisions) and be perceived as fair, if they are to maximize employee commitment.

NOTES

*   We thank Colin MacLeod, John Meyer, Deborah Rupp, and an anonymous reviewer for their very helpful comments on an earlier version of this chapter. Writing of this chapter was supported by research funding from the Social Sciences and Humanities Research Council of Canada, awarded to the first author.

1. In the contemporary literature, researchers sometimes use a four-factor model of justice (see Colquitt et al., 2001) in which the interactional justice construct is divided into 'informational' and 'interpersonal' justice to reflect information-sharing and respectful treatment, respectively. For our purposes in the present chapter, we use the broader and more common label of interactional justice, but note distinctions as needed.
2. In the early research, researchers often did not distinguish procedural and interactional justice as separate constructs, considering them instead to be related aspects of process fairness.
3. For reviews of the traditional paradigms, see Colquitt et al. (2005) and Bobocel and Gosse (2015).
4. A limited number of studies have included measures of normative and continuance commitment. In general, like affective commitment, justice is moderately positively related to normative commitment (e.g., Cohen-Charash and Spector, 2001; Meyer et al., 2002; Rupp et al., 2014). The relation between justice and continuance commitment is inconsistent, with some early evidence suggesting a negative relation (e.g., Cohen-Charash and Spector, 2001) but more recent evidence demonstrating no significant association (e.g., Rupp et al., 2014). More research is needed to establish theory and empirical evidence regarding how justice may relate to other dimensions of commitment.
5. Note that although Hausknecht and colleagues grounded their predictions in fairness heuristic theory, justice was assessed in terms of components rather than as overall justice.
6. Although not described earlier, Choi (2008) also found the same source–target matching effects, and the same cross-foci effect.
7. Researchers typically compute intra-class correlations to ensure significant within-group agreement and between-group differences before conducting cross-level analyses (e.g., Naumann and Bennett, 2000). Hence, climate estimates reflect valence of shared perceptions rather than strength of climate.
8. Lind and Tyler (1988) recognized the importance of both the structure of decision procedures (for example, whether input is solicited) and the manner in which authorities treat recipients (for example, respect) as determinants of process fairness perceptions, but they did not view these elements as fundamentally different. Thus, in research deriving from the relational and identity models, procedural justice is typically operationalized broadly to include both elements.

REFERENCES

Adams, J.S. (1965). Inequity in social exchange. In L. Berkowitz (ed.), *Advances in Experimental Social Psychology* (Vol. 2, pp. 267–299). New York: Academic Press.

Allen, N.J. and Meyer, J.P. (1990). The measurement and antecedents of affective, continuance, and normative commitment to the organization. *Journal of Occupational Psychology*, *63*, 1–18.

Ambrose, M.L. and Schminke, M. (2009). The role of overall justice judgments in organizational justice research: A test of mediation. *Journal of Applied Psychology*, *94*, 491–500.

Arshad, R. and Sparrow, P. (2010). Downsizing and survivor reactions in Malaysia: Modelling antecedents and outcomes of psychological contract violation. *International Journal of Human Resource Management*, *21*, 1793–1815.

Bianchi, E.C., Brockner, J., van den Bos, K., Seifert, M., Moon, H., van Dijke, M., and De Cremer, D. (2015). Trust in decision-making authorities dictates the form of the interactive relationship between outcome fairness and procedural fairness. *Personality and Social Psychology Bulletin*, *41*, 19–34.

Bies, R.J. and Moag, J.F. (1986). Interactional justice: Communication criteria of fairness. In R.J. Lewicki, B.H. Sheppard, and M.H. Bazerman (eds), *Research on Negotiations in Organizations* (Vol. 1, pp. 43–55). Greenwich, CT: JAI Press.

Blader, S.L. and Tyler, T.R. (2009). Testing and extending the group engagement model: Linkages between social identity, procedural justice, economic outcomes, and extrarole behavior. *Journal of Applied Psychology*, *94*, 445–464.

Blau, P.M. (1964). *Exchange and Power in Social Life*. New York: Wiley.

Bobocel, D.R. (2013). Coping with unfair events constructively or destructively: The effects of overall justice and self-other orientation. *Journal of Applied Psychology*, *98*, 720–731.

Bobocel, D.R. and Gosse, L. (2015). Procedural justice: A historical review and critical analysis. In R. Cropanzano and M. Ambrose (eds), *Oxford Handbook of Psychology: Justice in Work Organizations* (pp. 51–87), New York: Oxford University Press.

Brockner, J. (2010). *A Contemporary Look at Organizational Justice: Multiplying Insult Times Injury*. New York: Routledge.

Brockner, J., De Cremer, D., Van den Bos, K., and Chen, Y.R. (2005). The influence of interdependent self-construal on procedural fairness effects. *Organizational Behavior and Human Decision Processes*, *96*, 155–167.

Brockner, J. and Wiesenfeld, B.M. (1996). An integrative framework for explaining reactions to decisions: Interactive effects of outcomes and procedures. *Psychological Bulletin*, *102*, 189–208.

Byrne, Z. (April, 1999). How do procedural and interactional justice influence multiple levels of organizational outcomes? Paper presented at the annual meeting of the Society for Industrial and Organizational Psychology, Atlanta, GA.

Camerman, J., Cropanzano, R., and Vandenberghe, C. (2007). The benefits of justice for temporary workers. *Group and Organization Management*, *32*, 176–207.

Choi, J. (2008). Event justice perceptions and employees' reactions: Perceptions of social entity justice as a moderator. *Journal of Applied Psychology*, *93*, 513–528.

Cohen-Charash, Y. and Spector, P.E. (2001). The role of justice in organizations: A meta-analysis. *Organizational Behavior and Human Decision Processes*, *86*, 278–321.

Colquitt, J.A., Conlon, D.E., Wesson, M.J., Porter, C.O.L.H., and Ng, K.Y. (2001). Justice at the millennium: A meta-analytic review of 25 years of organizational justice research. *Journal of Applied Psychology*, *86*, 425–445.

Colquitt, J.A., Greenberg, J., and Zapata-Phelan, C. (2005). What is organizational justice? A historical overview. In J. Greenberg and J.A. Colquitt (eds), *Handbook of Organizational Justice* (pp. 3–56). Mahwah, NJ: Lawrence Erlbaum Associates.

Colquitt, J.A., Long, D.M., Rodell, J.A., and Halvorsen-Ganepola, M.D. (2014). Scale indicators of social exchange relationships: A comparison of relative content validity. *Journal of Applied Psychology*, *99*, 599–618.

Colquitt, J.A., Scott, B.A., Rodell, J.B., Long, D.M., Zapata, C.P., and Conlon, D.E. (2013). Justice at the millennium, a decade later: A meta-analytic test of social exchange and affect-based perspectives. *Journal of Applied Psychology*, *98*, 199–236.

Cropanzano, R. and Byrne, Z.S. (2000). Workplace justice and the dilemma of organizational citizenship. In M. Van Vugt, M. Snyder, T.R. Tyler, and A. Biel (eds), *Cooperation in Modern Society: Promoting the Welfare of Communities, States and Organizations* (pp. 142–161). New York: Routledge.

Cropanzano, R., Byrne, Z.S., Bobocel, D.R., and Rupp, D.E. (2001). Moral virtues, fairness heuristics, social entities, and other denizens of organizational justice. *Journal of Vocational Behavior*, *58*, 164–209.

Cropanzano, R. and Mitchell, M.S. (2005). Social exchange theory: An interdisciplinary review. *Journal of Management*, *31*, 874–900.

De Cremer, D., Tyler, T.R., and den Ouden, N. (2005). Managing cooperation via procedural fairness: The mediating influence of self–other merging. *Journal of Economic Psychology*, *26*, 393-406.

Eisenberger, R., Huntington, R., Hutchison, S., and Sowa, D. (1986). Perceived organizational support. *Journal of Applied Psychology*, *71*, 500–507.

Folger, R. and Konovsky, M.A. (1989). Effects of procedural and distributive justice on reactions to pay raise decisions. *Academy of Management Journal*, *32*, 115–130.

Gerstner, C.R. and Day, D.V. (1997). Meta-analytic review of leader–member exchange theory: Correlates and construct issues. *Journal of Applied Psychology*, *82*, 827–844.

Greenberg, I. (1990). Looking fair vs. being fair: Managing impressions of organizational justice. In B. Staw and L. Cummings (eds), *Research in Organizational Behavior* (Vol. 12, pp. 111–157). Greenwich, CT: JAI Press.

Hausknecht, J.P., Sturman, M.C., and Roberson, Q.M. (2011). Justice as a dynamic construct: Effects of individual trajectories on distal work outcomes. *Journal of Applied Psychology*, *96*, 872–880.

Holtz, B.C. and Harold, C.M. (2009). Fair today, fair tomorrow? A longitudinal investigation of overall justice perceptions. *Journal of Applied Psychology*, *94*, 1185–1199.

Johnson, R.E. and Chang, C.H. (2008). Relationships between organizational commitment and its antecedents: Employee self-concept matters. *Journal of Applied Social Psychology*, *38*, 513–541.

Jones, D.A. and Martens, M.L. (2009). The mediating role of overall justice and the moderating role of trust certainty in justice-criteria relationships: The formation and use of fairness heuristics in the workplace. *Journal of Organizational Behavior*, *30*, 1025–1051.

Lavelle, J., Rupp, D.E., and Brockner, J. (2007). Taking a multifoci approach to the study of justice, social exchange, and citizenship behavior: The target similarity model. *Journal of Management*, *33*, 841–866.

Leventhal, G.S. (1980). What should be done with equity theory? New approaches to the study of fairness in social relationships. In K. Gergen, M. Greenberg, and R. Willis (eds), *Social Exchange: Advances in Theory and Research* (pp. 27–55). New York: Plenum Press.

Li, A. and Cropanzano, R. (2009). Do East Asians respond more/less strongly to organizational justice than North Americans? A meta-analysis. *Journal of Management Studies*, *46*, 787–805.

Liao, H. and Rupp, D.E. (2005). The impact of justice climate and justice orientation on work outcomes: A cross-level multifoci framework. *Journal of Applied Psychology*, *90*, 242–256.

Liden, R.C., Wayne, S.J., Kraimer, M.L., and Sparrow, R.T. (2003). The dual commitments of contingent workers: An examination of contingents' commitment to the agency and the organization. *Journal of Organizational Behavior*, *24*, 609–625.

Lind, E.A. (2001). Fairness heuristic theory: Justice judgments as pivotal cognitions in organizational relations. In J. Greenberg and R. Cropanzano (EDS), *Advances in Organizational Justice* (pp. 56–88). Stanford, CA: Stanford University Press.

Lind, E.A. and Tyler, T.R. (1988). *The Social Psychology of Procedural Justice*. New York: Plenum Press.

Loi, R., Yang, J., and Diefendorff, J.M. (2009). Four-factor justice and daily job satisfaction: A multilevel investigation. *Journal of Applied Psychology*, *94*, 770–781.

Marzucco, L., Marique, G., Stinglhamber, F., De Roeck, K., and Hansez, I. (2014). Justice and employee attitudes during organizational change: The mediating role of overall justice. *European Review of Applied Psychology*, *64*, 289–298.

Masterson, S.S., Lewis, K., Goldman, B.M., and Taylor, M.S. (2000). Integrating justice and social exchange: The differing effects of fair procedures and treatment on work relationships. *Academy of Management Journal*, *43*, 738–748.

Mayer, D.M., Nishii, L., Schneider, B., and Goldstein, H. (2007). The precursors and products of justice climates: Group leader antecedents and employee attitudinal consequences. *Personnel Psychology*, *60*, 929–963.

Meyer, J.P. and Allen, N.J. (1991). A three-component conceptualization of organizational commitment. *Human Resource Management Review*, *1*, 61–89.

Meyer, J.P., Stanley, D.J., Herscovitch, L., and Topolnytsky, L. (2002). Affective, continuance, and normative commitment to the organization: A meta-analysis of antecedents, correlates, and consequences. *Journal of Vocational Behavior*, *61*, 20–52.

Michel, A., Stegmaier, R., and Sonntag, K. (2010). I scratch your back – You scratch mine. Do procedural justice and organizational identification matter for employees' cooperation during change? *Journal of Change Management*, *10*, 41–59.

Moorman, R.H. (1991). Relationship between organizational justice and organizational citizenship behaviors: Do fairness perceptions influence employee citizenship? *Journal of Applied Psychology*, *76*, 845–855.

Moorman, R.H. and Byrne, Z.S. (2005). How does organizational justice affect organizational citizenship behavior? In J. Greenberg and J.A. Colquitt (eds), *Handbook of Organizational Justice* (pp. 355–380). Mahwah, NJ: Lawrence Erlbaum.

Mossholder, K.W., Bennett, N., and Martin, C.L. (1998). A multilevel analysis of procedural justice context. *Journal of Organizational Behavior*, *19*, 131–141.

Naumann, S.E. and Bennett, N. (2000). A case for procedural justice climate: Development and test of a multilevel model. *Academy of Management Journal*, *43*, 881–889.

Ohana, M. (2014). A multilevel study of the relationship between organizational justice and affective commitment: The moderating role of organizational size and tenure. *Personnel Review*, *43*, 654–671.

Organ, D.W. (1988). *Organizational Citizenship Behavior: The Good Soldier Syndrome*. Lexington, MA: Lexington Books.

Organ, D.W. and Konovsky, M. (1989). Cognitive versus affective determinants of organizational citizenship behavior. *Journal of Applied Psychology*, *74*, 157–164.

Rhee, J., Park, T., and Hwang, S.H. (2011). Non-regular professionals' dual commitment in South Korea: Antecedents and consequences. *The International Journal of Human Resource Management*, *22*, 612–631.

Roberson, Q.M. and Colquitt, J.A. (2005). Shared and configural justice: A social network model of justice in teams. *Academy of Management Review*, *30*, 595–607.

Rupp, D.E. and Cropanzano, R. (2002). The mediating effects of social exchange relationships in predicting workplace outcomes from multifoci organizational justice. *Organizational Behavior and Human Decision Processes*, *89*, 925–946.

Rupp, D.E., Shao, R., Jones, K.S., and Liao, H. (2014). The utility of a multifoci approach to the study of organizational justice: A meta-analytic investigation into the consideration of normative rules, moral accountability, bandwidth-fidelity, and social exchange. *Organizational Behavior and Human Decision Processes*, *123*, 159–185.

Shao, R., Rupp, D.E., Skarlicki, D.P., and Jones, K. (2013). Employee justice across cultures: A meta-analytic review. *Journal of Management*, *39*, 263–301.

Simons, T. and Roberson, Q. (2003). Why managers should care about fairness: The effects of aggregate justice perceptions on organizational outcomes. *Journal of Applied Psychology*, *88*, 432–443.

Tajfel, H. and Turner, J.C. (1979). An integrative theory of intergroup conflict. In W.G. Austin and S. Worchel (eds), *The Social Psychology of Intergroup Relations* (pp. 33–47). Monterey, CA: Brooks-Cole.

Thibaut, J. and Walker, L. (1975). *Procedural Justice: A Psychological Analysis*. Hillsdale, NJ: Erlbaum.

Tyler, T.R. and Blader, S.L. (2003). The group engagement model: Procedural justice, social identity, and cooperative behavior. *Personality and Social Psychology Review*, *7*, 349–361.

Tyler, T.R. and Lind, E.A. (1992). A relational model of authority in groups. In M.P. Zanna (ed.), *Advances in Experimental Social Psychology* (Vol. 25, pp. 115–191). San Francisco, CA: Academic Press.

Van den Bos, K. (2001). Uncertainty management: The influence of uncertainty salience on reactions to perceived procedural fairness. *Journal of Personality and Social Psychology*, *80*, 931–941.

Van den Bos, K., Lind, E.A., and Wilke, H.A.M. (2001). The psychology of procedural and distributive justice viewed from the perspective of fairness heuristic theory. In R. Cropanzano (ed.), *Justice in the Workplace: From Theory to Practice* (Vol. 2, pp. 49–66), Mahwah, NJ: Lawrence Erlbaum Associates.

Van Dierendonck, D. and Jacobs, G. (2012), Survivors and victims, a meta-analytical review of fairness and organizational commitment after downsizing. *British Journal of Management, 23*, 96–109.

Viswesvaran, C. and Ones, D.S. (2002). Examining the construct of organizational justice: A meta-analytic evaluation of relations with work attitudes and behaviors. *Journal of Business Ethics, 38*, 193–203.

PART VI

COMMITMENT ACROSS CULTURES

26. Understanding commitment across cultures: an overview
S. Arzu Wasti

The purpose of this chapter is to critically evaluate the cross-cultural generalizability of commitment theories developed in North America and to provide a theoretical and methodological roadmap for future research on commitment in different contexts. While the issues covered are expected to apply to various conceptualizations of commitment, the three-component model (TCM) by Meyer and Allen (1991) is chosen as the reference model as it has established itself as the dominant paradigm, notwithstanding various theoretical and empirical challenges (e.g., Klein et al., 2012). Furthermore, the three components have been argued to be differentially useful in understanding commitment in different cultures (e.g., Wasti, 2003).

Integrating and refining prior research in the United States (US) (Becker, 1960; Mowday et al., 1979), the TCM was developed by Canadian scholars (Meyer and Allen, 1991) and, as with most academic knowledge produced in the North American context, was soon imported by researchers around the world. In the first decade of importation, a handful of studies explicitly tested the generalizability of the TCM to different parts of the world (e.g., Ko et al., 1997; Vandenberghe, 1996) and a minority of studies developed a priori hypotheses regarding cultural differences (e.g., Wasti, 2002). The majority adopted an imposed-etic approach, which assumes culture-specific or emic theories, constructs, and measures (usually developed in the US or Canada) to be universal or etic (see Wasti and Önder, 2009 for a review). A decade later, the growing adoption of the TCM outside of North America has enabled insightful meta-analyses on the role of macroeconomic as well as cultural variables (e.g., Meyer et al., 2012). More generally, commitment research not only enjoys a stronger theoretical basis as to how commitment might be experienced in different cultures and why, but also benefits from increased statistical sophistication to tackle the operationalization and analysis of such differences (e.g., Eisinga et al., 2010; Fisher, 2014).

Nonetheless, a cursory review of a selective sample of the non-North American organizational commitment research (that is, Social Science Citation Index publications in management, business, applied psychology, and industrial relations journals in 2014 that have 'commitment' in their title) suggests that many studies still fail to fully incorporate the role of the institutional and cultural characteristics of their study context to their research questions and methodology, as well as interpretation. Although statistical advances enable tests of measurement equivalence or confirmatory factor analyses (Chapter 32 in this volume), the possibility remains that the operationalization may be construct-deficient in the new context. Furthermore, such studies seem to suffer from errors of omission, as they tend to adopt research questions that are heavily inspired by the mainstream literature and neglect to incorporate contextually relevant or salient constructs to the research design.

It should be noted that the TCM itself represents the thinking that prevailed in organizational behaviour (OB) theory developed in North America in the late twentieth century (Wasti et al., 2016). This heritage is characterized predominantly by quantitative survey-based field research that develops and tests middle-range theories (Weick, 1974). Middle-range theories leave out the context and focus on a small number of constructs, such as the components of commitment, their proximal antecedents and outcomes. So by design, the TCM is an acontextual model that has not explicated its assumptions as to the characteristics of the cultural and institutional context it is embedded in. Naturally, as with other North American OB theories, the TCM was developed on the basis of certain implicit values and assumptions as to human nature, the meaning and purpose of organizations, the environments they exist in, and the like (Gelfand et al., 2008). In the following section, these assumptions and their cross-cultural generalizability are evaluated.

THE PREMISES AND THE GENERALIZABILITY OF THE TCM

Gelfand et al. (2008) observe that modern organizational psychology has developed within a context of industrialization, wealth, and social tranquility. Thus, one primary assumption underlying the TCM encompasses the macroeconomic context. Anchoring to Inglehart's (1997) discussion of materialist versus postmaterialist values, Gelfand et al. (2008) refer to the wealthy and industrialized context of Western science as postmaterialism. Postmaterialist values emphasize self-expression, subjective well-being, and quality of life; as opposed to the materialist values, which emphasize economic and physical security. The TCM is a product of a period of economic strength and stability, opportunity, and mobility. It is probably no coincidence the topic of organizational commitment, particularly affective commitment (AC), emerged and gained ground in the US. In contrast, in lower-income countries, where employees are dependent on the income provided by their organizations and have fewer options, organizations can afford to maintain transactional contracts (Wasti and Önder, 2009). In these contexts, material concerns may render continuance commitment (CC) the most relevant component, and 'hygiene factors' such as pay and job security can play a greater role in fostering commitment (Gelfand et al., 2008).

Another assumption of the TCM seems to be that organizations function under relatively strong legal systems, and in consequence organizations are also characterized by bureaucratic structures. The strength of the legal system determines the prevalence of formal, enforceable versus informal contracts. Weak legal systems, such as those in ex-communist or developing countries, enable authority structures that are particularistic (Fligstein, 1996). Particularistic organizations display concentration of power in the hands of a few individuals (for example, members of the same political party) and arbitrary use of power. Employees in these organizations depend on particular individuals rather than formal rules or procedures for recruitment, promotion, or other rewards. As argued by Pearce et al. (2000), employees in particularistic organizations are unlikely to be committed to the organization; however, they may be committed to the persons in the organization upon whom they depend.

The discussion up to now appears to make a distinction between 'developing versus developed' countries. However, even within developed nations, the TCM may not be easily transferable. The TCM has mostly been elaborated in a liberal market economy. With the imperative to keep labor costs down and sustain managerial prerogatives, liberal market economies tend to have fewer welfare policies (Hult and Svallfors, 2002). In contrast, in welfare economies such as Germany or Denmark, employees are granted extensive rights and protection against employers (for example, unemployment benefits, strong barriers to lay-offs and dismissals; Wasti et al., 2016). Nonetheless, research does not find higher levels of commitment in welfare economies (e.g., Hult and Svallfors, 2002). This is in line with Eisenberger et al. (1997), who reasoned that favorable organizational experiences would generate more positive attitudes if employees believed them to be at the discretion of the organization, not legally stipulated. Thus, the primary antecedents of organizational commitment identified in the North American literature (for example, voice, lack of alternatives, job security) seem to have less relevance in welfare economies.

The TCM also reflects certain assumptions regarding workways, defined as a culture's signature pattern of workplace beliefs and practices that represent a society's ideas about what is true, good, and efficient in the domain of work (Sanchez-Burks and Lee, 2007). Sanchez-Burks (2005) argued that American workplace norms are guided by 'Protestant relational ideology', which refers to a deep-seated sentiment that emotional, relational, and personal concerns ought to be put aside at work in order to direct one's attention to the task at hand. Relatedly, in the US social groups rarely bridge the work–non-work divide (for example, co-workers versus church friends; Sanchez-Burks, 2005). This divide facilitates the maintenance of 'professionalism' at the workplace as there is little spillover from the personal life domain in terms of relational norms or expectations.

Indeed, the commitment literature does not consider the multiplexity of relationships, which refers to whether or not personal friendships and instrumental resources are exchanged in the same relationship (Morris et al., 2000). However, evidence from collectivist cultures in East Asia and the Middle East suggests that workways are characterized by a much greater emphasis on relational, affective, and personal components (e.g., Sanchez-Burks and Lee, 2007; Triandis, 1995). In such cultures, the prevalent leadership style is paternalism (Aycan, 2001; Cheng et al., 2004). Paternalistic managers show holistic concern for subordinates' well-being, such as attending their personal events and helping to solve personal problems. Similarly, an employee's sense of obligation to their boss extends the boundaries of the office or workday (Aycan, 2001; Sanchez-Burks and Lee, 2007). In such cultures, not only would interpersonal commitments play a greater role than organizational commitment, but also the multiplexity of the relationships would have implications for what commitment means, how it develops and unfolds, as it straddles personal and professional life domains.

With respect to assumptions regarding human nature, the TCM assumes an individualist mindset, which entails a belief that personal choices are omnipotent (Markus and Kitayama, 1991). Like many research paradigms in OB, the TCM also presupposes that, for the most part, employees freely choose the best companies to work for, and are preoccupied with personal need fulfillment (Gelfand et al., 2008). These assumptions may not be relevant in collectivist contexts, where individuals adjust their preferences and behavior to fulfill their relational duties and obligations. Of all assumptions underlying the TCM, this one has been the most popular to be tested so far. Research from collectivist contexts has demonstrated the relative importance of normative commitment (NC) (e.g., Wasti, 2003), and in particular, the commitment towards the supervisor (e.g.,

Cheng et al., 2003). Furthermore, this research has underlined the role of ingroups such as family in employment decisions (e.g., Hom and Xiao, 2011; Wasti, 2002), which is in stark contrast to the mainstream research on commitment and turnover that tends to overlook the interrelationships between work and non-work commitments (Bielby, 1992).

Finally, the TCM is also couched in assumptions of looseness (Gelfand et al., 2011) and relatively lower levels of power distance (Hofstede, 1980). In a culture with large power distance, there is greater dependence on and acceptance of authority; whereas low power distance cultures are characterized by more egalitarian relationships (Hofstede, 1980). For instance, the primary antecedents of AC such as voice and empowerment reflect a low power distance mindset and have been shown to be less effective in high power distance countries (e.g., Robert et al., 2000). Cultural tightness or looseness is defined as the strength of social norms and the degree of sanctioning within societies (Gelfand et al., 2011). People in tight cultures are prevention-oriented, and dutiful. People in loose cultures do not engage in such self-regulation, so norms in general exert less influence on behavior. Gelfand et al. (2011) have found the US to be one of the looser countries, which may account for the relative lack of interest in NC and its implications in the mainstream literature. In tighter countries like Japan, in contrast, commitment has been shown to have stronger normative undertones, including peer pressure from co-workers (e.g., Near, 1989).

Any theory that originates and is mostly tested in a single context can be considered to have been only partially validated, with its full structure and variance remaining an empirical question (Aycan and Gelfand, 2012). By testing the TCM with research designs that explicitly address the assumptions outlined above, evidence for its generalizability and completeness can be obtained; if necessary, culture-specific adaptations and additions can be made to enhance its cross-cultural applicability. Furthermore, while the TCM is proposed to embody the above assumptions, processes that are prevalent in other cultural contexts may actually be present in North America as well but in a recessive or muted form (Aycan and Gelfand, 2012). For instance, multiplex work relationships may not be the norm in the US, but this may mean that they are muted on average or overlooked by researchers who were guided by different priorities or perceptions (Smith, 2012). Yet, there may be conditions in the US where understanding multiplexity and commitment is relevant. For instance, Ingram and Zou (2008) observed that workplace friendships are increasing in the US due to societal trends such as people living alone, and spending more time at work. Thus, understanding variance across cultures can help to better understand variance within cultures as well.

STUDYING CULTURE AND COMMITMENT

As in all areas of OB, cross-cultural commitment research proliferated after Hofstede's (1980) seminal work that offered four dimensions – namely individualism–collectivism, power distance, uncertainty avoidance, and masculinity–femininity – along which cultural differences could be described. Hofstede's (1980) neat typology brought about a wealth of studies focusing on cultural variables at an individual level of analysis. Studies typically sampled participants in two or more countries, and measured commitment and related psychological or organizational constructs. In earlier years, the observed differences were explained by passing or post hoc reference to Hofstede's (1980) nation-level value framework; later, individual-level hypotheses were advanced with reference to the burgeoning work on individualism and collectivism (e.g., Markus and Kitayama, 1991; Triandis, 1995). This latter period also drew on the conceptual and methodological refinements provided by the Schwartz Value Survey (Schwartz, 1992) as well as the GLOBE study (House et al., 2004).

While acknowledging the service that Hofstede's (1980) or comparable value frameworks have provided in putting the study of culture to the fore of mainstream OB, several concerns have been raised regarding the trajectory of comparative OB research (e.g., Fischer et al., 2005; Tsui et al., 2007). One concern is a level-of-analysis issue (e.g., Oyserman and Uskul, 2008). Researchers applying Hofstede's frameworks assume that individuals from countries that ranked high on individualism are highly individualistic, while individuals from countries ranked low in individualism are highly collectivistic. Moreover, Hofstede's scores represent a nation-level aggregation of individual-level values of a certain sample of individuals at a certain place and certain point in time, but they have been treated by researchers as representing consensus within nations and generalizability across contexts and over time (Oyserman and Uskul, 2008). All these assumptions are increasingly being empirically challenged (e.g., Fischer and Schwartz, 2011).

Researchers have tried to get around these problems by measuring individualism–collectivism values at the individual level as a potential mediator of the cross-cultural difference (Leung and van de Vijver, 2008). While the meditational analysis makes a firmer claim than reference to nation-level scores, Cohen (2007) notes that this alternative is not without problems on at least three grounds: (1) unless all else is measured, it does not rule out any other country-level variables that could have affected the results; (2) it requires individual-level measures of cultural orientations that demonstrate strong validity, for which the evidence is wanting; and (3) it reduces culture to an individual difference variable, thereby omitting the role of culturally conferred practices and institutional arrangements in shaping cognition, emotion, and behavior.

Indeed, Gelfand et al. (2008) note that the confusion regarding the level of culture is not surprising, given that discerning the appropriate level of culture is a complex issue. They argue that culture can be operationalized at the individual, group, organization, and nation level. Rather than advocating one 'right' definition or level, they advise researchers to consider different options for defining culture, use the definition that is most appropriate given a particular research question, and to provide an explicit rationale to why culture is at a particular level of analysis. In what follows, I outline some ways to explore how culture may affect organizational commitment by drawing on some recent discussions in the study of psychology and culture.

Individual-Level Analyses of Culture and Commitment

Gelfand et al. (2008) differentiate a number of conceptualizations of culture at the individual level. For instance, psychological culture refers to individuals' personal values, attitudes, or beliefs; whereas 'subjective cultural press' captures individual differences in perceptions of cultural values, attitudes, and/or norms. As mentioned, cross-cultural OB has largely employed the value conceptualization; however, relying extensively on this perspective to decipher cultural differences has been increasingly criticized (e.g., Kirkman et al., 2006). Recently, drawing on two different research traditions in cultural psychology, Leung and Morris (2015) proposed two alternative approaches to studying culture: the constructivist and the intersubjectivist approaches.

The constructivist approach posits that culture influences behavior through the culturally conferred schemas or cognitive lenses that people use to make sense of ambiguous information. The activation of a schema depends on three factors: accessibility, applicability, and judged appropriateness (Higgins, 1996). Thus, according to the constructivist account, many cultural patterns are situation-specific rather than context-general. The constructivist approach is useful in that it explicates how a person's situational motivations or specific experiences – such as working in a multicultural context, or a person's multiple cultural backgrounds, as in the case of biculturals – influences behavior. Leung and Morris (2015) note that the constructivist account seems to predict a level of behavior instability that seems counter to reliable observations of cultural stability. They argue that the enduring structures and institutions in a cultural context reinforce and sustain the culturally conferred schemas, thereby generating a level of regularity in the behaviors typical of a particular culture.

The intersubjective approach theorizes that the perceptions of descriptive (typical) or injunctive (approved) societal norms are an important motivational force because they enable coordination within the group, and guide members towards appropriate behavior in a given situation (Cialdini et al., 1991). Recent research has convincingly shown that cultural differences in cognitive biases or judgment patterns are driven more by perceived descriptive norms than by personal beliefs or values (e.g., Shteynberg et al., 2009). Leung and Morris (2015) note that norm-based accounts can also explain situation-specific cultural differences because norms are representations of typical responses to specific situations. Furthermore, they observe that norm accounts may serve better than schema accounts to explain the stability and persistence of cultural patterns of social behavior, as individuals within a culture mostly agree in their perception of societal norms, irrespective of their personal preference or adherence.

Leung and Morris (2015, p. 35) observe that 'the three psychological mechanisms – values, schemas, and norms – are usually pitted against each other as rival accounts of how culture influences individual behavior'. However, they argue that the three mechanisms may be complementary, and to that end they propose the situated dynamics framework. According to Leung and Morris (2015), this framework is akin to a moderated mediation model, with the three psychological mechanisms mediating the influence of culture on individual behavior, and different types of situational characteristics moderating the salience of each mechanism. Specifically, they propose that values play a more important role in accounting for cultural differences in weak situations where fewer constraints are perceived; schemas play a more important role when situational cues increase their accessibility and relevance; and norms play a more important role when social evaluation, social identity, and group membership are salient (Cialdini et al., 1991).

In its current conceptualization, the situated dynamics framework primarily offers predictions regarding the influence of culture on specific tasks (for example, negotiations, ethical decisions). Nonetheless, the framework has the potential to contribute to the study of commitment with its premise that the influence of culture cannot be fully understood without fully considering the situation (Leung and Morris, 2015). The term 'situation' here corresponds to the term 'social niche', which describes a collectively created and maintained set of constraints and incentives (Yamagishi, 2011, 2013). For instance, consider a finding such as Chinese employees showing a stronger commitment to their supervisor than, say, Americans. Rather than asserting that the collectivist Chinese employees have internalized loyalty values, one might also note that in Chinese organizations, selection is typically through *guanxi* networks or ingroup referrals (Aycan and Gelfand, 2012). Furthermore, once recruited, the relationship between the supervisor and the employee may in all likelihood become a multiplex one, and extend beyond the workplace and involve the continuous interaction of the close kin of both parties (Wasti and Tan, 2010). Thus, the prevalent workways of the Chinese culture would serve to increase the accessibility and relevance of schemas, and in particular, descriptive norms related to person-specific attachments as well as defection costs. Furthermore, China is a tight culture (Gelfand et al., 2011), where the salience of norms and the penalties for deviance are higher than in looser countries like the US. Thus, a fruitful direction for cross-cultural commitment research might involve understanding the differences in the attributes of situations or social niches across cultures (Bond, 2013).

Multilevel Analyses of Culture and Commitment

Multilevel modeling refers to the exploration of the relationship between variables at different levels such as societal, organizational, and individual, nested within each other, which is what cross-cultural research is essentially about. Fischer (2009) observes that a common component in most definitions of culture is that it is a shared meaning system that differentiates one society from another. Accordingly, he argues that the choice of composition models (Chan, 1998) should reflect this assumption. For instance, referent-shift models require individuals to answer items in relation to the higher-level unit of investigation (for example, people in this culture do X in situation Y), and direct consensus models consist of individual-level value scores. In both models, individual scores are averaged across members of a given culture based on the assumption that the values or perceptions are shared. Accordingly, to ensure that variables can be aggregated to a culture level, researchers should consider agreement (within-unit homogeneity) at an individual level, as well as cultural differences between countries (between-unit heterogeneity) (Fischer, 2009). Given the current discussion of values versus norms, Fischer (2009) advises to consider both referent-shift and direct consensus models.

It should be noted that the extant value frameworks (for example, Hofstede, Schwartz) have employed an additive or summary index model of aggregation. This approach fails to take within-nation variation into account and thus makes an untested assumption of sharedness, a common definition of culture (Fischer, 2009). To address these concerns, Fischer and Schwartz (2011) reanalyzed three available data sets (the Schwartz Value Survey, the Portrait Values Questionnaire, and the World Values Survey) and found rather modest evidence for within-country agreement, and between-country variance except for value items related to conformity. While this finding was deemed a strong blow to comparative research that hinged upon cultural value dimensions, subsequent discussions have questioned the necessity to posit shared values within cultures and have made a case for the usefulness, if not the sufficiency, of using these aggregate value scores (e.g., Morris, 2014; Schwartz, 2014).

In cross-cultural multilevel OB models, societal culture is primarily proposed to influence work attitudes and behavior indirectly through organizational practices (Fischer et al., 2005). Drawing on this reasoning, Wasti and Önder (2009) offered specific propositions with respect to commitment across cultures. For instance, they proposed that in low power distance cultures, job designs facilitating employee autonomy might be common. By increasing feelings of self-worth and fulfillment, such human resources (HR) practices may foster AC (Meyer and Allen, 1997). Another cross-level direct effect of relevance involves the influence of societal culture on the organizational context. Organizational context comprises size, ownership, and authority structure, that is, whether power is positional or personal, and its degree of centralization. In countries where the family structure is more traditional, the importance of family identity and the concomitant distrust of non-family members reinforce small-scale family business ownership (Whitley, 1992). Family organizations are characterized by informal authority structures, leading to particularistic HR practices, which are likely to foster commitment to particular individuals rather than to the organization (Wasti and Önder, 2009).

In addition to cross-level direct effects, Aycan and Gelfand (2012) propose testing cross-level moderator effects, that is, how societal culture moderates the impact of organizational practices on individual outcomes. For example, Fisher (2014) found that empowerment mitigated the negative relationship between overload and organizational commitment only in low power distance countries. Finally, societal culture may moderate the relationship between psychological states and behavioral outcomes (Aycan and Gelfand, 2012). Regarding commitment and outcomes, Wasti and Önder (2009) argued that both AC and NC to supervisor would be more predictive of turnover and discretionary behaviors than commitment to the organization in high as opposed to low power distance cultures. In collectivist or tight cultures, NC might be a better predictor of turnover than for individualist or loose cultures.

Multilevel models of cross-cultural commitment can also benefit greatly from the incorporation of socio-institutional and macroeconomic variables (Fischer et al., 2014; Tsui et al., 2007). Socio-institutional factors directly influence the HR system, as when laws stipulate standards as to minimum wage or hours of work, or unions protect employees against undue dismissal. Further, socio-institutional variables have an indirect impact on HR systems, through their influence on the organizational context. For instance, countries differ with respect to the prevalence of organizations that use capital- and skill-intensive technologies (Scott, 2006). Organizations using capital- and skill-intensive technologies, which are more widespread in developed economies, tend to have HR systems geared towards maintaining a skilled workforce able to use discretion in work-related matters. In contrast, in organizations that invest little in capital and employee skills, which are more prevalent in developing economies, the less formalized HR systems tend to comprise short-term employment, lower wages, and less benefits, triggering at best a CC mindset, particularly on the part of marginalized workers and those with limited opportunities elsewhere (Rousseau, 1995).

In terms of macroeconomic factors, in developing economies, alternative employment opportunities are typically scarce and employment contracts tend to be relatively short term, earnings are unstable, and organizations offer little more than basic pay (Hamilton and Kao, 1990). While Wasti and Önder (2009) proposed that this would limit employees to transactional psychological contracts and CC, Fischer et al. (2014) found that in lower-income countries employee-oriented practices are perceived to be more prevalent, presumably as compensation for the suboptimal material conditions. While Fischer et al. (2014) did not link organizational practices to employee attitudes, such findings can be fruitfully incorporated to research on commitment.

Some Methodological Issues

Beyond the theoretical ordeals, there is a multitude of methodological concerns that need to be tackled in cross-cultural research. As these have been discussed at great length elsewhere (e.g., Gelfand et al., 2002; Leung and van de Vijver, 2008; Schaffer and Riordan, 2003; van de Vijver and Leung, 1997), only some basics are highlighted here.

As in all research, the methodological issues in cross-cultural investigations revolve around sampling, instrumentation, and data analysis; however, there are additional validity threats that do not haunt monocultural studies with a similar design (Gelfand et al., 2002). Regarding sampling, two decisions are especially pertinent to cross-cultural research: the sampling of cultures and of subjects. Given the practical impossibility of randomly sampling a large number of cultures, researchers are urged to at least use purposive sampling of cultures in a theory-guided fashion and to employ the systematic contrast strategies (for example, sampling cohorts that differ in their duration of exposure to a cultural environment, such as first- and second-generation immigrants; replicating the findings across diverse pairs of cultural groups) proposed by Leung and van de Vijver (2008).

Related to sampling, cross-cultural research often implicitly assumes national culture is defined by socio-political boundaries; however, there is evidence for substantial within-nation or intraregional divergence in cultural values due to differences like geographic and climatic patterns, immigration patterns, concentration of ethnic communities, or differential rates of economic development (e.g., Dheer et al., 2014). To account for within-nation variance, participants can be asked to identify their ethnic or cultural identity and the effect of this variation can be empirically tested (Fischer et al., 2005). Peterson and Søndergaard (2011) noted that one of the main reasons for continued use of national borders was the limited availability of cultural and criterion data about within-nation regions. However, Dheer et al. (2014) have fruitfully made use of region-level data that is available in the World Values Survey (Inglehart, 1997) to identify subcultures in Canada and the US. It seems that future research using a regional approach might increase both specificity of prediction and sample size (that is, power) by including regions both within and across countries (Oyserman and Uskul, 2008).

To maximize the effectiveness of purposive sampling, it is important to align the macro- and meso-institutional contexts of the different samples while ensuring that they are far apart on the theoretical dimension of culture (van de Vijver and Leung, 1997). Culture is not the only predictive factor for organizational phenomena and the implications of relevant variables (for example, organizational structure and rewards, the industry) need to be accounted or controlled for (Gelfand et al., 2008). However, matched samples may not be representative of their cultural groups, or the impact of culture may be less evident in large organizations, organizations operating in high-tech industries, or multinational corporations (Gelfand et al., 2008; Fischer et al., 2005). An alternative strategy may be sampling organizations that maximize variability within a country but show some representation in terms of dominant subcultures and industry characteristics within the country (Fischer et al., 2005). In addition, the background characteristics of the subjects need to be aligned or measured, and accounted for statistically. Single-country studies may equally benefit from a detailed description of macro- and meso-institutional contexts and sample characteristics by way of explicating sources of alternative hypotheses.

With respect to instrumentation, a primary decision facing cross-cultural researchers is whether to develop a new instrument or to use an existing one. While the use of imported scales raises concerns about construct bias, as they may not be covering all aspects relevant to the construct in the new culture (Farh et al., 2006), there are often practical reasons to use an existing instrument. In such cases, researchers are recommended at least to use translation–backtranslation (Brislin, 1980), but ideally to ensure semantic equivalence (Schaffer and Riordan, 2003). Another concern is method bias (van de Vijver and Leung, 2001). In comparative studies, there should be uniformity across samples in terms of administration procedures, instrument formats, respondent familiarity with instruments, researcher–respondent rapport, and the like (Schaffer and Riordan, 2003). Single-country studies should also ensure that the participants are comfortable with the instrument and its administration.

Instruments need to be further evaluated in terms of whether the intended construct exists and can be measured in each of the cultural groups separately (the issue of bias and equivalence; e.g., van de Vijver and Leung, 1997; Chapter 32 in this volume) as well as whether the construct has the same meaning at individual and culture levels (the issue of isomorphism in multilevel studies; see Fischer et al., 2010). Depending on the research question, four types of equivalence may need to be statistically assessed (Fischer, 2009): functional equivalence (whether the construct has the same function across cultural samples), structural equivalence (whether the same items can be used to measure the construct), metric equivalence (whether the items have the same factor loadings across cultural groups), and full score equivalence (whether the items have the same anchor point across cultural groups). Single-country studies that use imported scales or develop new ones should also provide validation evidence for the scales in the context in which they are applied. Finally, given the potential for problems with the usage of an instrument for the first time in a new context, the burden of pilot testing is greatly justified and is recommended as a prerequisite to cross-cultural research (Schaffer and Riordan, 2003).

CONCLUDING REMARKS

Conducting cross-cultural research has many challenges and requires considerable financial and social capital (Peterson, 2001). Such an enterprise may not be desirable or feasible for all or at all times. Furthermore, comparative studies by nature focus on topics of relevance to multiple contexts, which may dictate some aspects of the research question or the methodology. In contrast, single-country studies have the luxury to focus on truly context-specific phenomena, and thereby contribute to global knowledge in unique ways (Tsui, 2004). If researchers outside of the mainstream could pose the question, 'If I were the first researcher to study commitment, what would strike me as the most imminent problem or interesting puzzle?', with respect to their local context, perhaps we would see more on the dynamics of interpersonal commitments as they straddle personal and professional life domains; the management of commitment in family firms; the meaning and maintenance of commitment in turbulent environments; the commitment of marginalized populations such as those in the grey sectors or grey economy, immigrants or minorities, and the like. Such investigations with an ethnographic mindset are extremely valuable to complement extant knowledge towards a more global science and should not be considered to be secondary, but rather an opportunity.

REFERENCES

Aycan, Z. (2001). Human resource management in Turkey: Current issues and future challenges. *International Journal of Manpower*, *22*, 252–261.

Aycan, Z. and Gelfand, M.J. (2012). Cross-cultural industrial and organizational psychology. In S. Koslowski and K. Klein (eds). *Handbook of Industrial and Organizational Psychology* (pp. 1103–1160). New Jersey: Blackwell.

Becker, H.S. (1960). Notes on the concept of commitment. *American Journal of Sociology*, *66*, 32–42.

Bielby, D.D. (1992). Commitment to work and family. *Annual Review of Sociology*, *18*, 281–302.

Bond, M.H. (2013). Refining Lewin's formula: A general model for explaining situational influence on individual social behavior. *Asian Journal of Social Psychology*, *16*, 1–15.

Brislin, R.W. (1980). Translation and content analysis of oral and written material. In H.C. Triandis and J.W. Berry (eds.), *Handbook of Cross-cultural Psychology* (pp. 389–444). Boston, MA: Allyn & Bacon.

Chan, D. (1998). Functional relations among constructs in the same content domain at different levels of analysis: A typology of composition models. *Journal of Applied Psychology*, *83*, 234–246.

Cheng, B., Chou, L.F., Wu, T.Y., Huang, M.P., and Farh, J.L. (2004). Paternalistic leadership and subordinate responses: Establishing a leadership model in Chinese organizations. *Asian Journal of Social Psychology*, *7*, 89–117.

Cheng, B.S., Jiang, D.Y., and Riley, J.H. (2003). Organizational commitment, supervisory commitment, and employee outcomes in the Chinese context: proximal hypothesis or global hypothesis? *Journal of Organizational Behavior*, *24*, 313–334.

Cialdini, R.B., Kallgren, C.A., and Reno, R.R. (1991). A focus theory of normative conduct: A theoretical refinement and reevaluation of the role of norms in human behavior. In M.P. Zanna (ed.), *Advances in Experimental Social Psychology* (Vol. 24, pp. 201–234). New York: Academic Press.

Cohen, D. (2007). Methods in cultural psychology. In S. Kitayama and D. Cohen (eds), *Handbook of Cultural Psychology* (pp. 196–236). New York: Guilford Press.

Dheer, R., Lenartowicz, T., Peterson, M.F., and Petrescu, M. (2014). Cultural regions of Canada and United States: Implications for international management research. *International Journal of Cross Cultural Management*, *14*, 343–384.

Eisenberger, R., Cummings, J., Armeli, S., and Lynch, P. (1997). Perceived organizational support, discretionary treatment, and job satisfaction. *Journal of Applied Psychology*, *82*, 812–820.

Eisinga, R., Teelken, C., and Doorewaard, H. (2010). Assessing cross-national in variance of the three-component model of organizational commitment: A six-country study of European university faculty. *Cross Cultural Research*, *44*, 341–373.

Farh, J.L., Cannella, A.A., and Lee, C. (2006). Approaches to scale development in Chinese management research. *Management and Organization Review*, *2*, 301–318.

Fischer, R. (2009). Where is culture in cross cultural research?: An outline of a multilevel research process for measuring culture as a shared meaning system. *International Journal of Cross Cultural Management*, *9*, 25–49.

Fischer, R., Ferreira, M.C., Assmar, E.M.L., Baris, G., Berberoglu, G., Dalyan, F., Wong, C.C., and Hassan, A. (2014). Organizational practices across cultures: An exploration in six cultural contexts. *International Journal of Cross Cultural Management*, *14*, 105–125.

Fischer, R., Redford, P., Ferriera, M.C., Harb, C., and Assmar, E.M.L. (2005). Organizational behavior across cultures: Theoretical and methodological issues for developing multi-level frameworks involving culture. *International Journal of Cross Cultural Management*, *5*, 27–48.

Fischer, R. and Schwartz, S. (2011). Whence differences in value priorities? Individual, cultural, or artifactual sources. *Journal of Cross-Cultural Psychology*, *42*(7), 1127–1144.

Fischer, R., Vauclair, M.C., Fontaine, J.R., and Schwartz, S.H. (2010). Are individual- and culture-level value structures different? Testing Hofstede's legacy with the Schwartz Value Survey. *Journal of Cross-Cultural Psychology*, *41*, 135–151.

Fisher, D.M. (2014). A multilevel cross-cultural examination of role overload and organizational commitment: Investigating the interactive effects of context. *Journal of Applied Psychology*, *99*, 723–736.

Fligstein, N. (1996). Markets as politics: A political-cultural approach to market institutions. *American Sociological Review*, *61*, 656–673.

Gelfand, M.J., Leslie, L. M., and Fehr, R. (2008). To prosper, organizational psychology should . . . adopt a global perspective. *Journal of Organizational Behavior*, *29*, 493–517.

Gelfand, M.J., Raver, J.L., and Holcombe, K. (2002). Methodological issues in cross-cultural research. In S. Rogelberg (ed.) *Handbook of Industrial and Organizational Psychology Research Methods* (pp. 216–46). New York: Blackwell.

Gelfand, M.J., Raver, J.L., Nishii, L., Leslie, L.M., Lun, J., et al. (2011). Differences between tight and loose cultures. *Science*, *332*, 110–104.

Hamilton, G. and Kao, C.S. (1990). The institutional foundation of Chinese business: The family firm in Taiwan. *Comparative Social Research*, *12*, 95–112.

Higgins, E.T. (1996). Knowledge activation: Accessibility, applicability, and salience. In E.T. Higgins and A.W. Kruglanski (eds), *Social Psychology: Handbook of Basic Principles* (pp. 133–168). New York: Guilford Press.

Hofstede, G. (1980). *Culture's Consequences: International Differences in Work Related Values*. Beverly Hills, CA: Sage.

Hom, P.W. and Xiao, Z. (2011). Embedding social networks: How *guanxi* ties reinforce Chinese employees' retention. *Organizational Behavior and Human Decision Processes*, *116*, 188–202.

House, R., Hanges, P., Javidan, M., Dorfman, P., and Gupta, V. 2004. *Culture, Leadership and Organizations: The Globe Study of 62 Societies*. Thousand Oaks, CA: Sage.

Hult, C. and Svallfors, S. (2002). Production regimes and work orientations: A comparison of six Western countries. *European Sociological Review*, *18*, 315–331.

Inglehart, R. (1997). *Modernization and Postmodernization: Cultural, Economic and Political Change in 43 Societies*. Princeton, NJ: Princeton University Press.

Ingram, P. and Zou, X. (2008). Business friendships. *Research in Organizational Behavior*, *28*, 167–184.

Kirkman, B.L., Lowe, K.B., and Gibson, C.B. (2006). A quarter century of culture's consequences: A review of empirical research incorporating Hofstede's cultural values framework. *Journal of International Business Studies*, *37*, 285–320.

Klein, H., Molloy, J., and Brinsfield, C. (2012). Reconceptualizing workplace commitment to redress a stretched construct: Revisiting assumptions and removing confounds. *Academy of Management Review*, *37*, 130–151.

Ko, J.W., Price, J.L., and Mueller, C.W. (1997). Assessment of Meyer and Allen's three-component model of organizational commitment in South Korea. *Journal of Applied Psychology*, *82*, 961–973.

Leung, K. and Morris. M.W. (2015). Values, schemas, and norms in the culture–behavior nexus: A situated dynamics network. *Journal of International Business Studies*, *46*, 1028–1050.

Leung. K. and van de Vijver, F.J.R. (2008). Strategies for strengthening causal inferences in cross-cultural research: The consilience approach. *International Journal of Cross Cultural Management*, *8*, 145–169.

Markus, H.R. and Kitayama, S. (1991). Culture and the self: Implications for cognition, emotion, and motivation. *Psychological Review*, *98*, 224–253.

Meyer, J.P. and Allen, N.J. (1991). A three-component conceptualization of organizational commitment. *Human Resources Management Review*, *1*, 61–89.

Meyer, J.P. and Allen, N.J. (1997). *Commitment in the Workplace: Theory, Research and Application*. Thousand Oaks, CA: Sage.

Meyer, J.P., Stanley, D.J., Jackson, T.A., McInnis, K.J., Maltin, E.R., and Sheppard, L. (2012). Affective, normative and continuance commitment levels across cultures: A meta-analysis. *Journal of Vocational Behavior*, *80*, 225–245.

Morris, M.W. (2014). Values as the essence of culture: Foundation or fallacy? *Journal of Cross-Cultural Psychology*, *45*, 14–24.

Morris, M.W., Podolny, J.M., and Ariel, S. (2000). Missing relations: Incorporating relational constructs into models of culture. In P.C. Earley and H. Singh (eds.), *Innovations in International and Cross-cultural Management* (pp. 52–90). Thousand Oaks, CA: Sage.

Mowday, R.T., Steers, R.M., and Porter, L.W. (1979). The measurement of organizational commitment. *Journal of Vocational Behavior*, *14*, 224–247.

Near, J.P. (1989). Organizational commitment among Japanese and US workers. *Organization Studies*, *10*, 281–300.

Oyserman, D. and Uskul, A.K. (2008). Individualism and collectivism: Societal-level processes with implications for individual-level and society-level outcomes. In F. van de Vijver, D. van Hemert, and Y. Poortinga (eds), *Multilevel Analysis of Individuals and Cultures* (pp. 145–173). Mahwah, N.J.: Erlbaum.

Pearce, J.L., Branyiczki, I., and Bigley, G.A. (2000). Insufficient bureaucracy: Trust and commitment in particularistic organizations. *Organization Science*, *11*, 148–162.

Peterson, M.F. (2001). International collaboration in organizational behavior research. *Journal of Organizational Behavior*, *22*, 59–81.

Peterson, M.F. and Søndergaard, M. (2011). Traditions and transitions in quantitative societal culture research in organization studies. *Organization Studies, 32*, 1539–1358.

Robert, C., Probst, T.M., Martocchio, J.J., Drasgow, F., and Lawler, J.J. (2000). Empowerment and continuous improvement in the United States, Mexico, Poland, and India: Predicting fit on the basis of the dimensions of power distance and individualism. *Journal of Applied Psychology, 85*, 643–658.

Rousseau, D.M. (1995). *Psychological contract in organizations: Understanding written and unwritten agreements*. Newbury Park, CA: Sage.

Sanchez-Burks, J. (2005). Protestant relational ideology: The cognitive underpinnings and organizational implications of an American anomaly. *Research in Organizational Behavior, 26*, 265–305.

Sanchez-Burks, J. and Lee, F. (2007). Cultural psychology of workways. In S. Shinobu and D. Cohen (eds), *Handbook of Cross Cultural Psychology* (pp. 346–369). New York: Lawrence Erlbaum.

Schaffer, B.S. and Riordan, C.M. (2003). A review of cross-cultural methodologies for organizational research: A best-practices approach. *Organizational Research Methods, 6*, 169–215.

Schwartz, S.H. (1992). Universals in the content and structure of values: Theoretical advances and empirical tests in 20 countries. In M.P. Zanna (ed.), *Advances in Experimental Social Psychology* (Vol. 25, pp. 1–65). San Diego, CA: Academic Press.

Schwartz, S.H. (2014). Rethinking the concept and measurement of societal culture in light of empirical findings. *Journal of Cross-Cultural Psychology, 45*, 5–13.

Scott, A.J. (2006). The changing global geography of low-technology, labor- intensive industry: Clothing, footwear, and furniture. *World Development, 34*, 1517–1536.

Shteynberg, G., Gelfand, M.J., and Kim, K. (2009). Peering into the 'magnum mysterium' of culture: The explanatory power of descriptive norms. *Journal of Cross-Cultural Psychology, 40*, 46–69.

Smith, P.B. (2012). Chinese management theories: Indigenous insights or lessons for the wider world. In X. Huang and M.H. Bond (eds), *The Handbook of Chinese Organizational Behavior: Integrating Theory, Research and Practice* (pp. 502–510). Cheltenham, UK and Northampton, MA, USA: Edward Elgar Publishing.

Triandis, H.C. (1995). *Individualism and Collectivism*. Boulder, CO: Westview Press.

Tsui, A.S. (2004). Contributing to global management knowledge: A case for high quality indigenous research. *Asia Pacific Journal of Management, 21*, 491–513.

Tsui, A.S., Nifadkar, S.S., and Ou, A.Y. (2007). Cross-national, cross-cultural organizational behavior research: Advances, gaps, and recommendations. *Journal of Management, 33*, 426–478.

Van de Vijver, F.J.R. and Leung, K. (1997). *Methods and Data Analysis for Cross-Cultural Research*. Thousand Oaks, CA: Sage.

Van de Vijver, F. and Leung, K. (2001). Personality in cultural context: Methodological issues. *Journal of personality, 69*(6), 1007–1031.

Vandenberghe, C. (1996). Assessing organizational commitment in a Belgian context: Evidence for the three-dimensional model. *Applied Psychology: An International Review, 45*, 371–386.

Wasti, S.A. (2002). Affective and continuance commitment to the organization: Test of an integrated model in the Turkish context. *International Journal of Intercultural Relations, 26*, 525–550.

Wasti, S.A. (2003). Organizational commitment, turnover intentions and the influence of cultural values. *Journal of Occupational and Organizational Psychology, 76*, 303–321.

Wasti, S.A. and Önder, Ç. (2009). Commitment across cultures: Progress, pitfalls, and propositions. In H.J. Klein, T.E. Becker, and J.P. Meyer (eds), *Commitment in Organizations: Accumulated Wisdom and New Directions* (pp. 309–343). New York: Routledge Taylor & Francis.

Wasti, S.A., Peterson, M.F., Breitsohl, H., Cohen, A., Jørgensen, F., Rodrigues, A.C., Weng, Q., and Xu, X. (2016). Location, location, location: Contextualizing commitment. *Journal of Organizational Behavior, 37*, 613–632.

Wasti, S.A. and Tan, H.H. (2010). Antecedents of supervisor trust in collectivist cultures: Evidence from Turkey and China. In M. Saunders, D. Skinner, N. Gillespie, G. Dietz and R.J. Lewicki (eds), *Organizational Trust: A Cultural Perspective* (pp. 311–335), Cambridge: Cambridge University Press.

Weick, K.E. (1974). Middle range theories of social systems. *Behavioral Science, 19*, 357–367.

Whitley, R. (1992). *Business Systems in East Asia. Firms, Markets and Societies*. Thousand Oaks, CA: Sage.

Yamagishi, T. (2011). Micro-macro dynamics of the cultural construction of reality: A niche construction approach to culture. In M.J. Gelfand, C.Y. Chiu, and Y.Y. Hong (eds), *Advances in Culture and Psychology* (Vol. 1, pp. 251–308). Oxford: Oxford University Press.

Yamagishi, T. (2013). From a measurement model to a dynamic causal model: Commentary on Schwartz. *Journal of Cross-Cultural Psychology, 45*, 30–36.

27. Commitment in Europe
Jörg Felfe and Jörg Wombacher

In Europe, declining birth rates and changing value orientations (for example, 'generation Y') are causing businesses to expend greater effort in attracting and keeping a highly qualified workforce. Hence there is growing interest in the concept of employee commitment as the psychological force that binds employees to their employer. This chapter aims to provide an overview of the situation of employee commitment in Europe. The following questions will be addressed: How committed are employees in Europe? Are there relevant differences across countries and regions, and how does Europe compare with other regions in the world? To what extent does culture account for these differences? What can be said in terms of antecedences and consequences of commitment in Europe, and are there specific research issues that have been addressed by European scholars? Answering these questions will contribute to a better understanding of the phenomenon from a specific European perspective.

LEVELS OF COMMITMENT

The following review of commitment levels in European countries and regions is based on cross-national comparison studies and meta-analytic reviews that include samples from a large number of European countries. Our focus is on affective organizational commitment (AOC) as the most widely studied and most beneficial component. Regional clusters will also be compared in terms of continuance and normative organizational commitment (COC and NOC). Although the overall picture is rather heterogeneous, some patterns of differences can be identified.

As much of the research is based on cross-sectional studies that were aggregated from the individual to the country level, a note of caution is in order prior to the review. Inferences about a country's commitment level based on aggregated data that is gathered from heterogeneous samples does not account for changes that may take place over time. Furthermore, cross-level inferences are predicated on the assumption that a specific sample or aggregate of samples are representative of the country. Isomorphism may be a reason to justify this inference (Fischer et al., 2010). However, factors other than country origin such as industry, demographics, economy, working conditions, and so on provide alternative explanations for the observed country differences. To reduce the risk of fallacious inferences, our review includes findings from representative cross-national surveys (for example, the European Social Survey) and from studies comparing commitment among national subsidiaries of international organizations that may be more homogeneous.

Differences between Countries

We identified a total of nine studies that address commitment differences among European countries (Table 27.1). Of these, four involve homogeneous samples (studies 1–4); three are based on international survey data (studies 5–7); and two are meta-analytic studies (studies 8 and 9). To facilitate comparison, means were converted into a scale indicating the percentage of maximum possible scores (Fischer and Mansell, 2009; Meyer et al., 2012). These scores range from 0 to 100. References to the studies will be made through their respective number in Table 27.1.

Studies 1 to 4 are based on homogeneous samples with respect to occupation or employer: study 1 (Vandenberghe et al., 2001) compared translators from 12 countries working for the European Commission, with small subsample sizes ranging from N = 21 to N = 61; study 2 (Glazer et al., 2004) compared commitment levels among nurses in Hungary, Italy, and the United Kingdom (UK); study 3 (Eisinga et al., 2010) included employees from universities in six European countries; and study 4 (Hattrup et al., 2008) obtained AOC data from workers of an automotive company with local operations in seven countries. Due to the relative equivalence of the sampled occupations and employing organizations, it may be argued that the observed cross-country differences are attributable to country origin rather than other factors. However, translation issues, use of unique occupations (nursing and university employees), and small sample sizes might limit generalizability. Cross-national comparisons are thus valid only within the study context. Another common thread is the considerable variation of commitment levels within countries. For example, the scores for the UK range from a low of 53.2 percent (university workers) to a high of 73.0 percent (translators). Similarly, Germany ranks top (75.8 percent) in the automotive sample, but comes second-last (57.1 percent) in the study of university employees. A more extensive study in Germany (Felfe and Franke, 2012; not shown in Table 27.1), which validated the German version of the Meyer and Allen (1997) scale among 10 000 employees, revealed considerable differences in commitment levels between private sector organizations (74.0 percent) and public organizations (66.0 percent), and between employees with leadership positions (75.0 percent) and those without (68.8 percent). These examples indicate that there is substantial variation of commitment levels within countries. Hence we next analyze more representative country data.

Studies 5, 6, and 7 are based on representative cross-country surveys conducted. Although retrieved from different sources (that is, the International Social Survey, ISS; Eurobarometer, EB; European Social Survey, ESS), the findings are comparable because the measures used to collect the data in each study bear close resemblance to items included in Allen and Meyer's (1990) AOC scale. Only the ESS data are based on a single-item measure. Study 5 (Hattrup et al., 2008) reports AOC levels of workers from 19 European countries using data from the 1997 Work Orientations II Module of the ISS. The observed commitment scores range from 57.4 percent for France to 71.0 percent for Portugal. Besides Portugal, high scores were also observed for Denmark (68.6 percent) and Switzerland (67.2 percent). Poland's score was rather low (59.6 percent), similar to that of France. Study 6 uses the 2004 ESS survey data with 18 522 employees from 26 European countries. The observed commitment scores range from 50.2 percent for Italy to 62 percent for Portugal. The ESS scores are thus lower, on average, than the ISS

Table 27.1 Affective commitment means for European countries

Study	Homogeneous samples				Representative surveys			Meta-analyses	
Author (date)	Vandenberghe et al. (2001)	Glazer et al. (2004)	Eisinga et al. (2010)	Hattrup et al. (2008)	Hattrup et al. (2008)	Koster (2011)	Six and Felfe (2006)	Fischer and Mansell (2009)	Meyer et al. (2012)
	1	2	3	4	5	6	7	8	9
K	14	3	7	6	15	19	13	76	184
N	580	958	723	4288	7078	18522	>6000	24754	120970
Austria			75.0			59.8	70.0		65.7
Belgium	70.4			58.7		61.8	71.6	55.8	53.7
Bulgaria					63.4			68.3	
Czech Rep			72.4		63.2	46.6			
Croatia								64.2	
Denmark	59.8				68.8	61.0	80.2	57.4	
Finland	68.2			59.2		55.0		66.5	43.4
France	73.2		70.8		57.4	54.0	67.8	66.5	55.9
Germany	70.4		75.8	57.1	64.4	60.8	69.0	57.8	51.7
Greece	71.0					56.8	69.8		60.3
Hungary			74.4		62.6	56.4		54.0	59.5
Ireland		59.5				57.2	75.0	40.0	41.9
Italy	67.0	53.7	71.0			50.2	64.8	58.8	58.9
Netherlands	68.8			58.1	65.0	54.8	72.2	60.5	67.0
Norway					65.4	57.6		59.6	70.9
Poland					59.6	49.2		64.3	57.2
Portugal	67.8				71.0	62.0	70.0	60.7	69.5
UK	73.0	53.2	65.8	57.3	63.6	53.8	70.8	60.7	54.8
Romania									63.6
Slovenia	61.6				62.8	52.8			
Spain	61.6				64.0	54.2	66.4	45.5	62.6
Sweden	62.8			56.5	61.8		73.6	58.2	46.1
Switzerland	67.2				67.2	61.8			76.0

Note: K = Number of independent samples from European countries; N = Cumulative sample size.

and EB scores, presumably because they are derived from a single-item measure that does not clearly differentiate between AOC and COC. COC levels are typically lower than AOC levels. Finally, study 7 (Six and Felfe, 2006) analyzes data from the 1995 standard Eurobarometer survey which included 6028 representative full-time employees. The observed AOC scores here range from 66.4 percent for Spain to 80.2 percent for Denmark.

Overall, there are seven countries that were included in all three studies: Denmark, France, Germany, the Netherlands, Portugal, Spain, and the United Kingdom. When examining these countries, two important observations can be made. First, the relative positions of the countries are rather similar in studies 5 and 6 (Spearman's rho = .93), and somewhat similar in studies 5 and 7 (Spearman's rho = .54). Denmark ranks consistently at the top, Germany in the middle, and France and Spain appear at the lower end. It is thus conceivable that the relative positions of these countries reflect real-world differences in their overall commitment levels. As stated before, however, there may be considerable variation within countries and over time.

A second point to be noted is the variation in the overall mean scores for the seven countries across the three studies. These means are 64.9 percent (study 5), 57.2 percent (study 6), and 70.9 percent (study 7) respectively. It is unclear whether these differences are due only to measurement and sampling issues, or whether they also reflect developments of commitment in Europe over time. It may be speculated that commitment in Europe has decreased over the period from 1995 (survey year of study 7) to 2004 (survey year of study 6). Clearly, however, more comparative research is needed, in order to draw a more reliable picture of how commitment in Europe has evolved.

In addition to the aforementioned studies, there are two international meta-analyses (studies 8 and 9) that also allow comparisons among European countries. Study 8 (Fischer and Mansell, 2009) investigated commitment across 49 countries, of which 19 were European. However, the commitment scores for most European countries were derived from only a few studies with small sample sizes, which precludes conclusions about these countries' overall commitment levels. Only the scores for Belgium (55.8 percent), Germany (57.8 percent), the Netherlands (60.5 percent), and the United Kingdom (60.7 percent) are calculated from a larger number of independent samples (10, 13, 7, and 14, respectively), and may be a more reliable estimation of commitment levels.

A more recent meta-analysis by Meyer et al. (2012; study 9) examined AOC among 20 European countries and more than 30 other countries. Unlike Fischer and Mansell (2009), Meyer et al. (2012) analyzed only those studies that used the three-component model (TCM), thus increasing the comparability of their findings both across countries and with the more representative survey findings above (that is studies 5, 6, and 7). A larger number of independent samples was available for Belgium (32 samples), France (10), Germany (20), the Netherlands (40), and the United Kingdom (25). The mean AOC for these countries was 53.7 percent for Belgium, 55.9 percent for France, 62.3 percent for Germany, 67.2 percent for the Netherlands, and 52.6 percent for the UK (Table 27.1). With the exception of Belgium, these countries were also included in the representative surveys. The observed relative positions are somewhat similar to those in study 5 (Spearman's rho = .60) and study 7 (Spearman's rho = .43). There is again a lower level in France, while the levels for Germany and the Netherlands are higher. Due to measurement equivalence it may be speculated that there are systematic differences across countries that are attributable to country-level characteristics.

Overall, it has to be stated that the results of the different studies are difficult to compare due to differences in measurement, sampling procedures, type of controls, and possible changes in commitment over time that cannot be captured by cross-sectional studies. As there seems to be some consistency when representative surveys are used, however, there is reason to believe that some of the observed cross-country variation is systematic and therefore attributable to country-level factors such as national culture and economic situation.

Differences between Regions

For a better overview, Meyer et al. (2012; study 9) clustered the countries based on the GLOBE cultural taxonomy (Hanges and Dickson, 2004). Compared to other regions in the world, Europe covers a wide range of clusters (that is, Nordic Europe, Germanic Europe, Eastern Europe, Latin Europe, and Anglo). As regards AOC, European clusters are found in both the top position (Germanic Europe with Austria, the Netherlands, Belgium, Switzerland, and Germany has a score of 66.8 percent) and the last position (Nordic Europe with Denmark and Sweden has a score of 49.0 percent). Moreover, all European clusters except for the Nordic cluster obtain higher AOC scores than the Anglo cluster (the United States, UK, Canada: 55.1 percent). However, it has to be acknowledged that the clusters are not homogeneous. For example, the relatively high score of Germanic Europe may be upwardly biased by Dutch (67.2 percent), Austrian (65.7 percent), and Eastern German samples (67.7 percent), while the Western German score was lower (51.7 percent). In their study among 10 000 German employees, Felfe and Franke (2012) obtained a mean level of 64.3 percent for overall German AOC, and this may be an appropriate reflection of the average German level combining East and West Germany.

In sum, employees in Nordic Europe show lower levels of AOC compared to other European regions and compared to the Anglo and Confucian Asia clusters. While the average level across all clusters is highest in Germanic Europe, Eastern and Latin Europe also show higher levels than the Anglo cluster. In other words, except for Nordic Europe, AOC seems to be higher in Europe than in the Anglo countries.

It is also important to examine differences in COC and NOC. Of the studies with homogeneous samples, for example, Vandenberghe et al. (2001) and Glazer et al. (2004) found some evidence of cross-national differences in COC, while Eisinga et al. (2010) found some differences in NOC. For a more comprehensive overview, Figure 27.1 displays the coefficients and commitment profiles for the GLOBE regions based on Meyer et al.'s (2012) meta-analysis. The results show specific patterns for AOC, COC, and NOC. Overall, the scores for COC are generally lower than for AOC, and there is also less variation in COC than in AOC and NOC. The Germanic and the Eastern European clusters show the highest levels of COC, and in the Nordic cluster COC is higher than that of the Anglo and Confucian Asian clusters. The lowest COC score was observed for Latin Europe. Felfe and Franke's (2012) study also found that COC levels were contingent on age (higher COC among older employees), were higher in public than in private organizations, and lower among leaders than non-leaders, indicating systematic variation within

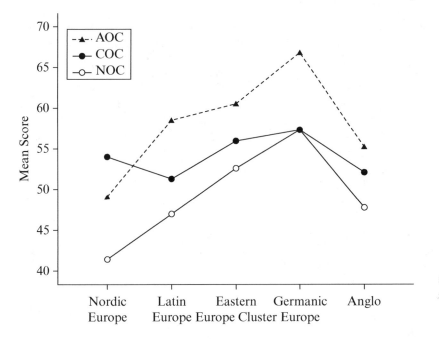

Source: Meyer et al. (2012).

Figure 27.1 Commitment profiles across European GLOBE clusters

countries. Overall, COC appears to be higher in European regions than in most other regions of the world.

With respect to NOC, Meyer et al.'s (2012) meta-analysis reveals generally lower levels than for the other two commitment forms. The lowest levels are found in Nordic and Latin Europe, whereas Eastern and Germanic Europe yielded higher levels. The score of the Germanic cluster is mostly represented by employees from the Netherlands (57.8) and therefore may be upwardly biased. In contrast, the results from Felfe and Franke with German employees clearly indicate a lower level (43.0) of NOC for Germany.

Overall, the comparison of profiles across European regions reveals that, except for Nordic Europe, there are relatively high levels of AOC, lower and more homogeneous levels of COC, and clearly lower levels of NOC. Germanic and Eastern Europe show higher levels than other European and non-European regions (Anglo and Confucian Asia). The Latin cluster is relatively similar to the Anglo and Confucian Asia clusters, albeit closer to the Anglo cluster with regard to NOC, and closer to the Confucian cluster with regard to AOC.

THE INFLUENCE OF CULTURAL VALUES, PERSONALITY, AND ECONOMY

As pointed out, there is some evidence of differences in commitment levels across countries worldwide and also between European countries and regions. Many studies have tried to explain these differences based on cultural values. A few studies have also investigated the effects of economic welfare and personality traits. In general, these effects can be examined at three levels of analysis: (1) the country level; (2) the individual level; and (3) in terms of the interaction between the country and the individual level. First, at the country level, it is assumed that members of the same culture are exposed to the same contextual influences. Hence there should be systematic differences between countries that can be studied at the country level (for example, there might be a higher level of NOC in collectivistic than in individualistic countries). Second, although a majority of individuals within a culture share the dominant values, there may be considerable variation within countries. Collectivistic individuals, for example, are found to have higher NOC than individualistic individuals (Felfe et al., 2006). Third, both the country and the individual level may interact (cross-level interaction): the relationship between cultural values and commitment, or between commitment and its antecedences and consequences on the individual level, may be affected by country-level characteristics (Felfe et al., 2008b). In the following, we summarize research on commitment relationships with cultural values and other explanatory factors. Our focus is on studies with European samples.

Country Level

There is no complete consensus on the implications of culture for commitment. Some authors have argued that AOC and COC should be positively related to collectivism because of the emphasis on social ties and group identity (e.g., Felfe et al., 2008b; Wasti and Önder, 2009). Others expect a positive relationship with individualism because employers put more effort into individual needs fulfillment, and individualistic values may enhance rational relationships (Fischer and Mansell, 2009; Gelade et al., 2006). As for NOC, there appears to be agreement that countries with collectivistic value orientations should show higher levels of commitment due to the importance placed on loyalty, obligation, and duty.

However, empirical research cannot provide consistent findings. Fischer and Mansell's (2009) meta-analyses including 18 European countries showed a positive relationship between collectivism and NOC, and between power distance and NOC. Collectivism was also positively associated with AOC, albeit only when considering GLOBE's 'in-group collectivism' and not Hofstede's (2001) individualism–collectivism scores. Similarly, large-scale surveys found no evidence of a relationship between country-level AOC and Hofstede's individualism–collectivism scores (Hattrup et al., 2008). In their worldwide employee opinion poll with N = 93055 participants from the automotive industry (including 16 European nations), Hausmann et al. (2013) found only a marginally positive relation between individualism and AOC after controlling for economic welfare (as measured by the Human Development Index), acquiescence bias, job satisfaction, and other variables. Based on their own and other studies, these authors concluded that there is limited support linking Hofstede's cultural dimensions to national differences in AOC.

Clearer support for both a positive relationship between AOC and measures of collectivism, and a negative relationship with individualism, is provided in Meyer et al.'s (2012) meta-analysis comparing 50 countries (including 20 European countries). Meyer et al. were able to show that correlations differed depending on how collectivism is conceptualized and measured: a significant correlation was found for Schwartz's 'embeddedness' and GLOBE's 'in-group collectivism' scores, but not for Hofstede's individualism–collectivism dimension. It was thus concluded that AOC levels differ between countries where collectivistic values center on family (for example, Spain, Italy), and countries where the values extend to larger institutions. As for the other two commitment forms, Meyer et al. (2012) found a positive relationship between NOC and both collectivism and power distance, but a non-significant relationship between COC and these variables.

All in all, with regard to national culture, it appears that there is a positive association between collectivism and both AOC and NOC, and between power distance and NOC, when using the Schwartz or GLOBE value taxonomies. Although the effects are rather small, they can be shown when controlling for different economic and job variables. As the number of European countries in these worldwide studies is substantial, it can be assumed that the findings also apply to Europe.

Besides cultural values, studies also compared countries in terms of the potential influence of economic welfare and personality traits on commitment. For example, Hausmann et al. (2013) used the Human Development Index (HDI) – which is a composite statistic of life expectancy, education, and income indices – as an indicator of economic welfare, and found generally lower levels of AOC in countries with high HDI scores. Likewise, Fischer and Mansell (2009) found that 'current income per capita' and 'economic growth per capita' were negatively associated with both AOC and NOC. The authors explained this finding by arguing that individuals in less economically developed countries are more likely to grow up with greater social interdependencies. The obligation of those who are employed to support family members is likely to increase normative pressures to stay with their employer. Similarly, affective ties become more important as the membership to relevant groups is important for job security and promotion. On the other hand, economic welfare is associated with more opportunities and individual independence which results in weaker affective ties and decreased affective commitment.

A contrasting argument is presented by Gelade et al. (2006) who analyzed secondary data (including 19 European countries). Although their study revealed no significant correlation between AOC and national income per capita, the authors argued that independence in more economically developed countries is associated with greater freedom to choose a satisfying job and employers that fulfill higher-order needs for self-esteem. Consequently, AOC should be stronger in countries with a developed economy, whereas poor economic conditions should enhance COC. In support for their argument, the authors were able to find a negative relationship between AOC and unemployment rates and a positive relationship with male economic activity rates. It was thus concluded that positive socio-economic conditions have a small positive effect on AOC.

Gelade et al. (2006) also investigated the relationships of personality with commitment at the country level. They found positive correlations between AOC with extraversion and happiness (life satisfaction), while the correlation with neuroticism was negative. Similarly, Hausmann et al. (2013) found that cultural positivity and life satisfaction positively predicted AOC, even after controlling for job satisfaction and job role (blue-collar, white-collar, or management) at the individual level. It was therefore concluded that AOC ratings reflect not only employees' attachment but also cross-cultural differences in constructs reflecting affectivity.

To provide a more specific picture of the discussed cross-country relationships within Europe, we reanalyzed the data reported in the aforementioned studies using European countries only. We correlated the culture, economic and personality variables used in the Hausmann et al. (2013) study with the commitment scores for the same European countries reported in the other studies (N = 9–14). The results are both convergent and divergent.

For individualism, rank correlations with commitment scores (AOC) were consistently negative, ranging from -.14 (Koster, 2011) to -.55 (Meyer et al., 2012). Collectivism and commitment thus seem to be positively associated within Europe. Furthermore, in support of the findings of Hausmann et al. (2013) and Gelade et al. (2006), coefficients for positivity with commitment scores were mostly positive, ranging from .13 (Meyer et al., 2012) to .38 (Felfe and Six, 2006). An examination of the rank coefficients for the HDI reveals mixed rank correlations. They were positive in four studies: Gelade et al. (2006): .27; Koster (2011): .11; Hattrup et al. (2008): .35; and Six and Felfe (2006): .36. Overall, these findings indicate a positive relationship between collectivism and commitment and a predominantly positive relationship with positivity across European countries. The relationship with the HDI is positive but less consistent.

Individual Level

As Meyer et al. (2012) noted, the correlations of commitment with individualism, collectivism, and power distance at the country level are very similar to those reported at the individual level. There are some individual-level studies with European samples that have analyzed these relationships. For example, Felfe et al. (2008b) found that collectivism was positively associated with AOC, COC, and NOC in Germany and Romania. Collectivism made a unique contribution to the explanation of commitment in both countries, even after controlling for other variables (remuneration, task content, climate, and leadership). There is thus evidence that collectivism is an independent predictor of commitment also at the individual level. Another study with German employees revealed that power distance is also related to commitment, albeit only to COC (Felfe et al., 2006). More recently, Felfe et al. (forthcoming) examined commitment in Austria, Germany, Slovenia, and Spain, and found that all three commitment forms were positively related with collectivism, while power distance is negatively related to AOC and positively related to NOC. Glazer et al. (2004) reported somewhat similar findings. They found positive relationships between AOC and collectivistic values (conservation and self-transcendence), and negative relationships between AOC and individualistic values (openness to change and self-enhancement; see Schwartz, 1992).

Overall, when considering European countries at the individual level, there is evidence for a positive relationship between collectivism and AOC, COC, and NOC. Power distance also seems to be positively associated with NOC and COC, but negatively with AOC.

Cross-Level

So far, the relationships between value orientations and commitment have been considered separately at the group level (that is, between countries) and at the individual level (that is, within countries). However the nature and strength of the individual-level relationships might vary from one country to another depending on aggregate country-level characteristics that function as moderators (for example, national culture). That is, there may be different individual-level associations between commitment and value orientations; commitment and antecedents; and commitment and consequences based on the moderating influence of the cultural context.

Value orientations and commitment

The culture–fit hypothesis posits that individuals with a higher collectivistic value orientation are better adjusted in a collectivistic context and, vice versa, that individuals with a higher individualistic value orientation are better adjusted in an individualistic context (Ward and Chang, 1997). For example, collectivistic employees are more willing to engage in closer relationships with their organization and develop higher commitment, and this tendency might be reinforced when the cultural context positively responds to group-oriented behavior and the effort to fulfill duties and obligations. Consequently, the emotional attachment of individuals is likely to increase when high value congruence is experienced. In support of the culture–fit hypothesis, Felfe et al. (2008b) showed that the relationship between collectivism and commitment at the individual level is stronger in Romania (more collectivistic) than in Germany (more individualistic), indicating some cross-level effects in Europe.

Antecedences of commitment

We now turn to the question of whether cultural differences affect the relationships between leadership and task content and commitment. On the individual level, Wasti (2003) showed for Turkish samples that the commitment of collectivistic employees was primarily predicted by satisfaction with the leader, while the commitment of individualistic employees was determined by satisfaction with work and promotion. Similarly, Felfe et al. (2008b) found that in Germany and Romania, transformational leadership was more closely associated with AOC for collectivistic employees. The greater impact of leadership on collectivistic employees should be even stronger in collectivistic societies where leaders generally play a more crucial role (Cheng et al., 2003; Chen and Francesco, 2000). In fact, Felfe et al. (2008b) found a stronger relationship between leadership and all commitment forms in China. Partly confirming these results, Jackson et al. (2013) reported in their international analysis (including European countries) that the relationship between transformational leadership and commitment in collectivistic countries was higher for COC and NOC but not for AOC. As for task content (intrinsic task motivation), Felfe et al. (2008b) found that the relationship between an intrinsically satisfying job task and AOC was stronger in Germany than in Romania (and even lower in China). This finding lends further support to the notion that a group or interaction-related variable (for example, leadership) is more important in a collectivistic context, while job conditions that fulfill individual growth and enhancement are more relevant in individualistic contexts.

Consequences and commitment

Generally there is strong evidence for meaningful relationships between commitment and work-relevant outcomes (e.g., Cooper-Hakim and Viswesvaran 2005; Meyer et al., 2002). In their recent study, Meyer et al. (2014) analyzed outcomes of AOC and reported negative correlations with withdrawal cognitions ($\rho = -.57$) and turnover intentions (ρ = −.15), and positive correlations with job performance (ρ = .25) and organizational citizenship behavior (OCB) (ρ = .35). Felfe and Franke (2012) revealed similar relationships for Germany. Moreover, they report that the relationship between AOC and perceived strain is negative (r = −.24), whereas the relationship between strain and COC is positive (r = .08). This pattern is also similar to Meyer et al.'s (2012) and Meyer and Maltin's (2010) findings. Adding to the bulk of international research, there are studies with European samples that addressed specific outcomes; for example, customer satisfaction (Felfe and Heinitz, 2010), performance in terms of errors and working speed (Schmidt, 2007).

In their most recent meta-analysis, Meyer et al. (2014) also examined whether the relationships between AOC and withdrawal cognition, turnover, and OCB were moderated by culture. They calculated the correlation between the mean correlation for a nation (AOC and outcome) and national culture values scores. The correlations between AOC and withdrawal cognition among 47 countries were correlated with individualism (r = .43), indicating that the negative relationship between AOC and withdrawal cognition (ρ = −.57) was lower in individualistic countries and stronger in collectivistic countries. The correlations for AOC and OCB were also correlated with individualism (−.34), indicating that the positive relationship (ρ = .35) was lower in individualistic countries and stronger in collectivistic countries. However, there were not enough European countries for systematic comparisons within Europe. There are only a few studies that exclusively focused on Europe. While Vandenberghe et al. (2001) found that relationships between commitment components and intent to quit were culturally invariant, Felfe et al. (2008b) showed that AOC was a stronger predictor for OCB and turnover intention in Romania than in Germany after controlling for task content, remuneration, and leadership. In their study with four European countries, Felfe et al. (forthcoming) also found a higher relationship between AOC and OCB in Spain (more collectivistic) than in Germany and Austria. Overall it can be concluded that, as for antecedences, collectivism seems to strengthen the relevance of AOC for outcomes.

SPECIFIC ISSUES

Besides the examination of commitment levels, antecedences, and consequences, European studies have addressed other specific topics. Due to space considerations our coverage is selective and only two of them can be outlined briefly. The first concerns commitment among the increasing number of contingent workers in the European labor force. The second looks at the relationship between commitment and conflict in organizations. Both fields underline the importance of conceptualizing commitment as a complex phenomenon with multiple targets (organization, team, form of employment) and components (TCM).

Form of Employment: Contingent Workers

Considering the growing number of contingent workers in Europe's workforce, Felfe et al. (2005) examined the relationships between commitment, transformational leadership, OCB, and strain among contingent workers in Germany. Acknowledging the dual commitment of temporary workers, they made a distinction between their commitment to the agency and to the hiring client company. The results revealed that specific characteristics of the agency organization are related to the commitment to the agency, whereas conditions within the client organization (task content, leadership at the client) are more correlated with the commitment to the client organization. Commitment to the client company is also a stronger predictor for OCB and for perceived strain than commitment to the agency. Commitment to the client was stronger than the commitment to the agency. Another German study confirmed this differential effect (Galais and Moser, 2009): commitment towards the client organization had positive effects on workers' well-being, while agency commitment had no effects.

Following the call of Gallagher and McLean Parks (2001, p. 204) 'that the growth of "contingent" or "alternative" forms of work relationships highlights the need for researchers to examine work-related commitments outside of the traditional employer–employee framework', Felfe et al. (2008a) extended the TCM by introducing 'commitment to the employment form' as a new commitment focus that reflects the attitudes toward a specific employment form (traditional–permanent, contingent–temporary, self-employment). As Felfe et al. (2008a) showed, commitment to the form of employment generally explains variance of organizational outcomes (strain, OCB, satisfaction), over and above organizational and occupational commitment. With regard to contingent work, Felfe et al. (2005) showed that commitment to contingent work was also positively related to OCB, and commitment to contingent work positively predicted commitment to the agency. Generally, commitment to the form of employment reflects an important attitude to the work situation besides commitment to the organization or occupation.

Commitment and Conflict Dynamics within Organizations

Just as contingent workers experience multiple commitments to different organizations, employees in larger organizations may develop multiple commitments to different entities within the organization (for example, commitment to the team or work group, and commitment to the overall organization in which the work group or team is nested). Riketta and van Dick (2005) have shown that distinguishing between these entities is of value because it allows differential predictions of outcomes. Besides direct effects on OCB and turnover, the pattern of dual commitment to the team and to the overall organization may also affect employees' reaction to conflicts in the organization: how will the conflict be managed if employees feel highly committed to their team but only poorly committed to the overall organization, and vice versa? Given today's trend toward more team-based structures, researchers have argued that organizations should mainly develop work group commitment. The question arises, however, whether a strong subunit commitment is always positive. It is conceivable that the otherwise beneficial effects of strong subunit commitment turn negative for the organization when conflicts occur. Accordingly, Johnson et al. (2009) requested more research on multiple commitment patterns whose behavioral consequences may reside in the pattern itself rather than just in the sum of its parts. Following this request, Wombacher and Felfe (in press) examined how conflicts between organizational subunits (for example, teams, departments) are managed based on employees' commitment to both their subunit and the overall organization. Findings from an experimental and a survey study indicate that a strong subunit commitment leads to organizationally disruptive conflict handling unless buffered and balanced by a strong organizational commitment. To ensure collaboration both within and across teams, organizations must strive to foster a sense of dual (organizational and team) commitment among their workforce.

SUMMARY AND DISCUSSION

To face the demographic challenges of today, European businesses need to maintain and develop their employees' commitment. This overview of what is currently known about commitment in Europe and how it may be affected by culture, leadership, working conditions, economy, and personality variables may contribute to a better understanding. Despite the methodological challenges underlying cross-country comparisons, there is converging evidence for stronger emotional attachments in countries whose populations are more collectivistic, wealthy, and satisfied in life. Moreover, many relationships between commitment and its antecedents and outcomes seem to be enhanced where an individual's value orientation fits that of the surrounding context. However, there is considerable variation of commitment within countries, and caution must be exercised when drawing inferences from the country level to organizations or employees.

Moreover, commitment is a complex phenomenon. While much is known about affective commitment, the other two forms (normative, continuance) are less well researched. For example, occupational health is an important issue that may be directly or indirectly influenced by these components. Particularly in larger organizations, commitment may be directed not only at the organization, but also at other foci (teams and work groups, or occupation). The examination of their interplay in terms of dual or multiple commitments may be fruitful for further research, and can lead to unique and sometimes unexpected findings. Despite the apparent drag in today's organizations toward more team-based structures, maintaining a sense of dual commitment may still be worthwhile as it can enhance conflict management and performance in an organization. When considering contingent workers, a meaningful distinction can be made in terms of commitment to the hiring agency and to the client company. As research that incorporates this complexity is still sparse, it is too early for an integrated European picture for anything other than AOC. We wish to encourage researchers to more fully incorporate this complexity by also using experimental research designs. Moreover, there is a need for more longitudinal analyses that can trace developments and changes in commitment over time. Only then can we draw a more reliable picture of the situation of commitment in Europe or elsewhere. Representative survey data such as from the Eurobarometer or International Social Survey are available for this purpose and can be used as proxies for Meyer and Allen's TCM measure if collecting primary data with original measures is too time-consuming or expensive.

REFERENCES

Allen, N.J. and Meyer, J.P. (1990). The measurement and antecedents of affective, continuance and normative commitment to the organization. *Journal of Occupational Psychology*, *63*(1), 1–18.

Chen, Z.X. and Francesco, A.M. (2000). Employee demography, organizational commitment, and turnover intentions in China: Do cultural differences matter? *Human Relations*, *53*, 869–887.

Cheng, B.S., Jiang, D.Y., and Riley, J.H. (2003). Organizational commitment, supervisory commitment, and employee outcomes in the Chinese context: Proximal hypothesis or global hypothesis? *Journal of Organizational Behavior*, *24*, 313–334.

Cooper-Hakim, A. and Viswesvaran, C. (2005). The construct of work commitment: Testing an integrative framework. *Psychological Bulletin*, *131*(2), 241–259. doi: 10.1037/0033-2909.131.2.241

Eisinga, R., Teelken, C., and Doorewaard, H. (2010). Assessing cross-national invariance of the three-component model of organizational commitment: A six-country study of European university faculty. *Cross-Cultural Research*, *44*, 341–373.

Felfe, J., Bergner, S., Jiminez, P., and Dunkl, A. (forthcoming). Personality, leadership, commitment and stress across Europe.

Felfe, J. and Franke, F. (2012). *Commit. Verfahren zur Erfassung von Commitment gegenüber der Organisation, dem Beruf und der Beschäftigungsform*. Bern: Verlag Hans Huber.

Felfe, J. and Heinitz, K. (2010). The impact of consensus and agreement of leadership perceptions on commitment, OCB and customer satisfaction. *European Journal of Work- and Organizational Psychology*, *19*, 279–303.

Felfe, J., Schmook, R., Six, B., and Wieland, R. (2005). Commitment bei Zeitarbeitern (Commitment among contingent workers). *Zeitschrift für Personalpsychologie*, *4*, 101–115.

Felfe, J., Schmook, R., and Six, B. (2006). Die Bedeutung kultureller Wertorientierungen für das Commitment gegenüber der Organisation, dem Vorgesetzten, der Arbeitsgruppe und der eigenen Karriere (The meaning of cultural value orientations for different commitment foci: Organization, leader, work group and career). *Zeitschrift für Personalpsychologie*, *5*, 94–107.

Felfe, J., Schmook, R., Schyns, B., and Six, B. (2008a). Does the form of employment make a difference? Commitment of traditional, temporary, and self-employed workers. *Journal of Vocational Behavior*, *72*, 81–94.

Felfe, J. and Six, B. (2006). *Die Relation von Arbeitszufriedenheit und Commitment* (The relationship between job satisfaction and commitment). In L. Fischer (ed.), Arbeitszufriedenheit (S. 37–60). Göttingen: Hogrefe.

Felfe, J., Yan, W., and Six, B. (2008b). The impact of individual collectivism on commitment and its influence on OCB, turnover, and strain in three countries. *International Journal of Cross-Cultural Management*, *8*, 211–237.

Fischer, R. and Mansell, A. (2009). Commitment across cultures: A meta-analytical approach. *Journal of International Business Studies*, *40*, 1339–1358.

Fischer, R., Vauclair, C.-M., Fontaine, J., and Schwartz, S.H. (2010). Are individual-level and country-level value structures different? Testing Hofstede's legacy with the Schwartz Value Survey. *Journal of Cross-Cultural Psychology*, *41*, 135–151

Galais, N. and Moser, K. (2009). Organizational commitment and the well-being of temporary agency workers – A longitudinal study. *Human Relations*, *62*, 589–620

Gallagher, D.G. and McLean Parks, J. (2001). I pledge thee my troth . . . contingently commitment and the contingent work relationship. *Human Resource Management Review*, *11*, 181–208.

Gelade, G.A., Dobson, P., and Gilbert, P. (2006). National differences in organizational commitment: Effect of economy, product of personality, or consequence of culture? *Journal of Cross-Cultural Psychology*, *37*, 542–556.

Glazer, S., Daniel, S.C., and Short, K.M. (2004). A study of the relationship between organizational commitment and human values in four countries. *Human Relations*, *57*, 323–345.

Hanges, P. and Dickson, M.W. (2004). The development and validation of the GLOBE culture and leadership scales. In R.J. House, P.J. Hanges, M. Javidan, P.W. Dorfman, and P. Gupta (eds), *Culture, Leadership, and Organizations: The GLOBE Study of 62 Societies* (pp. 122–151). Thousand Oaks, CA: Sage Publications.

Hattrup, K., Mueller, K., and Aguirre, P. (2008). An evaluation of the cross-national generalizability of organizational commitment. *Journal of Occupational and Organizational Psychology*, *81*, 219–240

Hausmann, N., Mueller, K., Hattrup, K., and Spiess, S.O. (2013). An investigation of the relationships between affective organisational commitment and national differences in positivity and life satisfaction. *Applied Psychology: An International Review*, *62*, 260–285.

Hofstede, G.H. (2001). *Culture's Consequences: Comparing Values, Behaviors, Institutions, and Organizations across Nations*. Thousand Oaks, CA: Sage Publications.

Jackson, T.A., Meyer, J.P., and Wang, X.-H. (2013). Leadership, commitment, and culture: A meta-analysis. *Journal of Leadership and Organizational Studies*, *20*, 84–106.

Johnson, R.E., Groff, K.W., and Taing, M.U. (2009). Nature of the interactions among organizational commitments: Complementary, competitive or synergistic? *British Journal of Management*, *20*, 431–447.

Koster, F. (2011). Able, willing and knowing: The effects of HR practices on commitment and effort in 26 European countries. *International Journal of Human Resource Management*, *22*, 2835–2851.

Meyer, J.P. and Allen, N.J. (1997). *Commitment in the Workplace: Theory, Research, and Application.* Thousand Oaks, CA: Sage Publications.

Meyer, J.P. and Maltin, E.R. (2010). Employee commitment and well-being: A critical review, theoretical framework and research agenda. *Journal of Vocational Behavior, 77*(2), 323–337. doi: http://dx.doi.org/10.1016/j.jvb.2010.04.007

Meyer, J.P., Stanley, D.J., Herscovitch, L. and Topolnytsky, L. (2002). Affective, continuance,and normative commitment to the organization:A meta-analysis of antecedents,correlates, and consequences. *Journal of Vocational Behavior, 61*(1), 20–52. doi:http://dx.doi.org/10.1006/jvbe.2001.1842.

Meyer, J.P., Stanley, D.J., Jackson, T.A., McInnis, K.J., Maltin, E.R. and Sheppard, L. (2012). Affective, normative, and continuance commitment levels across cultures: A meta-analysis. *Journal of Vocational Behavior, 80*, 225–245.

Meyer, J.P., Stanley, D.J., McInnis, K., Jackson, T.A., Chris, A. and Anderson, B. (2014). Employee commitment and behavior across cultures: A meta-analysis. Paris: ICAP.

Riketta, M. and van Dick, R. (2005). Foci of attachment in organizations: A meta-analytic comparison of the strength and correlates of workgroup versus organizational identification and commitment. *Journal of Vocational Behavior, 67*, 490–510.

Schmidt, K.-H. (2007). Organizational commitment: A further moderator in the relationship between work stress and strain? *International Journal of Stress Management, 14*, 26–40.

Schwartz, S.H. (1992). Universals in the content and structure of values: Theoretical advances and empirical tests in 20 countries. In P.Z. Mark (ed.), *Advances in Experimental Social Psychology* (Vol. 25, pp. 1–65). San Diego, CA: Academic Press.

Six, B. and Felfe, J. (2006). Arbeitszufriedenheit im interkulturellen Vergleich [Comparing job satisfaction across cultures]. In L. Fischer (ed.), *Arbeitszufriedenheit* (Job satisfaction) (pp. 243–272). Göttingen: Hogrefe.

Vandenberghe, C., Stinglhamber, S., Bentein, K., and Delhaise, T. (2001). An examination of the cross-cultural validity of a multidimensional model of commitment in Europe. *Journal of Cross-Cultural Psychology, 32*, 322–347.

Ward, C. and Chang, W.C. (1997). 'Cultural Fit': A new perspective on personality and sojourner adjustment. *International Journal of Intercultural Relations, 21*, 525–33.

Wasti, S.A. (2003). Organizational commitment, turnover intentions and the influence of cultural values. *Journal of Occupational and Organizational Psychology, 76*, 303–321.

Wasti, S.A. and Önder, Ç. (2009). Commitment across cultures: Progress, pitfalls and propositions. In H.J. Klein, T.E. Becker, and J.P. Meyer (eds), *Commitment in Organizations: Accumulated Wisdom and New Directions* (pp. 309–343). Florence, KY: Routledge/Taylor & Francis.

Wombacher, J. and Felfe, J. (in press). The role of team and organizational commitment in motivating employees' interteam conflict handling. *Academy of Management Journal.*

28. Employee commitment in China
Alex Newman and Dan Wang

Over the last three decades China has witnessed huge changes as a result of the opening-up and reform agenda pursued by the government authorities, which has led to a movement away from a centrally planned economic system to a free market social-ist system with 'Chinese characteristics' (Peck and Zhang, 2013). As part of the reform process the government authorities have removed the 'iron rice bowl' employment pro-tection provided to workers that was characteristic of the old system (Ding et al., 2000). Since the mid-1980s, legislative changes have been implemented that make it easier for organizations to hire and fire workers through the utilization of more flexible employ-ment contracts (Fleisher and Yang, 2003). Such changes have led to the dismantling of lifetime employment in the state sector and higher levels of unemployment (Ding et al., 2000; Warner, 1995). It has also led to greater competition in the labour market for skilled employees (Benson and Zhu, 2002).

Lower levels of employment protection have had a significant impact on the mindset of the younger generation of Chinese workers. They no longer expect to work for the same organization for life, are more open to changing jobs than in the past, and exhibit lower levels of commitment than the older generation (Fu et al., 2011). As a result vol-untary turnover rates in China have exploded over the last decade. For example, in 2012 Aon Hewitt's China Human Capital Intelligence Report showed that voluntary turnover rates were at 18.9 per cent (Sammer, 2013), a figure unheard of in the early years of the reform period.

Lower company loyalty and increased turnover rates have led researchers to investigate the antecedents of employee commitment in China in order to understand what may be done to assist organizations to retain staff. In addition, research has also been conducted to examine the benefits of employee commitment for organizations such as reduced turnover, higher performance and organizational citizenship behaviour (OCB). Although most empirical studies have focused on organizational commitment, work has also been conducted on supervisor commitment, union commitment, and work group commitment (e.g. Chan and Snape, 2013; Cheng et al., 2003; Felfe and Yan, 2009).

In this chapter we review empirical studies that have been conducted on employee com-mitment in China. These studies have typically used a cross-sectional survey methodol-ogy and have been conducted in a range of different organizational contexts (state-owned enterprises, private enterprises, foreign-invested enterprises, and public sector organiza-tions). The predominant focus of the review will be on organizational commitment as it has been the most widely studied out of all commitment foci. The Web of Science and Google Scholar were used to search for relevant peer-reviewed articles that focus on employee commitment and have 'China' or 'Chinese' in their title or abstract. We also used our own knowledge of the field and references in other articles to identify additional articles that may not have been caught by the systematic search. As a result, a total of 42 articles were identified for inclusion in our review. We restricted our review to studies published in English in peer-reviewed academic journals. Although this may limit our ability to look into indigenous concepts and arguments developed around commitment in China through an emic approach, we decided not to include articles in Chinese for two main reasons. First, our review of Chinese organizational behaviour journals indicated a general lack of academic rigour. Second, we found that authors in such journals typically borrowed concepts from the West to study domestic phenomena.

In the following sections we first highlight how commitment has been conceptualized and measured. After this, inconsistencies in the scales used to measure commitment foci in previous work are identified, especially organizational commitment. We also highlight work that suggests that organizational commitment might have distinct dimensions to those identified by studies in the West. Following this, work that has been conducted on the antecedents of organizational commitment is examined. Such antecedents include human resource management (HRM) practices, leadership, supportive relationships at work, positive organizational and team climates, and job satisfaction. Work on the outcomes of organizational commitment is then reviewed, and prior empirical findings that show how commitment interacts with other variables to predict outcomes of interest to organizations are highlighted. Such outcomes include enhanced job attitudes such as job satisfaction and turnover intentions, and higher levels of job performance, extra-role behaviours, and well-being. Following this, work on moderators of the relationship between organizational commitment and other variables such as the collectivism orientation and power-distance orientation of employees is reviewed. Finally, research that has been done on other forms of commitment is presented.

After reviewing extant work on organizational commitment in China, gaps in our existing knowledge are highlighted and potential avenues for future research suggested. We specifically ask researchers to be consistent in how they measure organizational commitment, and to conduct more work on other forms of employee commitment such as occupational commitment, supervisor commitment, and work group commitment, given that the overwhelming focus of research on employee commitment in China has been on organizational commitment. In addition, we call for more work to identify whether the factors which predict the development of commitment vary as a result of industrial contexts or generational differences. The need for more multilevel work to examine the relative influence of antecedents on organizational commitment at the individual, team, and organizational level, to establish how organizations may promote its development, is also highlighted.

CONCEPTUALIZATION AND MEASUREMENT OF ORGANIZATIONAL COMMITMENT

Organizational commitment has been measured in a number of ways in previous studies in the Chinese organizational context. One group of research studies has conceptualized organizational commitment as a unidimensional measure. For example, eight of the 42 studies identified in our review of the literature use full or abbreviated versions of the unidimensional Organizational Commitment Questionnaire (OCQ) (Mowday et al., 1979; Porter et al., 1974). Other studies have either developed their own unidimensional measures (Gamble and Huang, 2008) or adopted alternative measures (e.g. Hrebeniak and Alutto, 1972). However, a larger body of literature has conceptualized organizational commitment as a multidimensional construct. For example, 23 studies out of the 42 identified have utilized Meyer et al.'s (1993) multidimensional framework which conceptualizes organizational commitment as being composed of three distinct 'mindsets', namely affective organizational commitment (AOC), continuance organizational commitment (COC), and normative organizational commitment (NOC). Although many of these studies focus on one dimension of organizational commitment (in many cases, affective commitment), others have looked at differences between the three main dimensions in how predictive they are of employee work outcomes. Whereas some studies support the three-factor structure proposed by Meyer and colleagues (Chen and Francesco, 2003; Miao et al., 2013a; Miao et al., 2013b), other studies find alternative structures have a better fit (Cheng and Stockdale, 2003; Wang, 2004). For example, Wang (2004) established that continuance commitment separates into two factors – passive and active continuance commitment – and added a new dimension of value commitment to the multidimensional model. Value commitment refers to the extent to which an employee feels value congruence with the organization and is willing to exert concerted effort that benefits the organization (Wang, 2004). Similarly, Cheng and Stockdale (2003) found that continuance commitment separates into two factors: low alternatives and high sacrifices.

Chinese Culture and Organizational Commitment

The findings of recent meta-analytical work suggest that levels of AOC and NOC are typically higher in cultures such as China, where there are higher levels of in-group collectivism and power distance than in North America and Europe (Fischer and Mansell, 2009; Meyer et al., 2012). For example, Fischer and Mansell (2009) found that AOC was higher in countries with greater in-group collectivism, and that NOC was higher in countries with greater in-group collectivism and power distance. Similarly, Meyer et al. (2012) found that AOC and NOC were generally higher in countries such as China that have stronger collectivist values, and that NOC was higher in countries with stronger power/distance values. Neither of these studies found evidence of cultural effects on continuance commitment. These findings suggest that Chinese employees generally feel a greater sense of attachment and obligation to their organization than employees in more individualistic cultures such as the United States and Northern Europe.

Antecedents of Organizational Commitment

Twenty-seven studies were identified that examined antecedents of organizational commitment within the Chinese organizational context. Antecedents of organizational commitment examined by such studies include HRM practices, leadership, supportive relationships at work, positive organizational and team climates, and job satisfaction.

Human resource management practices
The use of high-performance work systems and high-involvement work practices by organizations has been shown to have a positive effect on organizational commitment in Chinese organizations. For example, Yu and Egri (2005) found that employee satisfaction with HRM practices in the areas of recruitment, employee selection, performance

management, training, compensation and job security, and working conditions were positively correlated with employees' AOC. Similarly, research by Qiao et al. (2009) revealed that the implementation of high-performance work systems was positively related to the organizational commitment of Chinese employees, especially those who are male and unmarried. Newman et al. (2011) found that employees' perceptions of their organization's training practices predicted higher levels of AOC and NOC in cases where participation in training was supported by their supervisor and co-workers. More recent work by Newman and Sheikh (2012) and Miao et al. (2013b) revealed that an organization's provision of extrinsic rewards (pay and other financial rewards) and intrinsic rewards (autonomy and role clarity) are positively associated with organizational commitment. Finally, Tang et al. (2003) found that the enforcement styles used in public sector organizations predicted civil servants' organizational commitment.

Leadership
Another body of research has looked at the role played by leaders in engendering the organizational commitment of their followers. Huang et al. (2006) established that the exhibition of participative leadership by supervisors was positively related to subordinates' OCBs, especially for employees with shorter organizational tenure. Similarly, Miao et al. (2013a) found that participative leadership was positively associated to subordinates' AOC and NOC through inducing higher levels of affective trust. Newman and Butler (2014) found that the transformational leadership of supervisors is positively related to subordinate AOC. They also investigated how employees' individual-level cultural orientations influenced the strength of the transformational leadership–AOC relationship. They found the relationship to be stronger for subordinates high in collectivism and uncertainty avoidance, and low in power distance. Finally, Miao et al. (2014) found that servant leadership is positively associated with subordinates' AOC and NOC through eliciting higher levels of affective trust.

Supportive relationships at work
Researchers have also established that supportive relationships at work are positively related to organizational commitment. For example, He et al. (2011) found that managerial support and co-worker support are positively related to employees' AOC. Similarly, Chan and Snape (2013) revealed a positive link between perceived organizational support and employees' AOC.

Positive team and organizational climates
There is a small and growing stream of research which identifies whether positive organizational and team climates promote higher levels of organizational commitment. Both Shafer (2009) and Fu and Deshpande (2012) found a positive association between employee perceptions of the ethical climate within their organization and their organizational commitment. Wong et al. (2002) found that employee perceptions of distributive and procedural justice climates are positively associated with organizational commitment, and this relationship is mediated by employee trust in the organization.

Job and pay satisfaction

Researchers have also found consistently strong evidence that job and pay satisfaction strongly predict higher levels of organizational commitment (Chan and Qiu, 2011; Froese and Xiao, 2012; Fu et al., 2011; Fu and Deshpande, 2012, 2014; Wang et al., 2002).

Other antecedents

A significant number of other antecedents of organizational commitment have been identified. Researchers have consistently found that organizational commitment increases with age (Fu et al., 2011; Newman and Sheikh, 2012; Wang et al., 2002), and that employees in more senior management positions exhibit higher levels of commitment, especially NOC (Chen and Francesco, 2000; Hofman and Newman, 2014). Empirical findings also indicate that employees who rate high in power distance and collectivism typically exhibit higher levels of AOC and NOC (Chan and Snape, 2013; Miao et al., 2013a; Wang et al., 2002). Recent research also suggests that an organization's implementation of corporate social responsibility initiatives is positively linked to employees' AOC and NOC (Hofman and Newman, 2014), and that the ethical behaviour of peers and managers is positively related to organizational commitment. Finally, research demonstrates that organizational commitment is typically higher in less-developed regions of China (Gamble and Tian, 2015), and that AOC and COC are typically higher in state-owned enterprises compared to foreign-owned enterprises, where value commitment is higher (Wang, 2004).

Outcomes of Organizational Commitment

Twenty-three studies out of 42 examined the outcomes of organizational commitment in the Chinese workplace. Outcomes of organizational commitment highlighted by these studies fall into three main groups; namely job attitudes (that is, turnover intentions, job and organizational satisfaction), job behaviour (that is, in-role and extra-role behaviours), and employee well-being. The findings of these studies also indicate that the strength of the relationships between AOC, NOC, and COC and these outcomes may differ.

Job attitudes

Research has shown that job attitudes such as turnover intentions and job satisfaction can be influenced by organizational commitment. For example, Chen and Francesco (2000) found that organizational commitment is negatively related to the turnover intentions of Chinese employees, and it is stronger for male than for their female counterparts. Similarly, based on a Taiwanese sample, Cheng et al. (2003) revealed a strong negative relationship between organizational commitment and turnover intentions. Cheng and Stockdale (2003) identified that all three dimensions of organizational commitment – namely AOC, NOC, and COC – predict turnover intentions. However, in contrast, Wong et al. (2002) and Yao and Wang (2006) found only AOC and NOC to predict turnover intentions and turnover behaviours, respectively; whereas Newman et al. (2011) confirmed a strong negative relationship between AOC and COC and turnover intentions for employees in the service sector. In addition, Wong et al. (2001) found that organizational commitment is more strongly related to the turnover intentions of Chinese employees than their Western counterparts. Empirical evidence also suggests that the organizational commitment of Chinese employees moderately predicts their willingness to stay (Gamble and Huang, 2008).

Research has also examined job satisfaction as another attitudinal outcome of the organizational commitment of Chinese employees. For example, Wong et al. (2001) found that organizational commitment was positively associated with the job satisfaction of employees, and its effects were stronger than in the West. Conceptualizing organizational commitment as a multidimensional construct, Cheng and Stockdale (2003) identified that AOC and NOC were strongly related to employees' job satisfaction. Similarly, both Cheng et al. (2003) and Wu and Norman (2006) established a positive relationship between organizational commitment and job satisfaction. Furthermore, Yao and Wang (2006) revealed that AOC predicted employees' job satisfaction strongly, and that the relationship gets stronger as allocentrism increases. Lu et al. (2010) also found a moderate positive relationship between AOC and job satisfaction, and demonstrated that AOC worked as a 'buffer' that moderates the negative relationship between work stressors (that is, interpersonal conflict, lack of autonomy) and job satisfaction. Recently, Yang et al. (2014) found that NOC was strongly related to job satisfaction.

Job behaviours

Apart from job attitudes, the literature suggests that organizational commitment is also positively related to employees' in-role and extra-role job behaviours. For example, researchers have established that organizational commitment influences job performance (Cheng et al., 2003; Francesco and Chen, 2004; Fu and Deshpande, 2014; Siu, 2003), and organizational citizenship behaviour (OCB) (Cheng et al., 2003; Francesco and Chen, 2004). Whereas Chen and Francesco (2003) found that AOC was positively and strongly related to in-role performance and OCB, they found that COC was negatively and weakly correlated to OCB. These findings are consistent with those from other meta-analytical work (Meyer et al., 2002) which shows that the relationships between COC and both job performance and OCB are weaker than those between AOC and NOC and such outcomes. In addition, studies have also established positive effects of organizational commitment on ethical behaviour in the workplace (Fu, 2014) and enforcement effectiveness; that is, the extent to which employees from the environmental bureau in a Chinese city perceived their work unit to be effective in implementing environmental regulations (Tang et al., 2003).

Employee well-being

A small stream of research has looked at employee well-being as an outcome of organizational commitment. For example, Donald and Siu (2001) found that organizational commitment strongly predicted employee well-being. In contrast, however, Tan and Akhtar (1998) established that higher levels of NOC might be positively associated with the willingness of employees to exert greater job effort, which in turn predicts burnout.

Relative importance of different dimensions of organizational commitment

The findings of previous studies typically indicate that AOC and NOC have a stronger positive effect on organizational outcomes than COC. For example, Chen and Francesco (2003) found that AOC was positively related to OCB, but COC was negatively related to it. In addition, Cheng and Stockdale (2003) identified that AOC and NOC are positively related to job satisfaction, but the relationship between COC and job satisfaction was non-significant. Recently, Gamble and Tian (2015) found that AOC and NOC were negatively related to employees' turnover intentions, while COC was positively related to their turnover intentions.

Moderators of the Relationship between Organizational Commitment and Other Variables

Although there has been a significant amount of research looking at relationships between organizational commitment and its antecedents and outcomes, a comparatively smaller number of studies have examined the factors which moderate such relationships. A few studies have begun to examine factors such as individually held cultural values, tenure, and organizational context which accentuate or attenuate the relationship between organizational commitment and its antecedents. For example, Newman and Butler (2014) found that the relationship between transformational leadership and AOC was stronger for individuals high in collectivism and uncertainty avoidance and low in power distance. These findings imply that individual-level cultural values of Chinese followers may promote their attitudinal response to transformational leadership. Huang et al. (2006) also found that participative leadership was more strongly associated with AOC for individuals with shorter tenure. Qiao et al. (2009) found that high-performance work systems are more strongly related to the organizational commitment of males compared to female employees. Lu et al. (2010) found that the link between job satisfaction and AOC was stronger for employees in private enterprises than it was for those in state-owned enterprises. They argue that this is because private enterprises recognize and promote employees mainly based on individual performance, but state-owned enterprises may consider a wider range of factors such as age and years in the organization.

Similar work has looked at factors such as individually held cultural values and gender which moderate the relationship between organizational commitment and its outcomes. Francesco and Chen (2004), for example, found that the relationship between AOC and both in-role and extra-role performance were weaker for collectivists. They argued that as collectivists are strongly motivated by group norms, their personal commitment to the organization will be less connected to performance than that of individualists. Chen and Francesco (2000) found that the relationship between organizational commitment and turnover intentions was stronger for males than females. They argue that this is because women may have more non-job-related reasons for leaving the organization than male employees.

Research on Other Commitment Foci

In addition to the wealth of literature on the antecedents and outcomes of organizational commitment, a small number of studies have looked at other commitment foci such as the work group, supervisor, and union. The examination of these foci is extremely important given that China is a culture high in power distance and collectivism, where loyalty to the supervisor and work group are higher than in cultures low in power distance and collectivism. For example, Felfe and Yan (2009) found that affective and normative work group commitment were positively related to employee OCBs and negatively related to their turnover intentions, and that these effects were stronger in a Chinese than a German sample. Cheng et al. (2003) found that supervisory commitment predicted work attitudes such as job satisfaction and turnover intentions as well as work behaviours such as OCBs and job performance. Van Vianen et al. (2011) found that employees' person–supervisor fit was positively related to organizational commitment through enhancing supervisor commitment, and that employee and supervisor fit perceptions were positively related to supervisor commitment through enhancing the quality of leader–member exchange (LMX). Snape et al. (2006) established that supervisor commitment was positively associated with altruism and interpersonal harmony, and negatively associated with withdrawal cognitions. In contrast, they found that only work group commitment was negatively associated with withdrawal cognitions. Finally, Chan and Snape (2013) revealed that perceived union support and horizontal collectivism were positively related to affective union commitment.

AGENDA FOR FUTURE RESEARCH

Through the extensive review of studies on employee commitment in China, we have provided insight on the measurement, antecedents and outcomes of employee commitment, as well as the moderators of the commitment–antecedents and commitment–outcomes relationships. Several gaps still remain in this area, which we present in this section, providing a platform to inform future research.

First, we believe that it is crucial for future research to maintain consistency in the approach used to measure commitment in the Chinese context. We recommend researchers adopt Meyer et al.'s (1993) framework of affective, normative, and continuance commitment as it has been widely validated in the Chinese context (Miao et al., 2013a, 2013b), and is the most popular commitment scale in use (Meyer et al., 2012). Methodologically, researchers should also seek to collect panel data on commitment, its antecedents and outcomes at multiple time points in order to establish causality between study variables (for more information, see Chapters 33 and 34 in this volume). In addition, researchers may consider adopting a person-centred approach, as opposed to the variable-centred approach used in prior empirical work, when conducting research on commitment in China. More specifically, following the example of recent research (Morin et al., 2015; Chapter 35 in this volume), researchers might examine the influence of different profiles of commitment on work attitudes and behaviours through the use of latent profile analysis.

As prior work on employee commitment in China has overwhelmingly focused on measuring the effects of organizational commitment on employee workplace outcomes, there is a critical need for research to examine the relative influence of other commitment foci such as occupational commitment, supervisor commitment, and work group commitment. For example, given that China is a collective society in which supervisory relationships and team dynamics are more important to employees than in more individualistic countries (Hwang, 2000), we might expect supervisor and work group commitment to have a stronger effect on workplace outcomes such as performance and organizational citizenship behaviour than organizational commitment. In examining the importance of different foci of commitment, researchers may consider using the recent unidimensional target-free measure of commitment developed by Klein et al. (2014) which may be applied to all workplace targets.

Research might also investigate generational differences in organizational commitment and the strategies organizations could use to enhance the commitment of different generational cohorts. For example, given that the younger generation of employees in China have been shown to have a greater need for high-involvement work practices and autonomy in their jobs than the older generation (Huang et al., 2006), we might expect such factors to have a greater influence on the commitment of such employees.

In the future, researchers may also consider conducting multilevel work to examine the relative influence of antecedents on different commitment foci at the individual, team, and organizational level. This will provide organizations with critical knowledge on the relative importance of employees' personal characteristics, leadership, and team dynamics, and organizational practices, to organizational commitment and other commitment foci. Research may also be conducted at different organizational levels to establish whether the organizational commitment of senior managers influences organizational commitment at lower levels of the organization (for example, mid- and low-level managers and employees). In addition, the relative effects of commitment at different levels of the organization on organizational-, team-, and individual-level performance outcomes should also be scrutinized. This will allow us to examine whether there are trickle-down effects of commitment from higher levels of the organization to lower levels.

Finally, given that prior research in China has focused on the positive relationship between employee commitment and workplace outcomes, future research might examine the potential negative relationship between employee commitment and employee outcomes. For example, in light of recent research which highlights the negative effects of being overcommitted (Kinman and Jones, 2008), future research might investigate the curvilinear relationship between commitment and workplace outcomes such as employees' job performance, burnout, and work–life balance. For instance, overcommitted employees might feel obligated to sacrifice their personal life and focus more on their work. As a result they may be overburdened by work and work-related stress, which might negatively affect their performance due to emotional exhaustion and a lack of work–life balance. Future research could seek to establish the threshold where commitment could begin to have a negative influence on the job performance of employees.

REFERENCES

Benson, J. and Zhu, Y. (2002). The emerging external labor market and the impact on enterprise's human resource development in China. *Human Resource Development Quarterly*, 13(4), 449–466.

Chan, A.W. and Snape, E. (2013). Are cultural values associated with organizational and union commitment and citizenship behavior? A study of Chinese manufacturing workers. *Asia-Pacific Journal of Management*, 30(1), 169–190.

Chan, S.H. and Qiu, H.H. (2011). Loneliness, job satisfaction, and organizational commitment of migrant workers: Empirical evidence from China. *International Journal of Human Resource Management*, 22(5), 1109–1127.

Chen, Z.X. and Francesco, A.M. (2000). Employee demography, organizational commitment, and turnover intentions in China: Do cultural differences matter? *Human Relations*, 53(6), 869–887.

Chen, Z.X. and Francesco, A.M. (2003). The relationship between the three components of commitment and employee performance in China. *Journal of Vocational Behavior*, 62(3), 490–510.

Cheng, B.S., Jiang, D.Y. and Riley, J.H. (2003). Organizational commitment, supervisory commitment, and employee outcomes in the Chinese context: Proximal hypothesis or global hypothesis? *Journal of Organizational Behavior*, 24(3), 313–334.

Cheng, Y. and Stockdale, M.S. (2003). The validity of the three-component model of organizational commitment in a Chinese context. *Journal of Vocational Behavior*, 62(3), 465–489.

Ding, D., Goodall, K., and Warner, M. (2000). The end of the 'iron rice-bowl': Whither Chinese human resource management? *International Journal of Human Resource Management*, 11(2), 217–236.

Donald, I. and Siu, O. (2001). Moderating the stress impact of environmental conditions: The effect of organizational commitment in Hong Kong and China. *Journal of Environmental Psychology*, 21(4), 353–368.

Felfe, J. and Yan, W.H. (2009). The impact of workgroup commitment on organizational citizenship behaviour, absenteeism and turnover intention: The case of Germany and China. *Asia-Pacific Business Review*, 15(3), 433–450.

Fischer, R., and Mansell, A. (2009). Commitment across cultures: A meta-analytical approach. *Journal of International Business Studies*, 40, 1339–1358.

Fleisher, B.M. and Yang, D.T. (2003). Labor laws and regulations in China. *China Economic Review*, 14(4), 426–433.

Francesco, A.M. and Chen, Z.X. (2004). Collectivism in action: Its moderating effects on the relationship between organizational commitment and employee performance in China. *Group and Organization Management*, 29(4), 425–441.

Froese, F.J. and Xiao, S. (2012). Work values, job satisfaction and organizational commitment in China. *International Journal of Human Resource Management*, 23(10), 2144–2162.

Fu, W. (2014). The impact of emotional intelligence, organizational commitment, and job satisfaction on ethical behavior of Chinese employees. *Journal of Business Ethics*, 122(1), 137–144.

Fu, W. and Deshpande, S.P. (2012). Antecedents of organizational commitment in a Chinese construction company. *Journal of Business Ethics*, 109(3), 301–307.

Fu, W. and Deshpande, S.P. (2014). The impact of caring climate, job satisfaction, and organizational commitment on job performance of employees in a China's insurance company. *Journal of Business Ethics*, 124(2), 339–349.

Fu, W., Deshpande, S.P., and Zhao, X. (2011). The impact of ethical behavior and facets of job satisfaction on organizational commitment of Chinese employees. *Journal of Business Ethics*, 104(4), 537–543.

Gamble, J. and Huang, Q. (2008). Organizational commitment of Chinese employees in foreign-invested firms. *International Journal of Human Resource Management*, 19(5), 896–915.

Gamble, J. and Tian, A. (2015). Intra-national variation in organizational commitment: Evidence from the Chinese context. *International Journal of Human Resource Management*, 26(7), 1–23.

He, Y., Lai, K.K., and Lu, Y. (2011). Linking organizational support to employee commitment: Evidence from hotel industry of China. *International Journal of Human Resource Management*, 22(1), 197–217.

Hrebeniak, L.G. and Alutto, J.A. (1972). Personal and role-related factors in the development of organizational commitment. *Administrative Science Quarterly*, 17(4), 555–573.

Hofman, P.S. and Newman, A. (2014). The impact of perceived corporate social responsibility on organizational commitment and the moderating role of collectivism and masculinity: Evidence from China. *International Journal of Human Resource Management*, 25(5), 631–652.

Huang, X., Shi, K., Zhang, Z., and Cheung, Y.L. (2006). The impact of participative leadership behavior on psychological empowerment and organizational commitment in Chinese state-owned enterprises: the moderating role of organizational tenure. *Asia-Pacific Journal of Management*, 23(3), 345–367.

Hwang, K.K. (2000). Chinese relationalism: Theoretical construction and methodological considerations. *Journal for the Theory of Social Behavior*, 30(2), 155–178.

Kinman, G. and Jones, F. (2008). Effort–reward imbalance, over-commitment and work–life conflict: Testing an expanded model. *Journal of Managerial Psychology*, 23(3), 236–251.

Klein, H.., Cooper, J.T., Molloy, J.C., and Swanson, J.A. (2014). The assessment of commitment: Advantages of a unidimensional, target-free approach. *Journal of Applied Psychology*, 99(2), 222–238.

Lu, L., Siu, O., and Lu, C.Q. (2010). Does loyalty protect Chinese workers from stress? The role of affective organizational commitment in the greater China region. *Stress and Health*, 26(2), 161–168.

Meyer, J.P., Allen, N.J., and Smith, C. (1993). Commitment to organizations and occupations: Extension and test of a three-component conceptualization. *Journal of Applied Psychology*, 78(4), 538–551.

Meyer, J.P., Stanley, D.J., Herscovitch, L., and Topolnytsky, L. (2002). Affective, continuance and normative commitment to the organization: A meta-analysis of antecedents, correlates and consequences. *Journal of Vocational Behavior*, 61(1), 20–52.

Meyer, J.P., Stanley, D.J., Jackson, T.A., McInnis, K.J., Maltin, E.S., and Sheppard, L. (2012). Affective, normative, and continuance commitment levels across cultures: A meta-analysis. *Journal of Vocational Behavior*, 80(2), 225–245.

Miao, Q., Newman, A., Schwarz, G., and Xu, L. (2013a). Participative leadership and the organizational commitment of civil servants in China: The mediating effects of trust in supervisor. *British Journal of Management*, 24(S1), 76–92.

Miao, Q., Newman, A., Schwarz, G., and Xu, L. (2014). Servant leadership, trust, and the organizational commitment of public sector employees in China. *Public Administration*, 92(3), 727–743.

Miao, Q., Newman, A., Sun, Y., and Xu, L. (2013b). What factors influence the organizational commitment of public sector employees in China? *International Journal of Human Resource Management*, 24(17), 3262–3280.

Morin, A.J.S., Meyer, J.P., McInerney, D.M., Marsh, H.W., and Ganotice, F. (2015). Profiles of dual commitment to the occupation and organization: Relations to wellbeing and turnover intentions. *Asia Pacific Journal of Management*, 32(3), 717–744.

Mowday, R.T., Steers, R.M., and Porter, L.W. (1979). The measurement of organizational commitment. *Journal of Vocational Behavior*, 14(2), 224–247.

Newman, A. and Butler, C. (2014). The influence of follower cultural orientation on attitudinal responses towards transformational leadership: Evidence from the Chinese hospitality industry. *International Journal of Human Resource Management*, 25(7), 1024–1045.

Newman, A. and Sheikh, A.Z. (2012). Organizational commitment in Chinese small- and medium-sized enterprises: The role of extrinsic, intrinsic and social rewards. *International Journal of Human Resource Management*, 23(2), 349–367.

Newman, A., Thanacoody, R., and Hui, W. (2011). The impact of employee perceptions of training on organizational commitment and turnover intentions: A study of multinationals in the Chinese service sector. *International Journal of Human Resource Management*, 22(8), 1765–1787.

Peck, J. and Zhang, J. (2013). A variety of capitalism . . . with Chinese characteristics? *Journal of Economic Geography*, 13(3), 357–396.

Porter, L.W., Steers, R.M., Mowday, R.T., and Boulian, V. (1974). Organizational commitment, job satisfaction, and turnover among psychiatric technicians. *Journal of Applied Psychology*, 59(5), 603–609.

Qiao, K., Khilji, S., and Wang, X. (2009). High-performance work systems, organizational commitment, and the role of demographic features in the People's Republic of China. *International Journal of Human Resource Management*, 20(11), 2311–2330.

Sammer, J. (2013). The changing cost of doing business in China. *Business Finance*, 11, January. http://businessfinancemag.com/hr/changing-cost-of-doing-business-china.

Shafer, W.E. (2009). Ethical climate, organizational-professional, conflict and organizational commitment. *Accounting, Auditing and Accountability Journal*, 22(7), 1087–1110.

Siu, O. (2003). Job stress and job performance among employees in Hong Kong: The role of Chinese work values and organizational commitment. *International Journal of Psychology*, 38(6), 337–347.

Snape, E., Chan, A.W., and Redman, T. (2006). Multiple commitments in the Chinese context: Testing compatibility, cultural, and moderating hypotheses. *Journal of Vocational Behavior*, 69(2), 302–314.

Tan, D.S.K. and Akhtar, S. (1998). Organizational commitment and experienced burnout: An exploratory study from a Chinese cultural perspective. *International Journal of Organizational Analysis*, 6(4), 310–333.

Tang, S.Y., Lo, C.W.H., and Fryxell, G.E. (2003). Enforcement styles, organizational commitment, and enforcement effectiveness: An empirical study of local environmental protection officials in urban China. *Environment and Planning A*, 35(1), 75–94.

Van Vianen, A.E.M., Shen, C.T., and Chuang, A. (2011). Person–organization and person–supervisor fits: Employee commitments in a Chinese context. *Journal of Organizational Behavior*, 32(6), 906–926.

Wang, L., Bishop, J.W., Chen, X., and Scott, K.D. (2002). Collectivist orientation as a predictor of affective organizational commitment: A study conducted in China. *International Journal of Organizational Analysis*, 10(3), 226–239.

Wang, Y. (2004). Observations on the organizational commitment of Chinese employees: Comparative studies of state-owned enterprises and foreign-invested enterprises. *International Journal of Human Resource Management*, 15(4), 649–669.

Warner, M. (1995). *The Management of Human Resources in Chinese Industry*. London: Macmillan.

Wong, C.H., Wong, Y., Hui, C., and Law, K.S. (2001). The significant role of Chinese employees' organizational commitment: Implications for managing employees in Chinese societies. *Journal of World Business*, 36(3), 326–340.

Wong, Y.T., Ngo, H.Y., and Wong, C.S. (2002). Affective organizational commitment of workers in Chinese joint ventures. *Journal of Managerial Psychology*, 17(7), 580–598.

Wu, L. and Norman, I.J. (2006). An investigation of job satisfaction, organizational commitment and role conflict and ambiguity in a sample of Chinese undergraduate nursing students. *Nurse Education Today*, 26(4), 304–314.

Yang, J., Liu, Y., Chen, Y., and Pan, X. (2014). The effect of structural empowerment and organizational commitment on Chinese nurses' job satisfaction. *Applied Nursing Research*, 27(3), 186–191.

Yao, X. and Wang, L. (2006). The predictability of normative organizational commitment for turnover in Chinese companies: A cultural perspective. *International Journal of Human Resource Management*, 17(6), 1058–1075.
Yu, B.B., and Egri, C.P. (2005). Human resource management practices and affective organizational commitment: A comparison of Chinese employees in a state-owned enterprise and a joint venture. *Asia-Pacific Journal of Human Resources*, 43(3), 332–360.

29. An examination of the social-institutional, cultural, and organizational antecedents of commitment in India

*Vidyut Lata Dhir, Nicholas L. Bremner and Sumita Datta**

Since gaining its independence in 1947, India has taken significant strides socially and economically. The liberalization of economic policies in the 1990s has resulted in a massive surge of competition from multinational corporations (MNCs). This increased competition has placed pressure on Indian firms to recognize the advantages of leveraging human capital (Dhir, 2013). Such efforts to maximize the performance and motivation of employees highlights the importance of employee commitment. Research has established consistent links between organizational commitment and desirable outcomes such as job performance, organizational citizenship behaviors (OCBs), well-being, and reduced turnover (Meyer et al., 2002). This makes commitment a key concept for Indian organizations to understand and foster in order to remain competitive. As India's economy continues to open up to the world, Western cultural values and management practices are likely to increasingly influence India's workforce. However, many attempts to apply Western management theories and practices in an Indian context have not had the intended effects (Kwantes, 2009). This poses a challenge for managers seeking to maximize human capital and raises important research questions about differences in the antecedents, outcomes, and experience of employee commitment in the workplace.

In order to understand employee commitment in an Indian context, it is important to consider the potentially far-reaching effects of cultural, social, and economic factors (Wasti and Önder, 2009). Since Hofstede (1980) published his seminal work on cultural dimensions of work-related values, additional frameworks have followed, along with an increased interest in understanding cultural differences in organizational commitment (Meyer et al., 2012). However, Wasti and Önder (2009) point out that many studies of organizational commitment conducted outside of North America have overlooked relevant contextual variables (for example, cultural norms, economic conditions, labor laws) and have adopted an 'imposed-etic' approach. This involves studying a construct in a new cultural context without regard for how relevant or applicable the theory, conceptualization, and/or measurement of the construct is to the new context. Given that much of the theory on organizational commitment was developed in Western countries (see Klein et al., 2009), it is important for researchers seeking to understand commitment in an Indian context to account for these differences in their research.

The purpose of this chapter is to help inform and guide future research on employee commitment in India. In an effort to do so, we briefly describe the changing workplace culture in India and review extant research in this context, contrasting it with Western commitment research. Next, we draw on Wasti and Önder's (2009) comprehensive model describing the influences of social-institutional and cultural factors on employee commitment and apply it to an Indian context. Specifically, we highlight cultural, societal, and organizational factors that are relevant to understanding commitment in India and should be considered for both research and practice. We conclude by discussing some of the implications for research and practice derived from this model.

THE CHANGING WORKPLACE CULTURE IN INDIA

Traditional culture in India is rooted in its joint family (that is, multiple generations of a family living under the same roof) and caste systems (A.K. Jain, 2015). These practices are representative of India's cultural values, which emphasize strong family ties and social status. In the language of Hofstede's (2001) cultural value framework, India leans towards collectivism (as opposed to individualism), greater power distance, and cultural tightness (Gelfand et al., 2006; A.K. Jain, 2015; Meyer et al., 2007). Collectivists identify strongly with their ingroup and are heavily influenced by social norms. Greater power distance is associated with obedience and dependence on authority figures, as well as greater acceptance of unequal distribution of power (Hofstede, 2001). Lastly, tight cultures have strong social norms and severe sanctions as a consequence of their violation (Gelfand et al., 2006).

However, India's economic liberalization has changed the country both culturally and socio-economically. India's new-found entrepreneurial freedom has led to increasing numbers of mergers and acquisitions, enabling organizations in a variety of industries to grow in size at an unprecedented rate. At the same time, MNCs have ascended in importance in India's economy. India's traditionally powerful public sector has lost much of its clout due to the government's privatization policies and has undergone the painful process of downsizing to remain viable. This led to the implementation of new exit policies such as 'voluntary retirement services', which sent a clear message to employees that the largely collectivistic notion of a long relationship with the organization was no longer a reality. Many of these changes have manifested themselves in the workplace culture of Indian organizations, which are now described as a mix of collectivism and individualism (A.K. Jain, 2015).

Increased competition and economic prosperity has also resulted in the migration of individuals from rural communities to metropolitan areas, affecting the structure of India's traditional family relationships. As India's middle class has grown in size and prosperity, the nuclear family structure has become more prevalent, along with a focus on values commonly espoused by Western societies such as personal achievement, self-interest, and wealth accumulation (Goswami et al., 2008). There have also been demographic changes in the Indian workforce. The average age of workers is decreasing: as of 2011 approximately 65 per cent of India's working population was 35 or under (Census of India, 2011), and many of these young, educated professionals possess different values than their older counterparts.

The factors outlined above offer a glimpse into the evolving context characterizing India's work environments, which are elaborated upon later in the chapter. The next section describes the existing commitment research in India and highlights some of the major differences between research conducted in this context and in the rest of the world.

ORGANIZATIONAL COMMITMENT RESEARCH IN INDIA

Arguably, Meyer and Allen's (1991) three-component model (TCM) of organizational commitment is the most widely adopted conceptualization of commitment by researchers internationally, including India. The TCM postulates that individuals can experience one or more of three distinct mindsets (or forms) of commitment towards various targets (or foci). The three mindsets are termed affective (AC), normative (NC), and continuance commitment (CC), and are characterized by emotional attachment, a sense of obligation, and perceived costs associated with leaving, respectively (see Chapter 3 in this volume). Each mindset binds the individual to a particular target or course of action, but for different reasons. Examples of foci include one's organization, supervisor, job, occupation, or initiatives such as organizational change (see Chapter 4 in this volume). However, this section will make apparent that Indian commitment research has almost exclusively focused on the organization as a focus of commitment.

As is apparent from the many chapters within this volume, the body of organizational commitment research conducted in Western countries is substantial. In contrast, research in India is in its relative infancy and has examined only a narrow range of antecedents, outcomes, and correlates of commitment, with the organization as the primary focus. Much of this research has involved one or more of the TCM commitment mindsets, and one of our objectives in this review is to highlight how findings in India relate to those obtained in North America. It should be noted that some studies reported findings that combined the AC, NC, and CC scores into a single index. This practice is contrary to the recommended use of the TCM (Allen and Meyer, 1990) and yields scores that are difficult to interpret. For this reason, we have omitted these studies from our review.

Antecedents of Commitment

Most studies addressing potential antecedents of organizational commitment have focused on comparisons in commitment levels based on demographic variables, as well as aspects of the job, work environment, or organization.

Demographic and organizational comparisons

Studies examining demographic differences in commitment have found that older employees tend to report higher AC and NC than their younger counterparts. Results are less consistent for CC (Dhir, 2013; B.P. Kumar and Giri, 2009; Natarajan and Nagar, 2011; Paramanandam, 2013). This mirrors Western research (Mathieu and Zajac, 1990) and highlights the difference in how the employment relationship may be viewed by different generations of employees. Additionally, it has been found that women generally report lower levels of organizational commitment than men (Vijaya and Hemamalini, 2012), which may be attributed to expectation that Indian women maintain their roles as homemakers even when employed at an organization (Agarwal, 2011). Finally, consistent with Western commitment research is the notion that individuals report greater AC and NC when they are in a higher income bracket (Paramanandam, 2013). Relatedly, employees with greater levels of education tend to report lower levels of CC, suggesting that they have better job prospects and mobility (Dhir, 2013).

Research in India has also focused on comparing commitment in different organizations based on their authority structure and size. Awasthy and Gupta (2010) studied commitment in three MNCs (from Korea, Sweden, and Anglo-America) and discovered through a series of interviews with Indian executives that those in the more decentralized Anglo-American MNCs tended to exhibit higher AC. They found that employees consistently reported high CC and low NC in all three MNCs. In support of this, Dhir (2013) found that all three components of commitment were higher for employees of small and medium-sized enterprises (SMEs) than employees of large-scale enterprises (LSEs). Among the three components, the difference in NC was the most pronounced. This contrasts with Western research where no relation was found between organizational size and commitment (Mathieu and Zajac, 1990).

Work experiences
Indian researchers have also examined employees' perceptions of, and attitudes towards, their jobs in relation to commitment. Studies examining job characteristics (for example, autonomy, role overload) and job satisfaction are relatively common and generally consistent with Western research, finding positive relationships with AC and NC (B.P. Kumar and Giri, 2009; Kwantes, 2009; Mishra et al., 2015).

Employees' psychological contracts (that is, perceptions of mutual exchange between employee and employer) have also been studied in Indian commitment research. Shahnawaz and Goswami (2011) found that in India's public sector, psychological contract breaches had the strongest negative relationship with employees' AC, but that the relationship was stronger for NC and CC in the private sector. Research has also found that interpersonal problems in the workplace and work–family conflict were negative predictors of all three commitment mindsets (Ahmed, 2013; Vijaya and Hemamalini, 2012).

Organizational variables
Variables related to characteristics of the organization have received the most attention in the commitment literature in India. Studies of organizational culture have used the OCTAPACE, which measures eight cultural dimensions, that is, openness, confrontation, trust, authenticity, proaction, autonomy, collaboration, and experimentation (Pareek, 2003, cited in Neelam et al., 2015); and the OCAI, which consists of two dimensions of culture, internal/external focus and flexibility/stability (Cameron and Quinn, 1999). All eight dimensions of the OCTAPACE have been found to relate positively to AC (Neelam et al., 2015). Additionally, it has been found that 'clan-like' cultures (high in internal focus and flexibility) tend to foster greater AC, NC, and CC (Padma and Nair, 2009).

With respect to human resource management (HRM) practices, Natarajan and Nagar (2011) found that employees who received four years of training from their organization reported higher NC than employees who received only one year of training. Additionally, high-quality HRM is positively related to all three organizational commitment mindsets, but is most strongly associated with NC (Bhatnagar, 2007). Western research results differ such that HRM practices tend to predict AC but not NC (Conway and Monks, 2009).

Finally, although transformational and various value-based leadership styles (for example, servant leadership, authentic leadership) have dominated Western research (see Chapter 22 in this volume), the roots of effective leadership in India are different. Some researchers have focused on a form of leadership called nurturant-task (NT) leadership, which Sinha (1980) describes as a blend of task-oriented authoritarian leadership and nurturing personalized leadership. Researchers have argued that NT leadership is necessitated in India because the Indian workforce is prone to be dependent on authority, prefer hierarchies, and prefer personalized relationships (Palrecha, 2008). Ansari (1986) and Palrecha (2008) supported this argument by finding that NT leadership was positively related to commitment, satisfaction, and productivity, as well as performance in Indian workers, respectively. That being said, there appear to be psychometric issues (that is, low reliabilities, poor factor loadings) with the existing measure of NT leadership (Palrecha, 2008).

Nonetheless, Western leadership constructs have been studied in India as well. Ramachandran and Krishnan (2009) found that transformational leadership was positively related to AC and NC among Indian employees, but was related only to AC among US employees. Chandna and Krishnan (2009) found that transformational leadership did not predict any of the three commitment mindsets in an Indian information technology (IT) company, but positively predicted NC and CC in a manufacturing organization indirectly through work beliefs (for example, work ethic, Marxist-related beliefs, leisure ethic). The authors explain that these results are likely due to a lack of personal communication from leaders in the IT organization.

Consequences of Commitment

Studies in India have much less frequently examined the consequences of commitment. This body of research has generally found relationships that are consistent with Western research, but has also revealed some interesting differences. For instance, Western research has generally found that AC explains the most variance in performance outcomes (Mathieu and Zajac, 1990; Meyer et al., 2002). However, research in India has found that the commitment mindset explaining the most variance (most often AC or NC) largely depends on context. For instance, Kansal (2012) found that only NC predicted service quality in the hotel industry. On the other hand, S. Jain and Swarup (2013) found that AC had a positive relationship with customer-oriented selling among employees of MNCs, but they did not measure NC or CC. In the retail sector, Jafri (2010) found that innovative work behavior was positively related to AC and negatively related to CC. Additionally, research in the automotive industry found positive relationships between all three components of commitment and organizational productivity (Dixit and Bhati, 2012).

Indian researchers have also examined OCB as an outcome of commitment and found results generally consistent with Western research. For instance, Dhir (2013) found that AC explained the most variance in OCB, followed by NC. On the other hand, others have found that NC is the stronger predictor of OCB (Gautam et al., 2005), and in some cases AC had no relationship with OCB (Mohamed and Anisa, 2012). Lastly, the negative relationship between organizational commitment and turnover intentions is well established in Western research (Meyer et al., 2002), and supported by Indian research (Shahnawaz and Goswami, 2011; Shukla et al., 2013).

Overall, interest in research on organizational commitment is growing in India. Results have generally been consistent with Western research, although NC appears to have stronger relationships than AC with several variables such as organizational size, psychological contract breaches, HRM practices, transformational leadership, and performance. Additionally, this review revealed significant limitations and areas of opportunity that will be discussed at the end of this chapter. The next section builds on the literature reviewed and draws attention to the differences in how commitment may be fostered and experienced in an Indian context.

EXPLORING THE INFLUENCE OF CULTURAL, CONTEXTUAL, ORGANIZATIONAL, AND INDIVIDUAL-LEVEL FACTORS ON COMMITMENT IN INDIA

As highlighted by Wasti and Önder (2009), studying commitment in a new cultural (that is, non-Western) context requires considering a variety of factors beyond those traditionally considered in cross-cultural research. Too often, differences found in cross-cultural research are attributed solely to differences in cultural values, and other important factors are overlooked. To help guide future commitment research in an Indian context, this section draws on Wasti and Önder's model of cultural and societal influences on commitment. We present a simplified version of this model in Figure 29.1, which focuses on several factors that are likely to be of relevance to commitment in India. Our model depicts India's societal-level culture and social-institutional factors (for example, legal and economic context) as influencing individual cultural values and the context of organiza-

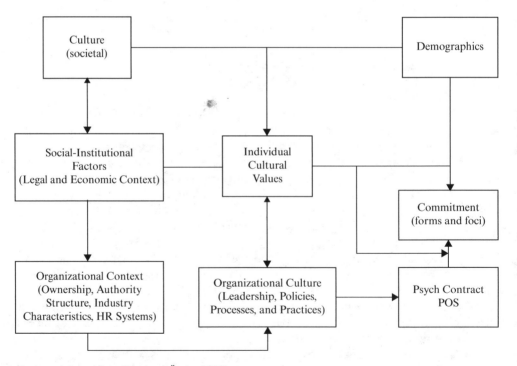

Source: Adapted from Wasti and Önder (2009).

Figure 29.1 An integrated model of cultural and social-institutional influences on commitment and its outcomes in an Indian context

tions in India. These factors then influence the cultural makeup of India's organizations, which is discussed in terms of how organizational culture and leadership mirror societal norms. All of these factors either directly or indirectly affect employees' psychological contracts (see Chapter 9 in this volume) and perceived organizational support (POS) (see Chapter 24 in this volume), which subsequently affect employees' forms and foci of commitment. Given that many of these relationships have already been proposed by Wasti and Önder (2009), we do not offer specific propositions. Instead, we highlight and discuss areas of the model in an Indian context in an effort to inform researchers seeking to design studies of commitment in India.

Social-Institutional Factors

Now one of the world's largest democracies, India has experienced a fairly stable political environment since its independence in 1947. India's government has guided the country towards greater industrialization and technological innovation, but there are still areas requiring significant growth that differentiate India from many Western countries. For example, the Indian industrial relations system has been criticized for failing to adapt to the globalization of India's economy, by concentrating too much power and authority in the state, stifling the bargaining rights of unions, and not acknowledging the needs of India's populations of informal and women workers (Hill, 2009). This context is different from the West, where the state has limited ability to confiscate wealth (Weingast, 1995), unions have ample collective bargaining rights, and movements supporting gender equality continue to gain momentum (Jackson, 1998). Although broad in scope, such socio-institutional factors are likely to have far-reaching consequences for organizations and their employees (Wasti and Önder, 2009).

Legal system

Laws currently governing labor and employment security in India were established in 1947 and have since undergone revisions that were subsequently reversed, leaving the laws relatively unchanged (Hill, 2009). Labor laws in India concentrate the bulk of power in the hands of the state, which has had an adversarial history with labor unions, making it difficult for employees to engage in collective bargaining or receive any form of representation. For this reason, unions may not be a viable focus of commitment for many Indian employees. The employment security afforded to Indian workers by the legal system has also fluctuated over time, and created a climate of instability (Hill, 2009). For example, although the state has taken steps to prevent large organizations from laying off workers, such organizations have been known to break into smaller units as a way around this.

An implication for organizations is that weak legal systems translate into authority structures in organizations that are inconsistent and particularistic (Wasti and Önder, 2009). Whitley (1992; cited in Wasti and Önder, 2009) states that family-run organizations, which are common in India, are often highly particularistic (a characteristic associated with favoritism and nepotism). As compared to family-run organizations, MNCs may treat employees more consistently because of their emphasis on importing Western management practices and structured HR systems. That being said, inconsistency and particularism is likely to be more prevalent across Indian organizations in general because of the country's labor laws.

Economic context

India has experienced significant economic growth since its liberalization and is on track for the creation of numerous jobs across the service, IT, and manufacturing industries (Das, 2015). However, the frequency of mergers and acquisitions mentioned earlier has created a turbulent environment affecting many workers. Mass layoffs involving tens of thousands of employees are commonplace in India, particularly in the IT industry. For example, Hewlett-Packard (HP) forecast 55 000 layoffs in 2015 and predicted the elimination of additional jobs after splitting into two companies (Bort, 2015). However, this instability varies across industry: Kwantes (2009) recognized the instability of IT engineers' positions and instead opted to collect data from mechanical and electrical engineers, who she argued work in much more stable industries.

Wasti and Önder (2009) argue that high levels of uncertainty associated with frequent economic crises will erode the consistency of HR systems and lead employees to focus on more transactional aspects of their employment relationship. It is also reasonable to expect that organizations in such an environment would avoid making any long-term investments in employees (such as training and development). While the provision of longer training has been shown to relate to higher NC among Indian employees (Natarajan and Nagar, 2011), avoiding such investments could lead employees to remain solely out of necessity (that is, experience high CC).

To summarize, the legal context in India likely promotes particularism in organizations, and the economic context of certain sectors likely fosters instability in employees' relationships with their organizations. Particularism is likely to polarize employees' commitment to the organization, whereas instability is likely to undermine AC and NC, and promote greater CC if employees have invested a great deal in the organization or have few employment alternatives.

Societal and Individual Cultural Factors

Indian society is based on strong family bonds where people depend on each other for moral and financial support. The strong norms and sense of interdependence fostered by India's joint family system are closely tied to the cultural values held by individuals. Although urbanization has begun to erode this system, it still represents a significant aspect of Indian society (Gore, 1990) that has implications for individuals' attitudes and behaviors as well as how organizations are run.

Wasti and Önder (2009) argue that organizations espousing collectivism, high power distance, and tightness foster more ingroup recruitment (for example, hiring family members), de-emphasize individual autonomy and rewards and recognition, create strong normative pressures to meet expectations, and have extensive onboarding and socialization processes. This is associated with a high concentration of power in organizations and is tied to India's caste system in the sense that employees are separated into two distinct 'classes': a privileged class with close ties to those with authority, and an underprivileged class of employee with less autonomy or recognition than the former (Wasti and Önder, 2009). Thus, similar to the influence of India's legal system, the values fostered by India's caste and joint family systems may also promote particularism in organizations.

This highlights the importance of understanding the salience and formation of in- and outgroups in Indian organizations. As mentioned before, managers of family-run enterprises may be more likely than those in other organizations (for example, MNCs) to play favorites and give preferential treatment to ingroup members, while offering little in the way of rewards and recognition to outgroup members. This is likely to foster competition among employees for good relations with those in positions of authority (Budhwar, 2003). In Western countries, employees who have high-quality relationships with their supervisor (that is, high leader–member exchange, LMX) experience greater psychological contract fulfillment, exhibit more extra-role behaviors (Henderson et al., 2008), and experience greater AC (Sherony and Green, 2002). In contrast, outgroup members in low-LMX relationships are likely to have unfulfilled or transactional psychological contracts, experience less support, and remain committed to their organization only out of necessity. The importance of such competition in India is made clear when it is considered that collectivists treat outgroups harshly in situations of disagreement or conflict (Wasti and Önder, 2009).

However, as India continues to open itself up to the world, Western cultural influences are increasingly likely to influence the attitudes of India's working population. Tayeb (1994) indicates that some Indian employees view work groups with an individualist mindset. Additionally, some Indian organizations are becoming a hybrid of traditional and Western values (A.K. Jain, 2015). Thus, instead of assuming all Indian employees hold traditional cultural values, and that these values are brought into the workplace unchanged, it is important for researchers to consider factors that may influence these values in employees. As an example, one of these factors that was raised earlier is age. Compared to older employees, younger employees generally possess less of a hierarchical mindset and espouse a mix of individualist and collectivist values (Agarwala, 2008). They are also more likely to move from one job to another, are more technologically skilled, less conscious of formalized rules and regulations, and more likely to choose a career that offers work–life balance (Dhir, 2013). This paints a very different picture of commitment for these individuals. They are less likely to foster personalized relationships at work and less likely to remain solely out of CC due to their perceived or actual mobility.

To summarize, traditional Indian values are more likely to be associated with particularism and personalized relationships than Western values. Given that culture in India is evolving and has resulted in differences in the values of both organizations and employees, researchers should be careful to assess these values and avoid generalizations about the values held by individuals and organizations.

Organization-Level Factors: Context and Culture

Both SMEs and large MNCs are growing rapidly as relevant organizational forms in India, and differ in ways that may affect employees' commitment (Dhir, 2013). In addition to size, these organizations are prone to differ in terms of ownership, authority structure, and industry characteristics. In turn, these factors affect variables such as the overall culture of the organization, the dominant leadership style of managers, and HR policies and procedures (Wasti and Önder, 2009). This section discusses the implications that these factors have for the commitment of employees in India.

Organizational context

The size, ownership, and authority structure of organizations are often closely related. In India, many SMEs are owned and operated by families. Family-managed SMEs are heavily influenced by family traditions, nationality, and the culture of their countries (Abbasi and Hollman, 1993). According to Saini and Budhwar (2004), these businesses have inherited traditions of hierarchy and control, reinforcing personalized superior–subordinate relationships and particularistic treatment of employees. On the other hand, larger organizations are similar to Western organizations and typically have more standardized processes and policies which result in more favorable and consistent treatment of employees (Fischer and Mansell, 2009; Wasti and Önder, 2009). The informal and centralized decision-making of SMEs concentrates power in the hands of a few individuals who often have full autonomy over how employees are treated. This authority structure, coupled with India's traditional values and the prevalence of a paternalistic management style (Budhwar, 2003), promotes an emphasis on organizational norms and social compliance. Such a focus is likely to bring management and (ingroup) employees closer together, which can promote greater identification with management and significant normative pressure to meet their expectations (Wasti and Önder, 2009). This could explain the higher levels of AC and NC in Indian SMEs.

Furthermore, employees of SMEs are often less educated and hold non-professional jobs, characterized by specialized routine tasks and little autonomy. The more specific individuals' experiences become in an organization, or the more specialized their work becomes, the less their ability to move from it is (Salancik, 1977). Thus, although employees of SMEs tend to report higher commitment, they do not necessarily perform better and are less likely to be competitive in the Indian job market. These factors are likely to promote a CC mindset characterized by a perceived lack of alternatives and mobility, and high costs of leaving the organization (Meyer and Allen, 1991; Wasti and Önder, 2009).

Organizational culture and leadership

Organizational culture represents the 'beliefs, ideologies, and values, and the ways these are transmitted through symbols, language, narratives (myths, stories), and practices (rituals and taboos) especially during socialization in the workplace' (Schneider et al., 2011, p. 373). Organizational cultures vary in strength and consistency, and have profound implications for employees' experiences at work. Given that leaders play a significant role in shaping and disseminating organizational culture, this section also discusses leadership in Indian organizations.

Wasti and Önder (2009, p. 325) state that 'organizations are open systems that perpetuate and reinforce societal norms'. Locally founded SMEs could be described as 'porous' in the sense that they are likely to incorporate and reinforce Indian cultural values (Abbasi and Hollman, 1993). On the other hand, managers of MNCs are likely to implement Western management practices intended to create a culture consistent with their overseas offices. In reality, managers' attempts to impose and adapt Western business practices have led to subcultures in many Indian organizations: one characteristic of the traditional Indian culture, and the other a fusion of Western and Eastern cultural values (A.K. Jain, 2015). The former type of culture is likely to operate in a manner similar to the culture of family-run SMEs. The latter type of culture is more likely to operate in a similar way to Western organizations, where personal achievement is valued and reinforced by HR policies (for example, individualized rewards and recognition) and employees are provided with empowerment and autonomy. The value of an organization's culture depends on its fit with the values of its employees (Biswas and Bhatnagar, 2013).

Cross-cultural leadership research has shown that many cultures do not possess the same underlying expectations of effective leadership (Den Hartog et al., 1999). For example, the leaders of family-run SMEs often adopt the NT leadership style, likely because it fits well in an Indian context where managers have a preference for being strict and demanding, but also caring and supportive, like the paternalistic head of an Indian family (Sinha, 1980). As suggested earlier, Indian employees may also perceive managers adopting Western leadership styles differently: potentially by reporting greater NC than their Western counterparts.

To summarize, researchers should carefully consider the type of organization being studied in terms of both contextual and cultural variables. Employees of Indian SMEs and MNCs in various industries could have very different expectations of their work environments and leadership, leading them to experience commitment in different ways.

Forms and Foci of Commitment in India

Aside from factors that influence commitment differently in India, the forms and foci of the TCM of commitment may also be perceived and experienced differently by Indian employees. For example, NC and CC may be more contingent upon obligations and costs associated with violating norms associated with one's ingroup (for example, family) rather than an obligation towards the organization or personal costs. While individuals in Western countries are comparatively less attached to their family, it is more common for individuals who are part of a joint family system to financially support their parents, grandparents, and/or siblings, to pool assets, and to live in the same space (Sharma, 2015). These factors and the values associated with them may color the nature of NC and CC towards one's job, organization, or occupation. For individuals who are a part of a joint family, the costs associated with leaving one's job, organization, or occupation would be interpreted as more shared or communal than personal.

Additionally, certain foci are likely to differ in their relevance for Indian employees. As mentioned earlier, union commitment may be irrelevant for many, due to India's legal context. Relatedly, although informal work represents only a small portion of the population in Western countries, the reverse is true in India, where only 10 percent of the working population is classified as possessing formal employment (Desai, 2013). This large population of workers with informal employment is overlooked by government services, has very low employment security, and is often subjected to poor working conditions (Joseph and Jagannathan, 2013). This population may experience commitment differently than employees with formal employment contracts. For example, commitment might be more likely to be directed at an authority figure than at the formal organization for such individuals. Unfortunately, there is little to no research in this area.

Limitations and Future Research

Future research should consider the existing gaps and limitations in Indian commitment research. For instance, research in India has been quite limited in the study of individual differences or dispositional factors such as personality (K. Kumar and Bakhshi, 2010), which have been quite common in Western research (e.g., Erdheim et al., 2006). This may be indicative of Indian culture where events are more likely to be attributed to situational factors than individual dispositions (Miller, 1984), and raises the question of whether individual difference variables will have weaker relationships with organizational commitment than what has been found in Western research.

Additionally, although Indian researchers have studied employee attitudes to a degree, comparative studies focusing on demographic and performance-related variables (for example, productivity) are more common. More attention could be paid to factors that highlight employees' perceptions of how they are treated by their organization. For example, POS and organizational justice have been frequently studied as antecedents of commitment in Western research (see Chapters 24 and 25 in this volume), but have received scant attention in India. Relatedly, employee well-being has garnered significant interest as an outcome of commitment among Western researchers (for a review, see Chapter 17 in this volume; Meyer and Maltin, 2010), but has not received much attention in Indian research. This raises questions about the relative importance of productivity and obedience versus employees' well-being in Indian organizations.

Mishra et al. (2015) have also highlighted the need for more longitudinal commitment research to understand how commitment develops over time in an Indian context. Further, the field would benefit from research examining the concept of commitment itself in an Indian context. As is common in many cross-cultural studies (Wasti and Önder, 2009), Indian researchers have often adopted frameworks developed in the West (for example, the TCM, transformational leadership) with little regard for how well they may translate in an Indian context. Finally, there is also a lack of direct cross-cultural comparisons between India and other countries.

Managerial Implications

As India continues to grow and flourish as a nation, leaders in business, government, and academia are called upon to find innovative ways of fostering employee commitment, well-being, and organizational performance. Arming decision-makers with the knowledge of important socio-economic, cultural, and contextual factors can help to foster management practices that benefit both organizations and employees.

SMEs can benefit by designing fair and consistent selection, training, performance appraisal, and compensation practices. They must position themselves as supportive champions of all employees by fostering a healthy and collegial work environment. When possible, MNCs should adopt a more decentralized and flexible organizational structure to develop more informal relationships which may help foster AC and NC. For MNCs to balance the management of local and expatriate employees, it is imperative to carefully balance fair and consistent HRM practices with a receptivity to the local culture.

With India emerging as a significant player in the global economy, there is a need for more collaborative research to understand the attitudes and behaviors of India's modern workforce. An understanding of organizational commitment represents an important starting point and can help India in achieving a productive and healthy workforce.

NOTE

* Vidyut Lata Dhir and Nicholas L. Bremner contributed equally to this chapter and both should be considered first authors. The authors would like to acknowledge the valuable contributions made by Malini Krishnan to this chapter.

REFERENCES

Abbasi, S. and Hollman, K. (1993). Business success in the Middle East. *Management Decisions*, *31*(1), 55–60.

Agarwal, P. (2011). A study of relationship between psychological contract and organizational commitment in Indian IT industry. *Indian Journal of Industrial Relations*, *47*(2), 290–305.

Agarwala, T. (2008). Factors influencing career choice of management students in India. *Career Development International*, *13*(4), 362–376.

Ahmed, M.A. (2013). Effects of interpersonal problems at work on organizational commitment. *Journal of Organisation and Human Behaviour*, *2*(2), 40–47.

Allen, N.J. and Meyer, J.P. (1990). The measurement and antecedents of affective, continuance and normative commitment to the organization. *Journal of Occupational Psychology*, *63*, 1–18.

Ansari, M.A. (1986). Need for nurturant-task leaders in India: Some empirical evidence. *Management and Labor Studies*, *11*(1), 26–36.

Awasthy, R. and Gupta, R.K. (2010). Organizational commitment of Indian managers in multinational companies. *Indian Journal of Industrial Relations*, *45*(3), 424–436.

Bhatnagar, J. (2007). Predictors of organizational commitment in India: Strategic HR roles, organizational learning capability and psychological empowerment. *The International Journal of Human Resource Management*, *18*(10), 1782–1811.

Biswas, S. and Bhatnagar, J. (2013). Mediator analysis of employee engagement: Role of perceived organizational support, P–O fit, organizational commitment and job satisfaction. *Vikalpa: The Journal for Decision Makers*, *38*(1), 27–40.

Bort, J. (2015, August 21). HP's layoffs will exceed 55,000 people, CFO says. *Business Insider India*. http://bit.ly/1IdcygP.

Budhwar, P.S. (2003). Human resource management in India. In P.S. Budhwar and Y.A. Debrah (eds), *Human Resource Management in Developing Countries* (pp. 75–90). New York: Routledge.

Cameron, K.S. and Quinn, R.E. (1999). *Diagnosing and Changing Organizational Culture*. Reading, MA: Addison-Wesley.

Census of India (2011). Main workers, marginal workers, non-workers and those marginal workers, non-workers seeking/available for work classified by age and sex. (B-1). New Delhi: Office of the Registrar General and Census Commissioner Retrieved from http://www.censusindia.gov.in/2011census/B-series/B-Series-01.html.

Chandna, P. and Krishnan, V.R. (2009). Organizational commitment of information technology professionals: Role of transformational leadership and work-related beliefs. *Tecnia Journal of Management Studies*, *4*(1), 1–13.

Conway, E. and Monks, K. (2009). Unravelling the complexities of high commitment: An employee-level analysis. *Human Resource Management Journal*, *19*(2), 140–158.

Das, P. (2015, March 4). Budget 2015: A booming job market awaits India. *Business Insider India*. http://bit.ly/1NfowWs.

Den Hartog, D.N., House, R.J., Hanges, P.J., and Ruiz-Quintanilla, S.A. (1999). Culture specific and crosscultural generalizable implicit leadership theories: Are attributes of charismatic/transformational leadership universally endorsed? *Leadership Quarterly*, *10*(2), 219–256.

Desai, M. (2013). Informal work. *Indian Journal of Industrial Relations*, *48*, 387–389.

Dhir, V.L. (2013). Organizational commitment and its role in managing responsibility in an organization. Unpublished doctoral dissertation. Shreemati Nathibai Damodar Thackersey Women's University, Mumbai.

Dixit, V. and Bhati, M. (2012). A study about employee commitment and its impact on sustained productivity in Indian auto-component industry. *European Journal of Business and Social Sciences*, *1*(6), 34–51.

Erdheim, J., Wang, M., and Zickar, M. J. (2006). Linking the Big Five personality constructs to organizational commitment. *Personality and Individual Differences*, *41*, 959–970.

Fischer, R. and Mansell, A. (2009). Commitment across cultures: A meta-analytical approach. *Journal of International Business Studies*, *40*, 1339–1358.

Gautam, T., Van Dick, R., Wagner, U., Upadhyay, N., and Davis, A.J. (2005). Organizational citizenship behavior and organizational commitment in Nepal. *Asian Journal of Social Psychology*, *8*(3), 305–314.

Gelfand, M.J., Nishii, L.H., and Raver, J.L. (2006). On the nature and importance of cultural tightness–looseness. *Journal of Applied Psychology*, *91*, 1225–1244.

Gore, M.S. (1990). *Urbanization and Family Change*. Bombay: Popular Prakashan.

Goswami, A., Dalmia, N., and Pradhan, M. (2008). Entrepreneurship in India. National Knowledge Commission, Government of India.

Henderson, D.J., Wayne, S.J., Shore, L.M., Bommer, W.H., and Tetrick, L.E. (2008). Leader–member exchange, differentiation, and psychological contract fulfillment: A multilevel examination. *Journal of Applied Psychology*, *93*, 1208–1219.

Hill, E. (2009). The Indian industrial relations system: Struggling to address the dynamics of a globalizing economy. *Journal of Industrial Relations*, *51*(3), 395–410. doi: 10.1177/0022185609104305

Hofstede, G. (1980). *Culture's Consequences*. London: Sage Publications.

Hofstede, G. (2001). *Culture's Consequences: Comparing Values, Behaviors, Institutions, and Organizations across Nations* (2nd edn). London: Sage Publications.

Jackson, R.M. (1998). *Destined for Equality: The Inevitable Rise of Women's Status*. Cambridge, MA: Harvard University Press.

Jafri, M.H. (2010). Organizational commitment and employee's innovative behavior: A study in retail sector. *Journal of Management Research*, *10*, 62–68.

Jain, A.K. (2015). Volunteerism and organizational culture: Relationship to organizational commitment and citizenship behaviors in India. *Cross Cultural Management*, *22*(1), 116–144.

Jain, S. and Swarup, K. (2013). Linkages of customer oriented selling with emotional intelligence and organizational commitment: Evidences from MNCs operating in India. *Drishtikon: A Management Journal*, *4*(1), 65–86.

Joseph, J. and Jagannathan, S. (2013). Three representations of insecurity in three narratives of unorganized workers. *Indian Journal of Industrial Relations*, *48*, 450–459.

Kansal, P. (2012). Linkage research model of Indian hotel industry. *Indian Journal of Industrial Relations*, *48*(2), 217–232.

Klein, K.J., Becker, T.E., and Meyer, J.P. (eds) (2009). *Commitment in Organizations: Accumulated Wisdom and New Directions*. New York: Routledge.

Kumar, B.P. and Giri, V.N. (2009). Effect of age and experience on job satisfaction and organizational commitment. *ICFAI Journal of Organizational Behavior*, *8*(1), 28–36.

Kumar, K. and Bakhshi, A. (2010). Dispositional predictors of organizational commitment: A theoretical review. *IUP Journal of Organizational Behavior*, *9*(1/2), 87–98.

Kwantes, C.T. (2009). Culture, job satisfaction and organizational commitment in India and the United States. *Journal of Indian Business Research*, *1*(4), 196–212.

Mathieu, J.E. and Zajac, D.M. (1990). A review and meta-analysis of the antecedents, correlates, and consequences of organizational commitment. *Psychological Bulletin*, *108*, 171–194.

Meyer, J.P. and Allen, N. (1991). A three-component conceptualization of organizational commitment. *Human Resource Management Review*, *1*, 64–89.

Meyer, J.P. and Maltin, E.R. (2010). Employee commitment and well-being: A critical review, theoretical framework and research agenda. *Journal of Vocational Behavior*, *77*, 323–337.

Meyer, J.P., Srinivas, E.S., Lal, J.B., and Topolnytsky, L. (2007). Employee commitment and support for an organizational change: Test of the three-component model in two cultures. *Journal of Occupational and Organizational Psychology*, *80*, 185–211.

Meyer, J.P., Stanley, D.J., Herscovitch, L., and Topolnytsky, L. (2002). Affective, continuance, and normative commitment to the organization: A meta-analysis of antecedents, correlates, and consequences. *Journal of Vocational Behavior*, *61*, 20–52.

Meyer, J.P., Stanley, D.., Jackson, T.A., McInnis, K.J., Maltin, E.R., and Sheppard, L. (2012). Affective, normative, and continuance commitment levels across cultures: A meta-analysis. *Journal of Vocational Behavior*, *80*, 225–245.

Miller, J.G. (1984). Culture and the development of everyday social explanation. *Journal of Personality and Social Psychology*, *46*, 961–978.

Mishra, S., Khan, S.M., and Mishra, P.C. (2015). An application of structural equation modelling to search antecedents' latent variables in organisational health, occupational role stress and social support for organisational commitment. *Journal of Organisation and Human Behaviour*, *4*(2–3), 39–45.

Mohamed, M.S. and Anisa, H. (2012). Relationship between organizational commitment and organizational citizenship behavior. *IUP Journal of Organizational Behavior*, *11*(3), 7–22.

Natarajan, N.K. and Nagar, D. (2011). Induction age, training duration and job performance on organizational commitment and job satisfaction. *Indian Journal of Industrial Relations*, *46*(3), 491–497.

Neelam, N., Bhattacharya, S., Sinha, V., and Tanksale, D. (2015). Organizational culture as a determinant of organizational commitment: What drives IT employees in India? *Global Business and Organizational Excellence*, *34*(2), 62–74.

Padma, R.N., and Nair, V.S. (2009). Organizational culture and its impact on organizational commitment in public and private organizations. *Global Management Review*, 4(1), 32–39.

Palrecha, R. (2008). The transformational leader model, the nurturant-task leader model, and the unique local leadership model: A quantitative and qualitative competitive test of three leadership models in India. Unpublished doctoral dissertation. Binghamton University, Binghamton, NY.

Paramanandam, P. (2013). Organisational commitment and functional role stress. *Journal of Organization and Human Behaviour*, 2(1), 34–39.

Pareek, U. (2003). *Training instruments in HRD and OD* (2nd edn). New Delhi, India: Tata McGraw-Hill.

Ramachandran, S. and Krishnan, V.R. (2009). Effect of transformational leadership on followers' affective and normative commitment: Culture as moderator. *Great Lakes Herald*, 3(1), 23–38.

Saini, D. and Budhwar, P. (2004). Human resource management in India. In P. Budhwar (ed.), *Managing Human Resources in Asia-Pacific* (pp. 113–139). London: Routledge.

Salancik, G. (1977). Commitment and the control of organizational behavior and belief. In B. Staw and G. Salancik (eds), *New Directions in Organizational Behavior*. Chicago, IL: St. Clair.

Schneider, B., Ehrhart, M.G., and Macey, W.H. (2011). Perspectives on organizational climate and culture. In S. Zedeck (ed.), *Handbook of Industrial and Organizational Psychology* (pp. 373–414). Washington, DC: APA.

Shahnawaz, M.G. and Goswami, K. (2011). Effect of psychological contract violation on organizational commitment, trust and turnover intention in private and public sector Indian organizations. *Vision: The Journal of Business Perspective*, 15(3), 209–217.

Sharma, S. (2015). Why Indians work: A cultural values perspective. *Indian Journal of Industrial Relations*, 50, 425–437.

Sherony, K.M. and Green, S.G. (2002). Coworker exchange: Relationships between coworkers, leader–member exchange, and work attitudes. *Journal of Applied Psychology*, 87(3), 542–548.

Shukla, A., Srinivasan, R., and Chaurasia, S. (2013). Impact of work related attitudes on turnover intention. *Indian Journal of Industrial Relations*, 49(1), 111–122.

Sinha, J.B.P. (1980). *The Nurturant Task Leader*. New Delhi: Concept.

Tayeb, M.H. (1994). Organization and national culture: Methodology considered. *Organization Studies*, 15, 429–446.

Vijaya, T.G. and Hemamalini, R. (2012). Relationship of work family conflict and enrichment with organizational commitment among sales person. *Journal of Strategic Human Resource Management*, 1(3), 32–38.

Wasti, S.A. and Önder, C. (2009). Commitment across cultures: Progress, pitfalls and propositions. In H.J. Klein, T.E. Becker and J.P. Meyer (eds), *Commitment in Organizations: Accumulated Wisdom and New Directions* (pp. 309–346). Florence, KY: Routledge.

Weingast, B.R. (1995). The economic role of political institutions: Market-preserving federalism and economic development. *Journal of Law, Economics and Organization*, 11(1), 1–31.

Whitley, R. (1992). *Business Systems in East Asia: Firms, Markets and Societies*. Thousand Oaks: CA, Sage.

30. Commitment in the Middle East
Aaron Cohen

Management and industrial psychologists have studied commitment in the workplace for many years (Cohen, 2003). Most of these studies focused primarily on organizational commitment (OC) and were conducted in Western cultures, mostly in North America. Work commitment among populations in Europe and South Asia was also studied and some significant findings have also accumulated for these areas. This review, however, focuses on commitment in a less-studied geographical area: the Middle East. In this turbulent region, the majority of the population are Arab and the dominant religion is Islam, a combination that results in a very traditional society (Cohen and Kirchmeyer, 2005). However, it should be noted that while Arabs constitute the dominant population in the Middle East, many also live and work in numerous countries outside the Middle East, particularly in Europe. This fact increases the importance of this population in the international workforce and thus the need to study and understand it.

Because of the relatively little research on Arabs' commitment in the Middle East, this chapter focuses mainly on Arabs in Israel, with the assumption that findings about the commitment of Arabs living in Israel can be widely generalized to Arabs in the rest of the Middle East and other countries. An understanding of commitment as pertaining to Arabs can potentially make several contributions. First, their commitment to the organization or other foci in the workplace may also be reflected in the manner in which they become committed to other entities outside the work domain. Studies of their commitment may enhance our understanding of the manner in which such an important population becomes attached and loyal to various other organizations. Second, our understanding of the concept of commitment may be increased if we understand the meaning and mechanisms of commitment among traditional societies and groups, since our current theories of commitment, such as the exchange theory, are based on Western conceptions. Commitment may have an entirely different meaning for members of traditional societies, particularly Arab or Muslim ones. Third, globalization has also heightened awareness of the need to understand not only organizational culture, but also the influence of national and international cultures on organizations (Sabri, 2013). Many large multinational organizations having their base in Western cultures operate in the Middle East or other countries that are characterized by traditional societies, such as Bangladesh, Indonesia, Pakistan, and more. Many organizations that operate in Western nations also have a diverse workforce, comprising, for example, many employees belonging to traditional societies, such as Arabs and/or Muslims, who are domiciled in Western countries, particularly in Europe. In the above two examples, management must take into consideration the culture of the host country and/or the culture of the minority groups in Western countries, which may have a perception of commitment that is different from that of employees who were born and raised in the Western culture. Their commitment may be affected by mechanisms different from those Western cultures (Cohen and Abed El Majid, 2014). Therefore, to be able to motivate these employees and increase their commitment levels, it is necessary to study their commitment and its sources. If our findings show that the concept of commitment is perceived differently by Arabs and Muslims, then Westernized theories have to be changed accordingly.

One could argue that a more representative perspective of Arabs' commitment can be learned by examining this concept in Arab countries. In principle, this is true. However, it seems that currently, in practice, it is difficult to research Arabs in many countries in the Middle East. Some Arab countries are collapsing, the boundaries between some other Arab states have become blurred, and the chaotic situation in many of them makes any thought of studies on work behavior and attitudes unrealistic. In some of the more stable Arab countries, such as the United Arab Emirates (UAE), Kuwait, and Saudi Arabia, many employees are not Arab. For example, in some studies in this region a typical sample was composed of 23.4 percent UAE nationals, 36.7 percent Arab expatriates, 34.6 percent Asians, and 5.1 percent Westerners (Yousef, 2000, 2001). A similar pattern was found in a sample of nurses in Saudi Arabia, where the majority of the nurses were not Arab (Al-Aameri, 2000). Therefore, conducting research on Arabs in Israel seems a more practical and realistic option for studying their commitment and for gaining some understanding of commitment in the Middle East. However, this chapter incorporates existing data from the more stable of the countries in the Middle East, such as Jordan.

The individual-level approach, which is based on personal values, is employed in this chapter for defining and examining culture. This approach seems to be more sensitive in terms of capturing culture (Cohen, 2007a, 2007b). This sensitivity is important since, within one nation, frequently more than one culture exists, as found in studies that compared commitment levels and values among different ethnic groups in Israel (Cohen, 2007a, 2007b; Cohen and Kirchmeyer, 2005). For example, while Arabs are in general collectivist, some may be more collectivist while others may be more individualistic (Triandis, 1995). In the present context, comparisons of Arabs and Jews in terms of their individual level of values provide us with more sensitive data regarding the concept of culture and its relationship to commitment. Nevertheless, a question remains concerning the model of values that should be used for studying commitment. Most of the studies reviewed in this chapter employed Hofstede's model of values (Hofstede, 1980) or Schwartz's model (Schwartz et al., 2001) of individual values.

ARABS IN ISRAEL: THE PERSPECTIVE OF INDIVIDUAL VALUES

Arabs living in Israel, representing about one-sixth of Israel's population, are a permanent, non-assimilating minority, clearly distinguished from Jews in terms of place of residence and culture. They speak their own language and adhere to their traditions (Cohen and Kirchmeyer, 2005). The culture of Israeli Arabs has been described as traditional collectivist. The collectivist orientation is expressed in values such as solidarity, cooperation, mutual trust, support, and a sense of belonging, which are believed to exist in the Arab society. In traditional societies, commitment in general is a complex attitude, influenced by the norms, sanctions, and pressures of the small group, family, and community. The values prized in such societies that are relevant to the workplace include a preference for more personal ties to supervisors, acceptance of more paternalistic treatment, and a sense that power relationships should be hierarchical. These factors may influence the attitudes and the behaviors of members of traditional societies as employees, resulting in greater commitment to the firm and, potentially, a higher level of performance (Abd El Majid and Cohen, 2015; Cohen and Abd El Majid, 2014).

In this chapter, Israeli Jews constitute the primary comparison group for Israeli Arabs, because I contend that the Israeli Jews represent a more Westernized culture. What is so distinct about the comparison between Arabs and Jews in Israel? What can be gained from such a comparison? The comparison by country presented in Hofstede's work (Hofstede Center, 2015) shows that Arab countries score higher than Israel on two dimensions: power distance and collectivism. The pattern where Arabs score high in these two dimensions was found in Turkey, Iran, Iraq, Jordan, Kuwait, Lebanon, Libya, Morocco, Saudi Arabia, Egypt, and Syria (Hofstede Center, 2015), as well as in Israel. With so many countries showing a pattern similar to that found in Israel, one can conclude that this is not a coincidence. In comparison with the Israeli culture, and probably any other Westernized culture, the Arab culture is characterized by higher levels of collectivism and power distance. In an empirical study, using Hofstede's cultural dimensions, the same pattern found by Hofstede was found among Israeli Arabs and Israeli Jews (Cohen, 2007a), with one minor exception: Israeli Arabs also scored higher than Israeli Jews in masculinity. Significant support for the pattern mentioned above was also found by Sabri (2013), who compared American employees in the United States (US) and Jordanian employees. Using Hofstede's dimensions of culture, he found that the Jordanian workers scored higher than the Americans mainly on the dimensions of power distance and collectivism. This chapter argues that the differences mentioned above probably influence the magnitude of commitment as expressed in attitudes and behavior.

GOALS OF THIS CHAPTER

This chapter covers several aspects of Arabs' commitment. First, the magnitude of different foci of commitment are described. In addition, the psychometric properties of commitment scales, particularly OC dimensions, are also reviewed. This chapter also discusses whether any differences exist in the magnitude of Arabs' commitment between different foci of commitment (organization, occupation, job, work group). Second, this chapter explores the determinants and the outcomes of commitment among Arabs. Meaningful differences between Israeli Arabs and Jews (as well as other groups) are expected to be found in the correlates of commitment, antecedents, and consequences. These differences should reflect the deep cultural differences between Arabs and Jews that are derived from their heritage, personal experiences, socio-economic level, and acculturation. This chapter concludes with a discussion that suggests a future research agenda for this important OC issue.

DIMENSIONS OF COMMITMENT: MAGNITUDE AND DISCRIMINANT VALIDITY

The study of OC has been profoundly influenced by Meyer and Allen's pioneering work on OC. Arguing that OC can be better understood as a multidimensional concept, Meyer and Allen proposed a three-dimensional model (Allen and Meyer, 1990; see Chapter 3 in this volume). They called their first dimension 'affective commitment', the second 'continuance commitment', and the third 'normative commitment'. Meyer and Allen's model has been considered the leading approach to OC (Cohen, 2003). However, in only a few studies has this conceptualization been applied in the Middle East, and many more studies are required. In other studies, particularly in the Israeli setting, multiple commitments in the workplace were studied and these are reviewed later.

Based on the individual value preferences described above, it can be expected that in a traditional society, such as the Arab society, similar importance would be ascribed to affective and normative commitments. Normative commitment should be important in the Arab society because, as mentioned above, Arabs are raised to value tradition, collectivism, and conformity (Cohen, 2007a; Cohen and Abd El Majid, 2014). Following the norms of their ethnic group, loyalty to their family throughout their lives is an important element of their being. As for Israeli Jews, the more Westernized society, it is expected (Cohen and Keren, 2008) that they would primarily value affective commitment because of its exchange nature. Israeli Jews will be affectively committed if the exchange with their work organization is perceived as fair and just. For Arabs, being committed to the organization is part of their nature. They are raised to value commitment to both work and non-work foci, and normative commitment is the dimension that best reflects it. However, the results from empirical findings regarding this expectation are mixed.

Meyer et al. (2012) found in their meta-analysis that normative commitment was relatively strong in the Middle East. However, the levels of affective OC among Arabs who were examined in Israel were found to be higher (Cohen, 1999, 2006, 2007a). This finding can be attributed to the fact that Israeli Arabs live in a Westernized society and over the years have internalized some of its values, particularly in the work setting. This means that their commitment to the organization is not unconditional. Having been exposed for many years to the Israeli Westernized culture and values, they expect something in return from the organization before becoming committed to it. Another possible explanation is that Arabs are more committed to any commitment foci in the workplace than employees representing the Westernized culture. Interestingly and not surprisingly, Meyer et al.'s meta-analysis showed that continuance commitment was lower in the Middle East than in many other countries. These findings show that commitment in the Middle East is more the normative than the affective type, and is definitely not the instrumental or calculative type.

In terms of the discriminant validity, findings showed that Arabs do understand the nature of affective and normative commitment, as well as distinguish between them. Cohen and Abd El Majid (2014) found a much better fit of the two-factor solution (affective and normative) than the one-factor solution in a sample of 1268 Arab teachers in Israel. The two-factor model revealed a better fit to the data than the one-factor model. Continuance commitment, however, was found to be a more complicated issue among Arabs in Israel. Some studies showed that Israeli Arabs had difficulty interpreting this form of commitment, including its two dimensions. This was demonstrated in very low reliability values for this dimension in some studies that measured this form (Cohen, 2010; Cohen and Abd El Majid, 2014), leading to its exclusion. Cohen (2010) and Cohen and Abd El Majid (2014) attributed this finding to the Arabs' status in Israel. Israeli

Arabs are a deprived minority with quite limited employment opportunities in the Israeli labor market. It may be that they find the specific items in the continuance commitment scale difficult to understand and interpret, since in their particular situation they simply cannot leave their organization because available options are lacking. For example, in practice, Arab teachers can work only in Arab schools. They would not be able to find employment in Israeli schools and would not easily find a job in an Arab city or village other than their own because of local preferences.

The specific items on the continuance commitment scale exemplify this argument. For example, the statement, 'I am not afraid of what might happen if I quit my job without having another one lined up' is quite unclear to many of them, because in many occupations they simply do not have an alternative. From a statistical point of view, we may obtain a very low variance in this case, leading to lower reliability. The same can be argued regarding the following statement: 'It would be very hard for me to leave my organization right now, even if I wanted'. Basically, most of the items on the continuance commitment scale are quite problematic for the Israeli Arabs whose employment options are very limited. Moreover, in most occupations, Israeli Arabs make significant sacrifices when they consider employment in the Israeli labor market.

Unlike the Arab samples, Israeli Jews were found to be capable of understanding the continuance commitment items (Cohen and Keren, 2008). Cohen and Liu (2011) found that among Jewish teachers, the three-factor solution for the three dimensions of OC showed a better fit than a one-factor solution. Findings also indicated that Israeli Jews perceive continuance commitment as being less important in terms of its magnitude than the affective and normative forms of commitment (Cohen and Keren, 2008; Cohen and Liu, 2011). Additional support for the deprivation argument was found in a study by Liu and Cohen (2010) that examined the three-dimensional model among Chinese employees, who also represent a traditional society. Their findings showed acceptable reliabilities of the continuance commitment scale and a significant relationship of this form of commitment with work outcomes, that is, with organization citizenship behavior (OCB). This finding may imply that for members of a traditional society not living in such a complex setting as the Israeli Arabs do, the continuance commitment dimension might be less of a problem.

Two interesting studies on the dimensions of OC were conducted in Jordan. Aladwan et al. (2013) examined the dimensions of Meyer et al.'s (1993) scales in a sample of 493 Jordanian employees, most of whom worked in the public sector. The findings revealed strong support for the existence of the three-factor dimensionality of the Meyer et al. scale, where the factors are affective, continuance, and normative commitment. They concluded that the findings in the Jordanian context support the conceptual framework, which consists of three factors, as mentioned above.

In another study, Suliman and Iles (2000) examined the dimensionality of Meyer and Allen's (1991) 24-item scales in Jordan. The study included 115 employees in a pilot study and 783 in the main study, mostly from industrial organizations. The findings of both samples supported the multidimensionality of OC. However, their analysis showed that, while there was a clear distinction between affective and continuance commitment, some items of the normative commitment scale loaded on the same factor as the affective commitment items. The findings led to the conclusion that some weakness of the normative commitment dimension exists in the Jordanian context. According to Suliman and Iles, this weakness suggests the need to develop a new normative commitment scale that considers the particular characteristics of the Arab culture. Future research should examine this issue.

The above findings raise the interesting question of whether the problems related to the dimensions of OC among Arabs are limited to the specific Israeli setting. What measures can be taken to resolve this issue? First, as Aladwan et al. (2013) mentioned, more studies of a similar nature should be performed in variant sectors and different countries that share the same or a similar culture and work conditions. Second, studies should be performed among Arabs in settings that do not limit their employment opportunities as the Israeli occupational situation does. Such studies would enable us to investigate whether it is the setting or the culture that affects Arabs' continuance commitment. In addition, studies in other Arab countries should control for the unique occupational situation. In Israel, Arab teachers have very limited employment alternatives, while Israeli Arabs in the healthcare industry have greater job opportunities. Whether different results are obtained in the two occupations would be of interest.

ANTECEDENTS AND OUTCOMES OF ORGANIZATIONAL COMMITMENT

Another important means of understanding commitment in the Middle East is to investigate the determinants and outcomes of commitment. This information is valuable for several reasons. First, it provides additional information regarding the discriminant validity of commitment dimensions and scales. Second, data on the determinants of commitment can shed light on the formation of commitment among Arabs in comparison to Jews, representing the more Westernized society. Third, data on the outcomes of commitment provide information about the predictive validity of commitment among Arabs and Jews.

Before reviewing the findings referring to the correlates of commitment, it should be noted that most of the studies comparing Arabs and Jews found that more variance in commitment, for any of the commitment foci, was explained by any given antecedent for Israeli Arabs than for the Jews. In addition, commitment foci were found to explain more variance of any outcome for the Israeli Arabs than for the Jews (Cohen, 1999, 2006, 2007b). This can be attributed to the assumption advanced here that commitment is a more important concept in traditional societies, such as the Arab one, than in Westernized societies, such as that of Israeli Jews. This does not mean that Arabs score higher on performance measures than Jews. Cohen's (2007b) findings showed higher performance levels among Israeli Jews than among Israeli Arabs. A brief review of OC correlates in the Israeli setting follows.

Values

An important set of antecedents that can provide information about the formation of commitment is individual values. Cohen (2010) found in a sample of 369 Arab teachers that among Schwartz's ten individual values, benevolence had a strong positive relationship with affective and normative OC. This finding strengthens the argument that in a collectivist society such as the Arab one, values representing collectivism, such as benevolence, play an important role in shaping the commitment. Similar findings were found by Wasti (2003) among Turkish employees. Her results indicated that normative commitment is less important for individuals who are highly idiocentric. Furthermore, social factors, operationalized as the disapproval of the family, were less important predictors of turnover intentions for idiocentric individuals but more important for individuals with strong allocentric values. Wasti concluded that these findings support the proposition that while the employment relationship may have normative implications for individuals who endorse allocentric values, such concerns are less influential in determining the behavior of idiocentric individuals who attend to, and regard highly, personal goals and preferences. According to Wasti (2003), these results might be interpreted in the context of the relatively collectivistic Turkish society, where highly allocentric values tend to be more normative and thus exhibit less variance. However, it should be noted that Wasti herself pointed out that the effects of allocentrism were particularly weak in her study.

This contention was supported by several other studies. Cohen found that benevolence had a very strong relationship with Israeli Arabs' affective and normative commitment (Cohen, 2010). Cohen and Abd El Majid (2014) found in a sample of 1268 Arab teachers that the values of tradition and benevolence were related to Arabs' affective and normative commitment. An important finding of this study is that the effect of individual values was sustained and became stronger even when transformational leadership was included in the equation. These two values had almost no relationship with the three dimensions of commitment among Israeli Arab teachers (Cohen and Liu, 2011) or Chinese employees (Liu and Cohen, 2010).

However, Cohen and Abd El Majid (2014), in a large sample of 1268 Arab teachers from 64 schools in Israel, found a relationship between individual values and the dimensions of OC that did not meet the above expectations. Specifically, their findings showed that achievement, a value representing openness to change, was positively related to OC. These outcomes were surprising, since the authors expected to find no relationship, or even a negative relationship, between values representing openness to change and self-enhancement and OC. Cohen and Abd El Majid (2014) suggested that this finding might indicate a possible process experienced by the Arabs in Israel. Israeli Arabs live in a society that consists predominantly of Jews and is considered relatively Westernized (Cohen, 1999, 2010; Cohen and Liu, 2011). It is possible, therefore, that values such as achievement, which are deemed to be more Westernized and are cherished by the Jewish Israeli society, will be also adopted by Arab teachers in Israel. Furthermore, Arab schools in Israel are subject to the same administrative rules and procedures as the Jewish schools and are evaluated based on the same standards and criteria. Thus, although Arabs in Israel still represent a traditional society, they are moving closer toward Westernized values. This is demonstrated in the study by the importance attributed by the teachers to the value of achievement. Another possible explanation for the above findings can be found in Leung and Morris's (2014) study, which raised the possibility that personal values might not influence behavior as much when the prevailing norms suggest that another course of action is more appropriate. Naturally, the explanation offered here should be tested in future research.

As for the Israeli Jews, Cohen and Liu (2011) found in a sample of teachers that normative OC was related positively to the value of stimulation. They also found that continuance OC was related positively to achievement, and affective OC was related positively to conformity and benevolence. In short, for the Israeli Jews examined in the above study, only affective commitment was related to values that represent collectivism. Findings similar to those for Israeli Jews were also found by Wasti (2002) and Wasti and Can (2008) among Turkish employees. Wasti found that affective commitment was a function of positive work experiences, associated with desirable work and personal outcomes, and that these relationships were not different across individuals with differing endorsement of collectivist cultural values. Wasti and Can (2008) found that collectivist values had almost no effect on the relationship between commitment to the organization, the supervisor, and the co-workers and outcomes such as OCB, stress, and turnover intentions.

The above findings seem to indicate that collectivist values are important for commitment in more traditional societies such as the Arab society. On the other hand, more Westernized cultures in the Middle East, such as the Turkish and Israeli Jewish cultures, are affected less by cultural values in general and collectivist values in particular. Future research in the Middle East should examine this issue further, particularly in mixed cultures where more traditional cultures such as the Arab one might be affected by Westernized ones, such as that of the Israeli Jewish or Turkish cultures.

Demographics

Concerning demographic variables, Cohen (2010) found among a sample of 369 Arab teachers that tenure in school (positively) and religiosity (negatively) were related to affective and not to normative OC. Gender was not related to either of the two dimensions (affective and normative). Cohen and Abd El Majid (2014) found in a sample of 1268 Arab teachers that age (negatively) and gender (female) were related to affective OC, while education was not. All three variables – age, gender, and education – were not related to continuance OC. Aladwan et al. (2013) found among Jordanian employees that gender was not related to affective and continuance commitment, but only to normative commitment (male). Age (positively) and education (negatively) were also related only to normative commitment. The participants' years of work experience were related negatively to affective and normative commitment, but not to continuance commitment. The above findings do not show any specific consistency in the relationship between demographic variables and commitment. It seems that the relationship between the demographic variables and commitment is not necessarily affected by culture.

Situational Determinants

In a few studies, situational determinants were studied. Khasawneh et al. (2012) found among 340 vocational teachers in Jordan a strong positive relationship between transformational leadership and OC, measured by the Organization Commitment Questionnaire (OCQ) (Mowday et al., 1982). Abd El Majid and Cohen (2015) also found a strong relationship between transformational leadership and affective and normative OC of Israeli Arab teachers. This relationship existed when demographic variables and individual values were included in the equations. Using the OCQ, a similar pattern of strong positive relationship was found between job satisfaction and OC in a sample of 922 bank employees in Lebanon (Dirani and Kuchinke, 2011). Finally, Al-bdour et al. (2010) examined the relationship between variables that represent internal corporate social responsibility practices and the three dimensions in a sample of 336 bank employees in Jordan. Their findings showed that the employees' high perceptions of the corporate practices in the field of social responsibility, which included training and education, health and safety, human rights, work–life balance, and workplace diversity, had a significant relationship with employees' affective and normative commitment, but not with continuance commitment. The authors concluded that the social exchange theory (Blau, 1964) is most suitable for explaining the reciprocal relationship between the corporate's social responsibility practices and employees' commitment to the bank in Jordan.

In summary, situational variables that are related to commitment in Westernized cultures are also related to it in the Middle East. It seems that leadership has a very strong effect on commitment in the Middle East, and future studies should explore this issue further. Is leadership related to commitment in the Middle East more strongly than in Westernized cultures? Is the reason for this the importance of the power distance value in traditional societies such as the Arab society in the Middle East? These questions offer many promising research agendas.

Organizational Citizenship Behavior (OCB)

Only a very few studies examined the relationship between Arabs' commitment and work outcomes, particularly those reported by the supervisor. Most of the data about this relationship were collected in Israel. Abd El Majid and Cohen (2015) found a very strong relationship between affective OC and OCB among a large sample of Arab teachers. This strong relationship was maintained when transformational leadership, individual values, and demographic variables were included in the equation. This finding, which is similar to those for Westernized societies, supports the importance of social exchange among Arabs. Therefore, it is not surprising that a similar relationship pattern was also found among Jewish teachers in Israel. Cohen and Keren (2008) found in a sample of 539 Jewish teachers that affective commitment was strongly and positively related to the altruism dimension of OCB and was also related to the civic virtue dimension of OCB, while normative commitment was not related to any of the OCB dimensions. Continuance commitment was negatively related to altruism, and none of the commitment dimensions was related to in-role performance.

In another sample of Israeli Jewish teachers, Cohen and Liu (2011) found that affective OC had a strong positive relationship with in-role performance and OCB, even when individual values were included in the equation. Continuance and normative commitment had no relationship with in-role performance and OCB. Liu and Cohen (2010) explained that the weak relationship of continuance and normative commitment with OCB is due to the fact that exchange relationships with their employer are critical for Western employees. These employees offer commitment in return for satisfaction with different aspects in the workplace, such as leadership, justice, and so on. Affective commitment is the key representation of such an exchange relationship, and this form of commitment has been found to be the primary determinant of many work outcomes, OCB included, in most Western cultures (Cohen, 2003; Cohen and Keren, 2008). In contrast, continuance commitment has been found to have only a weak or even sometimes negative relationship with many work outcomes in more Westernized cultures (Cohen and Keren, 2008). One of the possible conclusions from the above studies is that similar exchange mechanisms drive employees of the two cultures, Western and Arab (Abd El Majid and Cohen, 2015). Future research on commitment in the Middle East should explore this possibility further.

Multiple Commitments in the Workplace

Another aspect of commitment very rarely examined in the Middle East is multiple commitments and their correlates, that is, commitment to different foci in the workplace, such as the organization, the occupation, the job, the work group, the work itself, and more. In a comprehensive study that compared levels of commitment foci among teachers from different ethnic groups in Israel (non-religious Jews, Orthodox Jews, kibbutz members, Druze, and Arabs), Cohen (2007a) found that the Arab and Druze OC was significantly higher than that of secular Jews. In addition, the level of work involvement of Arabs and Druze was significantly higher than that of secular Jews. No significant differences were found between the groups regarding occupational commitment, job involvement, and group commitment. The absence of significant differences in group commitment is somewhat surprising. One would expect Arabs to have higher levels of group commitment, because collectivism is very important for them. More research is needed in order to gain an established understanding of the relative importance of different commitment foci among the ethnic groups.

Other studies have looked at the relationship between foci of commitment and work outcomes. One such interesting study (Cohen, 1999) compared the effect of several foci of commitment (affective OC, work involvement, group commitment, job involvement, and occupational commitment) on work outcomes (absence frequency, absence duration, OCB, life satisfaction, turnover intentions from the job, organization, occupation, and actual turnover) among Arab and Jewish hospital nurses in Israel.

The findings showed that the relation between foci of commitment and outcomes clearly differed across the two ethnic groups. Thus, culture was found to be an important moderator of the effects of commitment foci on work- and non-work-related outcomes. The findings indicated that Arab nurses were more committed than Jewish nurses to all commitment foci except for group commitment. The findings also showed that the Arabs' commitment had more favorable effects on their behavior and attitudes at work. For example, all five interactions with OC indicated a more favorable effect on outcomes among Arabs than among Jews. As for occupational commitment, the three significant interactions showed more favorable effects of this commitment on outcomes among Arab than among Jewish nurses (Cohen, 1999).

Cohen (1999) concluded, based on these findings, that the more traditional culture of Arab nurses, together with their status as a minority group, made them more committed employees than Jewish nurses. Moreover, their commitment affected their behavior more favorably than did the commitment of the Jewish nurses. According to Cohen (1999), commitment is a valuable attitude in traditional societies, and Arabs adhere to their traditional way of life to a greater extent than Americans, Japanese, and Jews. The Israeli Arabs' status as a deprived minority group operates only to increase the importance of commitment as a mechanism that assists them in coping with what some of them perceive as a hostile environment. For Arabs, it is their particular setting as a minority group that magnifies the importance of commitment and its relationship with outcomes. Future research should seek data whereby the above explanation may be tested. It should also attempt to find a context that will allow some separation between culture and status, namely, a cultural group that does not face the structural environmental constraints that the Arabs in Israel face. Arabs in some other Middle East countries may provide a suitable target population.

Another noteworthy finding in Cohen's (1999) study was that OC and occupational commitment had a more favorable effect on absence duration for Arab than for Jewish nurses. The findings showed in both cases that increase in commitment resulted in a strong increase in absence duration for Jewish nurses. According to Cohen, the different absenteeism results suggest that in the two groups absenteeism may result from different underlying processes. For Arabs, whose self-identities are assumed to be tied more to family and less to work roles, absence from work may be proactive in nature and represent another coping practice to manage their multiple identity domains. If so, with increasing family demands, Arabs may be expected to answer these demands more frequently; however, with increasing time pressures and responsibilities at work, such a practice could grow less effective for them by creating even more time pressure at work, and therefore absenteeism should become less prevalent. In contrast, for Jews, whose self-identities are assumed to be tied less to family and more to work roles, taking leave from work may be reactive in nature. If so, with increasing work demands, Jews could experience more unfavorable situations from which they feel the need to withdraw, and therefore absenteeism should become more prevalent.

In another study, Cohen (2006) examined the relationship between foci of commitment, cultural values, OCB, and in-role performance (as reported by the principals) among Israeli Jewish and Arab teachers. The findings showed that culture, measured at the individual level, had a strong effect on the relationship between commitment and OCB in three ways. First, ethnicity had a strong effect on the explained variance of OCB and in-role performance. The finding that ethnicity explained 7 percent of the variance of in-role performance is important in the sense that actual performance on the job is probably perceived differently by groups that represent different cultures. A second effect of culture was demonstrated by the relationship found between the four cultural dimensions (individualism/collectivism, uncertainty avoidance, masculinity/femininity, and power distance) and OCB. The third effect was demonstrated by the significant interaction effect of cultural values and commitment foci.

The findings of the interactions seem to support the notion that while ethnicity has a consistent effect on the relationship between foci of commitment and OCB and in-role performance (the effect of foci of commitment on OCB and in-role performance was positively stronger for Israeli Arabs than for Jews), variations in cultural values within each group were more complex. For example, foci of commitment had a stronger positive relationship with the outcome variables for those with high power distance than for those with lower power distance. Further, uncertainty avoidance interacted differently with commitment, producing a variety of outcomes in terms of their direction. Power distance was the cultural dimension that had the most interactions with foci of commitment. This finding demonstrates the importance of this value in the cultural setting of the Middle East. It should be mentioned that, in a cultural situation such as the one examined here, more interactions with collectivism were expected. However, the importance of collectivism was demonstrated mainly by its strong main effect on all outcome variables.

As for the effect of commitment foci, several findings of Cohen's (2006) study are worth noting. First, OC was related to in-role performance and OCB altruism above and beyond the effect of the two cultural constructs (ethnicity and values). This strengthens the value of OC as a concept that affects outcomes regardless of, and in addition to, the effect of culture. Second, the ANOVA findings showed that Arabs are more committed than Jews to their job and work group, and suggest that the proximity of the commitment foci affects the magnitude of commitment. Job and work group are more specific and tangible foci than the organization or the occupation. The proximity of the commitment foci seems to be more important to Israeli Arabs than to Jews in determining their level of commitment (Cohen, 2006).

As for Israeli Jews, Cohen (1998) found in a sample of Israeli nurses that occupational commitment was strongly related to outcomes such as turnover intentions from the organization, job, and occupation (higher level of commitment related to lower levels of turnover intentions), in addition to the effect of OC. Job involvement was related positively to self-reported absenteeism and to job tension. In the case of job tension, occupational commitment was also found to be related (negatively). Work involvement was not related to any of the outcomes. Similar findings were reported by Cohen and Freund (2005), who also showed the importance of occupational commitment, in comparison to OC and job involvement, in its relationship to withdrawal cognitions of 327 employees, most of whom were Jewish community center managers in Israel.

CONCLUSIONS AND FUTURE DIRECTIONS

Aladwan et al. (2013) accurately contended that the Middle East has provided little research about OC, which according to them is true for countries such as Jordan and other Arab countries. They concluded that it is not yet possible to chart an effective awareness of OC in this part of the world. While the above review provides some interesting insights into commitment in the Middle East, it seems that the unknowns about commitment in this area are significantly more numerous than the knowns. Therefore, every conclusion drawn here should be treated with caution and needs much stronger support through future research.

One tentative conclusion that may be drawn from the above review is that the dimension of affective OC is applicable to most cultures. In studies that examined both Israeli Arabs and Jews, this dimension was always interpretable and provided strong relationships with correlates for both groups. Normative OC was found to be a distinct dimension in the Israeli setting, but a study conducted in Jordan showed too much overlap of its items with affective OC (Suliman and Iles, 2000). Continuance OC was found to be uninterpretable in several studies among Arabs in the Israeli setting (Cohen, 2010; Cohen and Abd El Majid, 2014). Future research should further examine the dimensionality of commitment in the Middle East. It is important to consider whether the problems related to normative commitment arise in samples other than the Jordanian one. Future research should also examine whether continuance commitment can be applied to traditional cultures. As mentioned above, in more than one Arab sample the reliabilities of CC were below .60. Omitting items and performing CFA did not make a significant difference (Cohen, 2010; Cohen and Abd El Majid, 2014). An important issue that should be examined regarding continuance commitment is the extent to which the fact that Arabs in Israel have limited employment opportunities affected the problems related to its dimensionality. It is possible that the problems with the dimension of continuance commitment are related to the specific Israeli setting and not to culture (Cohen, 2010; Cohen and Abd El Majid, 2014). This issue should be explored further.

Findings that support the assumption that the Arab culture is more traditional were found in the relationship between traditional values and OC (Cohen, 2010; Cohen and Abd El Majid, 2014). The findings demonstrate that commitment is a valuable attitude in traditional societies, and Arabs are a group who adhere to their traditional way of life more than Americans, Japanese, and Jews in Israel. The Arab status as a minority group, no doubt a deprived one, operates only to increase the importance of commitment as a mechanism that assists them in coping with what some of them perceive as a hostile environment. In the case of Japanese employees, it is the organization that enhances the commitment of its employees by offering permanent employment, internal labor markets, quality circles, and company welfare programs. In the Arab case, it is their particular setting as a minority group that magnifies the importance of commitment and its relationship to work outcomes.

Based on the findings reviewed here, it seems that, among Arabs, collectivism and tradition still have a very strong relationship with attitudes, behaviors, and commitment. The principal mechanism that nurtures and preserves these values is socialization. In the Arab society, the notion that the family is the most important group in one's life is instilled from early childhood, and the individual should be committed to it (Sidani and Thornberry, 2010). The same is true of one's ethnic group, land, and so on. Arabs are taught that their family and community are more important than their individuality. Education for such values fosters the sense of commitment to other institutions as well such as organizations and occupations. In more Westernized cultures, one is taught that the individual is no less important than the collectives (community, family, and so on) existing in society. This leads to an entirely different perception of commitment.

It seems that, unlike in some other countries and particularly Western nations, the primary values of the Arab society are not changing, and the visible changes are mostly artificial. The Arabs seem to adopt the Westernized quality of life by using modern appliances and tangible objects such as cars, tools, television, and so on. However, as far as their values are concerned, it seems that tradition and religion have a much stronger effect on Arabs now than they did several years ago. Arabs value collectivism now even more strongly than previously (Abd El Majid and Cohen, 2015; Cohen and Abd El Majid, 2014). It should be noted, however, that future research should take into account the possibility that Arabs are not one group, characterized by uniform values and attitudes. Christian Arabs are much more modern and less extreme than Muslim Arabs. Druze are also another group that holds different values and patterns of behavior from those of the Muslims.

As for the future, it seems that there are different paths for Israeli Arabs and Arabs in other countries in the Middle East. In Israel, there are signs of stronger integration of Arabs and Jews in the labor market. For example, Arabs and Jews work together in the healthcare industry. In many hospitals in Israel, there are high proportions of Arabs in all healthcare occupations, including physicians. Working together is an important necessity in this industry. One can also find a mixed workforce in the police service, the construction sector, and some food industries. Arabs and Jews work together in many municipalities with high proportions of Arab citizens (Jerusalem, Haifa, and Nazareth). Despite the tension in Israel as a result of the Arab–Israeli conflict, a tendency exists to integrate the Arab population in all organizations. The proportion of Arabs in Israeli organizations will only increase, and the government is supporting the integration of Arabs in the workforce for economic reasons.

In other countries in the Middle East, the situation is much more complex. The region today is very unstable, and it is difficult to predict what kind of a Middle East we are going to have even within a few years. If the influence of Westernized values disappears because of the resurgence of the traditional forces in the area, commitment will become a stronger value, including in the work setting. However, this does not mean that it will enhance positive work attitudes and behaviors. If the traditional values lose their effect as Westernized ones become dominant, then commitment will become an attitude similar to the one that we know in the Westernized society. Some of this uncertainty was reflected in the ambiguous findings presented in this chapter. As for the future, commitment is an important concept, but it is far from being the main problem of this disturbed region.

REFERENCES

Abd El Majid, I. and Cohen, A. (2015). The role of the principal's values and perceived leadership style in developing citizenship behaviors and in-role performance among Arab teachers in Israel, *Leadership and Organization Development Journal*, 36(3), 308–327.

Al-Aameri, A.S. (2000). Job satisfaction and organizational commitment for nurses. *Saudi Medical Journal*, 21(6), 531–535.

Aladwan, K., Bhanugopan, R., and Fish, A. (2013). To what extent are Arab workers committed to their organisations? Analysing the multidimensional perspective of organisational commitment in Jordan. *International Journal of Commerce and Management*, 23(4), 306–326.

Al-bdour, A.A., Nasruddin, E., and Lin, S.K. (2010). The relationship between internal corporate social responsibility and organizational commitment within the banking sector in Jordan. *International Journal of Human and Social Sciences*, 5(14), 932–951.

Allen, N.J. and Meyer, J.P. (1990). The measurement and antecedents of affective, continuance and normative commitment to the organization. *Journal of Occupational Psychology*, 63, 1–18.

Blau, P. (1964). *Exchange, and Power in Social Life*. New York: John Wiley & Sons.

Cohen, A. (1998). An examination of the relationship between work commitment and work outcomes among hospital nurses, *Scandinavian Journal of Management*, 14(1–2), 1–17.

Cohen, A. (1999). The relation between commitment forms and work outcomes in Jewish and Arab culture. *Journal of Vocational Behavior*, 54(3), 371–391.

Cohen, A. (2003). *Multiple Commitments in the Workplace: An Integrative Approach*. Mahwah, NJ: Lawrence Erlbaum Associates.

Cohen, A. (2006). 'The relationship between multiple commitments and organizational citizenship behavior (OCB) in Arab and Jewish culture. *Journal of Vocational Behavior*, 69(1), 105–118.

Cohen, A. (2007a). An examination of the relationship between commitments and culture among five cultural groups of Israeli teachers, *Journal of Cross-Cultural Psychology*, 38(1), 34–49.

Cohen, A. (2007b). One nation, many cultures: A cross-cultural study of the relationship between personal cultural values and commitment in the workplace to in-role performance and organizational citizenship behavior, *Cross-Cultural Research*, 41(3), 271–300.

Cohen, A. (2009). A value based perspective of commitment in the workplace: An examination of Schwartz's basic human values theory among bank employees in Israel, *International Journal of Intercultural Relations*, 33, 332–345.

Cohen, A. (2010). Values and Commitment: A test of Schwartz's Human Values Theory among Arab teachers in Israel, *Journal of Applied Social Psychology*, 40(8), 1921–1947.

Cohen, A. and Abd El Majid, I. (2014). The role of principals' values and perceived leadership style in developing organizational commitment among Arab teachers in Israel. Paper presented at the 28th International Congress of Applied Psychology (ICAP), Paris, France.

Cohen, A. and Freund, A. (2005). A longitudinal analysis of the relationship between multiple commitments and withdrawal cognitions, *Scandinavian Journal of Management*, 21(3), 329–351.

Cohen, A. and Keren, D. (2008). Individual values and social exchange variables – Examining their relationship to and mutual effect on in-role performance and organizational citizenship behavior', *Group and Organization Management*, 33(4), 425–452.

Cohen, A. and Kirchmeyer, C. (2005). A cross-cultural study of the work/nonwork interface among Israeli nurses, *Applied Psychology: An International Review*, 54(4), 538–568.

Cohen, A. and Liu, Y. (2011). Relationships between in-role performance and individual values, commitment, and organizational citizenship behavior among Israeli teachers', *International Journal of Psychology*, 46(4), 271–287.

Dirani, K.M. and Kuchinke, K.P. (2011). Job satisfaction and organizational commitment: Validating the Arabic satisfaction and commitment questionnaire (ASCQ), testing the correlations, and investigating the effects of demographic variables in the Lebanese banking sector. *International Journal of Human Resource Management*, 22(5), 1180–1202.

Hofstede, G. (1980). *Culture's Consequences: International Differences in Work-related Values*. Beverly Hills, CA: Sage.

Hofstede Center (2015). Country comparison. http://geert-hofstede.com/ (accessed 12 February 2015).

Khasawneh, S., Omari, A., and Abu-Tineh, A.M. (2012). The relationship between transformational leadership and organizational commitment: The case for vocational teachers in Jordan. *Educational Management Administration and Leadership*, 1–15.

Leung, K. and Morris, M.W. (2014). Values, schemas, and norms in the culture behavior nexus: A situated dynamics framework. *Journal of International Business Studies*, 46(1), 1–23.

Liu, Y. and Cohen, A., (2010). Values, commitment, and OCB among Chinese employees *International Journal of Intercultural Relations*, 34, 493–506.

Meyer, J.P. and Allen, N.J. (1991). A three-component conceptualization of organizational commitment. *Human Resource Management Review*, 1(1), 61–89.

Meyer, J.P., Allen, N.J., and Smith, C.A. (1993). Commitment to organizations and occupations: Extension and test of a three-component conceptualization. *Journal of Applied Psychology*, 78(4), 538.

Meyer, J.P., Stanley, D.J., Jackson, T.A., McInnis, K.J., Maltin, E.R., and Sheppard, L. (2012). Affective, normative, and continuance commitment levels across cultures: A meta-analysis. *Journal of Vocational Behavior*, 80(2), 225–245.

Mowday, R.T., Porter, L.W., and Steers, R.M. (1982). *Employee–Organization Linkages: The Psychology of Commitment, Absenteeism, and Turnover*. New York: Academic Press.

Sabri, H.A. (2013). Existing and preferred organizational cultures in Arab and American organizations. *International Journal of Business and Management*, 1(1), 64–84.

Schwartz, S.H., Melech, G., Lehmann, A., Burgess, S., and Harris, M. (2001). Extending the cross-cultural validity of the theory of basic human values with a different method of measurement. *Journal of Cross-Cultural Psychology*, 32, 519–542.

Sidani, Y.M. and Thornberry, J. (2010). The current Arab work ethic: Antecedents, implications, and potential remedies. *Journal of Business Ethics*, 91(1), 35–49.

Suliman, A.M. and Iles, P.A. (2000). The multi-dimensional nature of organisational commitment in a non-western context. *Journal of Management Development*, 19(1), 71–83.

Triandis, H.C. (1995). *Individualism and Collectivism*. Boulder, CO: Westview Press.

Wasti, S.A. (2002). Affective and continuance commitment to the organization: Test of an integrated model in the Turkish context. *International Journal of Intercultural Relations*, 26(5), 525–550.

Wasti, S.A. (2003). Organizational commitment, turnover intentions and the influence of cultural values. *Journal of Occupational and Organizational Psychology*, 76(3), 303–321.

Wasti, S.A. and Can, Ö. (2008). Affective and normative commitment to organization, supervisor, and coworkers: Do collectivist values matter? *Journal of Vocational Behavior*, 73(3), 404–413.

Yousef, D.A. (2000). Organizational commitment as a mediator of the relationship between Islamic work ethic and attitudes toward organizational change. *Human Relations*, 53(4), 513–537.

Yousef, D.A. (2001). Islamic work ethic: A moderator between organizational commitment and job satisfaction in a cross-cultural context. *Personnel Review*, 30(2), 152–169.

31. Organizational commitment: a Latin American soap opera
Luis M. Arciniega

In Latin America, there is a long history of efforts by local managers to increase productivity and punctuality and to decrease absenteeism by using creative human resource management (HRM). In Havana cigar factories, for instance, supervisors faced serious problems guaranteeing the attendance of employees after lunchtime: the artisans of the classic hand-rolled cigars went home at noon for lunch, and considering that much of the traditional Cuban cuisine is based on beans, rice, pork, and spices, workers had a hard time returning to a workplace where the temperature could easily reach 100 degrees Fahrenheit in the early afternoon. As a response to the rampant absenteeism, managers of those small factories created a new position: the 'reader'. Men with good reading skills and charming voices were hired to read catchy novels to the employees. In a country where the literacy rate was low, having a reader in the workplace was the only access these employees had to these literary delights, and it gave them a reason to return to their jobs on time and in an alert state. Years later, in the mid-1930s, the readers were replaced by radio soap operas: professional actors, incidental sounds, and music increased the richness of the catchy radio dramas, and gave factory employees a strong reason to arrive on time after lunch. Radio soap operas helped managers to reduce absenteeism and to increase productivity. To this day, soap operas, now televised, remain an important source of income in economies such as Brazil, Colombia, and Mexico.

Latin American soap operas have found audiences worldwide, in distant countries such as Indonesia, Turkey, the Philippines, and even China, as well as several Arab countries. What do these diverse nations have in common? The answer is simple: as in most Latin American countries, these cultures are high on power distance and collectivism (Hofstede et al., 2005; House et al., 2004), their wealth it is not well distributed, and their average populations have weak reading comprehension skills (OECD, 2001).

Anthropologists say that popular songs, poems, and proverbs reflect the essence of a culture. Latin American soap operas certainly prove this rule: the plots of most of these narratives center around main characters dealing with the problems caused by power distance; for instance, a poor woman falls in love with a rich and powerful young man whose family spurns her.

This chapter does not intend to provide a comprehensive review of all studies related to commitment conducted in Latin America. Instead, it is intended to show a set of studies from representative countries of the region, dealing particularly with two common research questions of high relevance in these cultures: (1) do high-performance HRM practices have the same beneficial effects on organizational commitment in high power distance cultures as have been found in low power distance cultures?; and (2) what is the impact of the predominant paternalistic leadership style on the development of commitment? A formal search was conducted using the Institute for Scientific Information (ISI)

Web of Science database to select these studies, using the names of the largest countries in the region and organizational commitment as the search terms. A total of 36 empirical studies were identified. Due to the absence of documents from Argentina, a recent doctoral dissertation was considered for the review, in order to include at least one study from this key player in the region. An overview of the type of research on commitment conducted in Latin America would be incomplete without showing examples of studies done of state-run organizations, and of small and medium-sized enterprises, which is why the penultimate section of this chapter focuses on these topics. Finally, a global conclusion will be presented suggesting some actions regarding research.

POWER DISTANCE AND ITS CONSEQUENCES ON COMMITMENT

Over the last two decades, most of the global research on organizational commitment has concentrated on variables that influence the psychological attachment employees feel toward their organizations. A large proportion of this research focuses on the internal characteristics associated with the organization, such as policies and HRM practices, and systems granting or sharing power between employees at all levels of the organization. Most of this research was conducted in Canada, the United States, and some European countries (Meyer et al., 2002), where managers and supervisors conceive the process of sharing and granting power with lower-level employees as natural, and where there is mutual comfort with this concession. This approach is common in cultures with low power distance, but is not the rule in cultures with high power distance. Power distance is defined as the extent to which the less powerful members of an organization or a country expect and accept that power is unequally distributed (Hofstede et al., 2005). Table 31.1 shows some key figures for representative countries in the Latin American region, including the power distance indices from the classic study of Hofstede. It is important to mention that, in this index, Malaysia is at the top of the list with 104 units; Austria is at the very bottom with only 11. Table 31.1 also depicts the Gini index, a widely known figure that measures to what extent the income in a country is well distributed amongst its population. An index of 0 represents perfect equality, while an index of 100 suggests perfect inequality. Northern European countries are top performers in equality, with figures ranging in the mid-twenties, while developing countries fall in the mid-forties range, reaching the fifties in some cases.

In low power distance countries such as Austria, it is not only desirable but natural for employees to speak up to their superiors and to tell them what they think, in detail, even when they disagree. In higher-distance countries such as Guatemala, Brazil, and other Latin American countries, behavior tends to be different: employees of lower status behave submissively in front of their superiors, even if they disagree with their decisions or points of view; but when their bosses are not present, workers openly and loudly criticize them. Employees know it can be dangerous to publicly doubt the word of their superiors who hold all the power; 'This emphasis upon status differences makes it difficult for people at varying status levels to express themselves freely in discussion and argument' (Whyte, 1961, p. 64).

In order to implement a culture of continuous improvement in higher power distance

Table 31.1   National indices for some representative countries in Latin America

Country	Population in millions[1]	Power distance index[2]	Individualism index[2]	Freedom of press index[3]	Attendance at religious services[4]	% of Catholics[1]	Gini index[1]
Argentina	43.3	49	46	51	20.0	92.0	45.8
Bolivia	10.8	na	na	47	na	76.8	46.6
Brazil	200.3	69	38	45	49.9	64.6	51.9
Chile	17.5	63	23	31	23.5	66.7	52.1
Colombia	46.7	67	13	55	48.3	90.0	53.5
Costa Rica	4.8	35	15	17	na	76.3	50.3
Ecuador	15.9	78	8	64	48.9	74.0	48.1
Guatemala	14.9	95	6	60	na	na	55.1
Honduras	8.7	na	na	68	na	97.0	57.7
Mexico	121.7	81	30	63	46.2	82.7	48.3
Panama	3.7	95	11	49	na	85.0	51.9
Paraguay	6.8	na	na	59	na	89.6	53.2
Peru	30.4	64	16	47	39.7	81.3	45.3
Uruguay	3.3	61	36	24	12.3	47.1	45.3
Venezuela	29.3	81	12	81	na	96.0	39.0

Sources: 1. CIA (2015). 2. Hofstede et al. (2005). 3. Freedom House (2015). 4. World Values Survey (2015).

cultures, managers promoting upward communication practices with lower-level employees need to reduce the fears associated with presenting ideas that differ from those of the supervisors. Managers must also create incentives to promote a constant communication flow, since employees are accustomed to depending on their supervisors for direction and decision-making.

The literature in the field of cross-cultural management suggests that the contextual variables that could be the main roots in the development of a high power distance in a culture are: the longevity and robustness of its democratic institutions; the dominant religion and religiosity of its population; and the size of its middle class (Carl et al., 2004). In countries where democratic institutions are robust and long-standing, power distance tends to be lower, since power in general is not concentrated in the hands of few persons. Freedom of the press has been used as a proxy to measure the robustness of democracy in societies. Top-notch countries in the ranking of Freedom House (2015), such as Norway or Sweden, score low with 10 units having a 'Free Press' ranking; meanwhile, some Latin American countries score high and are considered under the status of 'Partly Free' such as Argentina, Brazil, or Chile, or even the worst 'Not Free' status, as the cases of Venezuela, Ecuador, and Mexico (see Table 31.1). Regarding religion and religiosity, it is said that countries with a large population that practices Hinduism, Islam, or Catholicism tend to be high on power distance. Individuals in these societies are predisposed to accept hierarchies emphasizing class roles (Carl et al., 2004). Latin America, as a subcontinent, has the largest concentration of Catholics in the globe. Table 31.1 depicts the proportion of the population in each country that practices this religion, as well as the proportion of the people attending religious services at least once a week. Finally, regarding the impact of the size of its middle class on a country's power distance, it has been suggested that a large middle class reacts more effectively against the excesses of power. More-educated people with higher levels of income, performing managerial or administrative jobs, are used to challenging and reacting to those excesses in an open manner. The Gini index is also used as a proxy to assess the size of the middle class. Scandinavian countries have lower indices (around 20) as a consequence of their large middle classes, while Latin American countries have higher indices (around 50), reflecting their small middle classes (see Table 31.1).

MANAGING FOR COMMITMENT IN HIGH POWER DISTANCE CULTURES

The following section describes a selected set of research projects conducted in Latin America, dealing with the key concern of whether high-performance human resource practices are key factors in fostering employee commitment.

The Case of a Large Mexican Holding Organization

This study, carried out by Arciniega and González (2006), is one of the very few conducted in Latin America assessing the impact of different variables associated with the implementation of high-performance HRM practices on organizational commitment and using a large sample from different companies. The model contained in the book by Meyer and Allen (1997, p. 106) served as the frame of reference for this research. This model proposes two main blocks of variables that can be considered as antecedents for the construct, and classifies them as distal and proximal. Distal variables are those associated with personal and organizational characteristics, socialization experiences, and environmental conditions. Proximal variables are work experiences, role states, and psychological contracts. Arciniega and González assessed a simplified version of that model, considering individual work values as the distal antecedents (that is, openness to change, conservation, self-enhancement, self-transcendence) and job experiences, measured through job satisfaction facets and some high-performance human resource practices, as the proximal antecedents. The study was conducted in eight different companies in northeastern Mexico, using a sample of 982 employees. Organizational commitment was measured using an 18-item questionnaire developed by Meyer et al. (1993).

The results of the study showed that in this large sample of Mexican employees, the key variable related to affective commitment was knowledge of organizational goals: that is, the extent to which the employee felt informed regarding the current and future plans of the firm, and also whether they were aware of how their daily work effort impacted the business unit's performance. The other key variables were: job security, satisfaction with development, the work value self-transcendence, and finally, perceived empowerment. Most of these predictors were consistent with the international meta-analyses (Meyer et al., 2002), but there was one unique finding: employees who placed high value on dealing with the concern for others and on altruism (that is, self-transcendence) were more likely to develop affective commitment.

Consistent with the widely known similarities between the predictors for the affective and normative components of commitment (see Chapter 3 in this volume), the two key antecedents for the normative dimension were exactly the same as for the affective component. The main antecedents for the continuance component were: empowerment, compensation, the work value 'conservation', communications practices, and the work value 'self-transcendence', but with a negative correlation, opposite to the relationship with the affective component.

This study offered two main findings. Firstly, a robust consistency with previous international results concerning the relationship of high-performance HRM practices and positive job experiences with organizational commitment (Meyer et al., 2002), suggesting that power distance is not an issue of concern when implementing this set of practices in a firm where the leaders and the organizational culture promote and accept these initiatives. Secondly, unique results regarding the influence of work values on organizational commitment, in particular the relationship between self-transcendence and affective commitment.

A Case in the Largest Private Company in Venezuela

In a similar vein to the study previously described, Arciniega and Menon (2013) assessed the connection between a continuous improvement project in a large bottling plant in Venezuela on the psychological empowerment and organizational commitment experienced by its employees. The study was conducted during a very contentious political and economic context (2008–2009), a relatively common scenario in Latin America over several decades. The company faced an exponential increase in its sales due to the boom in oil prices. As a result, many of its facilities had to increase their capacity in a very short time. To keep control of its operations and to comply with the quality standards, the firm decided to implement a system of continuous improvement. With the support of the company, the researchers conducted a cross-sectional study to assess the extent to which the formal practices involved in this process would be related to the social empowerment experienced by the employees, and more importantly, to their psychological empowerment, and in turn to their organizational commitment. The sample consisted of 313 employees. Affective and continuance commitment were assessed using an adapted version of Meyer et al.'s (1993) 18-item questionnaire.

The results show that the relationship between job characteristics and affective commitment is mediated by psychological empowerment. In particular, the results suggest that the key dimension of psychological empowerment that relates to affective commitment is goal internalization. Task feedback, in turn, seemed to be the job characteristic variable with the highest relationship with goal internalization. This study, conducted under adverse conditions in Venezuela, confirms the idea that high power distance is not an issue of concern when implementing practices related to the construction of a culture of continuous improvement, so long as the leadership and the organizational culture of the company are their overt sponsors.

Communication Matters: A Case from Argentina

There is another interesting research project conducted under an adverse political-economic scenario: a study carried out in Argentina over several months of monetary and foreign trade instability. The main goal of this study was to assess the relationships between the satisfaction experienced by employees in the service sector with the communication practices of their firms, and their affective and continuance commitment (Barresi, 2014). The study took place in two large multinational chains of supermarkets in the Greater Buenos Aires area. Business units were spread throughout the regions and in most cases operating on a 24/7 basis. This scenario was a fertile field for implementing effective organizational communication practices. Based on the large study of a global consultancy firm, the author suggests that formal communication practices allow employees to feel attached to the firm, and also that these are the best methods to develop a sense of awareness under the pressure of a changing and challenging business environment.

This study used a total sample of 372 employees: 204 working for the Carrefour Express stores chain, and 168 for the units of Maxi DIA. The following dimensions of communication were measured: formal communication management, organizational perspective, communication with the supervisor, communication in the employee's workplace, and informal horizontal communication. To operationalize organizational commitment, the Meyer et al. (1993) 18-item questionnaire was utilized.

Two main regression models were run. Regarding affective commitment, the model explained 41 percent of the variance, with only two significant predictors: formal communication practices with a standardized beta of .64, and communication with the supervisor with a coefficient of .17. The predictive power for the model of continuance commitment was very poor, being lower than 10 percent.

The results of this study suggest that formal communication practices have a high relation with the affective commitment experienced by the employees of this type of firm. Among these practices are: the ability of the firm to spread the mission and vision of the company at all levels of the organization; and the use of formal means of communications, such as an internal 24/7 video channel, and the monthly issue of a newsletter.

These studies are good examples of how employees' participation in continuous improvement efforts or sharing key information with them, considered in the ability–motivation–opportunity (AMO) theory, lead to the development of commitment (for a detailed discussion see Chapter 21 in this volume).

POWER DISTANCE + COLLECTIVISM = PATERNALISTIC LEADERSHIP?

As mentioned previously, from the perspective of the dimensions of Hofstede, Latin American countries are distinguished by their higher scores in power distance and collectivism. It is important to recall at this point that collectivism is one of the poles of a continuum, where individualism occupies the opposite extreme. Collectivistic societies are made up of individuals who are socialized throughout their lifetimes to integrate into strong cohesive groups that will protect and support them in exchange of unquestionable loyalty (Hofstede et al., 2005). On the contrary, in individualistic societies, the ties between persons are loose, and everyone is expected to look after themselves and their immediate family. Hofstede suggests that in cultures where individuals are dependent on ingroups, people are usually dependent on a figure of power, which explains why cultures high on collectivism are usually high in power distance as well. Table 31.1 shows the scores on both indices in some representative countries of Latin America. For reference, the most individualistic (least collectivistic) country in Hofstede's study was the United States (US), with a score of 91 points, and the least individualistic (most collectivistic) was Guatemala, with a score of 6.

A paternalistic leadership style is characterized by a leader acting in a way similar to a father with his sons. In the context of organizations, leaders provide protection and guidance to the employees, even beyond the border of their jobs, and in return they expect loyalty and respect. It is said that this peculiar leadership style is rooted in indigenous psychologies of Pacific Asian, Middle Eastern, and Latin American cultures, and it was seen as a natural mechanism of protection of the less powerful in the absence of social control that marked the feudal era (Aycan, 2006). In the case of Latin America, some authors suggest that the prevalence of this leadership style is a heritage of the colonial era when Spanish or Portuguese landlords provided protection to their workers in exchange for blind loyalty and intense work (e.g., Martinez, 2005). According to Aycan (2006), the paternalist leader creates a family atmosphere in the workplace, establishes close and individualized relations with subordinates, gets involved with personal issues of the subordinate beyond the work domain, expects loyalty from subordinates, and clearly maintains a line of status and authority. This paternalistic leadership style is also present in most Latin American soap operas, and is reflected in roles such as a tough but charismatic foreman in a Colombian coffee plantation, a sarcastic but charming overseer in a tequila *hacienda* in Mexico, or a bloody but loyal drug lord.

Cross-cultural studies conducted in the last decade have shown that paternalistic leadership has a positive influence on job attitudes, such as satisfaction and commitment, in countries high on power distance and collectivism (e.g., Aycan et al., 2000; Pellegrini et al., 2010). These cross-cultural studies were done in countries in North America, Europe, and Asia. Surprisingly, there has been an increasing stream of studies focused on this line of research conducted in different Latin American countries. Two of these studies will be described in the following paragraphs.

The Case of Paternalistic Leadership and White-Collar Workers in Chile and the US

This cross-cultural study using Chilean and the US-based employees had as its main goals assessing the influence of paternalistic style, delegation, organizational commitment, and job satisfaction, and identifying the differences in these countries (Lieberman, 2014). The basic rationale behind expecting differences was based on the fact that the US culture is low in collectivism and power distance, and Chile is high in both. For this reason it was expected that Chilean employees would feel more comfortable with a paternalistic style, and to the contrary, the participants from the US would appreciate more delegation. The author proposed, based on previous published findings, that a paternalistic style may be seen as a violation of privacy and as a mechanism for controlling people in the workplace in a country such as the US, while in Chile it could be seen as the only viable option to lead employees. Regarding delegation, the study suggests, based on previous research conducted in Chile, that the higher the level of the employee in the organizational chart, the higher demand for delegation would be. Regarding organizational commitment, it was expected that a paternalistic style would have a higher impact as a driver of affective commitment with the Chilean employees, and that in the US it would be delegation that had that impact on affective commitment instead.

The sample of this study was composed of 260 employees from Chile and 210 from the US. Both samples were diverse regarding educational and organizational levels, tenure, and age. Affective commitment was measured using an eight-item scale (Meyer et al., 1993). As expected, the paternalistic style was more valued in Chile than in the US, and the opposite happened with delegation. Contrary to the predictions, paternalistic style did not have a significant relationship with commitment in the Chilean sample; surprisingly, delegation had the highest standardized beta in the regression model for this sample. Regarding the US participants, only paternalistic style had a significant positive relationship. Additional analyses suggested that delegation mediated the relationship between paternalistic style and affective commitment.

The author argued that some differences in the composition of the samples could be the reason for the unexpected results. The US sample was composed of younger and more-educated people and 23 percent of them were of Latin American origin, a percentage higher than the overall population of the US: 15.1 percent (CIA, 2015).

Perceived Supervisor Support, Work–Family Conflict and Commitment in Brazilian White-Collar Workers

More research dealing with the impact of the paternalistic leadership style on employee attitudes such as work–family conflict (WFC) and organizational commitment was conducted in Brazil by a team based in the US (Casper et al., 2011). The authors developed their study based on the fact that Brazil is a country high on collectivism, that family is the most central element in this culture, and that women's participation in the workforce grew almost 40 percent as a consequence of the economic boom the South American country had for more than a decade. As a result of this surge in workforce participation, thousands of Brazilian women started to face work–family conflict. This scenario was a fertile field to explore gender differences on WFC, and to assess the relationship between supervisor's support, WFC, and organizational commitment.

In work–family conflict there are two causal relations: the pressure of work that can affect the family domain (work interference with family, WIF), or vice versa (family interference with work, FIW). The authors suggest that because Brazil is a collectivistic culture in which family is highly valued, when work interferes with family issues this conflict is likely to create a negative effect on the employees' attitudes towards their company. In other words, WIF will lead to low affective commitment, and workers in turn believe they remain mainly because they have to, and not because they want to, and their continuance commitment increases. The researchers also proposed that when employees perceive that their supervisors value their contributions and care about their well-being (perceived supervisor support, PSS), they value this support, and even when they are experiencing work–family conflict, they perceive this support as something positive from the firm which increases their affective commitment and decreases their continuance commitment to the company. Considering the dominance of the paternalistic leadership style in Brazil, it was expected that the effects of PSS would be higher than that reported in the literature for Anglo workers, because the paternalistic leader tends to care not only for the employee but also for their family. As a consequence when the employee faces work–family conflict, the leader cares for the problem in general, and the follower interprets this reaction as support from the firm, increasing their affective commitment towards it. In sum, it was expected that perceived supervisor support would moderate the relationship between WFC and organizational commitment. To validate their hypotheses, the authors sampled 168 Brazilian professionals from different sectors and different educational backgrounds. Affective and continuance commitment were measured through 16 items from Meyer and Allen's (1984) scale.

The results from the study showed a positive direct relationship between perceived supervisor support and affective commitment, and also between work interfering with family and continuance commitment. These results were consistent with international findings (e.g., Casper et al., 2007). The authors highlight that the impact of PSS on affective commitment was higher than encountered in previous studies conducted with Anglo samples, suggesting that the paternalistic leadership could have a key role in this relationship. Perhaps the most interesting result regarding the interactions between family interference with work (FIW) and perceived supervisor support in predicting organizational commitment was the fact that, when employees see that family issues are interfering with their work, and they perceive high support from their supervisors, higher support leads to higher continuance commitment. In general, the findings suggest that there are fewer negative consequences of work interference with family (WIF) on employee commitment in Brazilian employees than for their Anglo counterparts. Because Brazil is a culture where the boundaries between work and family are more permeable, the notion of competition between roles may be lower than in Anglo cultures where most of the research has been done in the past. As in previous studies, this research also shows that the expected influence of culture in the case of the dominant paternalistic leadership style on work–family conflict was not as important as originally expected by the researchers.

MANAGING FOR COMMITMENT IN LARGE STATE ORGANIZATIONS: THE CASE OF PETROBRAS

The previously described studies showed how human resource practices affect commitment and empowerment of employees of different types of organizations in the Latin American region. These studies provided good examples of how a firm can use its global partner or owner's know-how to improve its efficiency and its workforce commitment. It is also important to note that some organizations in the Latin American region are presently transitioning from large state-run companies to efficient world-class firms. One such case is Petrobras, the controversial Brazilian government energy company, whose name has become infamous due to corruption scandals.

In 1994 the government of Brazil introduced a new strategic plan that involved industrial restructuring, trade liberalization, and deregulation. In the case of the energy sector, the oil industry moved from a rigid system of state control to a neoliberal scenario where private companies were allowed to participate in different processes such as exploration, production, refining, and distribution, activities that had previously been totally controlled by the state-owned firm. Petrobras had to reinvent many aspects of its culture as a firm, including most of its human resource practices, with new pressures from the central government focused on reducing the costs of payroll. Changes included incentives for early retirement and a hiring freeze on new permanent positions. Fifteen years after these changes took place, a team of local researchers conducted a cross-sectional study in one of Petrobras' largest refineries to assess the impact of high-performance HRM practices on the levels of organizational commitment experienced by employees from different personal backgrounds, such as the type of contract with Petrobras (that is staff or temporary), gender, education, and job level (Sa Abreu et al., 2013).

The company implemented an integrated management system, establishing clearly defined macro and micro processes, procedures, and goals at all levels of the organization. This allowed the management of the firm to closely monitor performance, goal achievement, and the contribution of each employee to these metrics. The new HRM systems for attraction, compensation, promotion, and training were focused on these indicators. Regarding attraction and selection, the firm launched a nationwide campaign to recruit highly skilled candidates who had to take a comprehensive exam, and hired only the top 95th percentile of applicants. To increase knowledge of organizational goals, a periodic premium event was organized under the leadership of top management. For each business unit, all staff members gathered in order to see the progress of the strategic goals of their group.

The sample of this study consisted of 233 employees from all organizational levels of the refinery. The main goal of the study was to identify the individual characteristics of employees who reported the highest and lowest levels of the three components of organizational commitment. The researchers employed regression trees using the classification and regression tree (CART) method, where the algorithm splits the data into segments called nodes, which are as homogeneous as possible with respect to the dependent variable.

Regarding affective commitment, male employees with a permanent full-time contract and with a low level of education and a lower organizational level reported the highest level of affective commitment; while those with a temporary contract, with university studies, and a higher level in the organizational structure, reported the lowest levels of the affective dimension. Employees with ten or more years of tenure and a lower level of education reported the highest level of continuance commitment; as opposed to female employees with less than ten years of tenure and a university degree, who had the lowest.

Finally, the study showed that male temporary employees with a university degree were the highest on normative commitment. In contrast, female employees with a full-time permanent contract, no matter their tenure, reported the highest level of normative commitment. With regard to the relative importance of the personal characteristics in the conformation of the regression trees for each of the three components of commitment, the type of contract was the most relevant independent variable, followed by tenure and education level.

LOOKING INTO COMMITMENT IN SMALL AND MEDIUM-SIZED FIRMS

Considering the key role that small and medium-sized firms have in Latin American economies, and the lack of studies conducted outside of the US and Canada exploring the drivers of organizational commitment in this type of company, De Clercq and Rius (2007) conducted a study of 863 firms in Mexico with fewer than 500 employees. The study attempted to assess the relationships between employees' position and tenure, their perceptions of organizational climate, the firm's entrepreneurial orientation, and the organizational commitment experienced by their collaborators. This study, rooted in the social exchange theory, proposes that individuals in small and medium-sized organizations are more likely to feel committed to their companies and to exert considerable efforts in their daily work than those in larger organizations. Under this rationale, higher-level employees are more likely to build stronger social exchange relationships with their peers and organizations, develop greater perceptions of attachments and relational obligations to their employer, and thus show higher levels of normative and affective commitment. In the same vein, the study proposes that long-tenured employees are exposed to perceptions of support from their company for a longer time and are more likely to develop a feeling of gratitude and a moral obligation to remain in the company, and to do something beneficial for their firm in exchange for what they have received from it. As stated earlier, employees in high power distance cultures are accustomed to depending on their supervisors for direction and decision-making, and might be expected to have negative reactions to requests that they participate in decision-making processes or provide ideas to improve the processes in their companies. This narrative is challenged by De Clercq and Rius, who propose that employees in this type of culture might interpret this request from their firms as a sign of respect and consideration, and consequently increase their levels of affective and normative commitment. A unique contribution of this study is the proposal that employees will feel more committed to companies they perceive as capable of dealing with the increasing competition in a quickly changing environment, because they believe that the strong entrepreneurial orientation of the firm will increase their job security.

This study employed Allen and Meyer's (1990) original scale for measuring organizational commitment, and even when the hypotheses considered the affective and the normative dimensions as independent components, the researchers could not validate their original hypotheses because of a lack of discriminant validity between the two. Both dimensions were then collapsed into a general variable named 'organizational commitment'. The results suggest that the main influencer of organizational commitment of employees in the small and medium-sized firms that participated was 'psychological meaningfulness', that is, the employees' feelings about their contribution to the organization, their perception that their contributions were recognized, and the presence of challenging job goals. The employees' position came a distant second as a driver of organizational commitment. The results of this study are consistent with the ones conducted in both local and multinational large firms previously described in this chapter, suggesting that no matter the size of the company, the antecedents of commitment tend to be the same.

CONCLUSIONS

As stated in the introduction, this chapter was not intended to provide a comprehensive review of all studies related to commitment conducted in Latin America. Instead, it presented a selection of studies from representative countries of the region serving as a showcase of the type of research on commitment in Latin American countries that has been published in respectable academic journals.

Latin America is a fertile land for doing research on commitment. It is impressive that the Web of Science reports only 36 empirical studies conducted in the region dealing with organizational commitment. This trend is consistent with the findings showing that from 1963 to 2009, only 206 articles on business in Latin America appeared in leading academic journals (Nicholls-Nixon et al., 2011).

No matter the subarea of commitment research, there is a lot to do in this region. For example, there are just two published papers dealing with problems in measuring the construct: one suggesting that the affective and the normative dimensions are conceived as the same component in the minds of blue-collar workers (Betanzos Diaz et al., 2006), and another demonstrating that when running exploratory factor analyses (EFAs) on the 18-item version of the commitment questionnaire (Meyer et al., 1993), two items of the normative scale consistently appear in the factor associated with the affective dimension, in 95 out of 96 samples of 250 employees each (Arciniega and Gonzalez, 2012).

Regarding the studies reviewed in this chapter, it seems that even when the authors claimed that power distance and collectivism would have a relevant impact on the assessed variables, in general those dimensions did not have the expected effect; this is in line with the increasing body of research proposing that the variance within cultures is substantially higher than variance between cultures (e.g., Au, 1999; Tung, 2008). All this suggests a latent need to conduct large cross-cultural studies with more complex designs in order to explore whether these suggested differences really exist or not.

One final comment: during the last decade there has been an increasing number of business schools in Latin America trying to become accredited by international bodies such as the Association to Advance Collegiate Schools of Business (AACSB) or the European Foundation for Management Development (EFMD) Quality Improvement System (EQUIS). These kinds of organizations require that faculty members publish in academic journals indexed in international databases, such as the ISI Web of Science. Publishing in some of these journals requires having an updated training in using state-of-the-art multivariate statistical techniques, a training that many Latin American academics do not have. Instead, they know the context of organizations in their regions, and in many cases they have the ability to collect data in large companies in their area of influence. Meanwhile, many young doctoral students and recently graduated PhDs in the US, Canada, and the European Union are well trained in state-of-the-art statistical techniques, but find it extremely difficult to collect data in their countries. The necessity of increasing the number of academic publications, not only about commitment, but also about management in general, around the reality of the organizations in Latin America demonstrates an imperative need for collaboration between all involved stakeholders: organizations, employees, supervisors, universities, students, and obviously researchers. The potential synergies exist and could be consolidated with a little bit of work and perseverance. The actors are ready, it is time to start.

REFERENCES

Allen, N.J. and Meyer, J.P. (1990). The measurement and antecedents of affective, continuance, and normative commitment to the organization. *Journal of Occupational Psychology*, *63*, 1–18.

Arciniega, L.M. and González, L. (2006). What is the influence of work values relative to other variables in the development of organizational commitment? *Revista de Psicología Social*, *21*(1), 35–50.

Arciniega, L.M. and González, L. (2012). Exploring the flanks of loyalty: analyzing the structure and meaning of the normative dimension of organizational commitment. *Revista de Psicología Social*, *27*(3), 273–285.

Arciniega, L.M. and Menon, S.T. (2013). The Power of Goal Internalization: Studying psychological empowerment in a Venezuelan plant. *International Journal of Human Resource Management*, *24*(15), 2948–2967.

Au, K.Y. (1999). Intra-cultural variation: evidence and implications for international business. *Journal of International Business Studies*, *30*(4), 799–812.

Aycan, Z. (2006). Paternalism: towards conceptual refinement and operationalization. In U. Kim, K.S. Yang, and K.K. Hwand (eds), *Indigenous and Cultural Psychology: Understanding People in Context* (pp. 445–466). New York: Springer Science.

Aycan, Z., Kanungo, R.N., Mendonca, M.,Yu, K., Deller, J., Stahl, G. and Khursid, A. (2000). Impact of culture on human resource management practices: a ten country comparison. *Applied Psychology: An International Review*, *49*(1), 192–220.

Barresi, M. (2014). La percepción de la satisfacción con la comunicación y sus implicancias en el compromiso organizacional en la Argentina. Un estudio de impacto en dos grandes organizaciones multinacionales: Carrefour y DIA. Unpublished doctoral dissertation. Universidad Austral, Buenos Aires, Argentina.

Betanzos Dias, N., Andrade Palos, P., and Paz Rodríguez, F. (2006). Compromiso organizacional en una muestra de trabajadores mexicanos (Dimensions of organizational commitment among Mexican workers). *Revista de Psicología del Trabajo y de las Organizaciones*, *22*(1), 25–43.

Carl, D., Gupta, V., and Javidan, M. (2004). Power distance. In R.J. House., P.J. Hanges, M. Javidan, P.W. Dorfmann, and V. Gupta (eds), *Culture, Leadership and Organizations: The GLOBE Study of 62 Societies* (pp. 513–563). Thousand Oaks, CA: Sage.

Casper, W.J., Eby, L.T., Bordeaux, C., Lockwood, A., and Lambert, D. (2007). A review of research methods in IO/OB work–family research. *Journal of Applied Psychology*, *92*(1), 28–43.

Casper, W.J., Harris, C., Taylor-Bianco, A., and Wayne, J.H. (2011). Work–family conflict, perceived supervisor support and organizational commitment among Brazilian professionals. *Journal of Vocational Behavior*, *79*(3), 640–652.

CIA (2015). *Central Intelligence Agency: The World Factbook*. https://www.cia.gov/library/publications/the-world-factbook/.

De Clercq, D. and Rius, I.B. (2007). Organizational commitment in Mexican small and medium-sized firms: the role of work status, organizational climate and entrepreneurial orientation. *Journal of Small Business Management*, *45*(4), 467–490.

Freedom House (2015). Harsh laws and violence drive global decline: freedom of press 2015. https://freedomhouse.org/article/freedom-press-2015-harsh-laws-and-violence-drive-global-decline.

Hofstede, G., Hofstede, G.J., and Minkov, M. (2005). *Cultures and Organizations: Software of the Mind*. New York: McGraw-Hill.

House, R.J., Hanges, P.J., Javidan, M., Dorfmann, P.W. and Gupta, V. (2004). *Culture, Leadership and Organizations: The GLOBE Study of 62 Societies*. Thousand Oaks, CA: Sage.

Lieberman, L. (2014). The impact of a paternalistic style of management and delegation of authority on job satisfaction and organizational commitment in Chile and the US. *Innovar*, *24*(53), 187–196.

Martinez, P.G. (2005). Paternalism as a positive form of leadership in the Latin American context: Leader benevolence, decision making control and human resource management practices. In M. Elvira and A. Davila (eds), *Managing Human Resources in Latin America: An Agenda for International Leaders* (pp. 75–93). Oxford: Routledge.

Meyer, J.P. and Allen, N.J. (1984).Testing the 'side-bet theory' of organizational commitment: some methodological considerations. *Journal of Applied Psychology*, *69*(3), 372–378.

Meyer, J.P. and Allen, N.J. (1997). *Commitment in the Workplace: Theory, Research, and Application*. Thousand Oaks, CA: Sage.

Meyer, J.P., Allen, N.J. and Smith, C.A. (1993). Commitment to organizations and occupations: extension and test of a three-component conceptualization. *Journal of Applied Psychology*, *78*(4), 538–551.

Meyer, J.P., Stanley, D.J., Herscovitch, L., and Topolnytsky, L. (2002). Affective, continuance, and normative commitment to the organization: a meta-analysis of antecedents, correlates and consequences. *Journal of Vocational Behavior*, *61*(1), 20–52.

Nicholls-Nixon, C.L., Davila Castilla, J.A., Sanchez Garcia, J., and Rivera Pesquera, M. (2011). Latin America Management research: review, synthesis, and extension. *Journal of Management*, *37*(4), 1178–1227.

OECD (2001). Reading for change: performance and engagement across countries, results from PISA 2000. http://www.keepeek.com/Digital-Asset-Management/oecd/education/reading-for-change-performance-and-engagement-across-countries_9789264099289-en#page1.

Pellegrini, E.K., Scandura, T.A., and Jayaraman, V. (2010). Cross-cultural generalizability of paternalistic leadership: an expansion of Leader-Member Exchange theory. *Group and Organization Management*, *35*(4), 391–420.

Sa Abreu, M.C., Cunha, M.C., and Reboucas, S.M.P. (2013). Effects of personal characteristics on organizational commitment: evidence from Brazil's oil and gas industry. *International Journal of Human Resource Management*, *24*(20), 3831–3852.

Tung, R.L. (2008). The cross-cultural research imperative: the need to balance cross-national and intra-national diversity. *Journal of International Business Studies*, *39*(1), 41–46.

Whyte, W.F. (1961). *Men at Work*. Homewood, IL: Dorsey Press.

World Values Survey (2015). *Online Data Analysis*. Data file and code book. http://www.worldvaluessurvey.org/WVSOnline.jsp.

PART VII

METHODOLOGICAL ISSUES

32. A contemporary update on testing for measurement equivalence and invariance
Robert J. Vandenberg and Neil A. Morelli

For many commitment researchers, answering substantive research questions often requires very different study designs: studies where groups are compared (e.g., Stanley et al., 2013), where commitment is collected across time to evaluate potential change (e.g., Bentein et al., 2005), or where a person-centered approach is applied to identify commitment profiles (Meyer et al., 2013). But what do each of these studies have in common? They must all make the assumption that their measurements are invariant or equivalent across groups or time periods. Measurement equivalence/invariance (ME/I) is the assumption that the measurement properties of commitment scales are stable (that is, invariant or equivalent) between the groups, at the various points of repeated measurement, or among the commitment profiles emerging between commitment scales applied to different samples. ME/I is a critical assumption because if it cannot be met, the researcher may not be able to unambiguously interpret the findings of conceptual interest, as a lack of invariance implies that the measures have different meanings between groups, across time, or within the profiles (Vandenberg and Lance, 2000).

Given the importance of testing the ME/I assumption, especially due to the high number of group comparison and longitudinal study designs employed in commitment research, we would direct readers to the ME/I steps articulated in Vandenberg and Lance (2000), which has been cited nearly 3000 times according to Google Scholar (as of 30 June 2015; not excluding self-citations). However, while briefly summarizing the Vandenberg and Lance (2000) steps and applying them to a commitment literature example would have been selfishly convenient for the first author, we firmly believe that it is more helpful to commitment researchers for us to ask the following questions. In light of the wide-spread application of ME/I testing over the last 15 years, what has been learned? Are the steps as originally articulated in Vandenberg and Lance (2000) still applicable? What aspects of the ME/I testing process need modification in light of the accumulated evidence, and what should researchers be alert to in undertaking that testing process? By asking these questions we are not suggesting that the ME/I assumption is not a concern, and therefore that a commitment researcher no longer needs to test it. It is still very much a concern. Instead, our point is that there may be some modifications to the steps as originally proposed by Vandenberg and Lance (2000), and that there may be other options to consider when undertaking ME/I analyses. The purposes of this chapter, therefore, are to address the above questions by evaluating the accumulated ME/I evidence, and, as articulated in Aguinis and Vandenberg (2014), to address some methodological and analytical ME/I issues before the collection of data.

We first address whether or not all of the steps as articulated by Vandenberg and Lance (2000) are required to evaluate the stability of the measures' properties. Evidence strongly suggests only two of the original nine steps are needed to address stability, whereas the others depend on the researcher's conceptual goals for collecting data in the first place. We illustrate this recommendation using an empirical example that assumes the conceptual goal of the researcher is to test group mean differences between the latent commitment constructs.

Next, we discuss an issue rarely addressed in ME/I tests: the potential biasing effects of selecting the referent indicators in the confirmatory factor analysis (CFA) measurement models that in reality, and often unknown to the researcher, are not invariant between the groups. Failing to have invariant referent indicators negatively impacts the unambiguous interpretation of the results from the ME/I tests. Finally, we acknowledge that although Vandenberg and Lance (2000) took a CFA approach to testing ME/I, item response theory (IRT) has emerged over the last 15 years as an alternative analytical approach. Consequently, we provide an overview of IRT and its relative advantages and disadvantages compared to CFA for the commitment researcher who needs to choose the method most applicable to their research question and data. Space constraints limit the amount of detail we can include in each section. Therefore, we will provide key references to advanced treatments of each theme.

THE NECESSARY STEPS FOR ME/I TESTING

We strongly encourage interested readers to review the rationale and full explanation of each step originally published in Vandenberg and Lance (2000), but for convenience's sake we have provided the steps they identified via an extensive literature review. Based on that review, and as directly quoted from Vandenberg and Lance (2000, pp. 12–13), these steps are:

(a) An omnibus test of the equality of covariance matrices across groups or within a group across time, that is, a test of the null hypothesis of invariant covariance matrices (i.e., $\Sigma^g = \Sigma^{g'}$), where g and g' indicate different groups.

(b) A test of 'configural invariance,' that is, a test of a 'weak factorial invariance' null hypothesis (Horn & McArdle, 1992) in which the same pattern of fixed and free factor loadings is specified for each group. *Configural invariance must be established in order for all subsequent tests to be meaningful.*

(c) A test of 'metric invariance' (Horn & McArdle, 1992) or a test of a strong factorial invariance null hypothesis that factor loadings for like items are invariant across groups (i.e., $\Lambda^g = \Lambda^{g'}$). *(At least partial) metric invariance must be established in order for subsequent tests to be meaningful.*

(d) A test of 'scalar invariance' (Meredith, 1993; Steenkamp & Baumgartner, 1998) or a test of the null hypothesis that intercepts of like items' regressions on the latent variable(s) are invariant across groups ($\tau^g = \tau^{g'}$).

(e) A test of the null hypothesis that like items' unique variances are invariant across groups (i.e., $\Theta^g = \Theta^{g'}$). Tests (c) through (e) follow the same sequence as that recommended by Gulliksen and Wilks (1950) for tests of homogeneity of regression models across groups and should be regarded as being similarly sequential, so that tests of scalar invariance should be conducted only if (at least partial) metric invariance is established, and tests of invariant uniquenesses should proceed only if (at least partial) metric and scalar invariance has been established first.

(f) A test of the null hypothesis that factor variances are invariant across groups (i.e., $\Phi_j^g = \Phi_j^{g'}$). This was sometimes treated as a complement to Test (c), in which differences in factor variances were interpreted as reflecting group differences in the calibration of true scores (e.g., Schaubroeck & Green, 1989; Schmitt, 1982; Vandenberg & Self, 1993).

(g) A test of the null hypothesis that factor covariances are invariant across groups (i.e., $\Phi_{jj'}{}^{'g} = \Phi_{jj'}{}^{'g'}$). This was sometimes treated as a complement to Test (b), in which differences in factor covariances were interpreted as reflecting differences in conceptual associations among the true scores (e.g., Schmitt, 1982). Often, this and test (f) were combined in an omnibus test of the equality of the latent variables' variance/covariance matrices across groups (i.e., $\Phi^g = \Phi^{g'}$).

(h) A test of the null hypothesis of invariant factor means across groups or within a group across time (i.e., $\Phi^g = \Phi^{g'}$) which often was invoked as a way to test for differences between groups in levels on the construct of interest.

(i) Other, more specific tests that were discussed by only one or a few of the sources reviewed.

What follows is a review and update to the steps above. The articles from Ployhart and Oswald (2004), and Schmitt and Ali (2015) largely influenced this update. Therefore, we strongly recommend that the interested reader consult these resources for the logic and details underlying the following statements.

While Vandenberg and Lance (2000) did not directly state the following, it was certainly implied that to fully assess the measures' properties, all of the ME/I tests from the comparisons of the covariance matrices to the latent means should be undertaken (steps a through h). Schmitt and Kuljanin's (2008) review affirmed this unwritten implication. Specifically, they reviewed the research literature in a manner quite similar to the Vandenberg and Lance (2000) review, but limited it to 75 studies using ME/I testing procedures published after the year 2000. In summary, Schmitt and Kuljanin (2008) reported greater percentages across the board for most of the a though h invariance tests than what was originally reported in Vandenberg and Lance (2000). This finding was particularly true of the structural tests (that is, latent variances, latent means, and so on). The conclusion, therefore, was that the Vandenberg and Lance (2000) article was leading researchers to perform most of the invariance tests to draw conclusions about the quality of their studies' measures.

However, even as early as 2004, Ployhart and Oswald argued that undertaking the ME/I steps was really dependent upon the 'end game' or conceptual reasons for collecting the data from the groups in the first place. Specifically, the exact aim of their article was extending the covariance structure analysis (CSA) approach into testing for mean differences (conceptually expected differences) between the groups using the latent means and not the observed means (means and covariance structure analysis, MACS). Ployhart and Oswald (2004) noted five advantages of testing for mean differences this way, instead of employing a standard analysis of variance (ANOVA). First, all of the parameters are estimated simultaneously with a MACS, which permits the testing of conceptually justified alternative models (see Vandenberg and Scarpello, 1990, for an example). Such model testing is impossible using ANOVA. The second advantage is that MACS tests the latent mean differences disattenuated from measurement error (Ployhart and Oswald, 2004). Again, ANOVA cannot do this. Third, while ANOVA requires assumptions of variance homogeneity for between groups tests and sphericity for repeated measures tests, no such assumptions are required in the MACS approach (those assumptions can be modeled or accounted for if necessary). The fourth advantage with MACS is that the quality (that is, equivalence or invariance) of the measures can be evaluated using some ME/I procedures before completing the test of latent mean differences (Ployhart and Oswald, 2004). Finally, partial invariance strategies may also be used to reduce the biasing effects due to having some items that are truly not invariant in the set (Ployhart and Oswald, 2004).

Table 32.1   Time 1 affective commitment

Test	Chi-sq. – d.f.	CFI	Delta Chi-sq. – d.f. and Delta CFI
Configural	21.89 – 18	.99	Excellent Fit
Metric	24.33 – 23	.99	2.44 – 5 (nonsig.) and .00
Uniqueness	29.72 – 29	1.0	5.39 – 6 (nonsig.) and .00
Scalar Invariance	487.86 – 35	.79	na
Means Different	32.65 – 34	1.0	Could compare to Uniqueness 2.93 – 5 and .00
Factor Variance*	38.02 – 35	.99	5.55 – 1 and -.01

Once more, the ANOVA or any other general linear modeling does not have the latter capabilities.

The fourth advantage is the most pertinent to our discussion of what ME/I tests are really needed to draw conclusions about the quality of the properties underlying a given measure. Specifically, while Ployhart and Oswald (2004) do not state this directly, it can be implied by their MACS process that the only ME/I tests relevant to evaluating the measure's or measures' quality between the groups are the configural and metric invariance tests (see Table 2, pp. 36–37, and the discussion of that table). Indeed, they do not even include the tests of equal covariance matrices or of equal latent variable covariance in their proposed testing sequence (Vandenberg and Lance, 2000 tests a and g, above) leading up to testing for conceptually expected differences in latent means. While they include the other invariance tests, they do so only because they are integral to the MACS process for testing latent mean differences. That is, they were not included to evaluate the quality of the measures' properties per Vandenberg and Lance's (2000) original reasoning.

We illustrate Ployhart and Oswald's (2004) process in Table 32.1. The sample for this illustration was two groups of employees, one group who stated, 'Yes, I am currently searching for another job outside of this organization', and another who stated 'No, I am not currently searching for another job outside of this organization'. These employees were measured on the Meyer and Allen (1991) affective commitment scale, and the general hypothesis is that the latent means of affective commitment should statistically differ between the two groups.

In brief, the first two rows of Table 32.1 indicate that there was strong support for both configural and metric invariance. Per Vandenberg and Lance (2000), therefore, we can be confident that the two groups were using the same cognitive frame of reference (that is, configural invariance) when completing the commitment items, and they were anchoring the items to the latent variables in the same degree (that is, metric invariance). We will return to this point below, but it was uncertain to us from the Ployhart and Oswald (2004) article what role the test for the invariance of the uniqueness terms plays in the MACS procedure. However, it is worth noting that Schmitt and Kuljanin (2008) stated four years later that when testing for latent mean differences, the uniqueness invariance test is irrelevant. In any event, this question is moot in the current example because, as seen in Table 32.1, the invariance of the uniqueness terms was supported.

The scalar invariance test plays a vital part in the test for latent mean differences using the MACS approach. Namely, if the two groups truly differ in affective commitment, then those differences should be seen at the item level. If we constrain the scalar (the item intercepts or $\tau^g = \tau^{g'}$) to be invariant and in reality they are not, then model fit should be extremely poor. As seen in Table 32.1, this is exactly what happened. However, this is a good thing. Page constraints prevent a full discussion as to why the following happens (see Bollen, 1989; Cheung and Rensvold, 1999; Ployhart and Oswald, 2004), but imposing invariance constraints between the items intercepts (scalars) are needed in order to identify the latent means and the differences between them. The latent means are fixed to zero during the scalar invariance test. During the next step, one of the latent means in one group will remain fixed to zero (the 'yes' group), but the latent mean of the other group (the 'no' group) will be freely estimated. The observed parameter of the freely estimated latent mean is actually the difference between the two latent means. Since we are allowing the differences to emerge at this level, model fit should recover because the groups truly differ from one another (Ployhart and Oswald, 2004). As seen in Table 32.1, this is exactly what happened. Most importantly, the freely estimated latent mean had a *t*-value of 2.18 (p < .0001) indicating that the 'no' group was significantly greater than the 'yes' group on affective commitment. While a similar conclusion would have probably been reached with an ANOVA, we would have less confidence in that outcome given the advantages to the MACS approach specified by Ployhart and Oswald (2004). Furthermore, there have been cases where an ANOVA supported significant differences but the MACS approach did not (e.g., Vandenberg and Self, 1993). Finally, one can evaluate whether the assumption of homogeneity is supported; this is done by placing an invariance constraint between the factor variances (Ployhart and Oswald, 2004). If model fit is poor, then heterogeneity is supported. If model fit is good, as it was in this example, then homogeneity may be assumed.

In sum, there were two overall goals for reviewing the Ployhart and Oswald (2004) article. The first was to illustrate to commitment researchers that mean group comparisons can be completed through a structural equation modeling (SEM) framework, with some clear advantages for doing so. The second was to illustrate that not all of the ME/I tests are needed to evaluate the quality of the measures. In the current case, only the configural and metric invariance tests were addressing the latter, while the other ME/I tests either had no function or had a very specific role in the MACS approach for testing latent mean differences.

The article by Schmitt and Ali (2015) also systematically addressed the question concerning what ME/I tests are really needed to evaluate quality. However, their approach to the question focused on practical significance rather than statistical significance: how much invariance is needed before the parameter estimates are adversely impacted (that is, something was statistically significant before the ME/I tests and is not after it)? Configural invariance was not part of this question. It was not included because Schmitt and Ali (2015) reaffirmed the serious implications of not supporting configural invariance as stated by Vandenberg and Lance (2000). Namely, if it is not statistically supported, then this means that the groups were using a different conceptual frame of reference to respond to the same set of items, and therefore that measure cannot be used to compare and contrast the groups in any meaningful substantive manner.

As to the other tests, and what they mean by the practical significance of supporting or not supporting them, the reader is referred to Schmitt and Ali (2015, p. 343, Table 16.1) for a summary of their recommendations. However, their overall conclusion was that there would need to be a strong indication of a lack of invariance (statistical significance) before the parameter estimates, and the substantive conclusions made from them, are impacted on a practical level. For example, their conservative advice for metric invariance is that valid comparisons can be made if at least half the items are invariant (Schmitt and Ali, 2015). They provide similar advice for some of the other invariance tests and they also differentiate between comparing groups whose language is the same vs. comparisons with measures translated into different languages. The bottom line, as quoted from Schmitt and Ali (2015, p. 343), is that:

> Researchers should continue to analyze responses to their measures for a lack of invariance, but they should also focus on the degree to which findings of a lack of invariance are interpretable, have relevance for decisions that are made using the instrument, and the evaluation of substantive hypotheses regarding relationships among variables.

Our point here is that three of the original ME/I tests from Vandenberg and Lance (2000) may be unnecessary. First, testing the invariance of the covariance matrix (step a, at the start of the chapter) is not needed. As Schmitt and Kuljanin (2008) report, this step is hardly ever undertaken. This finding may indicate that many researchers already understand that this step is not really an omnibus test of ME/I as originally thought by Vandenberg and Lance (2000). With one exception, a similar conclusion may be drawn with the invariance test for item uniqueness terms (step e, above). As stated by Schmitt and Kuljanin (2008, p. 214), 'If a researcher has specific hypotheses about item uniquenesses or reliability (in the presence of latent factor invariance), this test would be appropriate. Otherwise it seems superfluous and is not required in most or all cases.' The third step worth ignoring is the test of invariance of factor covariances between groups (step g). As Schmitt and Kuljanin (2008) also noted, this step seems to be undertaken under the belief it needs to be established before testing for latent mean differences. On the contrary, invariance of the factor covariances does not need to be established, and therefore there is some question as to what it really gains us. Likewise, Schmitt and Ali (2015) do not consider it in their recommendations for practical significance.

Despite our suggested changes to Vandenberg and Lance's (2000) proposed ME/I test sequence, what remains clear from the literature is that the tests for configural (step b) and metric (step c) invariance are still a requirement to evaluate the quality of a set of measures between groups and/or across time within a group. Therefore, these tests remain critical even though there may not be as much practical impact for the lack of metric invariance as originally thought (Schmitt and Ali, 2015). Another observation that is very clear from the literature is that tests for scalar invariance (step d) and factor variance invariance (step f) are really dependent upon the research goal behind collecting the data. We used Ployhart and Oswald (2004) as a means to illustrate the latter.

One final point of divergence from Vandenberg and Lance's (2000) original prescription for ME/I testing is worth noting. Recent reviews such as that by Schmitt and Kuljanin (2008) have discovered a general increase in the frequency of partial invariance testing, especially when items are found not to be equivalent at the metric level. Although Vandenberg and Lance (2000) were cautious about atheoretical partial invariance testing, they still recommended that partial invariance testing be conducted as a standard matter of course. Instead, we find the situations and opportunities for partial invariance testing to be fewer than the Vandenberg and Lance testing sequence suggests (for example, testing for partial invariance is inappropriate when only composite scores are of substantive interest). We have also found that partial invariance testing, conducted at the item level, is extremely sensitive to a lack of invariance for the item selected as the reference indicator (Vandenberg, 2002). This phenomenon is explained in greater detail in the following section. For these reasons, we generally recommend that partial invariance testing be carefully conducted in specific circumstances, or not at all.

REFERENCE INDICATOR OR STANDARDIZATION PROBLEM

It is common knowledge that one indicator in a multi-item measure must be fixed to 1 when specifying that measure's factor model within a SEM modeling framework (the standardization procedure). This item is the reference indicator and serves to identify the factor model underlying a given measure. Under most circumstances, the selection of the reference indicator from a set of items belonging to the same latent variable is arbitrary (see Maruyama, 1997, pp. 181–184, as to why this is the case). However, undertaking ME/I tests between two or more groups is one circumstance where the reference indicator selection should be purposeful and planned (Johnson et al., 2009; Cheung and Lau, 2012; Rensvold and Cheung, 2001). When the same reference indicators are selected and fixed to 1 in each group, there is an assumption that those indicators are invariant, particularly metrically invariant. Recall that an outcome of metric invariance testing is to identify the problem items (not invariant) in a measure or set of measures, and forming a set of usable items (invariant) from the remainder (Rensvold and Cheung, 2001). As explained below, however, there are potentially serious problems to accomplishing the latter goal when the reference indicators are truly not metrically invariant, but this is unknown to the researcher – the typical case.

Ironically, Rensvold and Cheung (2001, p. 26) stated nearly 15 years ago that, 'we first described this problem and proposed a solution two years ago (Cheung & Rensvold, 1999; Rensvold & Cheung, 1998). It has attracted little attention to date, despite its obvious implications for a large number of published studies'. The irony underlying this quote is that little has changed 15 years later. While hardly scientific, we arbitrarily selected about 25 studies in the 2011–2014 timeframe from the more than 2800 Vandenberg and Lance (2000) citations. Not a single one addressed the reference indicator or standardization problem, as it is known, when undertaking the ME/I tests. Johnson et al.'s (2009) systematic literature review made the same observation.

Commitment researchers, particularly those using translated versions of measures in cross-cultural studies, should be very mindful of the standardization problem. Assuming configural invariance is supported, it is highly unlikely that full or scale-level metric invariance will be supported (see the Schmitt and Kuljanin, 2008, review on this issue, particularly material starting at the bottom of p. 215). Assuming that is the case, the researcher will engage subsequently in some partial or item-level invariance tests to identify which item or items contributed to the lack of scale-level invariance (Cheung and Rensvold, 1999; Vandenberg and Lance, 2000). As noted above, the goal for doing so is to identify a usable set of items, and it is here that the standardization problem may lead to wrong conclusions regarding the usability of a measure's items. To understand the problem, one needs to know how the reference indicator operates on the estimation of the factor load-ings for the other (non-reference) items underlying a given measure.

As explained by Johnson et al. (2009; see also Cheung and Rensvold, 1999, Appendix B; and Yoon and Millsap, 2007, pp. 440–441), the reference indicator defines the scaling constant and, as such, the magnitudes of the factor loadings for the other items are determined by that constant. Specifically, although the reference indicator is constrained to the value of 1, let us assume that its 'real' underlying standardized factor loading is .6 (λ_{RI}). Due to the constraint, all of the other factor loadings associated with items of the same measure are rescaled relative to the reference indicator by a magnitude of $1/\lambda_{RI}$ (the scaling constant), or in this example 1/.6 which is 1.67 (Johnson et al., 2009). Assuming the population factor loading for the second item in the measure is .7, the estimated factor loading for it will be 1.67*.7, or 1.17. Likewise, if the third item has a population loading of .5, its estimated loading will be .835.

Let us also assume that the example values above are for a three-item measure of com-mitment given to a group of employees of a United States (US)-based firm. The same commitment measure is then translated into German and administered to the firm's German affiliate. Assuming there is a conceptual reason for wanting to compare the two groups on commitment, the researcher first undertakes the series of ME/I tests, and to be consistent, uses the same reference indicator. As noted previously, it is presumed (but untested) by most researchers that the factor loading of the reference indicators are invari-ant to one another. If the loadings are truly invariant, then there is no problem. However, if they are truly not invariant, false conclusions concerning the invariance status of the other items may be drawn (that is, the standardization problem). Using the same values above but with the German λ_{RI} equaling .8, the scaling constant in this case is 1.25. This means the estimated factor loadings of the other two items will be .875 and .625, respec-tively. This is on average a 25 percent decrease from the original scaling constant. The scale-level or overall test for metric invariance would probably statistically support a lack of invariance when in reality the remaining two items are invariant. Further, undertaking the subsequent partial metric invariance step would probably support that one or both of the remaining items are not invariant. To illustrate the problem even further, instead of a population loading of .5 for the third item above, let us assume it is .667. Its esti-mated loading in the German sample will be .835 – the same estimate for the American sample. Again, while the overall metric invariance test will support a lack of invariance, the partial invariance test will probably identify the second item, and not the third item, as the source for the lack of invariance. The reality, though, is that the opposite is true.

It should be noted that Johnson et al. (2009) found that it is not the overall or scale-level test of metric invariance that is negatively impacted by selecting a reference indicator that is truly not invariant. It is the partial or item-level invariance testing that is adversely impacted. Specifically, and as illustrated in the examples above, Johnson et al. (2009) pointed out that the overall test correctly identifies that there is a lack of invariance when it is present among the items. However, the overall test does not identify the source for the lack of invariance. Those sources are uncovered through the partial or item-level invari-ance testing process, and it is at this level that false conclusions may be drawn about the item set's invariance status when the reference indicator is truly not invariant.

The standardization problem is a very serious issue and one that needs to be addressed by researchers taking the time to identify reference indicators within each measure that are truly invariant between the groups. However, this is much easier stated than it is to actually do. As far as the authors know, only two procedures have been proposed to find invariant reference indicators. Yoon and Millsap (2007) evaluated the simpler procedure. The reader is encouraged to read their full article for the details and underlying logic. In summary, though, the procedure includes specification searches among the modification indices in a model where the factor variance of a measure in one group is fixed to one, but is freely estimated in the other group(s). Further, the factor loadings are then constrained equal between the groups. The presumption is that large modification indices will point out items that are not invariant. In their evaluation, Yoon and Millsap (2007) found the procedure to be fairly accurate when there were a relatively small number of not-invariant items in the total item set, the differences were relatively large, and the sample size was also large. However, the procedure was fairly inaccurate in terms of identifying truly invariant items under other less than optimal conditions. Our conclusion is that while simple, it is a fairly weak procedure overall, and should not be used in identifying invariant reference indicators.

The second, more difficult procedure was first proposed by Rensvold and Cheung (1998; see also Cheung and Rensvold, 1999; Rensvold and Cheung, 2001). This procedure is called the factor-ratio test. Details of the procedure may be found in the latter sources, but in summary, the factor-ratio test systematically examines all possible combinations of referents and arguments within each group. As explained in the above sources, the referent is the item chosen as the reference indicator and the argument is the item in the measure that is being tested for metric invariance between the groups. Each factor ratio is evaluated using a chi-square difference test. The end result of the procedure is a set of items from a given measure that are invariant between groups. The reference indicator is selected from one of these items in each group so that the scaling constant is the same.

As reviewed by Yoon and Millsap (2007), historically there have been three major criticisms of the factor-ratio test. The first criticism is perhaps the most striking in that up until 2007 no simulation work had been performed to show how accurately the factor-ratio test procedure worked. Second, the test was criticized as being too tedious due to there being $p*(p-1)/2$ factor ratios. For a three-item measure, there are three factor ratios, but for a ten-item measure, the number is 45 (Yoon and Millsap, 2007). The number of factor ratios expands greatly depending on the number of dimensions in the model, and the number of items per dimension. The third criticism was that each test had to be calculated by hand as there were no known software packages that could calculate the tests in a convenient manner. However, each of these criticisms has been recently addressed.

To address the first criticism, French and Finch (2008) evaluated the accuracy of the factor-ratio test via a simulation in which they varied: (1) number of factors and items per factor; (2) sample sizes; and (3) number of not-invariant items per factor. In the end, the results were very supportive of Cheung and Rensvold's factor-ratio test; that is, the test's ability to detect items that are not invariant was quite strong across most conditions. However, that detection rate was negatively influenced by model complexity, and higher proportions of not-invariant items in a given item set. In other words, the factor-ratio test is less effective when the number of variables and items per variable are high (complex models), and when a given measure is highly contaminated with not-invariant items (French and Finch, 2008).

With respect to the second and third criticisms, Cheung and Lau (2012) addressed them by specifying all of the factor ratios (the $p*(p-1)/2$ as defined above) at once, and simultaneously completing all of the tests on them using the Mplus SEM software package (Muthén and Muthén, 1998–2012). They used a fairly complex measurement model to demonstrate how to do so. While the concern here is identifying a truly invariant referent indicator in the context of metric invariance testing, Cheung and Lau (2012) also extended the factor ratio tests beyond the latter to many of the other forms of invariance testing. Perhaps the most important aspect of the article, practically speaking, is that the authors provide all of the Mplus syntax in the article's appendices. Therefore, the interested researcher should be able to adapt their syntax for their own ME/I purposes. Our closing point in this section is that Cheung and Lau (2012) removed a great deal of the tediousness in undertaking the factor-ratio procedure for identifying a truly invariant set of indicators. Consequently, the means exist in turn to avoid the standardization problem.

IRT AND CFA APPROACHES

The prudent commitment researcher following the recommendation that ME/I tests of their measurement scales should be conducted to determine the quality of their measure(s) or answer substantive questions will likely wonder about the differences between a CFA-based approach, like the one described in Vandenberg and Lance (2000), or an IRT-based approach. To help orient the intrepid commitment researcher in this situation, we have provided a brief summary of the Tay et al. (2014) article. Their article provides the most up-to-date comparison of the IRT and CFA approaches to ME/I evaluation (see also Meade and Lautenschlager, 2004). In brief, as noted in Vandenberg and Lance (2000), the CFA approach assumes that the observed score (for example, a response to one item of a multi-item commitment measure) is a linear combination of a latent variable (the unobserved commitment construct), a factor loading (the relationship to the latent variable), a tau or intercept value (that value of the observed variable when the latent variable is at zero), and a error-uniqueness term (a residual value that is in part random/error and in part systematic/unique). An evaluation of the invariance of each of the latter parameters is basically an evaluation of the measure's equivalence and is represented by steps b through e above. Structural equivalence is undertaken by evaluating the invariance of the latent factor variances, the covariance between latent factors (assuming more than one scale is being evaluated), and the latent means (steps f–h above). Recall, once more (and ignoring the suggestion above that configural and metric invariance tests are all that is needed to evaluate measurement quality) that the assumption with the CFA approach as originally proposed by Vandenberg and Lance (2000) was that a researcher has conceptual reasons to compare two or more groups for hypothesis testing purposes, but before doing so wishes to establish that there is measurement and structural equivalence between the groups at the scale level (Vandenberg and Lance, 2000).

In contrast, the IRT approach grew out of a testing background (Meade and Lautenschlager, 2004; Schmitt and Kuljanin, 2008; Tay et al., 2014). That is, the goal was to detect the lack of ME/I among items in a test bank with the assumption that a not-equivalent test item (differential item functioning, DIF) is indicative of a test bias between the groups on that item, but not necessarily the test as a whole (Tay et al., 2014).

The cumulative impact of DIF across a set of test items could impact observed mean differences between groups on the test or what is known as differential test functioning (DTF). Regardless of its history in testing, it was recognized early on that the IRT approach could be used to evaluate the equivalence of other 'non-test' measures such as commitment (Meade and Lautenschlager, 2004). Unlike CFA, IRT assumes a log-linear relationship (logistic) of items to the underlying latent trait, and that each relationship may be described by a set of item parameters that are unique to each item (Meade and Lautenschlager, 2004; Tay et al., 2014). Two parameters of particular importance are the discrimination parameter, or a parameter, and the item location, or b parameter. The a parameter is the IRT equivalent to the CFA factor loading, λ. Unlike λ, however, which represents a linear association of the observed score to the latent variable, the a parameter is the slope of the item characteristic curve (ICC) that determines the relationship between the observed and latent variables (Meade and Lautenschlager, 2004). The b parameter has also been referred to as the IRT equivalent to the CFA item intercept, τ. However, this comparison can be somewhat misleading. First, for polytomous items (such as commitment items with a five-point agree to disagree anchor), there is more than one b parameter. Essentially, the b parameters can be used to determine a particular item's category response function or the probability that a person at a given level of the latent variable will respond to that item with a given response (1, 2, 3, 4, or 5; Meade and Lautenschlager, 2004; Tay et al., 2014).

A major difference between the two approaches concerns specifying the source for the lack of invariance (Tay et al., 2014). Given that CFA tests are sequential, the researcher knows the exact basis for the lack of invariance (for example, metric, factor variances). In contrast, all item parameters within IRT are estimated simultaneously, and therefore the concern is simply whether or not there is item equivalence. Another major difference between the two approaches is in the number of measures that can be compared. Within CFA, multiple measures may be compared at once, but only a single measure or dimension is typically evaluated within IRT (Tay et al., 2014). Page constraints restrict detailing all of the similarities and differences between the two approaches, but the interested reader is referred to Tay et al. (2014, pp. 6–7, Table 2) where a direct comparison is made between the CFA steps and IRT. As noted there, for example, there is no IRT equivalent to testing the invariance of uniqueness terms and factor covariances. However, there are some similarities between the two approaches with respect to the remaining steps. Ultimately, commitment researchers are encouraged to consider both approaches, and indeed it has been suggested that both approaches should be undertaken when conducting any evaluation of ME/I (Meade and Lautenschlager, 2004).

CLOSING COMMENTS

Similar to Vandenberg and Lance (2000), the underlying theme of our review of the ME/I testing process was that the tests described above are intended to detect potential problems with chosen commitment measures to determine if they can be used in a substantive manner. While this 'quality test' will most likely remain the primary motivation for undertaking ME/I tests in the foreseeable future, we argue that commitment researchers could use these tests in a substantively meaningful manner. For example, assume a commitment researcher is interested in evaluating how commitment emerges over time; specifically, before one enters the organization to some point after the socialization stage is presumed to end. Because the individual is not employed at baseline, no conceptual frame of reference yet exists for what it is like to be committed to a given organization. Therefore, a test for configural invariance may fail at this point in time. In this case, though, it may be a desired outcome, not a nuisance. After the individual is employed, evidence for the emergence of a cognitive frame of reference for commitment would be testing for configural invariance at multiple points after employment, and supporting it at some time point. Further evidence may be supported by relatively small factor loadings when configural invariance is first supported, but the loadings grow in strength and stabilize at other measurement occasions. In other words, tests for metric invariance may fail across time at first, but then are supported later when a stable conceptual frame of reference for commitment develops. The Vandenberg and Self (1993) study demonstrates this hypothetical scenario to some degree.

Taking an IRT perspective, one may also expect the slope of the item characteristic curve (*a* parameter) determining the relationship between the commitment items and their underlying latent variables to strengthen across time as the person moves from being a newcomer to a fully functioning employee. Similarly, a particular commitment item's category response function (*b* parameter), or the probability that a person at a given level of the latent variable will respond to that item with a given response, will also change as the commitment conceptual frame-of-reference emerges.

In closing, the goal of this chapter was not to dismiss Vandenberg and Lance's (2000) general concern that ME/I assumptions should be examined. That concern is still quite important. Rather, the goal was to reshape their original recommendations as to which tests are most critical in light of the evidence accumulated over the last 15 years. If the concern is with the quality of the underlying properties of a measure (or measures), then only the tests for configural and metric invariance are needed. Some of the other tests are not needed at all; while the evaluation of the other tests is really dependent upon the conceptual goals for collecting the data in the first place. Finally, we also note that even the tests for configural and metric invariance from a CFA perspective, and for the *a* and *b* parameters in an IRT framework, may be used in substantively meaningful ways.

REFERENCES

Aguinis, H. and Vandenberg, R.J. (2014). An ounce of prevention is worth a pound of cure: Improving research quality before data collection. *Annual Review of Organizational Psychology and Organizational Behavior, 1*, 569–595.

Bentein, K., Vandenberg, R., Vandenberghe, C., and Stinglhamber, F. (2005). The role of change in the relationship between commitment and turnover: A latent growth modeling approach. *Journal of Applied Psychology, 90*, 468–482.

Bollen, K.A. (1989). *Structural Equations with Latent Variables*. New York: John Wiley.

Cheung, G.W. and Lau, R.S. (2012). A direct comparison approach for testing measurement invariance. *Organizational Research Methods, 15*, 167–198.

Cheung, G.W. and Rensvold, R.B. (1999). Testing factorial invariance across groups: A reconceptualization and proposed new method. *Journal of Management, 25*, 1–27.

French, B.F. and Finch, W.H. (2008). Multigroup confirmatory factor analysis: Locating the invariant referent sets. *Structural Equation Modeling, 15*, 96–113.

Gulliksen, H. and Wilks, S.S. (1950). Regression tests for several samples. *Psychometrika, 15*, 91–114.

Horn, J.L. and McArdle, J.J. (1992). A practical and theoretical guide to measurement invariance in aging research. *Experimental Aging Research*, *18*, 117–144.

Johnson, E.C., Meade, A.W., and DuVernet, A.M. (2009). The role of referent indicators in tests of measurement invariance. *Structural Equation Modeling*, *16*, 642–657.

Maruyama, G.M. (1997). *Basics of Structural Equation Modeling*. Thousand Oaks, CA: Sage.

Meade, A.W. and Lautenschlager, G. (2004). A comparison of item response theory and confirmatory factor analytic methodologies for establishing measurement equivalence/invariance. *Organizational Research Methods*, *7*, 361–388.

Meredith, W. (1993). Measurement invariance, factor analysis and factorial invariance. *Psychometrika*, *58*, 525–543.

Meyer, J.P. and Allen, N.J. (1991). A three-component conceptualization of organizational commitment. *Human Resource Management Review*, *1*, 64–89.

Meyer, J.P., Stanley, L.A., Vandenberg, R.J. (2013). A person-centered approach to the study of commitment. *Human Resources Management Review*, *23*, 190–202.

Muthén, L.K. and Muthén, B.O. (1998–2012). *Mplus User's Guide* (7th edition). Los Angeles, CA: Muthén & Muthén.

Ployhart, R.E. and Oswald, F.L. (2004). Applications of mean and covariance structure analysis: Integrating correlational and experimental approaches. *Organizational Research Methods*, *7*, 27–65.

Rensvold, R.B. and Cheung, G.W. (1998). Testing measurement models for factorial invariance: A systematic approach. *Educational and Psychological Measurement*, *58*, 1017–1034.

Rensvold, R.B. and Cheung, G.W. (2001). Testing for metric invariance using structural equation models: Solving the standardization problem. In C.A. Schriesheim and L.L. Neider (eds), *Research in Management: Vol. 1. Equivalence in Measurement* (pp. 21–50). Greenwich, CT: Information Age.

Schaubroeck, J. and Green, S.G. (1989). Confirmatory factor analytic procedures for assessing change during organizational entry. *Journal of Applied Psychology*, *74*, 892–900.

Schmitt, N. (1982). The use of analysis of covariance structures to assess beta and gamma change. *Multivariate Behavioral Research*, *17*, 343–358.

Schmitt, N. and Ali, A. (2015). The practical importance of measurement invariance. In C.E. Lance and R.J. Vandenberg (eds), *More Statistical and Methodological Myths and Urban Legends* (pp. 327–346). New York: Routledge.

Schmitt, N. and Kuljanin, G. (2008). Measurement invariance: Review of practice and implications. *Human Resource Management Review*, *18*, 210–222.

Stanley, L.A., Vandenberghe, C., Vandenberg, R.J., and Bentein, K. (2013). Commitment profiles and employee turnover. *Journal of Vocational Behavior*, *82*, 176–187.

Steenkamp, J.E.M. and Baumgartner, H. (1998). Assessing measurement invariance in cross national consumer research. *Journal of Consumer Research*, *25*, 78–90.

Tay, L., Meade, A.W., and Cao, M. (2014). An overview and practical guide to IRT measurement equivalence analysis. *Organizational Research Methods*, *17*, 1–44.

Vandenberg, R.J. (2002). Toward a further understanding of and improvement in measurement invariance methods and procedures. *Organizational Research Methods*, *5*, 139–158.

Vandenberg, R.J. and Lance, C.E. (2000). A review and synthesis of the measurement invariance literature: Suggestions, practices and recommendations for organizational research. *Organizational Research Methods*, *3*, 4–70.

Vandenberg, R.J. and Scarpello, V. (1990). The matching model: An examination of the processes underlying realistic job previews. *Journal of Applied Psychology*, *75*, 60–67.

Vandenberg, R.J. and Self, R.M. (1993). Assessing newcomers' changing commitment to the organization during the first 6 months of work. *Journal of Applied Psychology*, *78*, 557–568.

Yoon, M. and Millsap, R.E. (2007). Detecting violations of factorial invariance using data-based specification searches: A Monte Carlo study. *Structural Equation Modeling*, *14*, 435–463.

33. Tracking change in commitment over time: the latent growth modeling approach

Kathleen Bentein

Whether commitment was conceptualized as an internal force that binds an individual to a target and/or to a course of action of relevance to that target, and experienced as a conscious 'mindset' of desire (affective commitment, AC), obligation (normative commitment, NC), or a perceived cost (continuance commitment, CC) (Meyer and Allen, 1991, 1997; Meyer and Herscovitch, 2001); as a psychological bond expressed by a dedication to and responsibility for a target (Klein et al., 2012); or strictly as an attitude defined by a combination of affect, cognition, and action readiness (Solinger et al., 2008), it has invariably been seen as likely to change over time under the influence of different categories of variables (for example, personal characteristics, work and socialization experiences). Further, commitment has been reported to have an impact, over time, on different consequences (for example, turnover, performance, organizational citizenship behaviors, employee health; for a review, see Meyer et al., 2002). Acknowledging that commitment is dynamic requires an appropriate method to capture change over time in commitment research. Within the current arsenal of statistical procedures available to researchers, latent growth modeling (LGM) has emerged as a powerful approach (Bollen and Curran, 2006; Chan, 1998; Duncan et al., 2006; Singer and Willett, 2003). Commitment researchers have begun to use this specific structural equation modeling application that models intra-individual change over time from data on longitudinally assessed variables.

This chapter reviews the commitment studies that have used the LGM approach to track intra-individual change in commitment and related variables, and outlines the preliminary insights of these studies. First, I will briefly present the LGM approach, along with its key features and principles, and provide interested readers with pertinent references.

THE LATENT GROWTH MODELING APPROACH

The LGM approach can be used to address a large variety of questions regarding the nature of change in a targeted variable (Chan and Schmitt, 2000). One set of questions focuses on the fundamental characteristics of intra-individual change over time in the targeted variable. They include: is there a non-zero change trajectory over time? What is the shape of this change trajectory (that is, linear or non-linear, increasing or decreasing)? And, is the change more or less rapid across time? A second set of questions pertains to inter-individual differences in the intra-individual change trajectory in the targeted variable over time, and to predictors, correlates, or consequences of these inter-individual differences. For instance: is the change more rapid for some individuals than for others? Is the change in one variable related to the change in another variable? And, are there measurable factors that would allow one to predict the rate of change? (Chan and Schmitt, 2000).

These two sets of questions refer to the two-level structure of LGM models, with level 1 corresponding to a test of intra-individual (or within-person) change; and level 2 a test of inter-individual (or between-person) differences in this intra-individual change. Willett and Sayer (1994, 1995) and Singer and Willett (2003) elegantly described how the multilevel model of change is mapped onto the general covariance structure analysis model. Without entering into these technical descriptions, I will present the LGM approach as a practical two-stage process. In the first stage, or the basic LGM model, an intra-individual trajectory of change is estimated based on repeated measures of the targeted variable taken on multiple occasions. In the second stage, or the augmented LGM model, additional variables (that is, time-invariant or time-variant) are incorporated in the previous LGM basic model as a predictor, correlate, or consequence of inter-individual differences in intra-individual change trajectory.

LGM models require repeated assessments of the targeted variable over time on the same sample of individuals. There should be at least three measurement waves (Bollen and Curran, 2006). The higher the number of waves, the greater the precision of the intra-individual trajectory estimates, and the greater the reliability for the measurement of change. With three measurement waves, one can estimate whether change is linear or not; while with five waves, one can test linear, quadratic, and cubic change, for example. Before estimating the intra-individual change trajectory of the targeted variable, it is also important to demonstrate, rather than simply assume, that the same construct was measured at each measurement time, and measured with the same precision, which corresponds to configural and metric invariances over time (see Chapter 32 in this volume for a complete discussion of measurement invariance).

Basic LGM Model

The goal of the basic (or unconditional) LGM model is to estimate an unobserved, or latent, trajectory from a set of repeated observed measures (Bollen and Curran, 2006). Basic LGM models are constructed as confirmatory factor analysis (CFA) models within the usual structural equation modeling framework, but latent factors are actually interpreted as chronometric (time) common factors representing individual differences over time rather than psychometric (measurement) common factors (McArdle, 1988).

As an illustration, in a linear model the two latent factors of the variable's change trajectory (also referred to as growth parameters) are the intercept and the slope. The intercept latent factor, labeled the Initial Status factor, contains information about the status of the variable at the start of the process, that is, the value of the variable at Time 1. The slope latent factor, labeled the Change factor, contains information about the rate of change of the variable over the time period of interest. The direction of change is indicated by the latent mean of the Change factor. A statistically significant positive value indicates an increase in the targeted variable across time, and a statistically significant negative value denotes a decrease in the variable. The latent variance of the Initial Status and Change factors provides information about inter-individual differences in intra-individual change (that is, true individual differences in the Initial Status and Change factors). Lastly, the covariance between the Initial Status and Change factors indicates how the status of the variable at the start of the process influences the rate of change of the variable over the time period of interest (Chan, 1998). Contrary to the usual CFA model, where the factor loadings are generally estimated, the LGM model fixes these loadings to specific a priori values. It is the choice of these loadings that determines the origin of the process and the shape of the change trajectory (Bollen and Curran, 2006).

Two alternative LGM model specifications are possible, depending on the operationalization of the focal variable (Lance et al., 2000). In first-order factor LGM models (FOF LGM models), the targeted variable is operationalized as a single composite variable (the observed mean of the variable) for each measurement time. In second-order factor LGM models (SOF LGM models), the targeted variable is modeled as a latent variable assessed by multiple indicators at each measurement occasion. There are several advantages of using a SOF LGM model rather than a FOF LGM model. Notably, the SOF can distinguish between disturbance variance due to the trajectory disturbance and the disturbance of the measurement item (Bollen and Curran, 2006). It also lets the researcher directly test the prerequisite assumption of measurement invariance (Chapter 32 in this volume). To determine an appropriate growth form of change trajectory that accurately describes intra-individual change over time in a targeted variable, alternate plausible basic LGM models are generally compared in nested model comparisons (Chan, 1998; Lance et al., 2000).

Augmented LGM Model

The basic LGM model is just the starting point for what can be achieved with the LGM approach; multiple extensions of this basic model exist. Even if all individuals in the sample share a common intra-individual trajectory of change for the targeted variable, the presence of inter-individual differences in the growth parameters (that is, significant variances of the Initial Status and Change factors) warrants a follow-up step in which this inter-individual heterogeneity is predicted by other variables. The first natural augmented LGM model can be estimated by incorporating time-invariant predictors of the growth parameters of the intra-individual change trajectory (Singer and Willett, 2003). This type of model allows one to test the hypothesis that the rate of change of the targeted variable is contingent on the values of the predictor.

A second classical augmented LGM model can be estimated by incorporating time-variant predictors of the growth parameters of the intra-individual change trajectory (Singer and Willett, 2003). This model is fitted by simply combining two basic LGM models, thereby allowing exploration of relationships among the two sets of individual growth parameters of these two variables (that is, Initial Status/Change/Quadratic factors from the two change trajectories).

Many other augmented LGM models exist, such as those modeling outcomes of the growth parameters of the intra-individual change trajectory (Lance et al., 2000), and those modeling intervening effects in which mediation processes are estimated (Pitariu and Ployhart, 2010). More recently, development of interaction LGM models that consider the interaction between the growth parameters of two time-variant predictors on the growth parameters of a time-variant outcome represents another important extension of the basic LGM model (Li et al., 2000; Wen et al., 2014).

The Multigroup LGM model (Bollen and Curran, 2006) lets researchers test whether trajectories of change in a targeted variable differ between two or more groups. In this approach, the growth parameters can be simultaneously, but separately, estimated for each group. This allows testing of group differences not only on the mean of growth parameters (Initial Status and Change factors, for example), but also on the variances and covariances of these parameters, and on the links between other variables and growth parameters.

Latent Class Growth Analysis and Growth Mixture Models (Nagin, 1999, 2005) represent another extension of the basic LGM model, in which individuals are classified into latent classes based upon similar patterns of change across time in a targeted variable. In this case, contrary to the multigroup LGM model, heterogeneity in growth parameters is believed to be due to membership in unobserved or unknown subpopulations, that is the latent classes. For more information and technical details on LGM, see Bollen and Curran (2006), Duncan et al. (2006), and Singer and Willett (2003).

CHANGE IN COMMITMENT OVER TIME

Since the first study by Lance et al. (2000), which introduced the Latent Growth Modeling (LGM) approach as 'an attractive alternative' for correctly examining intra-individual change in commitment dimensions, other researchers have begun to track intra-individual change in commitment and related variables using this approach (Bentein et al., 2005; Ng et al., 2010; Solinger et al., 2013). I will review the preliminary insights of all these commitment studies using the LGM approach, and suggest several ways that this work can be extended.

How Does Commitment Change Over Time?

To be able to answer the question, 'How does commitment change over time?', it is important to specify when. Only a few empirical studies have examined change in commitment at a specific period of time, and these studies have chosen to study the period of organizational entry. This is not surprising given that entry marks the very beginning of commitment, and that early commitment seems to be crucial for the development of lasting commitment (Kammeyer-Mueller and Wanberg, 2003; Wanous, 1980). Change in organizational commitment has thus been seen as an indicator of the success of a socialization process (Bauer et al., 2007; Kammeyer-Mueller and Wanberg, 2003).

Three studies (Bentein and Meyer, 2004; Lance et al., 2000; Vandenberghe et al., 2011) tested a model of organizational commitment across time with the LGM approach, during the first months of organizational entry (respectively, during the first 12, 6, and 8 months). They all found a decline in AC (or internalization, in the study by Lance et al., 2000, which is very conceptually similar to AC) during the entry period. This pattern of change for AC across time is congruent with the 'honeymoon-hangover effect' described in the literature (e.g., Boswell et al., 2009; Van Maanen, 1975): the initial 'honeymoon' period reflects the naïve optimism of newcomers and appears to be quickly followed by a 'hangover' period or 'reality shock' as newcomers start discovering the less attractive aspects of their jobs.

Yet it seems that change does not occur on all commitment dimensions. Although

Bentein and Meyer (2004) also observed a decreasing trajectory of NC during the period of organizational entry, both Lance et al. (2000) and Bentein and Meyer (2004) found a stable trajectory of CC (or compliance) across time. One possible explanation for this is related to the attributes underlying commitment mindsets (Bentein and Meyer, 2004; Bentein et al., 2005). Specifically, the psychological contract literature (e.g., Morrison and Robinson, 1997) supports the existence of two broad bases that underpin individuals' relationships to their organization: relational and transactional. The relational bases emphasize the part of the relationship linked to socio-emotional or social exchange elements of the workplace, while the transactional bases emphasize the part of the relationship linked to the exchange of tangible facets. Interestingly, Morrison and Robinson (1997) argued that the relational bases of the employment relationship are more sensitive than transactional bases to unforeseen changes in, or breaches of, obligations by the employer. Because the core of both AC and NC includes socio-emotional elements, these two dimensions might be considered representations of relational-based psychological contracts. These dimensions might be very sensitive, and responsive to encounters with organizational events that undermine them (for example, reality shocks, unmet expectations, and other events that break the psychological contract). In contrast, the attributes characterizing CC are more transactional and impersonal in nature in that they are externally anchored to the job market or to the tangible benefits accrued over time that result from longevity in the organization. Events causing fluctuations in CC will thus occur less frequently in the early stages of employment than those that may alter individuals' levels of AC and NC. In terms of change processes, the first six months in Lance et al. (2000) and 12 months in Bentein and Meyer (2004) might have been 'too early' to capture change in CC.

More recently, Solinger et al. (2013) went a step further in providing insight into the development of commitment during the organizational entry period. They argue that newcomers, as they encounter different socialization experiences over time and react to them differently, differ in the way they develop their commitment over time. Solinger et al. thus developed a theoretical taxonomy of distinct 'onboarding scenarios' that newcomers experience at entry, using commitment as an indicator. They tested their theoretical taxonomy through a Latent Class Growth Model on the first 25 consecutive weeks of employment commitment measures. They conceptualized commitment as an attitude consisting of positive affect, favorable cognitions, and readiness to take action on behalf of the organization. Their results confirm that individuals display distinct developmental trajectories of commitment at entry: they identified five groups of newcomers whose trajectories correspond to their theoretical taxonomy. Interestingly, their 'honeymoon-hangover' scenario, with a decreasing trajectory of commitment over time, corresponds to the trajectory found for AC in previous studies described above, and represents a sizable proportion of participants (25 percent). Yet this pattern of change in commitment during the organizational entry period is not the only one, and it seems that commitment is not always declining across time during the organizational entry period (here, the first six months).

Overall, the studies that model intra-individual change in commitment during the first months of employment with an LGM approach confirm that commitment changes over time during this period. Even Solinger et al. (2013) find that the three scenarios that are characterized by a relatively stable trajectory of commitment across time display some change over time, but of small amplitude. All of the researchers report true inter-individual differences in the growth trajectories observed for each commitment dimension (latent variances of growth parameters were all significantly different from 0; or newcomers were characterized by distinct patterns of change in commitment in the study by Solinger et al., 2013), suggesting that there is heterogeneity in the way individuals change in their commitment dimensions over time in the organizational entry period.

What is the Interplay among the Commitment Dimensions' Trajectories of Change?

Lance et al. (2000), Bentein and Meyer (2004), and Bentein et al. (2005) included different commitment mindsets in their LGM models, which enabled them to examine cross-domain relationships between them. In addition to AC and NC, Bentein et al. (2005) also included two distinct facets of CC: high sacrifice (HS) and lack of alternatives (LA). The results of these three studies provide interesting insights into the pattern of cross-domain associations among the Initial Status and Change factors of commitment mindsets during the organizational entry period (Lance et al., 2000; Bentein and Meyer, 2004), or during a not specifically identified period for the individual (Bentein et al., 2005).

First, past observations regarding static associations among commitment dimensions are upheld. Specifically, Bentein and Meyer (2004) found that AC and NC initial status variables and NC and CC initial status variables were positively related. Bentein et al. (2005) noted that AC, NC, and HS initial status variables were positively associated with each other, as were the initial status variables for HS and LA; LA had negative associations with both AC and NC. Lance et al. (2000) found that the Compliance (similar to CC) initial status variable and Internalization (similar to AC) initial status variable were unrelated. Thus, these results seem consistent with past (static) findings.

When the dynamic aspects of the dimensions were evaluated, some divergence from past research emerged. A first important observation concerning the interplay among the commitment dimensions is that the initial status of CC (Bentein and Meyer, 2004) or of its subdimensions (Bentein et al., 2005) is never associated with the rates of change in AC or NC; and that the initial status of compliance is also unrelated to the rate of change in internalization in the study by Lance et al. (2000). Interestingly, these findings might advocate against the retrospective rationalization process proposed as a significant factor that enhances the development of AC (Meyer and Allen, 1991). Accordingly, AC is partially shaped through a rationalization process: employees form their AC toward the organization based on their CC because affective attachment lets them rationalize their actions and feelings of being bound to the organization. These findings do not support this behavioral commitment perspective because the processes leading to change in AC and NC are completely independent from continuance commitment.

Bentein et al. (2005) and Bentein and Meyer (2004) also showed that change patterns in AC and NC were strongly interrelated. Bentein et al. (2005) found a positive association between the respective initial status factors of AC and NC, and between their respective change factors. Moreover, the initial status of AC was associated in the same way with the rate of change in NC as with its own rate of change; and the initial status of NC was associated in the same way with the rate of change in AC as with its own rate of change. Interestingly, some results also demonstrated asymmetry in the relationship between desire (AC) and obligation (NC). In Bentein and Meyer's (2004) study, the initial level of NC is positively related to the decline in both NC and AC, while the initial level of AC does not relate significantly to the decline in either AC or NC during the specific period of organizational entry. Bentein et al. (2005) performed complementary analyses examining the relative contribution of AC and NC to the actual probability of leaving the organization. They demonstrate that while declines in both AC and NC impact the probability of turnover, the decline in normative commitment is the strongest predicting factor. Together, these results might shed light on the controversy regarding the AC–NC distinction in the commitment literature, and suggest a predominance of the mindset of obligation (NC) over the mindset of desire (AC).

All three studies explore the change in commitment mindsets but consider these mindsets individually. Given that all commitment mindsets potentially coexist within individuals, Vandenberg et al. (2007, also described by Vandenberg and Stanley, 2009) propose to identify subgroups of individuals who are characterized by different combinations of change trajectories in all commitment mindsets. To adopt this person-centered approach (as opposed to a traditional variable-centered approach), they use a Latent Class Growth Model. They identify five distinct latent classes of individuals who share a similar combination of changes in commitment mindsets. Their results tend to confirm that AC and NC are more sensitive to events that occur in the environment because they change in all classes except one; HS changes in only three classes, and LA remains stable in all classes except one. Moreover, AC and NC appear to often change congruently across time, except in one class labeled the 'Stuck' class, while the change trajectories of HS and LA are more distinct from each other. It seems that the Stuck class is a specific combination of change trajectories in commitment dimensions that deserves our full attention. As the only class in which the mindsets of obligation and desire do not change congruently, it might shed light on the specific role of NC in the commitment process. Note that 42 percent of the participants (299 subjects out of 712) in the sample of Vandenberg et al. (2007) fall into this class, representing a large number of individuals. Taken together, these results confirm the existence of distinct combinations of change trajectories in commitment mindsets, and a more important role of the mindset of obligation (NC) than previously anticipated.

How is Change in Commitment Related to Predictors?

When intra-individual change in commitment is found, a key extension of the LGM approach is to integrate putative determinants and outcomes of longitudinal change within an augmented LGM model. Very few studies have explored the determinants of change in commitment. Lance et al. (2000) examined linkages between changes in commitment over the first six months and some specific antecedents. Consistent with their expectations, they found that both anticipatory met expectations and job choice difficulty have significant effects upon initial status and change in internalization (conceptually close to AC). Newcomers who expect to have their expectations met through their work experience start with higher levels of internalization and experience a greater decline in internalization than do individuals with lower anticipatory met expectations at organizational entry. Further, newcomers who experience difficulty in making their job-choice decision start with lower levels of internalization but experience lower rates of decline in internalization than do individuals with lower job choice difficulty at organizational entry. Their results also show that social aspects have a significant influence on change in internalization: the greater the experience with the agents through whom the socialization information is conveyed, the lower the rate of decline in internalization across time.

Solinger et al. (2013) explore the same type of determinants of change in commitment among newcomers. They examine whether their latent classes relate differently to the following covariates: person–organization fit (P–O fit), high met expectations, and contract breach. Their results confirm that their five latent classes differ, as expected, in terms of these three covariates: newcomers with high commitment report high P–O fit, high met expectations, and low contract breach. However, their results must be interpreted with caution because their three covariates, even if they can be theoretically considered as antecedents of change in commitment, are measured at the end of their study, after the 25 waves of commitment measurement.

Vandenberghe et al. (2011) also explored some determinants of longitudinal change in commitment during the organizational entry period. They used the stress literature as a framework for their hypotheses. Interestingly, they found that the initial level of commitment at entry is associated with an increase in 'role overload' over time, but that the increase in role overload is associated with a steeper decrease in AC over time. These results thus suggest that the same variable, role overload, might be experienced and perceived differently across time. The authors suggest that role overload may be initially appraised rather favorably as a challenge stressor; and later, as discrepancies between demands and resources emerge, as a hindrance stressor. Newcomers who experience a high level of AC at entry may thus construe their organizational role more broadly than those with a lower level of AC, which may then predispose them to experience heavy workload. As they experience frustration regarding the resources to cope with this workload, what is first perceived as a challenge might become an overload.

The last study that explores some determinants of longitudinal change in commitment over time is that of Ng et al. (2010). They hypothesize and find that perceptions of psychological contract breach are associated with AC across time. Specifically, the initial status of psychological contract breach is negatively related to the initial status of AC, and the rate of increase in psychological contract breach is positively related to the rate of decline in AC.

How is Change in Commitment Related to Consequences?

In studies of the consequences of longitudinal change in commitment, researchers have focused on turnover intention (Bentein and Meyer, 2004; Bentein et al., 2005; Lance et al., 2000; Vandenberg et al., 2007; Vandenberghe et al., 2011). The results of these studies mirror past research findings regarding associations among the static elements of the constructs: the initial status of AC, and of NC (when measured), has a negative association with the initial status of turnover intention. More importantly, these studies also showed that the greater the rate of declining change in AC (or NC), the greater the rate of increasing change in turnover intention.

Bentein et al. (2005) showed that decreasing changes in AC and NC predicted actual turnover behavior through the increasing change in turnover intention. Only the change in turnover intention had a significant association with turnover behavior, while the initial status of turnover intention was not significantly associated with turnover.

Bentein et al. (2005) also developed different scenarios to explore the relative role of the commitment dimensions and turnover intention in the prediction of actual turnover behavior. When they compared a first scenario, that represents what happens to the probability of turnover when both AC and NC decline (from 5 to 2 on the Likert answer scale), with a second scenario that represents what happens to the probability of turnover when both AC and NC stay at a very low level (at 1 on the Likert scale), holding turnover intention constant in both scenarios, the first scenario resulted in a predicted turnover probability of .30, while the second yielded a value of .03. It therefore seems that the dynamic nature of commitment increases the probability of leaving the organization, more so than low levels of commitment alone. Given the non-significant relationship between initial status of turnover intention and turnover behavior, these results suggest that a cognitive saliency factor might play a role in this process: it is not the fact of having low (or high) commitment or turnover intention that is important, but the fact that the individual experiences a decrease in this variable that makes this experience salient for them.

Vandenberg et al. (2007) also showed that each of their latent classes was associated with change in turnover intention, as the theory predicts. Only the results for the 'Socio-Emotionally Decreasing' class were unexpected in that turnover intention did not change over time for these individuals, whereas the decline of AC and NC would have suggested a corresponding increase in turnover intention. Their results highlight the importance of considering commitment dimensions together because it seems that turnover intention only changes when change in AC and NC was combined with change in one or both of the two other dimensions. In a series of logistic regressions, Vandenberg et al. (2007) also demonstrated that change in turnover intention predicts actual turnover in four of their five classes. Only in the increasing class did turnover intention not predict turnover behavior. This is the only class in which individuals increase their commitment over time, so this result might suggest that individuals are less sensitive to increasing change in commitment over time than to decreasing change in commitment.

Ng et al. (2010) showed that the declining change in AC was related to the declining change in innovation-related behaviors (generating, spreading, and implementing innovative ideas at work) over a six-month period. Further, they confirmed a mediation LGM model in which the Initial Status of affective commitment is a complete mediator of the effect of the Initial Status of psychological contract breach on the Initial Status of innovation-related behaviors; and the decline in affective commitment is a partial mediator of the effect of the increase in psychological contract breach on the decline in innovation-related behaviors. It thus seems that longitudinal change in commitment might play an important role as a mediator between psychological contract breaches and employees' proactive behaviors.

Finally, Vandenberghe et al. (forthcoming) examined the temporal relationship between AC to the organization and AC to the supervisor. Drawing from role theory (Katz and Kahn, 1978), they hypothesized and found that supervisors' roles are shaped by the expectations of the organization in which low-tenured employees are embedded, and that decreasing change in AC to the organization leads to decreasing change in AC to the supervisor. This is the first study to use LGM to track change in commitment to other targets than the organization.

AVENUES FOR FUTURE RESEARCH

To date, scant commitment research has used the LGM approach to capture inter-individual differences in intra-individual change; I have tried to present the preliminary insights of these studies. These findings need to be interpreted prudently because they often rely on a single study, and more research is needed to justify confidence in their generalizability. Based on these preliminary insights, I will now suggest several ways that this work can be extended.

As noted above, all the studies that have examined longitudinal change in commitment over time during a specific period concentrated on the period of organizational entry (Lance et al., 2000; Vandenberghe et al., 2011; Solinger et al., 2013). I suspect that the period of organizational entry is not the only one in which commitment is likely to change over time, and that there are other specific moments in the employee–organization relationship that deserve our attention. Specifically, the bond or the force binding the employee to the organization might be revised and reinterpreted when organizational changes are introduced purposefully (e.g., Fedor et al., 2006), when the context changes (mergers, acquisitions, or lay-offs; Brockner et al., 1992; Gopinath and Becker, 2000), or when the person is near or at the end of the employment relationship (Breitsohl and Ruhle, 2013; Solinger et al., 2016). I suspect that these important changes in the employee–organization relationship will also be characterized by specific trajectories of commitment change across time. Some of these trajectories might be discontinuous or non-linear, with a plateau effect, sudden break, or multiple downturns or upturns (Ployhart and Vandenberg, 2010). A variety of approaches exist for modeling more complex trajectories within the LGM framework, including adding squared, cubed, or higher-power parameters, or dividing time into different epochs, and allowing the trajectories to differ (in slope, for example) during each epoch (see Bollen and Curran, 2006, pp. 88–125; and Singer and Willett, 2003, pp. 189–242 for a description of these approaches).

Preliminary results showed not only that the rate of change in commitment might vary depending on the type of mindset, but also that the mindset types are associated to different degrees. Overall, changes in AC and NC seem to be strongly associated, while changes in LA and HS seem more independent. However, these preliminary results also support a more important role of change in NC, relative to change in AC, than previously anticipated; see Meyer and Parfyonova (2010) for an interesting review of NC, the poor relative of the tridimensional model of Meyer and Allen (1991, 1997).

The portrait of the interplay between commitment mindsets seems even more complex when authors adopt a person-centered approach (Vandenberg et al., 2007). For example, the proposition that any combination of mindsets serves as a 'context' for the other mindsets, and particularly for NC, which could be experienced as moral duty in an AC/NC-dominant profile or as an indebted obligation in a CC/NC-dominant profile (Gellatly et al., 2006; Meyer and Parfyonova, 2010), needs to be further refined to adequately explain all the possible classes of latent growth. The test of this proposed distinction between two facets of NC would, for example, necessitate a comparison between a class that experiences an increase in AC and NC combined with a decrease in HS and LA (AC/NC-dominant profile) and a class that experiences an increase in HS (and eventually LA) and NC combined with a decrease in AC (CC/NC-dominant profile). In fact, these two classes are theoretical and none of the latent growth classes found in Vandenberg et al. (2007) could be classified as a pure representation of one of these two classes. The reality is much more complex and diverse when intra-individual change is factored into the equation. AC and NC might evolve together in a different direction from HS and LA but decline across time, rather than increase, while HS and LA do not change (see Class 4); or AC might evolve in one direction and HS and LA in the other, while NC remains stable (see Class 5). Further research is thus needed to develop a strong theoretical framework that explains the complex interplay between the distinctive rates of change in the different commitment mindsets. As preliminary findings suggested, a cognitive saliency factor might play a role here. Change in one mindset might render this dimension very salient for the individual when they have to interpret or reinterpret the other mindsets of their bond with the organization. Future research is needed to test this nuanced hypothesis of a context effect depending not only on the nature of the mindset, but also on its rate of change across time.

We also know from the commitment literature that employees can develop commitment to many other targets than the organization, like the occupation, the project, the supervisor, and the team, and that these commitments might complement, substitute, or create a psychological conflict for the individual (Chapter 4 in this volume). Exploration of these processes of complementarity, substitution or conflict between forms of commitment toward different targets might also be better conceptualized across time (see Vandenberghe et al., forthcoming). For example, the process of substitution of commitment toward an abstract and distal focus such as the organization with commitment toward a more proximal and concrete focus such as the team (Becker, 2009) would be operationalized as a decreasing trajectory of organizational commitment concomitant with an increasing trajectory of commitment to the team. Future research is thus needed to test whether individuals experience significant changes in commitment toward different foci during specific periods of the employment relationship and to develop a theoretical framework of these processes of complementarity, substitution, or conflict between commitment targets over time.

Some preliminary results also suggest that individuals are less sensitive to increasing change in commitment over time than to decreasing change in commitment (Vandenberg et al., 2007). This implies that the pattern of relationships observed between longitudinal change in commitment and outcomes may differ depending on whether the change is an increase or a decrease: enhancing commitment may not pay off rapidly in terms of improving attitudes and behaviors at work, whereas a decline in commitment may have a more rapid negative effect on attitudes and behaviors at work. This differential pattern of relationships depending on whether the change is an increase or a decrease might also be observed between some antecedents and commitments. Consequently, future research might examine this asymmetry related to the direction of the change (increase versus decrease) in the relationships between commitments and its antecedents and outcomes more systematically.

PRACTICAL IMPLICATIONS

These research findings should encourage managers and organizations to consider timing when interpreting an employee's commitment. Preliminary results suggest that there may be 'risky periods' in the employee–organization relationship, such as the one following the honeymoon phase at entry and characterized by decline in AC and NC. Organizations should thus take a proactive attitude to support employees during these risky periods, for example by informing newcomers of the expected pattern of job attitudes they will experience in the entry period (Boswell et al., 2009).

Further, it seems that when things get worse, employees might experience a rapid reduction in commitment, but when the situation gets better it takes time to increase their commitment. This type of asymmetry between a decreasing change trajectory and an increasing trajectory is consistent with Brockner et al.'s (1992, p. 260) assertion that it may be 'easier to break, rather than build employees' organizational commitment'. Therefore, continued and regular organizational efforts aimed at maintaining a commitment climate may be particularly important to avoid dropping trajectories. Organizations might also want to explore specific actions that help to rebuild commitment among employees who experienced a decreasing trajectory of commitment (Solinger et al., 2016).

REFERENCES

Bauer, T.N., Bodner, R., Erdogan, B., Truxillo, D.M., and Tucker, J.S. (2007). Newcomer adjustment during organizational socialization: A meta-analytic review of antecedents, outcomes, and methods. *Journal of Applied Psychology*, 92, 707–721.
Becker, T.E. (2009). Interpersonal commitments. In H.J. Klein, T.E. Becker, and J.P. Meyer (eds), *Commitment in Organizations: Accumulated Wisdom and New Directions* (pp. 137–178). New York: Routledge/Taylor & Francis.
Bentein, K. and Meyer, J.P. (2004). Evolution of Commitment during Organizational Entry: A Latent Growth Modeling Approach. Paper published in the *Proceedings of 32nd Annual Conference of the ASAC (Administrative Sciences Association of Canada)*, ASAC CD-ROM.
Bentein, K., Vandenberg, R.J., Vandenberghe, C., and Stinglhamber, F. (2005). The role of change in the relationship between commitment and turnover: A latent growth modeling approach. *Journal of Applied Psychology*, 90, 468–482.
Bollen, K.A. and Curran, P.J. (2006). *Latent Curve Models: A Structural Equation Perspective*. New York: John Wiley & Sons.
Boswell, W.R., Shipp, A.J., Culbertson, S.S., and Payne, S.C. (2009). Changes in newcomer job satisfaction over time: Examining the pattern of honeymoons and hangovers. *Journal of Applied Psychology*, 94(4), 844–858.
Breitsohl, H. and Ruhle, S. (2013). Residual affective commitment to organizations: Concept, causes and consequences. *Human Resource Management Review*, 23(2), 161–173.
Brockner, J., Tyler, T.R., and Cooper-Schneider, R. (1992). The influence of prior commitment to an institution on reactions to perceived unfairness: The higher they are, the harder they fall. *Administrative Science Quarterly*, 37, 241–261.
Chan, D. (1998). The conceptualization and analysis of change over time: An integrative approach incorporating longitudinal mean and covariance structures analysis (LMACS) and multiple indicator latent growth modeling (MLGM). *Organizational Research Methods*, 1, 421–483.
Chan, D. and Schmitt, N. (2000). Inter-individual differences in intra-individual changes in proactivity during organizational entry: A latent growth modeling approach to understanding newcomer adaptation. *Journal of Applied Psychology*, 85, 190–210.
Duncan, T.E., Duncan, S.C., and Strycker, L.A. (2006). *An Introduction to Latent Variable Growth Modeling: Concepts, Issues and Applications* (2nd edn). Mahwah, NJ: Lawrence Erlbaum.

Fedor, D.B., Caldwell, S., and Herold, D.M. (2006). The effects of organizational changes on employee commitment: A multi-level investigation. *Personnel Psychology, 59*, 1–29.

Gellatly, I.R., Meyer, J.P., and Luchak, A.A. (2006). Combined effects of the three commitment components on focal and discretionary behaviors: A test of Meyer and Herscovitch's propositions. *Journal of Vocational Behavior, 69*, 331–345.

Gopinath, C. and Becker, T. (2000). Communication, procedural justice, and employee attitudes: Relationships under conditions of divestiture. *Journal of Management, 26*(1), 63–80.

Kammeyer-Mueller, J.D. and Wanberg, C.R. (2003). Unwrapping the organizational entry process: Disentangling multiple antecedents and their pathways to adjustment. *Journal of Applied Psychology, 88*, 779–794.

Katz, D. and Kahn, R.L. (1978). *The Social Psychology of Organizations* (2nd edn). New York: Wiley.

Klein, H.J., Molloy, J.C., and Brinsfield, C.T. (2012). Reconceptualizing workplace commitment to redress a stretched construct: Revisiting assumptions and removing confounds. *Academy of Management Review, 37*, 130–151.

Lance, C.E., Vandenberg, R.J., and Self, R.M. (2000). Latent growth models of individual change: The case of newcomer adjustment. *Organizational Behavior and Human Decision Processes, 83*, 107–140.

Li, F.Z., Duncan, T.E. and Acock, A. (2000). Modeling interaction effects in latent growth curve models. *Structural Equation Modeling, 7*, 497–533.

McArdle, J.J. (1988). Dynamic but structural equation modeling of repeated measures data. In J.R. Nesselroade and R.B. Cattell (eds), *The Handbook of Multivariate Experimental Psychology* (2nd edn) (pp. 561–614). New York: Plenum Press.

Meyer, J.P. and Allen, N.J. (1991). A three-component conceptualization of organizational commitment. *Human Resource Management Review, 1*, 61–89.

Meyer, J.P. and Allen, N.J. (1997). *Commitment in the Workplace: Theory, Research, and Application*. Newbury Park, CA: Sage.

Meyer, J.P. and Herscovitch, L. (2001). Commitment in the workplace: Toward a general model. *Human Resource Management Review, 11*, 299–326.

Meyer J.P. and Parfyonova, N.M. (2010). Normative commitment in the workplace: A theoretical analysis and re-conceptualization. *Human Resources Management Review, 20*, 283–294.

Meyer, J.P., Stanley, D.J., Herscovitch, L., and Topolnytsky, L. (2002). Affective, continuance, and normative commitment to the organization: A meta-analysis of antecedents, correlates, and consequences. *Journal of Vocational Behavior, 61*, 20–52.

Morrison, E.W. and Robinson, S.L. (1997). When employees feel betrayed: A model of how psychological contract develops. *Academy of Management Review, 22*, 226–256.

Nagin, D.S. (1999). Analyzing developmental trajectories: A semi-parametric, group-based approach. *Psychological Methods, 4*, 139–157.

Nagin, D.S. (2005). *Group-Based Modeling of Development*. Cambridge, MA: Harvard University Press.

Ng, T.W., Feldman, D.C., and Lam, S. (2010). Psychological contract breaches, organizational commitment, and innovation-related behaviors: A latent growth modeling approach. *Journal of Applied Psychology, 95*, 744–751.

Pitariu, A.H. and Ployhart, R.E. (2010). Explaining change: Theorizing and testing dynamic mediated longitudinal relationships. *Journal of Management, 36*, 405–429.

Ployhart, R.E. and Vandenberg, R.J. (2010). Longitudinal research: The theory, design, and analysis of change. *Journal of Management, 36*, 94–120.

Singer, J.D. and Willett, J.B. (2003). *Applied Longitudinal Data Analysis: Modeling Change and Event Occurrence*. New York: Oxford University Press.

Solinger, O.N., Van Olffen, W., and Roe, R.A. (2008). Beyond the Three-Component Model of Organizational Commitment. *Journal of Applied Psychology, 93*, 70–83.

Solinger, O.N., Van Olffen, W., Roe, R.A., and Hofmans, J. (2013). On becoming (un)committed: A taxonomy and test of newcomer on-boarding scenarios. *Organization Science, 24*(6), 1640–1661.

Solinger, O.N., Hofmans, J., Bal, P.M., and Jansen, P.G.W. (2016). Bouncing back from psychological contract breach: How commitment recovers over time. *Journal of Organizational Behavior, 37(4)*, 494–514.

Vandenberg R.J. and Stanley, L.J. (2009). Statistical and methodological challenges for commitment researchers: Issues of invariance, change across time, and profile differences. In H.J. Klein, T.E. Becker and J.P. Meyer (eds), *Commitment in Organizations: Accumulated Wisdom and New Directions* (pp. 383–418), New York: Routledge.

Vandenberg, R.J., Stanley, L.J., Vandenberghe, C., and Bentein, K. (2007). On the applicability of latent class growth analysis. Paper presented at the annual conference of Academy of Management, Philadelphia, PA, August.

Vandenberghe, C., Bentein, K. and Panaccio, A. (forthcoming). Affective commitment to organizations and supervisors and turnover: A role theory perspective. *Journal of Management*.

Vandenberghe, C., Panaccio, A., Bentein, K., Mignonac, K., and Roussel, P. (2011). Assessing longitudinal change of and dynamic relationships among role stressors, job attitudes, turnover intention, and well-being in neophyte newcomers. *Journal of Organizational Behavior, 32*, 652–671.

Van Maanen, J. (1975). Police socialization: A longitudinal examination of job attitudes in an urban police department. *Administrative Science Quarterly, 20*, 207–228.

Wanous, J.P. (1980). *Organizational Entry*. Reading, MA: Addison-Wesley.

Wen, Z., Marsh, H.W., Hau, K.T., Wu, Y., Liu, H., and Morin, A.J.S. (2014). Interaction Effects in Latent Growth Models: Evaluation of Alternative Estimation Approaches. *Structural Equation Modeling: A Multidisciplinary Journal, 21*, 361–374.

Willett, J.B. and Sayer, A.G. (1994). Using covariance structure analysis to detect correlates and predictors of individual change over time. *Psychological Bulletin, 116*, 363–381.

Willett, J.B. and Sayer, A.G. (1995). Cross-domain analyses of change over time: combining growth modeling and covariance structure analysis. In G.A. Marcoulides and R.E. Schumacker (eds), *Advanced Structural Equation Modeling: Issues and Techniques* (pp. 22–51). Hillsdale, NJ: Lawrence Erlbaum Incorporated.

34. Capturing the process of committing: design requirements for a temporal measurement instrument

*Woody van Olffen, Omar N. Solinger and Robert A. Roe**

One of the new developments in the organization sciences is the study of the temporal 'process nature' of various organizational phenomena (Tsoukas and Chia, 2002; Langley et al., 2013). Among commitment scholars, this is reflected in a rising interest in how commitment to the organization forms and changes over time (e.g., Judge and Kammeyer-Mueller, 2012; Klein et al., 2012; Solinger et al., 2013). This move toward a dynamic perspective is exciting and promising in terms of what might be learned about commitment. However, if we truly want to come to grips with the role of time and change, we need to set up our studies in such a way that theory, research design, and measurement practices are aligned (Collins, 2006; Edmondson and McManus, 2007). In this chapter we will argue that temporal process research comes with a new set of principles and practical guidelines (criteria) that are not necessarily in line with conventional thinking.

We argue that studying the dynamic nature of commitment requires a temporal process mindset regarding theory, design, and measurement. Temporal process thinking involves thoughts and ideas on how phenomena change, grow, vary, and terminate over time (Langley et al., 2013; Roe 2008a). In organizational behavior (OB), temporal thinking is still relatively uncommon as compared to thinking in terms of differences between subjects (henceforth: the variance or differential mode). Differential and temporal modes of thought translate into research approaches that influence decisions in all stages of inquiry (see, Shepherd and Sutcliffe, 2011; Roe, 2008a). Problems may arise when the application of differential conventions in conceptualization and measurement of constructs in the temporal domain is unwarranted (Roe et al., 2012). The clearest example of this is when a researcher interested in a temporal change process simply adopts a (validated) item designed to study individual differences in job satisfaction, such as, 'I am generally satisfied with my job'. Respondents may erroneously interpret 'generally' as generalizing over time instead of over job aspects. As a result, their response reflects the overall average satisfaction level they have experienced over time. Contrary to the researcher's intention, the result is a temporally unspecific measurement. It is much like repeatedly asking someone, 'How hungry are you, in general?' Such questions fail to capture real change in the phenomenon of interest and, thus, lack construct validity in the temporal domain, even though their construct validity in the variance domain is well established. To overcome this, we should explicate where and how our theory, design, and measurement practices might require translation from the differential mode to the temporal mode. For instance,

---

* We dedicate this chapter to the memory of Robert Roe (1944–2016). Robert was a driven pioneer and propagator of temporal research in OB. He was also a warm and inspiring colleague and mentor.

in temporal measurement it is usually a good idea to make the respondent aware of time in the question itself: 'I am satisfied, at this moment.'

In the following, we will work out the implications of the temporal process mode of thought for the measurement of change in commitment (or rather, the committing process). Next, we articulate a set of specific design implications for a proper committing process measurement instrument. We will close by reflecting on the possibilities of using this instrument in research and practice.

WHAT MAKES THE TEMPORAL PROCESS APPROACH DIFFERENT?

Temporal research can best be understood by referring to the well-known data-matrix of Cattell (1952), which has subjects, time moments and attributes as its dimensions. Differential commitment research, for instance, examines the variance and covariance of two or more attributes (say, commitment and fair treatment) in P subjects (individuals) at one or more moments in time, whereas temporal research examines the variance and co-variance of two or more attributes in one or more subjects across Q time-moments (Roe, 2014a, 2014b). Most studies on commitment have followed a traditional cross-sectional design; that is, a differential design with a single time moment. The focus of differential studies is typically on assessing variance in dependent variables at some point in time and on determining which part can be explained from independent variables. Temporal studies have a different focus: they intend to map or explain the variation of an attribute over time. Temporal research can be done in two contrasting ways, which yield quite different results. One, the temporal panel approach, essentially extends traditional cross-sectional work over time by studying individual differences measured at multiple time moments. This approach is exemplified by studies of commitment using cross-lagged panel analysis (e.g., Vandenberg and Scarpello, 1994; Vander Elst et al., 2014) or latent growth analysis (e.g., Bentein et al., 2005; Ng et al., 2010: see Chapter 33 in this volume). The second one, which is focal in the current chapter, is the temporal process approach. Its objective is to study individual change trajectories and to find out how these differ from each other. It examines how commitment and other phenomena unfold, looking at them as developing patterns or trajectories (rather than repeated cross-sections) and searching for explanations of their shape (Collins, 2006; George and Jones, 2000; Roe, 2008a). Compared to the differential approach, therefore, the focus shifts from explaining differences (in commitment) to mapping and explaining processes (committing); in other words, from 'being to becoming' (see, Tsoukas and Chia, 2002). This approach has, for instance, been followed by Solinger et al. (2013), yielding five 'families' of committing to a new job over time.

Temporal panel studies provide little or no information about alternative change trajectories other than a limited set of parameters (typically intercepts, trends, and curvature). Various analytical methods can be applied to estimate these. Cross-lagged panel analysis primarily focuses on causal order (often to follow up on established cross-sectional findings[1]) and does not consider change trajectories as a whole. Latent growth analysis fits a mathematical function of a fixed functional form to the overall ('mean') change trajectory in the sample, and subsequently looks for (co)variation in the parameters of that function that best describes the set of individual change trajectories. Thus, it puts constraints on individual-level trajectories, 'forcing' them to follow the sample-level trajectory. In contrast, the temporal process approach starts from the individual level and allows individual trajectories to take any form. Grouping is based on similarity, using, for instance, group-based modeling techniques. No a priori functional form is specified. In this way multiple and qualitatively very different trajectories can be found, such as the 'honeymoon-hangover' or the 'learning to love' committing trajectories (Solinger et al., 2013). Thus, temporal process research seeks to identify different (groups of) trajectory shapes and (eventually) examine how the prevalence of the shape and the shape itself relate to predictors (Nagin, 2005). (Latent) groups of shapes can be detected using analytical methods such as latent class growth modeling (LCGM) (see Andruff et al. 2009; Nagin 2005), growth mixture modeling (e.g. Chapter 35 in this volume) and functional data analysis (e.g., Solinger et al., 2016a). LCGM and growth mixture modeling are statistical techniques specifically aimed at identifying groups that display qualitatively different development trajectories (so-called 'latent classes').

Clearly, these two analytical approaches answer starkly contrasting research questions. The panel approach is mostly used for explanatory purposes, particularly to answer questions of causality using pairs of repeated measures of commitment and its various antecedents or consequents. As such it builds and extends existing theory and empirics. The temporal process approach, on the other hand, addresses the shape of trajectories as a whole. Unfortunately, however, for most OB phenomena good process theory, specifying 'typical' developments, is still lacking (see Navarro et al., 2015). Most temporal process research in OB is therefore descriptive and explorative,[2] charting the territory before explanation can start. The process of committing to the organization is a clear case in point: theoretical process models that predict the variations of trajectory forms in committing are, as yet, rather scarce and underarticulated (see Solinger et al., 2013).

It should be noted that the differential–temporal process distinction has roots in contrasting ontologies and epistemologies (Monge, 1990; Roe, 2008a; Tsoukas and Chia, 2002). The differential paradigm sees the world of people and organizations as essentially stable and tries to gain knowledge about 'what is' from diversity in stable characteristics. It typically treats change as error ('noise'; see Ployhart, 2008), and only exceptionally acknowledges it as an alteration in the configuration of characteristics. It also assumes that what is valid for the population (or sample) as a whole applies to every individual subject (Molenaar, 2008). In contrast, the temporal process paradigm sees the world as being in constant flux and tries to extract knowledge about 'what happens' from change trajectories of individual subjects. Here, change is the default and stability the exception. Stability is treated only as 'a special form of change' (Roe et al., 2012). These differences are reflected in the methodologies used and the findings obtained. That the top-down logic of differential methods and the bottom-up logic of temporal process research may produce diverging outcomes is well illustrated in a study by Li and Roe (2012) on the development of task conflict in teams: the overall linear pattern at the sample level matches the individual trajectories of only two out of 42 teams.

TIME SPECIFICATION IN THE TEMPORAL PROCESS APPROACH

A critical issue from a temporal perspective is that the flow of time has no 'natural' segmentation, so that in order to study phenomena one needs to select a certain time window. This can be done in countless ways. One may not assume that all 'cuts of time' will produce the same image of phenomena. Neither will a study of a phenomenon over time be generalizable to other time windows than the one selected first. Indeed, a recent review study shows that temporal process research of particular phenomena – that is, motivation and performance – reveals widely differing outcomes, depending on the time window adopted (Roe, 2014a). From a temporal process perspective, observations, measurements, relationships in empirical research are always premised on the time window adopted. At least three temporal parameters need to be explicitly specified (Roe and Inceoglu, 2016): length of time frame (L), the moment of onset (M), and number of observations (N).

Determining the length of time frame and the number of observations is an important challenge for researchers, and should ideally be informed by theory or previous research. However, in areas where research has been predominantly differential and studies have been temporally underspecified – as is the case with commitment – such guidance is lacking. One therefore cannot help but engage in exploratory research and use 'temporal zooming' (Roe, 2014a) to find out which combinations of L and N yield meaningful results. In order to cast a wide net it is helpful to use high-density repeated measurement (HDRM) (Solinger et al., 2013), which allows highly frequent, fine-grained ('dense') observations for a long period of time.

Equally important is finding an appropriate starting point (M) for the observation period. As Spain and colleagues have noted: 'Often . . . researchers wade into the stream of events with no real care as to when they do so. Put simply, Time 1 often is not really Time 1 but an arbitrary starting point for the study. Likewise, the studies often end at an equally arbitrary point in time' (Spain et al., 2010, p. 621). Particularly relevant for process research on committing is that M is linked to the start (or end) of a new employment relationship and that this is done for every subject in the study. If this point is ignored, a sample may comprise persons at very different stages in their relationship with the organization, including newcomers and those preparing to leave, and no meaningful image of the process of committing can emerge.

Planning a temporal process study within a sufficiently long time frame comes with considerable technical and motivational challenges. In the following, we spell these out and forward a number of options to deal with them in the design of an instrument to capture the committing process.

DESIGNING A PROPER MEASUREMENT INSTRUMENT FOR TEMPORAL PROCESS RESEARCH

While there are many instruments in the OB field that provide good measures of interpersonal differences, their capacity to capture changes over time is questionable. A critical issue is that the underlying notions of reliability and validity do not have the same meaning in differential and temporal measurement. In fact, these notions, which provide the standards for good measurement, derive from classical test theory[3] (CTT) (Gulliksen, 1950; Lord and Novick, 1968), which is clearly differential in nature. It assumes that every subject out of a pool of subjects has a single invariable 'true score'. Reliability in this context refers to the correlation between true score estimates from repeated or parallel versions of the same test calculated across different subjects. Importantly, reliability in this sense cannot be estimated for the scores produced by a single subject. The same is true for validity, being the correlation between a test and another (conceptually related) test. Besides, one must realize that instruments developed for differential use are typically biased against the measurement of change, the reason being that change is considered as a source of error that is minimized during test construction by removing items that are susceptible to change. Over the years, several researchers have realized that classical test theory has limited relevance for the measurement of temporal patterns (e.g., Collins, 2006; Molenaar, 2008). Temporal process research therefore needs alternative notions of reliability and validity that relate to change patterns or trajectories observed within a single subject or within each subject out of a pool of subjects, allowing for the possibility that they show different trajectories (Collins and Cliff, 1990; Molenaar, 2004). These notions will have to be translated into practical standards for constructing temporal process measurement instruments.

In order to arrive at a clear program of requirements for an instrument measuring the committing process, we follow a design methodology approach (Eekels, 2000; Roe, 2005; Roozenburg and Eekels, 1995). The differences between measuring commitment and measuring the committing process raise a number of issues that point to new and specific design requirements. Below, we describe each issue in detail and specify the resulting requirements. As these issues tend to be related, specific design requirements often support multiple issues simultaneously.

MEASUREMENT ISSUES AND ASSOCIATED INSTRUMENT DESIGN REQUIREMENTS

Issue 1:   Reliability of Mean Commitment Scores versus Reliability of Committing Patterns

Reliability is essentially a matter of replicability: an instrument is reliable to the degree that multiple measurements with the same or a parallel instrument yield similar results. In a differential setting this means if the rank order of scores – as assessed by a correlation coefficient – is the same. Instruments to measure commitment in the differential tradition typically pose several questions about the same content domain (here, commitment) in order to capture the highest possible fraction of true commitment variance over error variance (Nunnally and Bernstein, 1994). For such multi-item instruments reliability is typically expressed in Cronbach's alpha (which is the average of all possible split-half reliability coefficients). When a mean commitment score is reliable, we can be confident that the instrument picks up only real differences in commitment between individuals, not noise (including change). In the process research case, however, the focus of attention shifts to another issue, namely to the replicability of a particular string of commitment scores over time. When should an individual pattern be considered 'reliable'? Reasoning from a differential perspective, one might be tempted to focus on the reliability of the point-by-point commitment change scores over time; so-called 'reliable change' (Collins, 2006; Collins and Cliff, 1990; Salthouse et al., 2006; see also Fisher and To, 2012). A pattern might be seen as reliable when the proportion of true variance in change scores is high compared to error change (noise) in each and every one of these measured changes. However, this would ignore the fact that an observed pattern over time is not just a random collection of point-by-point changes, but a very specifically ordered one – a 'Gestalt' so to speak – and that it is this specific order of changes, this form, that we want to assess the reliability of. An ordered series of changes cannot be meaningfully reduced to 'a sum of differences' without losing critical information. Clearly, the concept of temporal reliability represents a challenge from the viewpoint of what we expect of a reliable measure, namely that it can be replicated. But how to replicate a pattern that develops uniquely in time? Several analogs of traditional differential reliability come to mind. First, by analogy of test–retest reliability, we could try to replicate the measurements of the same subject in a comparable time window. This would only work, however, when almost complete control over testing circumstances between time windows exists and no learning occurs. A second alternative is to develop a temporal process analog of parallel forms reliability in the differential domain. In the latter, we randomly divide the n items of a (long) standard test in two shorter subtests of $n/2$ items and calculate the correlation between the two. In the temporal domain, we could do a similar thing by randomly dividing the n points forming a pattern over time into two constituting patterns with $n/2$ observations, say: the odd and even observations along the x-axis. Temporal reliability would then be measured as the overlap between the two resulting patterns, as if we take two snapshots of the same process and compare their overlap. The extent to which the patterns do not overlap represents 'pattern level error', which should be minimized.

Instrument design requirements

High-density repeated measurement (HDRM) (see Solinger et al., 2013) ensures recording patterns consisting of a large number of points N within a chosen interval of length L starting at moment M. This facilitates the reliable capturing of processes, as described above.

Requirement 1: The instrument should take repeated measurements of commitment at high density.

In differential research, respondents are usually instructed explicitly to respond with a 'typical' or 'general' situation in mind. We need similar cues for the temporal process that the instrument should pick up. So, in order to articulate the instrument's purpose to capture 'fleeting' points as part of an evolving sequence, we could display the pattern thus far each time respondents are asked to add a new point. We call this feature historical response display.

Requirement 2: The instrument should display the committing process trajectory respondents are building up as they add points.

The trajectory that is building up could be verified by asking respondents: does the trajectory displayed so far provide an accurate picture of how your commitment has developed? If not, they may be allowed to alter the past pattern to bring it in accordance with their perceived progression. We are aware that this is a rather radical design choice, but it is intended, again, to ensure that respondents respond at the level of the pattern instead of an individual point. Such 'pattern level response' matches the intended theoretical level of measurement, namely that of the unfolding process. Moreover, it may help to improve the reliability of the resulting pattern because respondents are asked to agree with it again and again, thereby filtering out incidental response noise. Note that this feature is simply a temporal analog of the established practice of using slightly different but similar scale items to filter out 'noise' in conventional differential questionnaires. Having subjects repeatedly subscribe to the trajectory as it is forming has a number of advantages: (1) it reduces undue variation resulting from imperfections in memory;[4] (2) it makes even small adjustments meaningful because they are consciously scored relative to past scores; and (3) it lessens response routines and mindlessness as it forces the respondent to think about change and stability.

Requirement 3: The instrument should allow respondents to alter the ensuing committing trajectory at (every) measurement occasion (retrospective adjustment).

Note that all features of the instrument so far also add to construct validity as they all implicitly stress that it is the pattern – that is, the process of committing – that is being measured, rather than a string of quasi-unrelated points. Much research will need to be conducted to establish whether such procedures actually ensure the reliability of a pattern, as conceived above.

Issue 2:   Validity of Mean Commitment Scores versus Validity of Committing Patterns

Whereas temporal process reliability is about the replicability of committing patterns, temporal process validity deals with capturing the 'right' substantive meaning of each pattern: does it capture the right process? Construct validity of the committing trajectory, then, is the extent to which it actually represents the subjects' 'development of committing', the committing process, so to speak, and not the development of something else. The validity of temporal processes can be inferred, for instance, when theoretically related (concurrent) 'process constructs' show congruent changes over time (possibly with a time lag) while non-related (that is, discriminant) constructs do not. Such congruence can be assessed by calculating dynamic correlations (e.g. Roe, 2014a) or time-series analysis. Temporal validities could then be calculated between, for example, being treated fairly and committing, or committing and staying intentions. Validity can be explored further by looking at relations between certain morphologic characteristics of trajectories (for example, trend, amplitude, curvature). For instance, the occurrence and depth of dips in the committing trajectory might be predicted from certain work events: changes in the psychological contract or organizational downsizing might be followed by changes in committing, but incidents such as pay raises or breaks might be unrelated.

Instrument design requirements
In order to assess the validity of trajectories in the way described above, related phenomena must be measured simultaneously.

Requirement 4: The instrument should be able to pick up discriminant and concurrent processes and disturbances/incidents.

To ensure the content validity of questions aimed at measuring the committing process, they should linguistically reflect its temporal process nature. Items should therefore be phrased as verbs (Rescher, 1996; Roe, 2008a) and explicitly tied to the current time. So, instead of a general state-like question such as, 'In general, I have the feeling that I belong to this organization', we rather ask for agreement on a statement like: 'Right now, I am feeling included in this organization'.

Requirement 5: As the instrument must record a string of responses of committing in the here-and-now, it uses active and instant wording of items.

This 'in the moment wording' of items also likely adds to the reliability of the measured pattern, because temporally unspecific phrasing can introduce unreliability. In the extreme case, the question 'In general, how committed are you?' is temporally unspecific, and yields unreliable recordings of change. In this respect, the use of verbs and active phrasing, in combination with a specific time frame, is also preferred from a reliability standpoint (that is, it picks up real instead of noise variation). For instance, Solinger et al. (2013, 2016b) used three short questions stating: "'at THIS moment. . . : (1) what I feel about [my organization]: I am proud; (2) what I think about [my organization]: I belong to it; (3) What I do for my organization: I engage/participate.'"

Issue 3:   Interpersonal versus Inter-Temporal Sensitivity

An instrument needs to record relevant nuances and contrasts in committing in order to be useful and reliable. If it is capable of detecting even small contrasts, it is sensitive. However, a sensitive measure is only valid if it picks up the intended contrasts. In differential research domains the measure needs to be sensitive to interpersonal differences in commitment, while in temporal process domains it needs to be sensitive to changes in committing over time (Roe, 2008b). Only these kinds of measures provide the information necessary to investigate the development, growth, or decline of commitment. Higher sensitivity potentially translates into greater morphological richness of the resulting patterns. A measure of committing can be considered temporally sensitive if it registers any change since the last measurement occasion that is meaningful in the mind of the respondent, no matter how small that change is.

Instrument design requirements

Temporal sensitivity can be fostered by using a fine-grained rating scale. If test items have only few anchors, recording nuances and micro-changes over time is difficult. In differential research settings, precision is achieved by averaging. But even there evidence shows that the precision of measurement increases with the number of scale points, albeit with a certain optimum (Nunnally and Bernstein, 1994). Fine-grained measurement scales better capture the underlying continuous distributions of focal variables. In a multilevel context, evidence has demonstrated that five-point single-item Likert scales lead to underestimated Intraclass Correlation Coefficient, $ICC_{(1)}$ coefficients (that is, within-case variance is overestimated and/or between-case variance is underestimated (Beal and Dawson, 2007). Such effects disappeared with the use of finer response scales. Another finding was that the number of time points interacted with scaling method, such that underestimation of the reliability of within-case variance $ICC_{(2)}$ was worst for the combined use of coarse measures and few time moments, and non-existent with the use of fine scales and many time moments (Beal and Dawson, 2007). Clearly, then, fine-grained measurement aids reliability.

Following these leads, we would expect that 'instant' commitment on an intuitive 0–100 scale (see the Celsius thermometer) is easier to score and more sensitive to micro-changes than conventional five-point Likert-type scales (see, Fisher and To, 2012). An additional advantage is that it can also record the total absence of commitment (score 0), something which is not possible with conventional scales. This is in line with a temporal conception of commitment as a process phenomenon (committing) having a beginning and an end in time.

Requirement 6: The instrument should provide a continuous answering scale with commitment ranging from 0 to 100.

Issue 4:   Robustness against Noise versus Robustness against Reuse

Differential and temporal measurement differ in their loci of distortion against which measurement needs to be robust. In the differential research tradition, measurement noise is attributed to time- or situation-related influences (for example, effects of mood or context, and maturation or learning effects; McGrath and Tschan, 2004), which distort the true score distribution. Scale developers try to deal with these distortions, for instance by phrasing scale items in very general, acontextual and ahistoric ways whereby respondents are typically invited to state their 'typical', 'general', 'normal', or 'average' commitment towards something. The result is that – in line with the nature of differential constructs and the idea of a single, invariable true score in CTT – measures favor stability.

In sharp contrast to this, in temporal process research momentary changes are of substantive theoretical interest, so each measurement occasion should be as time-specific as possible. It is the here-and-now that should be captured and the interest is explicitly on how this is different from a previous measure. However, this requirement introduces new threats. Specifically, temporal process measures should instead be robust against distortion due to repeated use of the same measure (Roe, 2008b). Recorded values should be insensitive to repeated measurement; that is, not affect observed responses. The potential distortion that can take place when a test is administered and reused can be of a systematic and a non-systematic nature. Systematic distortion takes place when so-called response-shifts occur. This happens when – in the mind of the respondent – the scale is recalibrated or the commitment construct redefined as time progresses. These phenomena are also known as beta change and gamma change (see Golembiewski et al., 1976). As experiences and information accumulate over time, the respondent's interpretation of the scale anchors may change. For instance, a fixed commitment level may be scored a 4 in the first month of work, but a 3 in the third month when it is judged more critically against colleagues' commitment. Such 'recalibration' of the anchors is called 'beta change'. 'Gamma change' occurs when – in the respondent's mind – the inherent meaning of 'being committed' shifts over time; valid comparison over time then becomes impossible. Clearly, such systematic distortions – if they occur – threaten the validity of the measured trajectories. To detect them in temporal research, we refer to the general practical suggestions on safeguarding measurement validity (for example, Requirements 4 and 5, above).

This leaves us with the category of non-systematic distortions of patterns over time. These can have two sources: distortions that occur 'naturally' due to the passage of time and those that occur because of a particular method of measurement. Naturally occurring distortions are for instance mood or immediate-context effects (for example, a noisy environment). These distract respondents in a non-systematic way. They can be dampened by mood checks and proper respondent instructions (see below). Method-related distortions can occur when the time interval between measurements interacts with the fallibility of human memory (Roe, 2008a). As we intend to measure a reliable string of earlier responses vis-à-vis each other, bad recall of these previous answers can make the observed patterns unreliable. Design-wise, this problem may be averted by using historical response display (that is, Requirement 2) and by choosing an appropriately intensive frequency (see Requirement 1). If the repetitions are close in time (as they are in HDRM), observed responses can become routinized and habitual (for example, 'I am always scoring 5 on this item'), which compromises measurement validity. This should be addressed by avoiding measurements too close in time. Borrowing an example from aviation might help to clarify the issue. After an airplane takes off from the runway, the air is temporarily moving. This instability in the air is dangerous for subsequent planes, increasing the risk of crashing during take-off. Some time is needed for the air to stabilize before a next plane can take off. The instability in the air is called the 'vortex effect'.[5] Analogously, the 'vortex-effect' of temporal measurement is the impact on measurement validity and reliability of item X at time t as a result of its closeness in time to its predecessor X_{t-1}. A minimal 'cooling down' time (T_c) may be required before acceptable validity and reliability of X_t can be ascertained again (for instance, to avoid routinization). Self-report measures of commitment may be prone to a vortex effect as well, requiring a minimum amount of time in between administrations before a new, 'fresh', equally valid response can be expected. If the time between measurements is too short, the next answer may get 'caught up' in the vortex of the former, damaging its response validity. What a proper T_c value is for which type of items is as yet unknown, and can only be assessed in future process methodology research. It may also serve as a yardstick to distinguish between alternative measures and measurement methods.

Instrument design requirements
Naturally occurring distortions can be dealt with in at least two ways. First, the expected source of noise can be measured by incorporating it in the instrument. Examples of such measurable instant distortions of committing responses are the respondent's mood or temporary (personal) circumstances. Secondly, direct environmental disturbances can be minimized by ascertaining that administration takes place at a quiet place and time, for instance by instruction or by prompting respondents at appropriate (quiet) times.

Requirement 7: The instrument should avoid disturbance by concurrent and transient noise either by including (and controlling for) them or by giving instructions for proper 'low noise' administration.

The dangers of taking measurements too close in time can of course be avoided by building in sufficient time in-between. Respondents need ample time to 'refresh'. Note that this optimal time is likely to depend on the method of administration as well (see Issue 5, below). Short, rapidly administered (even fun) questionnaires probably create a smaller vortex than do lengthy, tedious questionnaires. Solinger et al. (2013), for instance, took weekly measures of commitment with a fast-capture (web-based) instrument.

Requirement 8: The instrument should avoid disturbance due to a vortex effect by allowing sufficient time in between measurements.

Issue 5: Single-Shot Respondent Compliance versus Sustained Respondent Involvement

When response compliance is predominantly concerned with obtaining a single, initial response, relatively little attention needs to be paid to the user-friendliness of measurement instruments. The same goes for a typical three- to four-wave temporal panel study with months in between measurement occasions. In contrast, in HDRM process studies involving, for instance, a year of weekly measures with multiple subjects, attrition poses a major threat because all respondents must remain motivated to cooperate many times for a long period of time. As a result, more attention needs to be paid to 'the user side' of measurement. Taking high-volume process measures requires a long-term relationship between the respondent on the one hand, and the instrument and researcher on the other. This implies that in temporal process research the respondent becomes a significant stakeholder in the construction of a proper measurement system. Critical issues that make a HDRM system appealing on the respondent side are low intrusiveness and a user-friendly interface, with features such as simplicity, comprehensibility, esthetic attractiveness, a positive 'feel', fun, meaningfulness, and proper incentives to keep responding.

Instrument design requirements
Low intrusiveness means that the 'response burden' must be low. Three to four minutes per measurement occasion should be the maximum.[6] This means that responses must be captured fast and easy. Traditional lengthy questionnaires do not fit this bill. Instead, only a few, clear, pointed questions should be used. Multi-process constructs such as organizational commitment are best measured by a single question per sub-process. For instance, to tap organizational commitment Solinger et al. (2013, 2016a, 2016b) followed the traditional tripartite view on attitudes (e.g., Rosenberg and Hovland, 1960) by using a cognitive ('I belong'), an affective ('I am proud'), and a behavioral item ('I engage').[7]

Another way of relieving the response burden is by making the responding process easy. This can be done by designing a user interface (that is, a responding medium such as a web-based console or a computer or smartphone with an app) that is user friendly, for instance by prompting the user, by using easily readable fonts, easy and colorful answering sliders, and an intuitively appealing order of questions.

Requirement 9: The instrument limits response burden by using few items (one per attribute) and a user-friendly responding interface.

A second way of building sustained respondent involvement is by making participation in the temporal research project attractive. Besides the use of extrinsic motivators (rewards) for continued participation, the design of the instrument itself can be used to mobilize other, more intrinsic motivators as well. Appealing, esthetic design of the interface is one possibility. Making participation fun is another. A real frontier in instrument design – also for research purposes – is 'gamification'. Various options, such as assembling points for every response, can be thought of.

Requirement 10: The instrument should be attractive to (re)use by adding esthetic and playful features.

DISCUSSION AND CONCLUSION

In this chapter we have shown that the increased scientific interest in temporal aspects of commitment necessitates a reconsideration of its conceptual basis, which in turn has important ramifications for the way commitment is to be measured over time. Adding to the latter are practical considerations of the need to take high-frequency measurements with respondents over a long time interval, with a clear and meaningful starting point that should be the same for all subjects. The game of doing research, so to speak, is altered considerably by these factors combined. Temporal researchers ask different things of their respondents, who are likely to ask something else (and more) in return. In short: their relationship changes.

In order to gather reliable and valid temporal data, we have therefore recommended a number of design features, some of which may be considered controversial, at least by traditional standards. Their adequacy and usefulness are up for future consideration, application, testing, and refinement. As we have argued, difficult trade-offs are involved such as between gathering many time points and sample attrition resulting from response burden. The solution we propose lies in developing fast-capture measures with sufficient face validity. Technological advances now bring such research instruments within reach, for instance by using mobile apps. The first two authors are themselves involved in a combined academic–commercial venture that has developed a mobile app[8] to capture and display weekly commitment measures of individuals in work communities such as teams, departments, and even entire organizations. This app was developed in cooperation with a serious gaming firm to add playful features, as advocated in the requirement program above. By making a research instrument easy to access and even fun to interact with, we hope to ascertain continued compliance. Clearly, care must be taken, on the other hand, that these features do not interfere with the reliability and validity of measurements. How to achieve this is something that is to be discovered as our experience with these new ways of measurement increases.

Another important trade-off exists in the need to truly capture responses at the level of patterns building up during the time window defined by L, M, and N. To this end, we advocated 'retrospective display' of previous responses, whereby respondents affirm a developing pattern again and again. We are aware, however, that this may in turn elicit biasing response mechanisms at the pattern level as well. Consistency may be sought, for instance, with implicitly held personal 'theories' on how change should unfold ('pattern-guessing'), confirmation bias, and naive extrapolation. All of these may bias responders towards consistency, positivity (if one's past trajectory is growing), and negativity (if one's past trajectory is declining). Investigating the positive and potential negative effects of pattern-based responding in an experience sampling measurement context is therefore another important objective for future research.

Temporal process research holds great promise for gaining a deeper understanding into questions of how the process of committing develops. It will help in uncovering typical patterns or scenarios of commitment in work communities, which will also aid timely intervention in management practice. Using the recommendations outlined above may help to build proper measurement instruments to reach those important goals.

NOTES

1. Which is logically incorrect; see below, and Thompson (2011).
2. In other areas of social science, temporal process theorizing and group-based methods are much more common. In particular, developmental psychology has a longer tradition by studying comparative developments between groups in drug use, depression, learning, delinquency, and so on.

3.   Modern psychometric theory (often referred to as item response theory, IRT) defines reliability and validity with reference to subjects' scores on a 'latent trait' (theta scores, rather than true scores on a particular test). Its application in OB is very rare. Besides, IRT also has a differential basis.
4.   Note that possible 'recall bias' in retrospective adjustment is expected to be weakened, as a record of previous responses is displayed 'black on white'. In other words: subjects are likely to be very conscious of adjusting points if they are allowed to. Clearly, however, just how much such adjustments are subject to recall bias should be the subject of further research. Relatedly, one might want to find the optimal retrospective time frame respondents that may be allowed to adjust, ranging from only the previous response to all previous responses. Alternatively, one may choose to separate the process of adding points and that of 'acknowledging' the final historical pattern, by asking the latter only after the last point was added. We thank an anonymous reviewer for suggesting this alternative.
5.   For example, in romantic relationships, posing the question 'Do you love me?' to your partner is likely to elicit ever less valid responses as frequencies and density in time of the question increase. It may even devolve into a proxy of indifference.
6.   This is the amount of time we thought it would take to get a cup of coffee from a nearby coffee machine in the workplace. Typically, this activity is not very intrusive.
7.   Clearly, the choice of items now becomes of paramount content validity interest. Selection may be based on linguistic analysis or high item–total scale correlations in a differential study. Note that items may need to be rewritten in immediate, active words (see Requirement 5).
8.   For an impression, see http://www.en-gager.com.

REFERENCES

Andruff, H., Carraro N., Thompson A., Gaudreau P., and Louvet, B. (2009). Latent class growth modelling: A tutorial. *Tutorials in Quantitative Methods for Psychology*, *5*(1), 11–24.
Beal, D.J. and Dawson, J.F. (2007). On the use of Likert-type scales: Influence on the aggregate variables. *Organizational Research Methods*, *10*(4), 657–672.
Bentein, K., Vandenberghe, C., Vandenberg, R., and Stinglhamber, F. (2005). The role of change in the relationship between commitment and turnover: A latent growth modeling approach. *Journal of Applied Psychology*, *90*(3), 468–482
Cattell, R.B. (1952). Three basic factor-analytic research designs: their interrlations and derivatives. *Psychological Bulletin*, *49*, 499–520.
Collins, L.M. (2006). Analysis of longitudinal data: The integration of theoretical model, temporal design, and statistical model. *Annual Review of Psychology*, *57*, 505–528.
Collins, L.M. and Cliff, N. (1990). Using the longitudinal Guttman simplex as a basis for measuring growth. *Quantitative Methods in Psychology*, *108*(1), 128–134.
Edmondson, A.C. and McManus, S.E. (2007). Methodological fit in management field research. *Academy of Management Review*, *32*(4), 1155–1179.
Eekels, J. (2000). On the fundamentals of engineering design science: The geography of engineering design science. Part 1. *Journal of Engineering Design*, *11*(4), 377–397.
Fisher, C.D. and To, M.L. (2012). Using experience sampling methodology in organizational behavior. *Journal of Organizational Behavior*, *33*, 865–877.
George, J.M. and Jones, G.R. (2000). The role of time in theory and theory building. *Journal of Management*, *26*(4), 657–684.
Golembiewski, R.T., Billingsley, K., and Yeager, S. (1976). Measuring change and persistence in human affairs: Types of change generated by OD designs. *Journal of Applied Behavioral Science*, *12*, 133–157.
Gulliksen, H. (1950). *Theory of Mental Tests*. New York: Wiley.
Judge, T.A. and Kammeyer-Mueller, J.D. (2012). Job attitudes. *Annual Review of Psychology*, *63*, 341–367.
Klein, H.J., Molloy, J.C., and Brinsfield, C.T. (2012). Reconceptualizing workplace commitment to redress a stretched construct: Revisiting assumptions and removing confounds. *Academy of Management Review*, *37*, 130–151.
Langley, A., Smallman, C., Tsoukas, H., and Van de Ven, A.H. (2013). Process studies of change in organization and management: Unveiling temporality, activity, and flow. *Academy of Management Journal*, *56*(1), 1–13.
Li, J. and Roe, R.A. (2012). Introducing an intrateam longitudinal approach to the study of team process dynamics. *European Journal of Work and Organizational Psychology*, *21*(5), 718–748.
Lord, F.M. and Novick, M.R. (1968). *Statistical Theories of Mental Test Scores*. Reading, MA: Addison-Wesley.
McGrath, J.E. and Tschan, F. (2004). *Temporal Matters in Social Psychology: Examining the Role of Time in the Lives of Groups and Individuals*. Washington, DC: American Psychological Association.

Molenaar, P.C.M. (2004). A manifesto on psychology as idiographic science: Bringing the person back into scientific psychology, this time forever. *Measurement, 40*, 201–218.

Molenaar, P.C.M. (2008). Consequences of the ergodic theorems for classical test theory, factor analysis, and the analysis of developmental processes. In S.M. Hofer and D.F. Alwin (eds), *Handbook of Cognitive Aging: Interdisciplinary Perspectives* (pp. 90–104). Thousand Oaks, CA US: Sage Publications.

Monge, P.R. (1990). Theoretical and analytical issues in studying organizational processes. *Organization Science, 1*(4), 406–430.

Nagin, D.S. (2005). *Group-Based Modeling of Development*. Cambridge, MA: Harvard University Press.

Navarro, J., Roe, R.A., and Artiles, M.I. (2015). Taking time seriously: Changing practices and perspectives in Work/Organizational Psychology. *Journal of Work and Organizational Psychology, 31*(3), 129–214.

Ng, T.W.H., Feldman, D.C., and Lam, S.S.K. (2010). Psychological contract breaches, organizational commitment, and innovation-related behaviors: A latent growth modeling approach. *Journal of Applied Psychology, 95*(4), 744–751.

Nunnally, J.C. and Bernstein, I.H. (1994). *Psychometric Theory* (3rd edn). New York: McGraw-Hill.

Ployhart, R.E. (2008). The measurement and analysis of motivation. In R. Kanfer, G. Chen, and R.D. Pritchard (eds), *Work Motivation: Past, Present, and Future* (pp. 18–61). New York: Routledge Taylor Francis.

Rescher, N. (1996). *Process Metaphysics: An Introduction to Process Philosophy*. New York: State University of New York.

Roe, R.A. (2005). The design of selection systems: Context, principles, issues. In A. Evers, O. Smit, and N. Anderson (eds), *Handbook of Personnel Selection* (pp. 73–97). Oxford: Blackwell.

Roe, R.A. (2008a). Time in applied psychology: The study of 'what happens' rather than 'what is'. *European Psychologist, 13*(1), 37–52.

Roe, R.A. (2008b). Time and the study of behavior in organizations: Implications for assessment, selection, and development. Paper presented at the SHL Seminar, Thames Ditton, UK.

Roe, R.A. (2014a). Performance, motivation and time. In A. Shipp and Y. Fried (eds), *Time and Work. Vol. 1: How Time Impacts Individuals* (pp. 63–110). London: Routledge/Taylor & Francis.

Roe, R.A. (2014b). Test validity from a temporal perspective: Incorporating time in validation research. *European Journal of Work and Organizational Psychology, 23*(5), 754–768. doi: 10.1080/1359432X.2013.804177.

Roe, R.A., Gockel, C., and Meyer, B. (2012). Time and change in teams: Where we are and where we are moving. *European Journal of Work and Organizational Psychology, 21*(5), 629–656.

Roe, R.A. and Inceoglu, I. (2016). Measuring states and traits in motivation and emotion: A new model illustrated for the case of work engagement. In D. Bartram, F. Cheung, K.F. Geisinger, D. Iliescu, and F.T.L. Leong (eds), *The ITC International Handbook of Testing and Assessment* (pp. 63–88). Oxford: Oxford University Press.

Roozenburg, N.F.M. and Eekels, J. (1995). *Product Design: Fundamentals and Methods*. Chichester: Wiley.

Rosenberg, M.J. and Hovland, C.I. (1960). Cognitive, affective, and behavioral components of attitudes. *Attitude Organization and Change: An Analysis of Consistency among Attitude Components, 3*, 1–14.

Salthouse, T.A., Nesselroade, J.R., and Berish, D.E. (2006). Short-term variability in cognitive performance and the calibration of longitudinal change. *Journal of Gerontology: Psychological Sciences, 61B*(3), 144–151.

Shepherd, D.A. and Sutcliffe, K.M. (2011). Inductive top-down theorizing: A source of new theories of organization. *Academy of Management Review, 36*(2), 361–380.

Solinger, O.N., Hofmans, J., Bal, P.M., and Jansen, P.G.W. (2016a). Bouncing back from psychological contract breach: How commitment recovers over time. *Journal of Organizational Behavior, 37*(4), 494–514.

Solinger, O.N., Hofmans, J., and Van Olffen, W. (2016b). The dynamic microstructure of organizational commitment. *Journal of Occupational and Organizational Psychology, 88*(4), 773–796.

Solinger, O.N., Van Olffen, W., Roe, R.A., and Hofmans, J. (2013). On becoming (un) committed: A taxonomy and test of newcomer onboarding scenarios. *Organization Science, 24*(6), 1640–1661.

Spain, S.M., Miner, A.G., Kroonenberg, P.M., and Drasgow, F. (2010). Job performance as multivariate dynamic criteria: Experience sampling and multiway component analysis. *Multivariate Behavioral Research, 45*(4), 599–626.

Thompson, M. (2011). Ontological shift or ontological drift? Reality claims, epistemological frameworks, and theory generation in organization studies. *Academy of Management Review, 36*(4), 754–773.

Tsoukas, H., and Chia, R. (2002). On organizational becoming: Rethinking organizational change. *Organization Science, 13*(5), 567–582.

Vandenberg, R.J. and Scarpello, V. (1994). A longitudinal assessment of the determinant relationship between employee commitments to the occupation and the organization. *Journal of Organizational Behavior, 15*(6), 535–547.

Vander Elst, T., Richter, A., Sverke, M., Näswall, K., De Cuyper, N., and De Witte, H. (2014). Threat of losing valued job features: The role of perceived control in mediating the effect of qualitative job insecurity on job strain and psychological withdrawal. *Work and Stress, 28*(2), 143–164.

35. Person-centered research strategies in commitment research
*Alexandre J.S. Morin**

Commitment is a vibrant field of research, encompassing unidimensional, multidimensional, and multifocal theories (see Chapters 2, 3, and 4 in this volume, respectively). Although a person-centered approach can inform all of these frameworks, Meyer and Allen's (1991) three-component model (TCM) is arguably the model that has been the most extensively investigated from a person-centered perspective and the focus of this chapter. The TCM defines commitment as a 'force that binds an individual to a target and to a course of action of relevance to that target' (Meyer et al., 2006, p. 666). This attachment is proposed to be maintained through three distinct mindsets: affective commitment (AC), normative commitment (NC), and continuance commitment (CC). Employees are assumed to experience each mindset to varying degrees in relation to multiple targets (for example, organization, colleagues, supervisors, occupation; Morin et al., 2009), so that individual profiles reflect a combination of AC, NC, and CC directed at various constituencies. Specific mindset–target combinations are hereafter referred to as a commitment component.

Variable-centered studies looking at interactions among commitment components showed that the relations involving specific components differed as a function of the strength of the other components (Gellatly et al., 2006). However, these studies are limited in their power to detect and interpret complex interactions among multiple components. A person-centered approach, aiming to identify distinct, and relatively homogeneous, subgroups presenting qualitatively and quantitatively distinct profiles on a set of commitment components, has been advocated as more appropriate for investigations of complex relations among multiple commitment components (Meyer et al., 2013b). A person-centered approach views individuals in a more holistic fashion, and affords the opportunity to address complex interactions among commitment components that would be difficult to detect using traditional variable-centered analyses (Meyer et al., 2013b; Morin et al., 2011b). However, person-centered approaches also require a paradigmatic shift in the way research questions are framed, moving away from a correlational approach centered on variables to a configurational approach centered on persons (Delbridge and Fiss, 2013).

This chapter aims to provide a broad introduction to a person-centered perspective of commitment research more generally, and to the analytical possibilities provided by mixture models more specifically. This chapter first briefly presents the underpinnings of the person-centered perspective, before proposing a user-friendly description of the various types of mixture models available to person-centered commitment researchers.

A PERSON-CENTERED APPROACH TO COMMITMENT RESEARCH

In the original formulation of the TCM, Meyer and Allen (1991) proposed that employees would present commitment profiles reflecting their relative levels of AC, NC, and CC to the organization. Building on this, Meyer and Herscovitch (2001) offered a set of propositions concerning eight hypothetical profiles of commitment reflecting distinct combinations of high or low scores on each mindset. Essentially, the logic of these propositions is that commitment mindsets can combine and be experienced in different ways, so that how any one is experienced or relates to other variables will depend on the context created by the other mindsets. For example, Gellatly et al. (2006) proposed that NC might be experienced as a moral imperative when combined with strong AC, but as an indebted obligation when combined with weak AC and strong CC. When multiple targets are considered, the notion that commitment to a specific target can contextualize commitment to the other targets has been addressed through the ideas that commitment to different targets may conflict with one another (Reichers, 1985) or that compatible commitments may reinforce one another (Meyer and Allen, 1997). When multiple targets and mindsets are combined, Meyer and Allen (1997) proposed that dependencies, or nesting, can develop among commitment targets, which may have implications for mindsets pertaining to each target. To illustrate, consider two groups of employees, both of which have a strong desire to continue working with their colleagues (strong group AC). The first group also enjoys working in their organization (strong organizational AC), evidencing compatibility. However, the second group has little desire to remain with the organization (weak organizational AC), suggesting conflict. The first group would be expected to stay in the organization and work group, and to perform up to or beyond the standards of both. The second group could be expected to develop a high level of CC to the organization, as this employment tie is their only way to remain working with their colleagues. This scenario illustrates how nested commitments can generate compatibility or conflict.

So far, studies have attempted to verify these propositions through the identification of profiles of employees' AC, NC, and CC to their organizations (for reviews, see Meyer et al., 2013b; Meyer and Morin, 2016), AC to two or more targets (e.g., Morin et al., 2011b), or AC, NC, and CC to more than one target (e.g., Meyer et al., 2015; Morin et al., 2016; Tsoumbris and Xenikou, 2010). This research has supported the idea that commitment components create a context for other commitment components, and that both compatibility and conflicts among commitments is possible. However, the use of different idiosyncratic reporting and labeling approaches makes it difficult to integrate results from multiple studies.

REPORTING AND LABELING

To facilitate the systematic comparison and integration of results across studies, a common profile labeling scheme and clear reporting guidelines seems to be required. Profiles of any kind can vary along three dimensions: (1) shape: the overall pattern, or configuration, of high and low scores on various indicators; (2) elevation: the average level of commitment across indicators within each profile; and (3) scatter: the degree of differentiation among indicators within each profile. So far, research has mainly used profile shape to determine labels, such as through the identification of the mindset(s) with the highest score as being 'dominant' (Meyer et al., 2013b). Shape-differentiated profiles are considered to be qualitatively differentiated. When all indicators (for example, mindsets) are at approximately the same level, labels such as 'uncommitted', 'moderately committed', or 'fully committed' are typically used and profiles are said to be quantitatively differentiated.

For illustration purposes, prototypical TCM profiles corresponding to these qualitative and quantitative differentiations are illustrated in Figure 35.1a. With the exception of the moderately committed profile, these profiles correspond to the eight theoretical profiles discussed by Meyer and Herscovitch (2001). A series of descriptive labels (in parentheses in Figure 35.1a) are also proposed to depict the psychological states reflected in these profiles, which may be more meaningful to practitioners: emotionally committed (AC-dominant), obligated (NC-dominant), trapped (CC-dominant), morally committed (AC/NC-dominant), indebted (CC/NC-dominant), and invested (AC/CC-dominant).

To add precision to the description of the profiles, qualifiers are proposed to describe profiles where the level of elevation is either high or low, and profiles that show a weak level of differentiation (scatter) across indicators. To reflect elevation, 'high' is used when all indicators are above the average and 'low' when all indicators are below average. To reflect scatter, the term 'weak' is used when there are relatively small differences between indicators within a profile. Note that in cases where elevation is high or low, scatter is nat-

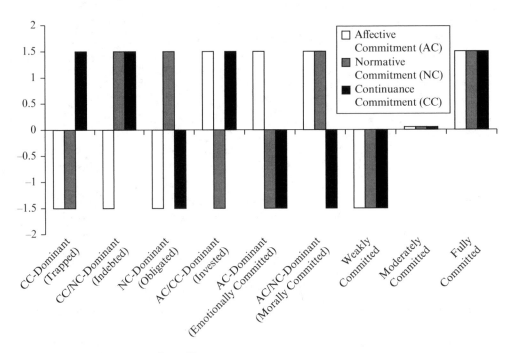

Figure 35.1a   Prototypical profiles

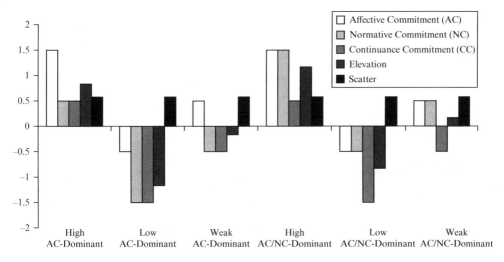

Figure 35.1b   Profiles differing in terms of elevation and scatter

urally restricted so that the qualifier 'weak' is not used in this situation. It is also possible to include indicators of elevation (the average level across indicators in a single profile) and scatter (the standard deviation across indicators in a single profile) to the graphical presentation of the profiles. Figure 35.1b illustrates variations in elevation and scatter for the AC-dominant and AC/NC-dominant profiles, and incorporates within-profile indicators of elevation and scatter to the graphical representation. These indicators of elevation and scatter were calculated as the mean and standard deviation of the indicators within each profile, and added to the figure (for a similar procedure, see Marsh et al., 2009). Profiles characterized by the same scatter but in which all mindsets are located above average (high), below average (low), or both above and below average (weak) are presented.

The application of this profile labeling scheme also involves systematizing the way results are reported. Typically, studies have reported either raw scores (Meyer et al., 2013a) or standardized scores (Morin et al., 2011b) of commitment components. The second approach is more naturally suited to the proposed profile labeling scheme. In measurement, raw scores can seldom be ascribed any substantive meaning due to the lack of meaningful unit of measurement. Even comparisons across scales from a single instrument are precarious unless one can demonstrate that the implicit unit of measurement is equivalent across these scales. Furthermore, many studies rely on idiosyncratic measures, or modified versions of validated questionnaires, making comparisons based on raw scores simply impossible. Standardized scores not only make scores interpretable as a function of the sample mean and standard deviation, but they also make the graphical presentation of results (and the identification of high/low scores) clearer, especially when histograms are used. However, standardized scores remain a function of sample means and standard deviations, which may differ across studies. Thus, a third and stronger alternative is to present scores based on normative data (Kam et al., 2016). Norms are currently available for 54 distinct countries for TCM measures of AC, NC, and CC to the organization (Meyer et al., 2012). Overall, my recommendation is to graphically represent the profiles using histograms based on standardized scores, or normed scores when available, while reporting raw scores (and sample means and variance) in supplementary tables to help contextualize sample characteristics.

MIXTURE MODELING APPROACHES TO PERSON-CENTERED ANALYSES

This chapter focuses on a mixture modeling approach to person-centered analyses (for a brief overview of alternative approaches, see the online supplements). Mixture modeling is a model-based approach to clustering, based on the assumption that a sample includes a mixture of subpopulations, and is part of the generalized structural equation modeling (GSEM) framework (Muthén, 2002). GSEM allows for the estimation of relations between any type of continuous and categorical observed and latent variables. Traditional latent variable models (for example, confirmatory factor analyses, CFA; and structural equation models, SEM) assume that all individuals are drawn from a single population and yield variable-centered results reflecting a synthesis of the relations observed in the total sample. GSEM relaxes this assumption by allowing all or part of any CFA/SEM model to differ across unobserved subgroups of participants. More precisely, GSEM identifies relatively homogeneous subgroups of participants differing qualitatively and quantitatively from one another in relation to: (1) their configuration of a set of observed and/or latent variable(s); and/or (2) relations among observed and/or latent variables. These subgroups are typically referred to as latent profiles, and represented in the model as a categorical latent variable (where the latent profiles represent the distinct categories).

Within GSEM, person-centered analyses present three key defining characteristics. First, they are typological: their results provide a classification system helping to categorize individuals into qualitatively and quantitatively distinct profiles. Second, they are prototypical: all participants have a probability of membership in all profiles based on their degree of similarity with each prototypical latent profile. These profiles are called latent because they are represented by a latent categorical variable where each category represents an inferred, unobserved, prototypical subpopulation. Finally, they are exploratory: solutions including different numbers of profiles are typically contrasted in order to select the optimal solution in a mainly exploratory manner. Even though it is possible to devise confirmatory mixture models when theory is advanced enough to provide clear expectations regarding the exact nature of the profiles to be expected (Finch and Bronk, 2011), these models still need to be contrasted with unconstrained exploratory models to show that their fit to the data remains comparatively acceptable. In practice, the optimal number of profiles is determined based on inspection of: (1) the substantive meaning and theoretical conformity of the solution; (2) the statistical adequacy of the solution; and (3) statistical indicators (additional details on model estimation and statistical indicators are provided in the online supplements).

Another key consideration is to demonstrate that the profiles are meaningful. It is important to keep in mind that it is technically impossible to empirically distinguish a LPA model including k profiles from a common factor model including $k - 1$ factors (e.g., Steinley and McDonald, 2007). Both have identical covariance implications and can be considered 'equivalent' models (e.g., Cudeck and Henly, 2003), and end up explaining equivalent variance. Similarly, it is hard to rule out the possibility that spurious profiles might emerge due to violations of the model's distributional assumptions even when none are present in the data (Bauer, 2007). Thus, in order to support a substantive interpretation, it remains necessary to embark on a process of construct validation to demonstrate that the profiles: (1) have heuristic value; (2) have theoretical conformity or value; (3) are meaningfully related to key covariates; and (4) generalize to new samples (Marsh et al., 2009; Morin et al., 2011b).

The following sections include a user-friendly description of the main categories of mixture models available to person-centered commitment researchers: latent profile analyses (LPAs), factor mixture analyses (FMAs), latent transition analyses (LTAs), mixture regression analyses (MRAs), and growth mixture analyses (GMAs). These models are graphically presented (and numbered) in Figure 35.2.

LATENT PROFILE ANALYSES (MODEL 1)

LPAs are the most common form of mixture model used in commitment research (Meyer et al., 2013b), and aim to describe subgroups of participants differing from one another on their configuration on a series of commitment components. While CFAs estimate continuous latent variables (factors) representing groupings of indicators, LPAs estimate categorical latent variables (profiles) representing groupings of persons (Lubke and Muthén, 2005). LPAs can accommodate a variety of continuous, ordinal, and categorical measurement scales (McLachlan and Peel, 2000), and take into account a multilevel structure (Henry and Muthén, 2010).

LPAs allow for the direct specification of alternative models whose adequacy can be compared with various relative fit indicators. For example, LPA models can be estimated while allowing profiles to be defined only on the basis of the indicators means, or also be defined while allowing the variance of the indicators to differ across profiles (Peugh and Fan, 2013). Contrary to cluster analyses, LPAs do not assume the variance of the indicators to be invariant (the same) across profiles. However, the invariance of the indicators' variances remains LPAs' default parameterization in some statistical packages, such as Mplus (Muthén and Muthén, 2014). Relaxing this default helps to obtain less-biased parameter estimates (Peugh and Fan, 2013), and provides a more flexible and realistic representation than relying on artificial constraints through which the level of inter-individual variability is forced to be equivalent from one profile to the other (Morin et al., 2011a). Correlated uniquenesses can also be included. However, LPAs typically assume the conditional independence of the indicators, which are expected to be unrelated to one another conditional on the latent profiles. GSEM makes it possible to relax this assumption through the inclusion of correlations among the residual variances of the indicators, which may even be beneficial to the estimation process under some highly specific conditions (Peugh and Fan, 2013). Nevertheless, this assumption should be relaxed only with caution, and on the basis of strong a priori expectations of residual associations among the indicators (for example, wording effects). Correlated uniquenesses drastically change the meaning of the model, which aims to parsimoniously summarize the indicators' covariance by a finite number of latent profiles. Method factors, providing an explicit

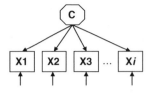

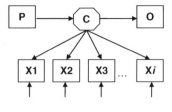

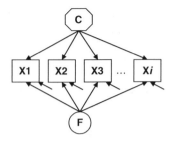

Model 1
Latent Profile Analyses

This model estimates *C* latent profiles differing from one another based on their configuration on *i* indicators (X1 to X*i*).

Model 2
Latent Profile Analyses with Covariates

This model integrates predictors (P) and outcomes (O) to Model 1. In this model, P influences the likelihood of memberships into the latent profiles, and the likelihood of membership into the latent profiles influences O.

Model 3
Factor Mixture Analyses

This model simultaneously estimate *C* latent profiles and F common factors from the same *i* indicators (X1 to X*i*). In this chapter, we discuss the use of F to control for global tendencies shared across indicators.

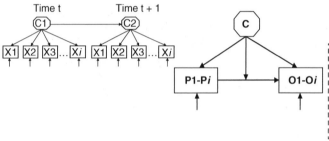

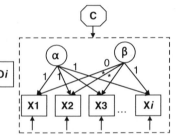

Model 1
Latent Transition Analyses

This model estimates *C* latent profiles at two separate time points (C1 and C2), and the probabilities for individuals to transition from C1 to C2 over time. Latent transition analyses can be used to assess the similarity of a latent profile solution over time. However, latent transition analyses do not require the mixture model estimated at C1 to be equivalent to the mixture model estimated at C2.

Model 5
Mixture Regression Analyses

This model estimates *C* latent profiles differing at the level of relationships (regressions) among a set of predictors (P1 to P$_i$) and outcomes (O1 to O$_i$). Mixture regression analyses identify subpopulations among which these relationships differ. Mixture regression analyses can be combined with latent profile analyses to identify profiles differing on the basis of both these relationships, but also the configuration of indicators.

Model 6
Growth Mixture Analyses

This model estimates *C* latent profiles presenting different longitudinal trajectories on one or more variables over *i* time points. Individual trajectories are estimated through a latent growth model (Bentein, this volume), any part of which is allowed to differ across profiles.

Figure 35.2　Key models described in this chapter

control for construct-irrelevant sources of covariance, should generally be preferred (Schweizer, 2012). GSEM also makes it possible to include method factors, so that the latent profiles can be estimated controlling for the effects of explicitly modeled residual associations (Lubke and Muthén, 2005; see the section below on FMAs).

LPAs are very flexible, and make it possible to directly assess the added value of alternative specifications (free estimation of indicators variance, correlated uniquenesses, and factor mixture models) in terms of improvements in the relative fit of the model. However, mixture models remain complex and computer-intensive, and have a tendency to converge on improper solutions, or fail to converge at all. When this occurs, it suggests that the model may have been overparameterized (for example, too many profiles, too many parameters freely estimated across profiles) and that more parsimonious models may be superior. My recommendation is to always start with theoretically 'optimal' models, and then reduce model complexity when necessary.

LPAs WITH COVARIATES (MODEL 2)

A key strength of LPAs is the possibility to directly include covariates (predictors, correlates, or outcomes) to the model. Directly including covariates helps to limit Type 1 errors by combining analyses, and has been shown to reduce biases in the estimation of the relations between covariates and the profiles (Bolck et al., 2004). With mixture models, it is particularly critical not to rely on two-step strategies (that is, exporting the most likely class membership of participants to an external data file, and relating this observed categorical variable to covariates using regressions or analyses of variance, ANOVAs), which ignore the prototypical nature of the profiles (that is, individuals' probability of membership in all profiles; Marsh et al., 2009). Covariates can be conceptualized as having an impact on profile membership (predictors), as being impacted by profile membership (outcomes), or as being related to profile membership with no assumption of directionality of the associations (correlates). Because these three types of covariates are included using different approaches, this distinction needs to be made a priori, on the basis of theoretical expectations and research background.

Predictors are included in the final model using a multinomial logistic regression representing the relation between the predictor and the likelihood of membership into the various profiles. In multinomial logistic regressions, each predictor has $k - 1$ (with k being the number of profiles) effects for each possible pairwise comparison of profiles. The regression coefficients reflect the expected increase, for each unit of increase in the predictor, in the log-odds of the outcome (the probability of membership in one profile versus another). Odds ratios (ORs) are also typically reported, and reflect the change in the likelihood of membership in a target profile versus a comparison profile for each unit of increase in the predictor (for example, OR = 2 means that each unit of increase in the predictor is associated with participants being twice more likely to be member of the target, versus comparison, profile).

Predictors are included to the model after the class enumeration procedure has been completed, and their inclusion or exclusion should not change the nature of the profiles (Marsh et al., 2009). Such a change would indicate a violation of the assumption that the direction of the relation goes from the predictors to the profiles, rather showing that predictors act as profile indicators (Marsh et al., 2009; Morin et al., 2011b). When this happens, alternative strategies involving estimating the model using starts values taken from the final unconditional model, or using 'auxiliary' approaches where the covariates are kept inactive, can provide valuable alternatives (Asparouhov and Muthén, 2014; Vermunt, 2010). These approaches are discussed and illustrated in the online supplements.

The typical way of including outcomes to the model involves including them as additional profile indicators. However, when multiple outcomes are considered, this method almost always results in a change in the nature of the profiles. Whenever this is the case, associations between inactive outcomes and the profiles can also be easily tested using a variety of auxiliary approaches (Asparouhov and Muthén, 2014; Lanza et al., 2013; Vermunt, 2010) illustrated in the online supplements.

Correlates are typically used for descriptive purposes and do not need to be directly included in the model. Thus, to properly assess the relations between correlates and prototypical latent profiles (that is, taking into account individual probabilities of membership in all classes), auxiliary approaches should be preferred. The AUXILIARY *(e)* approach implemented in Mplus, which relies on Wald chi-square test of statistical significance based on pseudo-class draws and tests the equality of correlates means across profiles (Asparouhov and Muthén, 2007; Bolck et al., 2004), does not assume any directionality in the associations between profiles and correlates.

FACTOR MIXTURE ANALYSES (MODEL 3)

GSEM allows for the simultaneous inclusion of continuous (factors) and categorical (profiles) latent variables within the same model. FMAs include factors and profiles estimated from the same indicators. A complete review of FMAs is beyond the scope of this chapter. FMAs can be used to investigate the underlying continuous or categorical nature of psychological constructs (Clark et al., 2013; Masyn et al., 2010), and to test the measurement invariance of psychometric measures across unobserved subpopulations (Tay et al., 2011). Of direct relevance to commitment research, FMAs can integrate a continuous latent factor to control for a generic tendency shared among indicators. For example, Morin and Marsh (2015) used FMAs to estimate profiles of strengths and weaknesses in terms of teaching competencies (that is, relations with students, marking), while controlling for global levels of effectiveness (that is, for the fact that there are good and poor teachers). Their results clearly showed that FMAs resulted in more clearly differentiated profiles than LPAs. Based on theory that posits that commitment will be expressed through distinct complementary mindsets (AC, NC, CC), there are no apparent reasons to expect the need to apply a similar control for global commitment levels in the estimation of mindset profiles. In contrast, it could be argued that global tendencies to commit in an affective, or normative, manner need to be controlled in multi-target research. Arguably, continuance commitment is not likely to reflect such a global tendency. For instance, Morin et al. (2011) used a similar FMA approach to identify profiles of AC directed to seven targets, while controlling for individual differences in the propensity to commit affectively.

TESTING THE SIMILARITY OF PROFILE SOLUTIONS ACROSS MEANINGFUL SUBGROUPS OF PARTICIPANTS

As noted previously, a key test of the meaningfulness of a profile solution involves verifying the extent to which this solution generalizes to different subgroups of participants, samples, and cultures. Arguably, evidence for generalizability in person-centered research is built on an accumulation of studies, from which it becomes possible to identify a core set of profiles emerging with regularity, together with a set of more peripheral profiles emerging more irregularly under specific conditions (for an extended discussion, see Solinger et al., 2013). So far, person-centered commitment research has been mainly limited to single-sample studies conducted in Western countries (but see Morin et al., 2016). Although a few studies (Meyer et al., 2013a; Meyer et al., 2015) have tested the extent to which profiles replicate across samples, they have done so based on qualitative visual comparisons of profile solutions (for a review, see Meyer and Morin, 2016). Thus far, there has yet to be a true quantitative comparison of commitment profile solutions across meaningful subgroups of participants (defined based on age, gender, profession, culture, and so on). Clearly, the systematic assessment of the generalizability of profile solutions, their development, and their consequences across subpopulations represents a key direction for future commitment research. However, a comprehensive framework to guide tests of the similarity of profile solutions is necessary (such as the CFA/SEM invariance framework; Chapter 32 in this volume). Previous research has proposed a preliminary three-step approach for latent class analyses (that is, categorical indicators) without covariates (Eid et al., 2003; Kankaraš et al., 2011). Table 35.1 extends this framework to models based on continuous indicators including predictors and outcomes (for details of implementation, see the online supplements). This framework extends to tests of longitudinal similarity (that is, LTAs) and MRAs.

LATENT TRANSITION ANALYSES (MODEL 4)

LTAs estimate LPA solutions at multiple time points, and the connections (that is, transitions) between the profiles across these time points (Collins and Lanza, 2010). In their simplest expression, LTAs estimate LPA solutions based on the same set of indicators and including the same number of profiles at both time points. However, LTAs can also be used to model the connections between any types of mixture models (Nylund-Gibson et al., 2014). The bulk of research on commitment profiles has been cross-sectional (Meyer et al., 2013b). This lack of evidence regarding the longitudinal stability of commitment profiles represents an important limitation. Indeed, the demonstration that commitment profiles are stable is critical to support the idea that person-centered results can be used to guide managerial strategies to select, promote, or differentially manage employees with specific profiles. LTAs allow for the investigation of two types of stability in latent profile solutions over time (Kam et al., 2016). A first involves the stability of the profile structure within a sample, over time (within-sample stability): Whether the same number of profiles presenting a similar configuration can be identified over time. This form of stability directly relates to the taxonomy of similarity tests presented in

Table 35.1 Taxonomy of similarity tests for profile solutions

		Description	LPAs	LTAs	MRAs
(1)	Configural Similarity	• Tests if the same number of latent profiles can be identified across groups or time points. • Configural similarity is required to pursue the sequence of similarity tests. • Failure to support configural similarity means that the latent profiles differ across groups or time points and need to be contrasted using a qualitative process.	X	X	X
(2)	Structural Similarity	• Prerequisite: Configural similarity. • Tests whether the indicators' within-profile levels are the same across groups or time points. • Configural and structural similarity are required to pursue the sequence of similarity tests. • If the number and/or structure of the profiles differ across groups or time points, all subsequent analyses must be conducted separately across groups or time points.	X	X	X
(3)	Dispersion Similarity	• Prerequisite: Configural and structural similarity. • Tests whether the indicators' within-profile variability is the same across groups or time points. • Latent profiles do not assume that all members of a profile share the exact same configuration of indicators. This step tests whether within-profile inter-individual differences are stable across groups or time points. • Not applicable when profile indicators are categorical.	X	X	X
(4)	Structural Similarity	• Prerequisite: Configural and structural similarity. • Tests whether the relative size of the profiles is similar across groups or time points.	X	X	X

	LPAs	LTAs	MRMs
(5) Predictive Similarity	X	X	X
• Prerequisite: Configural and structural similarity.			
• This step includes predictors of profile membership to the most similar (2–4) model.			
• Tests if the predictors–profiles relations are the same across groups or time points.			
• This test requires the direct incorporation of predictors to the model.			
• This step is only appropriate when predictors are included in the study.			
(6) Explanatory Similarity	X	X	X
• Prerequisite: Configural and structural similarity.			
• This step includes outcomes of profile membership to the most similar (2–4) model.			
• Tests if the profiles–outcomes relations are the same across groups or time points.			
• This test requires the direct incorporation of outcomes to the model.			
• This step is only appropriate when outcomes are included in the study.			
(7) Regression Similarity			X
• Prerequisite: Configural similarity.			
• Tests whether the regressions that define the mixture regression profiles are the same across groups or time points.			
• This step is only relevant to mixture regression analyses.			
• This step is the second step of the taxonomy for mixture regression analyses.			
• For mixture regression analyses this step is the second step of the sequence of similarity tests.			
Recommended order	**1**-2-3-4-5-6	**1**-**2**-3-4-5-6	**1**-**7**-**2**-3-4-5-6

Steps that are a prerequisite to subsequent steps are bolded.

Notes: LPAs = latent profile analyses. LTAs = latent transition analyses. MRMs = mixture regression analyses. Recommended order: steps that are prerequisites to subsequent steps are in bold.

501

Table 35.1 (also see the online supplements). A second form of stability pertains to the consistency of individual employees' profiles over time (within-person stability): whether individual employees correspond to the same profiles over time. Applying LTAs to mindset profiles of organizational commitment over an eight-month period, Kam et al. (2016) showed that the profiles presented a very high level of within-sample and within-person stability. Based on these promising results, further investigations of the temporal stability of commitment profiles should be seen as a future priority for person-centered commitment research.

MIXTURE REGRESSION ANALYSES (MODEL 5)

MRAs have very rarely been used in research so far (e.g., Morin et al., 2015), and never in commitment research. MRAs aim to identify latent profiles of participants differing from one another at the level of estimated relations (regressions) between constructs. Thus, whereas LPAs regroup participants based on their configuration on a set of commitment components, MRAs identify subpopulations in which the relations among constructs differ. For example, variable-centered research shows that AC predicts higher levels of wellbeing and retention (e.g., Morin et al., 2013). MRAs make it possible to investigate whether these relations differ in specific subpopulations. For example, MRAs could reveal a profile in which AC relates as expected to wellbeing and retention, a second profile in which AC relates only to retention, and a final profile in which AC presents a negative relation with wellbeing suggesting that there might be risks to extreme levels of AC (e.g., Morin et al., 2013). In the estimation of MRAs, the means and variances of the outcomes (representing the intercepts and residuals of the regressions) need to be freely estimated across profiles to obtain profile-specific regression equations. More complex applications are possible, such as combining LPAs and MRAs to profile employees based on both their configuration of indicators, and relations between indicators. For example, one could combine the previous example (where AC predicts retention and wellbeing) with LPAs (including AC, NC, and CC). MRAs may reveal that the first profile (both predictions in the expected direction) includes morally committed (AC/NC-dominant) employees, that the second profile (AC only predicts retention) includes trapped (CC-dominant) employees, whereas a third profile includes emotionally committed (AC-dominant; both predictions in the expected directions, with a stronger relation between AC and wellbeing than in the first profile) employees. The estimation of this type of MRAs requires the free estimation of the predictors' means and variances in the extracted profiles. Such models also reveal potential interactions among predictors, resulting in profiles in which the relations among constructs may differ as a function of predictors' levels (e.g., Bauer, 2005). Given the complexity of these models, my recommendation is the same as for LPAs: start with the estimation of theoretically optimal models. When these fail to converge on proper solutions, fall back to simpler models where, in order, the variances of the predictors, the means of the predictors, and the variances of the outcomes, are constrained to equality across profiles.

GROWTH MIXTURE ANALYSES (MODEL 6)

GMAs identify subgroups presenting distinct longitudinal trajectories on one, or many, commitment component(s) over time. GMAs are complex and could easily deserve a complete chapter. For this reason, a complete coverage of GMAs remains beyond the scope of this chapter, and readers are referred to Morin et al. (2011a) and Ram and Grimm (2009). However, GMAs are built from latent curve models (LCMs) (see Chapter 33 in this volume), and more extensively described in the online supplements. In LCMs, commitment components are assessed over multiple time points and trajectories at the sample level are estimated through intercept and slope(s) factors that differ between individuals. In their simplest expression, GMAs extract latent profiles differing on these growth factors (that is, presenting different intercept and slope factors). More complex GMAs may extract subgroups differing on all LCMs parameters, and may even allow for the extraction of subgroups with trajectories following distinct functional forms (linear, quadratic, and so on). For example, in a study of recently promoted employees' trajectories of AC to the organization, one might observe one profile showing a steady decline in AC over time (suggesting that the promotion had negative consequences), a second showing a linear increase (suggesting satisfaction with the new role), and a third group showing an initial decrease followed by an increase (suggesting initial difficulties of adaptation, followed by a successful mastery of the new role). So far, a single study has applied a restricted form of GMAs to the study of newcomers' organizational AC (Solinger et al., 2013). This study revealed five distinct longitudinal profiles of employees, characterized by a 'high match', 'moderate match', or 'low match' with the organization (that is, persistently high, moderate, or low AC, respectively), by a 'learning to love' profile (increasing AC level), or by a 'honeymoon hangover' profile (increasing AC level, followed by a decrease). Clearly, these results beg replication and investigation of possible interventions to favor the emergence of the most desirable profiles. Examining profiles of longitudinal trajectories of commitment components represents another key area for future commitment research. This approach is particularly well suited to investigations of the effects of interventions, changes, or life transitions (allowing for the identification of subgroups showing differential reactivity to the intervention).

One critical issue that often tends to be misunderstood in applied research is that LCM and GMA estimate longitudinal trajectories as a function of time. Thus, a strong assumption of these models is that the time can be assessed as a function of a meaningful referent (Metha and West, 2000). Unfortunately, typical organizational studies, where a sample of employees presenting a variety of age and tenure levels is recruited and followed over time, do not meet this assumption. Suitable applications require trajectories to be explicitly modeled as a function of age or tenure levels, or as a function of key transition points that similarly concern all participants (intervention or experiment, organizational change, retirement, change of employment, and so on). Otherwise, time effects will be confounded with other, unmodeled, effects of age, tenure, and so on that vary across employees.

A SHORT NOTE ON THE MYTHICAL SHARED METHOD BIAS

Over the past decades, multiple attempts have been made to debunk the myth that shared method variance induces some kind of bias in the estimation of relations among variables (e.g., Spector, 2006). Unfortunately, this myth remains well anchored in organizational research; so well anchored that it even resisted the equation-based demonstration that multivariate analyses are naturally protected against biases potentially emerging from shared method variance because they involve the estimation of each predictor's unique contribution (that is, not shared) to the equation (Siemsen et al., 2010). Unfortunately, no such demonstration has yet been published for mixture models. Still, and for similar reasons, these models are equally unlikely to be biased by shared method variance as the goal of mixture models is to explain the covariance among a set of indicators through the extraction of profiles that are distinct from one another. In mixture models, uncontrolled sources of shared influences are likely to result in only a slightly lower level of dispersion (that is, scatter) within the profiles, rather than in substantially different results. Although FMAs control for shared sources of influences as part of the global factor, they should not be used simply to control for shared method variance when there are no substantive reasons to assume that this additional latent factor would be meaningful in its own right. Indeed, such global latent factors are known to absorb a substantial level of meaningful covariance in addition to shared method variance (Richardson et al., 2009). Likewise, analyses of relations between profiles and covariates are inherently multivariate, and thus also naturally controlled for shared method variance (Siemsen et al., 2010).

CONCLUSION

Person-centered methodologies are well suited to testing multiple aspects of commitment theory not easily addressed using the more traditional variable-centered techniques. However, it is particularly important to keep in mind that person- and variable-centered approaches should be viewed as complementary, and that their combination is likely to provide an incredibly rich view of the reality under study. This chapter aimed to provide a simple introduction to the multiple possibilities provided by GSEM, with the hope of stimulating researchers to think creatively about the wide range of questions that can be addressed with these evolving methodologies. Clearly, it was neither possible, nor feasible, to present all possibilities provided by GSEM within a single non-technical chapter. Throughout this chapter, many additional possibilities were also highlighted, hoping to stimulate curiosity about this rich analytical framework. However, mixture models remain complex, and present multiple challenges to inexperienced researchers. It is thus strongly recommended that researchers start with simpler models (LPAs, LPAs with covariates, FMAs), before moving on to more complex models (multiple-group LPAs, or LTAs), and to even more complex models (MRAs and GMAs). Mixture models require a strong understanding of CFA/SEM, multiple group analyses, and tests of measurement invariance (Chapter 32 in this volume), and GMAs should be anchored in a solid understanding of LCMs (Chapter 33 in this volume).

Marsh and Hau (2007) noted an increasing state of disconnection between statistical developments and substantive research, so that it is becoming increasingly difficult for any single researcher to keep up both methodologically and substantively. This chapter is a preliminary effort to bridge this gap. However, the best way to achieve this objective is to revise our views on how research should be done, in particular the view that it is critical for the lead author to fully master all elements of the research. Perhaps a more collaborative approach to research, where statistical and substantive experts team up, represents a solution. When successful, such collaborative teams not only help to increase the quality of a single paper, but also help to significantly increase the level of both statistical and substantive thinking on the part of all team members.

NOTE

* Online supplements for this chapter can be accessed at statmodel.com/MixtureModeling.shtml, or upon request from the author.

REFERENCES

Asparouhov, T. and Muthén, B.O. (2007). Wald test of mean equality for potential latent class predictors in mixture modeling. Technical Report. Los Angeles CA: Muthén and Muthén

Asparouhov, T. and Muthén, B.O. (2014). Auxiliary variables in mixture modeling: Three-step approaches using Mplus. *Structural Equation Modeling, 21*, 1–13.

Bauer, D.J. (2005). A semiparametric approach to modeling nonlinear relations among latent variables. *Structural Equation Modeling, 4*, 513–535.

Bauer, D.J. (2007). Observations on the use of growth mixture models in psychological research. *Multivariate Behavioral Research, 42*, 757–786.

Bolck, A., Croon, M., and Hagenaars, J. (2004). Estimating latent structure models with categorical variables: One-step versus three-step estimators. *Political Analysis, 12*, 3–27.

Clark, S.L., Muthén, B.O., Kaprio, J., D'Onofrio, B.M., Viken, R., and Rose, R.J. (2013). Models and strategies for factor mixture analysis: An example concerning the structure of underlying psychological disorders. *Structural Equation Modeling, 20*, 681–703.

Collins, L.M. and Lanza, S.T. (2010). *Latent Class and Latent Transition Analysis: With Applications in the Social, Behavioral, and Health Sciences.* New York: Wiley.

Cudeck, R. and Henly, S.J. (2003). A realistic perspective on pattern representation in growth data: Comment on Bauer and Curran (2003). *Psychological Methods, 8*, 378–383.

Delbridge, R. and Fiss, P.C. (2013). Styles of theorizing and the social organization of knowledge. *Academy of Management Journal, 38*, 325–331.

Eid, M., Langeheine, R., and Diener, E. (2003). Comparing typological structures across cultures by multi-group latent class analysis. A primer. *Journal of Cross-Cultural Psychology, 34*, 195–210.

Finch, W.H. and Bronk, K.C. (2011). Conducting confirmatory latent class analysis using Mplus. *Structural Equation Modeling, 18*, 132–151.

Gellatly, I.R., Meyer, J.P., and Luchak, A.A. (2006). Combined effects of the three commitment components on focal and discretionary behaviors. *Journal of Vocational Behavior, 69*, 331–345.

Henry, K. and Muthén, B.O. (2010). Multilevel latent class analysis: An application of adolescent smoking typologies with individual and contextual predictors. *Structural Equation Modeling, 17*, 193–215.

Kam, C., Morin, A.J.S., Meyer, J.P., and Topolnytsky, L. (2016). Are commitment profiles stable and predictable? A latent transition analysis. *Journal of Management, 42*, 1462–1490. doi: 10.1177/0149206313503010.

Kankaraš, M., Vermunt, J.K., and Moors, G. (2011). Measurement equivalence of ordinal items: A comparison of factor analytic, item response theory, and latent class approaches. *Sociological Methods and Research, 40*, 279–310.

Lanza, S.T., Tan, X., and Bray, B.C. (2013). Latent class analysis with distal outcomes: A flexible model-based approach. *Structural Equation Modeling, 20*, 1–26.

Lubke, G.H. and Muthén, B. (2005). Investigating population heterogeneity with factor mixture models. *Psychological Methods, 10*, 21–39.

Marsh, H.W. and Hau, K-T. (2007). Applications of latent-variable models in educational psychology: The need for methodological-substantive synergies. *Contemporary Educational Psychology, 32*, 151–171.

Marsh, H.W., Lüdtke, O., Trautwein, U. and Morin, A.J.S. (2009). Classical latent profile analysis of academic self-concept dimensions: Synergy of person- and variable-centered approaches to theoretical models of self-concept. *Structural Equation Modeling, 16*, 191–225.

Masyn, K., Henderson, C., and Greenbaum, P. (2010). Exploring the latent structures of psychological constructs in social development using the Dimensional-Categorical Spectrum. *Social Development, 19*, 470–493.

McLachlan, G. and Peel, D. (2000). *Finite Mixture Models.* New York: Wiley.

Metha, P.D. and West, S.G. (2000). Putting the individual back into individual growth curves. *Psychological Methods, 5*, 23–43.

Meyer, J.P. and Allen, N.J. (1991). A three-component conceptualization of organizational commitment. *Human Resource Management Review, 1*, 61–89.

Meyer, J.P. and Allen, N.J. (1997). *Commitment in the Workplace: Theory, Research, and Application.* Thousand Oaks, CA: Sage Publications.

Meyer, J.P., Becker, T.E., and Van Dick, R. (2006). Social identities and commitment at work: Toward an integrative model. *Journal of Organizational Behavior, 27*, 665–683.

Meyer, J.P. and Herscovitch, L. (2001). Commitment in the workplace: Toward a general model. *Human Resource Management Review, 11*, 299–326.

Meyer, J.P., Kam, C., Goldenberg, I., and Bremner, N.L. (2013a). Organizational commitment in the military: Application of a profile approach. *Military Psychology, 25*, 381–401.

Meyer, J.P. and Morin, A.J.S. (2016). A person-centered approach to commitment research: Theory, research, and methodology. *Journal of Organizational Behavior, 36*, 584–612.

Meyer, J.P., Morin, A.J.S., and Vandenberghe, C. (2015). Dual Commitment to Organization and Supervisor: A Person-centered Approach. *Journal of Vocational Behavior, 88*, 56–72.

Meyer, J.P., Stanley, D.J., Jackson, T.A., McInnis, K.J., Maltin, E.R., and Sheppard, L. (2012). Affective, normative, and continuance commitment levels across cultures: A meta-analysis. *Journal of Vocational Behavior, 80*, 225–245.

Meyer, J.P., Stanley, L.J., and Vandenberg, R.J. (2013b). A person-centered approach to the study of commitment. *Human Resource Management Review, 23*, 190–202.

Morin, A.J.S., Madore, I., Morizot, J., Boudrias, J.-S., and Tremblay, M. (2009). The Workplace Affective Commitment Multidimensional Questionnaire. Factor structure and measurement invariance. *International Journal of Psychology Research, 4*, 307–344.

Morin, A.J.S., Maïano, C., Nagengast, B., Marsh, H.W., Morizot, J., and Janosz, M. (2011a). Growth mixture modeling of adolescents trajectories of anxiety: The impact of untested invariance assumptions on substantive interpretations. *Structural Equation Modeling, 18*, 613–648.

Morin, A.J.S. and Marsh, H.W. (2015). Disentangling shape from levels effects in person-centred analyses: An illustration based university teacher multidimensional profiles of effectiveness. *Structural Equation Modeling, 22*, 39–59.

Morin, A.J.S., Meyer, J.P., Creusier, J., and Biétry, F. (2016). Multiple-group analysis of similarity in latent profile solutions. *Organizational Research Methods, 19*, 231–254.

Morin, A.J.S., Meyer, J.P., McInerney, D.M., Marsh, H.W., and Ganotice, F. (2015). Profiles of dual commitment to the occupation and organization: Relations to wellbeing and turnover intentions. *Asia Pacific Journal of Management, 32*, 717–744.

Morin, A.J.S., Morizot, J., Boudrias, J.-S., and Madore, I. (2011b). A multifoci person-centered perspective on workplace affective commitment: A latent profile/factor mixture analysis. *Organizational Research Methods, 14*, 58–90.

Morin, A.J.S., Scalas, L.F., and Marsh, H.W. (2015). Tracking the elusive actual–ideal discrepancy model within latent subpopulations. *Journal of Individual Differences, 36*, 65–72.

Morin, A.J.S., Vandenberghe, C., Turmel, M.-J., Madore, I., and Maïano, C. (2013). Probing into Commitment's Nonlinear Relationships to Work Outcomes. *Journal of Managerial Psychology, 28*, 202–223.

Muthén, B.O. (2002). Beyond SEM: General latent variable modeling. *Behaviormetrika, 29*, 81–117.

Muthén, L.K. and Muthén, B.O. (2014). *Mplus user's guide.* Los Angeles, CA: Muthén and Muthén.

Nylund-Gibson, K., Grimm, R., Quirk, M., and Furlong, M. (2014). A latent transition mixture model using the three-step specification. *Structural Equation Modeling, 21*, 439–454.

Peugh, J. and Fan, X. (2013). Modeling unobserved heterogeneity using latent profile analysis: A Monte Carlo simulation. *Structural Equation Modeling, 20*, 616–639.

Ram, N. and Grimm, K.J. (2009). Growth mixture modeling: A method for identifying differences in longitudinal change among unobserved groups. *International Journal of Behavioral Development, 33*, 565–576.

Reichers, A.E. (1985). A review and reconceptualization of organizational commitment. *Academy of Management Review, 10*, 465–476.

Richardson, H.E., Simmering, M.J., and Sturman, M.C. (2009). A tale of three perspectives: Examining post hoc statistical techniques for detection and correction of common method variance. *Organizational Research Methods*, *12*, 762–800.

Schweizer, K. (2012). On correlated errors. *European Journal of Psychological Assessment*, *28*, 1–2.

Siemsen, E., Roth, A., and Oliveira, P. (2010). Common method bias in regression models with linear, quadratic, and interaction effects. *Organizational Research Methods*, *13*, 456–476.

Solinger, O.N., Van Olffen, W., Roe, R.A., and Hofmans, J. (2013). On becoming (un)committed: A taxonomy and test of newcomer onboarding scenarios. *Organization Science*, *24*, 1640–1661.

Spector, P.E. (2006). Method variance in organizational research: Truth or urban legend? *Organizational Research Methods*, *9*, 221–232.

Steinley, D. and McDonald, R.P. (2007). Examining factor scores distributions to determine the nature of latent spaces. *Multivariate Behavioral Research*, *42*, 133–156.

Tay, L., Newman, D.A., and Vermunt, J.K. (2011). Using mixed-measurement item response theory with covariates (MM-IRT-C) to ascertain observed and unobserved measurement equivalence. *Organizational Research Methods*, *14*, 147–176.

Tsoumbris, P. and Xenikou, A. (2010). Commitment profiles: The configural effects of the forms and foci of commitment on work outcomes. *Journal of Vocational Behavior*, *77*, 401–411.

Vermunt, J.K. (2010). Latent class modeling with covariates: Two improved three-step approaches. *Political Analysis*, *18*, 450–469.

CONCLUSION

36. Employee commitment: looking back and moving forward
John P. Meyer

One thing that becomes abundantly clear from this *Handbook* is that commitment theory is alive and well, and that the community of researchers interested in commitment is quickly spreading around the globe. Not surprisingly, with greater involvement comes increased diversity in perspectives, approaches to theory development, and research strategies. It is impossible in the space available to fully synthesize the richness of the content in the many chapters of this *Handbook*. Therefore, although I will touch on all of the themes reflected in the various parts, I will devote the most attention to the two most controversial issues: the conceptualization of commitment, and its distinction from related concepts. There are both advantages and disadvantages to controversy and, while I will speak to both, I will emphasize the former because I believe that controversy can be a major impetus for future research, which was one of my primary objectives in putting together this *Handbook*.

CONCEPTUALIZATION OF COMMITMENT

As is evident from Chapter 2 by Klein and Park and Chapter 3 by Allen in Part I, there has yet to be a time in the history of commitment theory when there was consensus on its definition and measurement. This continues to be true today and could remain so for years to come. What that says about the state of the field is subject to interpretation. Some may see it as evidence of stagnation and a threat to the relevance of the commitment literature as a guide to evidence-based management. Others may see the divergence of views as healthy and vital as a stimulus for future investigation. My objective in this book was to provide a voice to authors with these divergent views and to allow readers to draw their own conclusions. I was heartened by the fact that both Klein and Park (Chapter 2) and Allen (Chapter 3) acknowledged that the ultimate value of the unidimensional and multidimensional approaches to the conceptualization of commitment will depend on how well they stand up to empirical scrutiny and prove useful as a guide to practice. I wholeheartedly agree, and would like to take the opportunity here to share my thoughts on the issue.

Much of the debate around the dimensionality of commitment hinges on the definition of the construct itself. There are no rules in the behavioral sciences about how one should define a construct. If the construct is one that is widely used in everyday discourse, as is commitment, then presumably the definition should reflect the essence of that common use. However, even the dictionary definitions that reflect this common use offer considerable leeway. For example, the *Merriam Webster Dictionary* (http://www.merriam-webster.com/dictionary/dictionary) definition includes: 'an agreement or pledge to do something in the future' and 'the state or an instance of being obligated or emotionally impelled'. Likewise, the *Oxford English Dictionary* (http://www.oed.com/) definition includes: 'The state or quality of being dedicated to a cause, activity, etc.' and 'An engagement or obligation that restricts freedom of action.' With these definitions in mind, consider the following definitions reflecting the multidimensional and unidimensional perspectives, respectively.

> a mind-set that can take different forms and binds an individual to a course of action that is of relevance to a particular target (Meyer and Herscovitch, 2001, p. 310)

> a volitional psychological bond reflecting dedication to and responsibility for a particular target (Klein et al., 2012, p. 137)

There is nothing inherently wrong with either of these definitions and both fall within the bounds of those provided by two of the leading dictionaries. Interestingly, both describe an underlying core construct that applies across the potential targets, or foci, of commitment. The 'multidimensionality' of the construct in the three-component model (TCM) that served as the basis for Meyer and Herscovitch's (2001) definition is reflected in the purported ways that the 'force' can be experienced. The other most notable difference is in the relative emphasis on the implications for behavior within the definition itself. Meyer and Herscovitch focus much more specifically on the notion that a commitment binds an individual to a course of action; in the Klein et al. definition the 'bond' is with the target itself, although it is clear from the accompanying theory that there are behavioral implications.

The 'rules' of science kick in when we attempt to measure a construct and embed it within a nomological network of correlates, antecedents, and consequences (Hinkin, 1998; Schwab, 1980). Allen summarizes a large body of research conducted within the TCM framework that she presents as evidence supporting the reliability and validity of its measures and basic propositions. Both the measures (Allen and Meyer, 1990; Meyer et al., 1993; Powell and Meyer, 2004) and the model (Meyer et al., 2004; Meyer and Herscovitch, 2001; Meyer and Parfyonova, 2010) have undergone revisions over the years in response to research findings and efforts to link the model with other theories. Moreover, the approach taken to test the model has changed somewhat with the development of new person-centered data analytic strategies (see Meyer and Morin, 2016; Morin, Chapter 35 in this volume; Vandenberg and Stanley, 2009). Several of the unidimensional models reviewed by Klein and Park (e.g., Mowday et al., 1979) have also received considerable support and continue to guide research today. The Klein et al. unidimensional target-free (KUT) model recently introduced by Klein and colleagues (Klein et al., 2012; Klein et al., 2014) is also receiving considerable support.

Thus, from the perspective of science, things are progressing as they should: constructs are being defined, measures are being developed and evaluated, theory is being tested, and refinements are being made. As long as the two approaches continue to stand up to the rigors of science, there appears to be no clear basis for declaring a winner. And, given that they derived from different starting points (definitions and conceptual models), there is no immediately obvious strategy to bring the dissenting views in line. Does it really matter? The answer might depend on what the two approaches contribute from a practical perspective; after all, this is the basic objective of applied science.

Again, for the purpose of discussion, I focus here on the TCM and the KUT as proto-typical examples of the multidimensional and unidimensional perspectives, respectively. This is not to deny the potential practical value of other approaches, current or future. I also refer the readers to the Chapters 2 and 3 in this volume for more detail regarding the KUT model and TCM, respectively. Here I will simply raise a few of the potential benefits and risks that I see associated with efforts to apply each of these approaches.

Arguably the greatest strength of the TCM is the fact that it acknowledges that individuals can experience their commitments in different ways – with different 'mindsets' – and that the nature of the mindset matters. Initially, with a focus on organizational commitment, and turnover as the primary outcome variable, Allen and Meyer (1990; Meyer and Allen, 1991) argued that commitment could be experienced as a desire (affective commitment), obligation (normative commitment), or need (continuance commitment) to remain. Although differences in the strength of the bond to the organization were expected, the major difference across the mindsets was expected to be reflected in employees' willingness to exert discretionary effort on behalf of the organization while they remained in its employ. As the model was extended to other targets (for example, occupations, change initiatives), the differentiating factor continued to be the implications of the mindsets for behaviors beyond those included within the 'terms' of the commitment (Meyer and Herscovitch, 2001). More recently, the TCM has been investigated using a person-centered strategy (see Morin, Chapter 35 in this volume) that allows for the detection of commitment profiles reflecting more nuanced mindsets, again with the prediction that these will relate differently to important organization- and employee-relevant outcomes (see Meyer and Morin, 2016, for a review).

The TCM was developed initially as a means of integrating differing approaches to the conceptualization and study of commitment (see Meyer and Allen, 1991) and, in Klein and Park's words, is more 'inclusive'. The advantages of this inclusivity – the recognition that mindset matters – is offset by the added complexity required by having to distinguish among different forms of commitment. This complexity has increased with evidence that the three components combine to form profiles, each with its own characteristic mindset. Moreover, the fact that the TCM was developed to integrate divergent views of commitment means that many will question whether the components (for example, continuance) or profiles (for example, CC-dominant) reflecting some of these perspectives are truly commitment. Indeed, this was one of the questions raised by Klein and Park in advocating for a unidimensional approach. I will return to this issue later following discussion of the potential benefits and risks of a unidimensional approach.

As Klein and Park point out, the unidimensional approach has a long history and various unidimensional theories and measures have been developed over the years. Some overlap considerably, whereas others are quite different. Each has its strengths and limitations but the variations are too extensive to address in detail here. I will focus instead on the KUT model because it is the most recent, builds on the strengths of those models that preceded it, and is being rigorously investigated. One of the benefits of this model is a clear and concise definition of the construct to guide the development of a short measure that can be applied across many different targets. Existing theory and research pertaining to individual targets of commitment can be used to establish a nomological network of correlates, antecedents, and consequences to be investigated. Although it is too early to determine whether the availability of a common measure will facilitate research to address the many questions one might ask about compatibility, conflict, and synergy among multiple commitments (see Becker, Chapter 4 in this volume), the potential is there.

So, the unidimensional approach has clear benefits, but do these come at a cost? To arrive at a unidimensional conceptualization of commitment, Klein and colleagues had to make clear decisions about what should and should not be included in the definition. Appropriately, they excluded anything that could more properly be considered an antecedent, correlate, or consequence of commitment. As part of the refinement process, they omitted any reference to the implications of commitment for future behavior (that is, the behavior to which an individual might be bound by making a commitment); the 'bond' is to the target and not to a 'course of action'. This is certainly a legitimate decision but, as was the case with the TCM, it invites challenges from those who might view commitment differently. For example, some might question whether a commitment exists if it does not have explicit implications for behavior. As I noted in Chapter 1, this is arguably one of the reasons why commitments are important. It is also something that helps to distinguish commitment from related constructs, an issue I return to below. Another potential implication is that narrowing the definition of commitment so precisely runs the risk of introducing (North American) culture bias. Wasti (Chapter 26 in this volume) argues that even the TCM, with its inclusion of mindsets (for example, normative commitment) that might be more reflective of the way commitment is experienced in some non-Western cultures, still reflects a North American perspective.

To this point, I have emphasized the apparent differences between the TCM and the KUT model; but are there any similarities? If so, might these similarities justify continuing parallel streams of research that might, at a minimum, lead to the identification of a unifying set of guiding principles? The optimist in me suggests that the answer to both questions might be yes. In what follows I describe one possible scenario.

Klein et al. (2012) do not deny that employees form other kinds of psychological bonds with their employer (or other targets) and that these bonds can have implications for their behavior and well-being. Indeed, they identify four bond types that they arrange on a continuum – acquiescence (perceived absence of alternatives), instrumental (high cost or loss at stake), commitment (volition, dedication, and responsibility), and identification (merging of self with the target) – with adjacent bonds being more likely to co-occur. There is a clear resemblance between the acquiescence and instrumental bonds, respectively, and the two facets of continuance commitment that are often identified (lack of alternatives and high sacrifice; see Vandenberghe and Panaccio, 2012). The major difference is that Klein et al. do not treat these bonds as forms of commitment; Meyer and Allen (1991) do. Klein et al. have yet to clearly articulate how these other bonds might relate to behavior, either on their own or in interaction with commitment. If we ignore the labels for a moment, the result of recent person-centered investigations of the TCM offer some grounds for speculation (see Meyer and Morin, 2016). It is quite likely that individuals with acquiescence or instrumental bonds, in the absence of commitment, will remain with the organization as long as the absence of alternatives or potential costs of leaving persist, but are unlikely to exert more effort into their jobs than is required. They may also experience considerable stress as a result of their perceived lack of freedom to pursue other options. However, when combined with strong commitment, the negative effects of having strong acquiescence or instrumental bonds are likely to be diminished. Moreover, the explanation for the difference might be due to frustration versus satisfaction of the employees' need for autonomy (see Gagné and Howard, Chapter 5 in this volume).

As noted previously, among the limitations of the TCM is its potential complexity and the fact that some of the component and profile mindsets are not commonly acknowledged as reflecting commitment in the conventional sense. Many researchers choose to focus on affective commitment only, although some, particularly those in collectivist cultures, view normative commitment as a more appropriate conceptualization (see Wasti, Chapter 26 in this volume). Among other things (for example, survey length), these decisions presumably reflect the investigators' own beliefs about the nature of commitment. Interestingly, the results of person-centered studies suggest that the most desirable organizational and personal outcomes are associate with strong affective and normative commitment (e.g., Gellatly et al., 2006; Meyer et al., 2012). The benefits of this combination – what Meyer and Morin (2016) recently described as moral commitment – is that it combines the mindsets of desire and obligation. The desire component has obvious implications for maintenance of a relationship, and the obligation component might explain persistence during those periods when desire wanes. Indeed, it might be this combination that corresponds most closely to what people commonly think of as commitment. Although everyone hopes that others' commitment to them will be based on desire, they might count on the obligation 'just in case'. This might also be why some people are reluctant to make commitments: few of us object to doing things we want to do, but it is the concern about what happens if or when conditions change, and the desire begins to erode, that makes commitment a bit daunting.

In light of this speculation, one reason why the TCM and KUT might coexist harmoniously is that they share, and support, some common guiding principles. For example, both would acknowledge that, although turnover can be reduced through the use of inducements that make it costly for employees to leave (that is, increase continuance commitment or the instrumental bond), this is not advisable unless accompanied by strategies to foster commitment (Klein et al., 2012) or affective or moral commitment (Meyer and Allen, 1991; Meyer and Morin, 2016). Another is that recent person-centered studies are beginning to provide evidence that the affective–normative commitment combination (moral commitment profile) is optimal, whereas continuance commitment on its own (CC-dominant profile) is most detrimental. To reduce the complexity introduced by the application of the person-centered approach in the investigation of the TCM, it might be preferable to measure these two forms of commitment directly. Indeed, it is possible that the KUT measure currently, or with minor modification, might be a good measure of moral commitment. One advantage of simplifying measurement within the TCM framework is that it would also simplify the application of a person-centered approach to the investigation of multiple commitments. Only time will tell whether this scenario plays out. In the meantime, individuals should adopt the approach best suited to their research or practice agendas.

RELATED CONSTRUCTS

As I noted in Chapter 1 in this volume, there are a number of other constructs under investigation or being used in practice that seem quite similar to employee commitment. At the very least, they 'compete' with commitment as predictors of important organization-relevant (for example, turnover, job performance), and employee-relevant (for example, well-being) outcomes. The authors of the chapters in Part II of this *Handbook* describe in considerable detail these related constructs – motivation, engagement, embeddedness, identification, and psychological contracts – and their relations with commitment. All acknowledge the overlap, but view it more in terms of complementarity than redundancy; however, this view is not shared by everyone (for example, see Becker, Chapter 4 in this volume). What can we learn from these comparisons, and what are the implications for the future of commitment theory, research, and practice?

The answers to these questions might depend on whether they are viewed through the lens of the academic or the practitioner. I expect that the issue will be of greatest concern to academics so I will start there. As applied scientists we have been trained to define our constructs clearly and concisely, to use these definitions to develop reliable and valid measures, to clearly articulate how the constructs should relate to other variables within a theory-based nomological network, and to evaluate our measures and models using the most appropriate methods and statistical analyses. To the extent that our constructs are intended to predict or explain the same phenomena as other constructs, we should also demonstrate that our construct adds value (that is, has incremental validity). These are admirable objectives and important rules to live by. However, no matter how well the rules are followed, there are no guarantees that consensus among scholars will be achieved, at least in the short term. In my view, the theorists and researchers whose work is described in Chapters 5–9 are all 'playing by the rules' and have provided evidence that their constructs are at least somewhat distinct from commitment and make an incremental contribution to the prediction of common outcomes. Of course it must be kept in mind that commitment is only one of the 'competitive constructs' with which these theorists and researchers must contend. With this in mind, let us consider each of these related constructs.

Gagné and Howard (Chapter 5 in this volume), and Albrecht and Dineen (Chapter 6) differentiate commitment from work motivation and engagement, respectively, in terms of their focus: the organization versus the task or job. Indeed, this distinction is generally clear from a comparison of the items from relevant measures, and research tends to demonstrate that organizational commitment is a better predictor of retention and behaviors directed at the organization, whereas motivation or engagement is a better predictor of task performance. However, according to commitment theorists, employees can commit to targets other than the organization, including jobs and tasks (Becker, Chapter 4 in this volume). If so, what is the difference between commitment to a task and task motivation or engagement? One possibility that I alluded to in Chapter 1 is that commitment, more so than motivation or engagement, implies a long-term orientation. Motivation and engagement can ebb and flow, whereas commitments are presumably more stable (Meyer and Allen, 1997; Mowday et al., 1982).

If the relative stability of commitment is indeed a differentiating factor, what are the implications for its conceptualization and measurement? One possibility is that the items we use to measure commitment should address this stability (for example, 'I am in this relationship for the long term'). A second possibility is that we should restrict the targets of commitment to those where a relatively long-term relationship or persistence in a course of action is relevant. For example, while it makes sense to commit to the completion of a project, it might make less sense to commit to each of the tasks required to complete that project. Motivation to perform those tasks (or engagement in the task) might be sufficient. Viewed in this light, the moderate to strong relations between organizational commitment and autonomous work motivation (Gagné and Howard, Chapter 5 in this volume; Meyer et al., 2004) and work engagement (Albrecht and Dineen, Chapter 6 in this volume; Christian et al., 2011) make sense, and the difference in the 'target' serves to differentiate between the constructs.

As Holtom points out in Chapter 7, the major distinction between commitment and embeddedness is that the former reflects a psychological state, whereas the latter includes more objective indicators (that is, fit, links, sacrifices) that increase the likelihood that an individual will remain in the organization. Given that staying and leaving are opposite sides of the same coin, it is true that the two constructs serve similar predictive purposes. From a theoretical perspective, one might argue that the different facets of embeddedness are more distal causes of the decision to stay or leave. Commitment, as a psychological state, might serve as a mediator of the effect of these facets on the stay/leave decision. If so, however, it might be important to specify clearly how the facets relate to the different commitment mindsets (in the TCM) or bond types (in the KUT model). For example, although fit with the job might contribute to the development of affective commitment (TCM) or the commitment bond (KUT), sacrifice might contribute to continuance commitment (TCM) or an instrumental bond (KUT). In either case, the end result might be a decreased likelihood of exit, but the implications for job performance or citizenship behavior might be quite different. Thus, there may be mutual benefits to the integration of embeddedness and commitment theories; the benefit to commitment theory is a relatively direct measurement of important antecedents (for example, fits, sacrifices), whereas the benefit to embeddeness theory is a set of mediating mechanisms (commitment mindsets of bond types) to explain both the common and differentiated outcomes of different sources of embeddedness.

Despite the inclusion of 'identification' in many popular definitions of commitment (e.g., Mowday et al., 1982; Meyer and Allen, 1991), in Chapter 8, Van Dick makes it quite clear that organizational commitment and organizational identification are distinct constructs. Organizational identity as a construct has its origins in social identification theory (Tajfel and Turner, 1979) and self-categorization theory (Turner et al., 1987) and reflects the incorporation of the relationship with the organization as part of one's self concept. Although related to organizational commitment, most likely as an antecedent (Meyer et al., 2006), the operationalization of organizational identification in terms of self-perception clearly differentiates it from commitment as a 'force' or 'bond'. The fact that employees can identify with varying targets within and outside the organization allows it to be linked to commitments to multiple foci. Importantly, there are features of identification that make it a particularly attractive variable to include in commitment research. For example, the salience of different facets of one's identity (for example, organization, team, profession) can vary, and indeed be manipulated, and might be useful in the investigation of fluctuations in commitment levels (see van Olffen et al., Chapter 34 in this volume). This might allow researchers to determine whether commitment to a particular target (for example, organization) fluctuates in an absolute sense over time, or whether the fluctuation corresponds to the relative salience of the target of identification.

Finally, in Chapter 9, Hansen and Griep explain the relevance of psychological contracts for commitment. Although in some conceptualizations of the psychological contract, commitment is viewed as a part of the construct (for example, one of the terms of the employee's obligation), Hansen and Griep point out that commitment is more often, and appropriately, considered an outcome of the contract type (for example, transactional or relational) or evaluation of the contract (that is, fulfillment or breach). Psychological contract theory has undergone some important revisions that could offer new directions for commitment theory and research. For example, in what Hansen and Griep refer to as Psychological Contract Theory 2.0, it is recognized that contracts develop and change over time in a variety of ways, and that the existence and/or fulfillment of different terms within the contract can have non-linear relations with outcomes, including commitment. Moreover, although commonly considered an antecedent of commitment, Hansen and Griep acknowledge that the nature and strength of one's commitment might influence perception of the contract and/or responses to breach. They, like many other authors of this book, call for more research using methods and analytic procedures that allow for the investigation of dynamic processes as they unfold over time.

Although it is impossible in the space available to fully address the academic controversy surrounding the 'construct redundancy' problem, I strongly encourage interested readers to use the chapters in Part II of this *Handbook* as an entry point to these other literatures and to identify creative ways to determine whether and where there are redundancies and, more importantly, how the theories might be combined to address mutual concerns for improving organizational effectiveness and employee well-being. In the meantime, let us look briefly at the construct redundancy issue from a practical perspective.

I expect that there are very few HR professionals, let alone corporate executives, who lose sleep over whether it is better to have employees committed or engaged. They are far more concerned about the outcomes (for example, retention and performance) and the drivers they have available to achieve them (for example, compensation systems, job design, management strategy) than they are about the mediating mechanisms (for example, commitment, identification, engagement). Having recently been involved in the development and implementation of an 'engagement' survey in a large organization, I was intrigued by how little understanding (or concern) there was about the distinctions between commitment and engagement, culture and climate, or a variety of the other distinctions made by academics. It was also interesting to see how little space was allotted in the final survey to the measurement of the 'state' of engagement or organizational commitment (and both were included); far more space was allotted to the measurement of employees' perceptions of the conditions expected to shape that state, things like trust in management, involvement in decision-making, quality of interpersonal relationships, and clarity of communication. In other words, from a practitioner perspective the construct distinctions may not matter very much.

So whose lens should we look through in assessing the status of commitment theory and research: the academic's or the practitioner's? In my view, both are important. As academics we need to continue to use rigorous methods in evaluating our constructs and testing our theories. New constructs and theories will continue to come on line. Some will be generated internally within the academic community and others will develop in response to what is happening in practice; still others will come from a combination of the two. Employee engagement is a good example. Kahn introduced the concept to the academic community in 1990, but the major impetus for research came from its popularity among human resources (HR) consultants and their clients (see Macey and Schneider, 2008). To their credit, many academics saw the interest generated by practitioners as an opportunity and began to develop precise definitions of engagement, create measures, and conduct research to investigate the drivers and consequences of engagement (see Christian et al., 2011, for a review). As noted by Albrecht and Dineen (Chapter 6 in this volume), an important part of this academic endeavor was to determine whether, and how, engagement differs from commitment. Did the HR consultants notice, or care? I hazard a guess that some did and some did not. In either case, at the end of the day, the emphasis is likely to be on how employees perceive conditions within the organization and what the organization can do to improve them.

As an academic, I admit to taking some exception to Macey and Schneider's (2008, p. 3) comment that engagement was introduced by HR consultants and that academics were 'slowly joining the fray'. Indeed, in a commentary to their focal article in *Industrial and Organizational Psychology: Perspective on Science and Practice*, Marylène Gagné and I (Meyer and Gagné, 2008) noted that the ideas being promoted by these firms in support of their engagement initiatives are grounded in a solid body of theory and research pertaining to other constructs, including commitment. In a more recent article (Meyer, 2013), I reiterated that claim, but also noted that my concern was not that consultants were promoting engagement rather than commitment, but that in doing so they might be ignoring large bodies of work simply because it did not include the term 'engagement'. I would be equally concerned if, in the future, consultants ignored what is currently being learned about the nature, development, and consequences of engagement because the current buzzword has changed (for example, 'passion').

Reconciling the two perspectives, at least in my own mind, I see the major contribution of applied science as being the establishment of basic principles that can be used to guide practice with the ultimate objective of improving organizational effectiveness and employee well-being. The constructs we use matter to the extent that they help to establish principles. For example, if the implications of using a particular management strategy to achieve a desired outcome can be demonstrated to be greater if mediated by commitment to the organization as opposed to engagement in one's job, then the distinction may be important. That is, it might have implications for how the principle is enacted and monitored in the short term (for example, with a measure of engagement or organizational commitment). How important it is will depend on the relative difference in explanatory power. This is a question that academics are well suited to address (and is probably a question that only academics will ask). It is also a question that should be asked and pursued until a reasonable answer can be found. However, if a management strategy will have the desired effects regardless of whether it contributes to engagement or commitment (or both), we should applaud the HR consultants for 'taking it to the street' regardless of how it is packaged.

In sum, questions regarding construct uniqueness and relevance, like questions of construct dimensionality, are important and should be pursued as long as the answers have relevance to the attainment of one's ultimate goals. In my estimation, the work on employee commitment and all of the constructs identified in Part II are continuing to advance our understanding of employer–employee relations and should continue, probably with more interaction across fields than currently exists. My hope is that this *Handbook* will stimulate more cross-fertilization.

COMMITMENT FOCI

In Chapter 4, Becker traces the evolution of commitment research from its initial focus on organization commitment to today, where considerable attention is being given to commitment to other targets within (for example, supervisor, team, project) and outside (for example, union, occupation) the organization, and their interactions. This is a natural and important development, particularly in an era where relations between employers and employees are becoming more tenuous (Meyer, 2009). The chapters in Part III address some of the commitment targets that have received the most attention to date, including occupations and professions (Meyer and Espinoza, Chapter 10), social entities (Vandenberghe, Chapter 11), unions (Horsman et al., Chapter 12), and actions (Meyer and Anderson, Chapter 13). As is clear from these chapters, these commitments have direct relevance to the immediate target, but have indirect or spillover effects for organizations. Some, such as goal, project, or change commitments, will likely require special attention from management. Others, such as commitment to supervisors and teams, may be influenced more by the targets themselves, but are also likely to be affected by organizational policies and practices. Still others, such as occupational (professional) commitment and union commitment are likely to be managed (or at least influenced) primarily by the target, but organizations still need to be concerned about whether the goals and values of these targets are aligned with those of the organization to minimize conflict or create synergy.

There are many other potential targets of commitment that were not addressed specifically in Part III, including commitments to family and other non-work entities (for example, religious or social groups) or actions (for example, hobbies, charitable activities). While it is tempting to suggest that more research should be directed to the investigation of these commitments and their implications for, and interactions with, work commitments, there is also need for caution to avoid construct proliferation. Consistent with the discussion above, it is important to ask whether these entities or actions are really the targets of 'commitment'; that is, is the connection expected to be relatively stable and have binding implications for behavior? If so, then it makes sense to consider how the implications of such a commitment will relate to important organization- and employee-relevant outcomes. In this regard, family is probably a target of commitment that deserves more attention than it has garnered to date; commitment to hobbies might be less so.

CONSEQUENCES OF COMMITMENT

The authors of the chapters in Part IV make it clear why interest in employee commitment has been so strong over the last several decades. Employees who are committed are more likely to stay with organizations and attend regularly (Gellatly and Hedberg, Chapter 14), perform effectively and be good organizational citizens (Stanley and

Meyer, Chapter 15), refrain from engaging in counterproductive behaviors (Marcus, Chapter 16), and be happier and healthier (Chris et al, Chapter 17; Klein and Brinsfield, Chapter 18). The research findings reported in these chapters, many of them obtained from meta-analyses, seem quite compelling. Although the strength of relations with individual outcomes is modest, in combination they suggest that there are clear benefits to commitment for both employers and employees. However, it is somewhat disconcerting that much of the research on the consequence of commitment is cross-sectional and often involves self-report measures of both the commitment and the outcome (for example, turnover intention). There is certainly enough evidence from longitudinal studies and/or studies using other-source or objective indices of the outcomes to suggest that the relations are meaningful, but there is a need for more of this kind of research.

It is also apparent from this section that most of the research on consequences has focused on organizational commitment. Admittedly, this is due in part to the space constraints faced by the authors as well as the fact that there are other chapters in the book dedicated to commitments to other foci and their outcomes. Nevertheless, another important direction for future research is to examine how commitments to different foci combine to influence employees' behavior, performance, and well-being. Also apparent is the fact that most of the research has been conducted at an individual level of analysis. This is perhaps not surprising given that commitment is experienced by individuals. However, it can and should be studied at higher levels (for example, unit, organization) as well. Indeed, organizations may be more convinced about the need to invest in initiatives designed to promote commitment if they have evidence that it provides competitive advantage (that is, organizations with more committed employees outperform those with less-committed employees; Meyer, 2009). Jiang (Chapter 21 in this volume) provides some evidence that this is indeed the case in his review of the implications of high-performance work systems on both commitment and organizational effectiveness. Again, more higher- and cross-level research is warranted.

DRIVERS OF COMMITMENT

As I mentioned in my introductory chapter, theory and research pertaining to antecedents of commitment has progressed to the point that it can now be largely organized around well-grounded core principles. These principles served as the organizing structure for Part V of this *Handbook*. One of these principles is that individuals differ in their propensity for commitment, and/or their fit with the work environment (Bergman and Jean, Chapter 19; van Vianen et al, Chapter 20). Importantly, the selection of individual difference variables of relevance to the investigation of propensity and fit can be guided to a greater extent than in the past by theories of personality, attachment, values, and self-concept. Similarly, we have learned a great deal more about the many types of fit (or misfit) – person–organization, person–job, person–supervisor, person–team – and how these contribute to the development, maintenance, or decline in commitment. The remaining chapters in Part V focus on the work context, but again are grounded in strong theory pertaining to strategic human resource management (HRM) (Jiang, Chapter 21), leadership (Trivsonno and Barling, Chapter 22), empowerment (Laschinger et al., Chapter 23), perceived organizational support (Stinglhamber et al., Chapter 24), and organizational justice (Bobocel and Mu, Chapter 25). In some cases, these theory-based principles can be combined to achieve an even richer understanding of the commitment process. For example, perceptions of organizational justice and organizational support may be inextricably intertwined and be strongly influenced by strategic HRM practices. Similarly, the effects of HRM practices and transformational leadership might be explained in part by their contributions to employees' sense of psychological empowerment. Links can also be drawn to principles reflected in other well-developed theories discussed elsewhere in this *Handbook*, including need satisfaction as articulated in self-determination theory (Gagné and Howard, Chapter 5) and psychological contract fulfillment (Hansen and Griep, Chapter 9). One advantage of having a set of strong theory-based principles to draw from is that it helps to explain why specific 'best practices' have been shown to work. It also provides a way of evaluating whether these practices will generalize to other situations. For example, providing family-friendly benefits might help to strengthen commitment in organizations where most employees have, or expect to have, family responsibilities because it is a sign of organization support. It might not have the same effect in organizations with very young employees who do not, and may never, have such responsibilities; in this case, providing concierge services or ready access to gourmet meals that free up time might be a more appropriate way to demonstrate support.

While research pertaining to antecedents has come a long way since Reichers (1985) referred to it as a 'laundry list', it is still limited in a number of respects. Most notably, there are still fewer experimental or quasi-experimental studies than is desirable. Unlike outcome studies where commitment is the independent variable and cannot be easily manipulated, in antecedent studies manipulation should be possible, and those studies that use it (e.g., Barling et al., 1996) provide particularly convincing evidence for the effectiveness of theory-guided interventions. When manipulation is not possible, the use of more longitudinal studies, particularly those amenable to the advanced analytic techniques described in Part VII, would also help to provide stronger evidence that interventions designed to improve P–E fit, demonstrate organization support, or bolster perceptions of justice will indeed have the desired impact on commitment. Finally, organization-level research along the lines of those described by Jiang (Chapter 21) in his discussion of strategic HRM would help to demonstrate that organizations can achieve competitive advantage by creating work conditions that are conducive to the development of commitment.

COMMITMENT ACROSS CULTURES

Interest in employee commitment is no longer a North American phenomenon. Admittedly, most commitment theory originated there and the bulk of the research is still being conducted in the Western world. However, the amount of research being conducted in non-Western countries is increasing rapidly. This provides both challenges and opportunities. In the opening chapter in Part VI, Wasti (Chapter 26) aptly describes the complexities of conducting cross-cultural research and alerts researchers to the many factors – societal, socio-institutional, organizational – and the interplay among them that can influence the nature and focus of commitment, how it develops, and how it affects behavior. These complexities are echoed by many of the other authors in Part VI as they describe the research coming out of Europe (Felfe and Wombacher, Chapter 27), China (Newman and Wang, Chapter 28), India (Dhir et al., Chapter 29), the Middle East (Cohen, Chapter 30), and Latin America (Arciniega, Chapter 31). Although it is impossible to capture the complexity of what these authors discuss in their chapters, the findings they report are both encouraging and disappointing. They are encouraging in that much of what has been discovered in North American research seems to hold in other countries and cultures. Therefore, our theories seem to generalize to at least some extent. The disappointment comes from the fact that much of the research being conducted in these countries is what Wasti refers to as 'imposed etic'; that is, the theories used to guide the research, and the measures used to conduct it, are largely adapted from North America. Although this allows us to address the issue of generalizability, it does not allow exploration of the possibility that commitment is experienced in different, or additional, ways in other cultures. A useful starting point might be to conduct more qualitative research to determine whether there are ways that commitments are experienced in other cultures that are not apparent when viewed through a Western lens (see Wasti and Önder, 2009).

One of the more interesting complexities involved in conducting research in other countries, particularly countries in the developing world, is that they are in the process of change. Admittedly, this poses a challenge to researchers hoping to compare commitment across national boundaries (that is, does one use the traditional or evolving culture as the basis for comparison?). On the other hand, this situation also provides a natural laboratory for research involving within-country comparisons (that is, comparing employees and/or companies reflecting the old and new cultures). Conducting this research will be messy because there are likely to be many moving parts, but a community of commitment researchers conducting multiple studies in different countries using varying research strategies should be up to the task. It is important to go into this research recognizing that it is a marathon rather than a sprint.

METHODOLOGICAL ISSUES IN COMMITMENT RESEARCH

Throughout the preceding discussion, I have alluded to the need for more research using the many advances that have been made with regard to methodology and analysis. The authors in Part VII describe some of these advances and illustrate how they might be used to advance our understanding of the nature, development, and consequences of employee commitment. I strongly encourage readers to consider how the strategies described in these chapters might help to advance their research agendas. The procedures for testing for invariance described by Vandenberg and Morelli (Chapter 32) will be important to those who want to make meaningful comparisons across groups or over time, both of which I and other authors have strongly advised. As important as invariance testing is as a starting point in such research, it is important to keep in mind that evidence for both invariance and lack of invariance (or partial invariance) can be informative. While evidence for measurement invariance is necessary for some forms of comparison, evidence for lack of invariance could lead to potentially interesting and important lines of research to investigate its source. For example, if the psychometric properties of a measure differ across cultural groups, it could suggest that commitment is experienced differently by these groups. Of course there are many other possible explanations (for example, translation issues) that would need to be ruled out.

Understanding and being able to predict change in commitment and its covariates over time is essential to demonstrating the practical value of commitment theory. Two of the chapters in Part VII specifically address the investigation of change and describe analytic strategies that can be used in such investigations. Bentein (Chapter 33) describes how latent growth modeling analyses can be used to investigate how commitment changes over time, and how both the initial level of commitment and the rate of change in commitment can be predicted and used to predict other variables (for example, turnover). She provides some illustrative examples that generated findings that would have gone undetected with more traditional forms of analyses (for example, that rate of change in commitment is a better predictor of turnover than is level of commitment). Unfortunately, there are only a few such studies available to date and, like any other area of investigation, the value of the findings depends on replication. Therefore, like Bentein, I strongly encourage researchers to collect data that will allow them to utilize this powerful analytic tool to advance our understanding of the commitment process.

Van Olffen et al. (Chapter 34) describe an even newer 'temporal process' approach to the investigation of the development and consequences of commitment. Being a new and innovative technique, some of the recommendations made by the authors are admittedly controversial (for example, allowing participants to view and 'correct' the data collected at earlier time points). As I noted above, this can be a plus if it serves to stimulate creative thinking and innovative research. There are also implications for how the relevant constructs (in this case commitment) are conceptualized and measured. The one caveat I would offer here is that there may be limits to how much a construct and its measures can be modified to meet the requirements for analysis and still remain true to the underlying theory. Temporal process research requires relatively frequent measurement of the construct(s) under investigation and is based on the assumption that short-term change is meaningful. In applying this technique to the study of commitment, Solinger et al. (2013) used an 'attitudinal' measure based on the theoretical model proposed by Solinger et al. (2008). Such an approach might be less viable for the investigation of commitment as conceptualized in the TCM (Meyer and Allen, 1991) and KUT (Klein et al., 2012) where it is assumed that commitment is a relatively stable construct; indeed, if it was found that commitment fluctuates too rapidly, it would raise questions about the very nature of the construct. That said, I can envision applications even with the TCM or KUT if applied under conditions where commitment is in its formative stage (for example, newcomers) or is under pressure for change (for example, during a merger or acquisition). Similarly, the temporal process approach might be very useful in testing the recent suggestion that affective commitment may be more sensitive to changing environmental conditions than is normative commitment (Meyer and Morin, 2016).

Finally, Morin (Chapter 35) discusses the application of a person-centered research strategy in the investigation of commitment. This approach is not a substitute for the more traditional variable-centered approach, but rather a complementary strategy to be used where appropriate for the question under investigation. Indeed, it is well suited to testing hypotheses concerning the nature and implications of mindset profiles within the TCM, and bond profiles within the KUT, as well as the potential for compatibility and conflict among commitments to different foci. It may well have other implications including the investigation of configurations of antecedents of commitment (for example, profiles of the 'Big 5' personality traits; profiles of HRM practices) or outcomes (for example, configurations of in-role and extra-role behavior directed at multiple targets). Importantly, this and any of the other analytic strategies should be chosen for its appropriateness to the question under investigation and not as a hammer in search of a nail.

CONCLUSION

We have learned a great deal about commitment over the years and this should serve well to convince practitioners that employee commitment is important. It should also help to guide them in their efforts to foster greater commitment. Disagreements remain, some of them apparently quite fundamental, including the conceptualization of the construct. This can lead theorists and researchers to get bogged down in debate, or it can energize them to take new and creative approaches to conducting research. I recommend the latter and suggest that, if the focus remains on how our research can best contribute to creating a fulfilled and productive workforce, it might matter little whether the disagreements actually get fully resolved. Despite all we have learned, it is clear that we still have much more to learn and the authors in this *Handbook* have given us plenty of interesting and useful ideas for how we might proceed. They have also suggested strategies that could be useful for gaining greater confidence in what we think we already know. Admittedly, the powerful analytic strategies described in Part VII are complex, and contemplation of their use might push some researchers outside of their comfort zone. One potential solution to this dilemma is the formation of collaborative teams of researchers with complementary substantive and methodological expertise. Indeed, it is very likely that true advances in our understanding of the commitment process will require collaboration of one form or another. For example, addressing potential compatibility and conflict in multidimensional and unidimensional conceptualizations might require collaboration among advocates of the two approaches, perhaps accompanied by 'neutral' third parties. Understanding how commitment is similar to or different from related constructs (for example, engagement, entrenchment) might require collaboration among researchers with expertise pertaining to the relevant constructs. And, of course, understanding whether commitment is the same or different across cultures might require not only a team of individuals with knowledge of the differing cultures, but also individuals with expertise in the appropriate research methods and analytic techniques. It is my hope that this *Handbook* and the wealth of ideas presented by its authors will serve as a stimulus to such collaboration.

REFERENCES

Allen, N.J. and Meyer, J.P. (1990). The measurement and antecedents of affective, continuance and normative commitment to the organization. *Journal of Occupational Psychology*, 63(1), 1–18.
Barling, J., Weber, T., and Kelloway, E.K. (1996). Effects of transformational leadership training on attitudinal and financial outcomes: A field experiment. *Journal of Applied Psychology*, 81, 827–832.
Christian, M.S., Garza, A.S., and Slaughter, J.E. (2011). Work engagement: A quantitative review and test of its relations with task and contextual performance. *Personnel Psychology*, 64, 89–136.

Gellatly, I.R., Meyer, J.P., and Luchak. A.A. (2006). Combined effects of the three commitment components on focal and discretionary behaviors: A test of Meyer and Herscovitch's propositions. *Journal of Vocational Behavior*, *69*(2), 331–345.

Hinkin, T.R. (1998). A brief tutorial on the development of measures for use in survey questionnaires. *Organizational Research Methods*, *1*, 104–121.

Klein, H.J., Cooper, J.T., Molloy, J.C., and Swanson, J.A. (2014). The assessment of commitment: Advantages of a unidimensional, target-free approach. *Journal of Applied Psychology*, *99*(2), 222–238.

Klein, H.J., Molloy, J.C., and Brinsfield, C.T. (2012). Reconceptualizing workplace commitment to redress a stretched construct: Revisiting assumptions and removing confounds. *Academy of Management Review*, *37*, 130–151.

Macey, W.H. and Schneider, B. (2008). The meaning of employee engagement. *Industrial and Organizational Psychology: Perspectives on Science and Practice*, *1*, 3–30.

Meyer, J.P. (2009). Commitment in a changing world of work. In H.J. Klein, T.E. Becker, and J.P. Meyer (eds), *Commitment in Organizations: Accumulated Wisdom and New Directions* (pp. 37–68). New York: Routledge/Taylor & Francis.

Meyer, J.P. (2013). The science–practice gap and employee engagement: It's a matter of principle. *Canadian Psychology*, *54*, 235–245.

Meyer, J.P. and Allen, N.J. (1991). A three-component conceptualization of organizational commitment. *Human Resource Management Review*, *1*(1), 61–89.

Meyer, J.P. and Allen, N.J. (1997). *Commitment in the Workplace: Theory, Research, and Application*. Thousand Oaks, CA: Sage Publications.

Meyer, J.P., Allen, N.J., and Smith, C.A. (1993). Commitment to organizations and occupations: Extension and test of a three-component conceptualization. *Journal of Applied Psychology*, *78*(4), 538–551.

Meyer, J.P., Becker, T.E., and Vandenberghe, C. (2004). Employee commitment and motivation: A conceptual analysis and integrative model. *Journal of Applied Psychology*, *89*(6), 991–1007.

Meyer, J.P., Becker, T.E., and Van Dick, R. (2006). Social identities and commitments at work: Toward an integrative model. *Journal of Organizational Behavior*, *27*(5), 665–683.

Meyer, J.P. and Gagné, M. (2008). Employee engagement from a self-determination theory perspective. *Industrial and Organizational Psychology: Perspectives on Science and Practice*, *1*, 60–63.

Meyer, J.P. and Herscovitch, L. (2001). Commitment in the workplace: Toward a general model. *Human Resource Management Review*, *11*(3), 299–326.

Meyer, J.P. and Morin, A.J.S. (2016). A person-centered approach to commitment research: Theory, research, and methodology. *Journal of Organizational Behavior*, *37*, 584–612.

Meyer, J.P. and Parfyonova, N.M. (2010). Normative commitment in the workplace: A theoretical analysis and re-conceptualization. *Human Resource Management Review*, *20*, 283–294.

Meyer, J.P., Stanley, L.J., and Parfyonova, N.M. (2012). Employee commitment in context: The nature and implication of commitment profiles. *Journal of Vocational Behavior*, *80*(1), 1–16.

Meyer, J.P., Stanley, L.J., and Vandenberg, R.J. (2013). A person-centered approach to the study of commitment. *Human Resource Management Review*, *23*(2), 190–202.

Mowday, R.T., Porter, L.W., and Steers, R. (1982). *Organizational Linkages: The Psychology of Commitment, Absenteeism, and Turnover*. San Diego, CA: Academic Press.

Mowday, R.T., Steers, R.M., and Porter, L.W. (1979). The measurement of organizational commitment. *Journal of Vocational Behavior*, *14*, 224–247.

Powell, D.M. and Meyer, J.P. (2004). Side-bet theory and the three-component model of organizational commitment. *Journal of Vocational Behavior*, *65*, 157–177.

Reichers, A.E. (1985). A review and reconceptualization of organizational commitment, *Academy of Management Review*, *10*, 465–476.

Schwab, D.P. (1980). Construct validity in organizational behavior. In B.M. Staw and L.L. Cummings (eds), *Research in Organizational Behavior* (Vol. 2, pp. 3–43). Greenwich, CT: JAI Press.

Solinger, O.N., van Olffen, W., and Roe, R.A. (2008). Beyond the three-component model of organizational commitment. *Journal of Applied Psychology*, *93*, 70–83.

Solinger, O.N., van Olffen, W., Roe, R.A., and Hofmans, J. (2013). On becoming (un) committed: A taxonomy and test of newcomer onboarding scenarios. *Organization Science*, *24*(6), 1640–1661.

Tajfel, H. and Turner, J.C. (1979). An integrative theory of intergroup conflict. In W.G. Austin and S. Worchel (eds), *The Social Psychology of Intergroup Relations* (pp. 33–47). Monterey: Brooks/Cole.

Turner, J.C., Hogg, M.A., Oakes, P.J., Reicher, S.D., and Wetherell, M.S. (1987). *Rediscovering the Social Group*. Oxford: Blackwell.

Vandenberg, R.J. and Stanley, L.J. (2009). Statistical and methodological challenges for commitment researchers: Issues of invariance, change across time, and profile differences. In H.J. Klein, T.E. Becker, and J.P. Meyer (eds), *Commitment in Organizations: Accumulated Wisdom and New Directions* (pp. 383–416). New York: Routledge/Taylor & Francis.

Vandenberghe, C. and Panaccio, A. (2012). Perceived sacrifice and few alternatives commitments: The motivational underpinnings of continuance commitment's subdimensions. *Journal of Vocational Behavior, 81*, 59–72.

Wasti, S.A. and Önder, Ç. (2009). Commitment across cultures: Progress, pitfalls, and propositions. In H.J. Klein, T.E. Becker, and J.P. Meyer (eds), *Commitment in Organizations: Accumulated Wisdom and New Directions* (pp. 309–343). New York: Routledge/ Taylor & Francis.

Index

AACSB (Association to Advance Collegiate Schools of Business) 444
Abd El Majid, I. 421–2, 424, 425, 426
Abrahamson, E. 51
absence culture 200
absenteeism
    commitment-enhancing management policies 201–3
    defining 199
    evolving perspectives on 199–201
    Latin American commitment studies 433
    Middle Eastern commitment studies 427, 428, 429
    and organizational commitment framework 195–6
    and presenteeism 200–201
    and three-component model 201, 202–4
    and withdrawal mindsets 195, 200–201, 202, 203–4
absorption (in employee engagement) 71, 73, 75, 80–81
abusive supervision 311–12
Academy of Management Review 106
ACN (affective–continuance–normative) commitment profiles 32, 33–6, 37–8
ACS (Affective Commitment Scale) 32, 80, 109, 452
action commitments
    and commitment to change 178, 183–6, 187, 188
    conceptual model 179–82
    defining 179–80, 181
    and entity commitments 178, 179, 180, 181, 183, 188–9
    future research agenda 188–9
    and goal commitment 178, 180, 181, 182–3, 187, 188
    implications for practice 187–8
    and justice 186
    and motivational factors 179, 180, 181, 182, 184–5
    and multiple commitments perspective 44
    and self-efficacy 181, 182, 183, 184–5, 187
    and team performance 183, 187
    and three-component model 184, 185–6
    unidimensional and multidimensional constructs 179, 182, 183–4, 187, 188
action-readiness 70

affective commitment 71, 195–6
    and absenteeism 201, 202–4
    and action commitments 184, 185–6
    affective consequences of commitment 251–5
    Chinese commitment studies 393, 394, 395–7
    and compliance 250
    conceptualizations of 248–51, 256
    and counterproductive work behaviors 223, 224, 225, 226–7, 228–31, 232
    and cross-cultural commitment theories 364, 366, 370
    current conceptualizations 250–51
    and dissonance 254–5
    and emotional attachment 250–51
    and emotional contagion 255
    and employee empowerment 320, 322–3, 325
    and employee turnover 197, 198, 202–4
    European commitment studies 376, 377, 378–9, 380–81, 382–4, 385–6, 388
    future research needs 256–7
    and goal commitment 252, 254
    Indian commitment studies 405–7, 410, 412, 413, 414
    and individual differences 263, 264, 269
    and internalization 250
    and job embeddedness 64, 65, 92
    and job performance 210, 212, 213–14, 215–16, 217, 218
    and job satisfaction 249, 251–2
    and latent growth modeling 462, 465–6, 467–8, 469–70, 471–3
    Latin American commitment studies 436–7, 438, 439–41, 442, 443, 444
    and ME/I testing 452–3
    and measurement of organizational commitment 74
    Middle Eastern commitment studies 421, 422, 424–5, 426, 429
    and motivation 253–4
    and multidimensional construct 31–2, 33–4, 35–6, 37, 38
    negative affect 120, 126, 151, 236, 237, 249, 252, 254–5, 256
    and occupational commitment 136, 137, 138–41, 142–3, 144, 145, 146
    and organizational identification 109, 110, 111